Health Economics

Health Economics

Editor: Bella Moody

FOSTER
ACADEMICS
www.fosteracademics.com

www.fosteracademics.com

FOSTER ACADEMICS

Cataloging-in-Publication Data

Health economics / edited by Bella Moody.
p. cm.
Includes bibliographical references and index.
ISBN 978-1-63242-670-3
1. Medical economics. 2. Medical care, Cost of. I. Moody, Bella.
RA410 .H43 2019
338.4--dc23

Foster Academics,
118-35 Queens Blvd., Suite 400,
Forest Hills, NY 11375, USA

ISBN 978-1-63242-670-3 (Hardback)

Printed and bound in China.

Contents

Preface

Over the recent decade, advancements and applications have progressed exponentially. This has led to the increased interest in this field and projects are being conducted to enhance knowledge. The main objective of this book is to present some of the critical challenges and provide insights into possible solutions. This book will answer the varied questions that arise in the field and also provide an increased scope for furthering studies.

The field of economics dealing with the issues related to value, efficiency, behavior and effectiveness in the production and consumption of health and healthcare is known as health economics. Specialists in this field are called health economists. They delve into the functioning of the healthcare systems and health-affecting behaviors. They also evaluate financial information, including the costs, expenditures and charges. The existence of knowledge gap between the patient and the physician is a state of benefit for the physician, which is called asymmetric information. It is a major area of focus under this field. Some of the main branches associated with health economics include medical economics, behavioral economics and mental health economics. This book unfolds the innovative aspects of health economics which will be crucial for the progress of this field in the future. It provides significant information of this discipline to help develop a good understanding of health economics and related fields. The topics covered in this book offer the readers new insights into the field of health economics.

I hope that this book, with its visionary approach, will be a valuable addition and will promote interest among readers. Each of the authors has provided their extraordinary competence in their specific fields by providing different perspectives as they come from diverse nations and regions. I thank them for their contributions.

Editor

1

Health expenditure and economic growth -a review of the literature and an analysis between the economic community for central African states (CEMAC) and selected African countries

Serge Mandiefe Piabuo* and Julius Chupezi Tieguhong

Abstract

African leaders accepted in the year 2001 through the Abuja Declaration to allocate 15% of their government expenditure on health but by 2013 only five (5) African countries achieved this target. In this paper, a comparative analysis on the impact of health expenditure between countries in the CEMAC sub-region and five other African countries that achieved the Abuja declaration is provided. Data for this study was extracted from the World Development Indicators (2016) database, panel ordinary least square (OLS), fully modified ordinary least square (FMOLS) and dynamic ordinary least square (DOLS) were used as econometric technic of analysis. Results showed that health expenditure has a positive and significant effect on economic growth in both samples. A unit change in health expenditure can potentially increase GDP per capita by 0.38 and 0.3 units for the five other African countries that achieve the Abuja target and for CEMAC countries respectively, a significant difference of 0.08 units among the two samples. In addition, a long-run relationship also exist between health expenditure and economic growth for both groups of countries. Thus African Economies are strongly advised to achieve the Abuja target especially when other socio-economic and political factors are efficient.

Keywords: Human capital, Health expenditure, Economic growth, Abuja declaration

Background

Endogenous growth models [1] highlights the importance of human capital on economic growth and development. Health is an important determinant of economic development; a healthy population means higher productivity, thus higher income per head [2]. The importance of human capital to economic growth cannot be over emphasized [3–5] because it serves as a catalyst to economic development. The contribution of health expenditure on economic development emanates from the health led growth hypothesis [6]. It considers health to be capital; therefore investments on health can lead to an increase in labour productivity,, thus increase in incomes and subsequent increase in the wellbeing of the population. Bloom and Canning [7] highlights that when labour is healthy, their incentive to develop new skills and knowledge is higher because they expect to enjoy long term benefits. However, when the labour force is characterized by workers with poor health, they turn to have an adverse effect on productivity; this explains the disparity in development in different regions of the world [8]. Fifty percent of divergence in economic growth between developing countries and developed countries is attributed to ill-health and low life expectancy [2].

The economic wellbeing of every population is ameliorated by change in technology and part of this change is due to advances in medical science. Newhouse [9] highlighted that change in technology is one of the major reasons for increase in health expenditure. The assertion of Newhouse [9] was empirically verified in the United States of America by Fuchs [10], whereby 85% of

* Correspondence: P.Mandiefe@cgiar.org
World Agroforestry Centre (ICRAF), Yaounde, Cameroon

a sample of health economics scholars confirmed that technical change accounted for the rapid growth in health care expenditure in the country.

Health care expenditure in Africa and rationale for this study

The importance of health as a key aspect of development and economic wellbeing of individuals and nations is increasingly being recognized in the world. This can be seen from a series of reforms taken by African countries to increase investments in health in order to meet the health Millennium Development Goals (MDGs). African leaders have expressed this trust through actions such as the 2001 Abuja Declaration on an increase in government funding for health by allocating 15% of the government budget to the health sector, the 2006 Addis-Ababa Declaration on community health in the African Region and the 2008 Ouagadougou Declaration on primary health care and health systems in Africa. The High-Level Taskforce on Innovative International Financing for Health Systems (HLTF) recommended that by 2009 low income countries should allocate at least US$ 44 per capita to deliver an essential package of health services. More than a third of African countries have not been able to meet both the Abuja target and the HLTF recommendation except for Botswana, Rwanda and Zambia. It is equally important to note that Equatorial Guinea has not been able to attain the Abuja target but has significantly high health expenditure per capita [11]. Table 1 below shows the level of attainment of these targets by African countries.

Developing a sound system for financing health care is one of the key mechanisms to show the commitments and political will of leaders and their ability to translate these commitments into results. The desire to develop strong health financing systems is a common objective of all countries but the increasing cost of health care accompanied by the poor economic performance of developing countries and African economies in particular makes it difficult to meet this objective. The majority of African countries falls within the low and middle income range and they face a severe problem of scarcity of funds to provide quality health care services with the average total health expenditure in African countries being at US$ 135 per capita in 2010, which is only 4.2% of the US$ 3150 spent on health in an average high-income country [12].

Lack of investment in health and in actions to address the environmental and social determinants of health is a serious constraint to upgrading health outcomes in Africa, bearing in mind that the continent registers the bulk of global maternal and infant mortality [11], it equally registers the highest number of people with HIV/AIDS [11]. The perpetual increase in injuries and non-communicable diseases is putting many countries under the pressure of a double burden of disease [11].

Constraints of financing health care in Africa arise principally from the mechanisms and strategies employed in financing health care. More than 40% of total health expenditure is characterized by household out of-pocket payments which is a very regressive method of financing health care [11]. This is principally because reliance on this form of payment creates financial barriers to access health services and the risk of impoverishment is increased [13]. These flaws in health care financing accounts for inefficiencies and disparity in the allocation of health care services among nations and between rural and urban areas. The Abuja declaration came as a solution to this problem by setting targets for African countries; to invest at least 15% of government budget on health and to have less than 20% of the total health expenditure coming from out-of pocket spending. As of 2013, only Botswana can boast of meeting this target. The out-of-pocket spending in Botswana is only 8% of the total health expenditure against an average 50% for most low and middle income countries in Africa while Government expenditure on health stands at around US$ 446 per capita, which is higher than African Region's upper middle income average of US$ 228 per capita and comparable to that of the upper middle income countries in the world [11].

African countries equally suffer from shortage in human resources for health (HRH). The World Health Organisation [11] reports that 36 out of the 46 countries in Sub-Saharan Africa are facing a HRH shortage crisis. According to Nabyonga et al. [14], the current shortage of health workers (physicians, nurses and midwives) in Africa is estimated to be at least 817 992. In order to

Table 1 Level of attainment of Abuja and HLTF targets

	GGHE/GGE more than 15%	GGHE/GGE less than 15%
Total health expenditure per capita more than US$ 44	Botswana, Rwanda, Zambia (3 countries)	Algeria, Angola, Cameroon, Cape Verde, Congo, Côte d'Ivoire, Equatorial Guinea, Gabon, Ghana, Guinea-Bissau, Lesotho, Mauritius, Namibia, Nigeria, Sao Tome and Principe, Senegal, Seychelles, South Africa, Swaziland, Uganda (20 countries)
Total health expenditure per capita less than US$ 44	Madagascar, Togo (2 countries)	Benin, Burkina Faso, Burundi, Central African Republic, Chad, Comoros, DRC, Eritrea, Ethiopia, Gambia, Guinea, Kenya, Liberia, Malawi, Mali, Mauritania, Mozambique, Niger, Sierra Leone, Tanzania (20 countries)

GGE General government expenditure, *GGHE* General government health expenditure
Source: [43]

address these problems, many African countries will have to increase their human health resources by at least 140% and review their institutions to train additional health workers [11]. Countries will encounter a lot of challenges in achieving this goal amongst which are; inequitable distribution of the available workforce, brain drain, low remuneration, reliance on expatriates in some countries, failure to attract and retain qualified staff especially in rural areas [11].

The relationship between public health expenditure and economic growth have been highly investigated in developing and developed countries, but these researchers do not come to a general conclusion. Hashmati [15] used the Solow growth model to investigate the relationship between health expenditure and economic growth using a sample of Organisation for Economic Co-operation and Development (OECD) countries from 1970 to 1992, he came to a conclusion that there was a positive relationship between health expenditure and economic growth. Kar and Taban [16] used co-integration method to verify the relationship between health expenditure and economic growth in Turkey; they noticed a negative relationship between health expenditure and economic growth. A similar study was carried out in Turkey by Yumuşak and Yıldırım [17] over the period 1980–2005. Using the co-integration method, it was also confirmed that there exist a negative relationship between health expenditure and economic growth. Arısoy et al. [18] used the same methodology in Turkey but over a longer time frame (1960–2005) and came to a conclusion that there is a positive relationship between health expenditure and economic growth. A similar study in Turkey by Eryiğit et al. [19] from 1950 to 2005 equally confirmed a positive relationship between health expenditure and economic growth.

By using short-run and long-run causality tests to verify the relationship between health expenditure and economic growth, researchers still find it difficult to come to a common conclusion. Cetin et al. [20] studied 15 OECD countries from 1990 to 2006 and concluded that there is no relationship between health expenditure and economic growth. Elmi and Sadeghi [21] verified this relationship using a sample of developing countries from 1990 to 2009 and made use of panel co-integration causality vector error correction model (VECM). Their results showed that there is a short-run relationship running from GDP to health expenditure and a bi-directional relationship in the long-run.

The role played by health expenditure was explored by Baldacci et al. [22], who made use of a panel of 120 developing countries between 1975 and 2000 to show that health expenditure within a particular time frame affects growth within that same time frame; lagged periods do not have any effect. His major conclusion was that, the effect of health expenditure on growth is not a stock effect but a flow.

In that same year, Bloom et al. [23] estimated a production function, which aggregates capital stock, labour and human capital (education, experience and health) to conclude that there is a positive and statistical significant effect of health expenditure on economic growth. Kwak [24], inspired by the Solow model, evaluated the impact of health expenditure on economic growth by breaking health expenditure into public and private health expenditure. Members of the Organisation for economic co-operation and Development (OECD) and developing countries make up his sample and his findings revealed that public expenditure on health had relatively higher positive effects than private health expenditure.

Comparative analysis of public and private expenditure on health was equally considered by Guissan and Arranz [25] who used least square regression and white heteroskedastic test to evaluate the impact of health expenditure on economic growth of 24 OECD countries from 1970 to 1996. The major findings of this study were that health expenditure plays an important role in enhancing the general wellbeing of individuals due to a greater share of individual consumption and overall productivity.

Empirical evidence on the relationship between health expenditure and economic growth can equally be seen in the study of Aurangzeb [26] who used an augmented Solow Growth model for Pakistan during the period 1973–2003. The Johansen co-integration technique and error correction model (ECM) were applied to show a positive and significant relationship between economic growth and health expenditure in both the short- and long-run.

David et al. [27] used a sample of 104 countries over the period 1960–1990 to examine the relationship between health and economic growth by applying non-linear two-stage least squares estimates (2SLS), and they noticed that good health had a positive and statistically significant effect on economic growth. They equally highlighted that, the life expectancy effect in growth regressions appeared to be a real labour productivity effect other than life expectancy proxied for workers experience.

Aguayo-Rico and Iris [28] used a sample of countries from four continents: 13 European countries, 12 African countries, 16 American countries, and 11 Asian countries to examine the impact of health on economic growth over the period 1970–80 and 1980–90. They made use of ordinary least square (OLS) regression and discovered that health capital had a significant effect on economic growth, especially with a variable that captures all the determinants of health. Similarly, Dreiger and Reimers [29] employed recent panel data co-integration technics using a sample of 21 OECD countries over the period 1975–2001, to investigate the relationship between health care expenditure and economic growth. They found the existence of a long-run relationship between health expenditures, GDP per capita and proxies for medical progress.

Causality and co-integration relationships between health care expenditure and economic growth in developing countries was investigated by Mila and Sadeghi from 1990 to 2009 and they found a short-run causality from GDP to health care spending but no short-run causality from health spending to economic growth. In the long-run, there is a bilateral causality and relationship between economic growth and health spending. Their findings showed that income is an important factor across developing countries in the level and growth of health care expenditure in the long-run. They equally outlined that the health-led growth hypothesis in developing countries is confirmed.

Bakare and Sanmi [30] investigated the relationship between health care expenditures and economic growth in Nigeria. They made use of the ordinary least square multiple regression as their method of analysis. Their results showed a significant and positive relationship between health care expenditure and economic growth. They recommended that Nigerian policy makers should continuously increase the percentage of budget allocated for health every year.

Ogundipe and Lawal [31] equally examined the impact of health expenditure on economic growth in Nigeria. They equally made use of the OLS. They noticed a negative effect of total health expenditure on growth which is contrary to the findings of Bakare and Sanmi [30] in Nigeria. Oni [32], equally verified the relationship between health expenditure and economic growth in Nigeria, she made use of multiple OLS regression. Her results showed that labour force productivity, total health expenditure and gross capital formation are important determinants of economic growth in Nigeria while life expectancy rate has negative impact on growth for the period covered by the study.

Mandiefe and Tieguhong [33] examined the contribution of public health investments to the economic growth of Cameroon. They employed the Vector Error Correction Model (VECM) as the econometric model used in their estimations. Annual time series data from 1988 to 2013 was used. The results of the estimations showed that public health investments contribute to the economic growth of Cameroon only in the long-run. This implies that public health investments boost economic growth in the long-run through efficient allocation of resources. Hence, they recommended that: first, the government should increase its health investment to 10 or 15% of its GDP as recommended by the African Union and WHO respectively; second, to enhance the provision of health care services by the private sector and third, to ameliorate the quality of health care services rendered by granting competitive awards to health units that render quality health care services.

From the empirical evidence above, it can be noticed that there is divergence in the effect of health expenditure on economic growth. We also notice divergence in results between developed and developing countries. These studies also show divergence in results of the direction of causality between health expenditure and economic growth in the short-run and in the long-run. All these divergence views give enough reasons to investigate the impact of health expenditure on economic growth in selected African countries. A lot of empirical studies Erdil et al. [34], Baldacci et al. [22], Bloom et al. [23] have investigated the relationship between economic growth and public health expenditure using granger causality test and tests for long-run association but no study to the best of our knowledge have investigated the relationship between health expenditure and economic development in the CEMAC sub-region.

The review above shows that there is abundant literature on the relationship between health expenditure and economic growth, this paper will contribute to literature by analysing performing a comparative analysis. This paper seeks to analyse how efficient the Abuja declaration can lead to economic growth by comparing the contribution of health care expenditure to economic growth of countries that meet the target with countries of the CEMAC sub region that do not meet the target. It is important to note that to the best of our knowledge this is the first study to empirically investigate the policy implications of the 2001 Abuja declaration in Africa. This paper will fill this gap by verifying the direction of causality between economic growth and public health expenditure and also to verify if there is any long-run association between them. In this direction, this paper attempts to respond to the following research question: what is the effect of public health expenditure on economic growth and the direction of causality between them in the short and long-run?

The rest of the paper is structured as follows. The methodology is outlined in Section II while Section III discusses the data. Section IV presents the empirical results before we conclude with Section V.

Methods

Theoretical framework

The mechanism through which public health investments affect economic growth and economic development is inscribed in the endogenous growth models. These models highlight the importance of human capital to economic growth. Neo-classical growth models explain economic growth based on savings and growth of population. Solow [35] highlighted that countries with higher savings will have higher per capita income every other thing being equal. In Solow's model, the rate of savings and population are the principal determinants of per capita income across countries [15].

Buchanan developed a theoretical model in 1965, encouraging public authorities to increase public spending on health independent of demand. This theory highlights that inefficiency in the provision of health care should be observed not by lack of supply of health care services but by reduced quality such as congestion, infrastructure, unequal distribution of staff.

Numerous models were developed to incorporate the impact of human capital on economic development. Romer [36] and Barro [37] emphasized that human capital is a very important factor in boosting economic development. Indeed, the theoretical underpinnings of Barro are still very relevant in contemporary empirical human capital literature in Africa [38]. The augmented Solow model by [5], equally emphasized on the importance of human capital on economic growth. These endogenous models do not assume human capital as a constant. Rather, they are based on the ability of human capital to influence growth in the short-run and in the long-run. The theoretical model developed in this study highlights a functional relationship between economic growth and health expenditure which is one of the components of human capital.

$$\text{Economic growth} = f(\text{health expenditure, health indicators}) + (\text{trade, household consumption})$$

Thus the following econometric relation will be estimated in this study;

$$GDP\ per\ capita_{it} = \alpha + \beta_i health\ expenditure\ per\ capita_{it} + \gamma_i household\ consumption\ per\ capita_{it} + \delta_i life\ expectancy_{it} + \omega_i labour\ force_{it} + \varphi_i trade_{it} + \varepsilon_{it}$$

Where i = individual country component

t = time component from 1995 to 2015

β_i, γ_i, δ_i, ω_i, φ_i are coefficients for our different variables and ε_{it} error term

Health as human capital is captured through expenditure on health, the life expectancy of an individual at birth and the proportion of the population that makes up the labour force of the economy. This study also highlights the importance of trade to the economy: researchers hypothesised that with a healthy human capital, production will increase through higher productivity of labour, thus, when the business climate is favourable it can create higher value added to the goods and services produced. Household consumption is equally considered because a great proportion of household income is spent on consumption in developing countries and it in turn reflects the level of domestic demand which has a multiplier effect on industry value added and thus economic growth.

This study seeks to find evidence for causality between health expenditure and economic growth and to verify the existence of co-integration, thus long-run relationships between the variables of the study. It also seeks to verify if the impact of health expenditure on economic growth is higher in African countries that achieved the Abuja Accord than those of CEMAC countries that did not. The granger causality test, panel co-integration test and panel OLS, panel fully modified ordinary least squares (FMOLS) and panel dynamic ordinary least squares (DOLS) models are employed to corroborate results and avoid the problems inherent in one method. Unit root tests are used to check if a series is stationary or not. A series is stationary if its probability distribution does not change over time. The Augmented Dickey fuller (ADF) test developed by Im et al. [39] will be used in this study. The combined Im, Pesaran and Shin(IPS) and Fisher tests would be employed.

Testing for the existence of a long-run relationship between health expenditure and economic growth often require the use of the Johansen's procedure. However, the power of the Johansen test in multivariate systems with small sample size can be severely distorted. Thus, it is imperative to combine information from time series as well as cross-section data. Panel co-integration tests are employed. Several tests were developed by Kao [40] and Pedroni [41, 42] to examine the existence of co-integration in a multivariate framework. Their proposed statistics test the null hypothesis of no co-integration versus the alternative of co-integration. Unfortunately, pooling time series has resulted in substantial losses as far as permissible heterogeneity of the individual time series are concerned. It is paramount that in the process of pooling time series as much heterogeneity as possible among individual time series should be maintained. The process of testing for co-integration among variables should permit as much heterogeneity among the individual countries of the panel as possible. If pooled results rely on homogeneous panel co-integration theory, then common slope coefficients are imposed. Pesaran and Smith [43] highlighted that if a common estimator is used due to differences among the individual countries, then health expenditure and economic growth are not cointegrated. Pedroni [41] residual test is used in this study, seven tests would be used, and four for within-dimension panel and three for between-dimension group, the within-dimension panel tests also highlights the weighted statistics.

The granger causality test will be used to verify the direction of causality between the variables of the study, with special interest being given to the direction of causality between health expenditure and economic growth. The granger causality is very sensitive with number of lags used. The test has four possible outcomes: a) neither variable Granger causes the other, b) unidirectional causality from x to y, c) unidirectional causality from y to x, d) both variables Granger cause each other.

Several methods can be used for estimation in a panel framework with co-integration, amongst which we have: OLS, Fully Modified OLS (FMOLS), dynamic OLS(DOLS), and Pooled Mean Group (PMG). Analysis of the properties (the finite sample proprieties of the OLS estimator, the t-statistic, the bias-corrected OLS estimator, and the bias-corrected t-statistic) of the OLS estimator by Chen et al. [44] analysed shows that the bias-corrected OLS estimator does not generally improve over the OLS estimator. Other alternatives such as the FMOLS estimator or the DOLS estimator can be more appropriate in co-integrated panel regressions. FMOLS is well known in conventional time series econometrics because it is believed to eliminate serial correlation in the errors and endogeneity in the regressors. However, Kao and Chiang [45] demonstrated that both the Fully Modified OLS (FMOLS) and OLS both show signs of small sample bias and that the dynamic OLS (DOLS) estimator can outperform both estimators. Three estimators with error correction will be considered in this paper: Panel OLS, Fully Modified OLS (FMOLS) and dynamic OLS (DOLS) to examine the relationship between health expenditure and economic growth empirically.

Data

In order to achieve the research objectives for this paper, Time series data from 1995 to 2015 was extracted from the World Development Indicators [46] of the World Bank. Due to high out of pocket expenditures in developing countries, the [46]) data base may not capture fully this informal expenditure, however it is the most reliable source of data for this study. This is inspired by the work of Mandiefe and Tieguhong [33] that considered GDP per capita as an indicator of economic growth. Variables on health expenditure used in this study are health expenditure per capita (logged), and life expectancy. Household consumption per capita (logged), labour force (logged) and trade are the other control variables used in this study. All these variables were extracted from the World Development Indicators and analysed using Eviews version 8. The sample for this study is made up of six (06) CEMAC member states and five other Sub-Saharan African countries that achieve the Abuja declaration, this is rather a small sample compared to Countries in Africa, thus a generalisation may lead to faulty conclusions due to the small size of the sample. Table 2 shows the two set of countries that make up our sample.

Results and discussion

Results of ADF test

We see from Table 3 below that at level with trend and intercept the variables are not stationary. This means that the properties (Mean, variance, autocorrelation) of the time series data is not constant, therefore it is imperative to differentiate and test for stationarity again. At first difference, our results show that the time series properties are now constant. We see that the properties for the time series data for CEMAC countries and other Sub-Saharan African countries that spend more than 15% of the general government expenditure on health are stationary after first difference. We therefore say they are integrated of order one. This result highlights that there is a high possibility of a long-run relationship between economic growth and health expenditure, the probability that these variables are co-integrated is high. In order to verify this, the panel Pendroni's residual co-integration test is effectuated with results provided in Table 4.

Panel Co-integration results

We see from Table 3 that the variables are co-integrated, panel co-integration test developed by Pedroni [42] is employed to empirically verify if there is co-integration.

The results from the panel co-integration test for CEMAC countries shows that for the seven within-dimension and between-dimension tests with normal statistics, five are significant as for the weighted statistics, while of the four within dimension tests two are significant. As for the other Sub-Saharan countries respecting the Abuja target, five of the within-dimension and between-dimension statistics are significant while two of the weighted within-dimension statistics are significant. We can therefore conclude from these test statistics that there is co-integration between the variables. This means that co-integration panel regression is necessary.

Table 2 Countries that make up the sample

African Countries (GGHE/GGE more than 15%)	CEMAC Countries (GGHE/GGE less than 15%)
Botswana, Rwanda, Zambia Madagascar, Togo	Cameroon, Equatorial Guinea, Gabon, Chad, Central African Republic, Democratic republic of Congo

GGE General government expenditure, *GGHE* General government health expenditure
Source: Compiled by author

Table 3 Augmented Dickey Fuller Unit root test

CEMAC	Augmented Dickey Fuller test				Decision
	Level		First Difference		
	Trend & inter	Probability	Trend & inter	Probability	
GDP per capita	11.1034	0.5201	30.7002	0.0022	I(1)
Health expenditure per capita	3.76014	0.9874	26.3409	0.0096	I(1)
Household final consumption expenditure per capita (constant 2010 US$)	7.45014	0.8265	50.1558	0.0000	I(1)
Labour force, total	16.3967	0.1737	32.0656	0.0014	I(1)
Life expectancy at birth, total (years)	3.34533	0.4564	92.7717	0.0000	I(1)
Trade (% of GDP)	5.45676	0.4567	34.4610	0.0002	I(1)
Other african countries (>15% GGE)					
GDP per capita	10.9147	0.3642	40.3050	0.0000	I(1)
Health expenditure per capita	9.44517	0.4904	35.7159	0.0001	I(1)
Household final consumption expenditure per capita (constant 2010 US$)	4.52449	0.9206	28.1659	0.0017	I(1)
Labour force, total	6.89184	0.7356	16.7841	0.0793	I(1)
Life expectancy at birth, total (years)	5.78906	0.6789	76.0157	0.0000	I(0)
Trade (% of GDP)	16.0930	0.0970	42.7828	0.0000	I(1)

Source: Computed by author

Results of the granger causality test

The objective of this test is to verify the direction of causality between the variables of our study. The null hypothesis of this test states that there is no granger causality between the variables while the alternative states that there is causality and it equally indicates if the causality is unidirectional or bidirectional. Table 5 below shows the results of the granger causality test for CEMAC region and other Sub-Saharan countries.

Our results show that for the other Sub-Saharan countries there is a unilateral causality running from GDP per capita to health expenditure, health expenditure does not granger cause GDP per capita. As for the CEMAC region there is bidirectional causality between GDP per capita and health expenditure. This means that the multiplier effect of health expenditure as GDP per capita increases in the CEMAC region is higher than that of the other countries that respect the Abuja target. This implies that, increasing expenditure on health can be a very important mechanism to increase the quality of human capital and thus economic growth, however this is not a direct mechanism where increase health expenditure will translate to economic growth, the necessary institutional framework have to be efficient and corrupt free to spur economic growth. The theoretical assumption is that economic growth and health are components of a feedback system or circle as health generates wealth and wealth generates health, but this feedback mechanism is not perfectly responsive. This is principally because other country specific proxies are important parameters to the responsiveness of increased health

Table 4 Panel co-integration test results

Pedroni Residual Cointegration Test		CEMAC(HE < 15% GGE)		Other african countries(HE > 15% GGE)	
		Statistic	Weighted Statistic	Statistic	Weighted Statistic
Within-dimension (panel)	Panel v-Statistic	5.320171***	−1.934143	−0.079408*	−1.629980
	Panel rho-Statistic	1.101854	1.583020	1.390759	2.080915
	Panel PP-Statistic	−6.944674***	−3.660656***	−4.191776***	−1.824957**
	Panel ADF-Statistic	−1.735961**	−2.395129***	−3.924845***	−2.128257***
Between-dimension (group)	Group rho-Statistic	2.199777		2.590251	
	Group PP-Statistic	−4.895312***		−2.152590***	
	Group ADF-Statistic	−1.533469*		−2.641490***	

GGE General government expenditure, *GGHE* General government health expenditure, *HE* Health Expenditure

The test statistics are normalized so that the asymptotic distribution is standard normal. *, **, *** indicate rejection of the null hypothesis of non-co-integration at the 10, 5,and 1% significance levels, based respectively on critical values of 1.281, 1.644 and 2.326

Source: Computed by author

Table 5 Results of granger causality test

Null Hypothesis:	Other african countries (PHE > 15% GGE)			CEMAC (PHE < 15% GGE)		
	Obs	F-Statistic	Prob.	Obs	F-Statistic	Prob.
Health Expenditure does not Granger Cause LGDP	95	5.78615	0.0043	114	4.83873	0.0097
GDP per capita does not Granger Cause Health expenditure		2.04999	0.1347		13.5136	6.E-06
Household consumption does not Granger Cause GDP per capita	95	2.44313	0.0926	114	2.08910	0.1287
GDP per capita does not Granger Cause Household consumption		0.08120	0.9221		0.94095	0.3934
Labour force does not Granger Cause GDP per capita	95	3.76413	0.0269	114	6.57896	0.0020
GDP per capita does not Granger Cause Labour force		0.92280	0.4011		2.30750	0.1044
Life expectancy does not Granger Cause GDP per capita	95	0.93059	0.3981	114	0.10912	0.8967
GDP per capita does not Granger Cause Life expectancy		4.01096	0.0214		0.70521	0.4962
Trade does not Granger Cause GDP per capita	95	0.99131	0.3751	114	1.37170	0.2580
GDP per capita does not Granger Cause Trade		2.40805	0.0958		2.66348	0.0742
Household consumption does not Granger Cause Health expenditure	95	0.72830	0.4856	114	0.75915	0.4705
Health expenditure does not Granger Cause Household consumption		3.50142	0.0343		0.24121	0.7861
Labour force does not Granger Cause Health expenditure	95	4.42441	0.0147	114	11.4054	3.E-05
Health expenditure does not Granger Cause labour force		0.47943	0.6207		3.48352	0.0342
Life expectancy does not Granger Cause Health expenditure	95	1.05275	0.3532	114	0.38290	0.6828
Health expenditure does not Granger Cause Life expectancy		3.56348	0.0324		1.76211	0.1765
Trade does not Granger Cause health expenditure	95	1.15248	0.3205	114	1.58412	0.2098
Health expenditure does not Granger Cause Trade		0.29987	0.7417		0.39338	0.6757
Labour force does not Granger Cause Household consumption	95	3.07424	0.0511	114	1.31762	0.2720
Cause Household consumption does not Granger Cause labour force		0.39595	0.6742		1.63605	0.1995
Life expectancy does not Granger Cause Household consumption	95	1.79853	0.1714	114	0.97617	0.3800
Household consumption does not Granger Cause life expectancy		1.67952	0.1923		6.40920	0.0023
Trade does not Granger Cause Household consumption	95	1.76174	0.1776	114	2.22514	0.1129
Household consumption does not Granger Cause Trade		0.39271	0.6764		0.34313	0.7103
Life expectancy does not Granger Cause labour force	95	0.09075	0.9133	114	0.89907	0.4099
labour force does not Granger Cause life expectancy		8.89750	0.0003		8.63025	0.0003
Trade does not Granger Cause labour force	95	0.21222	0.8092	114	4.22751	0.0171
labour force does not Granger Cause trade		0.09455	0.9099		4.14838	0.0184
Trade does not Granger Cause life expectancy	95	1.88887	0.1572	114	2.75488	0.0680
Life expectancy does not Granger Cause Trade		1.16546	0.3164		0.01484	0.9853

Source: Computed by author

expenditure on economic growth. This explains the possibility of unilateral causality from economic growth to health expenditure for other sub-Saharan countries.

Our results equally show a unilateral relationship between labour force and GDP per capita, labour force granger cause GDP per capita but GDP per capita does not granger cause labour force. This holds for both the CEMAC region and the other five Sub-Saharan countries that achieve the Abuja target.

We see from above that the high expenditure on health in the five Sub-Saharan countries achieving the Abuja declaration have a unilateral relationship running from GDP per capita to life expectancy. However as for countries in the CEMAC region there is no relationship between GDP per capita and life expectancy. This means that countries respecting the Abuja declaration turn to enjoy faster economic growth because the quality of their human capital is improved by increased health expenditure.

Our granger causality test also highlights that health expenditure granger cause household consumption but household consumption does not granger cause health expenditure, this is true for the five Sub-Saharan countries that respect the Abuja target on health expenditure. There is no relationship between health expenditure and household expenditure for CEMAC member countries. We therefore see that when the government spends more on health, the quality of human capital is higher, thus productivity increases, income per head increases leading to increase in household consumption per head.

There is a bidirectional relationship between labour force and health expenditure for CEMAC countries but a unilateral relationship running from labour force to health expenditure for the five countries achieving the Abuja declaration running from labour force to health expenditure. We equally see a unilateral relationship running from health expenditure to life expectancy for the five countries achieving the Abuja declaration, thus any increase in health expenditure will effectively leads to increase in the standard of living and life expectancy of citizens in these countries, but this is not true for CEMAC member countries.

There is a unilateral relationship running from labour force to household consumption for both groups of countries while there is a bidirectional relationship between trade and labour force in CEMAC and no relationship for the five countries achieving the Abuja declaration. This highlights the importance of labour force for the growth of CEMAC economies, therefore, productivity would greatly be enhanced if there is appropriate investment in health infrastructure and personnel in this sub-region.

Panel regression results

This paper makes use of three panel regression models: panel OLS, fully modified OLS (FMOLS), dynamic panel OLS(DOLS). The results can be seen from Table 6 below. The results shows that globally all the three models for both groups of countries have a very high explicative power with more than 96% of the variance of the dependent variable explained by the independent variables. This can be seen from the R-squared and the adjusted R square.

In this regard, it is imperative to invest in health. Drawing conclusions from the DOLS model because it is best suited for co-integrated panel regressions, we see that a unit change in health expenditure will lead to an increase in GDP per capita by 0.38% for the five Sub-Saharan African countries that respect the Abuja target while a unit change in health expenditure will lead to a 0.30% increase in GDP per capita for CEMAC countries. We see that achieving the Abuja targets leads to increase in GDP of these countries at a higher pace 0.08%than those of CEMAC countries who do not meet the target.

A negative relationship between household expenditure and GPD per capita is also noticed. It can be seen for countries of the CEMAC sub region and the five Sub-Saharan African countries that achieve the Abuja target; a unit increase in household consumption leads to a fall in GDP per capita. This relationship is significant for the five Sub-Saharan African countries that achieve the Abuja target, but not significant for countries of the CEMAC sub-region.

The results shows that labour force has a significant positive impact on GPD per capita for all the three models and for both regions with a higher effect for the five Sub-Saharan African countries that achieve the Abuja target and that invest in human capital resulting in a healthy labour force.

Life expectancy has a negative but not significant effect on GDP per capita for CEMAC countries and a negative and significant effect on GDP per capita for the five Sub-Saharan African countries that achieve the Abuja target. Trade expressed as a percentage of GDP has a positive and significant effect on GDP per capita for CEMAC countries and a negative and significant effect on GDP per capita for the five Sub-Saharan African countries that achieve the Abuja target.

Discussion of results

The main results of this study shows that expenditure on health is co-integrated with economic growth, with a significant positive impact of expenditure on health for countries in the CEMAC sub region and the five other African countries that achieve the Abuja target. But the impact is higher for countries that achieve the Abuja target than CEMAC countries that do not achieve the target. These results confirm those of Baldacci et al. [22], who used a panel of 120 developing countries to show that health expenditure have a positive and significant impact on growth over a particular timeframe. He equally highlighted that health expenditure is a flow but not a stock. These results equally corroborates with that of Bloom et al. [23] who estimated a production function and concluded that there is a statistical significant positive effect of health expenditure on economic growth.

Evidence of co-integration between health expenditure and economic growth for both sets of studies goes in line with the works of Mandiefe and Tieguhong [33] who used the vector error correction model to verify if there is any short run or long run relationship between health expenditure and economic growth. Their results showed that there is no short-run relationship but there is a long-run relationship between the variables. These results are in contradiction to the works of Ogundipe et al. [31], who examined the impact of health expenditure on economic growth in Nigeria but noticed a negative and significant impact. The result of Ogundipe et al. [31] is equally contrary to that of Bakare and Sanmi [30] in Nigeria who came to a conclusion that expenditure on health have a positive and significant effect on economic growth.

The long-run relationship between health expenditures and other proxies of health like life expectancy and economic growth in this study corroborates with that of

Table 6 Panel Regression results

GDP per capita(dependent Variable)	CEMAC (HE < 15% GGE)			Other african countries (>15% GGE)		
	Panel OLS	FMOLS	DOLS	Panel OLS	FMOLS	DOLS
Health expenditure per capita	0.304995*** (4.777252)	0.207370* (1.779484)	0.304995*** (3.269052)	0.128414*** (2.797812)	0.156037*** (2.515290)	0.381941*** (17.48346)
Household final consumption expenditure per capita (constant 2010 US$)	−0.046588 (−0.516395)	−0.220483 (−0.992283)	−0.046588 (−0.353367)	0.522384*** (7.736917)	0.478174*** (5.119678)	−0.727531*** (−28.95947)
Labour force, total	0.582692*** (2.816049)	0.670658* (1.894656)	0.582692* (1.927009)	0.165731* (1.798202)	0.090819 (0.648487)	1.379817*** (29.15916)
Life expectancy at birth, total (years)	−2.196447** (−2.587529)	−1.681589 (−1.084255)	−2.196447 (−1.770634)	0.654035*** (4.384715)	0.933523*** (3.748145)	−0.757376*** (−6.573151)
Trade (% of GDP)	0.476166*** (4.935038)	0.456469*** (3.087371)	0.476166*** (3.377024)	−0.242128*** (−2.867136)	−0.348765*** (2.994127)	−0.632140*** (−30.47444)
Constant	4.279689* (1.927313)			−0.842740 (−0.776672)		
R-squared	0.974961	0.979337	0.974961	0.987795	0.987782	0.999997
Adjusted R-squared	0.972784	0.972372	0.972784	0.986639	0.986561	0.999991
Long-run variance		0.076700	0.087998		0.012616	6.82E-07

Note: Figures in parentheses are t-stat. of the estimates; and "***", "**", and "*" indicates 1, 5, and 10% significant levels, respectively
Source: Computed by author

Dreiger and Reimers [29] who used panel co-intergration regression on a sample of 15 OECD countries to conclude that there is evidence of long-run relationship between economic growth and health expenditure and other proxies of health. Mila and Sadeghi verified the relationship between expenditure on health and economic growth by examining the direction of causality and if there is any long-run or short run relationship between health expenditure and economic growth. The results showed a short-run causality running from GDP to health expenditure, but there is a bilateral long-run relationship between economic growth and health expenditure. These findings confirm the results of our study.

Contemporary debate of how life expectancy affects economic growth is expanded in this paper, divergent views and empirical results have emerged relative to this topic; Barro [47] used a sample of 84 countries to show that there is a positive and significant impact of life expectancy on economic growth. Bloom et al. [48] used a sample of 104 countries and concluded that increase in life expectancy leads to increase in GDP by 2.65 to 4%. These authors highlight that life expectancy have a positive impact on GDP per capita. The results of this study however shows a negative and significant impact of life expectancy on economic growth, this view is supported by other empirical studies like that of Acemoglu and Johnson [49] who showed that health care inovations increases population growth and life expectancy which instead reduces per capital GDP per head. Barro and Lee [50] used new income data set to show a negative and significant impact of life expectancy on economic growth.

The important role of human capital in every economy shows that health care expenditure assures good quality labour force which is translated by increase in economic output thus increase in economic growth. The regression results shows a positive and significant impact of labour force on economic growth, Thus economies with young and qualified labour force turn to stir faster economic growth. This result contradicts results from developed countries with ageing labour force life that of Canada, with a negative impact of labour force on economic growth [51]. Empirical investigations in developing countries reveal a positive relationship between labour force participation and economic growth [52].

The positive and significant impact of health expenditure on economic growth in this study confirms empirical works of Hashmati [15]; Bakare and Sanmi [30]; Aguayo-Rico and Iris [28]; Dreger and Reimers [29] who confirm a positive and significant relationship between health expenditure and economic growth. The result from this paper and relate studies contradicts that of [53, 54], who studied a sample of 49 African countries from 1996 to 2010 to verify the impact of expenditure on education and health on economic growth. Their results showed that expenditures on education and health have a negative impact on economic growth.

Conclusion

This paper reviews the application of the Abuja declaration of 2001, 15 years after signatories to this declaration accepted to allocate 15% of government expenditure on health. As of 2013 only five African countries had more than 15% of government expenditure allocated to the health sector. This paper compares these five countries with countries the CEMAC region where no country meets the required target. Co-integration tests, granger causality and panel data co-integration analysis were conducted to reveal interesting results.

Results from the study shows that there is co-integration between health expenditures, proxies of health and economic growth; therefore there is a long-run relationship between the variables of our study for both CEMAC countries and the five other countries that achieved the Abuja declaration. Bi-directional causality between economic growth and health expenditure was noticed for CEMAC countries while countries achieving the Abuja declaration portrayed a unilateral causality running from economic growth to health expenditure. This therefore means that income is an important element in explaining healthcare expenditure, thus increase in general level of income can stimulate increase in health expenditure [55]. This highlights the potential of the impact of a healthy labour force for CEMAC region on economic growth.

It is important to acknowledge that pumping money into the health sector does not automatically lead to economic growth, other accommodating conditions have to be in place for optimal response of health expenditure. Governance related issues should assure that health investments are directed to improving health standard of the population. Economic growth may increase by other country specific policies, not necessarily health expenditure, however this study underscores the importance of efficient health expenditure as a potential driver of economic growth. Potential positive benefits can quickly be felt when the governance framework of countries are transparent in financial management.

Indeed, from the results of this study, people who live in countries that spend more than 15% of their government expenditure turn to live longer than those living in countries of the CEMAC region that spend less than 15% of their government expenditure on the health sector. Therefore, it could be argued that higher expenditures on health may partly explain some reductions in the cases of untimely deaths due to lack of appropriate medical care. Increase in health expenditure leads to higher economic growth from this study, but this increase is not proportionate for CEMAC countries as compared to the five other African countries that achieve the Abuja declaration. Countries that achieve this declaration enjoy a higher increase in economic growth when a unit of expenditure on health is added than the CEMAC countries. Therefore a unit increase in expenditure on health would can potentially lead to an additional 0.08% increase in economic growth for countries that increase expenditure on health especially when they take necessary conditions to meet intended development objectives.

Policy implication

This study outlines the importance of achieving the Abuja declaration and goes further to extend literature on the possible positive impact of increasing health expenditure on economic growth. From the results acquired, the following policy implications are pertinent for African countries.

This study shows that health expenditure is a fundamental determinant of economic growth of every nation and that increasing expenditure on health leads to higher growth rates. African countries should endeavor to meet and surpass the target of the Abuja declaration of 2001. One possible measure that could be taken to raise funds to meet this target could be by increasing taxes on products such as cigarettes and other products of ostentation and rechanneling the extra revenue generated to investment in healthcare. One of the important drawbacks to funding of Sub-Saharan countries is poor governance, thus measures to assure a fluid target based expenditure is imperative. In countries where poor governance is alarming, as the World Bank states, increasing public spending both from external donors and the government does not necessarily lead to the desired development outcomes [11]. Performance based financing can be an important mechanism that potential donors and government agencies can use. It is also believed to increase transparency and accountability in achieving targets [56]. Meessen et al. [56] also argues that it improves the allocative efficiency of resources especially in low-income developing countries where resources are quite limited. Thus an efficient financing mechanism with greater emphasis on the processes leading to the performance goal.

Funding

Funding for this paper was provided by the Technical Training Research Centre for Development (TTRECED-Cameroon), TTRECED provided funds for all aspects of the paper.

Authors' contributions

SMP conceived the idea of the paper, wrote and did data analysis. JCT read through, he equally contributed to the discussion of the paper. Both authors read and approved the final manuscript.

Competing interests

I come through this present note to highlight that there is no conflict of interest and both authors accept the submission of this paper.

References

1. Romer PM. Endogenous Technological Change. J Polit Econ. 1990;98(5):S71–S102.
2. World Health Organisation. Make every mother and child count. The World Health Report. 2005.
3. Riley G, 2012, Economic Growth - The Role of Human & Social Capital, Competition & Innovation. http://www.tutor2u.net/economics/revisionnotes/a2-macro-economic-growth-capital.html. Accessed 16 Apr 2014.
4. Lucas R. On the Mechanics of Economic Development. J Monet Econ. 1988; 22(1):3–42.
5. Mankiw G, Romer D, Weil D. A contribution on the Empirics of Economic Growth. Q J Econ. 1992;107:407–37.
6. Mushkin S. Health as an Investment. J Polit Econ. 1962;70(5):129–57.
7. Bloom DE, Canning D, PiaMalaney. Demographic Change and Economic Growth in Asia. Suppl Popul Dev Rev. 2000;26:257–90.
8. Cole MA, Neumayer E. The impact of poor health on total factor productivity. J Dev Stud. 2006;42(6):918–38.
9. Newhouse JP. Medical Care Costs: How Much Welfare Loss? J Econ Perspect. 1992;6(3):3–21.
10. Fuchs V. Economics, Values, and Healthcare Reform. Am Econ Rev. 1996; 86(1):1–24.
11. World Health Organisation. Research for universal health coverage. The world health report 2013. 2013.
12. Global Health Expenditure Database [online database]. World Health Organization. http://apps.who.int/nha/database
13. Series steering group. Mobilisingfiancial resources for maternal health. 2006.
14. Nabyonga Orem et al. 2010. Abolition of user fees: the Uganda paradox. Health Policy and Planning 2011;26(2):ii41–ii51.
15. Hashmati A. On the causality between GDP and Health Care Expenditure in Augmented Solow Growth Model. Stockholm: Department of Economic Statistics Stockholm school of Economics; 2001.
16. Kar M, Taban S. The impacts of the disaggregated public expenditure on economic growth. Ankara University Faculty of Political Science. 2003;53(3): 145–69.
17. Yumuşak IG, D Yıldırım C. An econometric examination over the relation between health expenditure and economic growth. J Knowl Econ Knowl Manage. 2009;IV:57–70.
18. Arısoy İ, Ünlükaplan İ, Ergen Z. The relationship between social expenditures and economic growth: a dynamic analysis intended for 1960–2005 period of the Turkish economy. MaliyeDergisi. 2010;158:398–421.
19. Eryiğit SB, Eryiğit KY, Selen U. The long-run linkages between education, health and defence expenditures and economic growth: evidence from Turkey. Def Peace Econ. 2012;23(6):559–74.
20. Cetin M, Ecevit E, Sağlıkharcamalarınınekonomikbüyümeüzerindekietkisi. OECD ülkeleriüzerinebir panel regresyonanalizi. DoğuşÜniversitesiDergisi. 2010;11(2):166–82.
21. Elmi ZM, Sadeghi S. Health care expenditures and economic growth in developing countries: panel co-integration and causality. Middle-East J Sci Res. 2012;12(1):88–91.
22. Baldacci E, Clements B, Gupta S, Cui Q. Social Spending, Human Capital, and Growth in Developing Countries: Implications for Achieving the MDGs, IMF Working Paper No. 04/217. 2004.
23. Bloom DE, Canning D, Sevilla J. The Effect of Health on Economic Growth: A Production Function Approach. World Dev. 2004;32:1–13.
24. Kwak R. The Relative Role of Public and Private Health Expenditure for Economic Growth: A Solow Growth Model Expansion. Senior Honors Theses. 2009.
25. Guissan MC, Arranz M. Econometric models of private and public health expenditure in OECD countries. Q Rev Econ Finance. 2003;44(2):296–320.

26. Aurangzeb. Relationship Between Health Expenditure and GDP in an Augmented Solow Growth Model for Pakistan: An Application of Cointegration and Error Correction Modeling. Lahore J Econ. 2001;8(2):1–18.
27. David EB, David C, Jaypee S. The Effect of Health on Economic Growth: A Production Function Approach. World Dev J Great Brit. 2004;32(1):1–13.
28. Aguayo-Rico A, Irish A. Empirical Evidence of the Impact of Health on Economic Growth. Issues Pol Econ. 2005;25:112–114.
29. Dreiger C, Reimers H. Health Care Expenditures in OECD Countries: A Panel Unit Roots and Cointegration Analysis, Discussion Paper Series, IZA DP No. 1469. 2005.
30. Bakare AS, Sanmi O. Health Care Expenditure and Economic Growth in Nigeria: An Empirical Study. J Emerging Trends Econ Manage Sci. 2011; 2(2):83–7.
31. Ogundipe MA, Lawal NA. Health Expenditure and Nigerian Economic Growth. Eur J Econ, Finance Adm Sci. 2011;30:125–129.
32. Oni LB. Analysis of the Growth Impact of Health Expenditure in Nigeria. J Econ Finance (JEF). 2014;3(1):77–84.
33. Mandiefe SP, Tieguhong JC. Contribution of Public Health Investments to the Economic Growth of Cameroon. Bus Eco J. 2015;6:189. doi:10.4172/2151-6219.1000189.
34. E. Erdil, I. H. Yetkiner. A panel data approach for income-health causality, The Economics of Health Reforms (Eds. Yfantopoulos, J. N.), ISBN: 960-88672-0-7, Chapter 38, 701–724, 2009.
35. Solow R. A contribution to the theory of economic growth. Q J Econ. 1956; 70(1):65–94.
36. Romer PM. Increasing Returns and Long run Growth. J Polit Econ. 1986; 94(5):1002–37.
37. Barro RJ. Economic Growth in a Cross Section of Countries. Q J Econ. 1991; 106(2):407–43.
38. Ssozi J, Asongu SA. The Effects of Remittances on Output per Worker in Sub-Saharan Africa: A Production Function Approach. 2015. South African Journal of Economics. http://onlinelibrary.wiley.com/doi/10.1111/saje.12100/abstract?userIsAuthenticated=false&deniedAccessCustomisedMessage=.
39. Im K, Pesaran M, Shin Y. Testing for Unit Roots in Heterogeneous Panels. J Econ. 2003;115:53–74.
40. Kao, C. Spurious Regression and Residual-Based Tests for Cointegration in Panel Data. J Econometrics. 1999;90:1–44.
41. Pedroni, P. Panel Cointegration; Asymptotic and Finite Sample Properties of Pooled Time Series Tests, with an Application to the PPP Hypothesis: New Results. Working Paper, Indiana University; 1997
42. Pedroni P. Critical Values for Cointegration Test in Heterogeneous Panels with Multiple Regressors. Oxf Bull Econ Stat. 1999;61:653–70
43. Pesaran MH, Smith R. Estimating long-run relationships from dynamic heterogeneous panels. J Econ. 1995;68:79–113.
44. Chen W, Clarke JA, Roy N. Health and wealth: Short panel Granger causality tests for developing countries. J Int Trade Econ Dev. 2014;23(6):755–84.
45. Kao C, Chiang MH. On the estimation and inference of a cointegrated regression in panel data. Adv Econ. 2000;15:179–222.
46. World Bank. World Development Indicators 2016. Washington, DC: © World Bank; 2016. https://openknowledge.worldbank.org/handle/10986/23969 License: CC BY 3.0 IGO.
47. Barro RJ. The Determinants of Economic Growth: A Cross-Country Empirical Study. Cambridge: MIT Press; 1996.
48. Bloom DE, Canning D, Graham B. Health, Longevity, and Lifecycle Savings. CMH Working Group Paper No. WG1: 9, 2001.
49. Acemoglu D, and Johnson S. "Disease and Development: The Effect of Life Expectancy on Economic Growth", Journal of Political Economy. 2007;115(6): 925–985.
50. Barro RJ, Lee JW. A New Data Set of Educational Attainment in the World, 1950-2010, NBER Working Paper 15902. 2010.
51. Spencer S, Seldon A. 'Immigration', Blair's Britain 1997–2007. Cambridge: Cambridge University Press; 2007.
52. Duval R, Eris M, Furceri D. Labour Force Participation Hysteresis in Industrial Countries: Evidence and Causes, Working Paper, OECD Economics Department. 2010.
53. Eggoh J, Houeninvo H, Sossou G-A. Education, Health and Economic Growth in African Countries. J Econ Dev. 2015;40(1):93–111.
54. Hilaire EJ, Gilles AS. Education, health and economic growth in developing countries. J Econ Dev. 2015;40:93–111.
55. Besir S. Healthcare Expenditure and Economic Growth in Developing Countries. Advances in Economics and Business. 2016;4(2):76-86 doi:10.13189/aeb.2016.040202
56. Meessen B, Hercot D, Noirhomme M , Ridde V, Tibouti A, Tashobya CK et al. Removing user fees in the health sector: a review of policy processes in six sub-Saharan African countries, Health Policy and Planning, 2011;26(2):ii16-ii29

2

Analysis of multi drug resistant tuberculosis (MDR-TB) financial protection policy: MDR-TB health insurance schemes, in Chhattisgarh state, India

Debashish Kundu[1*], Nandini Sharma[2], Sarabjit Chadha[1], Samia Laokri[3], George Awungafac[4], Lai Jiang[5] and Miqdad Asaria[6]

Abstract

Introduction: There are significant financial barriers to access treatment for multi drug resistant tuberculosis (MDR-TB) in India. To address these challenges, Chhattisgarh state in India has established a MDR-TB financial protection policy by creating MDR-TB benefit packages as part of the universal health insurance scheme that the state has rolled out in their effort towards attaining Universal Health Coverage for all its residents. In these schemes the state purchases health insurance against set packages of services from third party health insurance agencies on behalf of all its residents. Provider payment reform by strategic purchasing through output based payments (lump sum fee is reimbursed as per the MDR-TB benefit package rates) to the providers – both public and private health facilities empanelled under the insurance scheme was the key intervention.

Aim: To understand the implementation gap between policy and practice of the benefit packages with respect to equity in utilization of package claims by the poor patients in public and private sector.

Methods: Data from primary health insurance claims from January 2013 to December 2015, were analysed using an extension of 'Kingdon's multiple streams for policy implementation framework' to explain the implementation gap between policy and practice of the MDR-TB benefit packages.

Results: The total number of claims for MDR-TB benefit packages increased over the study period mainly from poor patients treated in public facilities, particularly for the pre-treatment evaluation and hospital stay packages. Variations and inequities in utilizing the packages were observed between poor and non-poor beneficiaries in public and private sector. Private providers participation in the new MDR-TB financial protection mechanism through the universal health insurance scheme was observed to be much lower than might be expected given their share of healthcare provision overall in India.

Conclusion: Our findings suggest that there may be an implementation gap due to weak coupling between the problem and the policy streams, reflecting weak coordination between state nodal agency and the state TB department. There is a pressing need to build strong institutional capacity of the public and private sector for improving service delivery to MDR-TB patients through this new health insurance mechanism.

Keywords: Multi-drug resistant tuberculosis, Health insurance, RSBY, Universal health coverage, Financial protection policy, Inequity, Kingdon's multiple streams, Implementation, Poor, India

* Correspondence: debashishkundu@yahoo.com;
debashish.kundu@theunion.org
[1]International Union Against Tuberculosis and Lung Disease (The Union), South-East Asia Office, C-6, Qutub Institutional Area, New Delhi 110016, India
Full list of author information is available at the end of the article

Introduction

Public subsidies that target the poor and vulnerable are widely used in developing countries to increase their access to health care. Targeted subsidies can be provided through health insurance premiums, health equity funds, vouchers, conditional cash transfers; and are demand side health financing mechanisms for achieving universal health coverage (UHC) [1–3]. In many high and middle income countries, insurance based models are the main instruments used to ensure financial protection for the entire population, achieved through financial reforms in revenue collection, pooling and purchasing [4]. Such health financing reforms improve equity in the distribution of resources, leading to improvements in equity in utilization of services and financial protection [4] by ensuring robust implementation of the insurance schemes, acting as a vehicle for achieving universal health coverage (UHC).

In India, health system is pluralistic with asymmetric healthcare distributive network across public and private sector [5], with 66% of hospitals and 80% of ambulatory care provided by the private sector [6]. The high user fees charged by these private providers combined with low health insurance penetration have led to high levels of out-of-pocket (OOP) expenditure. These high OOP expenditures are particularly evident in the diagnosis and treatment of chronic diseases, often resulting in catastrophic health expenditure for poorer patients [5] thereby jeopardising India's progress towards UHC. One such chronic disease disproportionately prevalent amongst the poor is Tuberculosis (TB) [7]. Looking at financial risk protection in relation to TB can therefore highlight important general lessons to inform decisions toward effective policy-making in the context of achieving UHC [8].

The World Health Organization recommends addressing poverty in national TB control programmes by promoting equity and pro-poor policies in disease prevention and control activities [9]. The high cost of treatment and the need to take medication over a long period of time, especially for multi-drug resistant TB (MDR-TB) patients, makes treatment less accessible for the poor [10]. Moreover, implementation gap previously shown in the literature appeared to lead to increased risk of incurring catastrophic expenditure due to TB [11]. In India, 84,000 multidrug-resistant (MDR)-TB cases are estimated to emerge annually among notified pulmonary TB cases [12], while a similar volume of cases are expected to be managed by the private sector but remain un-notified [13]. MDR-TB is forecasted to increase by 12% among incident TB cases in India, and additional control efforts are urgently required, beyond diagnosis and treatment of MDR-TB [14], to prevent increasing risk of incurring catastrophic expenditure due to MDR-TB. Disease burden due to TB in India is 3.27% (2.58% - 4.21%) of total DALY's [15], which can be averted by expansion and robust implementation of tuberculosis services that are cost-effective in high-burden countries [16]. There is need to have greater emphasis on innovative patient support mechanism, which among many includes prevention of catastrophic health expenditure due to MDR-TB through health insurance mechanism [13].

Kingdon's agenda-setting framework, suggests that when conditions in three streams: Problem, Politics and Policy, come together to bring an issue into the policy agenda, a window of opportunity arises for policy change [17]. The issue has to be seen to address a clearly defined problem (in the problem stream) and then a policy solution to the problem has to be available (in the policy stream) [18]. The political environment has to be favourable in addressing the problem (in the political stream). Such coupling creates an open policy window [17, 18]. In Chhattisgarh, a "tribal" state (as notified by the Government of India) in central India, similar coupling of Kingdon's three streams for agenda setting had taken place that had led to the emergence of a financial risk protection policy for MDR-TB patients in the state. This is described as follows:

Policy stream

In 2011, the Programmatic Management of Drug Resistant (PMDT) programme was launched in the State of Chhattisgarh as per the national PMDT policy expansion vision. The state attained full coverage for treating the MDR-TB 'free of cost' with centres established to identify Drug Resistant (DR) -TB in all the medical colleges of the state as of December 2012. As per the national PMDT policy, all MDR-TB patients have to undergo pre-treatment evaluations. The drug resistant TB patient should be hospitalized at the DR-TB Centre for a period of seven days to undergo pre-treatment evaluation for identifying those patients who are at a greater risk of adverse effects and to establish a baseline for monitoring, as the drugs for management of MDR-TB patients (2nd line anti-tuberculosis drugs) are toxic in nature [19]. Drug Resistant-TB centre is ideally established in the medical college hospital, a tertiary level health centre for pre-treatment evaluation, treatment initiation and management of side effects. During the same year, 2012, TB was made a notifiable disease by the Government of India [20].

Problem stream

Drug-resistant TB is known to be fatal and is estimated to be 100 times more costlier to treat [21] than cases of drug-sensitive TB [22]. In the private sector, out of pocket (OOP) health expenditure by a MDR-TB patient due to user fees for staying in the hospital, laboratory investigations on account of pre-treatment and follow-up evaluations are estimated to be eighty times, three times and four times more expensive than in the public sector respectively. This will often force poorer households to incur catastrophic health expenditure leading to impoverishment if not protected by a financial protection mechanism [13]. User fees for laboratory investigations (both pre-treatment and follow-up investigations) can be catastrophic for a poor MDR-TB patient even in the public sector [13]. OOP health expenditure accruing to any household member with TB that exceeds one-fifth (20%) of household annual income is considered to be catastrophic for that household [23].

Politics stream

The government of Chhattisgarh, envisages achieving UHC by improving the affordability, availability and accessibility of quality health care to every resident of the state [24]. To this end, the state had initiated universal health insurance scheme (UHIS) after announcement of this initiative from the Chief Minister, political head of the government in the state, in 2012. The UHIS provides health insurance coverage and protection to all people to fund their medical treatment on voluntary and hospitalization basis. It is managed by the National Health Insurance Programme, known as the "Rashtriya Swasthya Bima Yojana (RSBY)" Or social security scheme for a family with a maximum 5 household (HH) members who either live below the poverty line (BPL) or are members of specific categories of unorganized workers. These categories include - Mahatma Gandhi National Rural Employment Guarantee Act (MGNREGA) workers, Building and Other Construction (BOC) workers, Beedi workers, Domestic workers, Licensed Railway Porters, Street Vendors, Sanitation Workers, Mine Workers, Rickshaw Pullers, Rag Pickers, Auto and Taxi Drivers [25]. In addition to this Chhattisgarh state also provides the "Mukhyamantri Swasthya Bima Yojana (MSBY)" Or Chief Minister's Health Insurance Scheme for every HH in the state, if not covered by RSBY. MSBY is also limited to a maximum 5 HH members, and consists mainly of HH who are above the poverty line (APL) [Fig. 1]. Chhattisgarh is the first state in the country to initiate the UHIS which provides health insurance coverage to all state residents to fund their medical treatment.

Window of opportunity (coupling of problem and politics stream) for emergence of MDR-TB financial protection policy

Leveraging the opportunity for inter-sectoral collaboration, the State Tuberculosis (TB) Control Programme in Chhattisgarh facilitated partnership with RSBY and MSBY for Multi Drug Resistant TB (MDR-TB) patients in the year 2012 through creation of MDR-TB benefit packages for absorbing user fees for all pre-treatment evaluations, admissions, follow-up evaluations, ancillary drugs and nutritional support across all RSBY and MSBY empanelled network hospitals (both private and public) in the state [13]. The MDR-TB benefit packages are [Table 1]: 1) MDR-TB pre-treatment evaluation, 2) MDR-TB follow-up evaluation, and 3) MDR-TB hospital stay; an innovative financial protection mechanism to absorb OOP expenses incurred by MDR-TB patients from diagnosis to treatment completion across the public and private sector [13]. Overall objectives for establishing the MDR-TB benefits packages as a financial protection policy were to achieve equity in utilization of

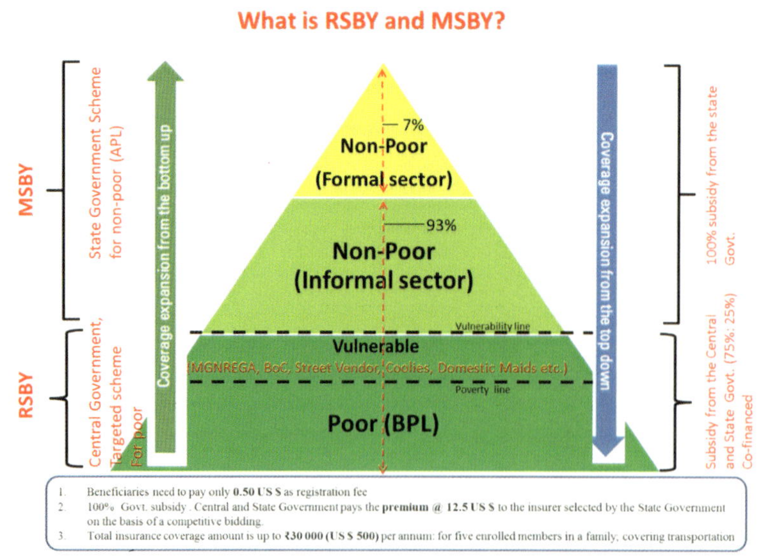

Fig. 1 Universal Health Insurance Scheme (UHIS) as managed by RSBY and MSBY (Developed from *Cotlear* et al., *2015)*

Table 1 Details of the innovative Rashtriya Swasthya Bima Yojna (RSBY) and Mukhyamantri Swasthya Bima Yojna (MSBY) MDR-TB benefit packages

MDR-TB benefit package name	Package details	Package Rate	Number of times/days claims can be processed (Package Cap)
Pre-treatment evaluations after diagnosis of MDR-TB	Chest X-ray, relevant haematological and biochemical tests: complete blood count (CBC), liver function tests (LFT), thyroid function tests (TFT), blood urea nitrogen (BUN), creatinine, urine (routine & micro-scopic), urinary pregnancy tests (UPT)	4000 (US$ 67[a])	Once
Follow-up evaluation	Chest X-ray, relevant haematological and biochemical tests: CBC, LFT, BUN, creatinine, urine (routine & microscopic)	3300 (US$ 55)	Maximum five times for creatinine and all other tests for maximum of twice
Hospital stay	Bed charges, doctors' consultation fees and any other additional/ ancillary drugs	5600 (US$ 93 @ US$ 13/ day)	Maximum 7 days' stay on pro-rota basis

MDR-TB multidrug-resistant tuberculosis

the packages in the sense that patients with equal needs should receive the benefit of the packages irrespective of their income (between poor and non-poor) [26]. Provider payment financial reform through fee for service was established by the creation of three MDR-TB benefit packages. Also, as per the insurance policy, the pre-treatment and follow-up packages are to be co-used with the hospital stay package, as utilization of the RSBY and MSBY health insurance scheme package for MDR-TB is based on hospitalization. The key financial reform steps taken for the MDR-TB patients in Chhattisgarh were:

1. Creation of RSBY and MSBY benefit packages [13] targeting the MDR-TB patients and integrating these packages with the list of other RSBY and MSBY disease packages in Chhattisgarh.
2. Piggy-backing on the already existing national health insurance programme - RSBY.
3. Contracting of the third party insurance agency (TPA) by the State Nodal Agency, to obtain pre-defined health services for the MDR-TB patients.

Initial experience with such a collaboration between Revised National TB Control Programme (RNTCP) and the UHIS through creation of benefit packages for patients with MDR-TB shows that such partnership can be set up and can in principle act to reduce OOP expenditure [13]. Previous studies have highlighted the mechanism emphasizing collaboration between RNTCP and health insurance schemes (RSBY and MSBY) for MDR-TB patients [13]. Exclusionary process that operates at all steps of implementation of the RSBY scheme due to issues of awareness, enrolment, utilization, delay in reimbursements to providers and fraudulent practices have been widely studied [27–31]. However, none of the existing studies have reported on the variation and inequities in utilization for specific benefits packages within the insurance scheme. Therefore, the aim of this study is to whether or not the implementation of the MDR-TB health insurance packages is effective in –

a. Benefitting those who needs them most, especially by equitable utilization of the packages by the poorest 20% quintile population [32];
b. Improving the private sector involvement in RNTCP.

By addressing these questions new insights will be gained on implementation of RSBY and MSBY MDR-TB benefit packages for both poor and non-poor MDR-TB patients, paving efficient and feasible ways to support progress towards India's journey to UHC.

Methods

Setting

The state of Chhattisgarh in central India (population 28 million, having 27 districts) has 80% of the population living in rural areas and 30% are considered "tribal". Out of 29 states in India, Chhattisgarh is the 10th largest and 17th most populated state in the country. Backward class of population, namely Scheduled Tribes (ST) and Scheduled Castes (SC), constitute 31.8% and 12% of the state's population respectively which belong to the most disadvantaged socio-economic groups in India [33]. The SC people are the one who were previously 'untouchables' and ST are community of people who lived in tribal areas (mainly forest) and are also known as 'Adivasis' [34]. Together the ST and SC population constitute 43% of the total population in the state [35] and have been traditionally marginalized. The state is also an insurgency hit (Left Wing Extremism or LWE) and poorest state in India, with 47.9% of people is living BPL, followed by 46.7% in Manipur and 45.9% in Odhisa. Of all states in India, the states of Chhattisgarh, Manipur, Odhisa, Madhya Pradesh, Jharkhand, Bihar and Assam figure among the poorest states where over 40% of people are below poverty line [36]. 24 out of 27 districts in Chhattisgarh are backward districts [37] with only three non-backward or economically rich districts. As per the National Sample Survey Organization (NSSO) nationwide household consumer expenditure survey, monthly per capita consumption expenditure (MPCE) is estimated to be below 10 US$ (600) per month in Chhattisgarh [38]. Besides, such socio-demographic characteristics, the state has higher number of health facilities in public sector than in private sector [39], and hardly any private health facilities in the tribal areas. Most of the RSBY and MSBY empanelled private health facilities are located in the urban areas [39].

How RSBY and MSBY health insurance schemes work?

Under the schemes each enrolled family is provided with a bio-metric smart card for paperless, cashless and portable transactions through smart cards. Each family is provided with a health insurance benefit of 500 US$ per family per annum on a family floater basis (upto 5 members in a family) and coverage of financial costs of the hospitalization expense. Hospitalization can be for both medical and surgical procedures (as per the predefined RSBY and MSBY package list for medical and surgical procedures). Conditions that are treated at home, congenital external diseases, drugs and alcohol induced illness, vaccination, war, nuclear invasion, suicide, naturopathy, Ayurveda, Unani and Siddha are excluded from the schemes (24). A key feature of RSBY health insurance scheme is portability - A beneficiary who has been enrolled in a particular district can use the smart card in any RSBY empanelled hospital across India. This makes the scheme truly unique and beneficial to the poor families who migrate from one place to the other [13, 25]. Beneficiaries of the scheme get cash less treatment in the government and private health institutions empanelled under the RSBY and MSBY as per their choice within the state and country. Additionally, transport expenses of ~ 2 US$ per hospitalization is paid to the beneficiary subject to a maximum of ~ 17 US$ per year per family. The beneficiaries need to pay only 0.5 US$ as registration fee for a year while the Central and State Government pays the fixed premium (12.5 US$) as per their sharing ratio (between Centre and State, 75:25 for RSBY, 0:100 for MSBY) to the private insurer selected by the state government on the basis of a competitive bidding [Fig. 1].

In India, 93% of workforce is in informal sector [18] where there is no formal employee and employer relationship arrangements, having both poor and non-poor [Fig. 1]. RSBY scheme for social security for the poor receives complete subsidy from the central and state Government. However, in case of MSBY, 100% subsidy is provided by the State Government of Chhattisgarh for non-poor [Fig. 1]. In every state, the State Government sets up a State Nodal Agency (SNA) that is responsible for implementing, monitoring supervision and part-financing of the scheme by coordinating with a private insurance company, hospital, district authorities and other local stake holders. Therefore the scheme has been designed as a business model, an organization with nexus of contracts or institutions, for the social sector with incentives built-in for each stakeholder [Fig. 2]. Design of this business model can be linked to the function of the health financing systems [4], wherein Central and State Governments collect revenue from the general tax system, which is pooled at the state level by the RSBY and MSBY state nodal agency to pay premiums to the selected private insurance company. The private insurance company reimburses the claims of the benefit packages from both private (accessed mainly by non-poor: APL) and public health facilities (accessed mainly by poor: BPL and unorganized workers) [Fig. 2]. So there is transfer of pooled resources to public and private service providers for giving fee for service [40] to the beneficiaries by the purchasers - state nodal agency and the insurance company, with weak regulation by the Government. Strategic purchasing through output based payments (a lump sum fee is reimbursed as per the MDR-TB package rates) to the providers (public or private health facilities empanelled under the schemes) by the third party health insurance agency (TPA) is the provider payment method used in RSBY and MSBY Universal Health Insurance Scheme. This business model design is seen as conducive both in terms of expansion of the scheme as well as for its long run sustainability [Fig. 2].

Data collection

Primary claims data on the uptake of 'RSBY and MSBY MDR-TB' packages under the routine national health insurance programme setting were collected from the server, accessible at the RSBY and MSBY State Nodal Agency of Directorate of Health Services, Raipur, from January 2013 to December 2015. This information was shared electronically with the principal investigator by the State Nodal Agency.

Data variables

The pre-defined data variables on patient code, package name, hospital name, hospital type (Public or Private), registration and discharge descriptions, scheme code (RSBY or MSBY), patient characteristics – age, sex, APL, BPL, unorganized worker, district and claim status, were collected.

Data processing and analysis

In total, 1159 records were checked by going through to identify any errors. 40 records for the Nuapada district

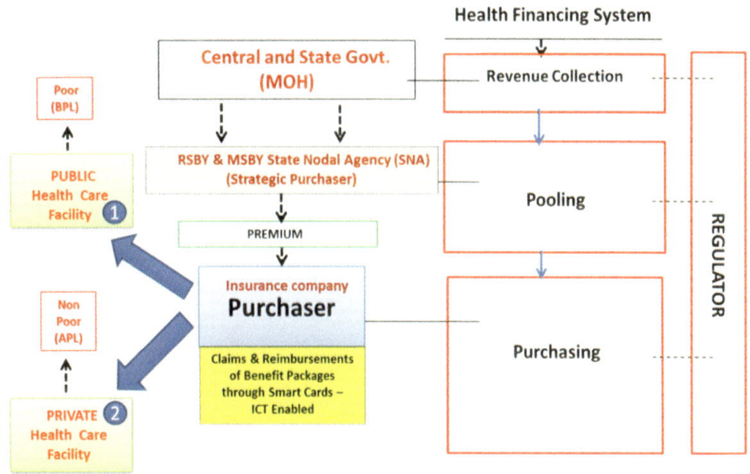

Fig. 2 RSBY and MSBY, a business model, an organization as a nexus of contracts/ institutions (Developed from Kutzin J. Health financing for universal coverage and health system performance: concepts and implications for policy, Bulletin of World Health Organization, 2013;91(8): 602–11; and concept of organization as a nexus of contracts by Bruno Messen, Institute of Tropical Medicine, Antwerp. 2016)

were excluded as this district in not part of Chhattisgarh state. Non-MDR-TB cases were also excluded from the data analysis. A final clean dataset was imported to Epi-Info version 7.1.5.2 software (CDC Atlanta, USA) for analysis. We performed descriptive statistics analysis using means, median and proportions. Where comparisons were needed, we used the Chi square test with α set at 5%. Trends in the utilization of the packages from 2013 to 2015 in public and private sectors were derived to bring out and compare differences in utilization. An extension of Kingdon's Multiple Streams for policy implementation framework [41] was applied to understand the implementation gap in the financial risk protection policy for MDR-TB patients.

Results

Utilisation of claims in public vs private sector

A total of 1159 RSBY and MSBY MDR-TB package claims were utilized by the beneficiaries [median age 43 years (IQR 30.5–55.5)], 67% claims from males, between 2013 to 2015. A total of 1044 (90.1%) claims were utilized by the beneficiaries in public health facilities as compared to 115 (9.9%) claims utilization in the private sector [Table 2]. 627 (54%), 278 (24%) and 254 (22%) claims were respectively processed under MDR-TB pre-treatment evaluation package, MDR-TB hospital stay package and MDR-TB follow-up evaluation package [Table 3]. Trends in utilization of MDR-TB hospital stay and follow-up evaluation packages showed better utilization of claims from the public sector [Figs. 3 and 4]. No claims were utilized under the MDR-TB follow up evaluation package from the private sector [Fig. 4].

Utilisation of claims by poor vs non-poor beneficiaries

Pooled (RSBY and MSBY) data on claims utilization of MDR-TB pre-treatment evaluation package showed that in the public sector, poor beneficiaries utilized five times more claims in 2015 than in 2013 mostly from the backward districts [Fig. 5]. In the private sector, non-poor beneficiaries utilized nineteen times more claims in the year 2015 compared to 2013 [Fig. 6]. Claims were utilized by non-poor fourteen times more in 2015 than in 2013 from non-backward or economically rich districts

Table 2 Key characteristics of the beneficiaries of all MDR-TB Packages (2013–2015)

Key Characteristics	RSBY $N = 911$ (%)	MSBY $N = 248$ (%)	Total $n = 1159$ (%)
1. Age			
< 15	46 (5.1)	14 (5.7)	60 (5.2)
15–34	239 (26.2)	80 (32.3)	319 (27.5)
35–54	373 (49.9)	91 (36.7)	464 (40.0)
55^{+}	253 (27.8)	63 (25.4)	316 (27.3)
2. Sex			
Male	624 (68.5)	154 (62.1)	778 (67.1)
Female	287 (31.5)	94 (37.9)	381 (32.9)
3. Socio-economic status			
Poor (1 + 2):	826 (90.7)	64 (25.8)	890 (76.8)
Non Poor (APL)	85 (9.3)	184 (74.2)	269 (23.2)
4. No. of claims utilized in public and private health facilities by the beneficiaries			
Public	822 (90.2)	222 (89.5)	1044 (90.1)
Private	89 (9.8)	26 (10.5)	115 (9.9)

Table 3 Claim utilization status by poor and non-poor beneficiaries in public and private sector as per the MDR-TB package types (2013–15)

Type of MDR-TB Package	Claim Utilization		
	Poor – N (%)	Non-Poor – N (%)	Total, n = 1159 (%)
a) MDR-TB Pre-treatment evaluation package utilization in			
Public	433 (87.6)	110 (82.7)	543
Private	61 (12.4)	23 (17.3)	84
Total	494 (100)	133 (100)	627 (54)
b) MDR-TB hospital stay package utilization in:			
Public	185 (88.9)	62 (88.6)	247
Private	23 (11.1)	8 (11.4)	31
Total	208 (100)	70 (100)	278 (24)
c) MDR-TB follow-up evaluation utilization in:			
Public	188 (100)	66 (100)	254
Private	0	0	0
Total	188 (100)	66 (100)	254 (22)

[Fig. 6]. In 2015, claims (313) surpassed the MDR-TB cases notified (215).

Factors associated with the use of RSBY-MDR TB pre-treatment evaluation package

In bivariate analysis, the odds of one-time use of RSBY pre-treatment evaluation package in non-poor patients was found to be 0.04 [95% CI (0.02–0.07, $p < 0.0001$)] times less in comparison with the poor. This association remained statistically significant in multivariate analysis [Odds ratio: 0.03, 95%CI (0.01–0.05)]. Age, sex, district type and the type of institution had no significant association with the use of RSBY-MDR TB package. The results of bivariate and multivariate analysis are presented in Table 4.

Discussion

RSBY and MSBY MDR-TB benefit packages were designed for financial risk protection of MDR-TB patients and to have equity in utilization of packages. These are the main goals of the health financing systems [40]. In the next section, extension of Kingdon's Multiple Streams (Problem, Policy and Politics streams) framework [41] is used to discuss the utilization of RSBY and MSBY MDR-TB benefit packages in terms of equity in benefitting the poor from these packages.

Problem stream

MDR-TB pre-treatment evaluation package vs. follow-up evaluation package

We found wide variations in claims utilization under the three MDR-TB packages with highest utilization in MDR-TB pre-treatment evaluation package - 627 (54%) and lowest utilization in MDR-TB follow-up evaluation package - 254 (22%). This finding indicates compromise

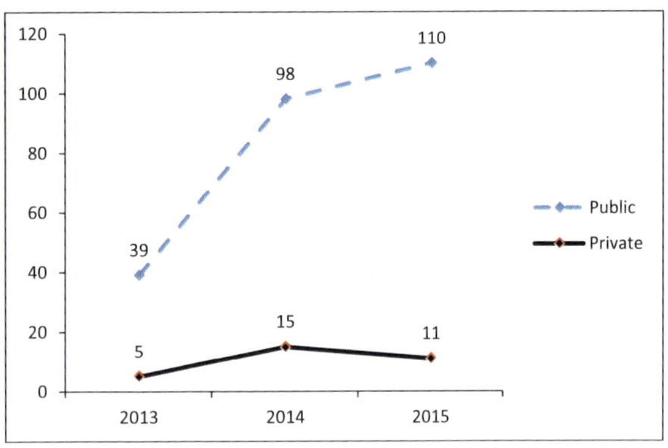

Fig. 3 Pooled (RSBY and MSBY) MDR-TB hospital stay package utilization in the public and private sector from 2013 to 2015

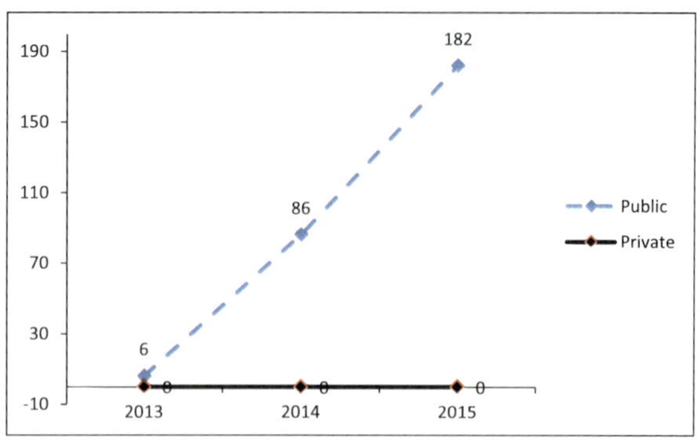

Fig. 4 Pooled (RSBY and MSBY) MDR-TB follow-up package utilization in the public and private sector from 2013 to 2015

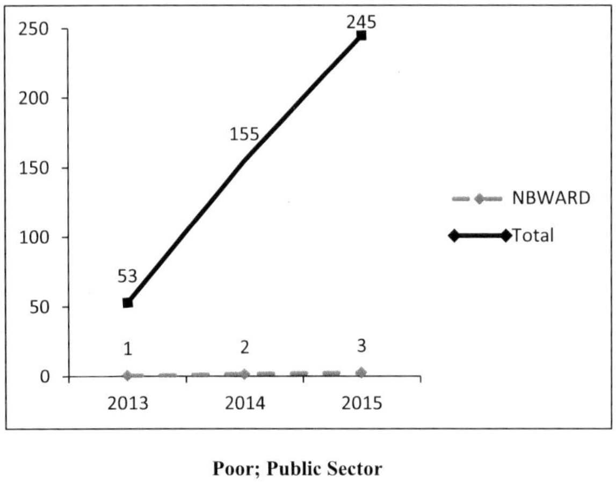

Fig. 5 Disaggregated pooled (RSBY and MSBY) data on claims utilization of MDR-TB pre-treatment evaluation package by poor in the public sector from 2013 to 2015

in continuity of care, wherein follow-up evaluation is of paramount importance to monitor the progress of the treatment until the patient is cured. Low utilisation of follow-up evaluation package could also be attributed to its low package cost, and hence, is less attractive for processing claims under this package in both public and private sector.

Public vs. private

A substantial difference in terms of the total number of claims processed between the public and private sector was noted with much greater involvement of public health facilities in the financial risk protection mechanism for MDR-TB patients. Public health facilities seemed to outperform the private health facilities, which can be attributed to a bigger number public health facilities presence in rural and tribal areas, and hence their empanelment by the state health insurance schemes. This could be one of the possible reasons for low utilisation of claims by the beneficiaries in the private sector, unlike in majority of the states in India where almost half of the TB patients are accessing treatment in the private sector [42]. Chhattisgarh is an exceptional state where presence of public health infrastructure is higher than the national average [43], as majority of tribal districts in the state are insurgency hit [44] without much presence of private health facilities. The private sector is present mainly in urban cities and remains reluctant to move to remote or rural areas as it can make more profit by being in urban areas [39]. Establishing linkages between MDR-TB packages and the universal health insurance scheme (RSBY and MSBY) was an attempt to invent newer ways of public private partnership that would engage and leverage the involvement of private sector healthcare providers in MDR-TB care on a national scale in India. It was envisioned that implementing this health insurance model for MDR-TB patients could go a long way towards averting the majority of OOP expenditure in the private sector, especially by linking diagnosis and supply of drugs for MDR-TB with the national TB control programme of Government of India [13]. Effective public health programme linkage with the public and private sector is of paramount importance not only for financial risk protection of MDR-TB patients, but also for comprehensive control of TB in the community.

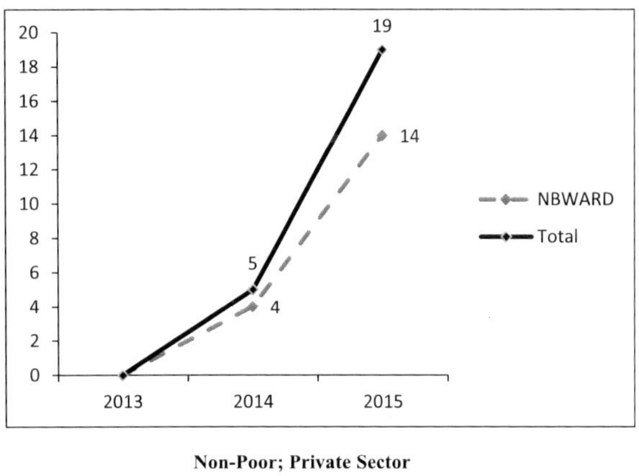

Fig. 6 Disaggregated pooled (RSBY and MSBY) data on claims utilization of MDR-TB pre-treatment evaluation package by non-poor in the private sector from 2013 to 2015

Poor vs non-poor

We found inequities in utilizing the packages under the RSBY and MSBY schemes by the non-poor and poor, which corroborate with evidence that voluntary health insurance schemes create similar inequities [45]. The non-poor MDR-TB patients were better able to access the private sector than the poor for utilizing claims under the MDR-TB pre-treatment evaluation package with an increasing trend and with drainage of public subsidy to the empanelled private health facilities. We also found gender inequity in utilising the claims as 67% of claims were utilised by the males. These disparities in utilizing the claims, which are unequal and inequitable, indicate lapse in proper implementation of MDR-TB benefit packages.

Policy stream

Policy vs practice

Variations in utilization of the MDR-TB benefit packages by public and private sector were also observed. Firstly, not a single claim was processed under the MDR-TB follow-up evaluation package from the private sector. A MDR-TB patient requires minimum of eleven follow-up evaluations during the course of MDR-TB treatment as

Table 4 Factors associated with the use of RSBY MDR-TB Pre-Treatment Evaluation Package by MDR-TB beneficiaries

Variable	Bivariate analysis		Multivariate analysis	
	Odds Ratio, OR (95% CI)	*p*-value	Odds Ratio, OR (95% CI)	p-value
Age in years				
0–14	Ref			
15–34	0.88(0.36–2.19)	0.786	0.62 (0.20–1.98)	0.423
35–54	1.55 (0.62–3.83)	0.344	1.06 (0.33–3.40)	0.921
≥ 55	1.18 (0.47–2.98)	0.719	0.61 (0.18–2.01)	0.418
Sex				
Male	0.95 (0.63–1.43)	0.815	0.97 (0.55–1.71)	0.910
Female	Ref			
Socio-Economic Status (SES)				
Poor	0.04 (0.02–0.07)	< 0.0001	0.03 (0.01–0.05)	< 0.0001
Non-Poor	Ref			
District Sub-types				
Most Backward & Left Wing Extremist Districts(MBLWE)	0.61 (0.26–1.41)	0.247	1.38 (0.63–3.01)	0.426
Backward & Left Wing Extremist (BLWE)	0.94 (0.48–1.85)	0.868	Ref	
Backward Districts (BWARD)	0.85 (0.41–1.77)	0.66	1.36 (0.69–2.67)	0.372
Non Backward Districts (NBWARD)	Ref		0.74 (0.18–3.03)	
Hospital Types				
Private	1.15 (0.63–2.10)	0.635	1.77 (0.59–6.12)	0.364
Public	Ref			
Year				
2015	3.09 (1.79–5.34)	< 0.0001	5.64 (2.57–12.39)	< 0.00001
2014	2.07 (1.14–3.75)	0.016	1.76 (0.79–3.91)	0.169
2013	Ref			

per the national Programmatic Management of Drug Resistant Tuberculosis (PMDT) guidelines [19]. Low utilization of MDR-TB follow-up evaluation package suggests that either the follow-up evaluations are not being done as per the schedule under the health insurance mechanism or not properly carried out under the routine programme setting or any other cause, and this needs to be investigated further. As per the policy of the benefit packages, its utilization under RSBY and MSBY schemes requires a hospital stay [24]. RSBY and MSBY MDR-TB packages are applicable for MDR-TB patients who are diagnosed as 'MDR-TB' cases by a RNTCP certified or any recognized laboratory on hospitalization basis. Ambulatory care is yet to be included and implemented in the mainstream health insurance [13]. However, utilization of MDR-TB hospital stay package was found to be sub-optimal 278 (24%). These aforementioned variations in utilizing the packages reflect on the weak implementation of MDR-TB benefit packages. The implementation gap previously shown in the literature lead to increased risk of incurring catastrophic expenditure due to TB [11]. Earlier studies on the mechanism of health insurance linkage with the TB control programme had recommended awareness campaigns, training and capacity building of joint programme staff for the success of this linkage [13]. Studies have suggested that key strategy to improve utilization of the RSBY scheme is by ensuring that the adequate information on entitlements and benefits reaches marginalized beneficiaries through proper awareness raising measures [13, 27–30].

Politics stream

The political stream is present, but is loosely coupled with the problem and policy streams. At the time of agenda setting (Kingdon 1992), state level politics (Chief Minister's political will to promote UHIS) influenced the formulation of the RSBY and MSBY MDR-TB financial protection policy. Similar influence was lacking in the implementation phase, as the implementation part of the programme was typically left to the programme officers.

Strengths and weaknesses of this study

There are important points that merit discussion on the strengths and weaknesses of this study. This is the first study which looked in detail how RSBY and MSBY MDR-TB benefit packages were used in the state of Chhattisgarh, India, disaggregated by poor and non-poor; in public and private sector; and across economically backward and rich districts, post its implementation suggesting weakness in it. We used fully electronic means of primary data collection and analysis. However, this study had certain limitations. Firstly, since the analysis is based on review of quantitative data received from State Nodal Agency (SNA), we do not know the quality of service received and patient satisfaction in utilising RSBY and MSBY MDR-TB packages. Secondly, we didn't have data on MDR-TB cases from private sector and MDR-TB treatment outcomes from public and private sector. Hence, we don't know impact of the intervention on adherence of MDR-TB treatment. To address these shortcomings future mixed methods (using both quantitative and qualitative) research for evaluating this intervention and for assessing quality of services for MDR-TB patients can be proposed [46]. Finally we only had data for MDR-TB patients and not all patients enrolled in the RSBY and MSBY schemes. So we were unable to undertake multivariate analysis to fully explore the differences in uptake of the packages between the different groups and facilities controlling for the various confounding factors. Examining this full dataset using multivariate regression techniques would be a key area for further research.

Conclusion and recommendation

An implementation gap was observed, reflecting weak coordination between state nodal agencies and the state TB department in the Chhatisgarh MDR-TB programme. This creates an opportunity for a policy entrepreneur to emerge, seize the window of opportunity and advocate change. Variations and inequities in utilization of MDR-TB packages; and low utilization of follow-up evaluation package could be the consequences of weak implementation of the MDR-TB benefit packages in the state of Chhattisgarh. Public health efforts should be consolidated in strengthening the vast presence of public health facilities in the state through proper institutional arrangements by establishing linkages with the national TB control programme for improving service delivery to the MDR-TB patients in order to achieve universal health coverage. Proper implementation of MDR-TB benefit packages through the health insurance mechanism could go a long way in contributing towards achieving universal health coverage in India, Sustainable Development Goal (SDG) 3 of the United Nations that articulates to ensure healthy lives and promote well-being for all, and progress towards achieving the end-TB strategy target of zero catastrophic costs due to TB by 2035. Complete engagement of the national programmes from the stage of planning to execution, and periodic programme review is necessary to ensure feasible and successful implementation of a policy intervention [47].

The following steps are recommended before scaling up this innovative initiative for financial protection of MDR-TB patients across the country based on literature review - 1) Creating awareness [13, 27–30] to empower the MDR-TB patients on their entitlements primarily at the health facilities level which are empanelled in the health insurance schemes. This can be achieved by adequate counselling from the field staff to the patients for reducing variations and inequities in utilisation of packages. 2) Joint programme review meetings [13, 27, 48] for ensuring close monitoring of MDR-TB and health insurance programme (UHIS), identifying and addressing critical bottlenecks, and to remove inequities by strengthening the public sector and regulating the private sector, are to be convened by the local stewards [27, 49] at state and district levels. 3) Training and capacity building of both RNTCP and RSBY and MSBY State Nodal Agency staff in the state [13] by the master trainers of these programmes for correct identification, enrolment, utilization and passing the benefits of the packages to the beneficiaries.

Acknowledgements

The authors acknowledge the assistance provided by the staff of the RSBY and MSBY State Nodal Agency, Directorate of Health Services, Government of Chhattisgarh. This paper is extracted from the thesis submitted by the first author in partial fulfilment of the requirements for the degree of Master of Science in Public Health, orientation in Health Systems Management and Policy, from the Institute of Tropical Medicine (ITM), Antwerp, Belgium. Gratitude is expressed to Professor Patrick Van Der Stuyft, Head of the Unit of General Epidemiology and Disease Control, ITM, Antwerp, Belgium for his guidance to improve this study and MPH thesis.

Ethical consideration

The study was a review of records and the data were anonymised, without involving patient interaction, so individual patient consent was deemed not required. The study is derived from the Master of Science in Public Health (MPH) thesis of the first author. The MPH thesis protocol was initially submitted to the Institutional Review Board (IRB) of Institute of Tropical Medicine (ITM), Antwerp, Belgium for ethical clearance. But, as the thesis protocol was based on pre-collected data, IRB ethical clearance was not necessary. Permission to use the data was provided by State Nodal Agency, Directorate of Health Services, Government of Chhattisgarh.

Funding

No funding was received to conduct this study.

Authors' contributions

Conceived and designed the experiments: DK, GA,NS. Analyzed the data: DK, GA, NS, SL, MA, SC. Contributed reagents/materials/analysis tools: DK, LJ, SL, MA, GA, NS, SC. Wrote the paper: DK, NS, LJ. All authors read and approved the final manuscript.

Competing interests

The authors declare that they have no competing interests.

Author details
[1]International Union Against Tuberculosis and Lung Disease (The Union), South-East Asia Office, C-6, Qutub Institutional Area, New Delhi 110016, India. [2]Department of Community Medicine, Maulana Azad Medical College, New Delhi, India. [3]Universite Libre de Bruxelles, Brussels, Belgium. [4]African Society of Laboratory Medicine; Ministry of Health, Cameroon, Yaoundé, Cameroon. [5]Center for Instructional Psychology and Technology, Faculty of Psychology and Education Science, KU Leuven, Leuven, Belgium. [6]Global Health and Development, Imperial College London; Centre for Health Economics, University of York, York, United Kingdom.

References

1. Ashford LS, Gwatkin DR, Yazbeck AS. Designing Health and Population Programs to Reach the Poor. World Bank, Heal Advis Serv. 2006:1–32. http://www.prb.org/pdf06/DesigningPrograms.pdf.
2. Victora CG, Wagstaff A, Schellenberg JA, Gwatkin D, Claeson M, Habicht JP. Applying an equity lens to child health and mortality: more of the same is not enough. Lancet. 2003;
3. Jacobs B, Ir P, Bigdeli M, Annear PL, Van Damme W. Addressing access barriers to health services: an analytical framework for selectingappropriate interventions in low-income Asian countries. Health Policy Plan. 2012;27(4):288–300.
4. Health KJ. Financing for universal coverage and health system performance: concepts and implications for policy. World heal organ bull world heal. Organ. 2013;91(8):602–11.
5. Bhattacharjee Ayona MD. India's Healthcare System Is Becoming More and More Unequal [Internet]. The Wire. 2017 [cited 2017 Jun 16]. Available from: https://thewire.in/146465/india-healthcare-system-inequality/
6. Prasad S. Preference of hospital usage in India. Ann Trop Med Public Heal Medknow Publications and Media Pvt Ltd. 2013;6(4):472.
7. Oxlade O, Murray M. Tuberculosis and Poverty: why are the poor at greater risk in India? PLoS One. 2012;7(11):1–8.
8. Laokri S. Collaborative Approaches and Policy opportunities for accelerated progress toward effective disease prevention, care, and control: using the case of poverty diseases to explore universal access to affordable health care. Front med. Frontiers. 2017 Aug 25;4:130.
9. World Health Organization. Addressing poverty in TB control - options for national TB control Programmes. World Health. 2005:4–80.
10. WPRO | World Health Organization: Tuberculosis in China a Disease of Poverty. WPRO. WPRO | WHO Western Pacific Region; 2016;
11. Laokri S, Weil O, Drabo KM, Dembelé SM, Kafando B, Dujardin B. Removal of user fees no guarantee of universal health coverage: observations from Burkina Faso. Bull World Health Organ. 2013 Apr 1;91(4):277–82.
12. Melorose J, Perroy R, Careas S. WHO global tuberculosis report 2017. Statew Agric L Use Baseline. 2017;2017:1. Available from: http://www.who.int/tb/publications/global_report/en/
13. Kundu D, Katre V, Singh K, Deshpande M, Nayak P, Khaparde K, et al. Innovative social protection mechanism for alleviating catastrophic expenses on multidrug-resistant tuberculosis patients in Chhattisgarh, India. WHO South-East Asia J Public Heal. 2015;4(June):69–77.
14. Sharma A, Hill A, Kurbatova E, van der Walt M, Kvasnovsky C, Tupasi TE, et al. Estimating the future burden of multidrug-resistant and extensively drug-resistant tuberculosis in India, the Philippines, Russia, and South Africa: a mathematical modelling study. Lancet Infect Dis. 2017 Jul;17(7):707–15.
15. IHME. Data Visualizations | Institute for Health Metrics and Evaluation [Internet]. 2017 [cited 2017 Sep 4]. Available from: http://www.healthdata.org/results/data-visualizations
16. Menzies NA, Gomez GB, Bozzani F, Chatterjee S, Foster N, Baena IG, et al. Cost-effectiveness and resource implications of aggressive action on tuberculosis in China, India, and South Africa: a combined analysis of nine models. Lancet Glob Heal. 2016 Nov;4(11):e816–26.
17. Kingdon JW. Agendas, alternatives, and public policies. 1995th ed. New York: New York : HarperCollinsCollege, ©1995.;
18. Shroff ZC, Roberts MJ, Reich MR, Cyrus Z, Roberts MJ, Agenda MRR, et al. Agenda Setting and Policy Adoption of India â€™ s National Health Insurance Scheme : Rashtriya Swasthya Bima Yojana Agenda Setting and Policy Adoption of India ' s National Health Insurance Scheme : Rashtriya Swasthya Bima Yojana. 2015;8604(April 2016).
19. Revised National Tuberculosis Control Programme (RNTCP). Guidelines on Programmatic Management of Drug Resistant TB (PMDT) in India. 2012;
20. Press Information Bureau Govt. of India. Notification of Tuberculosis [Internet]. National Informatics Centre. 2012 [cited 2017 Aug 27]. Available from: http://pib.nic.in/newsite/erelease.aspx?relid=83486
21. Ahmad S, Mokaddas E. Recent advances in the diagnosis and treatment of multidrug-resistant tuberculosis. Respir Med Elsevier Ltd. 2009 Dec;103(12):1777–90.
22. Ministerial Conference Amsterdam, 22–24 March, 2000. The stop TB initiative. The economic impacts of Tuberculosis 2000. Available from: http://www.stoptb.org/assets/documents/events/meetings/amsterdam_conference/ahlburg.pdf
23. Wingfield T, Boccia D, Tovar M, Gavino A, Zevallos K, Montoya R, et al. Defining catastrophic costs and comparing their importance for adverse tuberculosis outcome with multi-drug resistance: a prospective cohort study, Peru. PLoS Med. 2014;11(7)
24. Government of Chhattisgarh. RSBY and MSBY [Internet]. [cited 2016 Jun 10]. Available from: http://cg.nic.in/healthrsby/
25. Government of India. Rashtriya Swasthya Bima Yojna [Internet]. [cited 2016 Jun 10]. Available from: http://www.rsby.gov.in/about_rsby.aspx
26. O'Donnell O, Van Doorslaer E. Analyzing health equity using household survey data. Washington DC: The World Bank; 2008. p. 1–12.
27. Devadasan N, Seshadri T, Trivedi M, Criel B. Promoting Universal financial protection: evidence from the Rashtriya Swasthya Bima Yojana (RSBY) in Gujarat, India. Health res policy Syst. Health Research Policy and Systems. 2013 Jan;11(1):29.
28. Seshadri T, Ganesh G, Mh A, Kadammanvar M, Elias M, Pati MK, et al. CHAPTER 6 : Karnataka case study summary Karnataka : a land of inequities Health financing in India : focus Karnataka. 2012;(Census 2011).
29. Sabharwal N, Mishra V, Naik A, Holmes R, Hagen-Zanker J. How does social protection contribute to social inclusion in India ? 2014;(April):1–77.
30. Thakur H. Study of awareness, enrollment, and utilization of Rashtriya Swasthya Bima Yojana (National Health Insurance Scheme) in Maharashtra, India. Front public Heal. 2015;3(January):282.
31. Trivedi M, Saxena DB. Third angle of RSBY: service providers' perspective to RSBY-operational issues in Gujarat. J Fam Med Prim care Wolters Kluwer – Medknow Publications. 2013 Apr;2(2):169–72.
32. The World Bank. Poverty & Equity, Country Dashboard: India [Internet]. [cited 2016 Jun 10]. Available from: http://povertydata.worldbank.org/poverty/country/IND
33. United Nations in India. About Scheduled Castes and Scheduled Tribes [Internet]. [cited 2016 Jun 10]. Available from: http://in.one.un.org/task-teams/scheduled-castes-and-scheduled-tribes
34. Quora. What is the difference between scheduled caste (SC) and scheduled tribe (ST) ? How government has classified tribes and caste into it? [Internet]. [cited 2016 Jun 10]. Available from: https://www.quora.com/What-is-the-difference-between-scheduled-caste-SC-and-scheduled-tribe-ST-How-government-has-classified-tribes-and-caste-into-it
35. Shukla Alok. Paddy For Millers, Not People. Outlook. Raipur, Chhattisgarh; 2016 Mar;
36. PTI. Chhattisgarh Highest incidence of poverty: C Rangarajan panel. The economic Times 2014 Jul 8;
37. India PC. Riders for NREGA: Challenges of backward districts. Plan Comm India. 2003;(Report of the Task Force on "Identification of Districtsfor Wage and Self employment programmes").
38. MOSPI N 68th R. Household Consumption of Various Goods and Services in India 20ll-12. 2014.
39. Sulakshana Nandi. Is the National Health Insurance Scheme in Chhattisgarh Doing More Damage Than Good? [Internet]. The Wire. 2017 [cited 2017 Nov 14]. Available from: https://thewire.in/193696/national-health-insurance-scheme-chhattisgarh-damage-good/
40. Kutzin J. A descriptive framework for country-level analysis of health care financing arrangements. Health Policy. 2001 Jun;56(3):171–204.
41. Ridde V. "The problem of the worst-off is dealt with after all other issues": the equity and health policy implementation gap in Burkina Faso. Soc Sci Med. 2008 Mar;66(6):1368–78.
42. Satyanarayana S, Nair SA, Chadha SS, Shivashankar R, Sharma G, Yadav S, et al. From Where Are Tuberculosis Patients Accessing Treatment in India? Results from a Cross-Sectional Community Based Survey of 30 Districts. Pai M, editor. PLoS One. IIPS; 2011 Sep 2;6(9):e24160.
43. Bajpai V. Vikas. The challenges confronting public hospitals in India, their origins, and possible solutions. Adv public heal. Hindawi. 2014 Jul 13;2014:1–27.

44. Programme NRDW. State wise LWE districts [Internet]. Ministry of drinking water, Government of India. [cited 2016 Jun 10]. Available from: http://indiawater.gov.in/imisreports/Reports/BasicInformation/rpt_RWS_StatewiseLWEDistrict_D.aspx?Rep=2
45. OXFAM. Universal health coverage: Why health insurance schemes are leaving the poor behind. OXFAM Brief Pap. 2013;176(October):36.
46. Werner Soors; Jeroene De Man; Pascal Ndiaye; Fahdi Dkhimi; Remco Van de Pa; Bart Criel. Towards Universal Coverage in the Majority World. SHSOP, 32,. B. Criel, V. De Brouwere WVD and BM, editor. Antwerp: ITGPress, Nationalestraat 155, B-2000, Antwerp, Belgium; 2015. 1–231 p.
47. Kumar AM, Gupta D, Kumar A, Gupta RS, Kanchar A, Rao R, et al. HIV testing among patients with presumptive tuberculosis: how do we implement in a routine programmatic setting? Results of a large operational research from India. PLoS One. 2016;11(5):e0156487.
48. Kenyon TA, Mwasekaga MJ, Huebner R, Rumisha D, Binkin N, Maganu E. Low levels of drug resistance amidst rapidly increasing tuberculosis and human immunodeficiency virus co-epidemics in Botswana. Int J Tuberc Lung Dis. 1999 Jan;3(1):4–11.
49. Musgrove P, Creese A, Preker A, Baeza C, Anell A, Prentice T. Health Systems: Improving Perfomance. World heal Organ. 2000;78(1):1–215.

3

Income-related inequalities in diseases and health conditions over the business cycle

Tinna Laufey Ásgeirsdóttir* and Hildur Margrét Jóhannsdóttir

Abstract

How business cycles affect income-related distribution of diseases and health disorders is largely unknown. We examine how the prevalence of thirty diseases and health conditions is distributed across the income spectrum using survey data collected in Iceland in 2007, 2009 and 2012. Thus, we are able to take advantage of the unusually sharp changes in economic conditions in Iceland during the Great Recession initiated in 2008 and the partial recovery that had already taken place by 2012 to analyze how income-related health inequality changed across time periods that can be described as a boom, crisis and recovery. The concentration curve and the concentration index are calculated for each disease, both overall and by gender. In all cases, we find a considerable income-related health inequality favoring higher income individuals, with a slight increase over the study period. Between 2007 and 2009, our results indicate increased inequality for women but decreased inequality for men. Between 2009 and 2012 on the contrary, men's inequality increases but women's decreases. The overarching result is thus that the economic hardship of the crisis temporarily increased female income-related health inequality, but decreased that of men.

Keywords: Equality, Distribution, Health, Diseases, Income, Business cycles

JEL classification codes: I1, I14, I15, E3

Background

As the income gap between the richest and the poorest widens, the importance of monitoring health disparities across the income spectrum rises, and the debated amount of appropriate government spending on health care makes income-related health inequality an even more relevant subject to study. The importance of tracking how health is distributed along the income spectrum is made even clearer by the fact that the potential gains from publicly provided health care is not only improved public health but also minimized socio-economic health disparities.

Although studies on the income-related distribution of health in general have been extensive and the knowledge of the effects of business cycles on health has improved, the understanding of how business cycles affect income-related distribution of diseases and health disorders is much more limited. Using data from a survey on health and well-being conducted by the Directorate of Health in Iceland, this paper seeks to explain how the prevalence of thirty diseases is distributed across the income spectrum. Specifically, we examine this during a very turbulent economic period in Iceland, including a boom (2007), a subsequent bust (2009), and a period of partial recovery (2012). We thus take advantage of the unusually sharp change in economic conditions in Iceland during the Great Recession in 2008 and analyze how income-related health inequality changed across the different time periods.

As our study combines income inequality, health and business cycles, it can be seen as a contribution to at least two strands of literature; on the one hand, the relationship between income (income inequality) and health, and on the other hand, the relationship between business cycles and health. Therefore, the literature review is split in three parts; firstly, it discusses previous studies on the association between income inequality and health, secondly, it provides an insight into business cycles' effects on health and lastly, income-related health

* Correspondence: ta@hi.is
Department of Economics, University of Iceland, Oddi v/Sturlugotu, Reykjavík, Iceland

inequality and business cycles will be discussed followed by a brief discussion on the Icelandic context.

Health, income and inequality

A range of studies indicate a positive correlation between income and health, although the causality remains hard to determine [1–4]. Many economists refer to social factors such as education and labor-market participation as the most important determinants of this correlation and point out that educated individuals are better suited to understand health information and hence in a better position to reap the benefits of healthcare systems and choose a healthy life style than their less educated counterparts [5, 6]. Those same individuals also tend to have higher income, and many argue that higher income discourages risky health behavior and reduces the risk of health disorders, although health behavior has also been associated with income independent of education [7–9]. The reason here can for example be that incentives may be relatively greater to prolong life that is lived in relatively better economic circumstances.

The abovementioned hypothesized pathways focus on individual-level determinants of income-related health disparities. However, those may be suppressed or elevated by society-wide determinants, such as social, cultural and institutional settings. Although not conclusive at this point, a body of literature has indicated that in general, worse health can be found in societies with more unequal income distributions and numerous studies have concluded that more equal societies not only have better health [3, 4, 10] but also less health inequalities [11, 12]. Wilkinson and Pickett [4] argue that the association between income inequality and health is strongest when income inequality is measured across whole societies and that better health in more equal societies can be explained through stronger social relationships, social cohesion, trust, lower violence rates and less social distance.

Ásgeirsdóttir and Ragnarsdóttir [13] examine concentration indices for 26 European countries and find relatively extensive income-related health inequality in the Nordic countries, a result that has also been found by other researchers [14–18]. Ásgeirsdóttir and Ragnarsdóttir [13], shed light on the relationship between societal conditions and income-related health inequality, for example GDP. However, they do this cross-sectionally across countries. Although this is relevant, especially as Iceland is one of those Nordic countries examined, the focus of the current project is on rapidly changing ambient economic conditions within a country. In that regard it should be noted that Ásgeirsdóttir and Ragnarsdóttir [13] did not find a systematic pattern between countries' GDP and income-related health inequality. However, although GDP across countries may not be associated with the inequalities examined, this does not have to be the case for GDP levels over time within the same country – namely the business cycle. It may very well be that a variable that is generally positively associated with GDP across countries is counter-cyclical within a country. In fact health is a case in point, as population health generally increases with increased prosperity, while still being countercyclical by many estimates as discussed in the following section.

Health and business cycles

A wide range of studies has shown that recessions generally have a positive impact on public health [1, 9, 19–27]. Ruhm and Cawley [9] add that in accordance with these findings, mortality rates have proven pro-cyclical, driven by mortality that can be explained by life-style decisions, such as coronary heart disease and traffic accidents. Ruhm and Gerdtham [27] studied macroeconomic fluctuations and health in the OECD countries and reported that decreases in unemployment rate during the period 1960–1997 are associated with substantial increases in death caused by diseases such as cardiovascular disease, liver disease, influenza as well as deadly accidents and Ruhm [26] shows that over the period 1972–1991, temporary economic downturns in the United States reduced eight of ten sources of fatalities.

Ruhm and Cawley [9] suggest two mechanisms likely to explain these counter-cyclical health effects; firstly, they mention that less disposable income during recessions reduces unhealthy consumption (see also [28, 29]), secondly, they argue that during recessions, people tend to have more time for healthy behavior (e.g. exercise), since working hours are usually pro-cyclical (see also [30–32]). Others have pointed out that health can be seen as a production input, and hence when working hours are extended, people's health is affected, especially in cyclically sensitive sectors (such as construction), which indeed tend to be characterized by unhealthy or even dangerous working conditions [27, 33–35]. Ruhm [36] emphasizes that although the general results show that health improves in hard times, there are studies that indicate that mortality has become less pro-cyclical over the last few years (e. g. [37]) and even counter-cyclical [38, 39]. The important fact should also be mentioned that the results appear to be somewhat disease specific; Ruhm [26] shows that although physical health appears to be countercyclical, mental health has often been measured as pro-cyclical and Ruhm [36] finds that mortality due to cancer has over the last years become counter-cyclical, and suicide rates declined in economic upturns.

Income-related health inequality and business cycles: The Icelandic context

Although the effect of business cycles on income-related health inequalities has received much less attention, Ásgeirsdóttir's and Ragnarsdóttir's recent study [40] does focus on income-related inequality in health in Iceland using data from 2007 to 2009, a year pre and post the Icelandic economic collapse. Their results indicate pro-rich income-related health inequality and they find that the effects of the crisis substantially differ between males and females. For men, income-related health inequality increased after the crisis while for women it remained rather stable. They use data from surveys conducted in 2007 and 2009, but as a first attempt at this examination, they only use a very general one-variable health measure, namely self-assessed health. They call for further research examining this relationship using more specific measures of health. Such an analysis is presented in the current study.

Iceland's economy was hit hard by the Great Recession with considerable societal effects. Icelanders experienced, in a relatively short period of 5 years, an economic boom, followed by a sudden bust and then substantial recovery. These rapidly changing economic conditions make the years of 2007–2012 an ideal time period to examine the recession's effects on income-related health inequality in Iceland. Although only Ásgeirsdóttir and Ragnarsdóttir [40] have examined the business-cycle effects of the collapse on income-related health distributions, the special research opportunity created by those dramatic circumstances in Iceland has been taken advantage of in multiple studies examining the effect of the crisis on health [13, 41–44] and health behaviors [45–50]. Due to the incredibly low pre-crisis unemployment rate (of only 2% in October 2007) the large percentage increase in unemployment during the crisis still resulted in a lower rate (of 6% in October 2009) than in most other hard-hit countries such as Spain and Ireland [46, 51]. However, while these countries experienced a deflation during the crisis, in Iceland, on the contrary, prices rose due to a devaluation of the Icelandic Krona by about 36% in exchange markets [46]. This was evident both from the consumer price index which increased by roughly 12% between 2007 and 2008 and again 12% between 2008 and 2009 and from more than 10% drop in real wages between 2007 and 2010 [52]. While this obviously reduced people's purchasing power, it also had detrimental effects on Icelanders' debt obligations, especially those in foreign currencies [47]. Already by 2010, the CPI increase reverted back to its pre-crisis level (with annual increases of 3–5% between 2010 and 2012) and real wages to their pre-boom level [46, 47, 52]. This rapid recovery, which indeed was lauded in international news stories, has mainly been explained by three important factors: capital controls, a flexible labor market and flexible exchange rates [46, 53, 54].

Using data from the same survey as Ásgeirsdóttir and Ragnarsdóttir [40], as well as an additional wave of data from 2012, this paper seeks to extend the contribution of their study in two ways. Firstly, by extending the study period to include economic recovery. Secondly, by extending the depth of the analysis from one self-assessed health variable, to examining thirty different diseases and health disorders. These are eye disease (e.g. cataracts or glaucoma), irritable bowel syndrome, chronic fatigue syndrome, cold/flu, alcoholism (or substance addiction), chronic anxiety, chronic depression, anxiety, serious worries, sleeping difficulties, other mental disorders, shortness of breath, debility, myalgia, back/shoulder pain, arm pain, leg pain, frequent headaches, toothache, abdominal pain, rheumatoid arthritis, osteoarthritis, fibromyalgia, chronic back syndrome, chronic throat disease, diabetes, serious headaches, urinary incontinence, thyroid disease and high blood pressure. We examine the distribution of those diseases and conditions over the time period of interest by calculating concentration indices for each disease with respect to households' disposable income, both gender specific and overall and comparing the indices across years.

The additional data from 2012 strengthens the study in various ways. It allows us to determine whether or not the effects of the collapse in 2008 reversed with the recovering economy. This is important, as it sheds light on whether observed changes are likely to be due to the economic conditions or underlying time trends in health distributions. Also, a limitation of the first two waves is that no additional individuals were sampled, leading to an overall aging of the sample between waves. With the additional wave from 2012, new participants with the same age range as the first sample in 2007 were added, allowing us to examine to what extent the changes are driven by the aging of the sample. As indicated above, the contribution of this study is partly the detailed analysis across different health conditions and diseases, whereas Ásgeirsdóttir's and Ragnarsdóttir's [40] study only used one general measure of self-assessed health. It should also be mentioned that although the relation between some of those diseases and income has already been examined, the changes in the income-related distribution of those diseases has not been examined specifically across the business cycle.

Data

The data stems from the survey "Health and well-being", conducted by The Directorate of Health in Iceland in October 2007, 2009 and 2012. The survey includes variables on health, demographics and income. In October

2007, a stratified random sample of 9.711 Icelanders received the questionnaire with a net response rate of 60,8%. In 2009, every participant who had agreed to be contacted again received a questionnaire again. That year, the response rate was 69,3%, corresponding to 42,1% of the original sample participating in the first two waves of the survey. In 2012, a third wave of the survey was sent to 10,093 subjects, 3,659 respondents from the original sample and a new sample of 6,434 participants. The response rate of the new sample was 55,0%, resulting in 3,537 new answers and the response rate of the original sample was 88,7%, resulting in 3,246 individuals answering all three waves. Having eliminated observations with missing values on key variables, the final sample consisted of 9,963 observations on 6,446 individuals. For each regression, the final sample then depended on the number of missing values for the particular variables applied in the calculations.

We use thirty binary variables for health dummies, each representing a specific health disorder or disease mentioned above, taking the value 1 if an individual is suffering from the disease and 0 otherwise. The income variable is derived from the question: In what range do you estimate your household's income over the last 12 months? Fourteen response options ranged from "below 900 thousand" (7.064 USD) and "above 18 million" (141.287 USD) and the responses were coded as the midpoint of each interval. As the last option "above 18 million" had no upper bound, responses in that range were coded as 20,5 million.

In order to make households' income comparable between different household compositions, the OECD modified equivalence scale was applied. The equivalence scale addresses the concept of economies of scale within the household and hence the notion that a household's needs increase with every additional member, but not proportionally. To take this into account, each member was assigned a value (0–1) indicating his/her needs for resources relative to the others'; in particular, the first adult was assigned the value 1, every additional adult (over the age of 18) was assigned the value 0,5 and children were assigned 0,3. Although the OECD modified equivalence scale sets the child-adult cut-off at the age of fourteen, we categorized all individuals under the age of eighteen as children, due to data limitations. Subsequently, to obtain the equivalent household income variable used throughout the research, each household's income was divided by the sum of all its members' values making the income variable comparable between different household compositions as a measure of the financial means of the individual at hand [55].

Methods

The methodology was based on the concentration curve and the concentration index. The concentration curve is built on the idea of the Lorenz curve but instead of plotting the cumulative portion of the population against cumulative portion of total income, it plots the cumulative portion of a health variable against the cumulative portion of the sample, ranked by income [56–59]. In our case, in order to address the relationship between the distribution of particular diseases and the distribution of income, the x-axis represents the cumulated population, ranked by household income (poorest-richest) and the y-axis represents cumulated health (the absence of one of the thirty diseases of interest each time). Thus, a straight diagonal 45° line would represent perfect income-related health equality (line of perfect equality) where every income group has the same prevalence of a certain disease. A curve below the line of perfect equality indicates better health concentrated among those with higher income and a curve above the line of perfect equality indicates better health concentrated among those with lower income.

The concentration index, derived from the concentration curve, resembles the Gini coefficient and quantifies the health-income inequality graphed by the concentration curve. The concentration index is defined as twice the area between the concentration curve and the line of perfect equality. It ranges between – 1 and 1 where 0 indicates perfect equality and – 1 and 1 stand for perfect inequality, favoring low income groups (–1) and high income groups (1). Formally, the concentration index is calculated by the following formula:

$$CI = 1-2\int_0^1 L(s)ds$$

where $L\ (s)$ is the cumulative distribution of health, as a function of cumulative income, s. This can be computed by using the following formula, with individual level data:

$$CI = \frac{2}{n\mu}\sum_{i=1}^{n} y_i R_i - 1$$

with y_i (i = 1,...,n) as the health score of individual i, μ as the mean level of health and R_i as the relative rank by individual i's income [12, 18, 40, 57, 58].

Since our health variables are binary, calculations will be built on the Wagstaff Concentration Index (WCI), which is a slightly varied version of the concentration index. As Wagstaff [60] suggests for binary health variables, we normalize the CI by dividing it through by the reciprocal of the mean of the variable in question (1-μ):

$$WCI = \frac{2}{n\mu(1-\mu)}\sum_{i=1}^{n} y_i R_i - 1$$

The WCIs are calculated for each health variable each year, 2007, 2009 and 2012, followed by an inter-temporal comparison of the indices. As both health and labor-market outcomes can vary by gender, all estimations are run separately for males and females, as well as for the full sample. Having computed the WCIs of the 3 years we also compute the WCIs of the new-entry sample of 2012 (Sample 2), which had the same age range as the first sample (Sample 1) had in 2007. A comparison of the two samples gives us an idea of whether the changes in the WCIs of Sample 1 are partly driven by the aging over the 5 year period.

The WCI measurement does not take into account how unavoidable factors, such as age and sex, play a role in the inequality. This can be addressed using decomposition analysis, allowing us to partition the indices into unavoidable and avoidable inequality. Specifically, by decomposing the WCI into its various determinants, we isolate the unavoidable factors and calculate standardized WCIs by subtracting the unavoidable inequality due to gender and age. For each WCI, the decomposition is conducted using the following linear regressor model:

$$y_i = \propto + \sum_k \beta_k x_{k_i} + \varepsilon_i$$

where y_i stands for the health measure for individual i, x_{k_i} is a determinant of health for regressor k, and ε_i is the error term. The determinants used in the regression are equivalized household income, marital status, population density and number of people in household. Given y_i and x_{k_i} we can rearrange and write the WCI as:

$$WCI = \sum_k \left(\frac{\beta_k \bar{x}_k}{\mu}\right) WCI_k + \frac{GWCI_\varepsilon}{\mu}$$

where μ is the mean of the health measure y, $\bar{x}$ is the mean of the health determinant x_k, WCI_k is the WCI for x_k (the contribution from each determinant k to income-related health inequality) and the residual is $GWCI_\varepsilon$, the generalized WCI for the error term. The residual thus contains income-related health inequality not explained by variations in determinant x_k across the income spectrum [12, 18, 40, 57].

The data were analyzed in Stata 13.0 software [61].

Results

Tables 1, 2 and 3 show summary statistics for males, females, and full samples respectively. Calculations are based on those who answered all the waves (Sample 1), and the last column, 2012a, shows new-entrants in 2012 (Sample 2).

For the overall Sample 1, the frequency of the diseases and conditions increase over the period. For all 3 years, (and both samples) the summary statistics indicate higher prevalence of the diseases for women than for men.

This increase in disease prevalence is especially noteworthy between 2009 and 2012, thus on average, health is pro-cyclical between 2007 and 2009 but counter-cyclical between 2009 and 2012. This highlights the importance of having three waves to distinguish the effects of the changing economic environment from time trends, as well as the new sample of 2012 to shed light on the effects of the aging of the panel. Men's health is not affected by the economic collapse in a substantial way, the average frequency in the diseases rises by only 4, 9% between 2007 and 2009 and increases by 7, 3% between 2009 and 2012. Women's health is more volatile, with the average frequency increasing by 4, 2% between 2007 and 2009 and 11,5% between 2009 and 2012. Quite surprisingly, Sample 2 does not seem to be healthier than Sample 1 in 2012, despite the age difference. Although the trend in the average frequency of diseases is pro-cyclical between the first two waves and counter-cyclical between the latter two, the trends differ between diseases; for example, alcoholism is pro-cyclical over the whole period and mental illness (chronic anxiety, chronic depression and other disorders) has a counter-cyclical trend over the whole period.

Although the summary statistics are useful in order to study the impact of the recession on the prevalence of the diseases, our main results are listed in Tables 4, 5 and 6. These show the unstandardized and standardized Wagstaff Concentration Indices for each of the diseases/disorders. Table 4 represents the WCIs for men, Table 5 for women and Table 6 for the total sample. Again, the first three columns of the tables represent the WCI of Sample 1 (those who replied to the survey all three times) and the fourth column shows the WCI of Sample 2 (those who only replied in 2012).

On average, for both genders, better health is concentrated among those with higher income over the whole period. Our results show an increase in income-related health inequality among women over the years 2007–2009, but a decrease (to a lesser extent than the increase) between 2009 and 2012. For men, on the contrary, inequality increased over the first period but decreased over the second, less than it rose over the first. On the whole, income-related inequality increased for both men and women from 2007 to 2012, as the increase exceeded the decrease for both gender, and therefore the overall indices suggest a steady increase over

Table 1 Summary statistics for men

	2007			2009			2012			2012a[a]		
Health dummies[b]	Mean	SD	N	Mean	SD	N	Mean	SD	N	Mean	SD	N
Eye disease	0,0467	0,2111	857	0,0432	0,2035	879	0,0367	0,1882	871	0,0396	0,1952	959
Irritable bowel syndrome	0,0177	0,1318	849	0,0148	0,1208	879	0,0172	0,1300	874	0,0137	0,1162	951
Chronic fatigue syndrome	0,0722	0,2590	845	0,0772	0,2670	881	0,0625	0,2422	864	0,0916	0,2886	961
Cold or flu	0,0939	0,2918	863	0,0841	0,2777	892	0,0655	0,2476	870	0,0983	0,2979	946
Alcoholism	0,0199	0,1397	855	0,0192	0,1373	885	0,0239	0,1529	878	0,0391	0,1940	971
Chronic anxiety	0,0873	0,2824	848	0,0783	0,2688	881	0,0710	0,2570	873	0,0912	0,2880	965
Chronic depression	0,0434	0,2038	853	0,0407	0,1977	885	0,0368	0,1883	870	0,0465	0,2106	968
Anxiety	0,1474	0,3547	875	0,1620	0,3687	895	0,1813	0,3855	888	0,2182	0,4133	976
Serious worries	0,1824	0,3864	877	0,2134	0,4099	895	0,2097	0,4073	887	0,2510	0,4338	976
Sleeping difficulties	0,1899	0,3925	874	0,2147	0,4108	899	0,2120	0,4089	887	0,2441	0,4298	975
Other mental disorders	0,0215	0,1451	837	0,0170	0,1295	880	0,0161	0,1260	868	0,0187	0,1355	963
Shortness of breath	0,0548	0,2277	876	0,0713	0,2574	898	0,0772	0,2670	881	0,0781	0,2685	973
Debility	0,1479	0,3552	872	0,1737	0,3791	898	0,1859	0,3893	882	0,1711	0,3768	976
Myalgia	0,2345	0,4239	870	0,2220	0,4158	892	0,2568	0,4371	880	0,2916	0,4547	967
Back/shoulder pain	0,3836	0,4865	876	0,3621	0,4809	892	0,3957	0,4893	887	0,4413	0,4968	979
Arm pain	0,1707	0,3764	873	0,1629	0,3695	896	0,1808	0,3851	885	0,1988	0,3993	981
Leg pain	0,2176	0,4129	873	0,2310	0,4217	896	0,2537	0,4354	887	0,2838	0,4511	976
Frequent headaches	0,0905	0,2871	873	0,0936	0,2915	897	0,0857	0,2801	887	0,1160	0,3204	974
Toothache	0,0526	0,2233	875	0,0512	0,2205	899	0,0415	0,1996	891	0,0603	0,2382	978
Abdominal pain	0,1039	0,3053	876	0,1000	0,3002	900	0,1003	0,3006	887	0,1296	0,3361	972
Rheumatoid arthritis	0,0438	0,2049	844	0,0637	0,2444	879	0,0778	0,2680	861	0,0734	0,2610	926
Osteoarthritis	0,0985	0,2981	853	0,1110	0,3143	883	0,1154	0,3197	858	0,1138	0,3178	940
Fibromyalgia	0,0202	0,1408	841	0,0331	0,1789	877	0,0225	0,1483	845	0,0325	0,1775	922
Chronic back syndrome	0,1307	0,3373	857	0,1456	0,3529	879	0,1731	0,3785	861	0,2002	0,4004	934
Chronic throat disease	0,0200	0,1401	850	0,0239	0,1529	878	0,0266	0,1611	864	0,0267	0,1613	936
Diabetes	0,0340	0,1813	853	0,0385	0,1925	883	0,0628	0,2427	860	0,0611	0,2396	950
Serious headaches	0,0505	0,2192	851	0,0397	0,1954	881	0,0682	0,2522	880	0,0706	0,2563	963
Urinary incontinence	0,0607	0,2389	857	0,0646	0,2459	883	0,0997	0,2997	863	0,0908	0,2875	947
Thyroid disease	0,0141	0,1181	849	0,0216	0,1456	878	0,0275	0,1635	874	0,0249	0,1560	962
High blood pressure	0,1809	0,3851	857	0,2102	0,4077	880	0,2315	0,4220	864	0,2329	0,4229	953
Average	0,1011			0,1061			0,1138			0,1283		
Equivalized hh income[c]	5385	3068	890	4512	2429	913	4555	2510	908	4467	2486	1001

[a] 2012a shows Sample 2 (the new-entrants in 2012)
[b] Health dummies = 1 if the disease is present
[c] Equivalized hh income stands for equivalized household income where the OECD modified equivalence scale has been used to make income comparable between different household compositions

Table 2 Summary statistics for women

	2007			2009			2012			2012a[a]		
Health dummies[b]	Mean	SD	N	Mean	SD	N	Mean	SD	N	Mean	SD	N
Eye disease	0,0619	0,2412	1017	0,0531	0,2244	1054	0,0709	0,2568	1015	0,0474	0,2125	1140
Irritable bowel syndrome	0,0486	0,2152	1008	0,0612	0,2398	1046	0,0326	0,1776	1013	0,0469	0,2114	1131
Chronic fatigue syndrome	0,0663	0,2489	996	0,0973	0,2965	1048	0,1132	0,3170	1007	0,1427	0,3500	1135
Cold or flu	0,1278	0,3340	1033	0,0977	0,2970	1065	0,1049	0,3066	1020	0,0965	0,2954	1130
Alcoholism	0,0158	0,1246	1015	0,0104	0,1015	1057	0,0078	0,0882	1021	0,0141	0,1180	1133
Chronic anxiety	0,0985	0,2982	1015	0,1150	0,3192	1061	0,1179	0,3226	1018	0,1492	0,3564	1133
Chronic depression	0,0531	0,2244	1016	0,0604	0,2384	1059	0,0560	0,2300	1018	0,0756	0,2644	1138
Anxiety	0,2353	0,4244	1037	0,2630	0,4404	1061	0,2666	0,4424	1039	0,2973	0,4572	1164
Serious worries	0,2543	0,4357	1046	0,2696	0,4440	1072	0,2963	0,4568	1043	0,3251	0,4686	1169
Sleeping difficulties	0,2878	0,4529	1046	0,3096	0,4626	1069	0,3244	0,4684	1042	0,3547	0,4786	1170
Other mental disorders	0,0249	0,1560	1003	0,0314	0,1745	1051	0,0248	0,1556	1008	0,0498	0,2177	1124
Shortness of breath	0,1055	0,3073	1043	0,1052	0,3069	1065	0,1245	0,3303	1036	0,1301	0,3366	1168
Debility	0,2374	0,4257	1032	0,2908	0,4544	1059	0,3475	0,4764	1033	0,2925	0,4551	1152
Myalgia	0,4609	0,4987	1037	0,4459	0,4973	1063	0,4672	0,4992	1036	0,5098	0,5001	1171
Back/shoulder pain	0,5077	0,5002	1038	0,4948	0,5002	1061	0,5388	0,4987	1043	0,5575	0,4969	1173
Arm pain	0,2439	0,4297	1029	0,2453	0,4305	1064	0,2792	0,2792	1035	0,2737	0,4460	1162
Leg pain	0,3041	0,4603	1039	0,2992	0,4581	1063	0,3295	0,4703	1041	0,3239	0,4682	1164
Frequent headaches	0,2144	0,4106	1040	0,2008	0,4007	1066	0,2056	0,4043	1041	0,2537	0,4353	1163
Toothache	0,0499	0,2178	1043	0,0551	0,2284	1070	0,0539	0,2260	1038	0,0748	0,2632	1176
Abdominal pain	0,1704	0,3761	1039	0,1717	0,3773	1060	0,1792	0,3837	1038	0,2257	0,4182	1161
Rheumatoid arthritis	0,0820	0,2745	1000	0,1161	0,3205	1051	0,1162	0,3206	990	0,1057	0,3076	1116
Osteoarthritis	0,1815	0,3856	1014	0,2098	0,4074	1058	0,2314	0,4219	1007	0,1906	0,3930	1133
Fibromyalgia	0,0887	0,2845	992	0,1099	0,3130	1046	0,1429	0,3501	994	0,1317	0,3383	1116
Chronic back syndrome	0,2000	0,4002	1015	0,1907	0,3930	1054	0,2510	0,4338	1016	0,2376	0,4258	1132
Chronic throat disease	0,0318	0,1755	1007	0,0313	0,1742	1054	0,0419	0,2005	1002	0,0486	0,2151	1132
Diabetes	0,0247	0,1554	1011	0,0274	0,1634	1057	0,0386	0,1928	1010	0,0328	0,1781	1129
Serious headaches	0,1098	0,3128	1011	0,1067	0,3089	1059	0,1308	0,3373	1017	0,1764	0,3813	1134
Urinary incontinence	0,1708	0,3765	1019	0,1627	0,3693	1057	0,2261	0,4185	1026	0,1793	0,3837	1138
Thyroid disease	0,0663	0,2490	1010	0,0755	0,2644	1059	0,1068	0,3090	1021	0,0884	0,2841	1142
High blood pressure	0,1896	0,3922	1023	0,2054	0,4042	1066	0,2542	0,4356	1011	0,2181	0,4131	1151
Average	0,1571			0,1638			0,1827			0,1883		
Equivalized hh income[c]	4867	2877	1070	3938	2313	1091	4062	2259	1074	4123	2306	1197

[a] 2012a shows Sample 2 (the new-entrants in 2012)
[b] Health dummies = 1 if the disease is present
[c] Equivalized hh income stands for equivalized household income where the OECD modified equivalence scale has been used to make income comparable between different household compositions

Table 3 Summary statistics for both sexes

	2007			2009			2012			2012a[a]		
Health dummies[b]	Mean	SD	N	Mean	SD	N	Mean	SD	N	Mean	SD	N
Eye disease	0,0547	0,2275	1883	0,0483	0,2145	1945	0,0561	0,2301	1891	0,0437	0,2046	2103
Irritable bowel syndrome	0,0343	0,1820	1866	0,0398	0,1954	1937	0,0254	0,1573	1892	0,0316	0,1751	2086
Chronic fatigue syndrome	0,0697	0,2547	1851	0,0876	0,2828	1941	0,0901	0,2864	1876	0,1195	0,3244	2101
Cold or flu	0,1128	0,3164	1906	0,0909	0,2875	1970	0,0865	0,2812	1895	0,0971	0,2962	2080
Alcoholism	0,0176	0,1314	1880	0,0143	0,1189	1954	0,0152	0,1225	1904	0,0256	0,1580	2108
Chronic anxiety	0,0929	0,2904	1872	0,0983	0,2977	1954	0,0960	0,2947	1896	0,1223	0,3277	2102
Chronic depression	0,0484	0,2147	1879	0,0511	0,2203	1956	0,0470	0,2117	1893	0,0621	0,2414	2110
Anxiety	0,1944	0,3958	1924	0,2161	0,4117	1967	0,2271	0,4191	1933	0,2607	0,4391	2144
Serious worries	0,2207	0,4148	1935	0,2437	0,4294	1978	0,2558	0,4364	1935	0,2910	0,4543	2148
Sleeping difficulties	0,2439	0,4296	1931	0,2663	0,4421	1979	0,2730	0,4456	1934	0,3039	0,4600	2149
Other mental disorders	0,0233	0,1508	1849	0,0247	0,1553	1943	0,0207	0,1426	1880	0,0354	0,1848	2091
Shortness of breath	0,0834	0,2765	1931	0,0896	0,2857	1975	0,1025	0,3034	1922	0,1063	0,3083	2145
Debility	0,1968	0,3977	1916	0,2362	0,4248	1969	0,2729	0,4456	1920	0,2364	0,4250	2132
Myalgia	0,3575	0,4794	1919	0,3437	0,4751	1967	0,3708	0,4832	1920	0,4108	0,4921	2142
Back/shoulder pain	0,4512	0,4977	1926	0,4336	0,4957	1965	0,4737	0,4994	1936	0,5042	0,5001	2156
Arm pain	0,2111	0,4082	1914	0,2079	0,4059	1972	0,2338	0,4233	1925	0,2389	0,4265	2147
Leg pain	0,2656	0,4418	1924	0,2684	0,4432	1971	0,2954	0,4563	1933	0,3055	0,4607	2144
Frequent headaches	0,1584	0,3652	1925	0,1519	0,3590	1975	0,1499	0,3571	1934	0,1906	0,3928	2141
Toothache	0,0518	0,2217	1930	0,0530	0,2241	1981	0,0481	0,2140	1934	0,0681	0,2520	2158
Abdominal pain	0,1391	0,3461	1927	0,1390	0,3461	1971	0,1430	0,3502	1930	0,1816	0,3856	2137
Rheumatoid arthritis	0,0648	0,2462	1853	0,0917	0,2887	1941	0,0987	0,2983	1855	0,0909	0,2876	2046
Osteoarthritis	0,1438	0,3510	1877	0,1639	0,3703	1952	0,1786	0,3831	1870	0,1560	0,3629	2077
Fibromyalgia	0,0576	0,2330	1841	0,0745	0,2626	1934	0,0873	0,2824	1844	0,0867	0,2815	2041
Chronic back syndrome	0,1684	0,3744	1882	0,1712	0,3768	1945	0,2153	0,4111	1881	0,2208	0,4149	2070
Chronic throat disease	0,0263	0,1599	1866	0,0288	0,1673	1943	0,0348	0,1832	1870	0,0386	0,1927	2072
Diabetes	0,0288	0,1674	1873	0,0338	0,1807	1953	0,0506	0,2193	1876	0,0461	0,2097	2083
Serious headaches	0,0828	0,2757	1872	0,0763	0,2656	1952	0,1015	0,3021	1901	0,1280	0,3341	2102
Urinary incontinence	0,1203	0,3254	1887	0,1189	0,3237	1952	0,1684	0,3743	1894	0,1388	0,3458	2089
Thyroid disease	0,0428	0,2025	1869	0,0513	0,2207	1949	0,0705	0,2561	1900	0,0597	0,2371	2109
High blood pressure	0,1858	0,3891	1889	0,2088	0,4065	1959	0,2440	0,4296	1881	0,2253	0,4179	2108
Average	0,1316			0,1374			0,1511			0,1609		
Equivalized hh income[c]	5090	2974	1972	4195	2380	2019	4286	2386	1908	4282	2396	2203

[a] 2012a shows Sample 2 (the new-entrants in 2012)
[b] Health dummies = 1 if the disease is present
[c] Equivalized hh income stands for equivalized household income where the OECD modified equivalence scale has been used to make income comparable between different household compositions

Table 4 Wagstaff Concentration Indices for men

Disease	2007 WCI	2007 St. WCI[b]	2007 SE	2009 WCI	2009 St. WCI	2009 SE	2012 WCI	2012 St. WCI	2012 SE	2012a[a] WCI	2012a[a] St. WCI	2012a[a] SE
Eye disease	0,1100	0,0848	0,0035	0,2308	0,2296	0,0031**	0,1460	0,0970	0,0030	−0,0836	−0,0744	0,0028
Irritable bowel syndrome	0,0941	0,0710	0,0028	−0,0164	−0,0148	0,0023	0,1031	0,0806	0,0026	0,1064	−0,0240	0,0021
Chronic fatigue syndrome	0,1400	0,1405	0,0053*	0,1571	0,1534	0,0053*	0,3214	0,2976	0,0043***	0,3219	0,3775	0,0052***
Cold or flu	−0,0194	0,0026	0,0068	0,1625	0,1619	0,0060**	0,1882	0,2073	0,0056**	0,1439	0,1059	0,0061**
Alcoholism	0,0037	−0,0113	0,0025	0,2208	0,2200	0,0025	0,2637	0,2545	0,0026	0,1352	0,1327	0,0034
Chronic anxiety	0,1196	0,1170	0,0062	0,0414	0,0411	0,0057	0,2358	0,2295	0,0055***	0,2854	0,2815	0,0056***
Chronic depression	0,1975	0,2107	0,0044*	−0,0083	−0,0104	0,0037	0,2491	0,2455	0,0036**	0,4187	0,4242	0,0040***
Anxiety	0,1169	0,1287	0,0084**	0,0211	0,0185	0,0090	0,0287	0,0224	0,0093	0,1804	0,1691	0,0107***
Serious worries	0,1470	0,1544	0,0094***	0,0330	0,0307	0,0108	0,1479	0,1521	0,0108***	0,2289	0,2235	0,0116***
Sleeping difficulties	0,0359	0,0338	0,0096	0,0019	−0,0003	0,0098	0,0555	0,0412	0,0100	0,1217	0,1230	0,0105***
Other mental disorders	0,4514	0,4566	0,0030***	0,1147	0,1124	0,0027	0,4338	0,4058	0,0022**	0,3323	0,2680	0,0028**
Shortness of breath	0,1649	0,1639	0,0046**	0,1965	0,1908	0,0053*	0,0393	0,0287	0,0052	0,2241	0,2584	0,0052***
Debility	0,1845	0,1801	0,0082***	0,1115	0,1079	0,0082*	0,2546	0,2450	0,0085***	0,2195	0,2215	0,0076***
Myalgia	0,1025	0,0489	0,0109**	0,0265	0,0633	0,0109	0,0389	0,0736	0,0121	0,0367	0,0141	0,0128
Back/shoulder pain	0,0541	0,0696	0,0152	0,0101	0,0113	0,0147	0,0590	0,0711	0,0161	0,0650	0,0624	0,0165*
Arm pain	0,0958	0,0957	0,0085*	0,0888	0,0869	0,0080	0,0309	0,0427	0,0093	−0,0716	−0,0240	0,0088
Leg pain	0,0936	0,1028	0,0104**	0,1150	0,1131	0,0106**	0,1917	0,1938	0,0106***	0,0368	0,0621	0,0111
Frequent headaches	0,1314	0,1589	0,0064*	0,0033	0,0059	0,0067	0,2547	0,2501	0,0065***	0,1937	0,1480	0,0074***
Toothache	0,1623	0,1654	0,0049*	0,4457	0,4507	0,0053***	0,2318	0,2694	0,0047**	0,1072	0,0981	0,0054
Abdominal pain	0,1460	0,1723	0,0068**	0,0821	0,0820	0,0068	0,1527	0,1581	0,0067**	0,0890	0,0719	0,0074
Rheumatoid arthritis	0,2086	0,2071	0,0037**	0,1866	0,1821	0,0043*	0,1738	0,1454	0,0048**	0,1693	0,2408	0,0044**
Osteoarthritis	0,1753	0,1422	0,0055***	0,2129	0,2088	0,0053***	0,2311	0,2058	0,0055***	0,1205	0,1967	0,0050*
Fibromyalgia	0,3319	0,3133	0,0021**	0,3122	0,3086	0,0027**	0,3818	0,3794	0,0024***	0,1474	0,2060	0,0027
Chronic back syndrome	0,1485	0,1672	0,0075***	0,1379	0,1380	0,0074*	0,1934	0,2123	0,0087***	0,1121	0,1312	0,0085**
Chronic throat disease	0,0977	0,0996	0,0026	0,1448	0,1446	0,0025	0,1150	0,1500	0,0033	0,0290	−0,0083	0,0027
Diabetes	0,0012	−0,0457	0,0029	0,0140	0,0120	0,0029	0,0311	0,0245	0,0040	0,1350	0,1767	0,0038
Serious headaches	0,1120	0,1350	0,0048	0,0166	0,0160	0,0042	0,1029	0,1149	0,0060	0,0576	0,0459	0,0056
Urinary incontinence	0,2260	0,1768	0,0042***	0,2070	0,2047	0,0040***	0,0977	0,0686	0,0051	0,1568	0,1879	0,0043*
Thyroid disease	0,4220	0,4047	0,0020**	0,2709	0,2690	0,0022*	0,1218	0,1104	0,0028	0,1162	0,1167	0,0022
High blood pressure	−0,0811	−0,1006	0,0089*	0,0322	0,0296	0,0090	−0,0231	−0,0542	0,0093	0,0668	0,1115	0,0080
Average	0,1391	0,1349		0,1191	0,1189		0,1617	0,1574		0,1401	0,1442	

$^{*}p < 0{,}10$, $^{**} < 0{,}05$, $^{***} < 0{,}01$

[a] 2012a shows Sample 2 (the new-entrants in 2012)

[b] St. WCI stands for Standardized Wagstaff Concentration Indices where unavoidable inequality has been subtracted

Table 5 Wagstaff Concentration Indices for women

Disease	2007 WCI	2007 St. WCI[b]	2007 SE	2009 WCI	2009 St. WCI	2009 SE	2012 WCI	2012 St. WCI	2012 SE	2012a[a] WCI	2012a[a] St. WCI	2012a[a] SE
Eye disease	0,2389	0,1496	0,0038***	0,2601	0,2269	0,0031***	0,2620	0,1362	0,0041***	0,1141	0,1477	0,0031
Irritable bowel syndrome	0,0916	0,1128	0,0046	0,1449	0,1644	0,0049**	−0,0630	−0,1670	0,0033	0,0927	0,0727	0,0038
Chronic fatigue syndrome	0,2531	0,2363	0,0047***	0,2522	0,2507	0,0055***	0,1833	0,1840	0,0061***	0,2606	0,2706	0,0065***
Cold or flu	0,1003	0,1200	0,0069*	−0,0154	−0,0165	0,0062	0,0553	0,0216	0,0065	0,1028	0,1054	0,0059*
Alcoholism	−0,0713	−0,0729	0,0025	−0,0341	0,0356	0,0020	0,1940	0,1295	0,0017	0,2782	0,3541	0,0018
Chronic anxiety	0,2669	0,2874	0,0059***	0,3014	0,2969	0,0063***	0,2358	0,2966	0,0068***	0,3738	0,3232	0,0071***
Chronic depression	0,3160	0,3123	0,0042***	0,2466	0,2303	0,0046***	0,2766	0,2671	0,0026***	0,4741	0,4493	0,0046***
Anxiety	0,0775	0,0924	0,0102*	0,0318	0,0390	0,0108	0,0872	0,1256	0,0113**	0,2084	0,0349	0,0116***
Serious worries	0,0763	0,1137	0,0107**	0,1322	0,1514	0,0113***	0,0690	0,0950	0,0122*	0,2195	0,1855	0,0122***
Sleeping difficulties	0,0652	0,0547	0,0114*	0,0884	0,0831	0,0117**	0,0664	0,0751	0,0128*	0,0775	0,0573	0,0125***
Other mental disorders	0,1665	0,1513	0,0032	0,4848	0,5487	0,0035***	0,3178	0,3165	0,0033**	0,3793	0,3267	0,0041***
Shortness of breath	0,1611	0,1741	0,0059***	0,1311	0,1022	0,0058**	0,0753	0,1142	0,0064	0,2043	0,1656	0,0068***
Debility	0,1066	0,1332	0,0099**	0,1517	0,1514	0,0111***	0,1678	0,2200	0,0126***	0,0773	0,0498	0,0110*
Myalgia	−0,0210	−0,0007	0,0169	0,0668	0,0852	0,0164**	0,0189	0,0724	0,0176	−0,0011	−0,0372	0,0180
Back/shoulder pain	0,0247	0,0379	0,0179	0,0276	0,0390	0,0181	0,0370	0,0677	0,0193	0,0761	0,0528	0,0191**
Arm pain	0,0666	0,0612	0,0100	0,0227	0,0079	0,0098	0,0473	0,0617	0,0110	0,0410	0,0573	0,0098
Leg pain	0,0629	0,0528	0,0115*	0,0374	0,0324	0,0114	0,0706	0,0814	0,0121*	0,0973	0,0981	0,0116***
Frequent headaches	0,0495	0,0938	0,0098	0,0599	0,0840	0,0095	0,0147	0,0557	0,0100	0,1125	0,0843	0,0107***
Toothache	−0,0280	0,0138	0,0044	0,1387	0,1794	0,0046*	0,2997	0,3474	0,0046***	0,3100	0,3061	0,0054***
Abdominal pain	0,0292	0,0736	0,0086	0,1747	0,2143	0,0088***	−0,0127	0,0287	0,0087	0,1375	0,1020	0,0099***
Rheumatoid arthritis	0,1498	0,1115	0,0050***	0,1324	0,0892	0,0055**	0,2328	0,2165	0,0059***	0,0410	0,0962	0,0050
Osteoarthritis	0,2062	0,1668	0,0074***	0,1916	0,1433	0,0075***	0,1785	0,0939	0,0085***	−0,0236	0,0305	0,0066
Fibromyalgia	0,1602	0,1236	0,0054***	0,2446	0,2071	0,0056***	0,1648	0,1231	0,0068***	0,0934	0,0900	0,0060*
Chronic back syndrome	0,1691	0,1759	0,0086***	0,1213	0,1080	0,0080***	0,1836	0,1705	0,0099***	0,1297	0,1238	0,0090***
Chronic throat disease	0,1325	0,1819	0,0033	0,1909	0,1814	0,0029*	0,2395	0,2018	0,0036***	0,1538	0,1647	0,0037*
Diabetes	0,1458	0,1359	0,0024*	0,2517	0,2373	0,0025***	0,1578	0,2615	0,0031*	0,0944	0,0737	0,0024
Serious headaches	0,2498	0,2764	0,0066***	0,0794	0,1078	0,0066	0,0838	0,1885	0,0075	0,0952	0,0765	0,0086**
Urinary incontinence	0,1189	0,0958	0,0077**	0,1234	0,1081	0,0071***	0,1686	0,1302	0,0088***	0,1777	0,1721	0,0071***
Thyroid disease	−0,0039	−0,0216	0,0045	0,0925	0,0889	0,0045	0,1384	0,1936	0,0055**	−0,0201	−0,0159	0,0047
High blood pressure	0,1460	0,1014	0,0078***	0,1078	0,0720	0,0079***	0,1332	0,0081	0,0096***	0,0315	0,0791	0,0072
Average	0,1169	0,1182		0,1413	0,1416		0,1361	0,1372		0,1470	0,1366	

*$p < 0,10$, ** < 0,05, *** < 0,01

[a] 2012a shows Sample 2 (the new-entrants in 2012)

[b] St. WCI stands for Standardized Wagstaff Concentration Indices where unavoidable inequality has been subtracted

Table 6 Wagstaff Concentration Indices for both sexes

	2007			2009			2012			2012a[a]		
Disease	WCI	St. WCI[b]	SE	WCI	St. WCI	SE	WCI	St. WCI	SE	WCI	St. WCI	SE
Eye disease	0,1948	0,1377	0,0026***	0,2486	0,2339	0,0022***	0,2411	0,1484	0,0025***	0,0318	0,0504	0,0021
Irritable bowel syndrome	0,1238	0,0292	0,0027**	0,1617	0,1563	0,0027**	0,0128	−0,0172	0,0021	0,1216	0,0756	0,0022
Chronic fatigue syndrome	0,1940	0,1905	0,0035***	0,2187	0,1878	0,0038***	0,2620	0,0508	0,0037***	0,2651	0,2690	0,0042***
Cold or flu	0,0905	0,1080	0,0048**	0,0660	0,0649	0,0043	0,1224	0,1116	0,0043***	0,1217	0,1261	0,0042***
Alcoholism	−0,0116	−0,0499	0,0017	0,1214	0,2213	0,0016	0,2213	0,2303	0,0015	0,1421	0,1778	0,0019
Chronic anxiety	0,2074	0,2020	0,0042***	0,2052	0,1979	0,0042***	0,2579	0,2510	0,0044***	0,3461	0,2894	0,0045***
Chronic depression	0,2718	0,2558	0,0030***	0,1755	0,1560	0,0030***	0,2809	0,2623	0,0029***	0,4548	0,4283	0,0031***
Anxiety	0,1123	0,1006	0,0066***	0,0433	0,0190	0,0070	0,0867	0,0772	0,0073***	0,2020	0,1664	0,0078***
Serious worries	0,1192	0,1203	0,0071***	0,0982	0,0963	0,0078***	0,1212	0,1178	0,0081***	0,2294	0,1963	0,0084**
Sleeping difficulties	0,0673	0,0364	0,0075**	0,0679	0,0426	0,0076**	0,0779	0,0515	0,0081***	0,1068	0,0762	0,0082***
Other mental disorders	0,2786	0,2419	0,0022***	0,3731	0,4085	0,0022***	0,3841	0,3307	0,0020***	0,3773	0,2958	0,0025***
Shortness of breath	0,1905	0,1858	0,0038***	0,1748	0,1334	0,0039***	0,0751	0,0681	0,0042	0,2241	0,1876	0,0043***
Debility	0,1564	0,1427	0,0064***	0,1623	0,1169	0,0068***	0,2257	0,1969	0,0075***	0,1523	0,1152	0,0066***
Myalgia	0,0685	0,0489	0,0098**	0,0852	0,0633	0,0096***	0,0564	0,0736	0,0105	0,0389	−0,0098	0,0107
Back/shoulder pain	0,0559	0,0568	0,0117**	0,0388	0,0269	0,0114	0,0649	0,0789	0,0125**	0,0815	0,0576	0,0125***
Arm pain	0,0965	0,0728	0,0065***	0,0658	0,0292	0,0063**	0,0521	0,0535	0,0072*	−0,0025	0,0139	0,0066
Leg pain	0,0869	0,0718	0,0077***	0,0812	0,0574	0,0077***	0,1320	0,1247	0,0080***	0,0725	0,0840	0,0080***
Frequent headaches	0,1133	0,1177	0,0059***	0,0812	0,0769	0,0058**	0,1229	0,1080	0,0060***	0,1609	0,1086	0,0064***
Toothache	0,0716	0,0794	0,0033	0,2854	0,3236	0,0035***	0,2728	0,3016	0,0033***	0,2015	0,1907	0,0038***
Abdominal pain	0,0941	0,1076	0,0055**	0,1602	0,1556	0,0055***	0,0733	0,0608	0,0055*	0,1371	0,0976	0,0062***
Rheumatoid arthritis	0,1812	0,1330	0,0031***	0,1667	0,1086	0,0035***	0,2176	0,1657	0,0038***	0,1009	0,1478	0,0034**
Osteoarthritis	0,2072	0,1485	0,0046***	0,2124	0,1492	0,0045***	0,2101	0,1253	0,0050***	0,0461	0,0843	0,0041
Fibromyalgia	0,2224	0,1485	0,0030***	0,2944	0,2158	0,0031***	0,2288	0,1478	0,0036***	0,1361	0,1016	0,0033***
Chronic back syndrome	0,1751	0,1733	0,0057***	0,1384	0,1211	0,0055***	0,1931	0,2067	0,0066***	0,1309	0,1307	0,0062***
Chronic throat disease	0,1270	0,1231	0,0021	0,1692	0,1266	0,0020*	0,1870	0,2152	0,0024***	0,1328	0,1205	0,0023*
Diabetes	0,0650	0,0407	0,0019	0,1185	0,1124	0,0019*	0,0863	0,1123	0,0025	0,1050	0,1273	0,0022
Serious headaches	0,2270	0,2291	0,0041***	0,1083	0,0862	0,0039**	0,1122	0,1405	0,0048**	0,1081	0,0614	0,0051***
Urinary incontinence	0,1737	0,0945	0,0044***	0,1849	0,1307	0,0041***	0,1746	0,1043	0,0051***	0,1881	0,1601	0,0041***
Thyroid disease	0,0908	0,0178	0,0025	0,1673	0,1103	0,0026***	0,1646	0,1599	0,0031***	0,0347	0,0096	0,0026
High blood pressure	0,0284	0,0060	0,0059	0,0624	0,0556	0,0059**	0,0642	−0,0069	0,0067**	0,0486	0,0821	0,0054
Average	0,1360	0,1123		0,1512	0,1328		0,1594	0,1350		0,1499	0,1341	

*$p < 0,10$, ** < 0,05, *** < 0,01

[a] 2012a shows Sample 2 (the new-entrants in 2012)

[b] St. WCI stands for Standardized Wagstaff Concentration Indices where unavoidable inequality has been subtracted

the whole period, first driven by the increase in women's inequality and then by men's. Figure 1 graphs the main results by showing the average WCIs, both by gender and overall.

The panels in Fig. 2 graph the trends of the disease specific WCIs, separately for males and females, as well as overall. With only few insignificant exceptions, they all show income-related inequality favoring higher income groups (with WCIs ranging from around zero to 0,5).

Relatively high income-related inequality can be seen for the mental conditions - chronic anxiety (panel f), chronic depression (panel g), and other mental disorders (panel k) - and in all cases the inequality is higher for women than for men. For alcoholism or substance addiction (panel e) the WCIs for both genders have increased steadily over the entire period and are substantially higher for males than females. Toothache (panel s) and fibromyalgia (panel w) have also relatively high WCIs for both genders, and again higher for men than women. The income-related inequality in toothache has a clear trend with a rapid increase around the recession, but a slight recovery between 2009 and 2012.

The most stable WCIs are those connected to physical pain - such as myalgia (panel n), back/shoulder pain (panel o), arm pain (panel p), leg pain (panel q), and both headache variables (panels r and a1) - and these WCIs tend to have a slight decrease between 2007 and 2009 and a small increase between 2009 and 2012. A relatively steady WCIs can be found for arthritis, both rheumatoid arthritis (panel u) and osteoarthritis (panel v).

Discussions

Our findings contribute to existing studies on income-related inequality in health, and our research is – to our best knowledge – the first to look at the impact of an economic collapse on the income-related inequality in

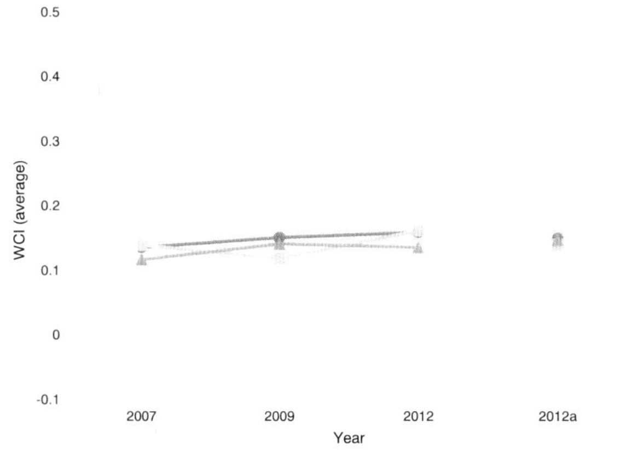

Fig. 1 Average concentration indices

specific diseases and disorders. As mentioned earlier, the current study can be seen as an extension of Ásgeirsdóttir's and Ragnarsdóttir's paper [40] on the impact of the economic collapse on income-related health inequality in Iceland over the period of 2007–2009. With additional data from 2012 we were able to study the impact over a longer period, and while they used a general health measure we measure health specifically for thirty different diseases.

A large proportion of government spending in Western countries goes to health care, which makes it important to monitor socio-economic inequality, in particular income-related health inequality. As our study provides a valuable insight into the distribution of various diseases along the income spectrum in Iceland we hope our results can be of practical value.

The unusually sharp changes in the economic conditions in Iceland over the short time period examined allowed us to study the business cycle's effects without being considerably affected by long-term changes in other variables which have caused methodological challenges in studies conducted over a longer time period. Furthermore, the timing of the collection of the data, which includes both income and health variables, enables us to take full advantage of these rapid changes as the first wave is collected a year before the economic collapse, the second wave a year after the collapse and the third 4 years after the crash, when the economy had already partly recovered.

Our results suggest a considerable income-related health inequality in Iceland over the years of 2007–2012. On average the higher-income individuals are healthier than their lower-income counterparts. On the whole, income-related health inequality increased steadily over the whole period, although the economic hardship of the crisis caused a temporary decrease in the case of males but an increase for women. For both genders, these temporal trends in the WCIs over the first period are reverted in the latter period during the recovery. It should also be mentioned that these opposing trends in the gender specific WCIs are most distinct in the trends of the mental health variables.

The gender differences in the WCIs highlight the importance of taking into account unavoidable factors by calculating standardized WCIs. For the full samples (both sexes), the standardized indices are substantially lower than the unstandardized ones. However, the differences between the standardized indices and the unstandardized are very small for the gender specific WCIs (where age is the only unavoidable factor). Clearly, the overall differences between the standardized WCIs and the unstandardized WCIs are driven by the large contribution of gender differences. In many cases, clear gender differences can also be observed in the impact of the recession on health, and our summary statistics reveal

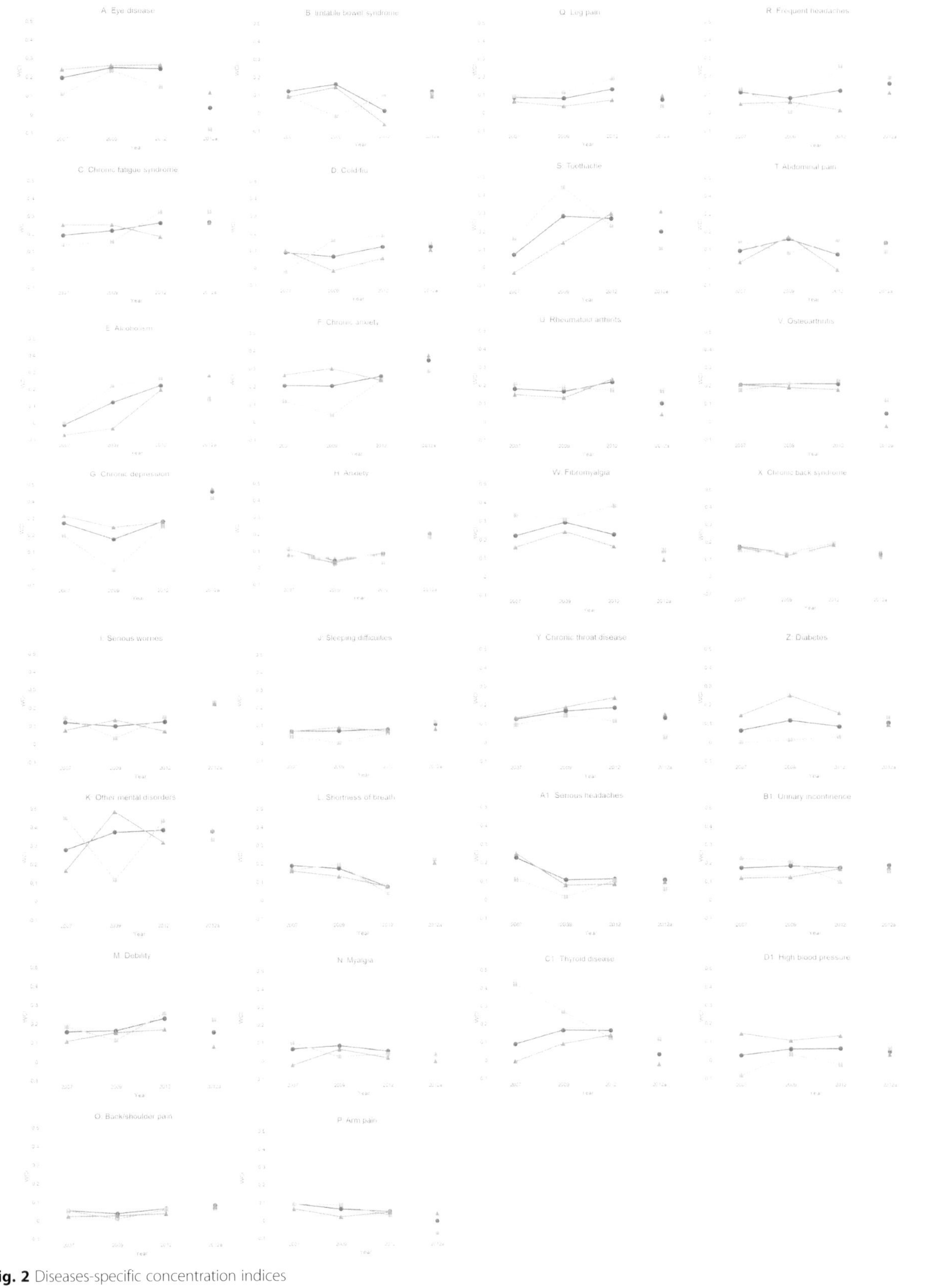

Fig. 2 Diseases-specific concentration indices

worse health and lower income for women than men over the whole period (results also found by Ásgeirsdóttir and Ragnarsdóttir [40]).

Furthermore, there are obvious gender differences in the trends of the WCIs; as mentioned above. During the economic downturn in the 2007–2009 period, women's income-related health inequality increased while that of men's decreased. During the recovery, in the 2009–2012 period, female inequality decreased and men's increased. Although we can only hypothesize about the reasons behind the gender differences in the WCI trends, the decrease in men's WCIs between 2007 and 2009 might be due to increased unemployment in cyclically sensitive sectors, such as construction industry, in which many studies have found counter-cyclical health trends as mentioned above. Increased unemployment in these sectors, which tend to be dominated by men, would then cause individuals to drop in the income ranking while improving in health, which lowers the WCIs. Our summary statistics support this hypothesis; physical health (especially physical health variables that are likely to be related to hard work such as myalgia, back/shoulder pain, arm pain, abdominal pain and serious headaches) improves during the recession (between 2007 and 2009). Regarding the increase in female income-related health inequality over the crisis period one might speculate whether these trends can be explained by different effects on different income groups: we suggest that women in higher income groups are more likely to follow Ruhm's and Cawley's [9] counter-cyclical health mechanisms mentioned above; during a recession they reduce their unhealthy consumption and increase healthy behaviors, such as exercise. Their lower income counterparts, on the other hand, might be more likely to be adversely affected by the recession, in particular less disposable income might affect their mental health. This hypothesis is also somewhat supported in our summary statistics; many of our physical health variables suggest that women's physical health improves during the crisis but their mental health clearly deteriorates. The lower average income of females, relative to men, could potentially explain why a decrease in income during the crisis had larger effects on women's mental health than men's. However, the reason for this gender difference remains unclear and would be an interesting avenue for future research. Importantly, the fact that the average income-related health inequality for both genders reverts back towards their pre-crisis levels as the economy recovers from the recession (over the 2009–2012 period) makes the observed changes even more likely to be due to the economic conditions.

Quite surprisingly, the changes in our gender specific WCIs over the first period (2007–2009) are not in accordance with those of Ásgeirsdóttir and Ragnarsdóttir [40] who concluded a decreased inequality for women, but an increased inequality for men. Here it should be noted that it is in our WCIs for mental health (such as chronic anxiety (panel f in Fig. 2), serious worries (panel i in Fig. 2), other mental disorders (panel k in Fig. 2) and sleeping difficulties (panel j in Fig. 2)) that drive the rise in women's WCIs and the decrease in men's is most distinct. In this respect it is important to bear in mind that Ásgeirsdóttir and Ragnarsdóttir [40] use a very general self-assessed health measurement and people's assessment is more likely to reflect physical health than mental health. This might partly explain the inconsistency between the results and highlights the importance of a more detailed analysis as the one presented here.

Our summary statistics show some consistency with the results of several studies mentioned earlier on the impact of business cycles on health; counter-cyclical physical health but pro-cyclical mental health [26, 27, 36]. In our results, such effects can be observed to some extent over the period 2009–2012. As Iceland's economy recovered rapidly from the recession, physical health deteriorated, but some of our mental health variables indicate an improvement. However, over the first period, the average frequency of diseases remains very stable. The negative impact of the crisis on mental health is consistent with studies on other hard hit European countries such as Greece [62] and Spain [63]. However, a recent study [64] shows that in these countries, the crisis had larger adverse effects on health in general than in Iceland and suggests that this is due to the stark differences in fiscal policies adopted during the recession.

When crudely observing cyclicality from the summary statistics, the aging of the sample needs to be kept in mind. Despite the lower age range, Sample 2 has slightly higher frequency in diseases on average than Sample 1 in 2012 which gives a reason to assume that aging is not an important determinant in the health deterioration. Still, the diseases most likely to be correlated with aging (both kinds of arthritis, fibromyalgia, debility, urinary incontinence, thyroid disease, high blood pressure and eye disease) have lower frequencies in Sample 2. Interestingly, higher frequency of diseases in Sample 2 is evident in all of the mental illness variables.

It is important to note that our study employs self-reported measures of the diseases and conditions of interest, which, although widely used, might pose problems to the reliability of the measurements. Differences in health assessment might e.g. be affected by differences in people's health awareness and evaluation, particularly since many of the health variables in question are conditions, rather than diseases. Moreover, one could even speculate whether such differences might be related to socio-economic status, which would further bias our measurements. Some conditions that have been of interest in previous research on business cycles and health are unfortunately omitted in this research, for example suicides, traffic accidents and infant mortality. How business cycles affect the distribution of those conditions across socioeconomic groups would however be of interest and we encourage future research on those topics.

The aging of the sample over the 5 year period can also be mentioned as a potential drawback to our study as the increase in the income-related inequality in health may partly be driven by the aging. One obvious reason for this is that as people grow older they are more likely to have worse health, and when they retire they tend to drop in their income ranking, which affects the income-related health inequality [65]. However, aging has also been found to increase the inequality before retirement. Deaton and Paxson [66] studied approximately 50.000 adults between the ages of twenty and seventy over the period of 1983 to 1994. They used self-reported health status as the health measurement and found that a correlation between health and income increases with age, particularly from the age of twenty up until retirement age. They provide several possible explanations for this; they mention how earnings are adversely affected by negative health shocks and hence progressively correlated with age. As people's health after retirement does not affect income, they suggest that the correlation may weaken in very old age. They also evaluate possible causalities running from income to health such as how poorer people become more exposed to various risk factors with age and have more limited access to health care than their richer counterparts. As Sample 2 constitutes a group of participants in the same age range as that of Sample 1 in 2007, the presentation of this newest sample can be seen as our way to partly address this problem. Although not evident for females on average, Sample 2 has a slightly lower WCIs than Sample 1 does in 2012, which might give a reason to conjecture that the aging of the sample increases the income-related health inequality.

Our results suggest that the increase driven by the aging of the sample is more likely to be found in physical illness than mental illness, and especially evident in both kinds of arthritis, fibromyalgia and physical pain. Our standardized WCIs support these findings as they show that the contribution of age is stronger for men than women and much larger in the latter period than the first. Especially, the contribution of age increases the WCIs of Sample 1 in 2012. Thus, the increase in men's income-related health inequality over the latter period is exaggerated by the aging of the sample. Consequently, as the overall increase in the income-related health inequality between 2009 and 2012 is driven by the biased increase in men's inequality, it also needs to be discounted.

Conclusions

By analyzing the period between 2007 and 2012 in Iceland, we show that the economic collapse increased female income-related health inequality but decreased that of men. These changes, which are largely driven by the trends in mental health inequality, reversed during the economic recovery period. Overall, we find a considerable income-related health inequality which increased steadily over the whole study period. Our results conform and contribute to a range of other studies on income-related inequality in health; they provide evidence of the effects of an economic collapse and a recovery on the distribution of thirty different diseases along the income spectrum. As many of the impacts and trends in the WCIs are still unexplained, a decomposition of all the WCIs would be a logical next step in order to provide a clearer picture of the main determinants of the income-related health inequality. Given the range of diseases and conditions examined within this study, such an analysis is beyond the scope of this paper, but encouraged.

Acknowledgements
We thank the Directorate of Health in Iceland for providing the data.

Funding
We are grateful for having received funding from The Icelandic Student Innovation Fund (application number 1536030091) and from The Icelandic Research Fund – Icelandic Center for Research (IRF grant number 130611–052) to support assistantship by Hildur Margrét Jóhannsdóttir.

Authors' contributions
The authors both collectively collaborated on all sections of the paper. Large portions of the work were executed by HMJ while supervised by TLA. Both authors read and approved the final manuscript.

Competing interests
The authors declare that they have no competing interests.

References

1. Ruhm CJ. Healthy living in hard times. J Health Econ. 2005;24(2):341–63. doi:10.1016/j.jhealeco.2004.09.007.
2. Wilkinson RG. Unfair shares: the effects of widening income differences on the welfare of the young. J Soc Policy. 1994;24(4):577–8. doi:10.1017/S0047279400025472.
3. Wilkinson RG, Pickett KE. Income inequality and population health: a review and explanation of the evidence. Soc Sci Med. 2006;62(7):1768–84. doi:10.1016/j.socscimed.2005.08.036.
4. Wilkinson RG, Pickett KE. Income inequality and health: A causal review. Soc Sci Med. 2015;128:316–26. doi:10.1016/j.socscimed.2014.12.031.
5. Berkman ND, Sheridan SL, Donahue KE, Halpern DJ, Crotty K. Low health literacy and health outcomes: an updated systematic review. Ann Intern Med. 2011;155(2):97–107. doi:10.7326/0003-4819-155-2-201107190-00005.
6. Kawachi I, Adler NE, Dow WH. Money, schooling, and health: Mechanisms and causal evidence. Ann N Y Acad Sci. 2010;1186:56–68. doi:10.1111/j.1749-6632.2009.05340.x.
7. Marmot MG, Rose G, Shipley M, Hamilton PJS. Employment Grade and Coronary Heart Disease in British Civil Servants. J Epidemiol Commun H. 1978;32(4):244–9.
8. Marmot MG, Smith GD, Stansfeld S, Patel C, North F, Head J, White I, Brunner E, Feeney A. Health Inequalities among British Civil Servants: The Whitehall II Study. Lancet. 1991;337(8754):1387–93.
9. Ruhm CJ, Cawley J. The economics of risky health behavior. Handb Health Econ. 2011;2:95–199. doi:10.3386/w17081.

10. Wagstaff A, van Doorslaer E. Income inequality and health: what does the literature tell us? Annu Rev Publ Health. 2000;21:543–67. doi:10.1146/annurev.publhealth.21.1.543.
11. Babones SJ. Income inequality and population health: correlation and causality. Soc Sci Med. 2008;66(7):1614–26. doi:10.1016/j.socscimed.2007.12.012.
12. Van Doorslaer E, Wagstaff A, Bleichrodt H, Calonge S, Gerdtham UG, Gerfin M, Geurts J, Gross L, Häkkinen U, Leu RE, O'Donnell O, Propper C, Puffer F, Rodriguez M, Sundberg G, Winkelhake O. Income-related inequalities in health: Some international comparisons. J Health Econ. 1997;16(1):93–112. doi:10.1016/S0167-6296(96)00532-2.
13. Asgeirsdóttir TL, Ragnarsdóttir DÓ. Determinants of relative and absolute concentration indices: evidence from 26 European countries. Int J Equity Health. 2013;12:53. doi:10.1186/1475-9276-12-53.
14. Bambra C, Eikemo TA. Welfare state regimes, unemployment and health: a comparative study of the relationship between unemployment and self-reported health in 23 European countries. J Epidemiol Commun H. 2009;63: 92–8. doi:10.1136/jech.2008.077354.
15. Eikemo TA, Bambra C, Huisman M, Kunst AE. Health inequalities according to educational level in different welfare regimes: a comparison of 23 European countries. Sociol Health Ill. 2008;30(4):565–82. doi:10.1111/j.1467-9566.2007.01073.x.
16. Eikemo TA, Bambra C, Joyce K, Dahl E. Welfare state regimes and income-related health inequalities: a comparison of 23 European countries. Eur J Public Health. 2008;18:593–9. doi:10.1093/eurpub/ckn092.
17. Mackenbach JP, Stirbu I, Roskam AJR, Schaap MM, Menvielle G, Leinsalu M, Kunst AE. Socioeconomic inequalities in health in 22 European countries. New Engl J Med. 2008;358:2468–81. doi:10.1056/NEJMsa0707519.
18. Van Doorslaer E, Koolman X. Explaining the differences in income-related health inequalities across European countries. Health Econ. 2004;13(7):609–28. doi:10.1002/hec.918.
19. Ariizumi H, Schirle T. Are recessions really good for your health? Evidence from Canada. Soc Sci Med. 2012;74(8):1224–31. doi:10.1016/j.socscimed.2011.12.038.
20. Granados JAT. Death Rates and Business Cycle Fluctuations in Spain at the End of the 20th Century: Further Empirical Evidence of the Mortality Increase During Economic Expansions. New York City: Mimeo, New School University; 2002.
21. Granados JAT. Increasing mortality during the expansions of the US economy, 1900–1996. Int J Epidemiol. 2005;34(6):1194–202. doi:10.1093/ije/dyi141.
22. Granados JAT. Recessions and mortality in Spain, 1980–1997. Eur J of Popul. 2005;21:393–422. doi:10.1007/s10680-005-4767-9.
23. Granados JAT. Macroeconomic fluctuations and mortality in postwar Japan. Demography. 2008;45(2):323–43. doi:10.1353/dem.0.0008.
24. Neumayer E. Recessions lower (some) mortality rates: evidence from Germany. Soc Sci Med. 2004;58:1037–47. doi:10.1016/S0277-9536(03)00276-4.
25. Ruhm CJ. Economic Conditions and Alcohol Problems. J Health Econ. 1995; 14(5):583–603. doi:10.3386/w4914.
26. Ruhm CJ. Are recessions good for your health? Q J Econ. 2000;115(2):617–50. doi:10.1162/003355300554872.
27. Ruhm CJ, Gerdtham UG. Deaths rise in good economic times: evidence from the OECD. Econ Hum Biol. 2006;4(3):298–316. doi:10.3386/w9357.
28. Gruber J, Frakes M. Does Falling Smoking Lead to Rising Obesity? J Health Econ. 2006;25(2):183–97. doi:10.3386/w11483.
29. Xu X, Kaestner R. The Business Cycle and Health Behaviors. No. 15737, NBER Working Papers. National Bureau of Economic Research. 2010. http://www.nber.org/papers/w15737. Accessed 12 Apr 2016
30. Courtemanche C. Longer Hours and Larger Waistlines? The Relationship Between Work Hours and Obesity. Forum Health Econ Pol. 2009;12(2):2–2. doi:10.2139/ssrn.975099.
31. Edwards R. Who is hurt by procyclical mortality? Soc Sci Med. 2008;67:2051–8. doi:10.1016/j.socscimed.2008.09.032.
32. Edwards R. American Time Use Over the Business Cycle. New York City: Mimeo, Queens College, CUNY; 2011.
33. Baker DB. The Study of Stress at Work. Ann Rev Publ Health. 1985;6:367–81. doi:10.1146/annurev.pu.06.050185.002055.
34. Karasek RA, Theorell T. Healthy Work: Stress, Productivity, and the Reconstruction of Working Life. New York: Basic Books; 1990.
35. Sokejima S, Kagamimori S. Working Hours as a Risk Factor for Acute Myocardial Infarction in Japan: A Case-control Study. British Med J. 1998;317(7161):775–780 http://www.jstor.org/stable/25180423 Accessed 1 Mar 2016
36. Ruhm CJ. Recessions, healthy no more? J Health Econ. 2015;42:17–28. doi:10.1016/j.jhealeco.2015.03.004.
37. Stevens AH, Douglas LM, Page M, Filipski M. The best of times, the worst of times: understanding pro-cyclical mortality. Am Econ J. 2011;7(4):279–311. doi:10.3386/w17657.
38. Economou A, Nikolaou A, Theodossiou I. Are recessions harmful to health after all?: Evidence from the European Union. J Econ Stud. 2008;35(4):368–84. doi:10.1108/01443580810903536.
39. McInerney M, Mellor JM. Recessions and seniors' health, health behaviors, and healthcare use: analysis of the medicare beneficiary survey. J Health Econ. 2012;31(5):744–51. doi:10.1016/j.jhealeco.2012.06.002.
40. Ásgeirsdóttir TL, Ragnarsdóttir DÓ. Health-income inequality: the effects of the Icelandic economic collapse. Int J Equity Health. 2014;13:1–23. doi:10.1007/s11150-013-9225-6.
41. Asgeirsdóttir TL, Eiríksdóttir VH, Bjarnadóttir RI, Kaestner R, Cnattingius S, Valdimarsdóttir UA. Low Birth Weight, Small for Gestational Age and Preterm Births Before and After the Economic Collapse in Iceland: A Population Based Cohort Study. PLoS ONE. 2013;8:12. doi:10.1371/journal.pone.0080499.
42. Asgeirsdóttir TL, Eiríksdóttir VH, Valdimarsdóttir UA, Hauksdóttir A, Lund SH, Bjarnadóttir RI, Cnattingius S, Zoega H. Pregnancy-Induced Hypertensive Disorders before and after a National Economic Collapse: A Population Based Cohort Study. PLoS ONE. 2015;10:9. doi:10.1371/journal.pone.0138534.
43. Ásgeirsdóttir TL, Jónsdóttir S. The Effect of Job Loss on Body Weight During an Economic Collapse. Eur J Health Econ. 2014;15(6):567–76. doi:10.1007/s10198-013-0494-z.
44. Ásgeirsdóttir TL, Ólafsdóttir Þ, Ragnarsdóttir DÓ. Business Cycles, Hypertension and Cardiovascular Disease: Evidence from the Icelandic Economic Collapse. Blood Press. 2014;23(4):213–21. doi:10.3109/08037051.2013.862913.
45. Ásgeirsdóttir TL, Berndsen HH, Guðmundsdóttir BÞ, Gunnarsdóttir BA, Halldórsdóttir HJ. The effect of obesity, alcohol misuse and smoking on employment and hours worked: evidence from the Icelandic economic collapse. Rev Econ Household. 2016;14(2):313–35. doi:10.1007/s11150-013-9225-6.
46. Ásgeirsdóttir TL, Corman H, Noonan K, Reichman N. Lifecycle Effects of a Recession on Health Behaviors: Boom, Bust, and Recovery in Iceland. Econ Hum Biol. 2016;20:90–107. doi:10.3386/w20950.
47. Ásgeirsdóttir TL, Corman H, Noonan K, Ólafsdóttir Þ, Reichman N. Was the Economic Crisis of 2008 Good for Icelanders? Impact on Health Behaviors. Econ Hum Biol. 2014;13:1–19. doi:10.1016/j.ehb.2013.03.005.
48. Ásgeirsdóttir TL, Ólafsdóttir Þ. Gender differences in drinking behavior during an economic collapse: evidence from Iceland. Rev Econ Household. 2015;13(4):975–1001. doi:10.1007/s11150-015-9283-z.
49. Ásgeirsdóttir TL, Ólafsdóttir Þ, Hrafnkelsson B. The Icelandic Economic Collapse, Smoking and the Role of Labor-Market Changes. Eur J Health Econ. 2014;16(4):391–405. doi:10.1007/s10198-014-0580-x.
50. Ásgeirsdóttir TL, Tryggvason Á. Hagsveiflur og vinnuslys á Íslandi 1986–2011. Stjórnmál og stjórnsýsla. 2014;10(2):399–426.
51. The World Bank. World development indicators: Google public data explorer. 2014. http://www.google.com/publicdata/explore?ds=d5bncppjof8f9_&met_y=ny_gdp_mktp_kd_zg& idim = country:USA:IND:GBR&hl = en&dl = en#!ctype = l&strail = false&bcs = d&nselm = h&met_y = ny_g dp_mktp_kd_zg&scale_y = lin&ind_y = false&rdim = region&idim = country:USA:IND:GBR:ISL:ESP:IRL &ifdim = region&hl = en_US&dl = en&ind = false. Accessed 2 Feb 2016
52. Statistics Iceland: Changes in CPI. Reykjavik: Statistics Iceland. 2016. http://px.hagstofa.is/pxis/pxweb/is/Efnahagur/Efnahagur__visitolur__1_visitalaneysluverds__1_neysluverd/VIS01000.px/Accessed 11 Apr 2016
53. Guðmundsson M. Iceland's crisis and recovery and current challenges. 2013. [Speech at a Conference organized by the French-Icelandic Chamber of Commerce; Islande, La Renaissance, Paris, 28 February 2013] http://www.bis.org/review/r130312d.pdf. Accessed 11 Mar 2016
54. Ólafsdóttir K. From recession to growth: Recovery in the labor market. [Guest lecture at Universita di Perugia, Perugia, 15 April 2013]. 2013. http://www.ec.unipg.it/DEFS/uploads/katrin-2-from_recession_to_growth-2.pdf. Accessed 6 Mar 2017.
55. OECD: Framework for Statistics on the Distribution of Household Income, Consumption and Wealth. Paris: OECD Publishing; 2013. doi: 10.1787/9789264194830-en
56. Kakwani NC. Measurement of Tax Progressivity: An International Comparison. Econ J. 1977;87(345):71–80. doi:10.2307/2231833.
57. Kakwani NC, van Doorslaer E, Wagstaff A. Socioeconomic Inequalities in Health: Measurement, Computation and Statistical Inference. J Econometrics. 1997;77(1):87–104. doi:10.1016/S0304-4076(96)01807-6.
58. O'Donnell O, Van Doorslaer E, Wagstaff A, Lindelow M. Analyzing Health Equity Using Household Survey Data. Washington: The International Bank for Reconstruction and Development/The World Bank; 2008. p. 95–114.

59. Wagstaff A, Paci P, van Doorslaer E. On the Measurement of Inequalities in Health. Soc Sci Med. 1991;33(5):545–57. doi:10.1016/0277-9536(91)90212-U.
60. Wagstaff A. The bounds of the concentration index when the variable of interest is binary, with an application to immunization inequality. Health Econ. 2005;14(4):429–32. doi:10.1002/hec.953.
61. StataCorp. Stata Statistical Software: Release 13. StataCorp, LP. Texas: 20 College Station; 2013.
62. Kentikelenis A, Karanikolos M, Papanicolas I, Basu S, McKee M, Stuckler D. Health effects of financial crisis: omens of a Greek tragedy. Lancet. 2011; 378(9801):1457–8. doi:10.1016/S0140-6736(11)61556-0.
63. Gili M, Roca M, Basu S, McKee M, Stuckler D. The mental health risks of economic crisis in Spain: evidence from primary care centres, 2006 and 2010. Eur J Public Health. 2013;23:103–8. doi:10.1093/eurpub/cks035.
64. Karanikolos M, Mladovsky P, Cylus J, Thomson S, Basu S, Stuckler D, Mackenbach JP, McKee M. Financial crisis, austerity, and health in Europe. Lancet. 2013;381(9874):1323–31. doi:10.1016/S0140-6736(13)60102-6.
65. Islam MK, Gerdtham U, Clarke P, Burström K. Does income-related health inequality change as the population ages? Evidence from Swedish panel data. Health Econ. 2010;19:334–49. doi:10.1002/hec.1479.
66. Deaton AS, Paxson CH. Aging and Inequality in Income and Health. Am Econ Rev, Papers and Proceedings. 1998;88(2):248–253. https://www.princeton.edu/~deaton/downloads/Aging_and_Inequality_in_Income_and_Health.pdf Accessed 13 Mar 2016

4

Economics of open tibial fractures: the pivotal role of length-of-stay and infection

Harm Hoekstra[1,2*], Bart Smeets[3], Willem-Jan Metsemakers[1], Anne-Cécile Spitz[4] and Stefaan Nijs[1,2]

Abstract

In order to define strategies to curb the continuing increase in healthcare costs, we describe the cost breakdown of open tibial fractures. Twenty-seven clinical and process variables were recorded retrospectively, and five main hospital related cost categories were defined. Three multivariate linear models were fitted to the data. Total healthcare costs of open tibial fractures were almost twice as high compared to closed fractures and mainly existed of hospitalization costs. Length-of-stay (LOS) was found to be the most important variable driving the healthcare costs of open tibial fractures. Deep infection lead to a 6-fold increase of LOS and 5-fold increase in total healthcare costs of open tibial fractures. Therefore, appropriate international consensus guidelines are required to improve not only the patient outcome (infection prevention) but also reduce overall healthcare cost by focusing on reducing the LOS.

Keywords: Costs analysis, Open tibial fractures, Healthcare financing

Background

Healthcare costs have increased significantly over the past decades. In Belgium, health expenditure currently accounts for approximately 10% of its GDP (gross domestic product), up from 8% in 2000 [1]. This puts Belgium on the top 10 list of OECD (Organization for Economic Co-operation and Development) countries with the highest healthcare expenditure, which is led by the United States with 16.4% [2]. The Belgian healthcare sector has been urged to find ways to keep the healthcare system viable. Therefore, multiple studies have focused on different facets of healthcare utilization and related costs. Recently, we reported an exploratory analysis of the healthcare costs associated with the treatment of AO/OTA (Arbeitsgemeinschaft fur Osteosynthesefragen/Orthopedic Trauma Association) type 44-B ankle fractures and defined strategies (e.g. immediate percutaneous intramedullary fibular fixation) to curb the continuing increase in healthcare costs [3]. Length-of-stay (LOS) was identified here as the main driver of the total healthcare costs.

In parallel, we want to understand the cost breakdown of open tibial fractures, since these fractures are associated with an increased complication rate (e.g. surgical site infection and nonunion) and treatment costs [4–6]. The distribution and treatment strategies of open tibial fractures vary considerably, due to its specific anatomic properties. Tibial fractures represent the most common open long-bone injuries with over 15% being open [7]. Nevertheless, we want to formulate strategies to reduce the cost of open tibial fractures.

Here we report a retrospective study of a large consecutive cohort of adult patients with either an AO/OTA type 41, 42 or 43 tibial fracture. We describe open tibial fractures in relation to patient demographics and operative characteristics. We define all hospital-related healthcare costs within the Belgium's healthcare system. Next, in order to define clear-cut clinical pathways and keep the healthcare system vital, we identify a subset of clinical variables that have a significant influence on costs and LOS, and determine whether these variables are actually related to the total healthcare costs. We hypothesized that Gustilo type 3 open tibial fracture patients will incur higher costs.

* Correspondence: harm.hoekstra@uzleuven.be
[1]Department of Trauma Surgery, University Hospitals Leuven, Herestraat 49, B-3000 Leuven, Belgium
[2]Department of Development and Regeneration, KU Leuven - University of Leuven, B-3000 Leuven, Belgium
Full list of author information is available at the end of the article

Methods

Patients

A total of 358 patients with an acute AO/OTA type 41, 42 and 43 tibial fracture were included in this study. All patients were treated at the Traumatology Department of University Hospitals Leuven between January 2009 and January 2014. Follow-up was until January 2016, allowing a maximum follow-up time of two years for all patients. Exclusion criteria were non-acute fractures (diagnosed more than 4 weeks after the accident), age < 18 years (*n*=29), other musculoskeletal trauma surgery during the follow-up (*n*=46), primary treatment elsewhere (*n*=23), , pathological fractures (*n*=1), and amputation (*n*=1) within 5 days after the accident. This study was conducted in compliance with national legislation and the guidelines of the ethics committee of University Hospitals Leuven. All tibial fractures related hospital stays and ambulatory consults of the selected patients were included in the analysis.

Study variables

Twenty-seven variables were retrospectively recorded from an electronic database (KWS – UZ Leuven); 20 clinical variables (gender, age, ASA-score [American Society of Anesthesiologists physical status score], cardiovascular risk factors [CVRF], AO/OTA bone segment, AO/OTA fracture type, AO/OTA fracture group, open fractures, antibiotic therapy, delayed-staged surgery, type of definite surgery, superficial infection, deep infection, nonunion, other complications, debridement (i.e. necrotectomy), hardware removal, re-osteosynthesis, other operations, and mortality) and 7 process variables (LOS to definite surgery, total length of antibiotic therapy, total LOS, number of operations, number of hospital admissions, number of surgical day care admissions, number of ambulatory consults).

Comorbidity was recorded using the ASA (American Society of Anesthesiologists physical status) -score. The cardiovascular risk factors (CVRF) include: age, current cardiovascular diseases (e.g., cerebrovascular accident, myocardial infarction, peripheral artery disease), diabetes, rheumatoid arthritis, smoking, use of blood vessel narrowing drugs (e.g., beta blockers and ergotamine), dyslipidemia, hypercholesterolemia, and hypertension. All fractures were classified according to the AO/OTA classification system [8]; fractures were classified according bone segment (41 - proximal tibia, 42 - tibia shaft, 43 - distal tibia), fracture type (A - extra-articular, B - partial articular, C - complete articular) and fracture group (1 - simple, 2 - wedge, 3 - complex). Open fractures were subdivided by the Gustilo-Anderson classification (type 1-3), which was determined at the time of initial debridement in the operating room [9]. Antibiotic therapy was categorized as either prophylactic (maximum of 5 days) or therapeutic [5]. Delayed-staged surgery includes all patients that were treated according to a delayed surgery protocol (i.e., external fixator prior to definite surgery). The type of definite surgery was categorized as intramedullary fixation (e.g. nailing), plate osteosynthesis, screw osteosynthesis, external fixator or arthrodesis (joint fusion). Surgical site infection was either classified as superficial or deep infections, which were defined according to Dellinger et al. and CDC (center for disease control) -guidelines. A superficial wound infection was one located above the fascia, with erythema and tenderness. A deep infection was defined as an infection involving deeper tissues as muscular fascia and bone, which could necessitate removal of the implant [10, 11]. Nonunion was assessed using follow-up radiographs and defined according to the US Food and Drug Administration guidelines as a not completely healed fracture within 9 months of injury and without progression towards healing over the past 3 consecutive months [12]. Other tibial related complications were wound problems, screw loosening, hardware migration, loss of reduction, peroneal nerve injury, and joint contracture. Nearly all other tibial related operations were bone grafting, (free) muscle flaps, and knee arthroplasty. LOS to definite surgery was defined as the number of consecutive hospital admission days until definite surgery. Total LOS was defined as the number of consecutive hospital admission days during the stay for the definite treatment. Surgical day care admissions include all operations (i.e. removal of hardware) performed in outpatients who did not require hospital admission.

Cost categories

Five main hospital related cost categories were defined: honoraria, materials, hospitalization (cost of daily patient care), daycare stay, and pharmaceuticals [3]. In summary: honoraria mainly consists of fees related to medical activities, mainly based on a fee-for-service principle (i.e. surgery, consults, and imaging). In the Belgium's healthcare system, honoraria are independent of the rank of the surgeon as activities are billed under the attending physician. Material related costs refer to the actual implants and other required materials. To analyze the performance impact due to differences in LOS, the patient's actual LOS was multiplied by the average national day based care fee (€410.84). The resulting sum was interpreted as the patient's hospitalization related costs. Costs for daycare stay include all operations (i.e. removal of hardware) performed in the outpatients that do not require hospitalization. Pharmaceuticals costs are all costs for received drugs and blood products.

The costs described in this paper relate to the Belgium's healthcare financing context and are exclusively hospital care-related. Furthermore, these costs comprise the majority of reimbursements paid to the

Table 1 Patient characteristics (n = 358)

Clinical characteristics	Gender	
	-Male	191 (53.4%)
	-Female	167 (46.60%)
	Age (years)	49 (36 – 62)
	ASA-score	
	-ASA 1	158 (44.1%)
	-ASA 2	158 (44.1%)
	-ASA 3	42 (11.7%)
	CVRF	198 (58.9%)
	AO/OTA bone segment	
	-41	122 (34.1%)
	-42	140 (39.1%)
	-43	96 (26.8%)
	AO/OTA fracture type	
	-A	119 (33.2%)
	-B	139 (38.8%)
	-C	100 (27.9%)
	AO/OTA fracture group	
	-1	162 (45.3%)
	-2	54 (15.1%)
	-3	142 (39.7%)
	Open fractures (Gustilo)	51 (14.2%)
	-1	26 (51.0%)
	-2	15 (29.4%)
	-3	10 (19.6%)
	Antibiotic therapy	
	-prophylactic	313 (87.4%)
	-therapeutic	45 (12.6%)
	Delayed-staged surgery	44 (12.3%)
	Type of definite surgery	
	-intramedullary nail	140 (39.1%)
	-plate osteosynthesis	144 (40.2%)
	-screw osteosynthesis	66 (18.4.1%)
	-external fixator	7 (2.0%)
	-arthrodesis	1 (0.3%)
	Superficial infection	7 (2.0%)
	Deep infection	12 (3.4%)
	Nonunion	18 (5.0%)
	Other complications	8 (2.2%)
	Debridement	19 (5.3%)
	Hardware removal	121 (33.8%)
	Re-osteosynthesis	14 (3.9%)
	Other operations	22 (6.1%)
	Mortality	11 (3.1%)
Process characteristics	LOS to definite surgery (days)	1 (0 – 3)
	Total length of antibiotic therapy (days)	1 (1 – 3)
	Total LOS (days)	7 (5 – 13)
	Number of operations	1 (1 – 2)
	Number of hospital admissions	1 (1 – 2)
	Number of surgical day care admissions	0
	Number of ambulatory consults	5 (3 – 8)

Categorical variables are presented as numbers and percentages, continuous variables as median with interquartile distributions

Abbreviations: ASA-score American Society, of Anesthesiologists physical status score, *CVRF* cardiovascular risk factors, *AO/OTA* Arbeitsgemeinschaft für Osteosynthesefragen/Orthopaedic Trauma Association, *LOS* length-of-stay

hospital (by any party involved) in financing the care for a specific patient either directly or indirectly.

Statistical methods

Continuous variables are presented as medians with interquartile distribution, whereas categorical variables are presented as numbers and percentages. Categorical variables were compared with the Pearson Chi-Square test. Comparison of continuous variables was performed using the Mann-Whitney U test.

In order to determine the variables that drive health-care costs and LOS of open tibial fractures, three multi-variate linear models were fitted to the data (in the form of $y = a + b_1x_1 + \cdots + b_nx_n$). Leave-one-out (LOO) cross validation was used to analyze generalizability [1]. For all categorical variables, binary dummy variables were introduced to represent the categorical values. For each categorical variable, the number of dummy variables introduced equals the number of different values the categorical value can take minus one.

The dataset with binary dummy variables included has a rather high dimensionality in relation to the number of available observations. As fitting a linear regression model directly on this dataset would lead to an unstable model, the dimensionality of the dataset was first reduced using Lasso regression for each of the three models. The variables that received a non-negative coefficient after the Lasso fit were then used to fit a multi-variate linear model. The choice for a linear model was made based on interpretability reasons.

Exploratory data analysis and subsequent building of the statistical model was done using R and the mlr framework [13, 14].

Results

Patient characteristics

Patient demographics, operative variables, and hospital stay-related variables are summarized in Table 1.

Table 2 Healthcare costs (n=358)

Category	Per patient	Total	Relative share
Honoraria	€1,596 (1,182 – 2,556)	€775,515	21 %
Materials (implants & screws)	€1,055 (544 – 1,528)	€446,313	12 %
Hospitalization	€2,876 (1,951 – 5,341)	€1,901,368	51 %
Daycare stay	€0 (0 – 86)	€36,931	1 %
Pharmaceuticals	€1,029 (870 – 1,789)	€553,071	15 %
Total	€6,962 (4,932 – 10,972)	€3,713,198	100%

The per patient costs show the median followed by interquartile range

Categorical variables are presented as numbers and percentages, and continuous variables as the median with interquartile distributions.

Healthcare costs

The distribution of the 5 main cost categories (honoraria, materials, hospitalization, daycare stay, and pharmaceuticals) and total costs are summarized in Table 2. The costs are presented as the median and interquartile distributions.

Descriptive statistics of open tibial fractures

A univariate comparison of clinical and process -related variables for patients with and without an open fracture is shown in Table 3. In addition, total costs for patients with open and closed tibial fractures are visualized in Fig. 1.

Which clinical parameters drive the healthcare costs of open tibial fractures?

In order to determine the importance of the clinical variables for driving healthcare costs, a multivariate linear model was fitted using total healthcare costs as the dependent variable. The resulting model (all variables costing model - *AV-CM*) had an R^2 of 0.98 and an adjusted R^2 of 0.97. Only the variable total LOS was deemed significant (Table 4, model AV-CM).

However, this high predictive value is mostly due to the fact that the LOS related variables are inherently correlated to healthcare costs due to Belgium's financing system. This is because a part of the actual reimbursement method involves, among other factors, multiplying the LOS with a daycare price. As hospitalization costs comprise a large part of the total costs it is to be expected that the LOS related variables are significant when fitting these variables to the total healthcare cost per patient.

Therefore, all stay related variables were excluded in a second model (non-stay related variables costing model – *NSRV-CM*), again with total costs as the dependent variable. The variables denoted with *excluded* in Table 4 model NSRV-CM were excluded. As a consequence, the performance of this second model decreased significantly. The model had a R^2 of 0.67 and an adjusted R^2 of 0.58 (Table 4, model NSRV-CM) shows the significant variables in this multivariate model: deep infection and CVRF.

Which clinical parameters drive the LOS?

Total LOS is the most important driver for healthcare costs (t = 30.56, AV-CM, Table 4). This brought up the question whether or not it is possible to identify the (non-stay related) variables that drive LOS. In subsequent analyses a multivariate linear model was built using LOS as a dependent variable and the non-stay related variables as independent variables. The model (LOS model – LS-M) had an R^2 of 0.54 and an adjusted R^2 of 0.46. The variable deep infection was found to be significant in the multivariate model (LS-M - Table 4).

How are the total healthcare costs of open tibial fractures, total LOS, deep infection, CVRF, and AO/OTA fracture type related?

Univariate analysis for open tibial fractures showed a 5-fold increase in the total healthcare costs (€48,702 [28,383-71,409] *vs.* €9,566 [6,781-15,094], $p<0.001$) (Fig. 2) and 6-fold increase of total LOS (60 [43-123] *vs.* 10 [7–18], p<0.001) in patients with a deep infection (*vs.* without deep infection).

The treatment costs and total LOS of open tibial fractures in patients with or without CRFV did not differ significantly (€13,321 [9,011-29,319] *vs.* €11,658 [6,992-13,804], p = 0.233) and 18 [9 – 34] *vs.* 11 [7 – 18], p = 0.138, respectively).

Despite open AO/OTA type 42 tibial fractures were the most important bone segment fractures driving the total healthcare costs and total LOS, open AO/OTA type 43 tibial fractures turned out to be significantly more expensive (€13,304 [9,150-31,571] *vs.* €8,116 [5,669-10,084], p = 0.026) (Fig. 3) with significantly longer total LOS (20 [9 – 44] *vs.* 8 [4 – 11], p =0.028) compared to open AO/OTA type 41 tibial fractures.

Do Gustilo type 3 open tibial fracture incur higher costs?

Univariate subanalysis for Gustilo type open tibial fractures showed significantly higher total healthcare costs (€16,163 [9,646 – 48,705] *vs.* €9,394 [7,157 –

Table 3 Comparison of clinical and process characteristics for open and *closed* tibial fractures (n = 358)

	Patients	Open (n = 51)	Closed (n = 307)	p
Clinical characteristics	Gender			0.079
	-Male	33 (64.7%)	158 (51.5%)	
	-Female	18 (35.3%)	149 (48.5%)	
	Age (years)	48 (29 – 60)	49 (37 – 63)	0.242
	ASA score			0.298
	-ASA 1	19 (37.3%)	139 (45.3%)	
	-ASA 2	23 (45.1%)	135 (44.0%)	
	-ASA 3	9 (17.6%)	33 (10.7%)	
	CVRF	26 (59.1%)	172 (58.9%)	0.981
	AO/OTA bone segment			<0.001***
	-41	6 (11.8%)	116 (37.8%)	
	-42	31 (60.8%)	109 (35.5%)	
	-43	14 (27.5%)	82 (26.7%)	
	AO/OTA fracture type			0.010**
	-A	22 (43.1%)	97 (31.6%)	
	-B	10 (19.6%)	129 (42.0%)	
	-C	19 (37.3%)	81 (26.4%)	
	AO/OTA fracture group			0.190
	-1	21 (41.2%)	141 (45.9%)	
	-2	12 (23.5%)	42 (13.7%)	
	-3	18 (35.3%)	124 (40.4%)	
	Antibiotic therapy			<0.001***
	-prophylactic	27 (52.9%)	286 (93.2%)	
	-therapeutic	24 (47.1%)	21 (6.8%)	
	Delayed-staged surgery	17 (33.3%)	27 (8.8%)	<0.001***
	Type of definite surgery			<0.001***
	-intramedullary nail	35 (68.6%)	105 (34.2%)	
	-plate osteosynthesis	14 (27.5%)	130 (42.3%)	
	-screw osteosynthesis	0	66 (21.5%)	
	-external fixator	2 (3.9%)	5 (1.6%)	
	-arthrodesis	0	7 (2.3%)	
	Superficial infection	0	0 (3.9%)	0.276
	Deep infection	7 (13.7%)	5 (1.6%)	<0.001***
	Nonunion	10 (19.6%)	8 (2.6%)	<0.001***
	Other complications	2 (3.9%)	6 (2.0%)	0.379
	Debridement	10 (19.6%)	9 (2.9%)	<0.001***
	Hardware removal	25 (49.0%)	96 (31.3%)	0.013*
	Re-osteosynthesis	8 (15.7%)	6 (2.0%)	<0.001***
	Other operations	10 (19.6%)	12 (3.9%)	<0.001***
	Mortality	1 (2.0%)	10 (3.3%)	0.619
Process characteristics	LOS to definite surgery (days)	0 (0 – 5)	1 (0 – 3)	0.950
	Total length of antibiotic therapy (days)	6 (4 – 11)	1 (1 – 2)	<0.001***
	Total LOS (days)	11 (7 – 25)	6 (4 – 13)	<0.001***
	Number of operations	2 (1 – 3)	1 (1 – 2)	<0.001***

Table 3 Comparison of clinical and process characteristics for open and *closed* tibial fractures (n = 358) *(Continued)*

	Patients	Open (n = 51)	Closed (n = 307)	p
	Number of hospital admissions	1 (1 – 2)	1 (1 – 2)	<0.015*
	Number of surgical day care admissions	0	0	0.883
	Number of ambulatory consults	7 (5 – 10)	5 (3 – 7)	<0.001***
Healthcare costs	Honoraria	€2,609 (1,484 – 4,013)	€1,494 (1,135 – 2,281)	<0.001***
	Materials (implants & screws)	€1,617 (1,070 – 2,501)	€1,002 (467 – 1,397)	<0.001***
	Hospitalization	€4,519 (2,876 – 10,271)	€2,465 (1,643 –5,341)	<0.001***
	Day care stay	€0 (0 – 177)	€0 (0 – 86)	0.588
	Pharmaceuticals	€1,448 (981 – 3294)	€978 (862 – 1,724)	<0.001***
	Total healthcare costs	€11,061 (7,135 – 19,883)	€6,632 (4,714 – 10,095)	<0.001***

Categorical variables are presented as numbers and percentages, continuous variables as median with interquartile distributions
*p < 0.05, **p ≤ 0.01, ***p < 0.001 (p < 0.05 is considered to be significant)
Abbreviations: CVRF cardiovascular risk factors, *LOS* length of stay

14,802], p = 0.044) (Fig. 4), longer total LOS (26 [9 – 72] *vs.* 11 [7 – 17], p =0.044), as well as prolonged use of antibiotics (11 [6 – 24] *vs.* 5 [4 – 7], p =0.017) for type 3 compared to type 1 open tibial fractures. Subsequently, most deep infections were observed in patients with Gustilo type 3 open tibial fractures.

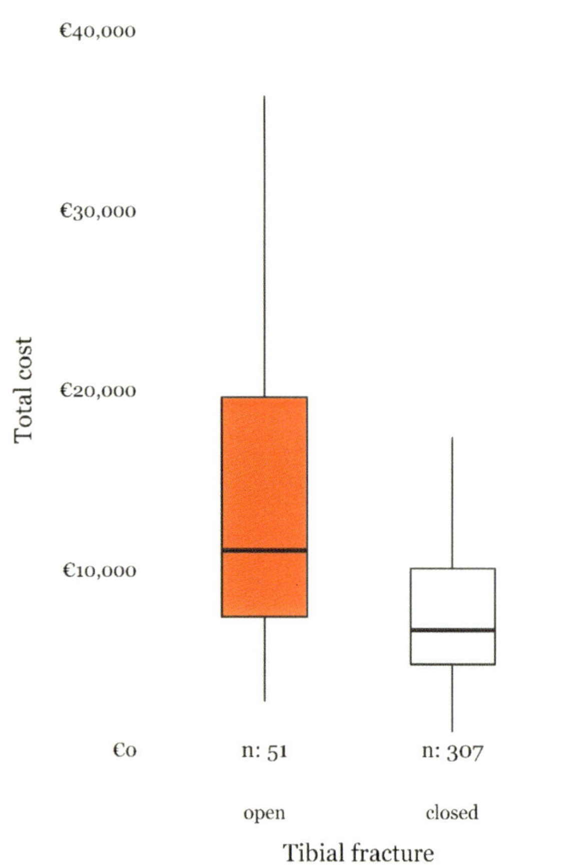

Fig. 1 Distribution of total healthcare costs for patients with and without open tibial fractures

Discussion

The goal of this study was to perform an exploratory analysis of treatment costs for open tibial fractures and define strategies in order to reduce these costs. A subset of clinical relevant variables was identified that drive the total healthcare costs and LOS. We hypothesized that Gustilo type 3 open tibial fracture patients incur higher costs.

Due to thin soft tissues layers covering the tibia shaft, open tibial fractures concerned here were predominantly AO/OTA type 42 fractures. These fractures were exclusively treated intramedullary. Open tibial fractures were approximately 8-times more frequently complicated by deep infection and nonunion in comparison with closed fractures. Subsequently, open tibial fractures required significantly more reinterventions (e.g. debridement, hardware removal, re-osteosynthesis). As a consequence, total healthcare costs of open tibial fractures were almost double as high compared to closed fractures. They mainly consisted of hospitalization costs. Total LOS was the most important variable driving the healthcare costs of open tibial fractures (t = 30.56). After exclusion of all process variables related to hospital stay, deep infection was identified as the most important clinical parameter driving the LOS (model LS-M) and total healthcare costs (model NSRV-CM) of open tibial fractures. In addition, CVRF were identified as significant driver of the total healthcare costs. Patients with open tibial fractures that were complicated by deep infection, showed a 6-fold increase in LOS and 5-fold increase in total healthcare costs. Despite the fact that open AO/OTA type 43 fractures were on average the most expensive tibial fractures, the multivariate analysis showed that the presence of an AO/OTA type 42 tibial fracture (in combination with other factors) was found to be a more important factor in driving the LOS and total healthcare costs. Gustilo type 3 open tibial fractures had a significantly higher total LOS and amount of healthcare costs, due to a higher rate of deep infection (30%).

Table 4 Model results (n = 51)

	Model	AV-CM		NSRV-CM		LS-M	
	Dependent variable	Total costs		Total costs		Length-of-stay	
	Variable	t-value	*p*	t-value	*p*	t-value	*p*
Clinical characteristics	Gender						
	-Male	.	.	.	.	.	.
	-Female	.	.	.	.	.	.
	Age	.	.	0.55	0.586	1.32	0.193
	ASA score						
	-ASA 1	.	.	.	.	.	.
	-ASA 2	.	.	.	.	.	.
	-ASA 3	.	.	0.92	0.362	.	.
	CVRF	.	.	2.09	0.043*	1.86	0.069
	AO/OTA classification						
	-bone segment 42 [a]	.	.	2.00	0.052	1.84	0.073
	-fracture type (A, B, C)	.	.	.	.	.	.
	-fracture group 3 [a]	.	.	0.77	0.446	0.89	0.380
	Open fractures	.	.	.	.	.	.
	Antibiotic therapy						
	-prophylactic	.	.	.	.	.	.
	-therapeutic	.	.	0.95	0.346	1.637	0.109
	Delayed-staged surgery	.	.	.	.	.	.
	Type of definite surgery						
	-intramedullary nail	.	.	.	.	.	.
	-plate osteosynthesis	.	.	.	.	.	.
	-screw osteosynthesis	.	.	.	.	.	.
	-external fixator	.	.	1.23	0.228	.	.
	-arthrodesis	.	.	.	.	.	.
	Superficial infection	.	.	.	.	.	.
	Deep infection	1.66	0.104	3.81	<0.001***	3.49	0.001***
	Nonunion	1.99	0.053	1.66	0.104	.	.
	Other complications	.	.	.	.	.	.
	Debridement	.	.	1.66	0.105	1.56	0.126
	Hardware removal	.	.	0.84	0.404	.	.
	Re-osteosynthesis	1.21	0.233	.	.	.	.
	Other Operations	.	.	.	.	.	.
	Mortality	.	.	.	.	.	.
Process characteristics	LOS to definite surgery	.	.	excluded	excluded	excluded	excluded
	Total length of antibiotic therapy	.	.	excluded	excluded	excluded	excluded
	Total LOS	30.56	<0.001***	excluded	excluded	excluded	excluded
	Number of operations	0.77	0.448	excluded	excluded	excluded	excluded
	Number of hospital admissions	1.18	0.246	excluded	excluded	excluded	excluded
	Number of surgical day care admissions	.	.	excluded	excluded	excluded	excluded
	Number of ambulatory consults	.	.	excluded	excluded	excluded	excluded
Model	R^2		0.98		0.67		0.54
	Adj R^2		0.97		0.58		0.46

$^*p < 0.05$ $^{**}p < 0.01$ $^{***}p \leq 0.001$ ($p < 0.05$ is considered to be significant)

[a] Categories which were not selected in the final models where dropped from this listing

Abbreviations: AV-CM all variables costing model, *NSRV-CM* non-stay-related costing model, *LS-M* length-of-stay model, *CVRF* cardiovascular risk factors, *LOS* length of stay

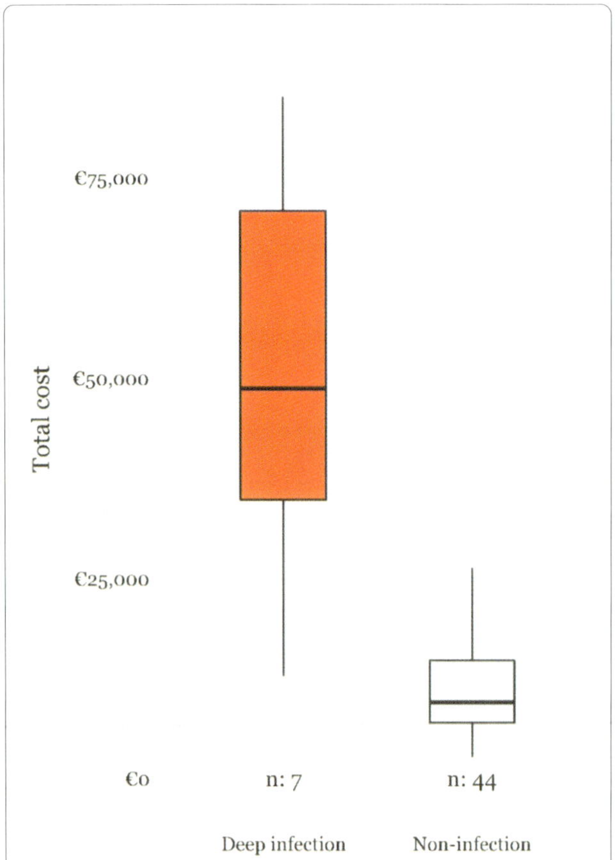

Fig. 2 Distribution of total healthcare costs for patients with deep infection of open tibial fractures

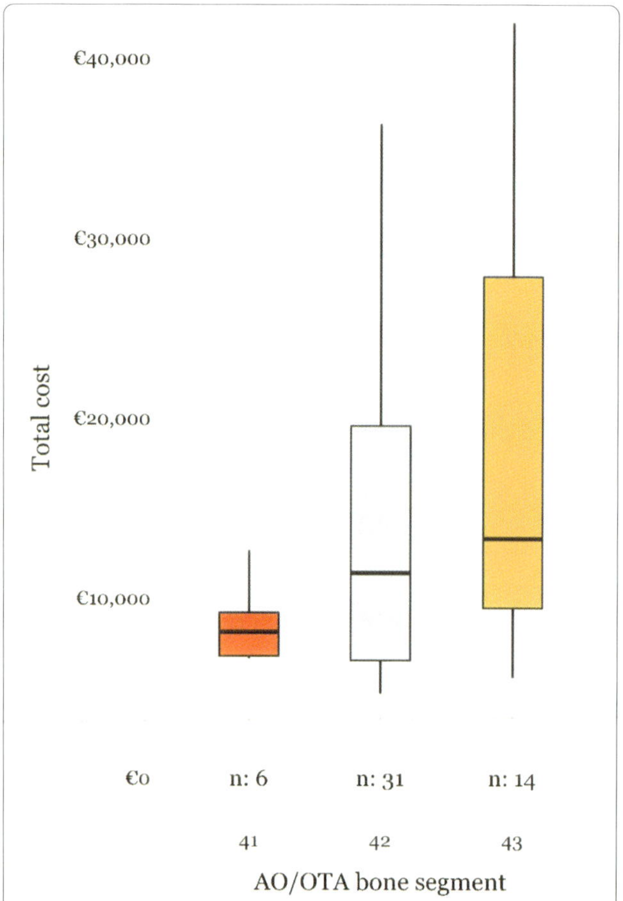

Fig. 3 Distribution of total healthcare costs for patients with AO/OTA type 41, 42 and 43 open tibial fractures

Our results are in line with Page et al. [15], who demonstrated that patients with open tibial fractures have significantly increased total healthcare costs in the year following their injury, primarily due to a prolonged LOS and a greater number of ambulatory consults. Moreover, the fact that the total healthcare costs were to great extent determined by hospitalization costs, which in turn were driven by LOS, is in accordance with our previous observations in AO type 44B ankle fractures [3]. Unfortunately, whether or not the patient had an open ankle fracture, was not taken into account in this study. The median total healthcare costs and LOS for AO type 44B ankle fractures were €5,021 and 5 days, whereas for open tibial fractures this was €6,962 and 7 days, respectively. In contrast, the LOS and total healthcare costs of AO type 44B ankle fractures were strongly driven by the age and a delayed-staged surgery protocol. Antonova et al. [16] reported in 2013, higher median total healthcare costs for the treatment of AO type 42 fractures of $13,364 during a 2-year follow-up. In disregard of inflation, total costs in Euro are estimated at approximately €10.800 (index period 2006). Furthermore, the healthcare costs for tibial diaphyseal nonunion were twice as high here. Unfortunately, the total healthcare costs for open tibial diaphyseal fractures were also not specified in this study.

Although the median total cost per patient for the treatment of open tibial fractures was approximately twice as a high compared closed tibial fractures, total cost for the treatment of open tibial fractures was €955,026 *vs.* €2,758,172 for closed fractures. Since the total number of open tibial fractures was limited (14.3% of all fractures), the impact of strategies to curb the total costs of open tibia fractures (25.7% of the total cost) was also limited. However, Belgium's hospitals are financed through a mixture of patient co-payments the health insurance system and the Ministry of Health [3], and therefore such strategies are certainly beneficial at the individual level. Another important limitation of these types of costing studies is the fact that it is often difficult to generalize the findings on an international scale. The difficulty in generalization stems from the fact that hospital financing is often very specific to a country. Currently no definitive way of internationally comparing costs for specific treatments exists. It might for example be the case - and it is in Belgium - that part of surplus funding for a given

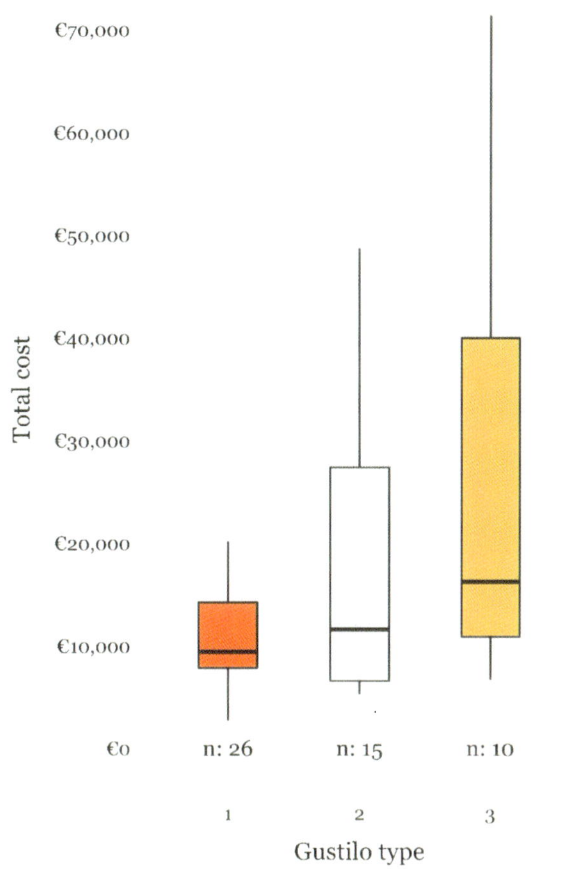

Fig. 4 Distribution of total healthcare costs for patients with Gustilo type 1, 2 and 3 open tibial fractures

treatment is used to make up for inadequate funding of another type of treatment. Without understanding the intricate details of hospital financing in that specific country one might come to the erroneous conclusion that treatment y is cheaper compared to a country with sufficient funding for this treatment. (Time-driven) activity-based costing as proposed by Kaplan and Porter might bridge this gap, but requires investments in order to make treatment costs more transparent and easily measurable [17]. The University Hospitals Leuven is currently developing such a model and future publications could present a further refined cost specification for ankle fractures.

Compared to the literature, our deep infection rate (3.4%) was rather low [18]. Patients with open tibial fractures were significantly more affected by deep infection and nonunion. Gustilo type 3 open tibial fractures were significantly more affected. This is in accordance with Khatod et al. [19], who found that the Gustilo grading system of open fractures is a significant prognostic factor to indicate infectious complications. Moreover, the average time to surgery in their study was also not significantly different in infected versus non-infected cases.

It is also important to notice that, especially in patients with open tibial fractures, we observed a strong variance in terms of costs. We assume that most likely the total LOS is not only a result of surgical strategy, patient characteristics and surgeon's decision, but is also a function of local guidelines, historically developed processes, habits and the individual preferences of the surgeon. Therefore, appropriate international consensus guidelines are required to improve not only the patient outcome but also reduce overall healthcare cost by focusing on reducing the LOS.

Deep infection was found to be the leading cause of the high total LOS and healthcare costs of open tibial fractures. Strict antibiotic guidelines and surgical protocols are adopted to minimize infection. Provided that the guidelines and protocols should be in the first place clinically beneficial, they may also serve as a tool to curb the total LOS and healthcare costs. Following the results of this study, we updated our treatment strategies for open fractures in order to improve patient outcome and reduce healthcare costs. First, current evidence states that long term systemic prophylactic antibiotic administration is not necessary [20]. Shortening this period will not only reduce healthcare costs but also reduce the change of creating bacterial resistance. Second, the time to definitive soft tissue coverage was shortened. A standardized protocol was developed with the colleagues from the department of plastic and reconstructive surgery to improve especially the logistic and planning of these procedures. Soft-tissue protocols consists of wound closure either with primarily or covered with adhesive drapes or VAC, preventing repeated debridement, and allowing rapid definite skin coverage. Finally, local prophylactic antibiotic strategies were improved. Current evidence indicates that locally delivered antibiotics or other antimicrobials could improve patient outcome [21–23]. Local delivery systems, like implant coatings, could be an asset in this field as well [24].

Please note, that the analysis presented here is based on an arguably limited sample of open tibial fractures, due to this a cautionary approach has to be taken when inferring properties about this sample and, in turn, about the population. This has been taken into consideration by limiting the number of variables in the multivariate model (see Methods) and by verifying the conclusion drawn below though bivariate analysis.

Conclusion

In conclusion, total healthcare costs for open tibial fractures were approximately twice as high compared to closed fractures and mainly consisted of hospitalization costs, i.e. the cost of daily patient care. This study shows that total LOS was the most important variable driving total healthcare costs of open tibial fractures. Guidelines on appropriate LOS can help to improve efficiency, decrease variability, and curb the total healthcare costs. Open tibial fractures complicated by deep infection presented the most significant increase in LOS and in total healthcare costs. Besides that infection prevention is essential in high-quality care, it can also be an important contribution to make trauma care more cost efficient. To that end, patients with open tibial fractures must be treated according to strict antibiotic and surgical guidelines. In cases of deep infection, updated antibiotic protocols make it possible to administer intravenous antibiotics in outpatients (OPAT) with the same level of outcome and a shorter LOS. Multiple possible preventive measures like local antibiotics and implant coatings can be addressed. Finally, as has been evident, trauma research faces the problem of studies publishing heterogeneous small sized patient cohorts, therefore (multicentre) randomized clinical trials on infection prevention are mandatory to ultimately ensure the quality as well as standardization of trauma protocols and hospitalization processes (i.e. LOS).

Endnote

[1]LOO cross validation showed a somewhat decreased performance on unseen data which was deemed acceptable due to the limited number of available observations.

Abbreviations

AO/OTA: Arbeitsgemeinschaft fur Osteosynthesefragen/Orthopedic Trauma AssociationLOSlength-of-stay; ASA-score: American Society of Anesthesiologists physical status score; AV-CM: All variables costing model; CVRF: cardiovascular risk factors; LS-M: LOS model; NSRV-CM: Non-stay related variables costing model

Funding

Not applicable.

Authors' contributions

HH collected the data, participated in the sequence alignment and drafted the manuscript. BS participated in the design of the study and performed the statistical analysis. WJM participated in the sequence alignment.ACS helped to collect the data. SN conceived of the study, and participated in its design and coordination and helped to draft the manuscript. All authors read and approved the final manuscript.

Competing interests

The authors declare that they have no competing interests.

Author details

[1]Department of Trauma Surgery, University Hospitals Leuven, Herestraat 49, B-3000 Leuven, Belgium. [2]Department of Development and Regeneration, KU Leuven - University of Leuven, B-3000 Leuven, Belgium. [3]Dataroots, B-1040 Brussels, Belgium. [4]Faculty of Medicine, KU Leuven - University of Leuven, B-3000 Leuven, Belgium.

References

1. OECD. (n.d.). OECD Statistics. Health expenditure and financing. Retrieved June 1, 2016, from http://stats.oecd.org/index.aspx.
2. OECD Health Statistics. WHO Global Health Expenditure Database; 2015. http://dx.doi.org/10.1787/health-data-en.
3. Smeets B, Nijs S, Nderlita M, Vandoren C, Hoekstra H. Health Care Usage and Related Costs in Fibular Plating for AO Type 44-B Ankle Fractures in a Belgian University Hospital: An Exploratory Analysis. J Foot Ankle Surg. 2016. doi:10.1053/j.jfas.2016.02.004.
4. Papakostidis C, Kanakaris NK, Pretel J, Faour O, Morell DJ, Giannoudis PV. Prevalence of complications of open tibial shaft fractures stratified as per the Gustilo-Anderson classification. Injury. 2011. doi:10.1016/j.injury.2011.10.015.
5. Metsemakers WJ, Handojo K, Reynders P, Sermon A, Vanderschot P, Nijs S. Individual risk factors for deep infection and compromised fracture healing after intramedullary nailing of tibial shaft fractures: A single centre experience of 480 patients. Injury. 2015;46(4):740–5. doi:10.1016/j.injury.2014.12.018.
6. Darouiche RO. Treatment of infections associated with surgical implants. N Engl J Med. 2004;350(14):1422–9. doi:10.1056/NEJMra035415.
7. Court-Brown CM, Rimmer S, Prakash U, McQueen MM. The epidemiology of open long bone fractures. Injury. 1998;29(7):529–34. doi:10.1016/S0020-1383(98)00125-9.
8. Marsh JL, Slongo TF, Agel J, Broderick JS, Creevey W, DeCoster TA, et al. Fracture and dislocation classification compendium - 2007: Orthopaedic Trauma Association classification, database and outcomes committee. J Orthop Trauma. 2007;21(10 Suppl):S1–133.
9. Gustilo RB, Mendoza RM, Williams DN. Problems in the management of type III (severe) open fractures: a new classification of type III open fractures. J Trauma. 1984;24(8):742–6.
10. Horan TC, Gaynes RP, Martone WJ, Jarvis WR, Emori TG. CDC definitions of nosocomial surgical site infections, 1992: a modification of CDC definitions of surgical wound infections. Infect Control Hosp Epidemiol. 1992;13(10):606–8.
11. Dellinger EP, Miller SD, Wertz MJ, Grypma M, Droppert BAP. Risk of infection after open fracture of the arm or leg. Arch Surg. 1988;123:1320–7.
12. MR B. Nonunions: evaluation and treatment. In: Browner BD, Levine AM, Jupiter JB, Trafton PG, editors. Skeletal Trauma: Basic Science, Management and Reconstruction. 3rd ed; 2003. p. 507–604.
13. Core R. Team, R: A Language and Environment for Statistical: Computing; 2013.
14. Bischl B, Lang M, Richter J, Bossek J, Judt L, Kuehn T, Studerus E, Kotthoff L, Julia S, Casalicchio G. mlr: Machine Learning in R. R package version 2.9. https://github.com/mlr-org/mlr.
15. Page PRJ, Trickett RW, Rahman SM, Walters A, Pinder LM, Brooks CJ, Pallister I. The use of secure anonymised data linkage to determine changes in healthcare utilisation following severe open tibial fractures. Injury. 2015; 46(7):1287–92. doi:10.1016/j.injury.2015.04.011.
16. Antonova E, Le TK, Burge R, Mershon J. Tibia shaft fractures: costly burden of nonunions. BMC Musculoskeletal Disorders. 2013;14(1):1. doi:10.1186/1471-2474-14-42.
17. Kaplan RS, Porter ME. How to solve the cost crisis in health care. Harvard Business Review. 2011;89(9). doi:10.1037/e632682011-011.
18. Patzakis MJ, Wilkins J. Factors influencing infection rate in open fracture wounds. Clin Orthop Relat Res. 1989:36–40. doi:10.1097/00003086-198906000-00006.
19. Khatod M, Botte MJ, Hoyt DB, Meyer RS, Smith JM, Akeson WH. Outcomes in open tibia fractures: relationship between delay in treatment and infection. The Journal of Trauma. 2003;55(5):949–54. doi:10.1097/01.TA.0000092685.80435.63.
20. Dunkel N, Pittet D, Tovmirzaeva L, Suva D, Bernard L, Lew D, Hoffmeyer P, Uckay I. Short duration of antibiotic prophylaxis in open fractures does not enhance risk of subsequent infection. Bone Joint J. 2013;95 B(6):831–7. http://doi.org/10.1302/0301-620X.95B6.30114.
21. Craig J, Fuchs T, Jenks M, Fleetwood K, Franz D, Iff J, et al. Systematic review and meta-analysis of the additional benefit of local prophylactic antibiotic therapy for infection rates in open tibia fractures treated with intramedullary nailing. International orthopaedics. 2014;38:1025–30.
22. Ostermann PA, Seligson D, Henry SL. Local antibiotic therapy for severe open fractures. A review of 1085 consecutive cases. J Bone Joint Surg Br. 1995;77:93–7.

5

Willingness to accept capitation payment system under the Ghana National Health Insurance Policy: do income levels matter?

Frank Gyimah Sackey* and Peter N. Amponsah

Abstract

This research was set to examine the factors influencing the willingness and the likelihood of Ghanaians to accept the capitation payment system under the National Health Insurance Scheme. Data was collected through the random sampling method in all the ten regions of Ghana. A probit estimation with marginal effects was adopted to examine the factors influencing the willingness and the likelihood while the generalized Blinder-Oaxaca decomposition was used to examine the extent to which individual characteristics influence the acceptance gap between high income and low-income earners. Our results indicated that, at the individual level, high income, being employed, awareness and smaller household size were the significant factors influencing the willingness and the likelihood to accept capitation. We also observed that the acceptance gap between high income and low-income earners was largely influenced by unexplained factors other than individual characteristics of high income earners. Since the willingness and the likelihood to accept capitation are mixed across regions and largely dependent on high incomes, the intention to roll out and implement the capitation system should be as a complementary payment system to the already existing one, being the diagnosis related grouping. We recommend that the current payment system, the diagnosis-related-grouping be maintained and complemented with capitation while measures to reduce, if not eliminate, the abuse associated with it be put in place.

Keywords: Capitation payment, Health insurance, Diagnosis-related grouping, Ghana

Background

The wealth of every nation is partly dependent on the health of its people. It is estimated that for every 10% increase in life expectancy at birth there is a corresponding rise in economic growth of 0.4%, and this economic growth leads to a further rise in life expectancy at birth [22]. According to Deaton [9], increase in growth leads to rise in incomes, which contributes to good health. Gupta and Mitra [14] observe that growth tends to reduce poverty and improves health status. They also find that growth and health status are positively correlated and have a two-way relationship. This finding suggests that better health enhances economic growth by improving productivity, and higher growth allows better human capital formation. For this reason, various governments try to put in place policies that will ensure improved health status of their citizenry. A major means of achieving this goal is to make health facilities available, accessible, and affordable. Therefore, health insurance policies have become a very important phenomenon.

Health insurance is an insurance product that insulates a person from financial loss due to accident, ill health and/or disability. Though these unexpected circumstances are not fixed and precise, their significance to society is that the condition of ill health arising from disease or injury prevents one from pursuing one's normal routine of living and affects one's survival. Therefore, health insurance has become a necessity; but it is not to everyone, especially the low-level income earners and poor homes in developing countries such as Ghana. Meeting the sustainable development goals (SDGs) involves making healthcare delivery accessible and affordable without compromising quality. Thus, in a bid to improving the health needs and accessibility, the government of Ghana introduced the Ghana National Health Insurance Scheme (NHIS) to provide financial

* Correspondence: franksackey@yahoo.com
Catholic University College of Ghana, Sunyani, Ghana

access to healthcare services of which the National Health Insurance Act, 2003 was passed by parliament. The scheme has moved from paying its accredited providers through the Fee-For-Service (FFS) to the Diagnosis- Related -Grouping (DRG) as a way of dealing with the abuse of the FFS system [10]. The DRG system, however, has also some weaknesses. For example, the DRG has been cited for not being able to successfully contain cost, especially for outpatient claims. In fact, outpatient claims account for 70% of the total NHIS claims and 30% total cost, which lead to a huge cost burden on the Authority (HIP, 2010). Such problems have led to the overhaul of its provider payment system with the introduction of the capitation payment which is currently being introduced as a pilot program in some selected regions across the country.

The NHIS law that established the National Health Insurance in Ghana provided for the institution of multiple payment methods including capitation. LI 1809, specifically mentions capitation as one of the provider payment methods to be considered for use under the NHIS. This has been the international best practices given the fact that no single provider method has been perfect. The proposed reform in Ghana does not do away with any of the already existing provider payment methods. Rather it introduces capitation for a specific level of care – the primary level of walk in outpatient care, which is the fundamental base of the health care systems, and reserves the DRG for services and Itemized Fee for medicines system to the higher levels of care. Under the proposed capitation system, the amount paid to providers will cater for selected OPD primary care cases.

The advantages of introducing per capita payments for first level outpatient primary care, as a complementary payment method to the already existing methods in the Ghana NHIS, include the following: It will reduce the current massive administrative and staff time costs of claims preparation, submission, vetting and reimbursement involved in using G-DRG and fee for services for medicines to pay for first line OPD care, It will improve the ability of the NHIA to forecast and budget, It will eliminate problems of delayed payment of claims – for the services in the per capita basket. This is because monies are now being paid in advance to providers. By tying clients to a PPP of their choice it reduces fragmentation of care and introduces continuity of care for clients. It will also enable proper implementation of a referral system. By enforcing the implementation of the gatekeeper system – which is already part of the policy of the Ministry of Health, it will reduce some of the current misuse of care and resultant costs and wastage. For example under the current system a client can visit several providers with the same condition – even on the same day, consuming staff resources and medicines at each point. This is a duplication and waste of scarce staff and financial resources. The sharing of risk between schemes/NHIA, providers and clients under a per capita system has a better potential to ensure the financial sustainability and preservation of the NHIS.

The major disadvantage of a per capita system is that the provider may be tempted to provide less than needed services to the client. A close monitoring of quality of care is therefore essential in a per capita payment system. It is also necessary to continuously monitor the per capita rate to make sure that it is and remains fair for the package of services covered. An examination of the costs to providers and the NHIS in terms of skill and staff time in claims processing suggested the need to revisit and work out a way of implementing the capitation payment method, which was proposed for use in Ghana at the time the LI 1809 that accompanied Act 650 was drawn but which remained unimplemented.

In summary the payment-method reforms involve: Introducing capitation (per capita payment) to replace DRG for service & FFS for medicines at the primary care level, retaining DRG for Services & Fee for service (FFS) for medicines at Specialist OPD clinics, Hospital referrals and inpatients (district, regional, specialist and teaching hospitals). The reforms are supported by: Accountability (financial management and reporting systems), strengthening of routine management information systems data completeness, quality, analysis and use, built in monitoring and evaluation for continuous quality improvement, improving clarity in stakeholder roles and relationships, and communication.

Ghana's objective in introducing capitation into its provider payment systems under the NHIS stem out of the already described advantages of capitation which are to: improve cost containment and viability of NHIS, share financial risk between schemes, providers and subscribers, introduce managed competition for providers and choice for patients (compatible with portability) to increase the responsiveness of the health system, improve efficiency and effectiveness of health services through more rational resource use, correct some imbalances created by the G-DRG, e.g., OPD supplier-induced demand, simplify claims processing, address difficulties in forecasting and budgeting, better provider-patient relationship.

The capitation system, which began in the Ashanti Region in 2012 on a pilot basis, has since been extended to the Volta, Upper East, Upper West, Brong Ahafo, Central, and the Western Regions (NHIA, 2015). The system has six main technical components: the package of services paid through the per capita rate, the base per capita, adjustment coefficients, enrolment/registration, financial management and reporting system, and quality monitoring system. These technical components would purportedly check and deal with all the problems associated with the payment system.

Besides eliminating the inefficiencies in the capitation payment system, the system has received protests from civil society organizations, politicians and service providers for its perceived negative effects on primary care delivery (Owusu-Sekyere and Bagah, 2014). In a press release, the Society of Private Medical and Dental Practitioners notified the public that it has suspended its services to the NHIS subscribers indefinitely. According to the medical and dental practitioners, the system is detrimental to quality of health care provision and a major threat to the survival of private health facilities [19]. Moreover, the Pharmaceutical Society of Ghana is reported to have sued the NHIA over capitation payment on grounds that it poses grave danger to patients given, among other factors, the recognition it (capitation payment) gives to persons outside the pharmacy profession (The Daily Guide, 2012). Hence, the capitation payment continues to be a subject of public discussion in Ghana.

According to a USAID report [21], some of the reasons for the rejection of the capitation system by the Ashanti region was the exclusion of primary care maternity services, i.e., antenatal care, normal delivery and post-natal care, the wide variation in primary care service quality and availability were not addressed. While proponents rationalize its importance and usefulness for health care delivery in Ghana, opponents call for its cessation [3]. The National Health Insurance Authority is currently sensitizing major stakeholders in the Brong Ahafo Region to enable them to understand the operation of the capitation system so that they assist in the dissemination of information to the people. Such sensitization and education may contribute to stakeholders' acceptance of the policy and its effectiveness in increasing accessibility, quality and sustainable healthcare delivery.

Statement of the problem

The capitation payment system under the NHIS has received opposition especially from providers and civil organizations. According to these groups the capitation system would adversely affect patient health outcomes because the financial risk transferred to providers may lead to under-provision of services and thereby reducing quality (Dodoo, 2013). This argument, however, does not provide any empirical evidence to support the claims. According to Agyei-Baffour, Oppong and Boateng [1], anytime there is an introduction of any new system or change, the fear of the unknown and protection of interests create anxiety among parties, and this apprehension may lead to misconception on the consequences of such new system. Also, according to Gibson et al. (2003), the resistance mainly arises from the limited attention paid to communicating the change to actors. However, such countries as the UK, Thailand and Chile have successfully implemented the capitation system of payment by increasing access and improving quality service delivery Allard et al. [2]. Therefore, it is important for policy makers to manage the interest of actors to arrive at desired policy goals and objectives.

Since 2012 when the pilot program for the capitation began in the Ashanti region, there have been various sensitization programs aimed at creating awareness. At the same time, resistance from providers has persisted. Whereas the resistance to the system comes from the providers, the opinions of the main people whom the policy seeks to protect and ensure that they received quality healthcare service have not been well engaged to determine their willingness to accept this system of payment. So, it is timely and relevant for this study to determine the public's willingness to accept the capitation as a system of payment under the National Health Insurance Scheme and the factors influencing this willingness or otherwise. In this regard, this study conjectures that the willingness of the people to accept capitation will depend on the citizens' individual and socio-economic characteristics, as well as their ability to afford and subscribe to this system of payment.

Objectives

Objectives for this paper include:

1. To determine the factors that influence the willingness to accept the capitation payment system under the Ghana National Health Insurance Scheme.
2. To examine the extent to which income levels influence the willingness to accept the capitation payment system under the Ghana National Health Insurance Scheme.

This study's outcomes and recommendations may inform policy makers about the various factors influencing people's willingness to accept and subscribe to the capitation payment system. This paper will also contribute immensely to the body of literature under health insurance for health practitioners, service providers, researchers, and policy makers generally.

The first part of this paper provides an overview of health insurance policy and states the problem regarding the capitation system of payment, the research objectives and significance of the study. The second section deals with the conceptual framework and literature on health insurance provision and schemes in Ghana. The next section discusses the method of collecting the data for the study and analyzing the data. The study proceeds with the econometric analysis of the data, as well as the presentation and discussion of results. Lastly, the study draws some conclusions and makes recommendations.

Review of literature

Health insurance

Health insurance is a way of pre-paying for the health services used by residents. In health insurance, payments made are spread over the subscribers and over time in the form of some agreed regular contribution. For an efficient health insurance system, the following issues need to be addressed; how money is collected from residents and pooled to pay for services, the services to be covered under the insurance or the benefit package and how these services are paid for on behalf of the citizens who are part of the insurance scheme (also known as the provider payment method. The provider payment method is therefore "the mechanism used for transferring funds from the purchaser of healthcare services to the providers".

Different methods are used to pay providers under a health insurance scheme. They include the Fee for Services (often itemized), the Diagnosis Related Groupings (DRG) and Capitation. There is no one method that is perfect as each method has its own advantages and disadvantages. Therefore a skillful mix of methods, taking into consideration the unique characteristics of the country, is required.

The fee for service

Under the Fee for Service provider payment method, the provider lists the different services which they have provided for the client and the cost of each service and requests payment. The advantage of the fee for service payment method is that the provider has no incentive to leave anything off the "shopping list". The disadvantage is that precisely for this reason, since the provider is also often the "owner" of the shop and the one choosing the items to be purchased for the client (because of the issues related to specialized knowledge); it is possible for the provider to provide unnecessary services to maximize profit. It does not mean that the provider will do this, but it is possible and hence, a known weakness of this system.

Experience all over the world over time shows that it is a system that can lead to cost inflation of costs and threaten the sustainability of health insurance. Countries that use Fee for Service successfully in their health insurance scheme, an example of which is Germany, often devise very complicated methods to counteract this tendency. Despite its well established disadvantage of causing cost inflation which can be a major threat to sustainability - and sometimes leading to unnecessary provision of services because it requires very little technical expertise to implement - fee for service is a common payment mechanism in many low income countries (Ghana National Health Insurance Authority).

Diagnosis related grouping (DGR)

With regards to the DRG payment method, related diagnoses are grouped together and the average cost of treatment in that group determined. Providers are therefore paid according to the diagnosis they give their client. Many developed countries including the USA and U.K, use DRG as part of their payment systems. Providers have to fill claims forms for reimbursement after providing the services. The claims made by the providers are then checked (vetted) for accuracy and genuineness before payment. The process is administratively complicated and makes a heavy demand on the time of both provider and scheme staff and the NHIA. The DRG for services also still holds some incentives for cost escalation though they are less, compared to the itemized fee for service. Since medicines at all levels remain under itemized fee for service, the potential of major cost escalation is also strong.

Capitation

Capitation is a provider payment mechanism in which providers in the payment system are paid, typically in advance, a pre-determined fixed rate to provide a defined set of services for each individual enrolled with the provider for a fixed period of time. The amount paid to the provider is irrespective of whether that person would seek care or not during the designated period.

The fixed amount is typically expressed on a Per Member Per Month (PMPM) basis. The member refers to NHIS subscribers assigned to the accredited providers. Under this payment system, the member or subscriber selects a preferred primary provider (PPP) to provide all the services under the capitation basket in exchange for the capitation rate. The total capitation amount is transferred to the provider at the beginning of the service period. The amount is calculated based on the total number of members who have selected a given provider (Ghana National Health Insurance Authority).

Capitation is a well-established provider payment method in several countries – high as well as middle income. In introducing capitation, Ghana is walking a tried and tested road that many other countries have already successfully walked. The British National Health Service has used capitation for decades. The British system has become more complicated over time with several generations of reform but the basic principle is one of capitation. Thailand, which is lauded internationally as a middle income country that now successfully covers virtually all its citizens with health insurance, uses capitation as the base of its provider payment system and reserves methods such as DRG for the higher referral level. Other examples of middle income countries successfully using capitation as one of their provider payment methods include Chile and Estonia, and have been successful in attaining universal or near universal coverage with health insurance.

Institutional framework

The Ghana health service

The Ghana Health Service (GHS) is a public service body established under Act 525 of 1996 as required by the 1992 Constitution. The GHS does not include teaching hospitals and private hospitals. It is an autonomous executive agency responsible for implementation of national policies under the control of the Minister for Health through its governing council – the Ghana Health Service Council. However, the GHS continues to receive public funds and thus remains within the public sector. Yet, its employees are no longer part of the civil service. Neither are the GHS managers required to follow all civil service rules and procedures. This independence of the GHS is designed primarily to ensure that its employees have a greater degree of managerial flexibility to carry out their responsibilities than would be possible if they had remained wholly within the civil service. The mandate of GHS is to provide and prudently manage comprehensive and accessible health service with special emphasis on primary health care at the regional, district and sub-district levels in accordance with approved national policies [12].

The objectives of the GHS involve: implementing approved national policies for health delivery in the country, increasing access to good quality health services, and managing prudently resources available for the provision of the health services. For the purposes of achieving these objectives, the GHS performs the following functions amongst others: provide comprehensive health services at all levels directly and by contracting out to other agencies, which includes developing appropriate strategies and setting technical guidelines to achieve national policy goals; undertake management and administration of the overall health resources within the service; promote healthy mode of living and good health habits by people; establish effective mechanism for disease surveillance, prevention and control; determine charges for health services with the approval of the Minister of Health; provide in-service training and continuing education; perform any other functions relevant to the promotion, protection and restoration of health [12].

Ghana introduced its National Health Insurance Scheme (NHIS) in 2003 through an Act of Parliament (Act 650) as a result of the inability of majority of Ghanaians, mostly the poor, to access health care under the Cash and Carry System of health care financing. It is said that only 21% out of 18% of Ghanaians who needed health care under the Cash and Carry System could afford to pay at the point of services. This estimate means that about 79% of people who needed healthcare could not afford (Send [18]).

In order to promote universal coverage and equity, the government of Ghana adopted the National Health Insurance Scheme (NHIS) in 2003, which was fully implemented in 2005. Under the law, there is a National Health Insurance Authority which licenses, monitors and regulates the operation of health insurance schemes in Ghana. The NHIS aims at ensuring equitable and universal access for all residents of Ghana to an acceptable quality package of essential health care services without out-of-pocket payment being required at the point of use [13]. Thus, the ultimate goal of the NHIS is the provision of universal health insurance coverage for all Ghanaians, irrespective of their socio-economic background. As at June 2009, about 67% of the Ghanaian population had subscribed to the NHIS [5].

The NHIS is based on District Mutual Health Insurance Scheme (DMHIS), which operate in all 170 districts of the country. The NHIS covers both the formal and informal sectors of the economy. According to McIntyre, Gilson and Mutyambizi [15], the implementation of the NHIS draws experience from the operations of the Community Based Health Insurance Scheme (CBHIS). The NHIS is financed by a national health insurance levy of 2.5% on certain goods and services, 2.5% monthly payroll deduction being part of the contribution to the Social Security and National Insurance Trust (SSNIT) for formal sector workers, government budgetary allocation, and donor funding. But the formal sector workers still have to pay a registration fee to a DMHIS for an identity card (ID) to be able to access health care services. Also, contributions from members of the informal sector are made to the NHIS with the minimum and maximum premium being GH 7.20 ($1.75) and GH 47.70 ($11.93), respectively [13]. However, the core poor, pregnant women, pensioners, people above the age of 70 and those below 18 years are exempted from premium payment. There is no other cost sharing or co-payments with the NHIS, except the premium paid.

The benefits' package of the NHIS consists of basic health care services, including outpatient consultations, essential drugs, inpatient care and shared accommodation, maternity care (normal and caesarean delivery), eye care, dental care, and emergency care. About 95% of the diseases in Ghana are covered under the NHIS. However, some services classified to be very expensive are on the exclusion list. Among these are cosmetic surgery, drugs not listed on the NHIS drugs list (including anti-retroviral drugs), assisted reproduction, organ transplantation, and private inpatient accommodation [8].

The provider payment method

There is no one perfect method; each method has advantages and disadvantages. Typically, therefore, most successful health insurance schemes use a combination of methods. A skillful mix of methods considering each country's unique context, including economics and history, is the best approach. Thus, effectively and efficiently managed health insurance schemes often provide for a mix of provider payment methods in a way that allows the advantages and disadvantages of the different methods to balance each other (NHIS, 2011). Capitation payment methods are able to control costs better than DRGs, but capitation can encourage providers to deliver less health care than optimal. On the other hand, DRG payments focus on technical efficiency to make better use of available resources and reduce average length of stay, but they also encourage hospitals to increase patient numbers [20].

In Ghana, provider payment methods in use currently are (a) Itemized Fee for Service (FFS) for noninsured clients for both services and medicines, (b) Diagnosis Related Groupings (DRG) for insured clients (services only), and (c) Itemized Fee for Service (FFS) for medicines of insured clients. However, these methods of payment have suffered abuses by service providers as well as subscribers. It has been observed that subscribers often patronize several health facilities with the same ailment within a period less than a month. Often, claims submitted by providers would have an individual with the same NHIS registration number appearing on more than one service provider's claim with the same ailment and similar drugs. Reasons like these have motivated the government of Ghana to implement the capitation payment system.

In 2010, the World Bank supported Ghana to introduce the capitation payment system as part of the National Health Insurance services. According to Ansong [4], the National Health Insurance Scheme in Ghana selected Ashanti region for the pilot of the capitation payment system because the region is situated in the middle of the country and has heterogeneous infrastructure and culture.

Empirical literature

Andoh-Adjei et al. [3] observed that health insurance subscribers in Ghana have high trust in their primary care provider for giving them quality care under capitation payment despite their negative attitude towards capitation payment. The study also added that subscribers are guided by proximity and quality of care considerations in their choice of provider. In contrast, Benoah [6] assessed the effects of the capitation payment system on health care delivery in Ashanti Region and found that the majority of subscribers (representing 90% of the respondents) admitted that they were not satisfied with the healthcare delivery under capitation. Hence, they did not see any improvement and effectiveness in healthcare delivery in the Ashanti region. This finding, however, is also different from the findings of Opoku, Nsiah, Oppong and Tetteh [17] who undertook a similar study within the same Ashanti region and observed that the capitation payment system has an efficient use of resource, creates competition among hospitals (quality service), and has turned hospitals to financial risk bearers.

However, an earlier study by Agyei-Baffour, Oppong and Boateng [1] on knowledge, perceptions and expectations of capitation payment system in a health insurance setting indicates that a majority (97.9%) of the clients had heard of the capitation payment. But, that knowledge did not reflect the clients' level of understanding of the system. About two-thirds (61.2%) disclosed that capitation was not important for them as clients were restricted to one Preferred Primary Provider (PPP) for a long period of time. Health providers also believed that people (34%) did not like the capitation payment system due to their misconception that it has been politicized. Others, constituting 26%, believed that the system did not give clients free choice of providers, and 17% held that capitation did not cover most drugs. Although awareness of the capitation was high among clients, attitudes toward the capitation payment system were somewhat poor.

The studies suggest that a good understanding of the capitation payment system is key to ensuring client and provider acceptance, as well as a smooth implementation of the system. It must be emphasized that almost all the studies about capitation payment system in Ghana have been on perception and expectations of the subscribers. None determined the extent to which subscribers' socio-economic and individual characteristics influenced their willingness to accept the capitation as a payment system under the Ghana Health Insurance Scheme. Thus, this study shifts the focus to examining the willingness of subscribers to accept the capitation payment system based on clients' individual and socio-economic characteristics.

Methods

Data

A sample of 1299 NHIS subscribers who have reached the working age and are either employed or unemployed from all the ten regions of Ghana were used for the study. The number of questionnaires administered for each region was chosen proportionately based on regional population as given by the 2010 Ghana Statistical Service Population Census [11]. The questionnaires were then administered randomly with the regional distribution as indicated in Table 1.

Table 1 Regional population and sample distribution

Region	Population	Sample size	Percentage
Ashanti	4,780,380	252	19.4
Greater Accra	4,010,054	211	16.24
Eastern	2,633,154	139	10.7
Northern	2,479,461	130	10.01
Western	2,376,021	125	9.62
Brong Ahafo	2,310,983	122	9.4
Volta	2,118,252	112	8.62
Central	2,201,863	116	8.93
Upper East	1,046,545	55	4.23
Upper West	702,110	37	2.85
Total	24,658,823	1299	100

Households were chosen at random, and questionnaires were administered to household heads. In the questionnaires, household heads were asked to answer questions with regard to their individual characteristics, their income levels, employment status, whether they have received education or sensitization about the capitation payment system and hence their perception and willingness to subscribe to the capitation payment system. Household heads were chosen for the study because they will, to a large extent, be responsible for the payment of their defendants under the payment methods.

To effectively examine the success of the capitation payment system, service providers and physicians were interviewed to solicit their views on the payment system. Thirty-three (33) were interviewed with at least three (3) providers from each region.

Descriptive analysis of data

Table 2 shows the descriptive analysis of the data. Out of the 1299 respondents used for the study, 571 (43.96%) were female while 728 (56.04%) were male. A total number of 765 (58.89%) were employed whereas 534 (41.11%) were unemployed or perceived themselves as unemployed though they were doing menial jobs for a living. In terms of their educational background, 689 (53.04%) of respondents had attained tertiary level of education, 255 (19.63%) had received secondary education, 328 (25.25%) had primary education but 27 (2.08%) had no formal education.

On whether respondents have any knowledge or awareness of the government's intention of implementing the capitation payment system under the Ghana National Health Insurance Scheme, 956 (73.60%) indicated that they have knowledge or awareness of the capitation policy while 343 (26.40%) did not. The mean age of the respondents was 38.44; the youngest was 20 years of age, and the oldest was 63 years. A total number of 448 (34.49%) lived in rural areas, categorized as towns with only Community-Based Health Planning and Services (CHPS) compound health facility, but 851 (65.51%) lived in the urban centers. With regard to their marital status, 516 (39.72%) were single whereas 65 (5%) were widows and 93 (7.16) were divorced. However, 625 (48.12%) were married.

The empirical model

The willingness to accept the capitation as a system of payment

The willingness to accept the capitation payment system of the NHIS is estimated by a linear model as follows:

$$W_i = \beta' X_i + \varepsilon_i \quad (1)$$

Where W_i is the willingness which is the outcome variable denoted by "1" if an individual i is willing to accept the capitation payment system and "0" if otherwise. The matrix X contains a set of variables picking up the respondent's individual, social and economic characteristics.

These are the explanatory variables consisting of age(respondent's age), income (the respondent's income level), sex (the gender of the respondent, denoted as "1" if male and "0" if female), household size (respondent's household size), education(level of education attained by respondent ranked as "4" if tertiary, "3" if secondary, "2" if primary and "1" if illiterate), marital status(marital status of the respondent ranked as "4" if married, "3" if divorced, "2" if widow and "1" if single), awareness(-whether respondent knows about capitation denoted as "1" if yes and "0" if otherwise), preference (if respondent prefer capitation to other form of payment denoted "1" if yes and "0" if otherwise), employed (employment status of the respondent denoted as "1" if employed and "0" if unemployed), location (area of residence of respondent denoted as "1" if urban and "0" if rural), region (a dummy for each of the ten regions). Eq. (1) shall be estimated using the linear probability model (LPM) with the stata version 12 software.

To determine the extent to which income level influences the willingness to accept capitation, income shall be differentiated by high and low-income earners. Here high-income earners shall be defined as individuals whose incomes are greater or equal to the average income based on the data while low incomes are those below the average. Therefore, the study seeks whether it is the individual characteristics of high income earners that influence their willingness to accept capitation or just their income levels. To do this we resort to the Blinder-Oaxaca decomposition [7, 16].

Table 2 Descriptive analysis of data

Variable	Description		Mean	Std. dev	Max	Min
Income	Average monthly income of respondent		1347.2	1404	200	8000
Household size	Number of persons living in the home of respondent		5.34	4.84	1	13
Education of respondent	Education	Number/percentage				
	Tertiary	680(53.04)				
	Secondary	255(19.63)				
	Primary	328(25.25)				
	Illiterate	27(2.08)				
SEX	Gender	Number/percentage				
	Female	571(43.96)				
	Male	728(56.04)				
Age	Age of respondent		38.44	8.32	20	63
Location	Location	Number/percentage				
	Rural	851(65.51)				
	Urban	448(34.49)				
Awareness	Knowledge	Number/percentage				
	No knowledge	956(73.60)				
	Aware	343(26.40)				
Employed	Employment	Number/percentage				
	unemployed	534(41.11)				
	employed	765(58.89)				
Marital status	Marital status	Number/percentage				
	Single	516(39.72)				
	Widow	65(5)				
	Divorced	93(7.16)				
	Married	625(48.12)				

The empirical model to be estimated is of the form:

$$\begin{aligned} Willingness = \alpha + \beta_1 Ylevel + \beta_2 hsize + \beta_3 edu \\ + \beta_4 sex + \beta_5 age + \beta_6 loc \\ + \beta_7 aware + \beta_8 empl + \beta_9 pref \\ + \beta_{10} region + \varepsilon_i \end{aligned} \tag{2}$$

Where *Ylevel*, is the income level, *hsize*, the household size, *edu*, the educational level attained, *sex*, the gender of respondent, *age*, the age of respondent, *loc*, residential area of respondent, *aware*, whether the respondent knows about the capitation, *empl*, employment status of respondent, *pref*, whether respondent prefers capitation to other forms of payment, *region*, region of residence of respondent and ε, being the error term. Ashanti region was used as the base category for the following reasons: the region is found in the middle belt of Ghana and has been a major destination center for people migrating from both the northern and southern part of the country. The region also has the largest population size. It was the region where the pilot program was first rolled out, and the fact those civil society organizations and some service providers in the region were in resistance to its implementation.

Determining the extent to which income levels influence the willingness to accept capitation

To determine the extent to which income levels influence the willingness to accept capitation, we rewrite Eq. (1) as follows:

$$W_{ij} = \beta_{ij} + \varepsilon_{ij} \tag{3}$$

In Eq. (3) the subscript ij reflects the belongingness to a particular group, e.g., high-income earners and low/non-income earners. Assuming that "*h*" is for high income earners and "*l*" is for low income earners with marginal effects β_h and β_l respectively, differences in the willingness to accept capitation will exist if $\beta_h \neq \beta_l$.

The necessary assumption being made is that the error ε_{ij} is independent of individual *i* belonging to group $j = h$ or $j = l$. Assuming β_h and β_l are the coefficient for employment for example then differences in acceptance will require that $|\beta_h| > |\beta_l|$or vice versa. The difference would be attributed to the fact that one group, e.g., high income earners, is endowed with a set of variables (characteristics) that makes high income earners likely to accept capitation than low income earners or vice versa. Thus $X_h \neq X_l$.

To properly quantify the extent to which the variables X_{ij} (endowments) and coefficient β_{ij} (unexplained factors) influence the decisions to accept capitation we resort to the Blinder-Oaxaca decomposition method. This method allows us to decompose the estimated acceptance gap between high income (A_h) and low/non-income earners (A_l) into two components as follows:

$$\hat{A}_h - \hat{A}_l = (\overline{X}_h - \overline{X}_l)\beta_l - \overline{X}_h(\hat{\beta}_h - \hat{\beta}_l) \quad (4)$$

The left hand of Eq. (4) measures the acceptance gap (estimate gap). The first term on the right-hand side of the equation picks up that part of the gap attributed to differences in endowments(characteristics), whilst the second term picks up the part attributed to coefficients (unexplained factors). Where the first part on the right-hand side is greater than the second part (in absolute terms), the decision to accept capitation by high income earners is largely influenced by their characteristics. On the other hand, where the second term on the right-hand side is greater than the first term (in absolute terms) then this acceptance gap is being largely influenced by unexplained factors. That means that high income earners' acceptance of that capitation is not influenced by their characteristics such as age, gender, employment status, marital status, etc., but just the fact that their incomes are high.

Results and discussion

Willingness to accept capitation

Table 3 shows the estimated effects of the likelihood that an individual and a region will accept the capitation payment system under the Ghana National Health Insurance Scheme. To allow for interpretation the study reports the marginal effects instead of coefficients.

At the individual level, the results show that increase in income increases the willingness and the likelihood of accepting the capitation by 8.5 percentage points. Awareness has become a very vital issue if any policy is to succeed as the targeted people need to be educated and informed about the policy and its implementation. In this study, where individuals are aware about the capitation and have knowledge of it, their willingness and the likelihood to accept the capitation increase by 25 percentage points. Compared to their unemployed counterparts, the employed are likely to accept the capitation while people from large households are less likely to accept the capitation system of payment. Of course, this is not surprising because the capitation is likely to drain incomes of bread winners of large households.

At the 10% level, people living in urban centers are more willing and likely to accept the capitation compared to their counterparts in the rural settings. This finding supports that of Andoh-Adjei et al. [3] that subscribers are guided by proximity and quality healthcare considerations. These attributes are found in the urban centers, where cluster of hospitals provide quality care and residents have ease of proximity.

At the regional level, and using the Ashanti region as the base category, the results indicated that people in the Greater Accra, Western, Central, Upper East and Upper West regions are more willing and likely to accept the capitation while the study did not find any significance in relation to the willingness and the likelihood to accept the capitation in the Eastern, Northern, Brong-Ahafo and Volta regions. Similarly, marital status, educational background, and gender as individual characteristics were not significant in determining the willingness and the likelihood to accept capitation.

Because the Ashanti region was used as the base category, the interpretation is that the people in the Ashanti region are not willing and are less likely to accept the capitation payment system. This finding supports those of Benoah (2013) and Agyei-Baffour, Oppong and Boateng [1] as well as that of USAID [21]. These findings for the various regions make the willingness and the likelihood to accept the capitation payment system mixed at the national level and as a national policy. With regard to the interviews conducted on the service providers, it was observed that eighteen (18) service providers, making up of thirteen private (13) service providers and five (5) public service providers, were against the implementation of the capitation system because they believe that their operations would be at risk because the per capita threshold payment amount would be the same irrespective of the resources used to treat patients. Thus, they are likely to spend more than the fixed per capita amount threshold given to them by the National Health Insurance Authority.

The remaining fifteen (15) service providers, constituting six (6) private service providers and nine (9) public service providers, were in favor of the payment system as they claimed that it would help increase health efficiency and deal with bloated bills sent to the National Health Authority for reimbursement. The outcome of the views of service providers is also mixed. While some providers welcome the capitation payment policy, others are also against its implementation.

Table 3 Willingness to accept capitation: probit estimation with marginal effects

Willingness	dF/dx	Std. Err	z	P > |z|	x-bar	[95% C.I.]
Log (Income)	.0850317	.015751	5.38	0.000	7.65901	.05416 .115903
Second Cycle	.0465709	.0433296	1.09	0.275	.196305	−.038354 .131495
Primary School	.0034488	.0380682	0.09	0.928	.252502	−.071164 .078061
Illiterate	.1024493	.1116649	0.95	0.340	.020785	−.11641 .321309
Sex	−.0170879	.0453663	−0.38	0.707	.397998	−.106004 .071828
Age	.004945	.0027895	1.77	0.076	38.4434	−.000522 .010412
Awareness	.2526399	.03664	6.98	0.000	.264049	.180827 .324453
Employed	.0954805	.0282816	3.39	0.001	.411085	.04005 .150911
Preference	.0113417	.0319956	0.35	0.723	.482679	−.051369 .074052
Widow	−.0178344	.0660746	−0.27	0.790	.050038	−.147338 .111669
Divorced	−.0587199	.0390965	−1.47	0.140	.30254	−.135348 .017908
Married	.0346609	.0453723	0.77	0.440	.250192	−.054267 .123589
Location	.0500246	.0300452	1.68	0.093	.344881	−.008863 .108912
Household size	−.0106649	.0036245	−2.94	0.003	5.34411	−.017769−.003561
Greater Accra	.2292637	.0518286	4.52	0.000	.163972	.020675 .271579
Eastern Region	.0198648	.0606954	0.33	0.741	.107005	−.177789 .068098
Northern Region	−.064766	.0558291	−1.11	0.267	.101617	−.245349−.016541
Western Region	.1459874	.0692565	2.19	0.029	.076212	−.08569 .212323
Brong Ahafo	.073684	.0591484	1.28	0.200	.094688	−.130942 .120848
Volta Region	.0791279	.0644581	1.26	0.206	.193995	−.183618 .036169
Central Region	.2694488	.0640492	4.25	0.000	.089299	.03834 .332441
Upper East	.4209035	.0707998	5.27	0.000	.04234	.177327 .513209
Upper West	.2635957	.0814817	3.27	0.001	.04388	.000961 .357182

Decomposing willingness among high and low-income earners

To examine the extent to which income levels influence the willingness and the likelihood to accept the capitation, this study resorted to a decomposition analysis. As to whether the individual characteristics of high income earners influence the willingness and the likelihood to accept capitation or otherwise, the study employed the generalized Blinder-Oaxaca decomposition and counterfactual analysis [7, 16].

Table 4 shows the overall results of the generalized Blinder-Oaxaca decomposition results. The results revealed a mean acceptance of 27% for low income earners and 50% for high income earners, leading to an acceptance gap of 23% in favor of high income earners. Dividing the explained (endowments) of 0.04 by the difference (gap) of 0.23, endowments (characteristics) accounted for only 18% of the acceptance gap. This 18% was the mean decrease in the acceptance gap if low income earners possessed the individual characteristics of high income earners. The unexplained (coefficients) of 0.19 showed that the unexplained factors amounted to 82% (0.19÷0.23) of the acceptance gap. Thus, applying the unexplained (coefficients) of high income earners to the low-income earners' characteristics, the acceptance gap will decrease by 82%. The results imply that the acceptance gap between the low income and high-income earners is not influenced by the individual characteristics

Table 4 Income levels and willingness: blinder-oaxaca decomposition and counterfactual analysis

Willingness	Coef.	Robust Std. Err.	z	P > |z|	[95% Conf. Interval]
Overall					
Low Income	.2701525	.0146612	18.43	0.000	.2414171 .2988879
High Income	.5013123	.0256303	19.56	0.000	.4510779 .5515468
Difference	−.2311598	.0295273	−7.83	0.000	−.2890323 -.1732874
Explained	−.0400858	.0140411	−2.85	0.004	−.0676059 -.0125657
Unexplained	−.191074	.0315304	−6.06	0.000	−.2528724 -.1292756

of high income earners but largely by the fact that they earn high income irrespective of their age, gender, education or marital status.

Conclusion and policy recommendations

The health of citizens contributes immensely to the wealth of every nation. Therefore, governments seek social policies that make health facilities available, accessible and affordable to the people. Health Insurance policy is one of such social policy interventions being implemented by Ghana as a way of making healthcare affordable. However, the Ghana Health Insurance Scheme has its challenges. A pilot of the capitation payment system in the Ashanti Region was a way of examining its effectiveness in dealing with abuses associated with the payment of claims under the FFS and the DRG. Although the pilot program has been extended to other regions, the capitation system has been abandoned recently in the Ashanti region.

For every policy to be effective its end users or the intended target groups need to be informed, sensitized and enlightened for them to understand, appreciate and embrace the policy wholly. It is also important to study their socio-economic background and individual characteristics and how these are likely to influence their willingness and likelihood of accepting such a policy. It is for these reasons that the present study sought to determine how the socio-economic as well as individual characteristics influence subscribers' willingness and likelihood of accepting the capitation payment system as a policy. The study also included a dummy for the regions to ascertain the regions' willingness. Another objective was to determine the extent to which income levels influence the willingness to accept the capitation system under the Ghana Health Insurance Scheme.

Using a linear probability model estimation with marginal effects, the study shows that high incomes, being employed, having smaller household size and awareness are the significant factors that increase the willingness and the likelihood of subscribers to accept the capitation payment system. At the regional level and using the Ashanti Region as a base category, the study reveals that people in the Greater Accra, Western, Central, Upper East and Upper West regions are likely to accept the capitation system as compared to the Ashanti Region. The findings do not show any significance with regard to the willingness to accept the capitation system for Eastern, Northern, Brong Ahafo and Volta regions.

In addition, the study used the generalized Blinder-Oaxaca decomposition and counterfactual analysis to determine the extent individual characteristics (such as age, gender, educational background, marital status, and high income) influence the willingness and the likelihood of accepting capitation. In this regard, the findings indicate that the willingness and the likelihood to accept the capitation by high-income earners are largely influenced by unexplained factors and not by age, gender, educational background, or marital status.

The study does not find any significance for the willingness to accept the capitation payment system for the Eastern, Northern, Brong Ahafo and Volta regions though the Volta and the Brong Ahafo regions have already been introduced to the pilot program. Also, the success or otherwise of the policy is largely hinged on the income levels of the people irrespective of the individual characteristics. Moreover, any policy that restricts public choice has negative consequences for welfare. The capitation system is a policy that restricts public choice because subscribers are limited to only one service provider. Besides, in the event of subscribers' emergency ill-health occurring in different vicinity, the subscribers cannot benefit from the health insurance under the capitation system.

Based on the findings and their implications, this study recommends that the capitation system should be rolled out as a complementary payment system to the ongoing payment system of the DRG and not as a replacement. The main purpose of the capitation as a policy measure is to address abuses under the National Health Insurance Scheme, which can be tackled by transforming the current payment system under the DRG and complementing it with the capitation payment system. In the DRG, subscribers have options and varied choices with regard to facilities and service providers. These elements add up to subscribers' preference for proximity and quality. Furthermore, the abuses which triggered the capitation policy can be addressed by introducing stringent measures such as automation and networking into the current system. This way, the abuses such as multiple claims can be identified and checked.

We recommend that both the DRG and the capitation payment systems be rolled out under the Ghana National Health Insurance Scheme. The capitation payment system should be adopted for general health practitioners providing primary health care while the DRGs should be used to reimburse providers for chronic and acute inpatient care. Thus DRG payment system should be operated under specialist hospitals while capitation payment system be used for primary health care.

In order to check exploitation of the DRG system for supernormal profits, payments should be "case-based" so as to increase efficiency and contain costs. For example, payments for chronic conditions relevant to specific medical condition and treatment should be according to groupings so that an average cost for such chronic conditions be determined in order to check any abuses.

As much as possible capitation for inpatients should be separated from outpatients' fixed annual payments and given different classification for payments and reimbursement. Moreover, incentives should be given to outpatient services to make such services more efficient to avert worsening inpatient situation or transferring patients to specialists' hospitals that may be costly.

Also, we suggest that prescription by physicians be separated from dispensing by pharmacists/pharmaceutical companies. Similarly, it should be mandatory for copies of prescription and dispensing forms to be submitted to the NHIA by patients for cross-checking and payment with regard to the DRG payment system so as to check the abuses and eliminate any supernormal profits by these parties. When these recommendations are implemented we expect that the two payment systems will be efficient in dealing with excessive cost problems that the NIA (insurer) faces in respect of DRGs and the risk of providing services over and above the per capita payment threshold that service providers receive in the case of capitation. The long hours spent by patients will reduce as patients will now know the type of ailment that should go to the general practitioners and the type that should come to the specialists.

In order to measure properly and deal with changes in the mode of reimbursement, we recommend that the NHIA come up with quality service ratings and quality metrics among peer service providers. The quality measures will inform changes in reimbursement to bring about competition for quality and efficient service delivery. There should be an annual assessment, as well as a review of payments and service delivery. If possible there should be a threshold increase in the yearly maximum reimbursement amount for outpatient visits. This mode of reimbursement can increase outpatient service utilization, which will benefit individuals. Annually, stakeholders must meet to examine and assess all the payment methods with regard to what is working or not and why.

Moreover, the NHIA must examine how it can handle revenue payments over and above revenues generated from premiums as a result of increases and changes in in-out patients. Such attention will inform the NHIA about the consequences and effectiveness of changes in reimbursements. However, where revenues from individual annual-premium-payments, monthly deductions from formal sector workers, and NHIA share from the value added taxation (VAT) are not enough to support the scheme, stakeholders should devise innovative ways of funding. For example, payment of road tolls could be increased to fund health insurance, and the informal sector may be persuaded to contribute to the scheme.

For further research, we propose an extensive qualitative research to elucidate why people prefer certain payment schemes to others. Such qualitative design may apply a flexible in-depth interviews to examine other individual and economic variables which may influence subscribers' perception and willingness to accept and subscribe to capitation and DRG payment schemes.

Abbreviations

CHPS: Community-Based Health Planning and Services; DRG: Diagnosis-Related-Grouping; FFS: Fee for Service; GHS: Ghana Health Service; NHIA: National Health Insurance Authority; NHIS: National Health Insurance Scheme; SSNIT: Social Security and National Insurance Trust

Acknowledgements

We would like to acknowledge the 2016/2017 final year students of Economics and Business faculty for their immense support in the administration of the questionnaires for the study.

Funding

We did not receive any funding for this study as the cost of the study was solely borne by us, the authors.

Authors' contributions

FGS was responsible for the empirical literature, methodology, analysis of data, discussion of results and conclusions, while, Rev. PNA was responsible for the introduction and theoretical literature and the editing of the entire article. Both authors read and approved the final manuscript.

Authors' information

Dr. Frank Gyimah Sackey, the corresponding author, is a senior lecturer and the Acting Dean for the School of Research and Graduate Studies of the Catholic University College of Ghana. He holds a PhD in Economics from the Universitat Rovira i Virgili and he is a Marti Franques Fellow of the Universitat Rovira i Virgili in Spain.

Rev. Fr. Dr. Peter Nkrumah Amponsah, the co-author, holds a PhD from the University of Southern Illinoi, at Carbon Dale, USA. He is a senior lecturer and the Dean of the Faculty of Social Sciences and Religious Studies of the Catholic University College of Ghana.

Competing interests

We confirm that this work is original and has not been published elsewhere, nor is it currently under consideration for publication elsewhere. We wish to state that there are no competing interests and therefore we have no conflicts of interests to disclose.

References

1. Agyei-Baffour P, Oppong R, Boateng D. Knowledge, perceptions and expectations of capitation payment system in a health insurance setting: A repeated survey of clients and health providers in Kumasi, Ghana. BMC Public Health. BMC series. 2013;10(1):13-1220.
2. Allard M, Jelovac I, Leger PT. Payment mechanism and GP self-selection: capitation versus fee for service. International Journal of Health Care Finance and Economics. 2014;14(2):143-60.
3. Andoh-Adjei, F.X., Cornelissen, D., Asante, A.F., Spaan, E., Velden, K.V.D. Does capitation payment under the National Health Insurance affect subscribers' trust in the primary care provider? A cross sectional survey of insurance subscribers in Ghana. BMC Health Service Research. 2016; 16:437: 1-11.
4. Ansong. National Health Insurance Authority to adopt capitation system of Payment 2013. http://www.africanelections.org/ghana/postelections/news/page.php?news=70. Accessed July 14 2017
5. Asenso-Boadi F. The interplay between district wide health insurance schemes and National Health Insurance Policies in Ghana. Accra; 2009.
6. Benoah, R.A. Assessing the effects of capitation payment system of NHIS and health care delivery in Ashanti region. Unpublished thesis submitted to College of Arts and Social Sciences, KNUST; 2015. Ghana.
7. Blinder AS. Wage discrimination: reduced form and structural estimates. The Journal of Human Resources. 1973;8:436-55.
8. Dalinjong PA, Laar AS. The National Health Insurance Scheme: perceptions and experiences of health care providers and clients in two districts of Ghana. Health Economics Review. 2012;2(13):1-13.
9. Deaton A. Health, inequality and economic development. Journal of Economic Literature. 2003;XLI:113-58.
10. Debpuur C, Dalaba MA, Chatio S, Adjuik M, Akweongo P. An exploration of moral hazard behaviors under the national health insurance scheme in northern Ghana: Aqualitative study. BMC Health Serv Res. 2015;15(1):469.
11. Ghana Statistical Service. Population and housing census. District Analytical Report: Sunyani West. Accra; 2010.
12. Ghana Health Service. *Organizational Structure*. http://www.ghanahealthservice.org/ aboutus.php? inf=Organisational%20 Structure. 2017. Accessed 02 May 2017.
13. Government of Ghana. National health insurance bill, memorandum. In: Accra; 2003.
14. Gupta I, Mitra A. Economic growth, health and poverty: an exploratory study for India. Development Policy Review. 2004;22(2):193-206.
15. McIntyre D, Gilson L, Mutyambizi V. Promoting equitable health care financing in the African context: current challenges and future prospects. Harare: Regional Network for Equity in Health in Southern Africa; 2005.
16. Oaxaca, R. Male-female wage differentials in urban labor markets. International Economic Review 1973; 14: 693-709.
17. Opoku, M., Nsiah, R., Oppong, P.A., Tetteh, E. The effect of capitation payment on the National Health Insurance Scheme in Ashanti region, Ghana. Available at: http://dx.doi.org/102139/ssrn.2479305; 2014.
18. Send Ghana. National health insurance scheme (NHIS); 2005 http://gh.sendwestafrica.org/our-programme/gelap/national-healthinsurance-scheme-nhis#.U0r-SFV_t-U. Accessed 2 May 2017.
19. The NHIA Capitation to be nationwide-CEO. The Ghanaian Times. p.9. February 14 2012.
20. Tolley DH, Manton GK. An evaluation of three payment strategies for capitation for medicare. The Journal of Risk and Insurance. 1987;54(4):678-90.
21. USAID. Lessons learned from the Ashanti capitation pilot: a synthesis of 3 evaluation reports. Submitted to the NHIA Capitation Project Team and the National Capitation Technical Sub-Committee. July, 2014.
22. World Health Organization. *The African regional health report*. WHO regional office for Africa. In: Luxemburg; 2014.

6

Results of a randomized controlled trial analyzing telemedically supported case management in the first year after living donor kidney transplantation - a budget impact analysis from the healthcare perspective

Klaus Kaier[1*], Silvia Hils[2], Stefan Fetzer[3], Philip Hehn[1], Anja Schmid[2], Dieter Hauschke[1], Lioudmila Bogatyreva[1], Bernd Jänigen[2] and Przemyslaw Pisarski[2]

Abstract

We analyze one-year costs and savings of a telemedically supported case management program after kidney transplantation from the perspective of the German Healthcare System. Recipients of living donor kidney transplantation (N = 46) were randomly allocated to either (1) standard aftercare or (2) standard aftercare plus additional telemedically supported case management. A range of cost figures of each patient's medical service utilization were calculated at month 3, 6 and 12 and analyzed using two-part regression models.
In comparison to standard aftercare, patients receiving telemedically supported case management are associated with substantial lower costs related to unscheduled hospitalizations (mean difference: €3,417.46 per patient for the entire one-year period, $p = 0.003$). Taking all cost figures into account, patients receiving standard aftercare are associated, on average, with one-year medical service utilization costs of €10,449.28, while patients receiving telemedically supported case management are associated with €5,504.21 of costs (mean difference: € 4,945.07 per patient, $p < 0.001$). With estimated expenditures of €3,001.5 for telemedically supported case management of a single patient, we determined a mean difference of €1,943.57, but this result is not statistically significant ($p = 0.128$). Sensitivity analyses show that the program becomes cost-neutral at around ten participating patients, and was beneficial starting at 15 patients. Routine implementation of telemedically supported case management in German medium and high-volume transplant centers would result in annual cost savings of €791,033 for the German healthcare system.
Patients with telemedically supported case management showed a lower utilization of medical services as well as better medical outcomes. Therefore, such programs should be implemented in medium and high-volume transplant centers.

Keywords: Telemedicine, Cost-of-illness, Cost-benefit

* Correspondence: Kaier@imbi.uni-freiburg.de
[1]Institute for Medical Biometry and Statistics, Faculty of Medicine and Medical Center – University of Freiburg, Stefan-Meier-Str 26, 79104 Freiburg, Germany
Full list of author information is available at the end of the article

Background

Successful solid organ transplantation can offer substantial improvements to patient quality of life. However, the recovery process after organ transplantations requires continuous effort and therapy to ensure and maintain satisfactory patient outcome and prevent graft loss [1]. Patient adherence to long-term medication is often insufficient for a variety of reasons, and many potential behavioral pitfalls have to be avoided [2–5].

Prevention of graft loss, beside its significance to individual patients, also represents a concern to the healthcare system as a whole due to the high number of patients on the German kidney waiting list and the permanent shortage of donor organs. In the literature there are different propositions on how to reduce occurrence of graft loss, however not all of them are equally effective in producing the desired results [6]. The continuing progress of communication technology provides healthcare professionals an expanding set of tools to potentially improve patient outcomes.

Our random controlled trial combines telemedically supported case management and monitoring of patient's vital data with video teleconferences between the patient and the Transplantation Center Freiburg [7]. The trial was registered with the German Clinical Trials Register (www.DRKS.de) under the identification number DKRS00007634.

The results of our random controlled trial show significant improvements in medical and disease-specific outcomes over the first year after transplantation as described in detail in Schmid et al. [8].

But beyond this medical dimension, telemedically supported case management also has an economic perspective. On the one hand costs of medical treatment increased due to necessary investments into the new telemedicine infrastructure and hiring and training of specialized personnel. On the other hand cost savings can be achieved due to prevention of medical emergencies, elimination of unneeded doctor visits and specialist consultations, and more appropriate therapy decisions. With regard to the resulting net cost effects of telemedically supported intervention prior evidence is mixed and sometimes flawed [9–12]. The benefits of telemedicine in delivering effective care coordination have been confirmed in chronic disease conditions such as cardiac insufficiency [13–15]. A new broad German study focus on telemonitoring for COPD using routine data from a major German sickness fund clearly demonstrates positive effects on healthcare costs [16].

We advance the debate on routine implementation of telemedicine in the health system using a case study from the clearly delimited field of kidney transplantation's aftercare. To best of our knowledge this is the first evaluation of a telemedicine and case-management intervention for transplantation patients with focus on economic (budget) impact in the German healthcare system, observing costs in the first year after transplantation. Furthermore we demonstrate that even if it is clear that a telemedicine intervention is dominant, i.e. preferable both medically and economically to standard care, the current reimbursement practice of German sickness funds still makes it difficult to implement the technique in a routine manner.

Methods

Data collection

A prospective, controlled, randomized and open project-study was realized as follows [7]: In September 2011, 50 patients who were scheduled for a living-donor kidney transplantation at the Transplantation Center Freiburg between October 2011 and March 2012 were randomly allocated to two groups receiving different aftercare programs during the first postoperative year.

The first group was offered standard aftercare in combination with telemedically supported case management. Daily, the patients completed a pre-defined medical questionnaire about their physical condition presented to them in their homes via an interactive web-based telemonitor. These data were monitored by medical staff with a special qualification for work with patients after kidney transplantation. If anomalous values occured, the medical staff contacted the patient by phone or video conference to discuss the following treatment process. The control group was offered standard aftercare without telemedically supported case management. Of the 50 randomized patients, two patients in each group dropped out, resulting in 46 available valid datasets.

One-year costs of medical service utilization

At three points (3, 6 and 12 months after transplantation), utilization of health care resources is recorded for every patient. For outpatient care visits at general practitioners (N = 194) and or medical specialists (N = 1829), standardized unit costs from Bock et al [2014] [17] were applied, representing costs from a societal perspective. For scheduled (N = 39) and unscheduled (N = 68) episodes of hospitalization, actual amounts of reimbursement were collected from the respective hospitals. Ambulatory visits at the outpatient department were priced according to the respective reimbursement (€270 per visit). All prices reflect 2015 values. Overall, six cost figures (*costs of general practitioner* out-patient care *visits, costs of medical specialist* out-patient care *visits, costs of scheduled in-hospital care, costs of unscheduled in-hospital care, costs of ambulatory visits at the out-patient department and total costs of care*) were calculated for each observation period and patient.

Costs of telemedically supported case management

Within the statutory health insurance in Germany, telemedically supported case management is not an element of standard care. A reimbursement by sickness funds is possible by using individual case requests, only. A hypothetical number of 20 patients receiving telemedically supported case management for a one year period is assumed to require an additional 50% nurse position (€28,500) with a suitably equipped work place (€500) and internal server provision (€1,024). In addition, patient-variable costs for a Touch-Screen-PC (€600) and software licenses (€300 per year) are claimed. To these fixed (€30,024 for 20 hypothetical patients) and variable (€900 per patient) costs of the one year telemedical support, an extra 25% for infrastructure expenses was added.

Statistical analysis

Skewed data is a major issue in statistical models of healthcare costs [18–20]. Beside the fact that the six cost figures were positively skewed, most of them were equal to zero during a considerable number of observation periods because patients did not see a physician and/or were not hospitalized in the respective time period. In order to accommodate these characteristics of the data, a two-part model approach was chosen for the regression analyses [21–24]. In two part models, a binary choice model is estimated for the probability of observing a zero versus positive outcome. Then, conditional on a positive outcome, an appropriate regression model is estimated for the positive outcome [25]. For part one of the applied models a logistic regression analysis was chosen to predict whether or not patients would utilize resources related to the respective costs figure. As recommended in the literature [20, 21, 24, 26–28], a generalized linear model (GLM) with the log link and gamma distribution was chosen for the second part. In order to first analyze the temporal development of the cost estimates between the two treatment groups, an interaction term between treatment group and observation period was used. The cluster option was used to address the fact that multiple monthly cost estimates are included in the dataset for the same patient. Then, the respective resource uses were summarized over the one-year period for each patient in order to analyze the treatment-related cost differences across the entire one-year period. Finally, a budget impact analysis [29] from the healthcare perspective is performed by combining the costs of a hypothetical number of 20 patients receiving telemedically supported case management with the actual results of summarized resource uses in the two groups. One-way sensitivity analyses are carried out to assess the impact that changes in a certain parameter will have on the analyses' results. Marginal means from all regression analyses are shown on the raw scale (€ per observation period). All analyses were performed using Stata 14 (Stata Corp., Texas. USA).

Results

Baseline characteristics

Table 1 provides an overview of baseline patient characteristics. The medical results of the RCT this study is a part of, including more detailed statistics, have been published elsewhere [8].

One-year costs of medical service utilization

Table 2 provides estimates regarding the different cost figures over the three observational periods. Between month 0 and month 3 after transplantation, the number of out-patient care visits is comparable between the two groups. Between month 3 and month 6, however, the group of patients with telemedically supported case management required fewer medical specialist consultations, which is associated with average cost savings of € 293.54 per patient (p = 0.036) for this period. Between month 6 and month 12 after transplantation, these cost savings increase to € 419.12 (p = 0.089). Over the entire one-year period, patients with telemedically supported case management substantially less frequently visited medical specialists, resulting in total cost savings of € 761.37 per patient (p = 0.048). As far as general practitioner visits are concerned, on the other hand, the costs are relatively identical between both groups (p = 0.879).

As a result of early diagnoses and short delay between the first onset of symptoms and initiation of treatment, telemedically supported case management is associated with substantial cost savings related to unscheduled hospitalizations. The associated cost savings are highest between month 3 and month 6 after transplantation and add up to savings of € 3417.46 (p = 0.003) for the entire one-year period. The costs of scheduled in-hospital care, in contrast, are less affected by telemedically supported case management (cost savings of € 964.31 over the entire

Table 1 Patient baseline characteristics after kidney transplantation (timepoint 0)

Characteristics	Standard	Telemedical
Median age in years (range)	51 (19–66)	46 (18–59)
Male sex	47,8%	60,9%
ABO-incompatible living kidney graft	26.1%	30.4%
HLA-Mismatches ≤ 4	43.5%	47.8%
First graft	82.6%	82.6%
Postoperative complications	52.2%	47.8%
Median graft GFR in ml	57.99	53.99
(range)	(13.60–82.92)	(38,48–81,95)

Table 2 Comparison of cost across the six cost figures

	Month 0-3	Month 3-6	Month 6-12	Total cost	*p*-value (total costs)
Costs of primary care physician visits:					
Standard	€13.39	€20.44	€35.94	€69.77	
Telemedical	€11.28	€21.85	€33.83	€66.95	
Difference	€2.11	-€1.41	€2.11	€2.82	0.879
Costs of specialist consultant visits:					
Standard	€650.31	€746.58	€1,053.31	€2,450.20	
Telemedical	€601.60	€453.04	€634.20	€1,688.83	
Difference	€48.72	€293.54	€419.12	€761.37	0.048
Costs of unscheduled in-hospital care:					
Standard	€2,376.24	€1,813.49	€1,245.33	€5,435.06	
Telemedical	€1,463.60	€190.78	€363.23	€2,017.60	
Difference	€912.64	€1,622.72	€882.10	€3,417.46	0.003
Costs of scheduled in-hospital care:					
Standard	€885.77	€338.14	€640.82	€1,920.36	
Telemedical	€843.79	€39.66	€72.60	€956.05	
Difference	€41.98	€298.47	€568.22	€964.31	0.073
Costs of amulatory visists at the university outpatient department:					
Standard	€246.52	€199.57	€211.30	€657.39	
Telemedical	€258.26	€246.52	€270.00	€774.78	
Difference	-€11.74	-€46.96	-€58.70	-€117.39	
Total costs of care:					
Standard	€4,172.23	€3,118.21	€3,158.84	€10,449.28	
Telemedical	€3,178.52	€951.84	€1,373.85	€5,504.21	
Difference	€993.71	€2,166.36	€1,784.99	€4,945.07	

one-year period, $p = 0.073$). On the other hand, patients with telemedically supported case management more often applied for ambulatory visits at the university outpatient department, resulting in additional costs of € 117.39 ($p = 0.035$) for the entire one-year period. Overall, telemedically supported case management is clearly associated with cost savings due to less frequent and/or less intense medical service utilization during the one-year period (see Fig. 1). These savings are highest between month 3 and month 6 after transplantation (€ 2166.36, $p < 0.001$) and add up to total savings of € 4945.07 ($p < 0.001$) for the entire one-year period. Overall, patients in the standard aftercare group are associated, on average, with €10,449.28 of on-year medical service utilization costs while patients with telemedically supported case management are associated with €5,504.21 of on-year medical service utilization costs.

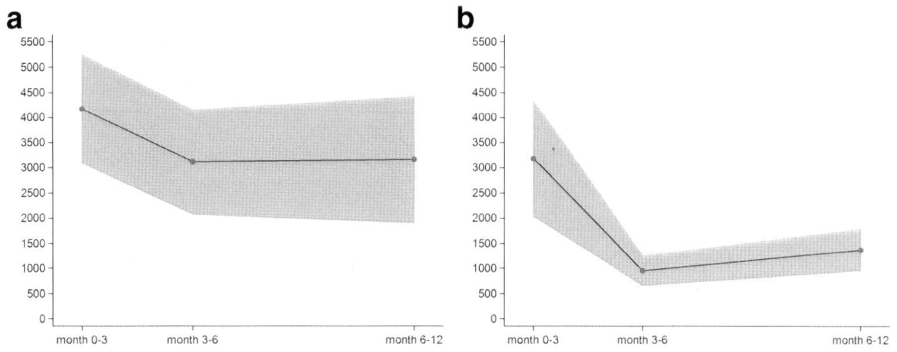

Fig. 1 Total costs of care. **a** standard aftercare and **b** telemedically supported case management

Budget impact analysis[1] of telemedically supported case management

The main objective of our study is to calculate the budget impact of the telemedically supported case management from the healthcare perspective. As a first step our analysis combines the costs of a hypothetical number of 20 patients receiving telemedically supported case management with the actual results of summarized resource uses in the two groups. As a result, costs of telemedically supported case management are estimated at €3,001.5 for a single patient. Although being hypothetical, this cost figure equals the amount of reimbursement from the different sickness funds using individual case requests. After combining this reimbursement (€3,001.5) with the costs of medical service utilization (€5,504.21, see above), the one-year costs in the telemedically supported case management group add up to €8,505.71. In comparison to the costs of medical service utilization in the standard aftercare group (€10,449.28, see above), telemedically supported case management may still be associated with lower costs (mean difference: €1,943.57), but this result is not statistically significant ($p = 0.128$).

As a first sensitivity analysis, we calculate the net savings of our telemedically supported case management program depending on the number of patients participating. Due to the effect of fixed cost degression the program becomes cost-neutral at around ten participating patients, and was beneficial at 15 patients (see Fig. 2). After an initial rapid increase, the increase of savings begins to level off, increasing from €67 at a program size of ten patients to €1318 at 15 patients, but only from €2318 to €2569 from 25 to 30 patients. The results are projected to become statistically significant ($p < 0.05$) at a program size of 30 patients. Please note that the results for more than 20 patients imply the assumption that an additional 50% nurse position may can provide telemedically supported case management to more than 20 patients.

As a second sensitivity analysis, we kept the share of personnel expenses (an additional 50% nurse position for 20 patients) flexible. We assumed a 2.5% nurse position necessary for every additional patient with telemedically supported case management (which is equal to €1,781.25). As shown in Fig. 2, the program now becomes beneficial even from a very low number of patients. Please note that these results imply the assumption that the nurse position may be easily increased and decreased relative to the number of patients with telemedically supported case management. All results of the sensitivity analyses are shown in Table 3.

Finally we transfer our results to the German healthcare system. We recommend that the program should be implemented in bigger transplant centers like Freiburg, with more than 30 living donor kidney transplantations a year. The program is highly feasible and, if implemented in this way, would result in significant savings of upwards of €3,000 per patient and year of telemedically supported case management. According to EuroTransplant, a total of 645 living kidney transplantations were conducted in 38 German transplant centers in 2015 [30]. Of these, 12 centers conducted more than 20 transplantations (n ~ 407 in total). According to our results, routine implementation of telemedically supported case management in these 12 centers would result in annual savings of €791,033 according to the procedure numbers of 2015 and the results of our base case scenario.

Discussion

Overall, the results of our study show that telemedically supported case management is associated with a substantially lower frequency of medical service utilization. As a result, one-year costs of care for these patients (€5,504.21) are roughly half the costs in the standard aftercare group (€10,449.28). Analysis of the different cost categories shows that the major drivers of these differences are episodes of unscheduled in-hospital care. This confirms the main rationale behind the study: An

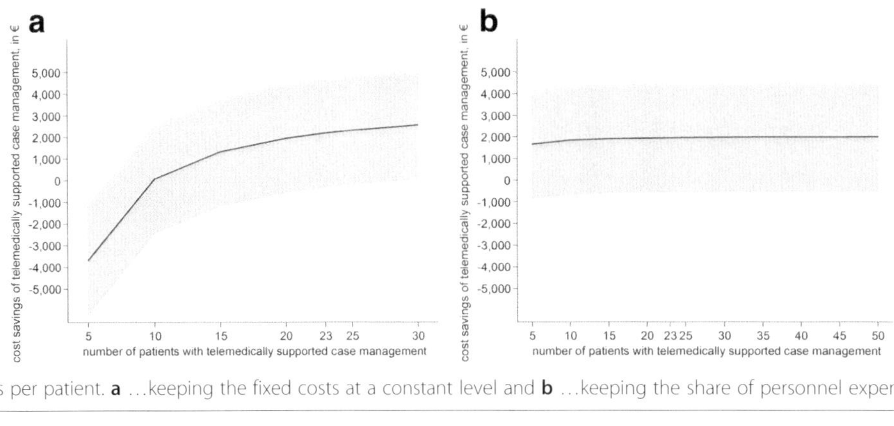

Fig. 2 Cost savings per patient. **a** ...keeping the fixed costs at a constant level and **b** ...keeping the share of personnel expenses flexible

Table 3 Budget impact analysis

	Hypothetical n	Standard	Telemedical	Difference	*p*-value
Sensitivity analysis 1: 5-30 patients, fixed costs at a constant level (in € and per patient)					
Base case	5 patients	€ 10449.28	€ 14135.21	-€3685.93	0.004
	10 patients	€ 10449.28	€ 10382.21	€ 67.07	0.958
	15 patients	€ 10449.28	€ 9131.21	€ 1318.07	0.301
	20 patients	€ 10449.28	€ 8505.71	€ 1943.57	0.128
	23 patients	€ 10449.28	€ 8260.95	€ 2188.33	0.086
	25 patients	€ 10449.28	€ 8130.41	€ 2318.87	0.069
	30 patients	€ 10449.28	€ 7880.21	€ 2569.07	0.044
Sensitivity analysis 2: 5-50 patients, keeping personal cost flexible (in € and per patient)					
Base case	5 patients	€ 10449.28	€ 8791.46	€ 1657.82	0.194
	10 patients	€ 10449.28	€ 8600.96	€ 1848.32	0.147
	15 patients	€ 10449.28	€ 8537.46	€ 1911.82	0.134
	20 patients	€ 10449.28	€ 8505.71	€ 1943.57	0.128
	23 patients	€ 10449.28	€ 8493.28	€ 1955.99	0.125
	25 patients	€ 10449.28	€ 8486.66	€ 1962.62	0.124
	30 patients	€ 10449.28	€ 8473.96	€ 1975.32	0.121
	35 patients	€ 10449.28	€ 8464.89	€ 1984.39	0.12
	40 patients	€ 10449.28	€ 8458.08	€ 1991.20	0.118
	45 patients	€ 10449.28	€ 8452.79	€ 1996.49	0.117
	50 patients	€ 10449.28	€ 8448.56	€ 2000.72	0.117

early diagnosis and short delay between the first onset of symptoms and initiation of treatment correlates with substantially lower medical service utilization. Our telemedicine intervention has shown to be effective at improving several important outcome measures of living donor kidney transplantation. The intervention has shown promise for better medical and disease-specific outcomes as well as saving costs – a win-win situation.

From the healthcare perspective, an implementation of the program in the 12 biggest transplant centers in Germany would result in annual net savings of €791,033 per year. However, the current reimbursement practice requires requests to be made for each case separately to each of the 117 German statutory health insurances. This may be seen as the main hurdle for implementing telemedically supported case management in other centers for the following reasons: Firstly, the high number of requests goes hand in hand with high negotiation and administrative costs. Secondly, from the point of view of the supplier of telemedicine aftercare infrastructure (in this case the transplantation center) the reimbursement and therefore the utilization of the investment is a priori uncertain. Thus, we propose to reimburse telemedically supported case management by sickness funds in a routine manner. Political action is needed in order to unlock these potential patient- and societal-level benefits.

Our study avoids several of the problems that are otherwise common in studies of the cost-efficacy of telemedicine [9, 10]. However, please note that the results of the present study are still subject to a number of limitations. First of all, 23 patients in each group is a very limited number of patients given the wide variation in cost measures. As a result, measures of significance in many cases do not reach the usual level of significance ($p < 0.05$) and results should be interpreted with the according caution. Also, the patient population was not large enough to properly control for socioeconomic background. For example, elderly patients might still be less comfortable with using telemedical devices, which could result in this or other patient populations receiving better results from traditional aftercare programs. On the other hand this means that taking such factors into account in the patient selection process, or making adjustments to our telemedical equipment and techniques to improve accessibility for any patients currently struggling to make best use of the equipment, might further improve the already significant impact of telemedical support on patient outcomes and costs we measured.

Secondly, collection of patient-level cost data during follow-up is a resource intensive exercise. In order to simplify this process, we decided to apply standardized unit cost for visits at primary care physicians, specialist or ambulatory visits at the university outpatient department

[17]. Presumably, this simplification might underestimate the true ambulatory expenditures as ambulatory care of transplant patients is exceptionally resource intensive. In addition, this simplification completely ignores medical treatment expenditures. Immunosuppressive regimes in renal transplant patients are costly, but adherence with medication may be considered of major importance for post-procedural outcomes [31]. Probably, adherence with medication is also improved by telemedically supported case management due to the fact that unnecessary changes in the drug therapy can be avoided. Recent regulatory changes towards an exclusion of immunosuppressive regimes from aut idem regulations in Germany underline the necessity of medication adherence among transplant patients [32, 33].

Conclusions

Our random controlled trial, covering about 7% of all living kidney transplantations conducted in Germany over the trial period, shows that the introduction of telemedically supported case management results not only in significant improvements in medical and disease-specific outcomes, but also a considerable potential for cost savings within the first year after transplantation, mainly by avoiding episodes of unscheduled in-hospital care.

Due to the effect of fixed cost degression we recommend that the program should be implemented in medium and high volume transplant centers. This would result in annual savings of almost €800,000 for the German healthcare system for living kidney transplantations alone.

From a broader perspective the major hurdle still standing in the way of widespread introduction of the telemedicine aftercare technique at the interface between the outpatient and inpatient sectors is the current reimbursement practice, in which requests have to be made for each case separately to each of the German statutory health insurances, representing a significant administrative hurdle. Hence, provision would have to be made for telemedically supported case management to be reimbursable by sickness funds in a routine manner.

Endnote

[1]Additional to our cost perspective the results also can be interpreted as net benefit to the patients, since their quality of life and health is improved by the earlier diagnosis and short delay between the first onset of symptoms and initiation of treatment resulting from the telemedical supported case management program.

Abbreviation

GLM: Generalized linear model

Acknowledgments

We gratefully thank Ilka Schlitter and Laith Al-Sayegh for their support in collecting the patient level cost data.

Funding

The project was funded by the European Union within the INTERREG IV Program (grant reference number "A 12 – Prométhée"). In 2011, the Transplantation Center Freiburg also received funding from Novartis for supporting the study. Neither funding body played any role in the design of the study and collection, analysis, and interpretation of data, or in the writing of the manuscript.

Authors' contributions

KK made substantial contributions to the conception and design of the work, provided data analysis and interpretation of the results and takes responsibility for the accuracy of the data analysis. He was responsible for drafting the manuscript, provided final approval of the version to be published and agrees to be accountable for all aspects of the work and ensuring that questions related to the accuracy or integrity of any part of the work are appropriately investigated and resolved. SH, AS and PP collected and had full access to all the data in the study and take responsibility for the integrity of the data. They made substantial contributions to conception and design of the work, revised the manuscript critically, provided final approval of the version to be published and agree to be accountable for all aspects of the work and ensuring that questions related to the accuracy or integrity of any part of the work are appropriately investigated and resolved. SF and PH made substantial contributions to conception and design of the work, took part in drafting the manuscript, revised it critically, provided final approval of the version to be published and agree to be accountable for all aspects of the work and ensuring that questions related to the accuracy or integrity of any part of the work are appropriately investigated and resolved. DH, LB and BJ substantially contributed to the realization of the study, revised the manuscript critically, provided final approval of the version to be published, and agree to be accountable for all aspects of the work and ensuring that questions related to the accuracy or integrity of any part of the work are appropriately investigated and resolved.

Competing interests

The authors declare that they have no competing interest.

Author details

[1]Institute for Medical Biometry and Statistics, Faculty of Medicine and Medical Center – University of Freiburg, Stefan-Meier-Str 26, 79104 Freiburg, Germany. [2]Transplantation Center, Department of General and Visceral Surgery, Medical Center, Faculty of Medicine, University of Freiburg, Hugstetter Str 55, 79106 Freiburg, Germany. [3]Faculty of Economics, Aalen University, Beethovenstraße 1, 73430 Aalen, Germany.

References

1. Sellares J, De Freitas DG, Mengel M, Reeve J, Einecke G, Sis B, Hidalgo LG, Famulski K, Matas A, Halloran PF. Understanding the Causes of Kidney Transplant Failure: The Dominant Role of Antibody-Mediated Rejection and Nonadherence. Am J Transplant. 2012;12:388–99.
2. Chisholm-Burns M, Pinsky B, Parker G, Johnson P, Arcona S, Buzinec P, Chakravarti P, Good M, Cooper M. Factors related to immunosuppressant medication adherence in renal transplant recipients. Clin Transpl. 2012;26:706–13.
3. Denhaerynck K, Steiger J, Bock A, Schäfer-Keller P, Köfer S, Thannberger N, De Geest S. Prevalence and Risk Factors of Non-Adherence with Immunosuppressive Medication in Kidney Transplant Patients. Am J Transplant. 2007;7:108–16.

4. Denhaerynck K, Burkhalter F, Schäfer-Keller P, Steiger J, Bock A, De Geest S. Clinical consequences of non adherence to immunosuppressive medication in kidney transplant patients. Transpl Int. 2009;22:441–6.
5. Gremigni P, Bacchi F, Turrini C, Cappelli G, Albertazzi A, Bitti PER. Psychological factors associated with medication adherence following renal transplantation. Clin Transpl. 2007;21:710–5.
6. De Bleser L, Matteson M, Dobbels F, Russell C, De Geest S. Interventions to improve medication-adherence after transplantation: a systematic review. Transpl Int. 2009;22:780–97.
7. Hils S, Schmid A, Hauschke D, Bogatyreva L, Pisarski P. Telemedically supported aftercare in living kidney recipients - an innovative project at the transplantation center Freiburg. In: Weimar M, Bos MA, Busschbach JJ, editors. Organ Transplantation: ethical, legal and psychological aspects. Lengerich: Global Issues, local solutions. Pabst Science Publishers; 2014. p. 93–101.
8. Schmid A, Hils S, Kramer-Zucker A, Bogatyreva L, Hauschke D, De Geest S, Pisarski P. Telemedically-supported case management of living-donor renal transplant recipients to optimize routine evidence-based aftercare: A single-center randomized controlled trial. Am J Transplant. 2016. [epub ahead of print].
9. Bergmo TS. Can economic evaluation in telemedicine be trusted? A systematic review of the literature. Cost Eff Resour Alloc. 2009;7:1.
10. Mistry H. Systematic review of studies of the cost-effectiveness of telemedicine and telecare. Changes in the economic evidence over twenty years. J Telemed Telecare. 2012;18:1–6.
11. Achelrod D. Policy expectations and reality of telemedicine - a critical analysis of health care outcomes, costs and acceptance for congestive heart failure. J Telemed Telecare. 2014;4:192–200.
12. Kitsiou S, Pare G, Jaana M. Systematic reviews and meta-analyses of home telemonitoring interventions for patients with chronic diseases: a critical assessment of their methodological quality. J Med Internet Res. 2013;15, e150.
13. Clark RA, Inglis SC, McAlister FA, Cleland JG, Stewart S. Telemonitoring or structured telephone support programmes for patients with chronic heart failure: systematic review and meta-analysis. BMJ. 2007;334:942.
14. Chaudhry SI, Phillips CO, Stewart SS, Riegel B, Mattera JA, Jerant AF, Krumholz HM. Telemonitoring for patients with chronic heart failure: a systematic review. J Card Fail. 2007;13:56–62.
15. DelliFraine JL, Dansky KH. Home-based telehealth: a review and meta-analysis. J Telemed Telecare. 2008;14:62–6.
16. Achelrod D, Schreyögg J, Stargardt T. Health-economic evaluation of home telemonitoring for COPD in Germany: evidence from a large population-based cohort. Eur J Health Econ. 2016. [Ebup ahead of print]
17. Bock JO, Brettschneider C, Seidl H, Bowles D, Holle R, Greiner W, König HH. Calculation of Standardised Unit Costs from a Societal Perspective for Health Economic Evaluation. Das Gesundheitswesen. 2015;77:53–61.
18. Mullahy J. Much ado about two: reconsidering retransformation and the two-part model in health econometrics. J Health Econ. 1998;17:247–81.
19. Mogyorosy Z, Smith P. The main methodological issues in costing health care services: a literature review. CHE Research Paper. **7**(2005)
20. Malehi AS, Pourmotahari F, Angali KA. Statistical models for the analysis of skewed healthcare cost data: a simulation study. Heal Econ Rev. 2015;5:1–16.
21. Li B, Cairns J, Fotheringham J, Ravanan R. ATTOM Study Group: Predicting hospital costs for patients receiving renal replacement therapy to inform an economic evaluation. Eur J Health Econ. 2015;17:659–68.
22. Buntin MB, Zaslavsky AM. Too much ado about two-part models and transformation?: Comparing methods of modeling Medicare expenditures. J Health Econ. 2004;23:525–42.
23. Belotti F, Deb P. TPM: Stata module to estimate two-part cross-sectional models. Stat Softw Components. 2013;S457538
24. Deb P, Manning W, Norton E. Modeling health care costs and counts. Los Angeles: Presentation at ASHEcon; 2014.
25. Belotti F, Deb P, Manning WG, Norton EC. twopm: Two-part models. Stata J. 2015;15:3–20.
26. Barber J, Thompson S. Multiple regression of cost data: use of generalised linear models. J Health Serv Res Policy. 2004;9:197–204.
27. Mullahy J. Econometric modeling of health care costs and expenditures: a survey of analytical issues and related policy considerations. Med Care. 2009;47:S104–8.
28. Jones AM, Lomas J, Rice N. Healthcare Cost Regressions: Going Beyond the Mean to Estimate the Full Distribution. Health Econ. 2015;24:1192–212.
29. Sullivan SD, Mauskopf JA, Augustovski F, Caro JJ, Lee KM, Minchin M, Orlewska E, Penna P, Barrios JMR, Shau WY. Budget impact analysis-principles of good practice: report of the ISPOR 2012 Budget Impact Analysis Good Practice II Task Force. Value Health. 2014;17:5–14.
30. DSO. Nierentransplantation. https://www.dso.de/organspende-und-transplantation/transplantation/nierentransplantation.html [2016].
31. Jürgensen JS, Arns W, Haß B. Cost-effectiveness of immunosuppressive regimens in renal transplant recipients in Germany: a model approach. Eur J Health Econ. 2010;11:15–25.
32. EB. Substitution von Arzneimitteln: G-BA legt Ausschlussliste vor. Dtsch Arztebl. 2014;111:A-1623
33. Gemeinsamer Bundesausschuss. Tragende Gründe zum Beschluss des Gemeinsamen Bundesausschusses über eine Änderung der Arzneimittel-Richtlinie (AM-RL): Abschnitt M und Anlage VII - Hinweise zur Austauschbarkeit von Darreichungsformen (aut idem) gemäß § 129 Absatz 1a SGB V: Bestimmung von Arzneimitteln, deren Ersetzung durch ein wirkstoffgleiches Arzneimittel ausgeschlossen ist (1. Tranche). 2014

7

Healthcare efficiency assessment using DEA analysis in the Slovak Republic

Robert Stefko[1], Beata Gavurova[2*] and Kristina Kocisova[2]

Abstract

A regional disparity is becoming increasingly important growth constraint. Policy makers need quantitative knowledge to design effective and targeted policies. In this paper, the regional efficiency of healthcare facilities in Slovakia is measured (2008–2015) using data envelopment analysis (DEA). The DEA is the dominant approach to assessing the efficiency of the healthcare system but also other economic areas. In this study, the window approach is introduced as an extension to the basic DEA models to evaluate healthcare technical efficiency in individual regions and quantify the basic regional disparities and discrepancies. The window DEA method was chosen since it leads to increased discrimination on results especially when applied to small samples and it enables year-by-year comparisons of the results. Two stable inputs (number of beds, number of medical staff), three variable inputs (number of all medical equipment, number of magnetic resonance (MR) devices, number of computed tomography (CT) devices) and two stable outputs (use of beds, average nursing time) were chosen as production variable in an output-oriented 4-year window DEA model for the assessment of technical efficiency in 8 regions. The database was made available from the National Health Information Center and the Slovak Statistical Office, as well as from the online databases Slovstat and DataCube. The aim of the paper is to quantify the impact of the non-standard Data Envelopment Analysis (DEA) variables as the use of medical technologies (MR, CT) on the results of the assessment of the efficiency of the healthcare facilities and their adequacy in the evaluation of the monitored processes. The results of the analysis have shown that there is an indirect dependence between the values of the variables over time and the results of the estimated efficiency in all regions. The regions that had low values of the variables over time achieved a high degree of efficiency and vice versa. Interesting knowledge was that the gradual addition of variables number of MR, number of CT and number of medical devices together, to the input side did not have a significant impact on the overall estimated efficiency of healthcare facilities.

Keywords: Healthcare system, Healthcare technical efficiency, Data envelopment analysis, Healthcare facility, Regional disparity

Background

The issue of healthcare in its broader concept falls within the public sector. The public sector is often viewed in terms of the efficient use of public resources. In the Slovak Republic [23, 24, 62], but also in other countries, several studies have been carried out to evaluate the efficiency of public organizations, including hospital facilities [26, 47, 58]. Potential users of performance measurement results in the healthcare system are governments, regulators, healthcare providers, and the general public. The significant systemic complexity of the healthcare sector determines the analytical level of research studies and the choice of adequate methods for assessing the efficiency of the healthcare sector. Their application is influenced by both the research objectives and the available database. Due to significant systemic changes in the healthcare sector related to the ongoing source of diagnosis and treatment processes, these changes should also be reflected in the outputs of these processes (increasing efficiency in the sector). Some methods may be sensitive to the implementation of so-called non-standard variables, in others the influence is minimal. The research question is to determine to what extent the standard application of methods using classical variables is sufficient for national and international comparison of the efficiency of the surveyed

* Correspondence: beata.gavurova@tuke.sk
[2]Faculty of Economics, Technical University of Kosice, Kosice, Slovakia
Full list of author information is available at the end of the article

units. In the context of the above, the goals of our contribution were set, with the result and process line. The primary objective of the contribution was to evaluate healthcare technical efficiency in individual regions on the basis of the theoretical backgrounds, practical experience and secondary research on the current state of healthcare facilities in Slovakia and quantify the basic regional disparities and discrepancies. The secondary objective is to quantify the impact of the non-standard variables in DEA related to the use of medical technologies (MR, CT) on the results of the evaluation of the efficiency of the healthcare facilities and their adequacy in the evaluation of the monitored processes. To evaluate the technical efficiency of healthcare facilities at the regional level, we used the extended DEA window analysis, under the conditions of constant (CCR model) as well as the variable return to scale (BCC model). The database was made available from the National Health Information Center and the Slovak Statistical Office, as well as from the online databases Slovstat and DataCube. The input and output variables have been compiled on the basis of a detailed analysis of the most commonly used variables in research studies and taking into account the theoretical rules for the construction of DEA models and limitations for sample size determination.

Data envelopment analysis and its analytical and application aspects in healthcare

DEA window analysis has been used by several types of research over the past two decades. Its particular application in the healthcare sector can be found in studies of Kazley and Ozcan [33] or Jia and Yuan [31]. In Slovakia, the issue of healthcare and the application of the DEA window analysis method were dealt with by Sendek et al. [60], who focused on assessing the efficiency of hospitals in the Czech and Slovak Republics using the BCC model. Many authors prefer the application of DEA methods due to several advantages like simultaneous use of multiple inputs and outputs (e.g. [13, 16, 27, 28, 34]), it does not require a mathematical specification of the production function (e.g. [13, 27, 28, 50]), it is most appropriate to investigate the impact of exogenous variables [32], suggests recommendations for an inefficient production unit [49]. On the other hand, its application spectrum is eliminated by several disadvantages, resp. limitations. The most important are results are sensitive to outlier values (e.g. [29, 45, 49, 57, 66]), it's just about measuring relative efficiency [28, 49, 56], limitation for the sample size [38].When choosing a DEA model, it is necessary to define initially if the input or output-oriented method will be used. The used methods are different for application to the healthcare sector. The output-oriented method is preferred by Araújo et al. [2], Hernandez and San Sebastian [28], Oikonomou et al. [51], Li and Dong [38], Karagiannis [32], Cheng et al. [13], Villalobos et al. [66]; Mujasi et al. [49], Mahate et al. [45], De Souza et al. [18]. The input-oriented method was used in studies presented by Grosskopf et al. [27], Kontodimopoulos et al. [34], Czypionka et al. [16], Rezapour et al. [57], Büchner et al. [10], Fragkiadakis et al. [22]. Opinions on DEA and its benefits vary. Hernandez and San Sebastian [28] stated that in the case of primary and secondary healthcare, inputs are uniform and low, and health outcomes could increase at efforts to achieve improved health promotion. They also point out that in many cases the needs for healthcare services are poorly met. In such situations, it would be unethical to reduce the amount of provided healthcare services to improve hospital efficiency. Cheng et al. [13] justify the choice of output orientation due to limited control of hospital managers over their inputs and controlled decisions on recruitment and investment by government departments. Oikonomou et al. [51] justified the choice of an output-oriented model because the demand for primary health care services has a tendency to expand and not to decrease. According to these authors, lowering inputs in the provision of health services is undesirable, while increasing outputs is feasible. Based on the study of literature, we decided to use an output-oriented model in our analysis, as the primary objective in the field of healthcare is the human health. When questioning hospital efficiency, it is important to focus attention on the quality of the services provided, on the quantity and satisfaction of patients and to focus on increasing patient satisfaction due to a better and better healthcare system. This will result in more treatment, more performance, more hospitalization, more release, and, as a result, an increase in quality of life and health, decreasing levels of disease mortality, late diagnosis and inadequate treatment. From a moral point of view, the healthcare system is specific and the aim of hospitals and healthcare facilities should not be to reduce inputs and costs but to concentrate on increasing outputs in the form of the above-mentioned objectives. For this reason, we prefer to use an output-oriented DEA model. The second important theoretical decision in DEA specification is the application of return to scale. The model assuming the constant return to scale was defined by Charnes et al. [12] and is marked as the CCR model. Second, the model assuming with the variable return to scale was described by Banker et al. [3] and is labelled as BCC. In the context of the defined goals, we decided to apply both approaches and compare the results achieved through both types of models.

Methods

Data Envelopment Analysis (DEA) is the dominant non-parametric approach to evaluate the efficiency of Decision-Making Units (DMU). From the point of view of assessing the efficiency of healthcare, DMUs can represent different levels of healthcare, including a complete healthcare system in the country, districts, hospitals, specific service providers, departments, or individual physicians. The efficiency of the DMU represents its distance from the efficiency frontier. The location and shape of the efficiency frontier depend on the user data and the used assumptions (a type of return to scale, input or output orientation). The efficiency frontier arises by plotting the relationship between the number of inputs and the outputs achieved in the two-dimensional space. This is a combination of individual tracking relationships between inputs and outputs. The construction of the efficiency frontier is based on the principle of the best estimate, so we only regard it as an approaching reality [15]. From a historical point of view, we consider Farrell and his work in 1957 to lay the foundations of the DEA method. Farrell [21], in his work, starts to measure efficiency by assuming that only one input enters the model and production unit produces only one output. However, as the authors of the first comprehensive model are considered Charnes et al. [12], who extended the original Farrell's model. This basic model is referred to by the initials of its authors, the CCR model, assuming that the production unit operates under the conditions of constant return to scale. The second basic model was developed by Banker et al. [3], named as the BCC model and is based on the assumption of the variable return to scale.

In the healthcare sector, there is imperfect competition, which is manifested by limited funding opportunities, market entry regulation, merger or market exit constraints resulting in inefficient management, so it is necessary to apply the BCC model in addition to the CCR model. DEA models can be input, or output oriented. While in the case of input-oriented models we try to find out the minimal level of inputs which is needed to produce a given level of outputs. Under the output-oriented models, we try to find out the answer which maximum level of outputs can be achieved by using the given level of inputs in order for DMUs to be considered effective.

In order to evaluate the technical efficiency of the healthcare system at the level regions of the Slovak Republic, we decided to apply the output-oriented models, CCR and BCC, based on the DEA window analysis. Output oriented CCR model can be formulated in the matrix form by the following formula:

$$\begin{aligned} &\text{Maximize} && g = \phi_q + \varepsilon(e^T s^+ + e^T s^-) \\ &\text{Under conditions} && X\lambda + s^- = x_q \\ &&& Y\lambda - s^+ = \phi_q y_q \\ &&& \lambda, s^+, s^- \geq 0 \end{aligned} \qquad (1)$$

where: ε – constant, q – evaluated DMU, y_q– output of evaluated DMUq, x_q– input of evaluated DMUq, $s^+$and $s^-$are slack variables for input and outputs.

As stated by Jablonský and Dlouhý [30] based on the model (1), the production unit is evaluated as effective if the optimal value of the function $g^* = 1$ and all complementary variables are equal to zero. If this value is above 1, the DMU cannot be considered as an efficient and the optimal value ϕ_q^* expresses the need for a proportional increase in inputs to achieve efficiency. Assuming that production units operate under the variable return to scale (increasing, decreasing, non-increasing, non-decreasing), we apply the BCC output-oriented model, where we add a convexity condition: $e^T\lambda = 1$.

When evaluating efficiency, we can sometimes encounter a limited number of DMUs. To overcome this problem, a so-called DEA window analysis was created. It allows us to compare the efficiency of a limited number of DMUs in individual periods and to analyze changes in efficiency over time. DEA window analysis generalizes the idea of moving averages to uncover the trend of DMU efficiency development over time. The moving average method is used to compile a different sample to determine the relative efficiency of each DMU. Based on the dynamic perspective, each DMU is considered as a separate unit in individual time periods in individual windows [15]. The input and output variables of DMU in the selected period are compared to that of other DMUs in all periods. We also compare the results of DMU from one period with the results of the same unit in the remaining periods. If the window is moved for the first time, at the same time the first period is deleted in each window and a new period is added. The benefit of this method is a comprehensive description of dynamic changes of the efficiency of each DMU, both horizontal and vertical. Of course, the main benefit is what we mentioned in the beginning, increasing the number of DMUs, which increases the discriminatory power in situations with a limited number of DMUs in the sample [31].

We assume a sample N (n = 1,...,N) DMUs during T (t = 1,...,T) periods of time. Each DMU uses r different inputs to produces s different outputs. If DMU_n^t is a combination of inputs and outputs for the Nth unit of the DMU in the T period, then the input vector X_n^t and output vector Y_n^t can be written as follows:

$$X_n^t = \begin{bmatrix} x_n^{1t} \\ \vdots \\ x_n^{rt} \end{bmatrix} \quad Y_n^t = \begin{bmatrix} y_n^{1t} \\ \vdots \\ y_n^{st} \end{bmatrix} \qquad (2)$$

If the window starts in time k ($1 \leq k \leq T$) and the width of the window is w ($1 \leq k \leq T\text{-}k$), then input matrix (X_k^w) and output matrix (Y_k^w) of each window will look like as follows:

$$X_k^w = \begin{bmatrix} x_1^k & x_2^k & \cdots & x_N^k \\ \vdots & \vdots & \ddots & \vdots \\ x_1^{k+w} & x_2^{k+w} & \cdots & x_N^{k+w} \end{bmatrix}$$

$$Y_k^w = \begin{bmatrix} y_1^k & y_2^k & \cdots & y_N^k \\ \vdots & \vdots & \ddots & \vdots \\ y_1^{k+w} & y_2^{k+w} & \cdots & y_N^{k+w} \end{bmatrix} \quad (3)$$

Appropriate determination of window size and window length are used by Cooper et al. [15] where we use the following labels: n = *number of DMU*, k = *number of periods*, p = *window length* ($p \le k$), w = *number of windows.* The following relationships apply to:

number of windows:

$$w = k - p + 1 \quad (4)$$

number of DMU in each window:

$$np/2 \quad (5)$$

number of different DMUs:

$$npw \quad (6)$$

Δ number of DMU (increase in number):

$$n(p-1)(k-P) \quad (7)$$

To derive the total number of different DMUs, Cooper et al. [15] mention the following relationship:

$$n(k-p+1)p \quad (8)$$

If we put the last equation equal to 0, we get a relationship for calculating the length of window:

$$p = \frac{k+1}{2} \quad (9)$$

To always reach an integer, the relationship applies:

$$p = \begin{cases} \frac{k+1}{2} & \text{, when } k \text{ is odd;} \\ \frac{k+1}{2} \pm \frac{1}{2} & \text{, when } k \text{ is even.} \end{cases} \quad (10)$$

In this paper, we will analyze the Slovak health care system. We have decided to monitor the DMU at the regional level as the best comparable minimum level of tracking. The smaller division into districts was not taken into account due to the lack of availability of microdata at the relevant regional level. The indicators monitored by multinational organizations are used as the smallest regional level of NUTS 3, which is the breakdown in the region when applying to Slovakia. In Slovakia, we have a total of eight districts. In the first step, DEA window analysis is performed to calculate the technical efficiency of healthcare facilities in the relevant regions. The selection of the DEA analysis is influenced by a number of sources that use the DEA method to assess the efficiency of medical devices. A review of the literature using the DEA method can be seen in the work of Worthington [68].

Due to the frequent criticism of the DEA method which is based on its nonparametric nature and is mirrored in a small statistical basis, one of the most important steps is the right choice of input and output variables. After the study of relevant literature, we decide to use five input and three output variables in our analysis. The specification of the variables used in the DEA, their summary overview and the brief definition are given in Table 1.

The number of beds is an indicator that reflects the size of the hospital. It is clear from this indicator that each added bed means an extra cost to the hospital for its purchase and future operation. On the other hand, the beds mean the possibility of providing basic hospital services, thus bringing the marginal profit to the hospital. Whether directly from the patient or from health insurance companies that reimburse hospitals for payments made for medications, consumed other medical supplies besides drugs themselves. The number of beds is one of the most commonly used indicators for comparing hospitals across the country. This fact was put forward by Wagstaff [67] in his study in the evaluation of Spanish hospitals in 1977–1981. Ley [37] had a sample of 139 Spanish hospitals, Valdmanis [64] compared US hospitals in Michigan, Byrnes and Valdmanis [8] compared the sample of 123 Californian hospitals, Kooreman [35] analysed nursing houses in the Netherlands, Zuckerman et al. [69] compared an extensive sample to 4149 American hospitals, Lopez-Valcarcel

Table 1 Specification of DEA model variables

Labels	Variable	Definition
Input variables		
x1	Number of beds	Total number of beds in the health facility
x2	Number of medical staff	Total number of medical staff, including the number of physicians and nurses
x3	Number of CT	Number of computed tomography (CT) devices
x4	Number of MR	Number of magnetic resonance (MR) devices
x5	Number of medical equipment together	Number of all medical devices
Output variables		
y1	Bed occupancy rate	Percentage use of the total number of beds
y2	Average nursing time in days	Ratio of treatment days to the total number of hospitalized patients

Source: Prepared by authors

and Perez [42] compared the efficiency of Spanish hospitals in 1991–1993 with the DEA and Stochastic Frontier Approach (SFA) method; Magnussen [44] evaluated the efficiency of Norwegian hospitals, Parkin and Hollingsworth [52] evaluated hospitals in Scotland, Linna [39] compared the results of the efficiency of the SFA, DEA and Malmquist methods on a sample of 43 Finnish acute care hospitals, Burgess and Wilson [9] compared 1545 US hospitals using DEA, Linna et al. [40] followed a sample of 48 Finnish acute care hospitals, Gerdtham et al. [25] compared 26 Swedish hospitals using SFA, and Maniadakis and Thanassoulis [46] analyzed the efficiency of 75 Scottish hospitals for a 5 year period. Several authors used a variable number of beds for international comparisons, such as Varabyova and Schreyögg [65], who compared OECD countries to each other. Dervaux et al. [17] compared the French and American hospitals, Samut and Cafri [59] compared 29 OECD countries between 2000 and 2010, Mobley and Magnussen [48] were using the DEA analysis to compare public, highly regulated Norwegian hospitals with a private, highly competitive unregulated system hospitals in California, USA.

The number of the medical staff represents the registered number of employees in natural persons, being the sum of the number of doctors, dentists, pharmacists, nurses, midwives, laboratory technicians, assistants, technicians and other health workers. With the authors Maestre et al. [43], Baray and Cliquet [4], we see the tracking of the basic indicator as the total number of employees without subdivision of employees into subgroups. According to these authors, the total number of employees is the basic indicator needed to monitor the economic outturn. The indicator also reflects the size of the patient's catchment area, which according to the geographical location of the hospital is used by the particular hospital [43]. Employee tracking alone has no telling value. Of course, the number of employees is largely affected by the increase in wage costs, with each additional employee in employment [4]. An indicator of the total number of employees was used in the studies by Byrnes and Valdmanis [8], Kooreman [35], Lopez-Valcarcel and Perez [42], Magnussen [44], Parkin and Hollingsworth [52], Maniadakis and Thanassoulis [46]. The total number of medical personnel, other technical personnel, and the number of non-medical personnel was used as an input variable by Cheng et al. [13] who used variable numbers of doctors, nurses, and the number of administrative and other staff. Czypionka et al. [16] used the variable of medical and non-medical staff, Varabyova and Schreyögg [65], and Li and Dong [38] used the variable of employees for the DEA model, Mahate et al. [45] distributed input variables to physicians, dentists, nurses, pharmacists, administrative and other workers to estimate technical efficiency. Fragkiadakis et al. [22] used inputs such as clinical staff, nurses and administrative staff, Rezapour et al. [57] used the total staff of hospitals in the aggregate variable: human resources. Blank and Valdmanis [6] used a variable to describe the efficiency of hospitals: employees and administrators, nurses, medical staff, other staff. Variable medical equipment denounces the overall technical equipment of hospitals and medical facilities and is expressed in pieces. In particular, we monitor the total number of technical devices including radiograph, mammography, positron tomograph, linear accelerators, electroencephalographs, ultrasound devices, brachytherapy devices, urethroscopes, bronchoscopes, endoscopes, laparoscopes, arthroscopes, tomographs, angiography, monitoring devices, ultraviolet and infrared emitters, colposcopes, laryngoscopes and pharyngoscopes, dialysis monitors, gamma cameras, isotopic irradiators, electromyographs, agnetic resonance, lithotriptors, cytoscopes, colonoscopes, sigmoidoscopes and rectoscopes, gastroscopes and duodenoscopes, cryogenic devices. Particularly, we focus on variable magnetic resonance (MR) and computed tomography (CT) devices, as they are the most widely used devices for the diagnosis of diseases and injuries in the human body. Some authors have used variable medical devices as a whole, like Grosskopf et al. [27] who used as inputs assets all buildings and facilities. Zuckerman et al. [69] used as an input variable the index of high-tech services. Puig-Junoy [54] used as one of the input variables the technological availability measured as a proportion of 33 technological items available in the intensive care unit expressed as a percentage. Bradford et al. [7] used the variable use of established and new technology. Dey et al. [19] used as a variable "capital facilities", defined as the provision of up-to-date technological equipment and equipment, also referred to in the second subcategory "maintenance" defined as reasonable and regular maintenance of medical equipment by the biomedical team of engineers. Chang and Lan [11] studied the impact of using new technologies on early diagnosis and treatment, Tsekouras et al. [63] monitored the impact of purchasing new high-tech medical devices to increase production efficiency, Kounetas and Papathanassopoulos [36] monitored the efficiency of Greek hospitals and the impact on efficiency by introducing advanced medical facilities, Rezaee and Karimdadi [56] used the input medical device, Oikonomou et al. [51] used the biomedical technology variable, which it divided by weight into a fully operational microbiological and imaging laboratory and a group of twenty diagnostic therapeutic and auxiliary devices, Ancarani et al. [1] examined the impact of the acquisition of relevant medical technologies and information technologies on the efficiency of hospital departments in three state hospitals in

Dubai. The impact of the introduction of information technology on the efficiency of the health system was also examined by Šoltés et al. [61]. Another group of authors focused on monitoring only individual MR or CT devices: Lo et al. [41], who monitored the effect of the MR, CT, röntgen, Chirikos and Sear [14] variable scan devices, used composite indices to measure efficiency, reflecting special MR tests and procedures. Retzlaff-Roberts et al. [55] used the number of MR devices per million population to confirm the growth and necessity of healthcare technologies, and Samut and Cafri [59] used input variables to count the MR and CT devices per 100,000 inhabitants.

Bed occupation is used by many authors in their studies, Kooreman [35], Linna [39], Chirikos and Sear [14], Perera et al. [53], Belciug and Gorunescu [5], Dy et al. [20], Rezaee and Karimdadi [56], Rezapour et al. [57]. An indicator of the use of the bed fund generally refers to the percentage utilization of the total number of hospital beds for a specified period, typically a calendar year [5]. As noted by Dy et al. [20], this indicator directly reflects the use of resources available to the hospital. Too low the value of the use of bedding is a warning signal for inefficient use of financial resources and hospital capacities, which should lead to a reduction in the number of beds with unchanged patient satisfaction, but to lower the cost of bed operation and maintenance [53]. The number of beds is directly related to the ownership of immovable property. Finding the optimal size of the use of bedding is key to effective hospital management. The Average Length of Stay (ALOS) tells you the length of the patient's length on the bed in the facility. It is calculated as a proportion of the total number of treatment days and the number of hospitalized patients. If the average treatment time would be reduced, the total costs would be reduced as the cost of treating the patient on the bed would be reduced. Also, the trend of lower-cost outpatient treatment is also reduced in even more complicated cases. On the other hand, there is a presumption that shorter stays are more demanding and therefore expensive. If the patient is discharged too quickly and healing is not possible, re-hospitalization may occur, which may even increase the cost. The variable average treatment time in days was used by Kooreman [35], Chirikos and Sear [14], Varabyova and Schreyögg, [65] to investigate the efficiency of DEA patients.

Results and discussion

The analysis was done using a narrower sample of years under review for the period 2008 to 2015. The reason for narrowing the sample is the consistency of data on medical devices and specific MR and CT devices reported since 2008. Therefore it was not able to use data since 2000. The total number of DMUs is 8 regions in each year (8 years). As the number of observations is only 56, which is a relatively low number, we decided to apply the DEA window analysis to expand the number of DMU units. The length of individual windows being calculated based on assumptions and relationships defined in the methodology. Altogether, eight models have been formulated. The following table shows the assignment of selected variables to defined models (Table 2).

For the calculation of the efficiency, data were collected for the reference period from 2008 to 2015. A summary of the basic descriptive statistics of the variables for each year separately and globally for the whole analysed period is shown in Table 3. From the descriptive statistics, we can see that in the case of the variable "number of beds" the maximum is approximately up to two times higher compared to a minimum in each year. This suggests that the size of the regional distribution is significant and the results in regions are different up to twofold when comparing the minimum and maximum in the sample. A similar but even more pronounced difference across regions can be seen in the variable "number of medical staff" where the maximum for the whole surveyed period is up to 2.87 times higher compared to the minimum. The biggest differences across the reporting period were recorded in two districts: Bratislava region (maximum) and Trnava region (minimum).

The variable "beds occupancy in days" is less volatile across the region compared to the previous two. For the whole analysed period the maximum is only 1.25 times higher compared to a minimum. The average minimum bed occupancy is 242 days per year, with a minimum value of 214 days and a maximum of 268. The most productive was the Nitra region in 2012 with a total of 268.4 days per year. The worst result of only 214.0 days per year was reached by the Trnava region in 2011. The average daily "nursing time" across all regions for the

Table 2 Specification of DEA models

Variables	m1	m2	m3	m4	m5	m6	m7	m8
Input variables								
x1	X	X	X	X	X	X	X	X
x2	X	X	X	X	X	X	X	X
x3					X	X		
x4			X	X				
x5							X	X
Output variables								
y1	X	X	X	X	X	X	X	X
y2	X	X	X	X	X	X	X	X

Notes m1, m3, m5, m7 - CCR models; m2, m4, m6, m8 - BCC models;
X - symbolizes that the variable is contained in model; x1 - number of beds; x2 - number of medical staff; x3 - number of CT devices; x4 - number of MR devices; x5 - the number of all medical devices; y1 – bed occupancy rate; y2 - average nursing time in days
Source: Prepared by authors

Table 3 Summary descriptive statistics of variables in calculating efficiency using DEA

		Variables						
		x1	x2	y1	y2	x3	x4	x5
2015	Min	2437	6022	221	7	7	2	813
	Max	5381	17,299	263	9	15	9	1720
	Average	3934	10,040	244	8	11	5	1149
	Median	3945	9264	249	8	11	4	1098
2014	Min	2408	6202	218	7	7	2	813
	Max	5554	17,248	267	8	15	9	1720
	Average	3952	9966	245	8	11	5	1149
	Median	3934	8995	248	8	11	4	1098
2013	Min	2373	6134	223	7	6	1	787
	Max	5563	17,054	264	8	15	10	2100
	Average	3954	9933	245	8	10	4	1182
	Median	3956	8787	251	8	10	3	1214
2012	Min	2348	6120	224	7	6	0	746
	Max	5356	17,127	268	8	15	9	2055
	Average	4030	9904	246	8	10	4	1277
	Median	3931	9056	249	8	10	3	1165
2011	Min	2533	6246	214	7	6	0	674
	Max	5736	17,163	263	9	16	11	1999
	Average	4119	9855	237	8	10	5	1232
	Median	3954	8790	242	8	9	3	1114
2010	Min	2637	6424	215	7	6	0	666
	Max	5934	16,472	258	9	18	11	1954
	Average	4392	9944	238	8	9	5	1196
	Median	4233	9040	243	8	8	4	1086
2009	Min	2568	6483	217	7	5	0	581
	Max	5988	16,031	251	9	13	10	1901
	Average	4440	9745	238	8	9	4	1122
	Median	4326	8977	241	9	9	5	1056
2008	Min	2558	6513	221	8	4	0	571
	Max	5930	15,405	251	9	14	10	2163
	Average	4460	9892	239	8	9	4	1100
	Median	4285	9539	242	9	9	5	974
2008–2015	Min	2348	6022	214	7	4	0	571
	Max	5988	17,299	268	9	18	11	2163
	Average	4162	9898	242	8	10	4	1193
	Median	4078	9475	244	8	9	4	1118

Notes x1 - number of beds in pieces; x2 - number of medical staff in persons; x3 - number of CT devices; x4 - number of MR devices; x5 - the number of all medical devices; y1 – beds occupancy in days; y2 - average nursing time in days
Source: Own calculations

whole of the monitored period was declining, so the regions reduced the caregiving time for the reference period 2008 to 2015. The highest average nursing times were in Kosice region in 2008 and the Nitra region in two consecutive periods 2009 and 2010. The shortest nursing time was 6.8 days in the Trnava region in 2014 and 2015. For the indicator, the number of MR devices, the differences can be again marked across regions. The lowest number of MR devices was recorded in the Trencín region in 2008 - 2012 and the highest number in the Bratislava region in 2011. The average in all regions is 4 MR devices. The number of CT devices is l higher compared to MR ones. The average over the monitored period is 10 CT devices. The most CT devices were in Bratislava in 2010 with a total of 18 CTs. The variable total number of medical equipment brings the largest difference between the maximum value of 2163 devices in the Bratislava region and the minimum of 571 devices in the Trencín region, both in 2008. As regards the median values of the variables in the monitored period, the following situations occurred. The number of beds fell from 4285 to 3945, a decrease of 8%. The number of health workers dropped from 9539 to 9264, a decrease of 3%. The use of beds in days increased from 242 to 249 days, an increase of 3%. Average nursing time in days decreased from 9 to 8, a decrease of 11%. The number of CT devices has increased from 9 to 11, which is a 22% increase. A drop from 5 to four MR devices represents a 20% drop. And finally, the number of medical equipment has risen from 974 units to 1098 units, an increase of 13%.

Estimated efficiencies for the years 2008–2015 using DEA analysis of different models are shown in Table 4. According to the m1 model, the Trnava, Trencin, Nitra and Banska Bystrica regions reached average efficiencies above the average of the whole sample. Below the average, there are the remaining regions, namely Zilina, Bratislava, Presov and Kosice region. The efficiency score equal to one can be seen in the Trnava region in 2008, 2011, 2012 and 2015. The Trencin region is efficient in 2011, 2012 and 2015. The third region that achieved efficiency equal to 1 is the Nitra region in 2009. The best average values reached the Trnava region with the value of 0.9929. On the other hand, the minimum average value was achieved in Kosice region (0.5262). The Kosice region recorded the biggest change, decreased by 13.74%. Besides Kosice region, the Zilina region (10.80%) and the Presov region (9.29%) also fell. The largest increase was recorded in the Banska Bystrica region (5.73%).

The m2 model compared to the m1 model reached higher average efficiency (0.9624). The average efficiencies above the average were also achieved by the Trencin and Trnava regions, as in the m1 model. Also, the Nitra region achieves efficiency at level 1, namely in 2009–2012, 2014 and 2015. According to the model m2, the Banska Bystrica, Zilina, Presov and Kosice region are

Table 4 Estimation of the efficiency of the DEA model average for whole analysed period (2008–2015) according different models

	m1	m2	m3	m4	m5	m6	m7	m8
Bratislava	0.5635	0.9618	0.5635	0.9618	0.5764	0.9618	0.5635	0.9618
Trnava	0.9929	0.9955	0.9947	0.9974	0.9983	1.0000	0.9954	0.9967
Trencin	0.9898	0.9922	0.9904	1.0000	0.9973	0.9982	0.9974	0.9986
Nitra	0.9427	0.9983	0.9430	0.9983	0.9713	0.9986	0.9653	0.9985
Zilina	0.6963	0.9325	0.6971	0.9436	0.6991	0.9325	0.6963	0.9325
Banska Bystrica	0.8545	0.9501	0.8563	0.9534	0.8546	0.9501	0.8558	0.9501
Presov	0.6651	0.9137	0.6661	0.9137	0.6716	0.9137	0.6728	0.9137
Kosice	0.5262	0.9553	0.5303	0.9605	0.6653	0.9557	0.5622	0.9553
Average	0.7789	0.9624	0.7802	0.9661	0.8042	0.9638	0.7886	0.9634

Source: Prepared by authors

located below the average. The most efficient were the Trnava, Trencin and Nitra regions with only minor deviations. Efficiency qual to one was reached by Trnava region in 2011, 2012 and 2015; Trencin region during the period 2011–2015; Nitra region during the period 2009–2012, 2014 and 2015 and Kosice region in 2008. The Trencin and Nitra regions were growing and the declines were reached in Bratislava, Zilina, Banska Bystrica, Presov and Kosice regions, with the biggest drop of Kosice region by 6.15%.

Model m3 has an average value of estimated efficiency over the whole reference period at 0.7802, which is significantly less than in the model m2 and more than the model m1. Fully efficient units were: Trnava region in 2008, 2011, 2012 and 2015; Trencin region in 2011,2012 and 2015; Nitra region in 2009. Above average were: Trencin, Trnava, Nitra and Banska Bystrica regions. Below the average were: the Zilina, Bratislava, Presov and Kosice regions. The increase in efficiency was recorded by the Bratislava, Trencin, Nitra and Banska Bystrica regions. The decline was recorded in Zilina, Presov and Kosice regions. The biggest loss of efficiency was reached by Zilina region, with a decrease around 11%. The most effective unit was the Trnava region with an average efficiency of 0.9947, while the least efficient unit was the Kosice region with an average efficiency of 0.5303.

The average value in model m4 of all regions for the whole surveyed period is 0.9661 and this results in the top three m1, m2 and m3 models. This is the highest average estimated efficiency. Above average there were Trencin, Trnava and Nitra regions. The Banska Bystrica region is no longer above the average of the Slovak Republic, but below it, along with the Zilina, Kosice and Presov region. For the first time, the model set the Trencin region as effective in every monitored year from 2008 to 2015. For this reason, the estimated value for the whole period for the Trencín region equals 1. In the Trnava region, as in the Trencin region, during the monitored period, there is zero change of efficiency. The declines were recorded in the Bratislava, Zilina, Banska Bystrica, Presov and Kosice regions. The most significant fall was recorded in the Zilina region with a total decrease of 7.34%.

The fifth is the m5, where the total average of the estimated efficiency for all regions is 0.8042 with a slight overall increase of 0.82%. Above average results, there were traditionally four regions, the same as in other previous models, namely Trencin, Trnava, Nitra and Banska Bystrica region. Under the average were Zilina, Presov, and Kosice regions. The highest average efficiency was reported by the m5 model in 2009, where the average efficiency in this year was 0.8130. On the other hand, the lowest efficiency was estimated on average for 2008 with average efficiency equal to 0.7783. The lowest efficiency is reached in the Bratislava region (0.5764). The highest performance on average was reached the Trnava region with an efficiency of 0.9983 without significant changes across the time period. An increase in the estimated efficiency was achieved by Bratislava, Banska Bystrica and Kosice regions. Kosice region recorded the most significant growth of 18.34%. The decline was recorded by the Nitra, Zilina and Presov regions, where the largest loss was in the Presov region (9.81%).

The m6 model, on average, has an estimated efficiency of 0.9638 across the whole reference period, with a slight decrease of 2.11%. The most effective unit with an estimated efficiency of 1 is Trnava region in 2008, 2010–2015. Another one is Trencin region in 2008, 2009, 2011–2015, and Nitra region with an efficiency of 1 in 2009–2015, and Kosice region in 2008. Above average were the Trnava, Trencin and Nitra regions. Below the average, there are Banska Bystrica, Zilina and Presov region. The decline in efficiency was in the Bratislava region by a slight 0.91%, in the Zilina region by 2.75%, in the Banska Bystrica by 2.06% in Presov by 6.43% and in Kosice region by 6.01%. The growth was only in one region, namely 1.12% in the Nitra region.

The average value of efficiency estimated by the m7 model for the whole period from 2008 to 2015 for the whole of Slovakia is 0.7886 with a total decline of 0.32%. As in all previous models, the above-average were Trnava, Trencin, Nitra and Banska Bystrica regions. Below the average were Zilina, Presov, Bratislava and Kosice regions. Efficiency equal to 1 was achieved by the Trnava region in 2008, 2011, 2012 and 2015; Trencin region in 2008, 2011, 2012 and 2015; and Nitra region in 2009. The increase in average efficiency for the whole analysed period was reached by the Bratislava region (3.68%), Nitra region (0.49%), Banska Bystrica region (6.75%) and Kosice region (12.70%). On the other side, the decline was recorded in the Zilina region (10,80%) and Presov region (12.82%).

The last model in the model group was the model m8. This model estimates the overall average efficiency for all regions over the observed period of 0.963394 with a fall of 2.13%. The Trencin, Trnava and Nitra regions are efficient throughout the whole period under review. Kosice region is efficient only in 2008. The increase in efficiency was reached by Nitra region (1.12%). In the other regions, there was a decline in efficiency, namely in the Bratislava region by 0.91%, in the Zilina region by 2.75%, in the Banska Bystrica region by 2.06%, in the Presov region by 6.43% and in the Kosice region by 6.15%.

After performing efficiency estimates using 8 models and partial analyzes each of them, we can conclude that every model created produces very similar results, no model speculated a special extreme value that would be inconsistent with other models. Therefore, we can conclude that the results shown and described in the previous sections are consistent with regard to the choice of input variables and roughly equally estimate the efficiency and inefficiency of Slovak regions. We note that the gradual substitution of the variables "number of MR devices ", "number of CT devices" and "number of all medical devices " to input side did not significantly affect the overall estimated efficiency of healthcare services in regions. Based on these findings, we consider that impact of selected input variables: x 1 - the number of beds and x2 - the number medical staff, and selected outputs: y1 – bed occupancy rate and y2 - average nursing time, was significant, and therefore the adding other variables affected the overall efficiency only in minimal way. The selection of the variables x1, x2, y1 and y2 is crucial for the evaluation of the efficiency of healthcare devices and we have confirmed this in the analysis. In the process of evaluation of the impact of medical technology (apparatus and equipment) on the efficiency, we recommend to add inputs or outputs which are directly results of the usage of medical technology in the field of treatment or prevention. In all models of DEA analysis, the regions of Trencin, Trnava and Nitra were repeated above the average. Banska Bystrica region was completing them, which was just above the average. In the m2, m4, m6 and m8 they were complemented by the Kosice region, but only in 2008, at the beginning of the monitored period and then gradually in each of the aforementioned models, the efficiency of the Kosice region had fallen over time. When we look at the development of variables, we repeat ourselves in the overriding values of the opposite of the other regions. Above average of whole sample during the whole analysed period, ie the highest average values, were at the x1 - Bratislava, Kosice and Presov regions. For variable x2 - the regions of Bratislava, Kosice, Presov and Zilina were above the total average. For variable y1 - the regions of Zilina, Kosice, Bratislava, Nitra and Banska Bystrica were above the overall average for this variable; y2 - regions of Bratislava, Nitra, Presov, Kosice and Banska Bystrica were above the y2 overall average; x3- Banska Bystrica, Bratislava and Zilina were above the total average; x4- Bratislava, Kosice, and Presov. were above the average; and for the last variable x5 the regions of Bratislava, Zilina and Kosice were above the average of whole sample for this variable. We see that Trencin and Trnava regions are not above the average in any input and output variables. What is important is whether they can provide adequate bad occupancy rate and average nursing time in days with the number of beds and the number of medical staff. In the deeper analysis and comparison of the number of beds and the use of beds, we can see that the regions with the highest number of beds are using them less than regions with fewer beds and therefore it is a clear recommendation to reduce the number of beds in Bratislava, Kosice, Zilina and Presov regions in order to increase the use of beds, as these regions have large surpluses of beds, resp., could increase the number of hospitals and thus their use. Another way is to increase their occupancy with unchanged bed counts. When looking at the ratio of the number of medical staff to the second observed variable "average nursing time in days", we get similar results as in the previous situation. In the Bratislava, Kosice and Presov regions, the proportion is too high, suggesting an optimal reduction in the number of medical staff. The same result is obtained by the proportional variations in the number of medical staff in the variable use of beds. Recommendations based on performance analysis are for Bratislava, Kosice, Zilina and Presov regions in terms of output orientations for increasing the use of beds with unchanged bed counts and the number of health workers. It also comes to our belief that the average time of care/treatment should be increased for Bratislava, Kosice, Zilina and Presov with unchanged beds and medical staff. This outcome is debatable, since increasing the average treatment time may mean making more demanding treatment procedures, hospitalization of which is demanding, which is desirable in terms of demand for health services. There is a tendency to reduce the average treatment time due to the shift of hospitalized performance to outpatient care and thus to the treatment of beds and the working time of healthcare workers. Unregulated reductions in average treatment time may lead to re-hospitalizations and re-operations, which reduces efficiency.

Conclusion

In the context of the ongoing globalization processes and pressures on the efficiency of healthcare systems in the countries, our study focused on analyzing and evaluating the efficiency of healthcare facilities in the various regions of the Slovak Republic in order to detect significant disparities. We applied the DEA method, used in many research studies to evaluate the efficiency of the sectors. Estimated efficiencies did not differ significantly in our models, but were consistent regardless of the change in input variables. The results of the analysis have shown that there is an indirect dependence between the values of the variables over time and the results of the estimated efficiency in all regions. The regions that had low values of the variables over time achieved a high degree of efficiency and vice versa. Interesting knowledge was that the gradual addition of variables "number of MR devices ", "number of CT devices " and "number of all medical devices " to the input side did not have a significant impact on the overall estimated efficiency of healthcare facilities. Technological advances in recent decades have brought many new diagnostic and therapeutic devices and healthcare practices that are also costly and which are expected to have significant health and economic benefits. For this reason, these processes need to be taken into account in systems for measuring and evaluating the efficiency of healthcare facilities. Our DEA method has not uncovered the impact of health technologies on health care efficiency, which significantly reduces its importance in the process of quantifying and evaluating efficiency in the future. In Slovakia, unlike in the rest of the world, the use of Health Technology Assessment (HTA) is totally absent. The efficiency of outputs from HTA is significantly increased by complementary use of adequate efficiency measurement methods, which would also take into account disparities and disproportions in the use of new health technologies in healthcare units on an aggregate scale. It is only possible to explicitly quantify the health and economic outcomes of their use and to set up a platform for national and international benchmarking. These specific facts encourage the realization of subsequent research aimed at finding, resp. designing appropriate systems to measure the efficiency of the healthcare system and their process interconnection. Their importance is particularly important in the process of creating stabilization and regulatory mechanisms in the health system and in the development of targeted policies.

Acknowledgements

This research paper is made possible through the support from VEGA Project No. 1/0945/17 Economic research on quantif. of marketing processes improving values for patients, multidimen. Analysis of the mark. Mix of HCF and quantif. of their importance in the process of establis. A system to measure the quality and efficiency.

Our thanks go out to the National Health Information Centre of the Slovak Republic for providing access to the central mortality database for the explored period as well as the other studied data along with the Statistical Office of the Slovak Republic.

Our acknowledgments also belong to the Ministry of Health of the Slovak Republic for its cooperation in creation of the new conceptions and methodologies and for its support of our research activities.

Funding

VEGA Project No. 1/0945/17 - Scientific Grant Agency of the Ministry of Education, science, research and sport of the Slovak Republic and the Slovak Academy of Sciences.

Authors' contributions

RS initiated the research and the manuscript. RS and BG proposed the study design, performed data collection, the literature research and the interpretation of the data. BG and KK participated in the design of the structure of the article, the interpretation of the data and literary research and the preparation of the manuscript. All the authors contributed to the article and approved the final form of the manuscript.

Competing interests

Authors declare that they do not have any competing financial, professional, or personal interests from other parties.

Author details

[1]Faculty of Management, The University of Presov, Presov, Slovakia. [2]Faculty of Economics, Technical University of Kosice, Kosice, Slovakia.

References

1. Ancarani A, Di Mauro C, Gitto S, Mancuso O, Ayach A. Technology acquisition and efficiency in Dubai hospitals. Technol Forecast Soc Chang. 2016;113:475–85.
2. Araújo C, Barros CP, Wanke P. Efficiency determinants and capacity issues in Brazilian for-profit hospitals. Health Care Manag Sci. 2014;17(2):126–38.
3. Banker RD, Charnes A, Cooper WW. Some models for estimating technical and scale inefficiencies in data envelopment analysis. Manag Sci. 1984;30(9): 1078–92.
4. Baray J, Cliquet G. Optimizing locations through a maximum covering/p-median hierarchical model: maternity hospitals in France. J Bus Res. 2013; 66(1):127–32.
5. Belciug S, Gorunescu F. Improving hospital bed occupancy and resource utilization through queuing modeling and evolutionary computation. J Biomed Inform. 2015;53:261–9.

6. Blank JK, Valdmanis VG. Environmental factors and productivity on Dutch hospitals: a semi-parametric approach. Health Care Manag Sci. 2010;13(1): 27–34.
7. Bradford WD, Kleit AN, Krousel-Wood MA, RE RN. Stochastic frontier estimation of cost models within the hospital. Rev Econ Stat. 2001;83(2): 302–9.
8. Byrnes P, Valdmanis V. Analyzing technical and allocative efficiency of hospitals. In: Data envelopment analysis: theory, methodology, and applications. Netherlands: Springer; 1994. p. 129–44.
9. Burgess JF, Wilson PW. Variation in inefficiency among US hospitals. INFOR, Can J Oper Res Inf Process. 1998;36(3):84–102.
10. Büchner VA, Hinz V, Schreyögg J. Health systems: changes in hospital efficiency and profitability. Health Care Manag Sci. 2016;19(2):130–43.
11. Chang L, Lan YW. Has the National Health Insurance Scheme improved hospital efficiency in Taiwan? Identifying factors that affects its efficiency. Afr J Bus Manag. 2010;4(17):37–52.
12. Charnes A, Cooper WW, Rhodes E. Measuring the efficiency of decision making units. Eur J Oper Res. 1978;2(6):429–44.
13. Cheng Z, Cai M, Tao H, He Z, Lin X, Lin H, Zuo Y. Efficiency and productivity measurement of rural township hospitals in China: a bootstrapping data envelopment analysis. BMJ Open. 2016;6(11):1–11.
14. Chirikos TN, Sear AM. Measuring hospital efficiency: a comparison of two approaches. Health Serv Res. 2000;34(6):1389–408.
15. Cooper WW, Seiford LM, Tone K. Data Envelopment Analysis A Comprehensive Text with Models, Applications, References and DEA-Solver Software. Springer; 2007 490 s. ISBN: 0387452818.
16. Czypionka T, Kraus M, Mayer S, Röhrling G. Efficiency, ownership, and financing of hospitals: the case of Austria. Health Care Manag Sci. 2014; 17(4):331–47.
17 Dervaux B, Ferrier GD, Leleu H, Valdmanis V. Comparing French and US hospital technologies: a directional input distance function approach. Appl Econ. 2004;36(10):1065–81.
18. De Souza PC, Scatena JHG, Kehrig RT. Aplicação da Análise Envoltória de Dados para avaliar a eficiência de hospitais do SUS em Mato Grosso. Physis: Revista de Saúde Coletiva. 2016;26(1)
19. Dey PK, Hariharan S, Clegg BT. Measuring the operational performance of intensive care units using the analytic hierarchy process approach. Int J Oper Prod Manag. 2006;26(8):849–65.
20. Dy MS, Kiley KB, Ast K, Lupu D, Norton SA, McMillan SC, Herr K, Rotella JD, Casarett DJ. Measuring what matters: top-ranked quality indicators for hospice and palliative care from the American Academy of hospice and palliative medicine and hospice and palliative nurses association. J Pain Symptom Manag. 2015;49(4):773–81.
21. Farrel MJ. The measurement of productive efficiency. J R Stat Soc Ser A (General). 1957;120(3):253–90.
22. Fragkiadakis G, Doumpos M, Zopounidis C, Germain C. Operational and economic efficiency analysis of public hospitals in Greece. Ann Oper Res. 2016;247(2):787–806.
23. Gavurová B, Šoltés V, Kafková K, Černý Ľ. 2013. Vybrané aspekty efektívnosti slovenského zdravotníctva. Jednodňová zdravotná starostlivosť a jej rozvoj v podmienkach Slovenskej republiky. Technická univerzita v Košiciach, Košice 2013. 276 s. ISBN: 978-80-553-1439-6.
24. Gavurová B, Šoltés V. 2013. Slovak Healthcare Effectiveness-Analysis of Comparative Aspects and Identification of Development Opportunities 2013.
25. Gerdtham UG, Löthgren M, Tambour M, Rehnberg M. Internal markets and health care efficiency: a multiple-output stochastic frontier analysis. Health Econ. 1999;8(2):151–64.
26. Gholami R, Higón DA, Emrouznejad A. Hospital performance: efficiency or quality? Can we have both with IT? Expert Syst Appl. 2015;42(12):5390–400.
27. Grosskopf S, Margaritis D, Valdmanis V. Competitive effects on teaching hospitals. Eur J Oper Res. 2004;154(2):515–25.
28. Hernandez AR, San Sebastian M. Assessing the technical efficiency of health posts in rural Guatemala: a data envelopment analysis. Glob Health Action. 2014;7
29. Ineveld M, Oostrum J, Vermeulen R, Steenhoek A, Klundert J. Productivity and quality of Dutch hospitals during system reform. Health Care Manag Sci. 2015:1–12.
30. Jablonský J, Dlouhý M. 2004. Modely hodnocení efektivnosti produkčních jednotek. 1. vyd. Praha: Professional Publishing, 2004. 184 s. ISBN 80-86419-49-5.
31. Jia T, Yuan H. The application of DEA (data envelopment analysis) window analysis in the assessment of influence on operational efficiencies after the establishment of branched hospitals. BMC Health Serv Res. 2017;17(1):265.
32. Karagiannis R. A system-of-equations two-stage DEA approach for explaining capacity utilization and technical efficiency. Ann Oper Res. 2015; 227(1):25–43.
33. Kazley AS, Ozcan YA. Electronic medical record use and efficiency. A DEA and windows analysis of hospitals. Socio Econ Plan Sci. 2008;43(3):209–16.
34. Kontodimopoulos N, Nanos P, Niakas D. Balancing efficiency of health services and equity of access in remote areas in Greece. Health policy. 2006; 76(1):49–57.
35. Kooreman P. Data envelopment analysis and parametric frontier estimation: complementary tools. J Health Econ. 1994;13(3):345–6.
36. Kounetas K, Papathanassopoulos F. How efficient are Greek hospitals? A case study using a double bootstrap DEA approach. Eur J Health Econ. 2013;14(6):979–94.
37. Ley E. Eficiencia productiva: Un estudio aplicado al sector hospitalario. Investicaionnes Económicas. 1991;15(1):71–88.
38. Li H, Dong S. Measuring and benchmarking technical efficiency of public hospitals in Tianjin, China a bootstrap–data envelopment analysis approach. INQUIRY: J Health Care Organization, Provision, and Financing. 2015; 52. 0046958015605487.
39. Linna M. Measuring hospital cost efficiency with panel data models. Health Econ. 1998;7(5):415–27.
40. Linna M, Häkkinen U, Linakko E. An econometric study of costs of teaching and research in Finnish hospitals. Health Econ. 1998;7(5):291–305.
41. Lo JC, Shih KS, Schen KL. Technical efficiency of the general hospitals in Taiwan: an application of DEA. Academia Econ Pap. 1996;24(3):275–96.
42. Lopez-Valcarcel BG, Perez BP. Changes in the efficiency of Spanish public hospitals after the introduction of program-contracts. Investicaionnes Económicas. 1996;20(3):377–402.
43. Maestre AM, oliveira MD, Barbosa-Póvoa AP. Location allocation approaches for hospital network planning under uncertainty. Eur J Oper Res. 2015; 240(3):791–806.
44. Magnussen J. Efficiency measurement and the operationalization of hospital production. Health Serv Res. 1996;31(1):21–37.
45. Mahate A, Hamidi S, Akinci F. Measuring the effect of size on technical efficiency of the United Arab Emirates hospitals. Global J Health Sci. 2016;9(3):116.
46. Maniadakis N, Thanassoulis E. Assessing productivity changes in UK hospitals reflecting technology and input prices. Appl Econ. 2000;32(12):1575–89.
47. Martini G, Berta P, Mullahy J, Vittadini G. The effectivness-effficiency trade-off in health care: the case of hospitals in Lombardy, Italy. Reg Sci Urban Econ. 2014;49:217–31.
48. Mobley LR, Magnussen J. An international comparison of hospital efficiency: does institutional environment matter? Appl Econ. 1998;30(8):1089–100.
49. Mujasi PN, Asbu EZ, Puing-Junoy J. How efficient are referral hospitals in Uganda? A data envelopment analysis and tobit regression approach. BMC Health Serv Res. 2016;16(1):230.
50. Nedelea IC, Fannin JM. Analyzing cost efficiency of critical access hospitals. J Policy Model. 2013;35(1):183–95.
51. Oikonomou N, tountas Y, Mariolis A, Souliotis K, Athanasakis K, Kyriopoulos J. Measuring the efficiency of the Greek rural primary health care using a restricted DEA model; the case of southern and western Greece. Health Care Manag Sci. 2016;19(4):313–25.
52. Parkin D, Hollingsworth B. Measuring production efficiency of acute hospitals in Scotland, 1991-94: validity issues in data envelopment analysis. Appl Econ. 1997;29(11):1425–33.
53. Perera R, Dowell A, Crampton P. Painting by numbers: a guide for systematically developing indicators of performance at any level of health care. Health Policy. 2012;108(1):49–59.
54. Puig-Junoy J. Technical efficiency in the clinical management of critically ill patients. Health Econ. 1998;7(3):263–77.
55. Retzlaff-Roberts D, Chang CF, Rubin RM. Technical efficiency in the use of health care resources: a comparison of OECD countries. Health policy. 2004; 69(1):55–72.
56. Rezaee MJ, Karimdadi A. Do geographical locations affect in hospitals performance? A multi-group data envelopment analysis. J Med Syst. 2015; 39(9):1–11.
57. Rezapour A, Azar FE, Zadeh NY, Roumiani Y, Faradonbeh SB. Technical efficiency and resources allocation in university hospitals in Tehran, 2009-2012. Med J Islam Repub Iran. 2015;29:266.
58. Rosenkratz AB, Doshi A. Characterizing the performance of the Nation's hospitals in the hospital outpatient quality reporting Program's imaging efficiency measures. J Am Coll Radiol. 2015;12(2):166–73.

59. Samut PK, Cafri R. Analysis of the efficiency determinants of health systems in OECD countries by DEA and panel Tobit. Soc Indic Res. 2016:1–20.
60. Sendek S, Svitálková Z, Angelovičová K. Efficiency evaluation of hospitals in the environment of the Czech and Slovak Republic. Acta Universitatis Agriculturae et Silviculturae Mendelianae Brunensis. 2015;63(6):2109–18.
61. Šoltés V, Balloni AJ, Gavurová B, Šoltés M. Economic aspects of a health system Electronization. Laboratory Management Information Systems: Current Requirements and Future Perspectives. 2014:32–50.
62. Šoltés V, Gavurová B. The functionality comparison of the health care systems by the analytical hierarchy process method. E+ M Ekonomie a Management. 2014;17(3):100–18.
63. Tsekouras K, Papathanassopoulos F, Kounetas K, Pappous G. Does the adoption of new technology boost productive efficiency in the public sector? The case of ICUs system. Int J Prod Econ. 2010;128(1):427–33.
64. Valdmanis V. Sensitivity analysis for DEAmodels. An empirical example using public vs. NFP hospitals. J Public Econ. 1992;48(2):185–205.
65. Varabyova Y, Schreyögg J. International comparisons of the technical efficiency of the hospital sector: panel data analysis of OECD countries using parametric and non-parametric approaches. Health Policy. 2013;112:70–9.
66. Villalobos M, Chacón M, Zitko P, Instroza-Ponta M. A new strategy to evaluate technical efficiency in hospitals using homogeneous groups of Casemix. J Med Syst. 2016;40(4):1–12.
67. Wagstaff A. Estimating efficiency in the hospital sector: a comparison of three statistical cost frontier models. Appl Econ. 1989;21(5):659–72.
68. Worthington AC. Frontier efficiency measurement in health care: a review of empirical techniques and selected applications. Med Care Res Rev. 2004; 61(2):135–70.
69. Zuckerman S, Hadley J, Iezzoni L. Measuring hospital efficiency with frontier cost functions. J Health Econ. 1994;13(3):255–80.

8

Determinants and the impact of the National Health Insurance on neonatal mortality in Ghana

Monica Lambon-Quayefio* and Nkechi S. Owoo

Abstract

The national health insurance was established to increase access to health care services and the maternal component was later introduced to improve the health outcomes of both mother and child. The main objectives of this study are to investigate the factors that affect neonatal deaths as well as examine the effect of the Ghana Health Insurance on neonatal deaths in Ghana. Using the most recent round of the Ghana Demographic and Health Survey, the study estimates the probit model with interaction effects to account for the heterogeneity in outcomes. Additionally, the study employs the propensity score matching approach to account for the possible endogeneity in the insurance enrolment decision. Results from the estimations, after controlling for relevant individual and household characteristics suggest that the national health insurance significantly reduces the likelihood of neonatal deaths. Estimates remain consistent even after more robust estimators are employed. Estimates from the interaction between place of residence and health insurance indicate that health insurance beneficiaries who reside in urban areas are at a higher risk of neonatal deaths compared to other women. Access to medical facilities proxied by distance to the nearest health post emerged as an important predictor of neonatal death. The study also suggests significant regional differences in neonatal deaths. We, therefore, conclude that the national health insurance may have the potential to substantially improve the health outcomes of neonates and have policy implications for increasing coverage to more mothers and their neonates, as well as coverage in critical neonatal services and drugs.

Keywords: Health insurance, Neonatal deaths, Health care access, Ghana

Background

The neonatal period- the first 28 days- is the most vulnerable period for the survival of every child. A new-born dies every 15 minutes in Ghana according to recent data from United Nations Children Emergency Fund (UNICEF, 2015). This reflects the relatively high levels of neonatal mortality recorded in the country. Globally, despite the accelerating progress made towards child survival, the decline in neonatal mortality has been slowest from the period 1990 to 2015. As such, the proportion of newborn deaths in child mortality has increased from about 37% in 1990 to 44% in 2013 (United Nations Interagency Group Child Mortality Estimation-UN-IGME, 2015).

After declining steadily from 122 deaths per 1000 live births in 1990 to 98 deaths per 1000 live births in 1998, the under-five mortality appeared to have stagnated at 111 deaths per 1000 live births between 2003 and 2008 [1]. The main reason for this reversal is the increased neonatal mortality (Ghana Newborn Health Strategy and Action Plan, 2014). Like the rest of the world, Ghana has experienced a stagnation in the declines in neonatal deaths. Data from the Ghana Health Service (GHS, 2010) show some inconsistency in the decline in neonatal mortality from 1993 through to 2015. The neonatal mortality rate was 41 deaths per 1000 live births in1993, declining to 30 deaths per 1000 live births, rising to 43 in 2003 and then falling again to 30 deaths per 1000 live births in 2008. UNICEF (2015) reports the 2013 neonatal mortality rate to be 29.3 and the 2015 rate to be 32 deaths per 1000 live births. The sluggish rate of neonatal declines since 1998 has resulted in the increase in neonatal deaths' contribution to infant deaths from 53% in 1998 to about 71% in 2014 (Ghana Demographic and Health Survey, 2014) as well as its contribution to child mortality.

* Correspondence: mplambon@gmail.com
Economics Department, University of Ghana, P.O.BOX LG 57, Accra, Ghana

Currently, neonatal mortality contributes about 40% of child mortality. As a result, neonatal mortality has become a very important component of infant mortality and child mortality and requires very exigent attention (Ghana National Newborn Health Strategy, 2014).Generally, aside other biological and medical factors, lack of access to modern health care services and medication are major contributing factors to child mortality [2]. High user fees and out-of-pocket payments which characterize most developing countries have generally been associated with low health care utilization. In developing countries like Ghana lack of access to health services due to financial constraints and/or physical access may result in delays in seeking treatment and encourage self-treatment, which are both associated with increased health complications [3]. In most cases, it hampers access to modern health services especially for young children [4].

In Ghana, the Newborn Health Strategy and Action plan whose goal is to reduce neonatal mortality from 30 to 21 deaths per 1000 live births by 2018 identified the issue of health financing for newborn care as one of the challenges which hinders improvement in the health of newborns. Although the national health insurance is currently designed to cover all pregnant women and children under 18 years (which includes newborns), not all services are covered by the scheme. This study, therefore, aims to investigate the risk factors of neonatal deaths and examine the potential role the national health insurance scheme can play in reducing the rate of neonatal mortality in Ghana. Since its establishment, only two studies have directly examined the effects of the health insurance on neonatal health. Both studies [5, 6] find a positive relationship between the national health insurance and new born health. Yet, these studies are very limited in terms of geographic coverage and measurement of new born health. The first study focused on only two districts out of the 216 districts in Ghana and employs post-natal checks as a proxy for new born health. Although the second study makes use of a nationally representative data, it also uses the continuum of maternal care as a proxy measure of new born health and does not account for endogeneity in the health insurance enrolment decision. To the best of our knowledge, no other study has examined the effect of the national health insurance scheme by simultaneously using more direct measures of neonatal mortality, using nationally representative data and accounting for endogeneity. This study, therefore, adds to the limited knowledge stock in the area of neonatal research.

This study may also have important implications for newborn health policy in Ghana. The Newborn Health Strategy and Action plan outlined strategies to substantially reduce out-of-pocket payments for essential drugs and tests for newborns as a way of reducing the financial barriers to accessing newborn health services. Another strategy is to increase advocacy efforts to improve the national health insurance's coverage on neonatal related health care. As such, findings from this research will provide the required empirical evidence to inform policy changes on increasing coverage to essential neonatal health needs. The remainder of the paper is organized in six sections as follows: the next section provides a brief historical background to the national health insurance, followed by section three which reviews existing literature on health insurance and child mortality. Section four describes the data while section five discusses the methodology used in the study. Section six provides the results and discussions while section seven concludes the paper with some policy recommendations.

Historical background to the National Health Insurance in Ghana

National health insurance in Ghana dates back to post-independence. Healthcare during the period was entirely free and was wholly financed by government tax revenue [7]. It insulated the poor and marginalized from financial distress. However, in 1970, free health care provision was no longer sustainable as a result of inadequacy of resources and budgetary constraints [8]. Consequently, a statutory dispensing fee of 30np (New Pesewa) was introduced by the National Liberation Council (NLC [7]. Also, upon the enactment of the Hospital Fees Decree 1969 which was later amended into the Hospital Fees Act 1971, a minimal user fee was charged to cover hospital procedures.

The economic decline coupled with inflationary pressures and growing unemployment in Ghana, at the time, made it heed to the then seemingly attractive proposals implementing a structural adjustment program in 1983. The goal of this program was to withdraw all forms of subsidies and then liberalize the economy. Consequently, the full cost recovery (also known as cash-and-carry) was introduced and adopted into the health system with the introduction of the Hospital Fees Regulation 1985 (L.I.1313). This extended the fees charged to include consultation, laboratory and other diagnostic procedures, medical, surgical and dental services, medical examinations and hospital accommodation [9]. Post-recovery programme's government expenditure on the health sector dropped to less than 20% that of the pre-1970.

Recognizing the importance of health care to the quality of human capital, Ghana made several attempts at finding alternatives that will abolish the cash and carry system. Various experimented alternatives proved unsuccessful, largely because of lack of resources and the inability of the government to pay for the budget of the health sector. Finally, the government took the decision to experiment with a social health financing initiative which led to the introduction of a health insurance scheme on a pilot basis in the 1990s. Afterwards, community health insurance (CHI) schemes and Mutual Health Organizations (MHO) sprang up in Ghana. They were mainly funded by faith-entities and international organizations [9].

The National Health Insurance

The development of the current National Health Insurance Scheme commenced with Ghana's resolve to access the highly indebted poor country (HIPC) initiative in March 2001. The government of Ghana was to allocate the funds towards projects that sought to reduce poverty and enhance economic growth. Simply, it highlighted the protection of the poor and marginalized, with special reference to women and children. As a result, in February 2003, some amount of the HIPC fund was allocated by the Ministry of Health to support the running and creation of Mutual health Organizations in most parts of the country. The national health insurance bill (Act 650) was eventually placed before the legislature for considerations. The bill required the formal and the informal sector to enroll together in government-sponsored district MHOs [8, 9].

The national health insurance scheme is financed from a pool of sources of which the individual premium payments ranging from GH7.2 to 48.0 (roughly USD 3.6 to 24) per person per year. These premiums are progressive which means the rich pays more than the poor. This source finances less than 5% of the NHIS expenditure (NHIA,2013). According to NHIA [10], the major source of funding is the value-added tax of 2.5% on all goods and services, which contributes approximately 60% to the NHIS revenue. Other funding sources include investment income or interest earned on National Health Insurance Fund reserves (17% of NHIS revenues), a 2.5% of social security contributions from formal sector workers (16% of NHIS revenues).

Almost all outpatient and inpatient services targeting over 90% of the disease burden including essential medicines (as included in the NHIS approved list) are offered to the insured without any co-payments. The insurance is cashless and the insured are not required to make any payment at the time of health care delivery. Payments for referrals up to the teaching hospitals are covered. However, HIV retroviral drugs, hormone, and organ replacement therapy, heart and brain surgery other than the ones caused accidents, diagnosis, and treatment abroad, dialysis for chronic renal failure and cancers are excluded from the insurance package [11].

Health service access and delivery under the NHIS

The National Health Insurance Scheme, which was implemented in 2004, has been accepted by Ghanaians as one of the best homegrown social intervention programs to be introduced in the country. Research reveals that the National Health Insurance Scheme has expanded access to health care for the majority of the population who, until its introduction, could not afford health care under the 'cash and carry' system. As at the end of December 2011, the total active membership of the scheme increased from 8.16 million in 2010 to 8.23 million in 2011 showing an increase of 0.8% over the 2010 figure and representing 33% of the population [9].

Moreover, upon the institution of the NHIS, outpatient utilization augmented by over twenty-eight fold from 0.6 million in 2005 to 16.9 and 25.5 million in the year 2010 and 2011 respectively. Similarly, Inpatient utilization increased over 30 fold from 28,906 in 2005 to 973,524 in 2009 but dropped to 724,440 in 2010. In 2011, however, inpatient utilization doubled, from 724,440 to 1.45 million. The Free Maternal Care (FMC) component was introduced in July 2008 to contribute to meeting the Millennium Development Goals (MDG) 4 and 5. Under this program, pregnant women are to receive free medical care. However, due to abuse of the system, the National Health Insurance Authority (NHIA) revised the implementation guidelines in 2010 to encourage pregnant women to register with the scheme before accessing health care [12]. Yet, it was revealed that the poor quality of the health care offered to NHIS card holders served as disincentive for pregnant women to register with the scheme [9].

Neonatal, infant and child health care under the NHIS

Though the NHIS insured beneficiaries against various health risks, the benefits of maternal and neonatal care under the scheme were central. In the second half of 2008, the revised free maternal care program was implemented under the NHIS, which mandated pregnant women to be enrolled onto the scheme (without payment of premiums) in order to enjoy the program benefits. The program allowed all expectant mothers to enjoy free health care services right from conception till after delivery. They could similarly access postnatal care at accredited heath facilities at no cost. The benefit package also included free neonatal coverage. Specifically, neonates enjoy free health services on the mother's card three months after delivery [13] Additionally, all babies had the right to free basic healthcare for a whole year [12, 14], and nationals below age 18 were also entitled to free health care under the scheme [15]. Consequently, a 30% reduction in infant mortality rate and another 13% decline in neonatal deaths were recorded between 2008 and 2011 [16, 17].

Literature review

Improving women's access to quality health care during pregnancy and infant and children's access to essential health care services is imperative for improved maternal and child health. The relationship between out of pocket payments for health care and child health outcomes have been documented by [18, 19]. There is however very little evidence about the relationship between health insurance and neonatal mortality because very few studies have measured these outcomes [20]. Globally, evidence from a systematic review by Spaan et al. [21] suggest that health insurance increases health care utilization. In Ghana, a number of studies [6, 22, 23] have confirmed the positive relationship between the health insurance and health care utilization, since its implementation in 2005 in terms of improvement in maternal and child health outcomes. Using a nationally representative data, Owoo and Lambon-Quayefio [24] confirmed a positive relationship between health insurance and antenatal visits. Brugiavini and Pace [25] and Mensah et al. [6] have also confirmed that women who are enrolled on the health insurance scheme are likely to deliver in institutions compared to women who did have health insurance. Access to and utilization of health care have been described by Comfort et al. [20] to be mediating factors of the impact of health insurance on health outcomes.

With respect to its link with newborn health and child mortality, most of the available evidence is based on studies from relatively more advanced countries which provide inconclusive findings. Some of these studies [26–29] have employed natural and quasi-natural experiments while others such as [5] have also relied on non-experimental econometric techniques in evaluating the effect of health insurance on child survival.

The Medicaid program in the United States was found to significantly reduce infant mortality and low birth weights, according to [30, 31] who used the instrumental variable approach to account for the endogeneity in the health insurance uptake decision. The State Children's Health Insurance program has also been linked with improved child health outcomes in the United States according to Joyce and Racine [32]. Similarly, in Taiwan, Chou et al. [33] relied on the difference in difference approach to evaluate the effect of health insurance on birth outcomes. Results showed a positive impact on birth outcomes and child mortality. However, these studies have focused more on post-neonatal mortality rather than on neonatal mortality. The limited evidence available on health insurance and neonatal mortality suggest a negative relationship. Using data for Brazil, Barros et al. [34] focused on gestational specific neonatal mortality and birthweight specific neonatal mortality and found that neonatal mortality decreased with coverage of health insurance.

Ghana specific studies on health insurance and neonatal health is even more limited. Mensah et al. [6] attempted to explore this relationship using the propensity score matching technique to account for the self-selection of women enrolling onto the national health scheme. The study finds a positive relationship between health insurance and newborn outcomes. The limitation of the study is two-fold. First, the study used post-natal care as a proxy for newborn health. However, whether or not mothers attend post-natal visits may not accurately capture the health status of neonates. Secondly, even though the study employed a rigorous estimation technique, the data employed focused only on two out of the 216 districts in Ghana. As a result, the findings from this study may not be nationally representative. Similarly, Browne and Kayode et al. [5] also used maternal continuum of care services such as antenatal care, skilled deliver and post-natal care as proxies for newborn health. However, Browne and Kayode et al. [5] do not account for the endogeneity in the health insurance enrolment decision. The objective of the study is two fold. The first is to examine the factors that influence neonatal deaths in Ghana, and the second is to estimate the impact of the Ghana's national health insurance on neonatal deaths. The first objective aims to update the neonatal mortality literature in Ghana's context, examining which factors significantly correlate with neonatal deaths, using more recent data. The second objective of the study adds to the limited evidence available on the association between health insurance and newborn health in two ways- using more direct measures of neonatal mortality and accounting for endogeneity, using a nationally representative data.

Data

The study makes use of the 2014 Ghana demographic and health survey which is a nationally representative data constituting over 12,000 households. The sampling for this data is based on a two-stage sampling technique. In the first stage, a total of 427 clusters were selected covering both the urban and the rural areas. From these clusters, 30 households were systematically selected in each of these clusters. Data is collected using three main questionnaires namely, the household questionnaire, the men's questionnaire and the women's questionnaire. Specifically, the analysis makes use of information from the women's questionnaire which captures demographic and socioeconomic information on women within their reproductive ages (15–49). The data includes information on birth history dating 5 years preceding the survey. The data also contains other relevant information such as details on education, wealth, employment, marital status as well as information on whether or not the household members have valid national health insurance. The main variable of interest in this analysis is whether or not the individual woman has a valid national health insurance card. Table 1 below provides a detailed description of the variables used in the study while Table 2 provides the summary statistics of the variables used in the analysis.

From the sample neonatal deaths make up about 4%. Disaggregating by national health insurance holders,

Table 1 Detailed description of study variables

Variable Name	Type	Constructed from:
Neonatal Death	Dummy (1-if age at death is 1 month;0 otherwise)	Age at death in months
Health Insurance Status	Dummy (1 if individual has a valid NHIS;0 otherwise)	Does individual hold a valid health insurance card?
No Valid NHIS (base)		
Valid NHIS		
Age of Mother	Continuous	Mother's current age
Mother's age		
Birth type	Dummy (1- twin birth; 0 single)	Child is twin
Single (base)		
Twin		
Birth Order of Child	Count	Birth order of child
Birth Order		
Sex of Child	Dummy (1 male;0- female)	Sex of Child
Child is Female(base)		
Child is Male		
Antenatal Care Visits	Continuous	Number of antenatal visits during pregnancy
Number of ANC visits		
Delivery type	Dummy (1- delivery by c-section; 0 – natural delivery)	Delivered by caesarian section
Natural birth (base)		
Caesarian birth		
Birth Interval	Dummy (1- > = 2 yrs.; 0- <2 yrs)	Preceding birth interval
Less than 2 yrs. (base)		
2 yrs. or more		
Distance to Health Facility	Dummy (1- distance a problem; 0 distance not a problem)	In getting medical help, is distance a big problem
Not a big problem (base)		
A big problem		
Place of Delivery	Dummy (1- delivered in a health facility; 0 otherwise)	Place of delivery
Non-Facility delivery (base)		
Facility delivery		
Distance to Health Facility		
Employment Status	Dummy(1 employed;0 unemployed)	Respondent worked in the last 12 months
Unemployed (base group)		
Employed		
Education:	Categorical	Highest educational level of individual
No Education (base group)		
Primary Education		
Secondary Education		
High Education		
Marital Status	Categorical	Current marital status
Single (base)		
Married		
Living together		
Formerly Married (widowed/divorced/separated)		
Wealth Quintiles	Categorical	Wealth index of household
Poorest (base group)		
Poor		
Middle		
Rich		
Richest		
Location	Dummy (1- urban; 0 rural)	Type of place of residence
Rural (base)		
Urban		
Region of Residence	Categorical	Region of residence
Greater Accra		
Western		
Central		
Volta		
Eastern		
Ashanti		
Brong-Ahafo		
Northern		
Upper East		
Upper West		

Table 2 Summary statistics

Study variables	Full sample		Valid Nhis		No Valid Nhis		Mean diff
	Mean	SD	Mean	SD	Mean	SD	*P*-value
Neonatal Death	0.04	0.19	0.04	0.19	0.04	0.19	0.642
Mother's Age	36.86	7.62	37.43	7.63	36.55	7.58	0.000
Twin	0.04	0.19	0.03	0.17	0.04	0.19	0.095
Birth order	2.95	1.93	3.09	2.02	2.83	1.86	0.000
Child is Male	0.51	0.5	0.53	0.5	0.52	0.5	0.208
Number of ANC Visits	6.26	2.82	5.97	2.73	6.54	2.67	0.00
Delivered by CS	0.1	0.31	0.1	0.3	0.11	0.32	0.349
Faciltiy Delivery	0.92	0.27	0.9	0.3	0.93	0.25	0.000
Birth Interval	0.86	0.34	0.87	0.34	0.87	0.33	0.465
Distance to Health Facility a Problem	0.33	0.47	0.38	0.48	0.3	0.46	0.000
Mother's Education							
No education	0.42	0.49	0.57	0.5	0.4	0.49	0.000
Primary	0.2	0.4	0.16	0.37	0.19	0.39	0.001
Secondary	0.35	0.48	0.25	0.44	0.38	0.49	0.000
Higher	0.02	0.15	0.02	0.14	0.03	0.17	0.014
Employment Status							
Employed	0.87	0.33	0.9	0.29	0.86	0.34	0.000
Marital Status							
Single	0.03	0.17	0.02	0.15	0.03	0.17	0.079
Married	0.69	0.46	0.75	0.43	0.73	0.45	0.011
Living Together	0.15	0.36	0.11	0.31	0.14	0.34	0.001
Formerly Married	0.13	0.34	0.12	0.32	0.11	0.31	0.339
Wealth Quintiles							
Poorest	0.32	0.47	0.47	0.5	0.32	0.47	0.000
Poor	0.23	0.42	0.16	0.37	0.22	0.41	0.000
Middle	0.2	0.4	0.16	0.36	0.2	0.4	0.000
Rich	0.14	0.35	0.09	0.29	0.15	0.36	0.000
Richest	0.11	0.31	0.12	0.33	0.12	0.33	0.911
Place of Residence							
Urban	0.397	0.49	0.42	0.49	0.37	0.48	0.000
Region of Residence							
Greater Accra	0.07	0.26	0.14	0.35	0.05	0.23	0.000
Western	0.1	0.3	0.05	0.21	0.1	0.31	0.000
Central	0.1	0.3	0.07	0.25	0.07	0.25	0.822
Volta	0.08	0.28	0.02	0.13	0.1	0.3	0.000
Eastern	0.1	0.3	0.07	0.25	0.1	0.3	0.000
Ashanti	0.11	0.31	0.01	0.09	0.1	0.3	0.000
Brong Ahafo	0.11	0.31	0.01	0.09	0.14	0.34	0.000
Northern	0.14	0.35	0.37	0.48	0.12	0.32	0.000
Upper East	0.1	0.3	0.02	0.15	0.12	0.32	0.000
Upper West	0.09	0.29	0.25	0.43	0.1	0.31	0.000
Observations	23,118		1941		13,055		

there seem to be no statistical difference in the proportions of neonatal deaths among individuals who had valid health insurance and those that did not. The average age in the study sample is about 37 years. The difference in age between those with health insurance and those without is statistically significant at 1%. Although statistically significant only at 10% the data shows a higher incidence of multiple births among individuals with no valid national health insurance. About half (51%) of the children considered in this sample are male. On the whole, the average number of antenatal sessions attended is 6. The data also suggests a significantly lower antenatal attendance for mothers with NHIS compared with mothers without. Generally, almost all the women (92%) in the study reported delivering at a health facility. Comparatively, there were less facility deliveries among individuals with the valid health insurance cards. Given its importance to delivery outcomes, the issue of whether distance to the nearest health facility is a problem was included in the analysis. On the whole about a third (33%) of the respondents in the sample complained that distance to the nearest health facility was a big problem. The problem seem to be more pronounced among respondents with valid health insurance. Of those with valid health insurance, about 38% of them expressed worry about distance to the nearest facility compared to the 30% who had no valid health insurance.

The education and household wealth of respondents are also important determinants of risk of death of neonates. The data categorizes individual women's education into four distinct groups namely no education, primary education, secondary education and higher education. As shown in the table, for all education categories considered in this study there are statistically significant differences between women with valid health insurance and those without. Overall, about 42% of the sample have no education. However, more than half (57%) of respondents with NHIS have no education compared to only 40% of women with no NHIS. Overall, 20% of the women in the sample have primary education. The proportion of women with NHIS who have primary education is about 16% compared to the 19% recorded among women with no valid health insurance. In general, approximately 35% of women in the study have secondary education. For women with valid nhis cards, the percentage of women with secondary education is about 25% while proportion is significantly higher for women with valid NHIS at 38%. Overall, only a few (2%) of the women have higher education. Among NHIS beneficiaries and non-beneficiaries, the proportion is approximately 2% and 3% respectively. Majority of the women (89%) reported as being employed. The proportions are similar among the sub groups of women with valid health insurance and no valid health insurance.

Based on information collected on ownership of various items and assets the survey generates wealth scores from which households are classified. According to the sample, women who belong to households categorized as being poorest, poor, middle, rich or richest categories are respectively 32%, 23%, 20%,14% and 11%. Consistently across the five quintiles, there are significant differences between women with valid health insurance and those with no valid health insurance. For instance, 47% of women who have valid NHIS are found in the poorest wealth category while 32% of women with no valid NHIS are also found in the poorest category. Similarly, for all the other four wealth categories, there are significantly higher proportions among women with no valid health insurance compared with women with valid health insurance. The study also controls for household location. The study accounts for the whether or not the respondents reside in the urban or rural area as well as region of residence in order to account for region specific characteristics.

Methods

The study employs two empirical techniques for each of the research objectives. The first objective of examining factors that influence neonatal deaths makes use of the probit model due to the binary nature of the dependent variable. The form of the probit model estimated is as follows:

$$Neonatal = \alpha NHIS + \beta Socioeconomic + \gamma Child + \varepsilon$$

Where *Neonatal* is a binary variable equal to 1 if the child died in the neonate stage and zero otherwise. *NHIS* is the variable of interest which captures whether or not the individual (mother) has a valid health insurance card or not. *Socioeconomic* is a vector that captures mother's demographic and socio economic characteristics such as age, education, wealth, marital status as well as region and area of residence. *Child* is a vector of child specific characteristics such as gender and birth order. The coefficient, α merely measures the probability of neonatal mortality if a mother has a valid health insurance and not necessarily the impact of the health insurance on neonatal death as this would provide biased measure due to the potential endogeneity in the health insurance uptake decision.

According to Berk [35] and Nichols [36], selection bias occurs when relevant covariates, whether observable or unobservable are omitted in the analysis. This omission creates a situation where the explanatory variables are correlated with the residuals, thereby producing biased estimates and consequently affecting the reliance of the probit estimates for causal inferences. For example, the probit estimates may be overstating the effects of health insurance on the probability of neonatal mortality even after controlling for other relevant covariates. In the NHIS enrolment decision and as argued by Wang et al., [37] in a related study, women who enroll in the NHIS may differ significantly from women who do not. For example, women who are at a higher risk of losing their neonates may be more likely to enroll on the health insurance scheme. Women's enrolment on the scheme is therefore not random. For example, some unobserved characteristics of women (perhaps specific health conditions) that make then more risky to lose their neonates also makes them risk averse. These may motivate them to enroll on the scheme. The unobserved heterogeneity in the characteristics of women in the sample may lead to unobserved selection bias.

Also, evidence from health care utilization studies, such as Arthur [38] and Dixon et al. [39] have indicated the rural-urban dichotomy in the utilization of maternal health care. As a result of this dichotomy, this study attempts to test the heterogeneity in the risk of neonatal death, by taking an interaction between the NHIS and whether or not the individual lives in the rural or urban areas.

The endogeneity problem is addressed by employing the Propensity Score Matching technique which is discussed below.

The Propensity Score Matching technique developed by Rosenbaum and Rubin [40] has been described as an alternative to obtaining unbiased estimates in assessing program effects [41, 42]. In this technique propensity scores which are defined as the probability of assignment to the treated group, conditional on observed covariates are estimated. This balancing score is estimated based on a logit or probit regression where the treated and control subjects are then grouped based on similar propensity scores. The propensity scores then allows for the estimation of the average treatment on the treated [43]. This precisely allows for measurement the effect of the intervention or treatment. Despite the advantage of being able to directly estimate the treatment or program effect, the propensity score matching technique makes an assumption that unobservable differences does not exist between the treated and control groups [44] and as such does not balance on the unobserved characteristics. Table 3 below provides details of the balancing process for the study variables . The results of the overidentification test also suggest that both control and treatment groups are balanced. Also, the balance plots in Fig. 1 below indicate that the control and treatment groups are fairly similar.

Following [6, 45, 46] the paper estimates the propensity scores on which women in the sample are matched into and put in two groups-women with valid health insurance and women without valid health insurance. The estimation adopted a maximum of two matches (based on the psmatch option). This means that for each score, a maximum of two matches are considered. The balancing test[2]results indicate that the treatment and control groups are very similar.

In the matching, model let ED = 1 represents a woman who has a valid national health insurance and ED = 0 represent a woman with no valid national health insurance. The treatment effect of valid health insurance is represented by TREAT for the individual women written as:

$$Treat_i = Y_i(1) - Y_i(0)$$

In this context, $Y_i(1)$ represents the risk of neonatal death if the mother has a valid national health insurance and $Y_i(0)$ represents the risk of neonatal death if the mother did not have a valid national health insurance. In this paper, the average treatment effect on the treated (ATET)[3] is estimated. The ATET evaluates the outcomes for those who received the treatment. In this case the, ATET estimates the risk of neonatal death for those who had a valid national health insurance. This is represented by the equation as:

$$ATET = E(Treat|ED = 1) = E(Y(1)|ED = 1) - E(Y(0)|ED = 1)$$

Given that the ATET directly focuses on the actual treatment participants, it evaluates precisely the gain from a program and therefore it can help determine whether or not the program or treatment was successful [47].

To check for sensitivity of results to different estimators, the paper employs other treatment effects estimators namely regression adjustment, inverse probability weights (ipw) and inverse probability weights with regression adjustment (ipwra).[4] These three estimators model for the non-random treatment assignment in different ways. Regression adjustment accounts for the non-random assignment by modeling the outcome (neonatal deaths in this case), ipw models the treatment assignment process and not specify a model for the outcome.

The IPWRA estimator accounts for the non-randomness in the treatment assignment by modelling both the outcome and the treatment. The estimator uses the ipw weights to estimate corrected regression coefficients that are then used to perform the regression adjustment. The IPWRA estimator is characterized by the double-robust property which ensures consistent treatment effects.

All three estimators pose the question "how would the outcomes (neonatal deaths) have changed if the mothers who had valid health insurance did not have" or "how would the outcomes have changed if the mothers who did not have valid health insurance ensured that they had valid health insurance?" The

Table 3 Propensity Score Balance Summary

A. Covariance Balance Summary				
	Raw		Matched	
Number of Observations	2905		5088	
Treated Observations	2544		2544	
Control Observations	361		2544	
Variable Name	Standardized Differences		Variance Ratio	
	Raw	Matched	Raw	Matched
Mother's age	−.1296483	.0364344	.9287937	1.009999
Child is Twin	−.0208939	−.1156947	.8807093	.5463699
Birth Order	−.1119146	.0710256	.8888037	1.199043
Male	−.0085316	−.0559324	.9982579	1.006856
# ANC Visits	.206661	−.1835419	.943477	.5885621
C-Section	.0540464	−.0597158	1.135394	.8804142
Birth Interval	−.0408154	.1321761	1.135338	.7049418
Facility Delivery	.2746749	.0830562	.7614058	.9029657
Distance to Health Facility a Problem	−.1786455	.1215717	.8775627	1.140062
Employed	−.2450663	−.1205648	1.515683	1.196728
Primary	.0234105	−.0090512	1.036952	.9856519
Secondary	.2972229	−.180736	1.146584	1.003001
Higher	.0924015	−.0616649	1.527182	.7932333
Married	−.1246425	.2719016	1.13	.8624613
Living Together	.1411103	−.2760325	1.319529	.7002463
Div/Wid/Sep	−.1245533	.0329835	.6440925	1.149318
Poor	.0742811	−.0427384	1.126954	.939822
Middle	.2025143	−.1443748	1.456805	.8293347
Rich	.2487801	−.0267813	1.756897	.9556369
Richest	−.0371579	.0262596	.926871	1.056912
Urban	−.1870417	−.0771981	1.079494	1.024072
Western	.1767931	−.1432928	1.761079	.7223761
Central	.0278805	−.0476522	1.091104	.8685413
Volta	.3894944	.088634	8.038964	1.302943
Eastern	.1335153	−.0792723	1.561523	.8110256
Ashanti	.3823853	.0773616	9.837706	1.275423
Brong-Ahafo	.538495	−.0802844	21.94662	.8581629
Northern	−.5721632	.042118	.4612771	1.108165
Upper East	.3371211	.1979067	3.502459	1.801891
Upper West	−.3843526	−.0066071	.4819179	.9822969
B. Over Identification Test				
Over identification test for covariance balance				
H_0: Covariates are Balanced				
Chi2 (31) = 22.0718				
Prob > chi 2 = 0.8807				

difference in these two counterfactual outcomes, also called potential outcomes precisely give the actual effect of the health insurance on neonatal deaths.

Results and discussion

The primary objectives of this study is to assess the key determinants of neonatal mortality and to determine the

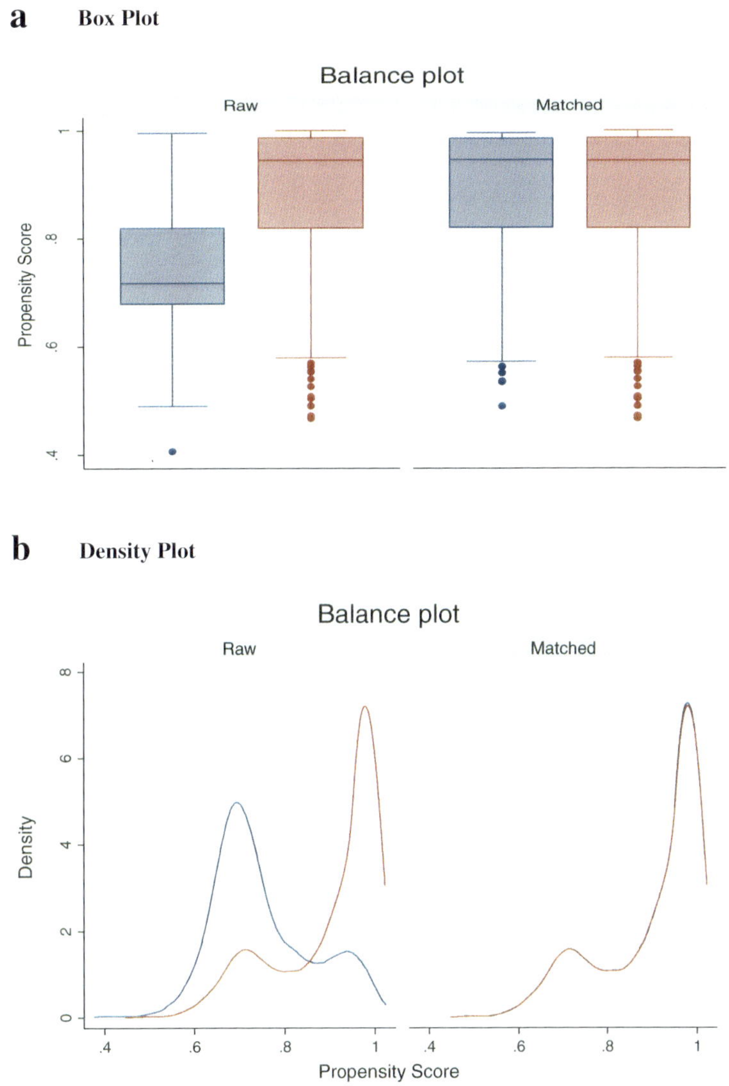

Fig. 1 Balance plots of control and treated samples

impact of the national health insurance on neonatal mortality. Results from the three models estimated are shown in Table 4 below. Table 5 below also shows results from the robustness checks when other estimators are employed. From Table 4, model one specifies a basic probit which does not account for the possibility of endogeneity in national health insurance uptake. Model two shows estimations from an interaction term between place of residence and the national health insurance. The last model, which is the main model of interest shows results from the propensity score matching estimation. The estimates shows that the national health insurance scheme has a significantly negative impact on the risk of neonatal deaths in Ghana. Specifically, the risk of neonatal death is reduced by about 5% for individual mothers who have valid national health insurance compared to others without a valid health insurance. This finding is consistent with those of Barros et al. [34] and Mensah et al. [6].

This finding can be explained by two possible paths- direct and indirect. Directly, the health insurance significantly reduces out of pocket payments during pregnancy until after the first post-natal check. As such any complication during pregnancy and delivery that may cause neonatal distress or deaths may be detected and treated. Also, given that infections are a major cause of neonatal mortality, early detection of infections especially within the period from delivery till the first post-natal may be treated, thus reducing the risk of death of neonates. Also, health insurance works indirectly through improved maternal health care utilization and practices which are likely to reduce neonatal deaths. As found by [5, 6, 24] the national health insurance increases antenatal care attendance,

Table 4 Estimation results: Probit, Probit with Interaction and PSM

Dependent Var: Neonatal Deaths	Model1 Probit	Model 2 Probit with Interaction	Model 3 PSM
Woman has Valid NHIS	−0.0144*	−0.0646***	
	(0.00795)	(0.0246)	
Mother's Age	−0.000490	−0.000528	
	(0.000586)	(0.000589)	
Child is Twin	0.000431	0.000148	
	(0.0146)	(0.0147)	
Birth Order	0.00282	0.00295	
	(0.00194)	(0.00194)	
Child is Male	7.20e-05	−3.80e-06	
	(0.00492)	(0.00492)	
Number of ANC Visits	9.29e-05	0.000106	
	(0.000970)	(0.000971)	
Delivered by CS	0.00497	0.00381	
	(0.00729)	(0.00737)	
Birth Interval	−0.00933	−0.00994	
	(0.00808)	(0.00800)	
Facility Delivery	0.00961	0.00942	
	(0.00731)	(0.00727)	
Distance to Health Facility a Problem	0.0107*	0.0117**	
	(0.00552)	(0.00554)	
Employed	−0.00617	−0.00520	
	(0.00603)	(0.00605)	
	(0.0175)	(0.0177)	
Married	−0.0137	−0.0141	
	(0.00863)	(0.00864)	
Living Together	−0.0224**	−0.0227**	
	(0.0103)	(0.0103)	
Divorced/Separated/Widowed	−0.0188	−0.0189	
	(0.0141)	(0.0141)	
Urban	−0.000404	−0.0286*	
	(0.00678)	(0.0150)	
Urban*Valid NHIS		0.0323**	
		(0.0154)	
Education Controls	Yes	Yes	
Regional Controls	Yes	Yes	
Wealth Quintiles	Yes	Yes	
Valid NHIS vs No Valid NHIS			−0.051***
			(0.007)
Observations	2905	2905	2905

Standard errors in parentheses*** $p < 0.01$, ** $p < 0.05$, * $p < 0.1$
Marginal effects presented in Models 1 and 2

Table 5 Regressions for Robustness Checks

	(Model 1) RA		(2) IPW		(3) IPWRA	
POmeans						
Valid NHIS = 0	0.0310***	(3.14)	0.0394**	(2.04)	0.0331***	(4.39)
Valid NHIS = 1	0.0172***	(6.67)	0.0164***	(6.64)	0.0164***	(6.64)
OME0						
Mother's Age	−0.00292	(−0.06)			−0.0199	(−0.41)
Child is Twin	2.270***	(2.89)			4.272***	(4.97)
Child is Male	−2.867*	(−1.80)			−5.079**	(−2.56)
# ANC Visits	−0.157	(−1.01)			−0.456***	(−2.68)
Delivery by CS	2.606***	(2.59)			3.997**	(2.44)
Birth Interval	−0.534	(−0.42)			−1.080	(−0.95)
Facility Delivery	−0.580	(−0.68)			−0.837	(−0.77)
Distance to Health Facility a Problem	2.464**	(2.48)			4.442***	(4.05)
Primary	−0.604	(−0.63)			0.206	(0.21)
Secondary	−0.531	(−0.59)			−0.842	(−0.80)
Higher	0.907	(0.56)			0.189	(0.07)
Poor	2.155**	(2.28)			3.491***	(2.70)
Middle	2.463*	(1.86)			2.756	(1.44)
Rich	4.465***	(2.80)			7.368***	(3.48)
Richest	2.654*	(1.72)			4.791**	(2.46)
Employed	−1.090	(−1.38)			−1.180	(−1.59)
Constant	−4.260*	(−1.83)			−4.581*	(−1.87)
OME1						
Mother's Age	−0.00449	(−0.20)			−0.00185	(−0.08)
Twin	−3.847***	(−15.51)			−3.973***	(−15.54)
Male	0.220	(0.70)			0.259	(0.82)
# ANC Visits	0.0278	(0.41)			0.0221	(0.31)
C-Section	−0.103	(−0.21)			−0.00225	(−0.00)
Birth Interval	−0.425	(−0.87)			−0.431	(−0.88)
Facility Delivery	0.552	(1.32)			0.535	(1.30)
Distance Problem	0.431	(1.29)			0.438	(1.30)
Primary	−0.0255	(−0.05)			−0.103	(−0.22)
Secondary	0.417	(1.10)			0.393	(1.06)
Higher	−3.861***	(−8.18)			−3.982***	(−8.54)
Poor	−0.438	(−0.99)			−0.417	(−0.95)
Middle	−0.410	(−0.92)			−0.397	(−0.91)
Rich	−0.707	(−1.28)			−0.692	(−1.24)
Richest	−0.395	(−0.69)			−0.450	(−0.78)
Employed	−0.307	(−0.86)			−0.347	(−0.96)
Constant	−3.981***	(−4.31)			−4.039***	(−4.28)
TME1						
Mother's Age			−0.0190**	(−2.38)	−0.0190**	(−2.38)
Twin			−0.219	(−1.03)	−0.219	(−1.03)

Table 5 Regressions for Robustness Checks *(Continued)*

	(Model 1) RA	(2) IPW		(3) IPWRA	
Birth Order		0.0652**	(2.44)	0.0652**	(2.44)
Male		0.00229	(0.03)	0.00229	(0.03)
# ANC Visits		0.0114	(0.73)	0.0114	(0.73)
C-Section		0.0101	(0.09)	0.0101	(0.09)
Birth Interval		0.0205	(0.16)	0.0205	(0.16)
Facility Delivery		0.0487	(0.56)	0.0487	(0.56)
Distance Problem		0.0553	(0.73)	0.0553	(0.73)
Employed		−0.242***	(−2.63)	−0.242***	(−2.63)
Primary		−0.142	(−1.39)	−0.142	(−1.39)
Secondary		0.0209	(0.21)	0.0209	(0.21)
Higher		0.308	(1.54)	0.308	(1.54)
Married		−0.0584	(−0.34)	−0.0584	(−0.34)
Living Together		0.00554	(0.03)	0.00554	(0.03)
Wid/Div/Sep		−0.355*	(−1.73)	−0.355*	(−1.73)
Poor		−0.00304	(−0.03)	−0.00304	(−0.03)
Middle		0.0667	(0.51)	0.0667	(0.51)
Rich		0.351**	(2.31)	0.351**	(2.31)
Richest		0.0376	(0.21)	0.0376	(0.21)
Urban		−0.162	(−1.63)	−0.162	(−1.63)
Western		0.942***	(5.99)	0.942***	(5.99)
Central		0.661***	(4.48)	0.661***	(4.48)
Volta		1.684***	(7.40)	1.684***	(7.40)
Eastern		0.826***	(4.95)	0.826***	(4.95)
Ashanti		1.645***	(6.71)	1.645***	(6.71)
Brong_Ahafo		2.083***	(7.60)	2.083***	(7.60)
Northern		0.0603	(0.42)	0.0603	(0.42)
U_East		1.379***	(7.61)	1.379***	(7.61)
U_West		0.188	(1.30)	0.188	(1.30)
Constant		1.202***	(3.27)	1.202***	(3.27)
Observations	2905	2905		2905	

t statistics in parentheses * $p < .1$, ** $p < .05$, *** $p < .01$

increases the probability of facility delivery and skilled delivery as swell as reduced complications during delivery. These together are likely to significantly reduce the risk of losing babies in the first month of life.

Although the probit models (together with interaction term model) do not provide impact evaluation estimates, they provide some useful information on the determinants of neonatal mortality. As expected, the probit estimations suggest a negative relationship between health insurance and the probability of neonatal deaths. Also, distance to the nearest health facility is an important determinant of neonatal mortality. Respondents who reported that distance to the nearest health facility is a problem are significantly more likely to experience neonatal deaths. The risk of death of neonates from individual mothers who complained about the distance to the health facility is approximately 1.1% higher. Most health facilities, especially in the rural areas, are located in district capitals and in relatively bigger towns. This coupled with the generally bad road network and conditions in these remote areas may make it relatively difficult to access critical health services for neonates, especially in times of emergencies, thereby increasing the risk of deaths. Especially in the rainy season when vehicles are unable to ply the roads, it makes traveling to the hospital even more precarious.

With respect to marital status and risk of neonate death, those who are married and those living-together are associated with a reduced risk of neonatal death. Individual women who are married have a 1.4% reduced risk of death while those living together have a reduced risk of 2.3% compared to single women. In order to evaluate the possible heterogeneity in effects of the national health insurance and neonatal death, an interaction between national health insurance and place of residence was taken. Results from the interaction estimation suggest that respondents who live in the urban areas and also have valid health insurance are associated with a significantly higher risk (3%) of neonatal deaths compared to others who reside in the urban areas and do not have valid cards and others who live in the rural areas. A possible explanation for this finding is that due to the increased maternal health care utilization as a result of the introduction of the health insurance scheme, there is a lot of 'pressure' on the hospital facilities, which renders the health care received relatively poor. This generally creates very long waiting queues which generally discourage pregnant women from patronizing essential health care services which may lead to better health outcomes of their babies. Also, the financial challenges of the health scheme has resulted in non-payment of claims by the health centers. As such, card holders are denied services. These may work together to deteriorate the neonatal outcomes in the urban centers.

Surprisingly maternal and household factors such as education and household wealth were not statistically significant predictors of risk of neonatal death. The results also indicate that there are statistically significant differences in the risk of neonatal deaths among the regions. For instance, the risk of neonatal death for respondents who reside in the Western region is approximately 3% higher than those from the greater Accra region. Similarly, Ashanti region and Brong-Ahafo regions are also associated with 3% higher risk of neonatal deaths compared to the capital region, greater Accra.

Conclusion

The study employs both the probit and the propensity score matching technique to estimate the impact of the national health insurance on neonatal deaths. While the probit estimate provides correlates of the risk of neonatal deaths, the propensity score matching approach employed in this context empirically compares the probability of neonatal death among individuals who have active national health insurance to the probability of neonatal deaths among individulas who do not have active or valid health insurance. Our results show that neonates of mothers with valid health insurance cards are significantly less likely to die. Results from this study, therefore, suggest that the national health insurance has the potential to significantly reduce the risk of neonatal deaths. Through the national health insurance health care services in general and, neonatal health services in particular, become more affordable to the population. As a result, health officials are able to avert any health risks of neonates that are likely to result in neonatal deaths. On the contrary, however, the results also indicate that distance to health facilities increases the risk of neonatal deaths. With a valid health insurance, neonates may still be at risk of death if the distance to the nearest hospital is a problem. Also, results from the interaction between health insurance and urban residence suggest that individuals in the urban areas who have national health insurance are significantly more likely to lose their babies in the infant stages. A possible reason for this finding is that most urban health facilities are over-stretched in terms of patients served and given the recent financial challenges of the national health insurance scheme, individuals who have the health insurance are either turned away or are given relatively substandard health care services.

These, therefore, suggest that although the national health insurance scheme may offer some potential to achieving the objectives of the Ghana National New-Born Health strategy of significantly reducing neonatal deaths by the year 2018, requisite infrastructure and appropriate policy changes need to be put in place. First, there is the need to review and extend coverage of the national health insurance beyond the first postnatal care as is the case in its present state as well as other essential drugs needed for critical neonatal health care. Secondly, it may be very beneficial for the national health insurance authority to intensify its efforts in solving the financial challenges the scheme is currently facing in order to honour its financial obligations. This may provide the necessary environment for neonates to receive the optimal healthcare services required to live past the first 28 days of their lives.

Endnotes

[2]Balancing Summary statistics, plots and over identification test provided in appendix Fig. 1

[3]The ATET was estimated using the teffects STATA command with the psmatch option.

[4]Results of these estimators are shown in the appendix in Table 3

Abbreviations

ATET: Average Treatment Effect on the Treated; CHI: Community Health Insurance; FMC: Free Maternal Care; GDHS: Ghana Demographic and Health Survey; HIPC: Highly Indebted Poor Country; IPW: Inverse Probability Weights; IPWRA: Inverse Probability Weights with Regression Adjustment; MDG: Millennium Development Goals; MHO: Mutual Health Organizations; MICS: Multiple Indicator Cluster Survey; MOH: Ministry of Health; NHIA: National Health Insurance Authority; NHIS: National Health Insurance Scheme; UNICEF: United Nations International Children Emergency Fund; UN-IGME: United Nations Interagency Group Child Mortality Estimation

Authors' contributions

ML-Q conceived the idea for the study. Both ML-Q and NO undertook the analysis. ML-Q did the write-up of the analysis. Both authors read and approved the final manuscript.

Competing interest

We would like to state that we the authors have no competing interests.

References

1. UNDP Ghana Report. Ghana Millennium Development Goals Report. 2010.
2. Schoeps A, Lietz H, Sie A, Savadogo G, De Allegri M, Muller O, Souares A. Health insurance and child mortality in rural Burkina Faso. Glob Health Action. 2015;8. doi:10.3402/gha.v8.27327.
3. Hadley J. Sicker and poorer: the consequences of being uninsured. The Henry J. Washington, DC: Kaiser Family Foundation; 2002.
4. Xu K, Evans DB, Kawabata K, Zeramdini R, Klavus J, Murray CJ. Household catastrophic health expenditure: a multicountry analysis. Lancet. 2003;362: 11–17. [PubMed].
5. Browne JL, Kayode GA, Arhinful D, Fidder SAJ, Grobbee DE, Klipstein-Grobush K. Health Insurance determines antenatal, delivery and postnatal care utilization: evidence from the Ghana Demographic and Health Surveillance data. BMJ Open. 2016;6:e008175. doi:10.1136/bmjopen-2015-008175.
6. Mensah J, Oppong J, Schmidt C. An evaluation of the Ghana national health insurance scheme in the context of the health MDGs. Health Econ. 2010;19(S1):95–106.
7. Senah KA, Hansen E, Ninsin, KA. 'Problems of health care delivery system, The State, Development, and Politics in Ghana, 1989. London: CODESRIA. 1989;242–67.
8. Yirbuor E. National Health Insurance and quality health Care in the Lawra District: University for Development Studies; 2011.
9. Owusu-Sekyere E, Bagah DA. Towards a Sustainable Health Care Financing in Ghana: Is the National Health Insurance the Solution? Public Health Research. 2014;4(5):185–94.
10. NHIA. NHIA annual report 2013. Accra, Ghana: NHIA; 2013.
11. Saleh K. The health sector in Ghana. Washington, D.C: The World Bank; 2013.
12. NHIA. National Health Insurance Authority Annual Report 2010. Accra: National Health Insurance Authority; 2010.
13. Dzakpasu S, Soremekun S, Manu A, et al. Impact of free delivery care on health facility delivery and insurance coveragein Ghana's Brong Ahafo region. PLoS One. 2012;7:e49430.
14. Smith M. and Fairbank A. An Estimate of Potential Costs and Benefits of Adding Family Planning Services to the National Health Insurance Scheme in Ghana and the Impact on the Private Sector. Accra: Banking on Health Project. 2008.
15. Gobah F. K. and Liang Z. The national Health InsuranceScheme in Ghana: Prospects and Challenges: a Cross-Sectional Evidence, Global Journal of Health Science. 2011;3(2)
16. Measure GDHS. 2008. http://www.measuredhs.com/what-we-do/survey/survey-display-301.cfm.
17. Ghana Statistical Service. Ghana Multiple Indicator Cluster Survey with an Enhanced Malaria Module and Biomarker,2011, Final Report. Accra, Ghana: Ghana Statistical Service. 2011.
18. Jacobs B, Price N. The impact of the introduction of user fees at a district hospital in Cambodia. Health Policy Plan. 2004;19(5):310–21.
19. Lagarde M, Palmer N. The impact of user fees on access to health services in lowand middle-income countries (review). Cochrane Database Syst Rev. 2011;13(4):CD009094. doi:10.1002/14651858.CD009094.
20. Comfort AB, Peterson LA, Hatt LE. Effect of health insurance on the use and provision of maternal health services and maternal and neonatal health outcomes: a systematic review. J Health Popul Nutr. 2013;31(4 Suppl 2):S81–S105.
21. Spaan E, Mathijssen J, Tromp N, McBain F, ten Have A, Baltussen R. The impact of health insurance in Africa and Asia: a systematic review. Bull World Health Organ. 2012;90:685–92.
22. Witter S, Garshong B. Something old or something new? Social health insurance in Ghana. BMC International Health & Human Rights. 2009;9(1):20.
23. Blanchet NJ, Fink G, Osei-Akoto I. The effects of Ghana's National Health Insurance Scheme on health care utilisation. Ghana Medical Journal. 2012; 46(2):76–84.
24. Owoo N. and Lambon- Quayefio M.P. "National Health Insurance, Social Influence and Antenatal Care Use." Health Economics Review. 2013;3:9.
25. Brugiavini A, Pace N. Extending Health Insurance: Effects of the National Health Insurance Scheme in Ghana. RSCAS Working Papers 2011/27, European University Institute. 2011.
26. Gruber J. "Health Insurance for Poor Women and Children in the U.S.: Lessons from the Past Decade." In Tax Policy and the Economy Vol. 11, edited by J. M. Poterba. Cambridge, Massachusetts: MIT Press. 1997;169–211.
27. Gruber, J. "Medicaid. 2000" National Bureau of Economic Research Working Paper 7829, 2000b.
28. Currie J. "Child Health in Developed Countries." In Handbook of Health Economics 30 Vol. 1B, edited by A. J. Culyer and J. P. Newhouse. Amsterdam: North-Holland. 2000;1054–1090.
29. Dubay L, Joyce T, Kaestner R and Kenney GM. "Changes in Prenatal Care Timing and Low Birth Weight by Race and Socioeconomic Status: Implications for the Medicaid Expansions of Pregnant Women." Health Services Research. 2001;36:373–398.
30. Currie J, Gruber J. Health insurance eligibility, utilization of medical care, and child health. Q J Econ. 1996a;111:431–66.
31. Currie J, Gruber J. Saving babies: the efficacy and cost of recent expansions of medicaid eligibility for pregnant women. J Political Econ. 1996b;104:1263–96.
32. Joyce T, Racine A. CHIP shots: association between the State Children's health insurance programs and immunization rates. Pediatrics. 2005;115(5): e526–34.
33. Chou S-Y, Grossman M, Liu J-T. The impact of National Health Insurance on Birth Outcomes; A Natural Experiment in Taiwan. Cambridge. NBER Working Paper No. 16811; 2011.
34. Barros FC, Victora CG, Barros AJ, Santos IS, Albernaz E, Matijasevich A, et al. The challenge of reducing neonatal mortality in middleincome countries: findings from three Brazilian birth cohorts in 1982, 1993, and 2004. Lancet. 2005;365:847–54.
35. Berk RA. An introduction to sample selection bias in sociological data. American Sociological Review. 1983;48:386–98.
36. Nichols A. Causal inference with observational data. Stata Journal. 2007;7:507.
37. Wang W, Temsah G, Mallick L. The impact of health insurance on maternal health care utilization: evidence from Ghana, Indonesia, and Rwanda. Health Policy Plan. 2017;32(3):366–75. doi:10.1093/heapol/czw135.
38. Arthur E. Wealth and antenatal care use: implications for maternal health care utilisation in Ghana. Heal Econ Rev. 2012;2(1):14. doi:10.1186/2191-1991-2-14.
39. Dixon J, Tenkorang EY, Luginaah IN, Kuuire VZ, Boateng GO. National health insurance scheme enrolment and antenatal care among women in Ghana: is there any relationship?. Tropical Medicine & International Health. 2014;19: 98–106. [PubMed]
40. Rosenbaum PR, Rubin DB. The central role of the propensity score in observational studies for causal effects. Biometrika. 1983;70:41–55.
41. Dehejia RH, Wahba S. Causal effects in non-experimental studies: reevaluating the evaluation of training programs. J Am Stat Assoc. 1999;94:1053–62.
42. Smith JA, Todd PE. Reconciling conflicting evidence on the performance of propensity-score matching methods. Am Econ Rev. 2001;91:112–24.
43. Imbens GW. Nonparametric estimation of average treatment effects under exogeneity: a review. Rev Econ Stat. 2004;86:4–29.
44. Joffe MM, Rosenbaum PR. Propensity scores. Am J Epidemiol. 1999;150:327–33.
45. Giedion U, Diaz BY, Alfonso EA. The Impact of Subsidized Health Insurance on Access, Utilization and Health Status: the Case of Colombia. Washington, DC: The World Bank. 2007.
46. Trujillo AJ, Portillo JE, Vernon JA. The impact of subsidized health Insurance for the Poor: evaluating the Colombian experience using propensity score matching. Int J Health Care Finance Econ. 2005;5(3):211–39.
47. Heckman J, LaLonde R, Smith J. The economics and econometrics of active labor market programs. In: Ashenfelter O, Card D, editors. Handbook of labor economics, vol. III. Amsterdam: Elsevier; 1999. p. 1865–2097.

9

Health care service provision in Europe and regional diversity: a stochastic metafrontier approach

Katharina Schley

Abstract

In the last decades, demographic change coupled with new and expensive medical innovations have put most health care systems in developed countries under financial pressure. Therefore, ensuring efficient service provision is essential for a sustainable health care system. This paper investigates the performance of regional health care services in six West European countries between 2005 and 2014. We apply a stochastic metafrontier model to capture the different conditions in the health care systems in the countries within the European Union. By means of this approach, it is possible to detect performance differences in the European health care systems subject to different conditions and technologies relative to the potential technology available. The results indicate that regional deprivation plays a key role for the efficiency of health care provision. Furthermore, a pooled model which assumes a similar technology for all countries cannot sufficiently account for differences between countries. Surprisingly, the Scandinavian regions lag behind other regions with respect to the metafrontier.

JEL Classification: C23, D61, I12, I18, R10

Keywords: Health production, Health efficiency, Stochastic frontier analysis, Metafrontier analysis

Background

Demographic and social changes likely rise the burden of chronic diseases, like cancer, cardiovascular diseases, and diabetes. Along with new and expensive treatment options this puts the health care systems around the world under financial pressures. As a result of an increasing number of patients health care budgets in many countries inflate. Already, health expenditure grows more rapidly than the economy in many countries [7] comprising the sustainability of health care funding.

The increasing demand for new and innovative treatments and an increasing request for better value for money for patients at constant budgets raised the topic of *value based care* [31, 32]. In this sense, Porter [31] diagnoses a need to restructure the delivery of care to obtain sustainable health care budgets. Along these lines, the evaluation of the allocation and utilisation of medical resources is likely an important lever for the assessment of the performance of health care systems.

Correspondence: kschley@uni-goettingen.de
University of Goettingen, Humboldtallee 3, 37073 Göttingen, Germany

Several attempts have been made to analyse cross-country differences in the performance of health care services. A pioneer work is by Evans et al. [15]. The authors analyse the efficiency of 191 countries based on data provided by the World Health Organisation (WHO). Greene [19] challenged the work by Evans et al. [15] demonstrating that considerable unobserved heterogeneity due to cultural and economic characteristics leads to an underestimation of systematic health care differences. Accordingly, Greene [19] respecified the model introducing fixed effects parameters. His 'true' fixed effects model is able to distinguish between unobservable cross-country heterogeneity not associated with inefficiency and inefficiency itself. For the European Union, few studies have analysed the performance of health care systems. For instance, Asandului et al. [2] analyse the efficiency of a cross-section of 30 European countries by means of a Data Envelopment Analysis. They show that some countries lie on the production frontier while most are underneath. The analysis of the regional variation of health outcomes and performance of health care services at the national level has recently gained increasing interest ([11, 17, 20, 29, 33], for example).

So far, very little attention has been paid to the evaluation of performance differences in a cross-country context at the regional level. This would increase the understanding of underlying factors of cross-country performance differences as many countries are faced by regional variations in health outcomes and the availability of medical infrastructure. Even though, national governments decide in general on health policy measures municipalities and other regional level bodies are responsible for the provision of medical services further highlighting the need for a regional level analysis. Furthermore, potential sources of inefficiency such as an over or under use of services are likely located at the regional level [17]. Against this background, the aim of this study is to evaluate the efficiency and performance of health care services at the regional level in (Western) Europe. For this purpose, we apply a stochastic metafrontier model [4, 28]. The metafrontier model is essentially a two step approach. In the first step, country specific frontiers are estimated. In a second step, the metafrontier production function, which is a deterministic parametric function enveloping the individual frontiers, is calculated. This approach has the advantage that cross-country differences in the utilised technology are taken into account. The general frontier model assumes that all producers use the same technology. Based on this, one would assume that in the health care setting all health care systems are subject to the same rules and regulations. Bos and Schmiedel [5] relate this to the benchmark paradox. In the European framework, this is not the case as the design of the European health care systems is heterogeneous. In general, though, the health care systems in the European Union have access to similar health care inputs and the same technology which is taken into account by means of the metafrontier. Moreover, it is possible to distinguish between the regional efficiency in relation to the country's own frontier and the metafrontier. For the analysis, we combine regional administrative information from six European countries (Austria, France, Germany, Italy, Scandinavia and Spain) for an extended time frame covering the period from 2005 to 2014.

To preview some results, we find that regional deprivation plays a key role for the efficiency of health care provision. Furthermore, we show that the efficiency scores of the health care systems in a pooled model, which assumes a common technology for all countries, differ from the efficiency scores with respect to the metafrontier.

The next section describes the stochastic frontier model and the metafrontier approach and introduces the data. Empirical results are discussed in the Section Results and discussion. The last section concludes. The appendix provides a detailed description of the data (Appendix A).

Methods

In this section, we describe the empirical model to assess the stochastic health frontier and metafrontier approach. Moreover, we introduce the data and the variables.

The stochastic frontier model

The *stochastic frontier analysis* (SFA) has become a common approach to asses production potentials and inefficiencies in the production of goods and services in, for example, farms, firms and hospitals. In contrast to standard non-parametric approaches which treat any deviation from a production function as inefficiency [8], the parametric SFA model allows to differentiate random deviations from the efficient frontier and inefficiency. We base the formalisation of a one-step SFA model on an approach proposed by Wang and Schmidt [37]. By quantifying production frontier parameters and exogenous influences on inefficiency simultaneously, we avoid the risk of biased estimation results inherent in two-step approaches based on estimated efficiency scores [37].

The health frontier

In order to evaluate performance differences in the regional provision of health care services, we define the European regions as producers of health (DMUs). In a strict sense, the regions themselves do not convert inputs into outputs. However, they can be considered as (health) producers in a wider sense as they provide a framework for the provision of health care services [21]. The pooled SFA model for health production in region i at time t reads as

$$y_{it} = \boldsymbol{x}'_{it}\beta + v_{it} - u_{it}, \tag{1}$$

$$v_{it} \sim \mathcal{N}(0, \omega^2), \tag{2}$$

$$u_{it} \sim \mathcal{N}^+(0, \sigma^2) \qquad i = 1, \ldots, N, \quad t = 1, \ldots, T. \tag{3}$$

In (1), y_{it} is the log output and $\boldsymbol{x}_{it}$ is a K-dimensional vector of the log input factors of region i at time t. Stochastic deviations from the health frontier are captured by v_{it}, which is conventionally assumed to be normally distributed with zero mean and variance ω^2. The inefficiency term u_{it} follows a half normal distribution with mean zero and variance σ^2. To include demographic and socio-economic characteristics which might influence the individual inefficiency of health care provision in each region, the model fulfills the so-called scaling property [37]

$$\sigma = \exp\left(\boldsymbol{z}'_{it}\delta\right). \tag{4}$$

In (4), $\boldsymbol{z}_{it}$ is a R-dimensional vector of the individual explanatory variables of the variance of the inefficiency term u_{it} for each country j. By virtue of the scaling property, the shape of the distribution of the inefficiencies u_{it}

is the same for all regions [37]. This is intuitively appealing, as in general all regions have the same possibilities to reach the efficiency frontier. Demographic and socio-economic characteristics shape the deviations from the health frontier. The model in (1) - (4) is estimated by means of Maximum-Likelihood methods.

In efficiency analyses the main interest lies on the estimation of technical efficiency which is the ratio of the observed output and the maximum feasible output on the production frontier [8]. It is measured as

$$\mathrm{TE}_{it} = \frac{y_{it}}{\tilde{y}_{it}} = \frac{\boldsymbol{x}'_{it}\beta + v_{it} - u_{it}}{\boldsymbol{x}'_{it}\beta + v_{it}}, \tag{5}$$

where $\tilde{y}_{it}$ is the maximum feasible output which lies on the production frontier.

Metafrontier model

The general (pooled) stochastic frontier model assumes homogeneous technologies for all individuals. In case of a comparison of health care systems across countries, this assumptions is far fetched. Even though, similar inputs and technologies are available to all the usage pattern, however, differs within the European countries due to different rules and regulations. A common production frontier cannot sufficiently account for these differences. In a metafrontier approach, it is possible to evaluate how efficient each country works in producing health and to compare the productivity and efficiency across nations without assuming similar technologies. The metafrontier approach is essentially a two step procedure developed by Battese et al. [4] and O'Donnell et al. [28]. In a first step, the group-specific (country-specific) frontiers are estimated by means of a stochastic frontier model as in (1) - (4) for each country separately. Accordingly, the estimated model parameters β and δ of the pooled SFA model in (1) and (4) change to β^j and δ^j for each country j. In a second step, a metafrontier is enveloped over the individual frontiers. Battese et al. [4] show that the metafrontier optimization can be solved by a linear programming problem for log-linear production functions according to

$$\begin{aligned} &\min_{\beta^*} L \equiv \sum_{i=1}^{N}\sum_{t=1}^{T}(\boldsymbol{x}'_{it}\beta^* - \boldsymbol{x}'_{it}\hat{\beta}^j) \\ &\text{s.t. } \boldsymbol{x}'_{it}\beta^* \geq \boldsymbol{x}'_{it}\hat{\beta}^j. \end{aligned} \tag{6}$$

In (6), β^* is a vector of the metafrontier parameters and $\hat{\beta}^j$ is a vector of the estimated country specific stochastic frontier parameters. As the $\hat{\beta}^j$ are assumed to be fixed in the linear programming problem, (6) is equivalent to $\min_{\beta^*} L \equiv \bar{\boldsymbol{x}}'\beta^*$, where $\bar{\boldsymbol{x}}$ is a vector of the means of all input variables for all observations [4].[1] The standard errors for the metafrontier parameters can either be obtained by bootstrap or simulation.

To compare the efficiency scores of the countries across different technology sets (frontiers), the technical efficiency with respect to the metafrontier can be calculated according to

$$\mathrm{TE}^*_{it(j)} = \frac{y_{it(j)}}{y^*_{it}} = \frac{\boldsymbol{x}'_{it(j)}\beta_{(j)} + v_{it(j)} - u_{it(j)}}{\boldsymbol{x}'_{it}\beta^*}, \tag{7}$$

where y^*_{it} is the output on the metafrontier. $TE^*_{it(j)}$ is the ratio of the observed output of region i at time t to the metafrontier output.

The ratio of the output of the prodcution function for country j relative to the potential output of the metafrontier for a given set of input variables is the metatechnology ratio (MTR) which is given by

$$\mathrm{MTR}_{it(j)} = \frac{\mathrm{TE}^*_{it(j)}}{\mathrm{TE}_{it(j)}}. \tag{8}$$

The MTR captures the difference between the productivity between the group and the metatechnology (the technology available to all countries). Figure 1 illustrates the concept of the metafrontier graphically. The production model is set to a single input - single output framework with three convex country frontiers labelled Country 1, 2, and 3. The metafrontier envelopes the three country frontiers. It is assumed to be a deterministic smooth function with values no less than the individual country functions. Point A indicates a point of production of region i at time t. The figure illustrates the technical efficiency of region i with respect to its group frontier ($\overline{0A}/\overline{0B}$) and the respective technical efficiency TE^*_{it} of region i to the metafrontier ($\overline{0B}/\overline{0C}$). Further, it shows the distance between the respective country's production set and the metafrontier ($\overline{0B}/\overline{0C}$) [24, 28].

Data and variables

Region-specific data on mortality, health care infrastructure and other characteristics are extracted from Eurostat online database.[2] Annual data cover the period from 2005 to 2014. The panel is unbalanced due to the non-availability of data for certain regions and years. The overall number of observations in the study is 1149 (see Appendix A for a detailed description of the data). We base the regional analysis on the NUTS-2 (Nomenclature des unités territoriales statistiques) regions.

Health production

It is hardly possible to directly measure the health of the population. The health status of the population can merely be approximated by measures such as life expectancy, mortality or morbidity. As specific measures of morbidity are not available at regional level, we use an age and sex standardised mortality rate (SMR) to resemble the population's health status (see Appendix A for detailed

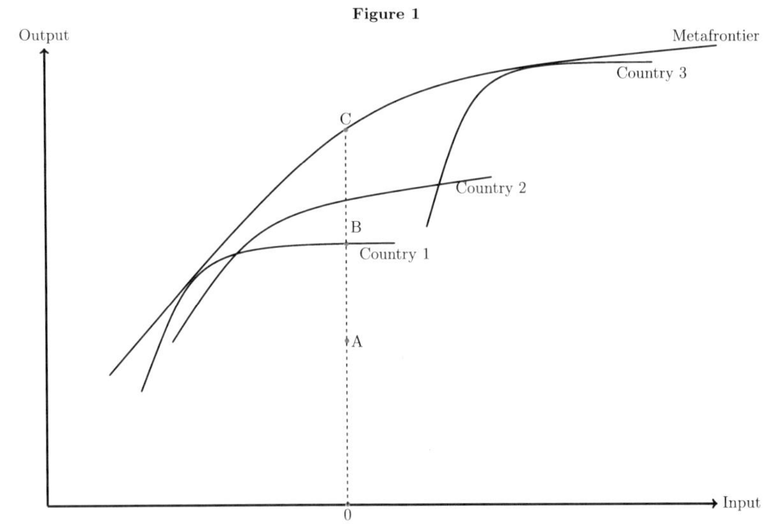

Fig. 1 Metafrontier model. The graph shows the group specific frontiers for three groups (Country 1 to 3) and the metafrontier. Own presentation based on O'Donnell et al. [28]

information on the construction of the standardised mortality rate). The standardised mortality rate takes differences in the age and sex distribution of the population into account. By means of the standardisation, we calculate an indicator of the population's health status that reflects the number of deaths that would have occurred if the European regions would have the same age and sex composition. To account for the health status of the population, we consider the inverse of the SMR. Panel (a) of Fig. 2 shows the spatial distribution of the average SMR. An visual inspections reveals a slight North-South gradient of the SMR for most countries with higher mortality rates in the South. In Italy and Spain the mortality rates appear to be lower in the South of the respective countries. Further, the SMR diverges between the regions in East and West Germany.

Health care infrastructure

The inclusion of health care inputs corresponds to the related literature [2, 6, 17, 23]. In our stylized specification of the country specific SFA model, we concentrate on the number of physicians (*doctors*) and the number of hospital beds (*beds*) both per 100,000 inhabitants as input variables representing the outpatient and inpatient sector, respectively as no data on the utilisation of health care services is available at such a high spatial resolution. Panels (b) and (c) of Fig. 2 display the average regional distribution of physicians and hospital beds, respectively. The spatial distribution of physicians does not exhibit a clear spatial pattern in Austria, Germany, Italy and Scandinavia. In France, the number of physicians is relatively low in the North. The area around Paris is an exception with a higher supply of physicians in comparison to the surrounding regions. The North of Spain is characterised by a higher supply of outpatient care. An eyeball inspection of Panel (c) reveals the highest densities of hospital beds in Finland. The supply of inpatient care exhibit a North-South gradient in Italy, Spain and Sweden with higher densities in the North of each country. Furthermore, the South of France and Austria and the North-East of Germany are characterised by slightly higher densities of hospital beds.

We further include the population density (*popdens*) to capture the degree of urbanisation of the region. Empirical evidence has shown a relationship between health and the population density of a region. However, a simple rural/urban differentiation does not sufficiently describe the relationship between health and location (see for instance Fassio et al. [16] and Adair [26]).

Socio-economic and demographic profiles

Besides the health care infrastructure demographic and socio-economic factors play an important role for the production of health and health outcomes [6]. In a health production framework those demographic and socio-economic factors can illustrate the utilisation of the health care infrastructure [20]. Due to varying regional utilisation structures, inefficiencies in the provision of health care services may arise. Possible sources of inefficiency include inaccurate and unnecessary medical treatments due to a lack of understanding and an over or under use of medical services [17, 20]. To control for different patterns in the utilisation of and the access to health care services we include the GDP per capita in (national) purchasing power parities, education, the share of the elderly and the population density in the inefficiency scaling function (as z_{it} in (4)) similar to Herwartz and

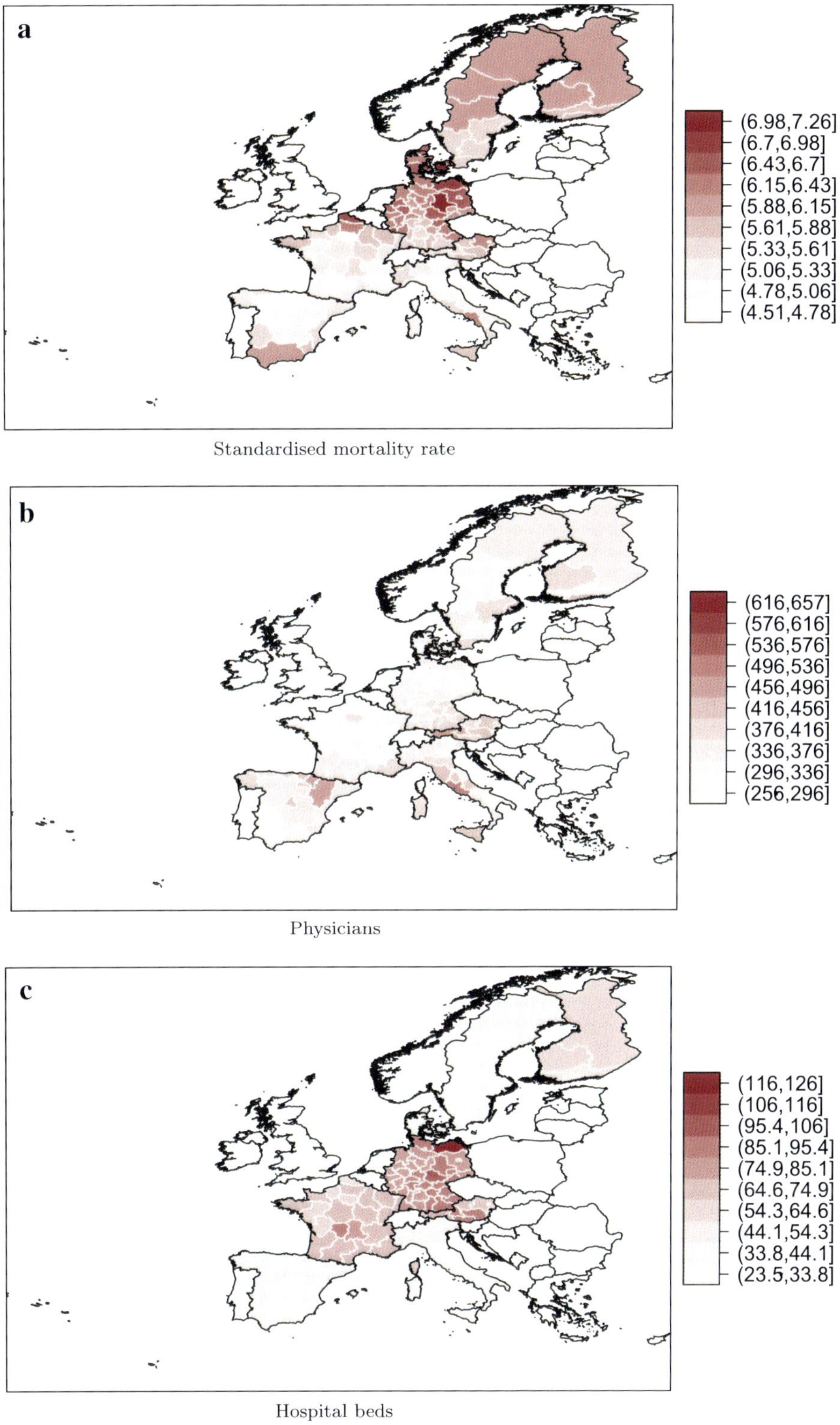

Fig. 2 Health care output and inputs. The figure presents the spatial distribution for the average standardised mortality rate (**a**) and physician density per 100,000 inhabitants (**b**) and the number of hospital beds per 10,000 inhabitants (**c**)

Schley [20]. The relationship between health and income is based on several factors. On the one side, income differences are directly related to differences in individual's and population's health status due to different conditions of life both at the individual and at the population level [25]. Empirical evidence has shown that regional (and individual) deprivation increases the risk of poor health [35]. As health care can be seen as a luxury good [30], regional deprivation does not only describe a direct link between health and income. Additionally, regional deprivation might account for access barriers to medical services [20]. We therefore include the GDP per capita (*gdp pc*) to describe regional deprivation.

The empirical literature has shown that a positive relationship between health and education exists [1, 12]. Higher education is related to a healthier life style which includes a healthy diet and exercises. Further, higher education is likely related to an improved understanding of medical treatments. To approximate education, we include the proportion of employees with a university degree as share of all employees (*education*). Both income and education can be seen to describe the access to and the utilisation of the regional health care services. To account for differences in the utilisation patterns associated with age, we include the share of the elderly (*age65*) as older age is related to an intensified need of medical treatment.

Additionally, we include the population density (*popdens*) in the inefficiency scaling function to control for factors influencing the efficiency of service production based on the location. As all countries offer a general coverage of the population by means of statutory health insurances or a taxed based National Health Services we do not control for price related access barriers.

Table 1 displays means, pooled standard deviations as well as within and between standard deviations. Cross-sectional heterogeneity across different NUTS 2 regions is more pronounced than the time heterogeneity. The stochastic frontier model for the production of health care in the European regions is estimated for all variables in the production function and *gdp p.c.* and *popdens* in logarithmic form.

Table 1 Descriptive Statistics. The table documents descriptive statistics for the 125 NUTS-2 regions from 2005 to 2014. The overall number of observations is 1149. In the second column the pooled sample means are reported, the third column contains the unbiased pooled standard deviations. In the last two columns the between and within sample standard deviations are presented, respectively

	Mean	SD	Between SD	Within SD
SMR	5.71	0.69	0.61	0.34
doctors	370.23	77.71	62.72	44.83
beds	600.19	236.59	235.98	29.12
popdensity	311.13	684.23	660.49	26.45
gdp p.c.	27647.00	6787.16	6556.47	1674.96
education	24.73	7.54	7.49	2.40
age65	0.19	0.03	0.03	0.01

Results and discussion

In the following, we discuss estimation and inferential results for the group specific stochastic frontier models and the metafrontier model. First, we discuss the relationship between the health care infrastructure and overall health. Second, we examine the extend to which demographic and socio-economic characteristics shape deviations from the health frontier. Third, we analyse the regional distribution of efficiency scores and how efficiency levels change with respect to the metafrontier estimation. If not mentioned otherwise, the discussion of estimation results refers to the nominal 5% significance level.

Elasticities of health care service provision

Table 2 documents the estimation results for the SFA model for pooled and group specific frontiers and the metafrontier model. Comparing the results of the group specific frontiers and the pooled model, which analyses the data for all countries simultaneously, shows that applying a joint model for all countries does not sufficiently capture the differences in health care production across the countries as the model parameters differ across models. To check the appropriateness of the metafrontier model, we apply a Likelihood Ratio (LR) test to test if technological differences between the countries are statistically significant.[3] Particularly, the test statistic for the LR test is $LR = 1214.8$ and χ^2 distributed with 50 degrees of freedom. We can therefore reject the null hypothesis of identical group frontiers.

The results of the group frontiers indicate a positive relationship between the number of physicians and health care outcomes. Solely, the estimated effect for doctors in Italy is negative. Somewhat surprising, the number of hospital beds negatively relates to population's health. This counter-intuitive effect might relate to an inappropriate distribution of health care infrastructure. Similarly, Herwartz and Schley [20] find a negative association between the supply of hospital beds and health outcomes in the German districts. Noticing the negative connection between inpatient care and health outcomes is in line with the supply-sensitivity of medical care. Accordingly, the supply and availability of medical resources influences its utilisation [36]. In other words, in regions with an increased level of inpatient care the hospital admission rates are relatively higher with likely adverse effects on health [36]. In line with this, Fisher et al. [18] find for the US that increased regional mortality rates are associated with a relatively high level of health care expenditure.

At first glance, the negative association of the population density and health seems counter-intuitive. However, as others have shown (see for instance [10, 16]) a low population density relates to an improved quality of life.

Table 2 Stochastic frontier and metafrontier estimation results (t-statistics in parentheses). This tables documents the estimation results from the regression model in (1) - (4) using data from 2005 to 2014. The second columns shows the regression results for a pooled model for all countries. The last column gives the metafrontier parameter results as in (6). The t-statistics for the metafrontier parameters are based on simulated standard errors (simulation with 500 replications)

	Pooled	Austria	France	Germany	Italy	Scandinavia	Spain	Metafrontier
Output elasticities (x_{it})								
Intercept	0.013	-0.042	0.034	0.01	0.053	-0.04	0.065	0.152
	(1.42)	(-3.63)	(4.18)	(1.62)	(5.68)	(-5.91)	(4.05)	(11.31)
ln(*doctors*)	0.092	0.261	0.465	0.219	-0.07	0.539	0.161	0.125
	(4.11)	(3.90)	(12.33)	(5.59)	(-2.44)	(11.31)	(4.54)	(3.46)
ln(*beds*)	-0.109	-0.275	-0.551	-0.258	-0.149	-0.213	-0.148	-0.209
	(-13.67)	(-4.91)	(-16.46)	(-5.75)	(-3.46)	(-8.62)	(-2.88)	(-6.99)
ln(*popdens*)	-0.006	-0.071	-0.049	-0.058	-0.034	-0.079	-0.016	-0.035
	(-1.47)	(-8.25)	(-6.53)	(-7.19)	(-3.17)	(-8.41)	(-2.21)	(-4.19)
Effects on inefficiency (z_{it})								
Intercept	-1.49	-0.134	3.421	-1.193	1.455	-8.408	1.119	
	(-1.87)	(-0.07)	(3.73)	(-1.36)	(1.69)	(-1.72)	(1.47)	
ln(*gdp p.c.*)	-1.83	-5.878	-2.449	-3.344	-1.38	-1.765	-1.056	
	(-4.2)	(-4.43)	(-2.97)	(-4.78)	(-3.48)	(-0.67)	(-1.21)	
education	-0.031	-0.019	-0.089	-0.128	-0.39	-0.139	-0.12	
	(-2.2)	(-0.34)	(-3.29)	(-6.04)	(-5.20)	(-2.10)	(-3.69)	
age65	-4.26	-25.972	-22.513	2.791	5.303	23.964	0.303	
	(-1.03)	(-2.60)	(-4.00)	(0.63)	(1.03)	(1.18)	(0.06)	
ln(*popdens*)	0.564	-0.937	0.343	-0.451	0.092	-1.954	0.212	
	(4.03)	(-1.65)	(1.73)	(-1.70)	(0.54)	(-4.00)	(2.16)	
σ_V	0.994	0.932	0.953	0.943	0.966	0.924	0.984	
$\gamma = \sigma_u^2/\sigma^2$	0.318	0.92	0.882	0.72	0.846	0.731	0.842	
log-likelihood	968.757	138.016	350.592	525.984	228.379	153.657	179.541	
no of observations	1149	90	218	368	177	116	180	

A note of caution is in order regarding the interpretation of the empirical results due to the potential of estimation bias as a result of reversed causality. For instance, more health care services could possibly be available in regions with a higher need, i.e. poorer population's health. Nevertheless, the health care sector is a highly regulated market in which fundamental market mechanisms might fail [9]. For example, the regional planning of health care services is based on allocation formulas in Germany which do not or only implicitly take morbidity into account [20]. Moreover, it is noteworthy that regulators do not know mortality and morbidity rates at the time of structural planning weakening the potentials of endogeneity bias (see also [20]).

The effect of socio-economic factors on the efficiency of health care services

In order to identify how the access to and the utilisation of the health care systems shapes the efficient provision of medical services, we examine the relationships of demographic and socio-economic variables and the efficiencies of health care service provision. Interestingly, many estimated coefficients in the medium panel of Table 2 are significant.

Income positively relates to the efficient provision of medical services. The estimated coefficients attached to *gdp p.c.* lack statistical significance in Scandinavia and Spain. This result is intuitively appealing as low income families are likely confronted with access barriers resulting in a lower utilisation of and satisfaction with the health care system [13]. Furthermore, we diagnose a positive relationship between the proportion of university graduates in the overall number of employees and efficiency. The effect lacks statistical significance only in Austria. Education helps to improve the execution of medical treatments and might enhance the utilisation of preventive care which might reduce inefficiencies in the health care sector. Additionally, as empirical literature has shown, people with higher educational achievements might have a lower burden of disease due to healthier lifestyle choices [1, 12]. Initially, the positive association of the number of senior citizens and the performance of health care systems in Austria and France seems somewhat surprising. One would expect that more comorbidities linked with old age would likely decrease the efficient provision of health care services. Similarly, Eibich and Ziebarth [14] find a direct positive correlation between the share of the elderly and well-being at the individual level possibly related to the provision of improved health care resources in regions with an older population.

The relationship between the population density and inefficiency depends on the specified country frontier. We diagnose a negative association between efficiency and the population density in the pooled model and the model for Spain. In Scandinavia, the relationship is reversed. The effects lack significance for all other countries.

Taken together, the results provide important insights into how demographic and socio-economic factors shape the efficient provision of health care services. The results highlight that allocation rules for medical infrastructure should take those factors into account (see for instance Smith [34] for the case of the UK). Furthermore, reducing access barriers possibly increases the efficiency of health care service provision by promoting the utilisation of preventive care. Additionally, raising the awareness in health care personnel (i.e. physicians and nurses) for the needs of specific (deprived) population groups likely decreases inefficiency by possibly improving the communication leading to a better understanding of medical treatments (see also Herwartz and Schley [20]).

Metafrontier estimates

The different parameter estimates in the group specific frontiers indicate that differences in the production technology of the respective health care systems exist. To investigate if those country specifics trigger differences in the efficiency of the health care provision, we analyse the health care systems by means of a metafrontier approach. The last row of Table 2 reports the parameter estimates and t-statistics based on simulated standard errors (see Battese et al. [4]). In line with the parameter estimates attached to the elasticities of the pooled model and the group frontiers, the results reveal a positive association of physicians and health. We find a negative relationship between hospital beds and the populations density and health.

Regional distribution of efficiency scores

Table 3 documents the average efficiency scores[4] for the pooled model, the country-specific frontiers, the MTR and the technical efficiencies with respect to the metafrontier. Note that the efficiency scores of the country-specific frontiers cannot be compared across groups as they are calculated with respect to different technologies [28].

For the sampled countries, the technical efficiency scores for the pooled model range from 0.6518 in Ciudad Autónoma de Ceuta, Spain and 0.9985 in Övre Norrland, Sweden with an overall average of 0.9696. In the pooled model the regions in Scandinavia perform the best while the Italian regions exhibit relatively low efficiency scores. These results are intuitively appealing as the Scandinavia social security systems enjoy an excellent reputation. Panel (a) of Fig. 3 shows the regional distribution of the average technical efficiency scores of the pooled model. A visual inspection reveals a limited regional variation of efficiency across countries.

The average efficiency scores of the country-specific frontiers are slightly lower compared to the pooled model. The relatively high group-specific efficiencies indicate that the regional health care systems use the available resources efficiently.

In the next step, we compare the MTR and the TE scores with respect to the metafrontier (TE^*). The MTR measures how close the country-specific frontier is to the metafrontier. Higher (lower) values of the MTR imply a smaller (larger) technology gap between the country specific individual frontier and the metafrontier. The MTR ranges from 0.7071 (Sjælland, Denmark) to unity (Övre Norrland in Denmark, Länsi-Suomi in Finland, and Basilicata in Italy). The MTR values equal to unity indicate that the individual country frontiers are tangent to the metafrontier. The TE^* range from 0.5719 in Ciudad Autónoma de Ceuta, Spain to 0.9979 in Länsi-Suomi, Finland. The overall mean is 0.8375. Panel (b)

Table 3 Technical efficiency (TE) and metatechnology ratio (MTR) for group frontiers and metafrontier. This table documents the average technical efficiencies for the respective countries for the pooled model in the first column, the average efficiencies for the group specific models in the second column, the average MTR in the third column and the average TE with respect to the metafrontier (TE*) in the rightmost column for 2005 to 2014

	TE (pooled model)	TE (country specific)	MTR	TE*
Austria	0.9700	0.9403	0.8668	0.8146
France	0.9746	0.9461	0.8938	0.8462
Germany	0.9669	0.9577	0.8785	0.8412
Italy	0.9583	0.9377	0.9097	0.8552
Scandinavia	0.9867	0.9662	0.8563	0.8249
Denmark	0.9725	0.9997	0.7883	0.7881
Finland	0.9933	0.9904	0.8883	0.8795
Sweden	0.9911	0.9421	0.8772	0.8234
Spain	0.9592	0.9207	0.8959	0.8244

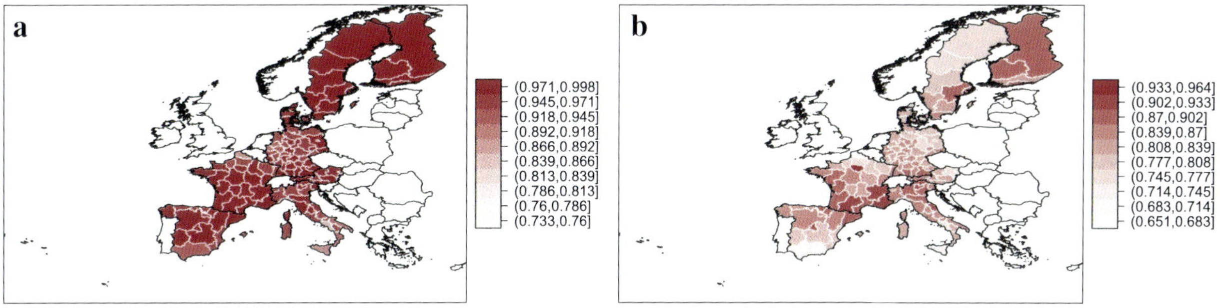

TE pooled model TE*

Fig. 3 Spatial distribution of the average technical efficiency scores for the pooled model (**a**) and the TE* with respect to the metafrontier (**b**)

of Fig. 3 displays the regional distribution of the efficiency scores with respect to the metafrontier. The graph highlights some interesting regional pattern with higher efficiencies in the North of Finland, Italy and Spain and the South of France and Germany. Somewhat surprisingly, the MTR results hint at a large technology gap in Scandinavia. In combination with high country-specific efficiency scores, the results indicate that the regions in Scandinavia would profit from rising the production potentials as the productivity with respect to their own frontier is already very high. Similar to the results of others (see for instance Joumard and Nicq [22]) this might highlight failing market mechanisms within a highly regulated health care system. For Italy and Spain, which on average perform the worst with respect to the pooled (and country specific) frontiers, the results imply that a better management of and an improved access to and utilisation of the available resources could likely lead to efficiency gains.

One can interpret the metafrontier as highlighting long-run production potentials [27]. Accordingly, the relatively low TE* hint at substantial scopes of improvement in the regional provision of health care services in Europe.

Conclusion

The health care systems around Europe are faced by challenges regarding the demographic change along with expensive medical innovations. In regard of those developments an efficient use of the scarce financial resources is necessary. Based on the different health care systems in Europe, the European governments adopt different strategies to deal with this and to guarantee an efficient use of the financial resources.

This paper analyses the efficiency of health service provision across several European countries by means of a stochastic metafrontier approach. The application of a metafrontier has the advantage that it is possible to distinguish between regional efficiency in relation to the country's own frontier and an European metafrontier.

The results show that a single European stochastic frontier model cannot sufficiently capture the heterogeneous conditions of health care provision in Europe. The comparison of the spatial distribution of the efficiency scores from a pooled European model assuming a homogeneous technology hints at significant efficiency differences across countries. The Scandinavian countries achieve on average the highest efficiency scores in a pooled model. Surprisingly, the regions in Scandinavia lag behind other regions with respect to the metafrontier highlighting potentials for rising the productivity in these regions by, for instance, easing some regulatory burdens. The relatively lower efficiency scores in Italy and Spain hint at substantial opportunities to rise the populations' health by improving the management of and the access to the available resources.

Endnotes

[1] For a more detailed discussion of the minimization problem in (6) see Battese et al. [4] and O'Donnell et al. [28].

[2] For Germany, we approximate the number of physicians and hospital beds by the respective number on federal state level as no information on NUTS-2 level is available.

[3] The test statistic for the LR test is $LR = -2\,[\ln(L(H0)) - \ln(L(H1))]$, where $\ln(L(H0))$ is the log-likelihood value of a stochastic frontier model estimated by pooling the data for all countries, and $\ln(L(H1))$ is the sum of the log-likelihood values of the country specific stochastic frontier models. The test statistic is χ^2 distributed. The degrees of freedom are the difference between the number of parameters estimated in the individual stochastic frontier models and the number of parameters estimated in the pooled model.

[4] The point estimates of technical efficiency for region i at time t are defined according to Battese and Coelli [3] as $\mathrm{TE}_{it} = E(exp(-u_{it}|\epsilon_{it})$ where ϵ_{it} is the composite error term of the production function, i.e. $\epsilon_{it} = v_{it} - u_{it}$.

Appendix A: Data description

Sample

The data cover the period 2005 to 2014. We analyse the health care systems at the NUTS-2 (Nomenclature des unités territoriales statistiques). The data is mainly drawn from the Eurostat database. For Germany, the infrastructural variables were not available at NUTS level. We approximate the number of hospital beds and physicians by the respective number of the federal states.

Standardised mortality rate

Annual data on sex and age specific number of deaths and inhabitants on district level are provided by the Eurostat online data base. As the regions' population differ in age and sex composition we use the direct standardisation to obtain a standardised mortality rate. The mortality rate then represents the expected number of deaths if the age and sex structures in all districts were identical. We use the European standard population 2013 for the standardisation.

Health care infrastructure

The number of physicians and hospital beds are provided by Eurostat. Both variables are measured per 100.000 inhabitants.

Socio-economic and demographic characteristics

The data on socio-economic and demographic characteristics are drawn from the Eurostat data base. The population density is the number of inhabitants per $1.000m^2$. The gdp p.c. is the regional gdp per capita in (national) purchasing power parities. Education is approximated by the share of employees with a university degree. We calculate the share of the elderly based on the population statistics provided by Eurostat.

Abbreviations

LR: Likelihood ratio; MTR: Metatechnology ratio; NUTS-2: Nomenclature des unités territoriales statistiques; SFA: Stochastic frontier analysis; SMR: Standardised mortality ratio; TE: Technical efficiency; WHO: World Health Organisation

Acknowledgments

I sincerely thank two anonymous referees, the members of my working group and the participants of the "13. DIBOGS-Workshop" in Hamburg for helpful advices and discussions. Financial support by the German Research Foundation (DFG) via the research training group 1644 "Scaling Problems in Statistics" is gratefully acknowledged.

Funding

The research project was supported by the German Research Foundation (DFG) via the research training group 1644 "Scaling Problems in Statistics".

Competing interests

The authors declare that they have no competing interests.

References

1. Aka B, Dumont J-C. Health, education and economic growth: Testing for long-run relationships and causal links in the United States. Appl Econ Int Dev. 2008;8(2):101–10.
2. Asandului L, Roman M, Fatulescu P. The efficiency of healthcare systems in Europe: A data envelopment analysis approach. Proc Econ Finance. 2014;10:261–8.
3. Battese GE, Coelli TJ. Prediction of firm-level technical efficiencies with a generalized frontier production function and panel data. J Econ. 1988;38(3):387–99.
4. Battese GE, Prasada Rao DS, O'Donnell CJ. A metafrontier production function for estimation of technical efficiencies and technology gaps for firms operating under different technologies. J Prod Anal. 2004;21(1): 91–103.
5. Bos JW, Schmiedel H. Is there a single frontier in a single European banking market?. J Bank Finance. 2007;31(7):2081–102.
6. Chakrabarti A, Rao DN. Efficiency in Production of Health: A stochastic frontier analysis for Indian states. In: Tavidze A, editor. Global Economics: New Research. Nova Science Publishers; 2007. p. 105–28.
7. Chevreul K, Durand-Zaleski I, Bahrami S, Hernández-Quevedo C, Mladovsky P. France: Health system review. Health Syst Trans. 2010;12(6): 1:291.
8. Coelli TJ, Rao DSP, O'Donnell CJ, Battese GE. An Introduction to Efficiency and Productivity Analysis. New York: Springer Science & Business Media; 2005.
9. Correia I, Veiga P. Geographic distribution of physicians in Portugal. Eur J Health Econ. 2010;11(4):383–93.
10. Cramer V, Torgersen S, Kringlen E. Quality of life in a city: The effect of population density. Soc Indicators Res. 2004;69(1):103–16.
11. Cullen MR, Cummins C, Fuchs VR. Geographic and racial variation in premature mortality in the U.S.: Analyzing the disparities. PloS ONE. 2012;7(4):e32930.
12. Cutler DM, Lleras-Muney A. Education and health: Evaluating theories and evidence. NBER Working Paper. 2006;12352:1:36.
13. Dubay L, Kenney GM. Health care access and use among low-income children: Who fares best?. Health Aff. 2001;20(1):112–21.
14. Eibich P, Ziebarth NR. Examining the structure of spatial health effects in Germany using hierarchical Bayes models. Reg Sci Urban Econ. 2014;49: 305–20.
15. Evans DB, Tandon A, Murray CJL, Lauer JA. The comparative efficiency of national health systems in producing health: An analysis of 191 countries. Br Med J. 2001;323(7308):307–10.
16. Fassio O, Rollero C, De Piccoli N. Health, quality of life and population density: A preliminary study on "contextualized" quality of life. Soc Indic Res. 2013;110(2):479–88.
17. Felder S, Tauchmann H. Federal state differentials in the efficiency of health production in Germany: An artifact of spatial dependence?. Eur J Health Econ. 2013;14(1):21–39.
18. Fisher ES, Wennberg DE, Stukel TA, Gottlieb DJ, Lucas FL, Pinder EL. The implications of regional variations in Medicare spending. Part 1: The content, quality, and accessibility of care. Ann Internal Med. 2003;138(4): 273–87.
19. Greene W. Distinguishing between heterogeneity and inefficiency: Stochastic frontier analysis of the World Health Organization's panel data on national health care systems. Health Econ. 2004;13(10):959–80.
20. Herwartz H, Schley K. Improving health care service provision by adapting to regional diversity: An efficiency analysis for the case of Germany. Health Policy. 2018;122(3):293–300.
21. Jacobs R, Smith P, Street A. Measuring Efficiency in Health Care: Analytic Techniques and Health Policy. Cambridge and New York: Cambridge University Press; 2006.
22. Joumard IAC, Nicq C. Health Care Systems: Efficiency and Institutions, Volume No. 769. 2010.
23. Kathuria V, Sankar D. Inter-state disparities in health outcomes in rural India: An analysis using a stochastic production frontier approach. Devel Policy Rev. 2005;23(2):145–63.

24. Lakner S, Muñoz TB, Aedo ER, Brümmer B. Technical efficiency in the Chilean agribusiness sector - A stocahstic meta frontier approach. Agribusiness. 2013;33(3):287–471.
25. Lynch JW, Smith GD, Kaplan George A, House JS. Income inequality and mortality: Importance to health of individual income, psychosocial environment, or material conditions. Br Med J. 2000;320(7243):1200–4.
26. McDade TW, Adair LS. Defining the "urban" in urbanization and health: A factor analysis approach. Soc Sci Med. 2001;53(1):55–70.
27. Mohi Uddin M, Brümmer B, Johanes Peters K. Technical efficiency and metatechnology ratios under varying resource endowment in different production systems: A stochastic metafrontier model in Bangladesh dairy farms. China Agric Econ Rev. 2014;6(3):485–505.
28. O'Donnell CJ, Prasada Rao DS, Battese GE. Metafrontier frameworks for the study of firm-level efficiencies and technology ratios. Empir Econ. 2008;34(2):231–55.
29. Ozegowski S, Sundmacher L. Understanding the gap between need and utilization in outpatient care - The effect of supply side determinants on regional inequities. Health Policy. 2014;114(1):54–63.
30. Parkin D, McGuire A, Yule B. Aggregate health care expenditures and national income. J Health Econ. 1987;6(2):109–27.
31. Porter ME. A strategy for health care reform - Toward a value-based system. N Engl J Med. 2009;361(2):109–12.
32. Porter ME, Teisberg EO. Redefining Health Care: Creating Value-based Competition on Results. Boston: Harvard Business Press; 2006.
33. Rettenmaier A, Wang Z. Regional variations in medical spending and utilization: A longitudinal analysis of US Medicare population. Health Econ. 2012;21(2):67–82.
34. Smith PC. Resource allocation and purchasing in the health sector: The English experience. Bull World Health Organ. 2008;86(11):884–8.
35. Stafford M, Marmot M. Neighbourhood deprivation and health: Does it affect us all equally?. Int J Epidemiol. 2003;32(3):357–66.
36. The Darthmouth Atlas of Health Care. Supply-Sensitive Care. 2018. http://www.dartmouthatlas.org/keyissues/issue.aspx?con=2937. Accessed 22 Feb.
37. Wang H-J, Schmidt P. One-step and two-step estimation of the effects of exogenous variables on technical efficiency levels. J Prod Anal. 2002;18(2):129–44.

10

Socioeconomic inequality of diabetes patients' health care utilization in Denmark

Camilla Sortsø[1,2], Jørgen Lauridsen[1*], Martha Emneus[2], Anders Green[2,3] and Peter Bjødstrup Jensen[2]

Abstract

Understanding socioeconomic inequalities in health care is critical for achieving health equity. The aim of this paper is threefold: 1) to quantify inequality in diabetes health care service utilization; 2) to understand determinants of these inequalities in relation to socio-demographic and clinical morbidity factors; and 3) to compare the empirical outcome of using income level and educational level as proxies for Socio Economic Status (SES).

Data on the entire Danish population of diabetes patients in 2011 ($N = 318,729$) were applied. Patients' unique personal identification number enabled individual patient data from several national registers to be linked. A concentration index approach with decomposition into contributing factors was applied. Differences in diabetes patients' health care utilization patterns suggest that use of services differ among patients of lower and higher SES, despite the Danish universal health care system. Especially, out-patient services, rehabilitation and specialists in primary care show different utilization patterns according to SES. Comparison of the empirical outcome from using educational level and income level as proxy for patients' SES indicate important differences in inequality estimates. While income, alike other measures of labor market attachment, to a certain extent is explained by morbidity and thus endogenous, education is more decisive for patients' ability to take advantage of the more specialized services provided in a universal health care system.

JEL Classifications: I10, I12, I14, I18

Background

Persistent differences in health by socio-economic status (SES) have long been a serious health policy concern in many European countries [9, 10, 43]. Evidence on the contributing factors to inequality in health in general and disease specific inequality may guide future efforts to reduce unequal distributions of for instance health care [9, 10]. This study presents – to our knowledge - first time evidence on the composition of socioeconomic inequality in diabetes patients' health care utilization patterns.

Diabetes Mellitus is one of contemporary time's most burdensome chronic diseases [52]. It is well known that socio-economic inequality exists in diabetes with higher incidence and mortality among lower socio-economic groups [1, 4, 18, 25, 31, 37]. Despite universal coverage health care systems, social inequalities have been evidenced in most European countries [43]. Several Danish reports have underlined that large differences exist in compliance to treatment, especially preventive efforts and retention of life style changes among chronic patients [11–13]. Access to health care, hence, is not only a question of equal potential access, as in a universal health care system like the Danish. The concept of "realized access" [20] reflects patients' actual use of the available services. In health care systems with universal coverage, realized access may be constrained by financial and organizational barriers to the use of benefits, such as required co-payments or other out-of-pocket payments, restrictions on specialty referrals, or lack of proximity to health care facilities [20]. Differences in use of health care within patient groups of same need provide insight into patients' ability to take advantage of the services provided in a universal health care system. Such knowledge can guide future effort to increase success of

* Correspondence: jtl@sam.sdu.dk
[1]Centre of Health Economics Research (COHERE), Department of Business and Economics, University of Southern Denmark, Campusvej 55, DK-5s30 Odense M, Denmark
Full list of author information is available at the end of the article

early detection, secondary prevention and treatment. This is highly important, not only for patients' quality and length of life, but also for societies to control the costs of the increasing diabetes populations [21, 38].

Several studies have assessed the level of socioeconomic inequalities in health using concentration indices and concentration curves [33, 43, 44, 47]. Taking advantage of the detailed Danish registers, we apply data on individual patient level on all Danish diabetes patients [41]. We have previously documented that diabetes patients of lower SES experience higher morbidity and mortality [39, 40]. Access to comprehensive data on patients' morbidity patterns is unique, allowing for investigation of novel associations between SES, morbidity and health care utilization patterns investigating the inquiry whether patients' health care usage reflects their need defined through morbidity.

The present study sets out three research inquiries 1) to quantify socioeconomic inequality in diabetes health care and pharmaceutical usage (reflected through cost accounts), 2) to decompose these inequalities by quantifying the contribution attributable to individual demographic determinants and individual morbidity characteristics, and 3) to compare the empirical outcome from using educational level versus income level as proxy for patients' SES. Thus, the outline of the paper is as follows. Next to this introduction, Section 2 briefly presents the econometric methods applied. Following this, Section 3 describes data collection and preparation, while the results are presented in Section 4. Finally, Section 5 provides a discussion of the results, while Section 6 rounds off with concluding remarks.

Methods

Similar to previous studies initiated by Wagstaff *et al.* [49] we use the concentration index as our measure of relative socioeconomic inequality in healthcare costs. A concentration curve $L(s)$ plots the cumulative proportion of the population (ranked by socioeconomic status (SES), beginning with lowest SES) against the cumulative proportion of costs. If $L(s)$ coincides with the diagonal everyone is equally off. However, if $L(s)$ lies below the diagonal, then inequality in healthcare costs exists and favors those with high SES. The further $L(s)$ lies from the diagonal, the larger the degree of inequality. The concentration index, C, is defined as twice the area between $L(s)$ and the diagonal and takes a value of 0, when everyone is equally off regardless of SES. The minimum and maximum values of C are –1 and +1, respectively; these occur in the (hypothetical) situation where costs are concentrated in the hand of the least disadvantaged and the most disadvantaged person, respectively. Thus, the larger negative value of C, the more costs concentrate among low SES groups. A computational formula for C was given by Kakwani et al. [27] as $C = \frac{2}{N\mu}\sum_{i=1}^{N} y_i R_i - 1$, where $\mu = \frac{1}{N}\sum_{i=1}^{N} y_i$ is the mean of observed costs, N the sample size, y_i observed costs, and R_i the fractional rank defined according to Kakwani et al. as $R_i = \frac{i-1}{N} + \frac{1}{2}$. Following the same authors, C can be conveniently computed as the covariance of y_i and R_i, i.e. $C = \frac{2}{\mu}\,\text{cov}_w(y_i, R_i) = \frac{2}{N\mu}\sum_{i=1}^{N}(y_i-\mu)\left(R_i-\frac{1}{2}\right)$.

A straightforward way of decomposing the predicted degree of inequality into the contributions of explanatory factors was proposed by Wagstaff et al. [48]. Adapting their approach to the present case, we use a traditional linear regression that links healthcare costs to the determinants, leading to a decomposition of the concentration index of predicted costs as $\hat{C} = \sum_k \frac{\beta_k \bar{x}_k}{\hat{\mu}} C_k$, where $\hat{\mu}$ is the mean of predicted costs, $\bar{x}_k$ the mean of the determinant x_k, and C_k the concentration index of x_k (defined analogously to C).

In order to assess sampling variability and to obtain standard errors for the estimated quantities, in particular for the concentration indices and the contributions, i.e. the $\frac{\beta_k \bar{x}_k}{\hat{\mu}} C_k$ parts, we apply a "bootstrap" procedure ([14];) in a four-step manner much similar to van Doorslaer et al. [44]: First, a random sub-sample of the size of the original sample is drawn with replacement. Second, the entire set of calculations, as specified above, are performed on this sample. Third, this whole process is repeated 1,000 times, each leading to replicate estimates. Fourth, using the obtained 1,000 replicates, standard deviations and t statistics can be computed for all calculated quantities.

Data

The study is part of the Diabetes Impact Study 2013 [21, 22, 38–40]. Data was collected from the Danish National Diabetes Register (NDR) [6], the Danish National Patient Register [34], the Danish National Prescription Registry [29], the Danish National Health Service Register [3], the Danish Civil Registration System [5], and social registers at Statistics Denmark (SD).

The study population covers all patients registered in NDR diagnosed before 1st of January 2012 and alive 1st of January 2011, described in detail elsewhere (1), leaving $N = 318{,}729$ patients. The analytical time is a window of one calendar year (2011) in a cross-sectional design. This design does not by definition allow for causational conclusions over time to be drawn, but it enables identification of differences between groups and hence cost pattern exploration [26].

The variables for the study may conveniently be grouped in three overall groups: Patients SES and demographic characteristics; health care usage, and patients' need for health care.

Patients' socioeconomic, demographic and morbidity characteristics are summarized and described in details in Table 1. Patients' *annual gross income* is applied as ranking variable, since this measure is the most common measure of SES in the literature analysing inequality through concentration indices [43–45]. Several studies, including those mentioned here, use household rather than individual income, given that the former is a more comprehensive expression of the patients' economic abilities. Household information, including household income, was not included in the present study. Furthermore, patients' *highest attained educational level*, based on the Danish Educational Nomenclatura with 13 educational groups, is applied as ranking variable as well, since this measure is frequently used in public health literature due to its simplicity and universality [19]. When education is used as a ranking variable, the full nine level definition is used, and otherwise a three level definition. Following what has been used in previous studies, included demographic variables are *age, gender, ethnicity* (*Dane, immigrant* or *descendant*), *civil status* (*married/partnership, unmarried, widowed/longest living partner* or *divorced/separated*), *region of residence, degree of urbanity of residence*, and *labour market status* (*unemployed, early retired, retired, not in job for other reasons*). Finally, relevant and available morbidity characteristics were added, including *incidence in 2011, complication group (CG0, CG1* or *CG2)* and *mortality* (alive or not in 2011) measures. Alike what has been discussed elsewhere, there may be endogeneity problems connected to in particular labour market status, as this affects not only health but also income rank. However, we expect the endogeneity problems to be less profound when using education as SES measure, given that education is taken relatively early in the life course and thus precedes present labour market status.

Turning to **health care usage**, overall volume of treatment related health care, including pharmaceuticals, received by the individual patient, are approximated by the costs of these services through hospital and health insurance statements. This implies that number or type of services is not considered but merely total costs by sectors. Measurements of health care and pharmaceutical consumption in the categories defined, as well as choices of appropriate cost units, are described in details in Table 2. Specifically, a total of nine health care cost components were available, made up of three components summarizing hospital inpatient care (*total inpatient services, inpatient services for stays longer than the average patient in the Diagnosis Related Grouping (DRG) group,* and *inpatient services for rehabilitation*), three components summarizing outpatient care (*total outpatient services, outpatient services for stays longer than the average patient in the DRG group,* and *outpatient services for rehabilitation*), two components summarizing primary care (*services in general practices* and *services for privately practising specialists*), and one component summarizing *prescribed pharmaceutical consumption.*

Patients' need for health care should ideally be measured by health care professionals' clinical assessment of the individual patient. Unfortunately, such data are unavailable, and instead we apply clinically defined morbidity patterns to proxy patients' need. Patients are classified into three complication groups (*complication group 0 – CG0, complication group 1 – CG1,* and *complication group 2 – CG2*), according to the progression of their diabetes. While CG0 indicates patients without registered complications, CG1 covers those with moderate or minor problems, and CG2 those with severe complications; see Table 3 and Green et al. [21] for details.

Results

Table 4 presents concentration indices using income as ranking variable. Contributions of socioeconomic, demographic and morbidity determinants to the predicted inequality (the former in percentage of the latter) is presented as well. As income is used as ranking variable, education serves as a control variable only, and thus is applied in the simpler three categories version. Regression coefficients and concentration indices for each of the determinants are given in Table 7 in Appendix.

Overall, the magnitudes of the figures in the table are modest, reflecting the Danish universal health care system with equal access to treatment [50]. Observed and predicted concentration indices for most of the cost variables are negative meaning that costs concentrate among patients of lower income groups. This is illustrated in Fig. 1, where concentration indices to the left are interpreted as costs accumulating among lower SES groups, while the right-side contributions are interpreted reversely.

In the decomposition analysis, we included patients' morbidity patterns, degree of complications at time of analysis, and whether the patient was diagnosed or died in the current year (2011). Ideally, patients' morbidity patterns should explain inequality in the distribution of health care costs, if costs were allocated exactly according to patients' need. This, of course, is an unrealistic expectation, since morbidity indicators cannot capture patients' exact need, and since costs of services cannot proxy the exact received number of services needed. From Fig. 1 it is clear that especially in-patient health care services inhibit inequality, favoring patients with lower incomes. This corresponds well to these patients

Table 1 Definition of socioeconomic, sociodemographic and morbidity characteristics

Characteristics	Definitions	Categories
Socioeconomics		
Highest educational level attained	Highest educational level attained at date of data extraction, based on the main groups in the Danish educational Nomenclature with 13 educational groups based on years of education.	Variable with 3 or 9 categories: 1) Primary education (<11 years) 2) Middle high education (11 to 15 years 3) Higher education (16+ years) 1) Primary education 2) Upper secondary education 3) Vocational education and training 4) Qualifying educational programmes 5) Short cycle higher education 6) Vocational bachelor's education 7) Bachelor programmes 8) Master programmes 9) PhD programmes
Income level	Annual gross income 2011 (DKK)	
Demographics		
Gender	Gender	1) Male 2) Female
Age	Age in mid-year	Continuous
Civil status	Marital status	1) Married or in civil partnership 2) Unmarried 3) Widow or longest living partner 4) Divorced or cancelled partnership
Ethnicity	Based on registrations in the Central Person Register 2011.	1) Ethnic Dane 2) Immigrant 3) Descendant
Region of residence	Residence 2011 in relation to the five Danish regions	1) "Capital Region of Denmark" 2) "Region Zealand" 3) "Region of Southern Denmark" 4) "Central Denmark Region" 5) "North Denmark Region"
Urbanity	Residence in type of geographic area in relation to urbanity	1) City 2) Suburbs 3) Outer areas/country side
Occupational status	Affiliation to the labour market	1) Affiliated to the labour market (employed or self-employed) 2) Unemployed (maternal leave, job seeker allowance) 3) Unemployed (unemployment benefit) 4) Education 5) Early retirement 6) Retired 7) Child
Morbidity		
Incident 2011	Patient diagnosed in calendar year 2011	0) Diagnosed in year ≠ 2011 1) Diagnosed in 2011
Complication group at present	Complication group at 31st of December 2011	1) CG0 2) CG1 3) CG2
Complication group at diagnosis	Complication group at diagnosis	1) CG0 2) CG1 3) CG2
Mortality 2011	Death in 2011	0) Alive 2011 1) Death 2011

experiencing higher morbidity and mortality [39, 40]. Looking at the decomposition of inequality for in-patient care, (Fig. 2), it is seen that morbidity patterns explain a large part of predicted inequality. Especially, the morbidity indicators severe complications at time of analysis and death in 2011 have marked influences on

Table 2 Definition of nine health care usage cost components

Cost component	Cost unit
Inpatient and outpatient services delivered in Danish hospitals registered in the National Patient Register divided into the following components: 1) Inpatient services 2) Inpatient services for stays longer than the average patient in this DRG-group 3) Inpatient services for rehabilitation 4) Outpatient services 5) Outpatient services for stays longer than the average patient in this DAGS-group 6) Outpatient services for rehabilitation	Diagnosis Related Grouping (DRG) system and Danish Ambulant Grouping System (DAGS) tariffs - year 2012 [35]. The DRG-tariff system is developed for administrative purpose and based on rough average costs across hospitals for specific diagnostic groups. Excludes interest and depreciation of buildings and equipment while other overhead costs are included
Primary care services delivered by general practitioners and privately practicing specialists such as: dentists, physiotherapists, chiropractors, chiropodists who are registered in the National Health Service Register divided into the following components: 1) Services in general practices 2) Services for privately practicing specialists	Reimbursement fees between the National Health Insurance scheme and private practicing physicians are used as cost units. General Practitioners are compensated by regions through a combination of per capita fee (app. 30% of total) and fee for service (app. 70%) [32]. To reflect this payment scheme in the unit cost, 43.8% of the fee for service in general practice was added on top. Overhead costs covered by capitation fee were hence not distributed across numbers of visits, as would have been most appropriate, but by resource burden.
Prescribed pharmaceuticals dispensed by Danish pharmacies and registered in the Danish national prescription register. (Pharmaceuticals consumed in hospitals are included in DRG-tariffs. Over-the-counter drugs are not included in the statements).	Total sales price includes patient out of pocket payments since costs of prescribed pharmaceuticals are shared between the patient and the primary health care sector by a copayment scheme where patients are reimbursed according to their need. These costs were aggregated since total costs are measured regardless of who pays. 20% VAT was subtracted.

inequality in that costs accumulate among patients with these morbidity characteristics, who are also those with the lowest educational level. Among immigrants and elder (75+), the pattern, however, is opposite with costs accumulating to a higher extent among the higher income groups.

As shown in Table 4, concentration indices for outpatient rehabilitation and specialist treatment in primary care are positive, contrary to the other cost variables. However, contributions from determinants are not significant and thus not illustrated.

Turning to the socioeconomic determinants, especially the higher income patients are receiving outpatient services, whereas the lower income patients are receiving more inpatient services and services in general practice.

According to patients' ethnicity, negative regression coefficients (Table 7 in Appendix), imply that immigrants accumulate lower costs than do ethnic Danes. Given that immigrants have lower incomes (as shown by

Table 3 Patient need for health care, as defined by complication state classification

Complication group	Health state[a]
Complication group 0 (CG0)	Diabetes without registered complications
Complication group 1 (CG1)	Moderate or minor complications, problems with eyes, heart, kidney and nervous system, minor amputations below the ancle, bypass operation and some eye operations
Complication group 2 (CG2) –	Severe complications: blindness, amputation above the ancle, severe heart failure, kidney transplant or dialysis

[a]ICD codes defined for each complication group is given in Table 6 in Appendix

the negative concentration indices of Table 7 in Appendix), this observation conflicts with the general observation of costs being concentrated among low income groups. However, a potential explanation may be that costs are relatively more concentrated among the higher socioeconomic groups of immigrants than is the case for ethnic Danes. This somewhat surprising tendency, which is observed for in-patient as well as out-patient care and for pharmaceuticals, even when all other demographics and morbidity patterns are taken into account, may be explained by immigrants experiencing language and cultural barriers hindering them in taking full advantage of the Danish universal health care system [12].

For labor market affiliation, the pattern is much similar across cost variables. Especially, being retired contributes highly to the level of inequality with magnitudes around 20-25% of the predicted inequalities in costs. Only children and patients under education have lower costs than patients in job whereas all the other categories in general incur higher costs, especially early retired. Turning to age and gender, it can be seen that these also contribute markedly to inequality. Given that young people are of better health, it is not surprising that they generate lower costs, and it is also to be expected that they have lower incomes, as many of them are studying or in the beginning of their labor market career. However, for the elder group, a potential interpretation may be that elder with low incomes are disfavored with respect to treatment cost.

From differences across the regions, a pattern is seen, which is also reflected in the level of urbanity, where especially residents in the country side use less resources

Table 4 Decomposition of inequality in health care and pharmaceutical usage ranked by income

Ranked by income	SECONDARY CARE										PRIMARY CARE				PHARMACEUTICALS	
	INPATIENT						OUTPATIENT									
	Care		long stays		Rehabilitation		Care		Rehabilitation		General pracitice		Specialist			
Number of observations	318,684		318,684		318,684		209,530		8,089		318,684		318,684		318,684	
Mean	20996.5	***	718.561	***	236.955	***	16836.740	***	3954.549	***	3069.671	***	2108.611	***	7489.03	***
C (observed)	−0.176	***	−0.230	***	−0.202	***	−0.036	***	0.024	***	−0.063	***	0.003	**	−0.038	***
C (predicted)	−0.180	***	−0.245	***	−0.207	***	−0.043	***	0.011	*	−0.064	***	−0.026	***	−0.040	***
C (unexplained)	0.004	*	0.016	**	0.004		0.006	***	0.013	***	0.001		0.029	***	0.002	**
Determinants (reference group)	C	Sig.	C	Sig.	C	Sig.	C	Sig.	C	Sig.	C	Sig.	C	Sig.	C	Sig.
SES																
Income	0.06		−0.81		0.28		−3.41		−3.72		1.10	*	99.38		−2.81	
Educational level (high education)																
Primary education	3.67	***	2.73		0.81		−14.15	***	29.22		14.78	***	97.09		2.46	
Medium education	−1.21	***	−1.18		0.39		2.26		−5.93		−4.89	***	1.99		2.45	***
Age and gender (Males0-14) (Females0-14)																
M15-29	−0.66	***	−0.86	***	0.18	**	−3.55	***	2.49		0.16	***	1.88		−0.82	***
M30-44	6.73	***	6.29	***	−1.76	**	24.22	***	−25.07		−6.20	***	−11.23		9.30	***
M45-59	20.45	***	20.20	***	−9.69	***	71.29	***	−58.47		−32.51	***	28.93		49.04	***
M60-74	1.80	***	1.97	***	−1.09	***	3.93	***	−8.11		−3.93	***	7.23		5.58	***
M75+	−10.65	***	−9.91	***	9.75	***	−45.51	***	40.92		26.83	***	−36.67		−33.88	***
F15-29	−0.53	***	−0.55	***	0.16	**	−1.74	***	2.06		1.05	***	−4.84		−1.25	***
F30-44	5.83	***	5.69	***	−2.43	***	17.72	***	−24.96		−10.59	***	54.68		17.01	***
F45-59	22.60	***	19.94	***	−10.61	***	78.07	***	−98.23		−42.88	***	205.85		50.83	***
F60-74	2.18	***	2.04	***	−1.25	***	4.53	***	−17.74		−4.14	***	17.25		4.66	***
F75+	−13.21	***	−11.54	***	10.23	***	−50.92	***	47.46		24.59	***	−49.24		−27.46	***
Labour market affiliation (in job)																
Not in job (maternity leave, job seeker allowance)	−0.29	***	−0.36	***	−0.30	***	−0.84	***	4.34		−0.69	***	2.88		−0.10	
Not in job (unemployment benefit)	1.86	***	0.54		0.84	***	2.68	***	−4.15		4.40	***	−21.52		2.81	***
Education, training	−0.63	**	−1.34	***	0.40	***	1.98	**	5.89		−0.87	***	4.43		1.60	*
Early retired	5.95	***	5.47	***	2.98	***	23.32	***	0.74		8.56	***	−114.36		40.97	***
Retired	22.60	***	18.74	***	14.34	***	74.14	***	−63.97		33.23	***	−349.57		71.38	***
Child	−1.18	***	−2.30	***	0.91	***	2.30		7.16		0.73	***	14.16		−3.47	***

Table 4 Decomposition of inequality in health care and pharmaceutical usage ranked by income *(Continued)*

Marital status (married)														
Unmarried	0.10	*	−0.35	**	−0.07		0.36	**	1.29	0.25	***	−4.49	−0.75	***
widowed/longest living partner	0.22		0.99	**	0.88	***	−1.91	***	−0.71	−0.11		20.81	0.71	***
Divorced/cancelled partnership	−0.29	***	−0.48	***	−0.40	***	0.78	**	−1.53	0.00		−5.02	−1.20	***
Ethnicity (Ethic Dane)														
Immigrant	−2.37	***	−2.09	***	−2.07	***	−5.93	***	−10.37	0.79	***	35.59	−13.87	***
Descendant	−0.05		−0.13	***	−0.05	**	−0.17		0.09	0.01		0.93	−0.31	***
Region of residence (Capital Region of Denmark)														
Region Zealand	0.02		−0.08		0.00		−0.13		4.30	0.04		3.82	−0.03	
Region of Southern Denmark	−0.64	***	−1.55	***	2.58	***	1.84	***	68.74	1.57	***	34.67	−0.76	***
Central Denmark Region	0.03		0.11		−0.15		−0.01		−36.14	−0.16		1.31	0.05	
North Denmark Region	−0.28	***	−0.35	***	0.64	***	−1.43	***	0.15	1.10	***	21.02	0.08	
Degree of urbanity of residence (cities)														
Suburbs	−0.01		0.02		0.00		−0.05		1.16	0.06	*	1.03	0.07	*
Country side	−0.35	**	−0.02		−0.79	***	−3.56	***	−16.87	1.92	***	25.08	0.46	*
Morbidity indicators														
Incident in 2011	0.18	***	0.01		0.23	***	−0.40	***	3.18	2.55	***	−26.42	3.42	***
Complication group CG1 (CG0) *	−0.67	***	−0.63	***	−0.45	***	−3.90	***	17.93	−0.23	***	2.67	−3.53	***
Complication group CG2 (CG0)*	26.30	***	20.01	***	23.68	***	57.50	***	−69.18	8.06	***	−116.38	50.73	***
Death in 2011	59.76	***	77.45	***	37.84	***	34.38	***	15.37	−8.04	***	152.06	−20.36	***

*CG0 = no complications, CG1 = minor complications, CG2 = severe complications

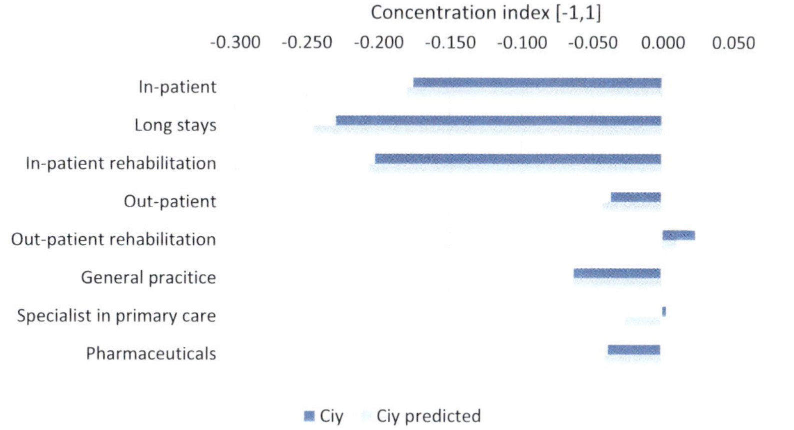

Fig. 1 Concentration index (observed and predicted by determinants) of income-related inequalities in cost outcomes Legend: Ciy = Observed concentration index for the outcome variable Ciy predicted = Concentration index predicted by the included determinants for the outcome variable

than patients resident in cities, and where costs are more concentrated among patients from higher income levels.

Turning to marital status, divorced patients generally have better income, as indicated by the positive concentration index (Table 7 in Appendix), and they accumulate more in-patient services but less pharmaceutical costs and general practice costs compared to married. The latter corresponds well with an expectation of divorced being more reluctant or hesitating to see a doctor. The former supports an expectation of divorced patients being in worse conditions when hospitalized and more depending on hospital care, given lack of care from a spouse at home.

Education as ranking variable

Table 5 mirrors Table 4, just with the nine categories educational level used as rank variable instead of income. Likewise, Table 8 Appendix in supplementary materials mirrors Table 7 in Appendix.

Turning to the regression coefficients (Table 8 in Appendix), some (although minor) differences across regions are found. Thus, the Capital Region and Zealand Region have higher costs for in-patient, out-patient, special care in primary care and pharmaceuticals than the three other regions, whereas the opposite is true for services in general practice. Overall, this pattern is also reflected in the level of urbanity, where especially residents in country side use less resources than patients' resident in cities, and where costs are more concentrated among patients from higher income levels. This might be explained by the Capital region and cities having more resources to seek up patients and invest in secondary prevention efforts targeting all patients also those

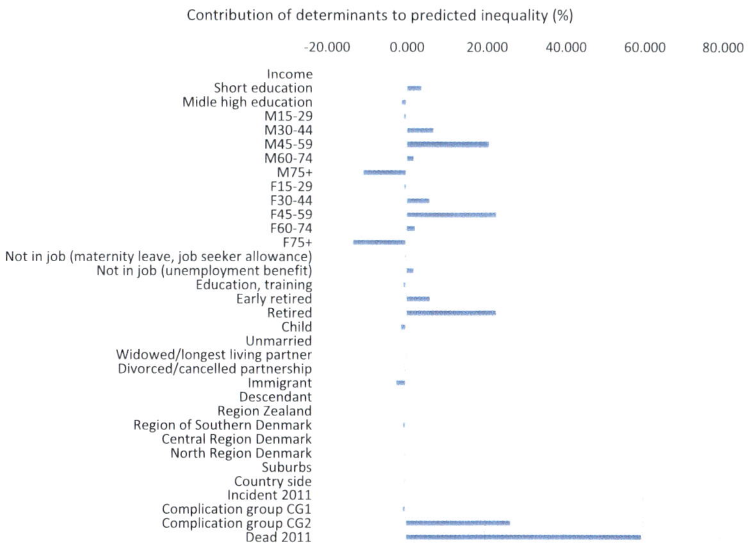

Fig. 2 Decomposition of income-related inequality in in-patient care costs

Table 5 Decomposition of inequality in health care and pharmaceutical usage ranked by education

Ranked by education	SECONDARY CARE										PRIMARY CARE				PHARMACEUTICALS	
	INPATIENT						OUTPATIENT									
	Care		long stays		Rehabilitation		Care		Rehabilitation		General practice		Specialist			
Number of observations	318,684		318,684		318,684		209,530		8,089		318,684		318,684		318,684	
Mean	20998.880	***	719.892	***	236.974	***	16830.080	***	3959.272	***	3069.761	***	2108.322	***	7488.065	***
C (observed)	−0.044	***	−0.047	***	−0.064	***	0.006	*	0.027	***	−0.045	***	0.015	***	−0.036	***
C (predicted)	−0.043	***	−0.048	***	−0.062	***	0.005	*	0.028	***	−0.045	***	0.017	***	−0.036	***
C (unexplained)	0.000		0.002		−0.002		0.001		0.000		0.000		−0.002	***	0.000	
Determinants (reference group)	C		C		C		C		C		C		C		C	
SES																
Income	0.06		−1.33		0.28		11. 8		0.48		0.48	*	9.62		−0.95	
Educational level (high education)																
Primary education	43.98	***	37.37		7.60		363.57		65.54	*	61.19	***	199.47	***	7.99	
Medium education	−11.41	***	−14.11		2.60		−34.53		−15.47		−15.48	***	−1.73		5.62	**
Age and gender (Males0-14) (Females0-14)																
M15-29	−2.24	***	−3.86	**	0.50	**	34.63		2.29		0.19	***	1.74	***	−0.70	***
M30-44	5.87	***	7.41	*	−1.23	**	−74.59		−4.28		−1.85	***	−3.02	***	2.08	***
M45-59	15.98	***	21.08	**	−6.01	***	−167.99		−13.05		−8.69	***	−2.67		9.86	***
M60-74	20.02	***	29.27	**	−9.48	***	−241.32		−18.19		−14.92	***	5.54	*	15.95	***
M75+	−0.31		−0.37		0.22		−3.22		−4.34		0.27		−0.11		−0.26	
F15-29	−1.81	***	−2.51	*	0.43	**	18.00		1.86		1.22	***	−1.10	***	−1.10	***
F30-44	5.09	***	6.66	*	−1.68	***	−54.11		−4.28		−3.16	***	4.38	***	3.81	***
F45-59	17.68	***	20.85	**	−6.55	***	−180.17		−21.80		−11.47	***	17.85	***	10.23	***
F60-74	24.17	***	30.07	**	−10.89	***	−278.22		−40.58	*	−15.70	***	21.88	***	13.36	***
F75+	−0.38		−0.45		0.23		−3.60		−5.08		0.24		−0.15		−0.21	
Labour market affiliation (in job)																
Not in job (maternity leave, job seeker allowance)	−0.64	***	−1.04	*	−0.51	***	3.47		1.08		−0.52	***	1.12	***	−0.06	
Not in job (unemployment benefit)	0.92	***	0.35		0.33	***	−3.96		−0.84		0.74	***	−1.78	***	0.36	***
Education, training	−0.98	**	−2.83	**	0.52	**	−7.67		1.50		−0.48	***	1.52	**	0.68	*
Early retired	20.88	***	25.70	***	8.21	***	−242.75		1.00		10.30	***	−54.05	***	37.18	***
Retired	26.66	***	29.38	**	13.32	***	−254.03		−12.14		13.41	***	−53.57	***	21.77	***
Child	3.72	***	9.54	*	−2.23	***	16.49		−3.98		−0.78	***	−7.75	***	2.78	***
Marital status (married)																
Unmarried	−0.22		1.04		0.13		2.24		0.02		−0.19	***	1.21	***	0.42	***

Table 5 Decomposition of inequality in health care and pharmaceutical usage ranked by education *(Continued)*

widowed/longest living partner	0.96		6.21	**	3.29	***	48.90		6.44		−0.19		13.59	***	0.90	***
Divorced/cancelled partnership	0.90	***	1.96	**	0.99	***	6.64		0.00		0.00		2.07	***	0.96	***
Ethnicity (Ethic Dane)																
Immigrant	6.77	***	7.63	**	4.67	***	−42.78		4.97		−0.78	***	−14.18	***	10.31	***
Descendant	0.10		0.30	*	0.08	*	−0.61		0.31		0.00		−0.26	**	0.15	***
Region of residence (Capital Region of Denmark)																
Region Zealand	0.54	***	−2.35	*	−0.04		6.83		2.77		0.34	***	5.76	***	−0.15	*
Region of Southern Denmark	−2.47	***	−7.99	**	7.77	***	−21.85		47.04	*	2.08	***	19.42	***	−0.77	***
Central Denmark Region	−0.93	***	−4.68	**	3.46	***	13.59		−19.07		1.70	***	8.27	***	−0.37	***
North Denmark Region	−2.22	***	−3.80	**	4.00	***	39.02		6.71		2.99	***	19.12	***	0.16	
Degree of urbanity of residence (cities)																
Suburbs	−0.36	*	0.74		0.04		2.65		−1.93		0.52	***	2.19	***	0.44	***
Country side	−2.21	**	−0.19		−3.92	***	69.52		−22.51	*	4.21	***	16.68	***	0.75	
Morbidity indicators																
Incident in 2011	0.25	***	0.04		0.25	***	3.22		1.63		1.19	***	−5.53	***	1.20	***
Complication group CG1 (CG0) *	0.13		0.15		0.07		8.98		1.05		0.02		−0.09		0.18	
Complication group CG2 (CG0)*	29.52	***	29.86	***	20.87	***	−217.68		−5.92		3.12	***	−19.41	***	14.79	***
Death in 2011	8.81	***	15.21	**	4.37	***	−28.03		−0.08		−0.41	***	2.94	***	−0.78	***

*CG0 = no complications, CG1 = minor complications, CG2 = severe complications

belonging to lower SES groups, who might be more difficult to address.

Concentration indices based on educational versus income ranks are shown in Fig. 3. It is seen that costs for outpatient rehabilitation and specialists in primary care concentrates among the higher socioeconomic groups, but with relatively stronger associations when ranking according to education. This may indicate that educational level is more decisive than income for usage of outpatient services, rehabilitation and specialist in primary care among diabetes patients.

Decomposition of inequality of costs for specialists in primary care (Fig. 4) shows that especially for women 45+, residents in the countryside and other regions than the Capital Region, costs concentrate among higher educated patients. For early retired and retired, the opposite pattern is seen with costs concentrating among the lower educated patients, since these patient groups on average have lower educational level than patients in job (as indicated by negative concentration indices in Table 8 in Appendix) and consume more resources since they are more morbid (cf. the positive regression coefficients in Table 8 in Appendix). The same applies for patients with severe complications and for immigrants. For the latter, the explanation is, however, reversed, as immigrants have higher educational level and consume less resources (Table 8 in Appendix). Therefore, their contribution to inequality is in the direction of costs accumulating among the lower educational groups. That immigrants have a higher average educational level than ethnic Danes is counterintuitive. One explanation might be that only the highest educated among immigrants are diagnosed at all, another that the preventive effect of education is not the same among ethnic Danes and immigrants.

Concentrating on ethnicity, the observed pattern for specialist treatment is likewise observed for all three types of in-patient care and pharmaceutical usage. For general practice, the pattern is opposite indicating that immigrants of lower educational levels have higher usage of these services than do ethnic Danes (Table 8 in Appendix).

Turning to morbidity indicators, severe complications and dead in 2011 generally explain more of income inequality than of educational inequality. While between 62 and 97% of income related inequality in costs for in-patient and out-patient care was explained by having severe complications or dying in 2011, the figures are 25–45% for educational level. For out-patient care, as much as 92% of costs accumulating among lower levels of income were explained from these two morbidity indicators. For education on the contrary, as much as 245% of inequality with costs accumulating among higher educated are explained from these two morbidity indicators.

For labor market affiliation, similar patterns are observed across the two tables, however with larger magnitude of contributions of the determinants for income inequality than educational inequality. For age and gender, patterns overall agree across the two tables.

Discussion

Based on our study of the population of Danish diabetes patients, we demonstrate modest inequality in diabetes patients' health care and pharmaceutical usage, reflecting that the Danish universal health care system is generally not inequitable. Our results, however, indicate that the amount of inequality explained by patients' morbidity patterns varies greatly across type of services showing different levels of realized access. This corresponds to previous findings concerning income-related inequality in health care utilization in Denmark [23]. Types of services showing inequality, however, differ from previous findings, suggesting that different utilization patterns are

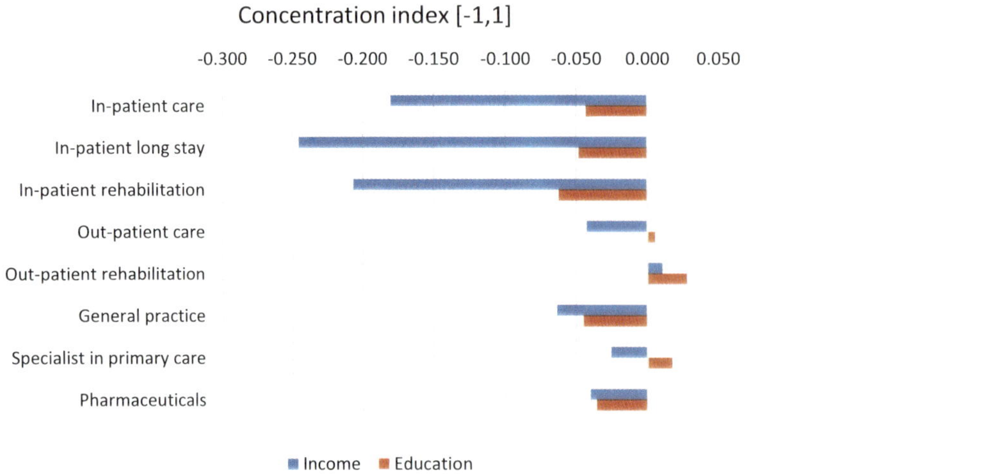

Fig. 3 Concentration indices of health care and pharmaceutical usage based on ranking by income and educational level respectively

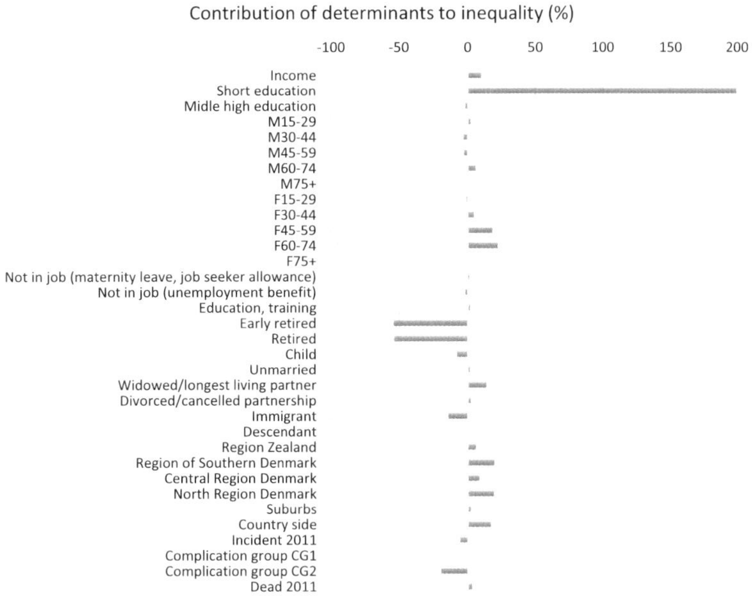

Fig. 4 Decomposition of education related inequality in costs for specialists in primary care

at stake within a specific chronic disease area. This indicates a need of disease specific investigations within the large public health diseases, aiming at informing future strategic efforts and national guidelines. Results indicate that patients of higher SES, especially when SES is measured by educational level, are favored or are more proactive in receiving services when they are seriously ill, and that they likewise are more willing to accept rehabilitation services and seek specialist care, when diagnosed with diabetes. In the Danish health care system, general practice, which is formed by private practice physicians serving under a contract with the government and the regions, serves as gate-keeper with referrals required for specialist treatment [50], which might be perceived as a barrier. Our findings supplement existing literature on differences in especially preventive services and maintenance of life style changes [11]. According to demographic determinants, results point to higher costs among higher income groups among immigrants, elder 75+ years and residents in outer areas. For immigrants, this finding illustrate lower realized access, which along with the findings concerning morbidity in this group stress the importance of reducing the barriers for these patient groups for fully taking advantage of the Danish health care system. Our results demonstrate that confounding is present between income and selected characteristics, in particular age, labor market attachment and diabetes complications, and that attention must be paid to these by properly controlling for them, as is done in the above regression. Also, given the potential endogeneity between income and labor market attachment (in the sense that labor market affiliation is a potential outcome of income), it is recommendable to either substitute or supply with analyses using education rather than income as measure of SES status. However, while lifestyle factors are not accounted for in the study, education may not be a fully true SES measure and thus not "fairly" compared to income as SES.

The present study does not investigate how to change inequality components, however, it does show where the largest potentials for socio-economic related inequality reduction lie, thus providing an important basis for future research and efforts to reduce inequality in diabetes and in health as such. Given marked prevalence increase in diabetes in Denmark as well as globally [21, 51], our findings indicate that inequality in diabetes will also increase. This only stresses the importance of recognition and prioritizing of inequality aspects within chronic disease and diabetes.

The study adds empirical insights regarding choice of proxy for SES. Important differences of applying income and education as proxy for patients' SES are noted, which may be ascribed to endogeneity of income, i.e., that income, alike other measures of labor market attachment, to a certain extent is determined by morbidity. Our results indicate that education is more decisive than income for patients' realized access. Hence, education as rank variable might be preferable in analyses of utilization patterns. Application of both education and income, however, may be recommended since the two enables a more nuanced and comprehensive understanding of results. Furthermore, when using education as proxy for SES, several reservations remain as discussed by inter alia Cutler and Lleras-Muney [9] and Cuther et al. (2011). One reservation regards as to whether there is a direct link or merely indirect links via for example lifestyle, which correlates with education. Furthermore, the health effect of an additional year of schooling may be far from constant. Also, the effect of age at educational attainment is pointed out: The lower age at educational attainment, the lower effect of education on health later in life, given that one should expect a diminishing effect of education over the lifespan. The education effect on health may also vary with gender and ethnicity. Finally, unobserved matters like genetic conditions or other intergenerational patterns are pointed out by the authors. For example, children from low SES families may have less educational outcome on health.

There are certain limitations of the study, which should be noticed. Data on patients' need evaluated from a physician or self-assessed by the patient would enhance the study, as would data on patients' life style choices. Next, since diabetes is highly influenced by risky health behaviour [36], observed associations might to a certain degree be explained by life style choices [37]. Furthermore, in our regressions, we chose not to include interactions aiming at easing interpretation of results. Also, in the concentration index calculations, tied ranking was applied within each educational level. This might potentially bias results as compared to what would be obtained by a continuous outcome variable. This was investigated by Clarke and Van Ourti [8], who included income level as an approximation for a ranking variable within each of the educational categories. Our results indicate downward as well as upward impacts of applying a grouped rank variable as compared to a continuous variable. Mainly, we find that the grouped variable underestimates the concentration indices. For outpatient care we find that the sign shifts from positive to negative. The concentration index for outpatient care was only significant on a 10% level. The results of Clarke and Van Ourti indicated the largest impact of grouped ranking variable in cases where the concentration index was insignificant. This might indicate that the positive sign for outpatient care can be questioned, however, the positive sign for ambulant rehabilitation remains with all ranking variables. Furthermore, it should be noted that while we use patients' personal income as a convenient measure of the individual SES, household income (equivalized for household composition) may alternatively be applied as a measure of the full economic capacity of the patient. While the latter summarizes the SES of the household, assuming the SES of the patient to be equal to the SES of the household, the former may be more adequate for more complex household compositions. Anyway, we appreciate that inclusion of household income rather than individual income would more precisely express the economic ability of the patient.

Finally, it should be noted that the methodology behind the study, was developed in the early 2000s [43, 44, 48]. Since then, different authors suggested alternative approaches to address certain aspects. Thus, corrections to the concentration index were suggested by Wagstaff [46] and Errygers [15]. Wagstaff showed that that the upper and lower bounds of a binary variable whose inequality is investigated depend on the mean of this variable, while Errygers showed that this is the case for any variable with bounds. Thus, when a health variable has bounds, the concentration index will depend on the mean, and comparisons between populations with different health means therefore become problematic. Other methods considering that socio-economic inequality is bivariate by nature and measuring the correlation between health and socio-economic status were suggested by Erreygers and Kessels [16], Kessels and Errygers [28], and Erreygers and Kessels [17]. To these, Heckley et al. [24] added a Recentered Influence Function (RIF) regression approach, where a two-dimensional decomposition of determinants of health as well as of determinants of the socio-economic variable (income in the present paper), together with a feed-back between these two, was suggested. Furthermore, the choice of concentration index involves a value judgement as discussed by e.g. Allanson and Paetrie [2] and Kjellson et al. [30]. Thus, a choice must be made between absolute and relative measures, and between measures of health or ill-health in case the index has both a lower and an upper bound. As shown by van Doorslaer and Koolman [42] and Clarke et al. [7], the choice of index can influence the ranking.

Conclusion

Even in a universal health care system, our results, which are based on the population of Danish diabetes patients, indicate differences in realized access with patients of higher SES, especially higher educational level, to a larger extent enjoying offers of especially out-patient services, rehabilitation and specialists in primary care. Health care usage of patients of lower SES hereby not always corresponds to their need. Especially elder people, divorced, people outside the labour market and immigrants are vulnerable when belonging to lower SES groups and would benefit from being targeted directly. Results indicate that different utilization patterns are at stake within a specific chronic disease as diabetes, compared to general health care utilization patterns. Methodologically, our findings underpin important differences of using income and educational level, respectively, as proxy for SES. Our results indicate that education is more decisive than income for patients' realized access whereas income-related inequality in health care usage to a higher extent is explained by morbidity. Several of these findings may underpin universal structures behind inequality in diabetes, and in chronic disease in general, which are valuable beyond the specific case of Denmark.

Appendix

Table 6 Grouping of diagnoses and interventions used for classifying hospital activities by complication states of relevance for diabetes, and with respect to diagnostic specificity for diabetes

Diagnosis or procedure	Qualifying for complication state[a]	Specificity for diabetes[b]
Diabetes in pregnancy, childbirth and the puerperium	0	1
Diabetes, without indication of chronic complication	0	1
Hypoglycaemiccoma NOS	0	0
Screening for diabetic retinopathy	0	1
Drug treatment or instruction specific for diabetes	0	1
Acute myocardial infarction	1	0
Diabetes with complication, not further specified	1	1
Diabetes with complications in peripheral vascular system	1	1
Diabetes with eye complication	1	1
Diabetes with footulcer	1	1
Diabetes with microangiopathy	1	1
Diabetes with neurological complication	1	1
Diabetes with peripheral angiopathy	1	1
Diabetes with renal complication	1	1
Diabetic cataract	1	1
Diabetic polyneuropathy	1	1
Diabetic retinopathy not otherwise specified	1	1
Diseases of the lens	1	0
Polyneuropathy	1	0
Proliferative diabetic retinopathy	1	1
Uraemia	1	0
Simplex diabetic retinopathy	1	1
Cataract, retinopathy in diabetes	1	1
Diabetic angiopathy in extremities	1	1
Diabetic nephropathy, Kimmelstiel-Wilson syndrom	1	1
Neuropathy, diabetic polyneuritis, diabetes	1	1
Amputation at or below ankle level	1	0
Coronary bypass operation	1	0
Surgery for eye complication	1	0
Teatment of ulcer of lower limb	1	0
Diabetes with gangraene	2	1
Diabetes with multiple complications	2	1
Diabetic maculopathy	2	1
Dialysis	2	0
Diseases of the retina	2	0
Heart failure	2	0
Kidney transplantation	2	0
Renalfailure	2	0
Stroke	2	0
Blindness	2	0
Diabetic gangraene	2	1
Gangrena of lower limb	2	0
Intracerebral haemorrhage	2	0
Amputation above ankle level	2	0

[a]Value indicates classification state (0, 1 or 2, respectively)
[b]Values 1 and 0 indicate that item is specific for diabetes and unspecific for diabetes, respectively

Table 7 Decomposition of inequality in health care costs ranked by income, regression coefficient (B) and concentration index (CI) for each determinant

Ranked by income		SECONDARY CARE										PRIMARY CARE				PHARMACEUTICALS	
		INPATIENT						OUTPATIENT									
		Care		long stays		Rehabilitation		Care		Rehabilitation		General practice		Specialist			
Variable (reference group)		Mean		Mean		Mean		Mean		Mean		Mean		Mean		Mean	
Income	b01**	0.00		0.00		0.00		0.00		0.00		0.00		0.00	*	0.00	
	ci01***	0.34	***	0.34	***	0.34	***	0.34	***	0.31	***	0.34	***	0.34	***	0.34	***
Education (high education)																	
low education	b02	1656.98	***	54.93		4.80		−1036.59	***	−287.87	*	349.09	***	−262.41	***	86.52	
	ci02	−0.19	***	−0.19	***	−0.19	***	−0.20	***	−0.19	***	−0.19	***	−0.19	***	−0.19	***
medium education	b03	1025.82	***	44.26		−4.24		−322.94		−137.91		216.14	***	−8.86		−159.67	***
	ci03	0.11	***	0.11	***	0.11	***	0.10	***	0.08	***	0.11	***	0.11	***	0.11	***
Age and gender (Males0-14) (Females0-14)																	
M15-29	b04	−613.27	***	−35.70	***	2.24	**	−450.36	***	−114.50	***	7.93	***	−17.02	***	−59.22	***
	ci04	−0.16	***	−0.16	***	−0.16	***	−0.17	***	−0.14		−0.16	***	−0.16	***	−0.16	***
M30-44	b05	−423.91	***	−17.71	***	1.44	**	−244.19	***	−58.19	***	20.43	***	−7.84	***	−45.28	***
	ci05	0.39	***	0.39	***	0.39	***	0.41	***	0.36	***	0.39	***	0.39	***	0.39	***
M45-59	b06	−283.26	***	−12.50	***	1.75	***	−181.37	***	−20.66		23.57	***	−1.83		−52.54	***
	ci06	0.38	***	0.38	***	0.38	***	0.38	***	0.35	***	0.38	***	0.38	***	0.38	***
M60-74	b07	−227.19	***	−11.16	***	1.79	***	−147.29	***	−15.57		26.02	***	2.06	*	−54.51	***
	ci07	0.02	***	0.02	***	0.02	***	0.01	***	0.03	**	0.02	***	0.02	***	0.02	***
M75+	b08	−228.72	***	−9.51	***	2.72	***	−175.53	***	−26.77	**	30.16	***	2.68	***	−56.25	***
	ci08	−0.21	***	−0.21	***	−0.21	***	−0.19	***	−0.18	***	−0.21	***	−0.21	***	−0.21	***
F15-29	b09	−492.86	***	−22.93	***	1.95	**	−220.61	***	−91.68	***	51.24	***	10.34	***	−90.40	***
	ci09	−0.13	***	−0.13	***	−0.13	***	−0.14	***	−0.07		−0.13	***	−0.13	***	−0.13	***
F30-44	b10	−366.93	***	−16.01	***	1.99	***	−178.72	***	−57.76	***	34.93	***	10.76	***	−82.82	***
	ci10	0.32	***	0.32	***	0.32	***	0.34	***	0.23	***	0.32	***	0.32	***	0.32	***
F45-59	b11	−313.06	***	−12.33	***	1.91	***	−198.61	***	−33.74	**	31.09	***	10.80	***	−54.44	***
	ci11	0.48	***	0.48	***	0.48	***	0.39	***	0.40	***	0.48	***	0.48	***	0.48	***
F60-74	b12	−274.92	***	−11.52	***	2.05	***	−169.68	***	−32.91	***	27.37	***	8.50	***	−45.58	***
	ci12	0.02	***	0.02	***	0.02	***	0.01	***	0.03	**	0.02	***	0.02	***	0.02	***
F75+	b13	−283.56	***	−11.09	***	2.86	***	−196.36	***	−31.08	***	27.64	***	3.61	***	−45.60	***
	ci13	−0.16	***	−0.16	***	−0.16	***	−0.15	***	−0.12	***	−0.16	***	−0.16	***	−0.16	***

Table 7 Decomposition of inequality in health care costs ranked by income, regression coefficient (B) and concentration index (CI) for each determinant *(Continued)*

Labour market affiliation (in job)																	
Not in job (maternity leave, job seeker allowance)	b14	5656.97	***	310.30	***	76.42	***	2065.49	***	796.35	**	705.00	***	344.42	***	147.77	
	ci14	0.09	***	0.09	***	0.09	***	0.11	***	0.13	***	0.09	***	0.09	***	0.09	***
Not in job (unemployment benefit)	b15	7714.01	***	100.31		45.45	***	1793.17	***	355.39		955.25	***	518.71	***	900.41	***
	ci15	−0.44	***	−0.44	***	−0.44	***	−0.43	***	−0.42	***	−0.44	***	−0.44	***	−0.44	***
Education, training	b16	−3160.16	**	−297.82	***	25.81	***	1328.96	**	−1347.85	**	−227.81	***	−165.51	***	621.87	*
	ci16	−0.90	***	−0.90	***	−0.90	***	−0.91	***	−0.85	***	−0.90	***	−0.90	***	−0.90	***
Early retired	b17	12395.85	***	509.88	***	80.83	***	8147.46	***	−67.01		932.87	***	1113.52	***	6599.71	***
	ci17	−0.15	***	−0.15	***	−0.15	***	−0.14	***	−0.10	***	−0.15	***	−0.15	***	−0.15	***
Retired	b18	7303.15	***	271.48	***	60.31	***	4240.48	***	431.49	*	562.26	***	511.90	***	1784.64	***
	ci18	−0.21	***	−0.21	***	−0.21	***	−0.20	***	−0.18	***	−0.21	***	−0.21	***	−0.21	***
Child	b19	−7903.27	***	−687.25	***	79.26	***	1970.06		−2358.20	*	257.09	***	−591.64	***	−1792.82	***
	ci19	−0.98	***	−0.98	***	−0.98	***	−0.98	***	−0.99	***	−0.98	***	−0.98	***	−0.98	***
Marital status (marriaged)																	
Unmarried	b20	−793.18	*	118.66	**	7.18		−967.62	***	91.72		−98.20	***	−144.60	***	435.56	***
	ci20	0.03	***	0.03	***	0.03	***	0.02	***	0.09	***	0.03	***	0.03	***	0.03	***
widowed/longest living partner	b21	546.13		110.96	**	28.94	***	−1280.55	***	−317.43	*	−14.08		−242.16	***	138.57	***
	ci21	−0.09	***	−0.09	***	−0.09	***	−0.06	***	0.01		−0.09	***	−0.09	***	−0.09	***
Divorced/annuled partnership	b22	1960.90	***	143.55	***	35.08	***	−729.78	**	−89.68		0.94		−154.77	***	625.22	***
	ci22	0.04	***	0.04	***	0.04	***	0.05	***	0.08	***	0.04	***	0.04	***	0.04	***
Ethicity (Ethic Dane)																	
Immigrant	b23	−4598.66	***	−180.16	***	−52.24	***	−1906.88	***	556.50	**	80.42	***	−332.02	***	−2082.04	***
	ci23	−0.21	***	−0.21	***	−0.21	***	−0.22	***	−0.18	***	−0.21	***	−0.21	***	−0.21	***
Descendant	b24	−2601.88		−272.86	***	−32.93	**	−1257.39		1008.95		19.62		−241.26	***	−1152.62	***
	ci24	−0.24	***	−0.24	***	−0.24	***	−0.25	***	−0.01		−0.24	***	−0.24	***	−0.24	***
Region of residence (Capital Region of Denmark)																	
Region Zealand	b25	1518.98	***	−218.02	***	−1.39		−1508.86	***	−1203.57	***	146.81	***	−559.62	***	−121.78	*
	ci25	0.00		0.00		0.00		0.00		−0.03		0.00		0.00		0.00	
Region of Southern Denmark	b26	−2690.03	***	−289.19	***	140.30	***	1281.61	***	−2932.85	***	343.49	***	−731.81	***	−246.01	***
	ci26	−0.04	***	−0.04	***	−0.04	***	−0.03	***	−0.05	***	−0.04	***	−0.04	***	−0.04	***
Central Denmark Region	b27	−2483.33	***	−418.62	***	154.80	***	−1992.48	***	−2226.42	***	697.56	***	−766.99	***	−293.93	***
	ci27	0.00		0.00		0.00		0.00		0.04	***	0.00		0.00		0.00	

Table 7 Decomposition of inequality in health care costs ranked by income, regression coefficient (B) and concentration index (CI) for each determinant *(Continued)*

North Denmark Region	b28	−3087.03	***	−173.55	***	91.92	***	−3236.22	***	−1330.41	***	632.16	***	−916.56	***	69.90	
	ci28	−0.03	***	−0.03	***	−0.03	***	−0.03	***	0.00		−0.03	***	−0.03	***	−0.03	***
Urbanity (Cities)																	
Suburbs	b29	−750.90	*	52.07		1.25		−439.30		971.95	***	170.91	***	−162.38	***	278.42	***
	ci29	0.00	*	0.00	*	0.00	*	0.00		0.01		0.00	*	0.00	*	0.00	*
Country side	b30	−791.07	**	−1.76		−23.64	***	−1447.17	***	975.13	***	230.68	***	−206.41	***	82.10	*
	ci30	−0.04	***	−0.04	***	−0.04	***	−0.04	***	−0.03	***	−0.04	***	−0.04	***	−0.04	***
Morbidity indicators																	
Incident in 2011	b31	−1287.16	***	−4.70		−21.37	***	1873.66	***	293.34		−949.62	***	−1000.48	***	−1880.24	***
	ci31	0.05	***	0.05	***	0.05	***	0.02	***	0.11	***	0.05	***	0.05	***	0.05	***
Complication group CG1 (CG0) *	b32	8924.98	***	370.12	***	77.74	***	3043.54	***	1104.35	***	158.60	***	192.82	***	3609.95	***
	ci32	0.01	***	0.01	***	0.01	***	0.04	***	0.05	***	0.01	***	0.01	***	0.01	***
Complication group CG2 (CG0)*	b33	29216.04	***	993.73	***	342.16	***	11567.27	***	2064.34	***	469.02	***	662.58	***	4359.56	***
	ci33	−0.13	***	−0.13	***	−0.13	***	−0.10	***	−0.07	***	−0.13	***	−0.13	***	−0.13	***
Death in 2011	b34	87725.75	***	5083.04	***	722.43	***	8603.19	***	−912.07	***	−617.85	***	−1014.66	***	−2310.90	***
	ci34	−0.68	***	−0.68	***	−0.68	***	−0.53	***	−0.53	***	−0.68	***	−0.68	***	−0.68	***

*CG0 = no complications, CG1 = minor complications, CG2 = severe complications
** b*N* = Regression coefficient of variable N
***ci*N* = Concentration index of variable N

Table 8 Decomposition of inequality in health care costs ranked by education, regression coefficient (B) and concentration index (CI) for each determinant

Ranked by education		SECONDARY CARE										PRIMARY CARE				PHARMACEUTICALS	
		INPATIENT						OUTPATIENT									
		Care		long stays		Rehabilitation		Care		Rehabilitation		General pracitice		Specialist			
Variable (reference group)		Mean		Mean		Mean		Mean		Mean		Mean		Mean		Mean	
Income	b01	0.00		0.00		0.00		0.00		0.00		0.00	*	0.00	*	0.00	
	ci01	0.11	***	0.11	***	0.11	***	0.11	***	0.10	***	0.11	***	0.11	***	0.11	***
Education (high education)																	
low education	b02	1671.70	***	57.60		5.09		−1044.36	***	−302.94	*	349.05	***	−260.11	***	91.10	
	ci02	−0.58	***	−0.58	***	−0.58	***	−0.58	***	−0.57	***	−0.58	***	−0.58	***	−0.58	***
medium education	b03	1055.65	***	47.62		−3.79		−334.48		−145.09		215.94	***	−6.32		−152.72	**
	ci03	0.25	***	0.25	***	0.25	***	0.25	***	0.28	***	0.25	***	0.25	***	0.25	***
Age and gender (Males0-14) (Females0-14)																	
M15-29	b04	−620.08	***	−35.51	***	2.27	**	−454.78	***	−112.13	***	7.99	***	−16.68	***	−58.14	***
	ci04	−0.14	***	−0.14	***	−0.14	***	−0.13	***	−0.16	*	−0.14	***	−0.14	***	−0.14	***
M30-44	b05	−426.18	***	−17.70	***	1.47	**	−247.64	***	−56.56	***	20.41	***	−7.58	***	−45.05	***
	ci05	0.08	***	0.08	***	0.08	***	0.10	***	0.08	**	0.08	***	0.08	***	0.08	***
M45-59	b06	−284.55	***	−12.48	***	1.77	***	−183.38	***	−19.55		23.57	***	−1.65		−52.41	***
	ci06	0.07	***	0.07	***	0.07	***	0.07	***	0.10	***	0.07	***	0.07	***	0.07	***
M60-74	b07	−229.27	***	−11.19	***	1.80	***	−149.42	***	−14.46		26.00	***	2.20	*	−54.49	***
	ci07	0.05	***	0.05	***	0.05	***	0.06	***	0.07	***	0.05	***	0.05	***	0.05	***
M75+	b08	−229.99	***	−9.48	***	2.74	***	−177.51	***	−25.93	**	30.16	***	2.81	***	−56.25	***
	ci08	0.00		0.00		0.00		0.00		0.03		0.00		0.00		0.00	
F15-29	b09	−500.86	***	−23.04	***	1.98	**	−224.03	***	−88.97	***	51.19	***	10.54	***	−90.45	***
	ci09	−0.11	***	−0.11	***	−0.11	***	−0.11	***	−0.08	*	−0.11	***	−0.11	***	−0.11	***
F30-44	b10	−369.02	***	−15.98	***	2.02	***	−181.68	***	−56.30	***	34.92	***	10.99	***	−82.49	***
	ci10	0.07	***	0.07	***	0.07	***	0.08	***	0.05	**	0.07	***	0.07	***	0.07	***
F45-59	b11	−314.80	***	−12.28	***	1.93	***	−200.69	***	−32.70	**	31.10	***	10.98	***	−54.35	***
	ci11	0.09	***	0.09	***	0.09	***	0.08	***	0.11	***	0.09	***	0.09	***	0.09	***
F60-74	b12	−276.81	***	−11.50	***	2.07	***	−171.59	***	−31.94	**	27.36	***	8.67	***	−45.62	***
	ci12	0.07	***	0.07	***	0.07	***	0.06	***	0.08	***	0.07	***	0.07	***	0.07	***
F75+	b13	−284.82	***	−11.08	***	2.87	***	−198.21	***	−30.10	***	27.64	***	3.74	***	−45.61	***
	ci13	0.00		0.00		0.00		0.00		0.02		0.00		0.00		0.00	

Table 8 Decomposition of inequality in health care costs ranked by education, regression coefficient (B) and concentration index (CI) for each determinant *(Continued)*

Labour market affiliation (in job)																	
Not injob (maternity leave, job seeker allowance)	b14	5647.67	***	310.49	***	75.85	***	2050.64	***	801.14	*	705.60	***	343.97	***	146.35	
	ci14	0.05	***	0.05	***	0.05	***	0.05	***	0.04		0.05	***	0.05	***	0.05	***
Not in job (unemployment benefit)	b15	7754.26	***	102.21		45.48	***	1755.88	***	345.08		954.64	***	520.03	***	905.78	***
	ci15	−0.05	***	−0.05	***	−0.05	***	−0.06	***	−0.11	**	−0.05	***	−0.05	***	−0.05	***
Education, training	b16	−3047.98	**	−296.37	***	26.77	***	[illegible]239.85	**	−1327.45	**	−226.53	***	−163.62	***	634.89	**
	ci16	−0.36	***	−0.36	***	−0.36	***	−0.38	***	−0.27	***	−0.36	***	−0.36	***	−0.36	***
Early pensioner	b17	12424.47	***	516.77	***	80.95	***	8113.88	***	−61.04		932.31	***	1111.59	***	6598.69	***
	ci17	−0.13	***	−0.13	***	−0.13	***	−0.13	***	−0.12	***	−0.13	***	−0.13	***	−0.13	***
Pensioner	b18	7360.21	***	273.17	***	60.90	***	4243.02	***	430.83	*	563.12	***	510.89	***	1791.89	***
	ci18	−0.06	***	−0.06	***	−0.06	***	−0.06	***	−0.05	***	−0.06	***	−0.06	***	−0.06	***
Child	b19	−8016.24	***	−679.84	***	79.79	***	1363.83		−2312.99	*	257.14	***	−578.69	***	−1788.10	***
	ci19	0.76	***	0.76	***	0.76	***	0.75	***	0.66	***	0.76	***	0.76	***	0.76	***
Marital status (marriaged)																	
Unmarried	b20	−762.99	*	119.34	**	7.51		−983.54	***	87.62		−98.00	***	−144.59	***	436.33	***
	ci20	−0.02	***	−0.02	***	−0.02	***	−0.01	***	0.00		−0.02	***	−0.02	***	−0.02	***
widowed/longest living partner	b21	498.17		111.25	**	28.21	***	−[illegible]264.30	***	−328.09	**	−14.91		−243.26	***	139.54	***
	ci21	−0.11	***	−0.11	***	−0.11	***	−0.11	***	−0.12	***	−0.11	***	−0.11	***	−0.11	***
Divorced/annuled partnership	b22	1959.70	***	144.38	***	35.48	***	−722.93	**	−93.74		0.99		−155.19	***	624.10	***
	ci22	−0.03	***	−0.03	***	−0.03	***	−0.03	***	0.00		−0.03	***	−0.03	***	−0.03	***
Ethicity (Ethic Dane)																	
Immigrant	b23	−4583.20	***	−184.46	***	−52.36	***	−1395.54	***	566.97	**	80.27	***	−331.87	***	−2081.26	***
	ci23	0.15	***	0.15	***	0.15	***	0.14	***	0.11	***	0.15	***	0.15	***	0.15	***
Descendant	b24	−2549.32		−270.53	***	−33.09	**	−1229.19		1017.49		19.23		−236.49	***	−1134.00	***
	ci24	0.11	***	0.11	***	0.11	***	0.12	***	0.13		0.11	***	0.11	***	0.11	***
Region of residence (Capital Region of Denmark)																	
Region Zealand	b25	1529.58	***	−219.20	***	−1.67		−1514.75	***	−1215.46	***	146.88	***	−560.24	***	−125.67	*
	ci25	−0.02	***	−0.02	***	−0.02	***	−0.02	***	−0.02		−0.02	***	−0.02	***	−0.02	***
Region of Southern Denmark	b26	−2687.59	***	−291.85	***	140.25	***	1267.48	***	−2931.74	***	344.33	***	−731.61	***	−251.59	***
	ci26	−0.03	***	−0.03	***	−0.03	***	−0.03	***	−0.04	***	−0.03	***	−0.03	***	−0.03	***
Central Denmark Region	b27	−2496.60	***	−422.31	***	154.16	***	−20[illegible]2.19	***	−2215.80	***	696.83	***	−767.81	***	−298.20	***
	ci27	−0.01	***	−0.01	***	−0.01	***	−0.02	***	0.03	***	−0.01	***	−0.01	***	−0.01	***

Table 8 Decomposition of inequality in health care costs ranked by education, regression coefficient (B) and concentration index (CI) for each determinant *(Continued)*

North Denmark Region	b28	−3077.69	***	−177.70	***	91.88	***	−3251.57	***	−1313.66	***	631.06	***	−916.52	***	63.75	
	ci28	−0.06	***	−0.06	***	−0.06	***	−0.06	***	−0.06	***	−0.06	***	−0.06	***	−0.06	***
Urbanity (Cities)																	
Suburbs	b29	−769.59	*	52.32		1.32		−421.47		975.00	***	171.33	***	−162.57	***	278.79	***
	ci29	−0.03	***	−0.03	***	−0.03	***	−0.03	***	−0.01		−0.03	***	−0.03	***	−0.03	***
Country side	b30	−794.58	**	−1.55		−23.33	***	−1437.32	***	979.44	***	229.74	***	−206.84	***	79.69	
	ci30	−0.06	***	−0.06	***	−0.06	***	−0.06	***	−0.05	***	−0.06	***	−0.06	***	−0.06	***
Morbidity indicators																	
Incident in 2011	b31	−1291.89	***	−5.98		−21.65	***	1862.19	***	307.23		−950.00	***	−999.99	***	−1878.38	***
	ci31	0.02	***	0.02	***	0.02	***	0.02	***	0.07	***	0.02	***	0.02	***	0.02	***
Complication group CG1 (CG0) *	b32	8970.85	***	371.90	***	78.17	***	3050.01	***	1100.95	***	159.51	***	193.67	***	3614.41	***
	ci32	0.00		0.00		0.00		0.01	***	0.00		0.00		0.00		0.00	
Complication group CG2 (CG0)*	b33	29218.30	***	994.70	***	342.29	***	11571.10	***	2057.79	***	469.32	***	662.94	***	4362.94	***
	ci33	−0.03	***	−0.03	***	−0.03	***	−0.03	***	−0.01		−0.03	***	−0.03	***	−0.03	***
Death in 2011	b34	87694.00	***	5094.08	***	720.90	***	8658.61	***	−921.76	***	−618.34	***	−1012.35	***	−2311.31	***
	ci34	−0.02	***	−0.02	***	−0.02	***	−0.05	***	0.00		−0.02	***	−0.02	***	−0.02	***

*CG0 = no complications, CG1 = minor complications, CG2 = severe complications
** b*N* = Regression coefficient of variable N
***ci*N* = Concentration index of variable N

Abbreviations

C: Concentration Index; CG0: Complication Group 0; CG1: Complication Group 1; CG2: Complication Group 2; DD2: Diabetes Database 2; DRG: Diagnosis Related Grouping; NDR: Danish National Diabetes Register; SD: Statistics Denmark; SES: Socio-Economic Status; WHO: World Health Organization

Acknowledgements

This study has been conducted by ApEHR in cooperation with the Danish Diabetes Association and supported by a Ph. D. program from COHERE supported by The Danish Centre for Strategic Research in Type 2 Diabetes, DD2. A consortium of sponsors from the pharmaceutical industry comprising Astra Zeneca/BMS, Novo Nordisk, Merck, Sanofi Aventis and Bayer has provided an unrestricted grant to ApEHR for the conduct of this research. We thank Terkel Christiansen for valuable commenting.

Funding

Camilla Sortsøs research was financed by an unrestricted grant from The Danish Centre for Strategic Research in Type 2 Diabetes, DD2. Anders Greens, Martha Emneus' and Peter Bjødstrup Jensens research was financed by an unrestricted grant from a consortium of sponsors from the pharmaceutical industry comprising Astra Zeneca/BMS, Novo Nordisk, Merck, Sanofi Aventis and Bayer.

Authors' contributions

CS: First draft of introduction, literature review, description of data. calculation and presentation of results, first draft of discussion and conclusion. JTL: Description of methodology, preparation of programming, calculation and presentation of results, contribution to introduction, discussion and conclusion. AG: Preparation and description of data, contribution to introduction, discussion and conclusion. ME: Preparation and description of data, contribution to introduction, discussion and conclusion. PBJ: Preparation and description of data, contribution to introduction, discussion and conclusion. All authors have read and approved on the final version of the paper prior to submission.

Competing interests

Neither the Danish Diabetes Association, the DD2 Centre nor the consortium of sponsors from the pharmaceutical industry has had any influence on the conduct of the study.

Endnotes

Not applicable.

Author details

[1]Centre of Health Economics Research (COHERE), Department of Business and Economics, University of Southern Denmark, Campusvej 55, DK-5s30 Odense M, Denmark. [2]Institute of Applied Economics and Health Research (ApEHR), Copenhagen, Denmark. [3]Odense Patient data Explorative Network (OPEN), Odense University Hospital and University of Southern Denmark, Copenhagen, Denmark.

References

1. Agardh E, Allebeck P, Hallqvist J, Moradi T, Sidorchuk A. Type 2 diabetes incidence and socio-economic position: a systematic review and meta-analysis. Int J Epidemiol. 2011;40(3):804–18.
2. Allanson P, Paetrie D. On the choice of inequality measure for the longitudinal analysis of income-related health inequalities. Health Econ. 2013;22:353–65.
3. Andersen JS, Olivarius NDF, Krasnik A. 2011. The Danish National Health Service Register. Scand J Public Health. 2011;39(suppl 7).
4. Brown AF, Ettner SL, Piette J, Weinberger M, Gregg E, Shapiro MF, et al. Socioeconomic position and health among persons with diabetes mellitus: a conceptual framework and review of the literature. Epidemiol Rev. 2004;26:63–77.
5. Bruce Wirta S, Hodgkins P, Joseph A. Economic burden associated with chronic constipation in Sweden: a retrospective cohort study. ClinicoEconomics and outcomes research : CEOR. 2014;6:369–79.
6. Carstensen B, Kristensen JK, Marcussen MM, Borch-Johnsen K. 2011. The National Diabetes Register. Scandinavian journal of public health. 2011;39(suppl. 7):58-61.
7. Clarke PM, Gerdtham U-G, Johannesson M, Bingefors K, Smith L. On the measurement of relative and absolute incomwe-related inequality. Soc Sci Med. 2002;55:1923–8.
8. Clarke P, van Ourti T. Correcting the Bias in the Concentration Index When Income is Grouped 2009. 2009.
9. Cutler D, Lleras-Muney A. Education and Health: Evaluating Theories and Evidence. In: Making Americans Healthier. In: House J, Schoeni R, Kaplan G, Pollack H, editors. Social and Economic Policy as Health Policy. New York: Russell Sage Foundation; 2008.
10. DM Cutler DM, Lleras-Muney A, Vogl T, et al. Oxford Handbook of Health Economics. Oxford: Oxford University Press; 2011. p. 124–63. Socioeconomic status and health: dimensions and mechanisms.
11. Danish Health Authority [Sundhedsstyrelsen]. Kronisk sygdom - Patient, sundhedsvæsen og samfund. Danish Health Authority: Forudsætninger for det gode forløb. Copenhagen; 2005.
12. Danish Health Authority [Sundhedsstyrelsen]. Strategi for indsatsvedrørende diabetes blandt etniske minoriteter. Copenhagen: Danish Health Authority; 2007.
13. Danish Health Authority [Sundhedsstyrelsen]. Ulighed i sundhed - Årsager og indsatser. Copenhagen: Danish Health Authority; 2011.
14. Efron B, Tibshirani R. 1993An Introduction to the Bootstrap. London: Chapman & Hall; 1993.
15. Errygers G. Correcting the concentration index. J Health Econ. 2009;28:504–13.
16. Erreygers G, Kessels R. 2013. Regression-based decompositions of rank-dependent indicators of socioeconomic inequality of health. Working Papers 2013007, University of Antwerp, Faculty of Applied Economics.
17. Erreygers G, Kessels R. 2015. Socioeconomic status and health: A new approach to the measurement of bivariate inequality. Working Papers 2015017, University of Antwerp, Faculty of Applied Economics.
18. Espelt A, Borrell C, Roskam AJ, Rodriguez-Sanz M, Stirbu I, Dalmau-Bueno A, et al. Socioeconomic inequalities in diabetes mellitus across Europe at the beginning of the 21st century. Diabetologia. 2008;51(11):1971–9.
19. Eze CO, Onwuekwe IO, Agu CE, Kalu UA. 2013. The prevalence of orthostatic hypotension in type 2 diabetes mellitus patients in a diabetic clinic in Enugu South-East Nigeria. Nigerian journal of medicine : journal of the National Association of Resident Doctors of Nigeria. 2013;22(3):175–80.
20. Gold M. 1998. Part I: The Concept of Access and Managed Care.Beyond Coverage and Supply: Measuring Access to Healthcare in Today's Market. Health Services Reserach 1998;33(3).
21. Green A, Sortsø C, Jensen P, Emneus M. 2015a. Incidence, morbidity, mortality and prevalence of diabetes in Denmark, 2000–2011: results from the Diabetes Impact Study 2013. J Clin Epidemiol. 2015;7:421–30.
22. Green A, Sortsø C, Jensen PB, Emneus M. Validation of the Danish National Diabetes Register. Clin Epidemiol. 2015b:7; 5–15.
23. Gundgaard J, Lauridsen J. 2013. Explaining the Source of Income-Related Inequality in Health Care Utilization in Denmark. COHERE: 2013.
24. Heckley G, Gerdtham U-G, Kjellson G. A general method for decomposing the causes of socioeconomic inequality in health. J Health Econ. 2016;48:89–106.
25. Imkampe AK, Gulliford MC. Increasing socio-economic inequality in type 2 diabetes prevalence–repeated cross-sectional surveys in England 1994–2006. Eur J Public Health. 2011;21(4):484–90.

26. Juul S. Epidemiologi og evidens. København: Munksgaard Danmark; 2004. p. 2004.
27. Kakwani N, Wagstaff A, van Doorslaer E. Socioeconomic inequalities in health: Measurement, computation and statistical inference. Journal of Econometrics. 1997;77:87–103.
28. Kessels R, Errygers G. Research Paper 2014–013. Department of Economics: University of Antwerp; 2014. A unified structural equation modeling approach for decomposition of rank-dependent indicators of socioeconomic inequality of health.
29. Kildemoes H, Sørensen H, Hallas J. The Danish National Prescription Registry. Scand J Public Health. 2011;39(7 Supp):38–41.
30. Kjellson G, Gerdtham U-G, Petrie D. Lies, damned lies, and health inequality measurements. Understanding the value judgement. Epidemiology. 2015;26:673–80.
31. Kristensen F, Sigmund H. Health Technology Assessment Handbook. Copenhagen: National Board of Health; 2007. p. 2007.
32. Kristensen T, Olsen KR, Sortsø C, Ejersted C, Thomsen JL, Halling A. Resources allocation and health care needs in diabetescare in Danish GP clinics. Health Policy. 2013;113:206–15.
33. Lauridsen J, Pradhan J. Socio-economic inequality of immunization coverage in India. Health Economics Review. 2011;2011:1(11).
34. Lynge E, Sandegaard JL, Rebolj M. The Danish National Patient Register. Scandinavian journal of public health. 2011;39(suppl- 7).
35. Ministry of Health. DRG-leksikon 2012. 2012. [Available from: http://sundhedsdatastyrelsen.dk/da/afregning-og-finansiering/takster-drg.
36. Nocon M, Keil T, Willich SN. Education, income, occupational status and health risk behaviour. J Public Health-Uk. 2007;15(5):401–5.
37. Robbins JM, Vaccarino V, Zhang H, Kasl SV. Socioeconomic status and diagnosed diabetes incidence. Diabetes Res Clin Pract. 2005;68(3):230–6.
38. Sortsø C, Emneus M, Green A, Jensen P, Eriksson T. Societal costs of diabetes mellitus 2015 and 2040 - forecasts based on real world cost evidence and observed epidemiological trends in Denmark. Modern Economy. 2015;6:1150–66.
39. Sortsø C, Green A, Jensen P, Emneus M. Societal costs of diabetes mellitus in Denmark. Diabet Med. 2016;33:877–85.
40. Sortsø C, Lauridsen J, Emneus M, Green A, Jensen PB. COHERE discussion paper 2/2016. Odense: University of Southern Denmark; 2016. Decomposing Inequality in Diabetes Patients' Morbidity Patterns, Survival and Health Care Usage in Denmark.
41. Thygesen LC, Daasnes C, Thaulow I, Hansen HB. Introduction to Danish (nationwide) registers on health and social issues: structure, access, legislation and archiving. Scandinavian journal of public health. 2011;39 (suppl. 7).
42. Van Doorslaer E, Koolman X. Equity II Project Working Paper #1. Rotterdam: Erasmus University; 2000. Income-related inequalities in health: some evidence from European Community Household Panel.
43. van Doorslaer E, Koolman X. Explaining the differences in income-related health inequalities across European countries. Health Econ. 2004;13(7):609–28.
44. van Doorslaer E, Koolman X, Jones AM. Explaining income-related inequalities in doctor utilisation in Europe. Health Econ. 2004;13(7):629–47.
45. van Doorslaer E, Masseria C, Koolman X, 2. Inequalities in access to medical care by income in developed countries. CMAJ : Canadian Medical Association journal = journal de l'Association medicale canadienne. 2006;174:177–83.
46. Wagstaff A. The bounds of the Concentration Index when the variable of interest is binary, with an application to immunization inequality. Health Econ. 2005;14:649–53.
47. Wagstaff A, van Doorslaer E. Overall versus socioeconomic health inequality: a measurement framework and two empirical illustrations. Health Econ. 2004;13(3):297–301.
48. Wagstaff A, van Doorslaer E, Watanabe N. On decomposing the causes of health sector inequalities, with an application to malnutrition inequalities in Vietnam. J Econom. 2003;112:219–27.
49. Wagstaff A, Paci P, van Doorslaer E. On The Measurement Of Inequalities in Health Social Science Medicine 1991;33(5):545–57.
50. Vallgårda S, Krasnik A, et al. In: Vallgårda S, Krasnik A, editors. Sundhedsvæsen og sundhedspolitik. Munksgaard Danmark: København; 2007.
51. WHO. Global status report on non-communicable diseases 2010. Description of the global burden of NCDs,their risk factors and determinants. WHO; 2011.
52. WHO. 2015. Diabetes Fact sheet 2015 [Available from: http://www.who.int/mediacentre/factsheets/fs312/en/.

11

Policy makers, the international community and the population in the prevention and treatment of diseases: case study on HIV/AIDS

Kjell Hausken[1*] and Mthuli Ncube[2]

Abstract

A four-period game is developed between a policy maker, the international community, and the population. This research supplements, through implementing strategic interaction, earlier research analyzing "one player at a time". The first two players distribute funds between preventing and treating diseases. The population reacts by degree of risky behavior which may cause no disease, disease contraction, recovery, sickness/death. More funds to prevention implies less disease contraction but higher death rate given disease contraction. The cost effectiveness of treatment relative to prevention, country specific conditions, and how the international community converts funds compared with the policy maker in a country, are illustrated. We determine which factors impact funding, e.g. large probabilities of disease contraction, and death given contraction, and if the recovery utility and utility of remaining sick or dying are far below the no disease utility. We also delineate how the policy maker and international community may free ride on each other's contributions. The model is tested against empirical data for 43 African countries. The results show consistency between the theoretical model and empirical estimates. The paper argues for the need to create commitment mechanisms to ensure that free riding by both countries and the international community is avoided.

Keywords: Disease, Policy, Game, Funding, Prevention, Treatment, Resource distribution, Free riding, Risky behavior

JEL classification: C72, D72, D74, I10, H51

Background

The global burden of disease is substantial. The prevalence of diseases wax and wane, and vary across countries and through time regarding the need to distribute funds. This paper focuses on diseases where funds are allocated for prevention and treatment, after which nature chooses a population fraction that contracts the disease. Treatment causes some to recover while others remain sick or die.[1] This papers tries to answer a few questions, as a way to get to some policy solutions: Why do some countries free ride on their responsibility to treat their citizens? Why do some donors prefer to focus on funding preventions when treatment is also a form of prevention? Which factors determine which population fraction contracts the disease? To what extent is the amount of funding committed consequential in changing the population fraction contracting the disease? Are the current mechanisms in place to make sure both policy makers in affected-countries and donors commit to funding both treatment and prevention of diseases?

In order to answer these questions and get to some solutions, the paper uses a game-theoretic approach involving policy makers, international donors, and people living with diseases. The behavior of the parties is driven by reactions to each other's actions, which results in outcomes that the questions above imply. The paper goes to the heart of the need to create more binding commitment-mechanisms to counter free riding by affected countries and also donors, in the financing of disease prevention and treatment. The paper also fleshes

* Correspondence: kjell.hausken@uis.no
[1]Faculty of Social Sciences, University of Stavanger, 4036 Stavanger, Norway
Full list of author information is available at the end of the article

out the behavioral incentives for those living with diseases and those who could contract it, pointing to the need for to meet their side of the bargain.

The paper assumes that policy makers and donors have accepted the *duty of rescue* and the people also have a *duty to respond* to rescue efforts, see Collier et al. [9]. Collier et al. [9] discuss the implications of the duty of the rescue principle on treatment and prevention choices, and the size of lifecycle financial liabilities for disease intervention and its fiscal implications. Other approaches, such as *accountability for reasonableness*, lend support to prioritization decisions by policy makers and donors in their interventions, see Daniels and Sabin [11]. Accountability for reasonableness seeks to establish a framework for prioritization and fair allocation of responsibilities in decision-making, unlike considerations of cost-effectiveness and comparative effectiveness research.

Historically in disease development, individuals moved first spreading the disease, through mechanisms such as infection, air transmission, food distribution, and lifestyle imitation. Policy-makers and others moved thereafter reacting to the disease. Finally individuals moved again, either increasing or decreasing their risky behavior. In this paper we do not focus on the history, but on what to do as we move into the future. To design a tractable model we thus omit the first step and start by considering what a policy maker should do here and now as we move into the future. A four-period game-theoretic model with complete information is conceptualized. First, a policy maker associated with the government in a country distributes funds between disease prevention and disease treatment. The fraction of funds distributed to disease prevention impacts whether individuals contract the disease. Second, observing the policy maker's available funds and distribution, the international community provides an analogous distribution between prevention and disease treatment. The international community[2] is considered to move second since in many countries, with adequate funds and distribution, intervention by the international community is not needed. In contrast, in other countries either lacking funds or inadequate distribution suggests the need for the international community to intervene.

From the model we are able to generate various properties which we discuss. Furthermore, from the outcomes of the model, the paper argues for the need to create commitment-mechanisms to ensure that free riding by both countries and donors is avoided. Although a cooperative game with binding agreements between the players would be desirable, such a game is hard to implement and sustain. Hence in this paper we develop the more fundamental non-cooperative game, with no binding agreements between the players, to illustrate the dilemmas. The paper also argues for commitment to funding both prevention and treatment, by policy makers and donors. Without these mechanisms the game will result in countries with limited resources only focusing on prevention, which is not desirable. The model also shows why more funding is needed, and how that can reduce the probabilities of disease contraction, and death from the disease.

The paper also addresses fiscal sustainability and debt sustainability issues. If, for example, donors free ride, how could a country meet its future unfunded debt from disease liabilities. The fiscal stability of any country, with or without resources is threatened.

The model is tested using HIV data for 43 African countries which are classified according to the model's characteristics. We test the model using regression analysis. Policy implications, suggestions and predictions and presented.

Health policy decisions are usually analyzed "one player at a time", which has various disadvantages associated with sectorial analyses and non-holistic analyses which may not capture phenomena comprehensively. Sectorial analyses may be incorrect when relevant cause-effect relationships are shut out from consideration. In this paper we bring the relevant players together in a game-theoretic approach to account for their different interests in a holistic approach.

Examples of disease prevention are awareness campaigns so that people are knowledgeable and take precautions e.g. by taking vaccines against disease contraction, or using condoms to avoid HIV contraction. Examples of disease treatment are hospital beds and medicines to treat diseases, and ameliorate the adverse effects of diseases, given that disease contraction has occurred.

Resource allocations between prevention and treatment are sometimes seen as being in competition. Literature abounds on decision-making for resource allocation for disease treatment and prevention. For HIV see Paltiel and Stinnett [27], Marseille et al. [25], Gonsalves [14], Kumaranayake et al. [23], Canning [6], Alistar and Brandeau [1], Boily et al. [4], Bärnighausen et al. [5], Bertozzi et al. [3], and the HIV Modelling Consortium Treatment as Prevention Editorial Writing Group [17], among others. There is also quite some focus on cost-effectiveness analysis of prevention measures, see Walker [29], Hogan et al. [18], Goldie et al. [13], Cohen et al. [8], Creese et al. [10], Galárraga et al. [12], and Granich et al. [15]. See Izazola-Licea et al. [19] and Hecht et al. [16] regarding financing the response to HIV/AIDS, and Coates et al. [7] regarding behavioral strategies for reducing transmission of the disease.

Some of the literature has focused on the incentives for resource allocation by corporations to develop drugs for either prevention (vaccinations) and treatment. See

Alistar and Brandeau [1] for decision making for HIV prevention and treatment. Private incentives for developing treatment drugs seem far stronger than those for developing vaccines for prevention, see Thomas [28], Kremer and Glennerster [20], Kremer and Snyder [21, 22], Kremer and Snyder [22], inter alia. Countries with high disease prevalence may be forced to allocate large budgets to disease treatment which may leave little left for disease prevention. This paper throws light on such resource allocations. See Mamani et al. [24] for a game theoretic model of international influenza vaccination coordination, and Moxnes and Hausken [26] for mathematical modeling of acute virus influenza A infections.

The rest of the paper is organized as follows. Section 2 presents the model. Section 3 analyzes the model. Section 4 compares the model with empirics. Section 5 concludes.

Methods: The model

A four-period complete information game is considered as shown in Fig. 1. There are three players, i.e. the policy maker in a country equipped with funds *f*, the international community equipped with funds *F*, and nature. In period 1 the policy maker distributes an amount *p* of its funds to disease prevention, which implies that the remaining amount *f-p* gets distributed to disease treatment. In period 2, having observed the policy maker's strategic choice in period 1, the international community distributes an amount *p* of its funds to disease prevention, which implies that the remaining amount *F-P* gets distributed to disease treatment. In period 3, affected by the policy maker's choice p in period 1 and the international community's choice P in period 2, nature chooses the population fraction q that contracts the disease. In practice, this means that each individual in the country observes the choices p and P and thereafter chooses a degree of risky behavior that affects the probability q that the individual contracts the disease.

If the disease contraction probability q is large, the policy maker and international community are more likely to distribute more funds f and F. The disease contraction probability q is assumed to decrease convexly in the prevention efforts p and P, and funds f and F, expressed probabilistically as

$$q = q(p, \chi P, f, F, \delta_1, nature), \; \partial q/\partial p < 0, \; \partial q/\partial P < 0, \; \partial^2 q/\partial p^2 > 0, \; \partial^2 q/\partial P^2 > 0, \; \partial q/\partial f < 0, \; \partial q/\partial F < 0, \; \partial^2 q/\partial f^2 > 0, \; \partial^2 q/\partial F^2 > 0, \; 0 \le q \le 1 \tag{1}$$

where $\chi \ge 0$ expresses the efficiency of the international community relative to the country's policy maker of converting funds into disease prevention or treatment, nature expresses that nature in the form of individuals make strategic choices based on the parameters and strategic choices in periods 1 and 2, and δ_1 is a set of parameters specific for the country that impacts disease contraction. Examples of such parameters pertain to governmental systems, infrastructure, climate, culture, employment rate, income, education, etc. If $\chi > 1$, the international community converts funds more effectively than the policy maker into prevention, and conversely if $0 \le \chi < 1$. The inequalities in equation (1) state that more funds p and *P* distributed to disease prevention, decreases the probability of disease contraction.

If the individual does not contract the disease, i.e. remains healthy, his/her utility is E. In contrast, if the individual contracts the disease and gets sick, the distributions f-p and F-P, implied by the strategic choices in period 1 and 2, come into play. The probability x that the average individual, having contracted the disease, remains sick or dies is assumed to decrease convexly in the disease treatment efforts f-p and F-P, and funds f and F, i.e.

$$x = x(\varepsilon(f-p), \varepsilon\chi(F-P), \delta_2, nature), \; \partial x/\partial p > 0, \; \partial x/\partial P > 0, \; \partial^2 x/\partial p^2 < 0, \; \partial^2 x/\partial P^2 < 0, \; \partial x/\partial f < 0, \; \partial x/\partial F < 0, \; \partial^2 x/\partial f^2 > 0, \; \partial^2 x/\partial F^2 > 0, \; 0 \le x \le 1 \tag{2}$$

where $\varepsilon \ge 0$ is the cost effectiveness of treatment relative to prevention, nature expresses that nature in the form

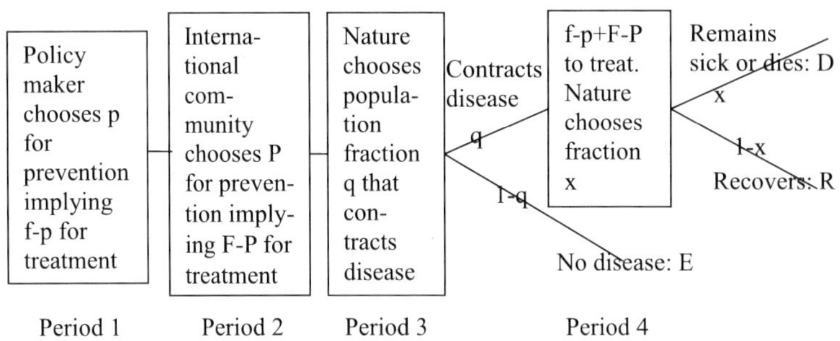

Fig. 1 Four-period game for policy maker, international community, and nature

of individuals make strategic choices based on the parameters and earlier strategic choices, and δ_2 is a set of parameters specific for the country that impacts getting sick or dying. The set δ_2 may be similar to the set δ_1 in equation (1), but may differ to the extent that the mechanisms for getting sick or dying differ from the mechanisms of disease contraction. If $\varepsilon > 1$, funds distributed to treatment are utilized more effectively than funds distributed to prevention, and conversely if $0 \leq \varepsilon < 1$. The inequalities in equation (2) state that more funds f-p and F-P distributed to disease treatment decreases the probability of getting sick or dying. Each individual receives utility D if he/she remains sick or dies, and utility R if he/she recovers,[3] where D < R < E.

Using Fig. 1, the average individual's expected utility is

$$\begin{aligned} v &= (1-q)E + q((1-x)R + xD) \\ &= E-q(E-R)-qx(R-D) \end{aligned} \tag{3}$$

Modeling the policy maker's funds f means accounting for the population size. Assuming n individuals in the country, and inserting equation (3), the policy maker's expected utility is

$$u = nv-af = n(1-q)E + nq((1-x)R + xD)-af \tag{4}$$

where a is the unit cost of converting funding into utility for the n individuals. Analogously, the international community's expected utility, inserting equation (3), is

$$\begin{aligned} U &= nv-AF \\ &= n(1-q)E + nq((1-x)R + xD)-AF \end{aligned} \tag{5}$$

where b is the unit cost of converting funding into utility for the n individuals.

Summing up, f, F, χ, ε, δ_1, δ_2, a, b, E, R, D are all exogenous parameters. Although funding f and F are exogenous in the model, these are allocated from national and international budgets which means that they in practice are chosen. As we discuss the model we will to some extent account for the possibility that f and F are chosen through mechanisms not specified in the model. In the model, the policy maker has one strategic choice variable, i.e. distribution p to prevention. Analogously, the international community has one strategic choice variable, i.e. distribution P to prevention. Nature in equations (1) and (2) means that nature in the form of individuals additionally impact the probability q of disease contraction and the probability x of remaining sick or dying given that the disease has been contracted.

Methods and Results: Interpreting and analyzing the model

The game is solved with backward induction. For period 2, differentiating the international community's expected utility U in (5) gives

$$\frac{\partial U}{\partial P} = -n\underbrace{\frac{\partial q}{\partial P}}_{<0}(E-R)-n\underbrace{\frac{\partial q}{\partial P}}_{<0}x(R-D)-nq\underbrace{\frac{\partial x}{\partial P}}_{>0}(R-D) = 0 \tag{6}$$

and

$$\frac{\partial^2 U}{\partial P^2} = -n\underbrace{\frac{\partial^2 q}{\partial P^2}}_{>0}(E-R)-n\underbrace{\frac{\partial^2 q}{\partial P^2}}_{>0}x(R-D)-2n\underbrace{\frac{\partial q}{\partial P}}_{<0}\underbrace{\frac{\partial x}{\partial P}}_{>0}(R-D)-nq\underbrace{\frac{\partial^2 x}{\partial P^2}}_{<0}(R-D) < 0 \tag{7}$$

where the signs below the derivatives are from equations (1) and (2). Since $\partial q/\partial P < 0$, the first two terms in equation (6) are positive. Since $\partial x/\partial P > 0$, the third and last term in equation (6) is negative. Hence functional forms for q and x exist that enable an interior solution for P, i.e. 0 < P < F. This interior solution is such that the international community distributes a final amount P to prevention, and the remaining amount F-P to treatment. The first term in equation (6) expresses that increased distribution P to prevention causes decreased disease contraction probability q, which is multiplied with the utility difference E-R between no disease and recovery. The second term in equation (6) also expresses that increased P causes decreased q, but this derivative is multiplied with the probability x of remaining sick or dying, and multiplied with the utility difference R-D between recovery and being sick or dying. These first two terms considered in isolation show that the international community increases its expected utility U by increasing its distribution P to prevention. Without something to constrain the value of P, the international community would choose maximum $P = F$. The third term provides this constraint. That is, the third term in equation (6) expresses that increased distribution P to prevention causes increased probability x of remaining sick or dying. This derivative is multiplied with the disease contraction probability q and the utility difference R-D between recovery and being sick or dying. This third term thus provides a counterweight to the first two terms. The international community cannot be expected to choose maximum P = F for prevention which may give an unacceptably high probability x since no funds are distributed to treatment. This reasoning shows how the international community can be expected to strike a balance between prevention P and treatment F-P. Functional forms of q and x also exist that cause the second derivative in equation (7) to be negative, thus ensuring a solution P = P*(p). Inserting this into equation (4) and differentiating the policy maker's expected utility u to determine the first period solution gives

$$\frac{\partial u}{\partial p} = -n\underbrace{\frac{\partial q}{\partial p}}_{<0}(E-R)-n\underbrace{\frac{\partial q}{\partial p}}_{<0}x(R-D)-nq\underbrace{\frac{\partial x}{\partial p}}_{>0}(R-D) = 0 \quad (8)$$

where $q = q(p, \chi P^*(p), \delta_1, nature)$ and $x = x(\varepsilon(f-p), \varepsilon\chi(F - P^*(p)), \delta_2, nature)$ and

$$\frac{\partial^2 u}{\partial p^2} = -n\underbrace{\frac{\partial^2 q}{\partial p^2}}_{>0}(E-R)-n\underbrace{\frac{\partial^2 q}{\partial p^2}}_{>0}x(R-D)-2n\underbrace{\frac{\partial q}{\partial p}}_{<0}\underbrace{\frac{\partial x}{\partial p}}_{>0}(R-D)-nq\underbrace{\frac{\partial^2 x}{\partial p^2}}_{<0}(R-D) < 0 \quad (9)$$

The reasoning for the policy maker in period 1 to strike a balance between prevention p and treatment f-p is analogous to the reasoning for the international community in period 2 to strike a balance between prevention P and treatment F-P.

Property 1: If the policy maker and the international community distribute unusually much funds p and P to prevention, the probability q of disease contraction is low, and most individuals receive the no disease utility E. Those few that contract the disease, have a high probability x of remaining sick or dying causing minimum utility D since limited funds f-p and F-P are distributed to treatment.

Proof: Property 1 follows from inserting $\partial q/\partial p < 0$ and $\partial q/\partial P < 0$ into equation (3) which causes 1-q in the first term to be close to 1 and q in the second term to be close to 0.

Individuals differ with respect to risky behavior. Some may choose risky behavior regardless of prevention efforts p and P, and some of these will statistically contract the disease. This prevents q from ever reaching zero. Those that contract the disease are likely to remain sick or dying since limited funds are distributed to treatment. Conversely, some may choose safe behavior regardless of prevention efforts p and P. These are unlikely to contract the disease (except e.g. through receiving contaminated blood or being attacked with a contaminated needle). Aside from these two extremes, many individuals may vacillate between risky and safe behavior, to be impacted by p and P. The second part of Property 1 follows from inserting $\partial x/\partial p > 0$ and $\partial x/\partial P > 0$ into equation (3) which causes 1-x to be small and x to be large in the second term.

Property 2: If the policy maker and the international community distribute limited funds p and P to prevention, and thus substantial funds f-p and F-P to treatment, the probability q of disease contraction is high, and few individuals receive the no disease utility E. The many that contract the disease, have a high probability 1-x of recovering causing utility R since substantial funds f-p and F-P are distributed to treatment.

Proof: Property 2 is the opposite of Property 1, and follows from equation (3).

The balance to be struck between prevention and treatment also depends on the nature of the disease partly expressed with the utilities E,R,D, e.g. whether it is deadly, how long it lasts, whether individuals somehow recover themselves, and whether and through which channels it spreads to other individuals. For deadly diseases that spread easily, prevention seems more called for than for minor diseases which enable individuals to function close to normally.

Property 3: If the cost effectiveness parameter ε of treatment relative to prevention is larger than 1, distributing more funds towards treatment is more appropriate.

Proof: Follows from equation (2) and the discussion thereafter.

Diseases vary greatly in how they suggest prevention or treatment as the appropriate strategy. In the early history of HIV, when treatment options were few or absent expressed with ε close to zero, prevention was the preferred strategy since disease contraction in some cases was a death sentence. As treatment options become more readily available, and at an affordable price, so that ε increased, more funds to treatment seem appropriate to enable those having contracted the disease to recover and live their lives despite disease contraction.

Property 4: If the country- specific parameter δ_1 is such that the disease contraction probability q is high, more funds to prevention seems appropriate. Conversely, if the country specific parameter δ_2 is such that the probability x of remaining sick or dying is high, more funds to treatment seems appropriate.

Proof: Follows from equation (1) and the discussion thereafter for δ_1, and from equation (2) and the discussion thereafter for δ_2.

Property 4 suggests that different conditions in different countries may impact the balance policy makers and the international community strike between prevention and treatment.

Property 5: If the efficiency χ of the international community relative to the country's policy maker of converting funds into disease prevention or treatment is large, then the international community can be expected to contribute relatively more than the policy maker, especially if conditions require more funds.

Proof: Follows from equation (1) and the discussion thereafter, and from equation (2).

Conditions vary greatly across countries regarding how funds are converted into disease prevention or treatment. Especially some third world countries, even if monetary funds are somehow available, may lack the competence, infrastructure, governmental institutions, equipment, transport capabilities, medicine, etc. to convert funds into prevention or treatment. In such instances, the international community, with more readily access to some of these capabilities expressed with large χ, may contribute more. However, the reverse may also occur. Local and cultural traditions, language, fear or non-acceptance of outsiders, etc. may hinder or block international community entry, thus expressing low χ, where the policy maker can be expected to contribute more.

Property 6: The unit costs a and A, for the policy maker and international community respectively, of converting funding into utility for the n individuals impact their contributions.

Proof: Follows from equation (4) for a and equation (5) for A.

Whereas χ in Property 5 expresses the funds conversion efficiency of the international community relative to the policy maker, the parameters a and A express how efficiently funds are converted into utility, and also provide scaling of the last terms af and AF in equations (4) and (5) relative to the first term nv.

Property 7: As the recovery utility R and the utility D of remaining sick or dying decreases to be substantially below the no-disease utility E, decreasing the disease contraction probability q becomes more important and funding f and F increases.

Proof: Follows from Fig. 1, the derivatives in equations (1) and (2), and the expected utilities in equations (4) and (5).

Property 7 illustrates the importance of accounting especially for the three utilities E, R and D at the end of period 4 in Fig. 1.

Property 8: The policy maker or the international community may choose to free ride on their contributions p and P, f-p and F-P, and f and F, and even finance other needs, in the hope that the other player with contribute more to the funding needs of HIV.

Proof: Differentiating equation (3) gives the positive derivatives

$$\frac{\partial v}{\partial f} = -\underbrace{\frac{\partial q}{\partial f}}_{<0}(E-R) - \underbrace{\frac{\partial q}{\partial f}}_{<0}x(R-D) - q\underbrace{\frac{\partial x}{\partial f}}_{<0}(R-D) > 0, \quad (10)$$

$$\frac{\partial v}{\partial F} = -\underbrace{\frac{\partial q}{\partial F}}_{<0}(E-R) - \underbrace{\frac{\partial q}{\partial F}}_{<0}x(R-D) - q\underbrace{\frac{\partial x}{\partial F}}_{<0}(R-D) > 0$$

Differentiating the expected utilities u and U in equations (4) and (5) with respect to the other player's funding, i.e. F and f respectively, and inserting equation (10), also gives positive derivatives, i.e.

$$\frac{\partial u}{\partial F} = \frac{\partial}{\partial F}(nv-af) = n\frac{\partial v}{\partial F} > 0,$$

$$\frac{\partial U}{\partial f} = \frac{\partial}{\partial f}(nv-AF) = n\frac{\partial v}{\partial f} > 0 \quad (11)$$

Since both players benefit from increased funding by the other player, incentives for free riding exist.

Even if a policy maker has available funds, to prevention or treatment or both, he may choose to withhold these funds for strategic reasons in period 1, in order to induce the international community to contribute the required funds in period 2. Conversely, the international community may announce a small amount of F funds for a given country in the hope that the policy maker may live up to his commitment and provide the required funds.

Methods and Results: Comparing the model with empirics

In this section we test aspects of the model against data from Africa, the region that is most affected by HIV and accounts for 78% of all people living with HIV. First we classify countries according to various characteristics. Second we run regressions in order to determine which characteristics matter in disease contraction.

Introduction

In 2015 more than 36.7 million people lived with HIV/AIDS worldwide.[4] Since its outbreak, 78 million people have become infected with HIV and 35 million people have died worldwide, of which 1.1 million died in 2015 alone. The situation is particularly acute in Africa where in 2015, 25.5 million were living with HIV. Eastern and southern Africa accounts for 46% of new HIV infections worldwide. In Africa 800.000 people died from AIDS-related illnesses in 2015. With more prevention measures, this number would be lower. But, with adequate treatment many can today live successfully with diseases such as HIV/AIDS.

With the advent of antiretroviral treatment (ART), HIV is no longer a death sentence but a chronic condition, with almost 13 million people in low and middle income countries now receiving ART. Treatment activities using ARTs are also preventative measures, as an individual who is well is not only alive and productive, but will also not transmit the disease. Prevention measures may also involve programs aimed at changing people's behavior or changing cultural norms. While the trajectory of the HIV epidemic has begun to change with declining number of new infections and mortality levels, the cost trajectory has continued upwards, driven by lifetime treatment needs, longer living cohorts of individuals receiving treatment, expanded treatment guidelines, and rising prevention costs in HIV-affected countries which have expanding populations. The global resource need, which was US$ 3.8 billion in 2002, was US$19.1 billion in 2013. Recent estimates in Atun et al. [2] point to about US$22-24 billion being needed per annum, to fund HIV intervention programs.

The economic, social and health benefits of HIV investment have been well researched. Increased labor productivity, reduced orphan care costs, deferred treatment and end-of-life care have been estimated to produce substantial economic gains. Similarly, expanded services have been shown to benefit populations by strengthening health systems and releasing system capacity to treat other conditions. Adding to the mix are cross-sectorial benefits and social protection realized with prudent investment in HIV prevention and treatment. Those benefits nevertheless remain tenuous due to a chasm in financing. Prior modeling suggested that annual resource needs could reach US$35 billion by 2030.

While the resource needs are enormous, in many low-income countries, especially in Africa, domestic sources remain very low, with HIV co-financing dependent on external sources. There is also evidence of free riding by affected countries. However, the donor sources are now being constrained by the fiscal constraints from the global economic crisis. Inefficiencies in channeling and utilization of available funds, also adds to resource constraints. Clearly, there is a need to create mechanisms for commitment to funding by both affected countries and donors in order to avoid 'free riding' by both parties.

Domestic financing remains constrained in sub-Saharan Africa. In Nigeria, for example, domestic financing accounted for US$123 million in 2014 compared to US$451 million. From external financing for the same year. In Uganda external financing was US$446 million, nine times more than the US$53 million from domestic resources. In Malawi, external financing accounted for 98% of overall resources spent on HIV intervention.

Country classification

Table 1 classifies countries according to the characteristics in (1) that determine the empirically estimated disease contraction probability q_e, i.e. country characteristics δ_1 (high δ_1 expresses high disease contraction probability), the policy maker's funds f, and the policy maker's empirically estimated fraction p_e distributed to disease prevention. Furthermore, the rightmost three columns in Table 1 classifies countries according to the characteristics in (2) that determine the empirically estimated probability x_e that the average individual remains sick or dies, i.e. country characteristics δ_2 (high δ_2 expresses high probability that an individual remains sick or dies), the policy maker's funds f, the policy maker's empirically estimated fraction p distributed to disease prevention, and the international community's empirically estimated funds provision F.

From Table 1 we see that countries with high resource mobilization, as measured by tax revenues to GDP ratio, f, are Angola, Botswana, Ghana, Lesotho, Mozambique, Namibia, South Africa, Swaziland and Zimbabwe. The bulk of the countries are in the intermediate stage of tax resource mobilization capacity. The countries with higher levels of tax mobilization capacity also have a higher HIV prevalence rate. These are also the countries with the highest levels of HIV contraction probability q_e. This perhaps means that those countries with no extractive resource endowment, such as Swaziland and to some extent Lesotho, have no more room to raise taxes and require innovative finance solutions or indeed further external aid.

The probability of remaining sick or dying from HIV-related illness is highest (above 0.2%) in Botswana, Lesotho, South Africa, Swaziland, Namibia, Mozambique, Malawi, Zambia and Zimbabwe. This pattern corresponds to the probability of contracting the disease. The rest of the countries have moderate probability of death from the disease.

Looking at resource allocation between prevention and treatment, countries that are allocating more to prevention, i.e. high p_e, are Angola, Chad, Ghana, Kenya, Liberia, Madagascar, Togo, Senegal, Mozambique, and Niger. Data on the split in resources between treatment and prevention of HIV is scarce.

Regarding external support from donors, Table 1 shows how they are contributing in each country. Contributions would be driven by many factors but one of them would be disease prevalence and capacity to manage the use of the resources. Countries with high and intermediate disease contracting probability receive a higher than average quantity of external aid.

Testing the model using regression analysis

This section analyzes the model econometrically, starting with the disease contraction probability q in equation (1), expressed as incidence. We wish to determine which country characteristics matter, and we estimated a regression equation of HIV incidence (probability of contracting HIV), against country characteristics variables such as GDP per capita, literacy, Voice & accountability indicators, government effectiveness, inequality, and poverty levels. GDP per capita is expected to have a negative relationship with HIV incidence in the sense that poorer countries with low GDP per capita are likely to have weaker health delivery systems and therefore higher levels of HIV incidence. Literacy levels, particularly higher education, is also expected to have a negative relationship with HIV incidence due to the fact that education and campaigns on prevention measures is likely to be more effective in countries with higher literacy levels. Voice & accountability indicators are expected to have a negative relationship with prevalence due to the fact that a higher level of freedom of expression is a good medium for prevention campaigns. On accountability, the higher this indicator the more likely a country will

Table 1 Population size *n*, policy maker's funds f, and the ratio δ_1 impacting the disease contraction probability q for 43 countries. Policy makers' empirically estimated strategic choice p_e that impact the empirically estimated disease contraction probabilities q_e, where Int means Intermediate and Lo/I means Low/Int. Additionally, the ratio δ_2 impacting the probability x that the average individual remains sick or dies, and the empirically estimated strategic choice F_e that impact the empirically estimated probabilities x_e that the average individual remains sick or dies[a]

Country	n[b]	f[c]	δ_1^d	p_e^e	q_e	δ_2^f	F_e^g $ mill(%) 2009-2011	x_e^h (%)
Angola	21256000	High(18.8%)	Low	0.342′	Low	Low	20.45(0%)	0.061
Benin	9742000	Int(15.4%)	Low	0.134″	Low	Low	27.80(1%)	0.031
Botswana	2096000	High(35.2%)	High	0.096′	High	High	123.14(3%)	0.286
Burkina Faso	17323000	Int(11.5%)	Low	-	Low	Low	35.63(1%)	0.035
Burundi	9023000	Int(17.4%)	Low	0.203″	Low	Low	26.79(1%)	0.055
Cameroon	20930000	Int(18.3%)	Low	-	Low	Int	22.00(1%)	0.167
Chad	12948000	Int	Low	0.294″	Low	Int	15.12(0%)	0.108
Congo, Dem Rep	74618000	Int(13.2%)	Low	-	Low	Low	56.44(0%)	0.043
Cote d'Ivoire	23919000	Int(15.2%)	Low	-	Low	Int	80.54(2%)	0.130
Egypt	84605000	Int(15.8%)	Low	-	Low	-	-	-
Equatorial Guinea	1837000	Low(1.7%)	Int	-	Int	Low	1.06(1%)	0.054
Eritrea	4980000	-	Low	-	Low	Low	15.53(0%)	0.02
Ethiopia	86614000	Int(11.6%)	Low	-	Low	Low	367.59(8%)	0.054
Gabon	2204000	Int(10.3% + Oil)	Lo/I	0.167″	Low	Low	2.94(0%)	0.091
Gambia	1794000	Int(18.9%)	Low	-	Low	-	6.76(0%)	-
Ghana	26441000	High(20.8%)	Low	0.281′	Low	Low	51.80(0%)	0.045
Guinea	11861000	Low(8.2%)	Low	0.135″	Low	Low	8.49(0%)	0.042
Guinea-Bissau	1699000	Int(11.5%)	Lo/I	-	Lo/I	Int	6.24(0%)	0.118
Kenya	43291000	Int(18.4%)	Int	0.270′	Int	Int	425.86(10%)	0.132
Lesotho	1887000	High(15%)	High	-	High	High	52.70(1%)	0.795
Liberia	3881000	Int(13%)	Low	0.313′	Low	Low	12.90(0%)	0.052
Madagascar	21852000	Int(10.7%)	Low	0.515″	Low	Low	10.15(0%)	0.027
Malawi	15316000	High(20.7%)	High	0.113′	High	High	146.23(3%)	0.300
Mali	16678000	Int(15.3%)	Low	-	Low	Low	22.04(1%)	0.030
Mauritania	3461000	Int(12.9%)	Low	0.144″	Low	-	0.61(0%)	-
Mauritius	1273000	Int(19%)	Low	-	Low	-	1.58(0%)	-
Morocco	32950000	Int(13.4%)	Low	-	Low	Low	-	0.003
Mozambique	24491000	High(22.3%)	High	0.422″	High	High	240.32(5%)	0.314
Namibia	2170000	High(28.8%)	High	-	High	High	114.22(3%)	0.230
Niger	17493000	Int(11%)	Low	0.421″	Low	Low	11.52(0%)	0.017
Nigeria	177096000	Low(6.1%)	Low	-	Low	Int	401.22(9%)	0.136
Rwanda	10780000	Int(14.1%)	Low	-	Low	Low	187.99(4%)	0.056
São Tomé and Príncipe	194000	Int(17.4%)	Low	0.046″	Low	-	0.30(0%)	-
Senegal	13567000	Int(19.2%)	Low	0.383′	Low	Low	25.34(1%)	0.015
Sierra Leone	5823000	Lo/I(10.5%)	Low	-	Low	Low	17.83(0%)	0.052
South Africa	52982000	High(26.9%)	High	-	High	High	595.11(14%)	0.453
Swaziland	1077000	High(39.8%)	High	-	High	High	50.58(1%)	0.557
Tanzania	45950000	Int(12%)	Int	-	Int	Int	341.80(8%)	0.174
Togo	6675000	Int(15.5%)	Low	0.257″	Low	Int	14.20(0%)	0.105
Tunisia	10889000	Int(14.9%)	-	-	-	-	-	-

Table 1 Population size *n*, policy maker's funds f, and the ratio δ_1 impacting the disease contraction probability q for 43 countries. Policy makers' empirically estimated strategic choice p_e that impact the empirically estimated disease contraction probabilities q_e, where Int means Intermediate and Lo/I means Low/Int. Additionally, the ratio δ_2 impacting the probability x that the average individual remains sick or dies, and the empirically estimated strategic choice F_e that impact the empirically estimated probabilities x_e that the average individual remains sick or dies[a] *(Continued)*

Uganda	35363000	Int(16.1%)	High	-	High	Int	284.60(7%)	0.178
Zambia	14129000	Int(16.1%)	High	-	High	High	255.15(6%)	0.212
Zimbabwe	13098000	High(49.3%)	High	0.152"	High	High	98.95(2%)	0.298

Notes: *f* is tax revenues as % of GDP. Low is 0-10%, Intermediate is 10.1-20%, and High is over 20%;' and" denote 2011 and 2012 figures, respectively. - means data is not available. Figures for donor funding F are in US$ mill and percentage of total donor funding is in parenthesis. Figures for probability of remaining sick or dying x are in % probability; The ranges for δ_2 are Low(less than 0.1%), Intermediate(between 0.0 and 2%) and High(above 2%)

[a]The data is sourced from World Health Organization(2014), UNAIDS (2014), The Global Fund for HIV/AIDs, Malaria and TB (2014), and the World Bank Statistical Data Base

[b]Data sourced from World Population Prospects, Economic and Social Affairs, United Nations, 2015

[c]Data sourced from the World Bank Data Base (2015)

[d]Constructed from data from the World Health Organization (WHO), 2015, and using a scale

[e]Data sourced from The Global Fund and UNAIDS, 2015

[f]Constructed from data from the World Health Organization (WHO), 2015, and using a scale. The ranges for δ_2 are Low(less than 0.1%), Intermediate(between 0.0 and 2%) and High(above 2%)

[g]Data sourced from the Global Fund, 2015

[h]Estimated from data from the World health Organization (WHO), 2015

improve service delivery. Higher general governance effectiveness is expected to have a negative relationship with incidence due to higher quality of service delivery to the population. Inequality levels are also expected to impact prevalence levels. The more unequal the society, the higher the prevalence level. Likewise, higher poverty levels are likely to be associated with a higher prevalence level, as the poor have lower access to medical care and are generally more vulnerable to disease. This is for 43 countries in Africa.[5]

Table 2 shows that only Inequality, International spending on HIV, Adult literacy, and Constant are significant. The most significant variable is international funding on HIV by financial donors. The Adult literacy rate is also quite significant and has a positive coefficient. However, this is the opposite of what is expected, but perhaps implies that middle-income countries, typically with a higher adult literacy levels, are exhibiting higher incidence levels due to other factors other than adult literacy. The countries just happen to be middle-income in classification. The inequality measure, i.e. the Gini coefficient, has a positive coefficient which is quite significant. This means that the more unequal the society, the higher the prevalence rate, as there is a large percentage of the population with poor access to health. Furthermore, inequality is quite high in some middle-income countries, which are showing higher levels of HIV incidence.

Table 2 Testing determinants of HIV incidence q in equation (1)

Variable	Coefficient	Std Error	t-Value	Significance level
Constant (Intercept)	1.012	0.558	1.814[b]	0.087
GDP per capita (current US$)	0.000	0.000	−0.603	0.555
Voice & Accountability	0.001	0.149	−0.009	0.993
Government Effectiveness	0.082	0.222	0.369	0.716
Adult Literacy Rate (%)	0.008	0.005	1.656	0.116
International Funding (US$1000)	0.022	0.006	3.656[a]	0.002
Poverty Head Count at US$1(%)	0.002	0.004	−0.598	0.558
GINI (Inequality)	0.023	0.014	1.698	0.108

[a]and [b]mean significance at the 5% and 10% levels, respectively

The coefficient for GDP per capita is not significant, which means that the level of income for the country is no predictor for its level of HIV incidence. Some poor countries have low incidence rates, while some middle-income countries have some of the highest incidence rates in the world, such as Botswana, South Africa and Swaziland. Voice & accountability is not a driver of HIV incidence, as some of the countries with a relatively free environment for public expression exhibit high incidence rates, such as South Africa. Again, government effectiveness, which is a proxy for the quality if heath systems, is shown not to be a factor in driving the incidence rate. Equally, the level of poverty, as measured by headcount ratio, does not explain differentials in the incidence rate.

We continue with the probability x of remaining sick or dying in equation (2). Again we ran a regression to determine if indeed variables like the level of prevalence, population size, incidence rate, level of domestic funding and level of international funding were significant drivers of x. Table 3 shows that the incidence rate is the most significant determinant of likelihood of dying from HIV. Indeed, countries with a high incident rate exhibit a high probability of HIV death. The level of domestic funding also is significant. Here the negative sign shows that countries with low domestic funding seem to have a higher HIV death rate. This may imply that they need to

Table 3 Testing determinants of probability x of dying from HIV in equation (2)

Variable	Coefficient	Std Error	t-Value	Significance level
Constant	0.024	0.12	2.094[a]	0.048
Prevalence Level	−0.003	0.04	−0.871	0.393
Population Size (n)	3.629E-10	0.000	1.262	0.220
Incidence Rate	0.354	0.046	7.773[a]	0.000
International Funding	−5.001E-11	0.000	−0.644	0.526
Domestic Funding	−2.921E -10	0.000	−2.038[a]	0.053

R-Squared = 0.978, Adjusted R-Squared = 0.947; [a]means significance at the 5% level

commit more resources to HIV. Population size and the prevalence level do not seem to as highly correlated with HV death rates. Table 3 shows that a country's HIV incidence rate is highly correlated with HIV deaths (t-Value = 7.773), as expected since HIV incidence is a necessary precursor to HIV deaths.

Next we consider international community funding F. From Table 4, the most significant driver of F is population size n. Table 3 shows that the higher the population size, the higher the aid flows. This may perhaps mean that the formula for allocating funds by donors relies too heavily on size of the country than the level of disease burden. If this is the case, this may need to be corrected.

In terms of drivers of policy maker funding f, the prevalence rate, followed by the incidence rate, are major factors, as shown in Table 5. This makes sense, as one expects countries with high prevalence and incidence rate that feeds prevalence, to distribute more funding to HIV. The econometric results show that the drivers of the theoretic model do determine the outcomes.

Policy implications, suggestions and predictions

In this section we use the model and properties to generate policy implications and predictions.

First, when the policy maker has limited funding, the country has a large population, the disease contraction probability is large, and when the probability that an

Table 4 Determinants of international community funding F

Variable	Coefficient	Std Error	t-Value	Significance level
Constant	6822084.868	27527999.14	0.248	0.806
Prevalence(No)	6562456.103	10037639.62	0.654	0.519
Population Size(n)	2.643	0.503	5.244[a]	0.000
Incidence Rate(No)	21186583.86	115023421.114	−0.184	0.855
Domestic Funding	0.451	0.352	1.282	0.211

R-Squared = 0.757; Adjusted R-Squared = 0.572; [a] means significant at the 5% level

Table 5 Determinants of policy maker funding f

Variable	Coefficient	Std Error	t-Value	Significance level
Constant	7408274.859	14835660.7	−0.499	0.622
Prevalence(No)	11851648.1	4955483.549	2.392[a]	0.024
Population Size(n)	0.252	0.388	−0.650	0.522
Incidence Rate(No)	97496309.5	59244152.819	−1.646	0.112
International Funding	0.132	0.103	1.282	0.211

R-Squared = 0.642; Adjusted R-Squared = 0.412; [a]means significant at the 5% level

individual remains sick or dies is large, then the international community is more likely to contribute funds. This has largely been the case in countries such as Kenya or Mozambique or Uganda with low resources but high disease burden. This raises the issue of whether countries with small populations should be penalized and receive meager donor resources. One example is resource constrained Swaziland with a small population, and a high disease burden and incidence rate.

Second, if the international community announces willingness to provide funds, then the policy maker will free ride. This raises the issue of whether free riding by policy makers should be allowed, whether it should be regulated, etc. A few countries in Africa have abdicated on their duty of rescuing their citizens, and delegated HIV intervention to international donors. Country ownership of programs has been seen to help building domestic systems for service delivery. A further issue to consider is whether to broaden and deepen tax-bases and other revenue resources from affected countries. The relevance and strength of commitment mechanisms to regulate free riding practices by affected countries should be analyzed.

Third, if the policy maker has substantial available resources, e.g. Botswana with substantial revenues from natural resources, then an incentive exists for the international community to free ride and not provide funding. The wisdom of such free riding should be questioned. The international community has the capacity of imposing higher standards. The efficiency in converting funds into outcomes and utility is something that the international community has been emphasizing through pronouncements in the Paris Declaration and Aid-effectiveness pronouncements. Furthermore, even the countries with large resources are carrying the future debt from funding the liability of HIV. This debt needs to be financed, and even large domestic resources may not be enough.

Fourth, the probability of contracting the disease falls to its minimum when the policy maker distributes all his resources to disease prevention, and reaches a maximum when the policy maker distributes no resources to disease prevention. Obviously, when disease prevention works, it seems to make sense to distribute more resource towards it. However, the marginal cost of increasing coverage of prevention programs may rise as the policy maker adds more people to the programs. Especially including people in rural areas with poor road access may cause general service delivery costs to increase.

Finally, the probabilities of disease contraction, and remaining sick or dying given contraction, depend on the fractions of funds distributed to prevention versus treatment. More funding causes lower probabilities. One determining factor is the relative marginal costs of prevention versus treatment. One recommendation is to distribute funds to both activities by accounting for the relative marginal costs of provision, by equating the two marginal costs.

Discussion and Conclusion

We have developed a four-period game between a policy maker and the international community on how to fund prevention and treatment of diseases, exemplified with HIV. We account for the behavior of individuals who engage in risky versus safe behavior which may or may not cause disease contraction. This approach is to our knowledge the first of its kind and extends earlier research where this phenomenon has been analyzed "one player at a time", instead of scrutinizing strategic interaction. The policy maker chooses in period 1 which fraction of his funds to distribute to disease prevention, and the remaining fraction is distributed to disease treatment. In period 2 the international community chooses an analogous distribution to prevention and treatment, or may choose not to provide funds. In period 3, nature determines who contracts the disease. Finally, in period 4, nature chooses, among those that have contracted the disease, who recovers and who remains sick or dies.

We find, first, that distributing substantial funds to prevention, by the policy maker or the international community, intuitively decreases the disease contraction probability, but those that contract the disease has a high probability of remaining sick or dying due to the limited funding to treatment. This illustrates how funding impacts how individuals behave in the face of a deadly disease. Second, and conversely, distributing substantial funds to disease treatment increases the disease contraction probability, but those contracting the disease recover with a higher probability. Third, if the cost effectiveness of treatment relative to prevention is higher, more emphasis on treatment is appropriate. Fourth, country specific conditions impact the appropriate relative channeling of funds into prevention versus treatment. Fifth, if the international community converts funds into disease prevention and treatment more efficiently than the policy maker, then relatively more funds from the international community may be expected in countries needing efficient funds conversion. Sixth, the policy maker's and international community's unit costs of converting funds into utility for the population impact their relative contributions. Seventh, more funding can be expected if the recovery utility and utility of remaining sick or dying are far below the no disease utility. Eighth, the policy maker and international community may free ride on each other's contributions.

The disease contraction probability intuitively is minimal when the policy maker distributes all his funds to disease prevention, and maximal when no funds are distributed to disease prevention. Thus, for example, a large utility difference between no disease and recovery causes the policy maker to distribute a large fraction of his funds to disease contraction causing a low disease contraction probability. Furthermore, a large unit cost for the international community in converting funding into utility causes large disease contraction probability.

From outcomes of the model, the paper argues for the need to create commitment-mechanisms to ensure that free riding by both countries and the international community is avoided. This means replacing a non-cooperative game with a cooperative game. Examples of such commitment mechanisms are in the Global Fund for HIV/AIDS, TB, and Malaria. Such commitment mechanisms require countries to co-finance, which may be effective, as countries never fully co-finance. We furthermore argue for commitment to funding both prevention and treatment, by policy makers and the international community. Without commitment mechanisms the game may result e.g. in countries with limited resources suboptimally focusing only on prevention, or only on treatment. The model further illustrates the mechanisms for determining appropriate funding levels, acknowledging limited return on investment, and how more funding can reduce the probabilities of disease contraction and death from the disease.

We classify countries according to characteristics and strategic choices that determine the empirically estimated disease contraction probability. We also tested for the drivers for expressions for the fraction of resources distributed to disease prevention, the disease contraction probability, the probability that an individual remains sick or dies, and additional funding by the international community provides. We estimate the regression equations. The results largely confirm the various theoretical relationships. We discuss the policy implications of the outcomes (assertions) of the model. Future research should look more thoroughly into a "commitment technology" in the form of a global governance mechanism that forces policy makers and donors to both commit to funding prevention and treatment, and not to free ride.

Endnotes

[1]Examples are diseases which are infectious, airborne (pathogens may be viruses, bacteria, or fungi), non-communicable (e.g. heart disease, cancer), foodborne (consuming food with pathogenic bacteria, toxins, viruses, prions, parasites, etc.), or involve lifestyle (e.g. sedentary lifestyle, diets with refined carbohydrates, trans fats, alcohol, drugs, etc.).

[2]We use the word international community to cover private and public financial donors, which also can come from within the given country from actors not associated with the country's policy maker.

[3]Recovery from a chronic disease such as HIV is impossible, but both prevention and treatment may ensure that the disease does not progress into AIDS causing death.

[4]http://www.amfar.org/about-hiv-and-aids/facts-and-stats/statistics–worldwide/, retrieved January 18, 2017.

[5]Angola, Benin, Botswana, Burkina Faso, Burundi, Cameroon, Chad, Congo, Democratic Rep., Cote d'Ivoire, Egypt, Equatorial Guinea, Eritrea, Ethiopia, Gabon, Gambia, Ghana, Guinea, Guinea-Bissau, Kenya, Lesotho, Liberia, Madagascar, Malawi, Mali, Mauritania, Mauritius, Morocco, Mozambique, Namibia, Niger, Nigeria, Rwanda, São Tomé and Príncipe, Senegal, Sierra Leone, South Africa, Swaziland, Tanzania, Togo, Tunisia, Uganda, Zambia, Zimbabwe.

Authors' contribution

All authors have contributed to all parts of the paper. Both authors read and approved the final manuscript.

Competing interests

The authors declare that they have no competing interests.

Author details

[1]Faculty of Social Sciences, University of Stavanger, 4036 Stavanger, Norway.
[2]Blavatnik School of Government & Fellow, St Antony's College, University of Oxford, Radcliffe Observatory Quarter, Oxford OX2 6GG, UK.

References

1. Alistar SS, Brandeau ML. Decision Making for HIV Prevention and Treatment Scale up: Bridging the Gap between Theory and Practice. Medical Decision Making. 2012;32(1):105–17. doi:10.1177/0272989x10391808.
2. Atun R, Chang AY, Ogbuoji O, Silva S, Resch S, Hontelez J, Bärnighausen T. Long-term financing needs for HIV control in sub-Saharan Africa in 2015–2050: a modelling study. BMJ Open. 2016;6(3): .doi:10.1136/bmjopen-2015-009656.
3. Bertozzi S, Padian NS, Wegbreit J, DeMaria LM, Feldman B, Gayle H, Isbell MT. HIV/AIDS prevention and treatment. Disease control priorities in developing countries. 2006;2:331–70.
4. Boily M-C, Mâsse B, Alsallaq R, Padian NS, Eaton JW, Vesga JF, Bartlett J. HIV Treatment as Prevention: Considerations in the Design, Conduct, and Analysis of Cluster Randomized Controlled Trials of Combination HIV Prevention. PLoS Medicine. 2012;9(7):e1001250. doi:10.1371/journal.pmed.1001250.
5. Bärnighausen T, Salomon JA, Sangrujee N. HIV Treatment as Prevention: Issues in Economic Evaluation. PLoS Medicine. 2012. doi:10.1371/journal.pmed.1001263.
6. Canning D. The Economics of HIV/AIDS in Low-Income Countries: The Case for Prevention. Journal of Economic Perspectives. 2006;20(3):121–42. doi:10.1257/jep.20.3.121.
7. Coates TJ, Richter L, Caceres C. Behavioural strategies to reduce HIV transmission: how to make them work better. The Lancet. 2008;372(9639): 669–84. doi:10.1016/S0140-6736(08)60886-7.
8. Cohen D, Shin-Yi W, Farley T. Cost-Effective Allocation Of Government Funds To Prevent HIV Infection. Health Affairs. 2005;24(4):915–26.
9. Collier P, Sterck O, Manning R. The Moral and Fiscal Implications of Anti-Retroviral Therapies for HIV in Africa (Vol. 2015-05): Centre for the Study of African Economies, University of Oxford. 2015.
10. Creese A, Floyd K, Alban A, Guinness L. Cost-effectiveness of HIV/AIDS interventions in Africa: a systematic review of the evidence. The Lancet. 2002;359(9318):1635–42. doi:10.1016/S0140-6736(02)08595-1.
11. Daniels N, Sabin J. Accountability for Reasonable Priority Setting. In: Akabayashi A, editor. The future of bioethics: international dialogues. Oxford: Oxford University Press; 2014.
12. Galárraga O, Colchero MA, Wamai RG, Bertozzi SM. HIV prevention cost-effectiveness: a systematic review. BMC Public Health. 2009;9 Suppl 1:S5. doi: 10.1186/1471-2458-9-S1-S5.
13. Goldie SJ, Yazdanpanah Y, Losina E, Weinstein MC, Anglaret X, Walensky RP, Freedberg KA. Cost-Effectiveness of HIV Treatment in Resource-Poor Settings — The Case of Côte d'Ivoire. The New England Journal of Medicine. 2006;355(11):1141–53. doi:10.1056/NEJMsa060247.
14. Gonsalves G. HIV/AIDS prevention and treatment. The Lancet. 2002; 360(9326):87. doi:10.1016/S0140-6736(02)09344-3.
15. Granich R, Kahn JG, Bennett R, Holmes CB, Garg N, Serenata C, Zhang C. Expanding ART for Treatment and Prevention of HIV in South Africa: Estimated Cost and Cost-Effectiveness 2011-2050 (Expanding ART for HIV Treatment and Prevention). PloS One. 2012;7(2):e30216. doi:10.1371/journal.pone.0030216.
16. Hecht R, Stover J, Bollinger L, Muhib F, Case K, de Ferranti D. Financing of HIV/AIDS programme scale-up in low-income and middle-income countries, 2009–31. The Lancet. 2010;376(9748):1254–60. doi:10.1016/S0140-6736(10)61255-X.
17. HIV Modelling Consortium Treatment as Prevention Editorial Writing Group. HIV Treatment as Prevention: Models, Data, and Questions—Towards Evidence-Based Decision-Making. PLoS Medicine. 2012;9(7):e1001259. doi:10.1371/journal.pmed.1001259.
18. Hogan DR, Baltussen R, Hayashi C, Lauer JA, Salomon JA. Cost effectiveness analysis of strategies to combat HIV/AIDS in developing countries. BMJ. 2005;331(7530):1431. doi:10.1136/bmj.38643.368692.68.
19. Izazola-Licea JA, Wiegelmann J, Arán C, Guthrie T, De Lay P, Avila-Figueroa C. Financing the response to HIV in low-income and middle-income countries. JAIDS Journal of Acquired Immune Deficiency Syndromes. 2009;52:S119–26.
20. Kremer M, Glennerster R. Strong medicine : creating incentives for pharmaceutical research on neglected diseases. Princeton: Princeton University Press; 2004.
21. Kremer M, Snyder CM. Why are drugs more profitable than vaccines? vol. 9833. Cambridge: National Bureau of Economic Research; 2003.
22. Kremer M, Snyder CM. Preventatives versus Treatments. USA: Department of Economics, Harvard University; 2015.
23. Kumaranayake L, Watts C, Dixon S, Mc Donald S, Roberts J. Resource allocation and priority setting of HIV/AIDS interventions: addressing the generalized epidemic in sub-Saharan Africa. Journal of International Development. 2001;13(4):451–66. doi:10.1002/jid.797.
24. Mamani H, Chick SE, Simchi-Levi D. A game-theoretic model of international influenza vaccination coordination. Management Science. 2013;59(7):1650–70.
25. Marseille E, Hofmann PB, Kahn JG. HIV/AIDS prevention and treatment - Reply. Lancet. 2002;360(9326):87–8. doi:10.1016/s0140-6736(02)09345-5.
26. Moxnes JF, Hausken K. Mathematical modelling of acute virus influenza A infections. Mathematical and Computer Modelling of Dynamical Systems. 2012;18(5):521–38.
27. Paltiel AD, Stinnett AA. Resource allocation and the funding of HIV prevention Handbook of economic evaluation of HIV prevention programs. New York: Springer; 1998. p. 135–52.
28. Thomas P. Big shot : passion, politics, and the struggle for an AIDS vaccine. New York: Public Affairs; 2001.
29. Walker D. Cost and cost-effectiveness of HIV/AIDS prevention strategies in developing countries: is there an evidence base? Health Policy and Planning. 2003;18:4–17.

12

Regret-sensitive treatment decisions

Yoichiro Fujii[1*] and Yusuke Osaki[2]

Abstract

The threshold approach to medical decision-making, in which treatment decisions are made based on whether the probability of sickness exceeds a predetermined threshold, was introduced by (Pauker and Kassirer, N Engl J Med 293: 229-234, 1975) and (Pauker and Kassirer, N Engl J Med 302:1109-1116, 1980). This study generalizes the threshold approach using regret theory. Regret theory is one of the established alternatives to expected utility theory (EUT), and partly overcomes the descriptive limitations of EUT. Under regret theory, agents suffer disutility from regret or enjoy utility from rejoicing by comparing the chosen alternative with the forgone one. We examine the effect of regret and rejoicing on the threshold approach by setting the EU case as a benchmark, and show conditions under which regret and rejoicing monotonically change the threshold probability. The threshold probability is lowered by regret and rejoicing under the reasonable condition in the sense that the condition can explain observed choices that EU fails to describe. This suggests that agents opt to undergo medical treatment by the feeling of regret and rejoicing. This result might explain the social problems that occur in relation to the public provision of medical services in many OECD countries such as medical expenditure rising faster than government forecasts. The results also imply that regret sensitivity might cause inequality of benefits from public medical services. Finally, we offer a solution to this problem.

Keywords: Medical decision-making, Non-expected utility, Public medical service, Regret and rejoicing, Treatment threshold

JEL classification numbers: D81, I12

Background

In their semsinal research, Pauker and Kassirer [1, 2] introduced an important normative criterion into medical decision-making under risk named the "treatment threshold."

Under the treatment threshold approach, medical decision-making is related to the probability of sickness at which agents are indifferent between treatment and no treatment. This probability is referred to as the "threshold probability." If the probability of sickness is higher (lower) than the threshold probability, agents should (should not) undergo medical treatment. Since Pauker and Kassirer's work, a number of studies have examined applications of the treatment threshold.[1] However, most of these studies are based on expected utility theory (EUT), which has been the dominant tool in medical decision-making under risk.

Empirical observations of decision-making under risk often contradict EUT (e.g., Allais [3] and Kahneman and Tversky [4]), and many preference representations have been proposed to explain these observations. Bell [5] and Loomes and Sugden [6] incorporated both regret and rejoicing into preference representations in what they termed "regret theory." In regret theory, agents not only gain utility from the chosen alternatives, but also suffer disutility from regret or enjoy utility from rejoicing by comparing the chosen alternative with the forgone one.[2] Regret theory can be viewed as one of the "bold" alternatives to EUT.[3] That is, regret theory has accumulated numerous empirical studies, developed axiomatic foundations for preference representation, and been applied to various economic analyses.[4]

Somewhat surprisingly, regret theory has received scant attention in the field of medical decision-making. Thus, the present study bridges the gap between the importance of regret theory and its lack of application to medical decision-making. Agents often face difficulties in medical decision-making because their decisions can

* Correspondence: fujii@eco.osaka-sandai.ac.jp
[1]Faculty of Economics, Osaka Sangyo University, Nakagaito 3-1-1, Daito-shi, Osaka 574-8530, Japan
Full list of author information is available at the end of the article

have a serious impact on their lives. This suggests that the forgone alternatives play an essential role in medical decision-making in addition to the chosen alternatives. Regret theory can formally incorporate the effect of the forgone alternatives into medical decision-making. It enables us to examine how regret and rejoicing influence the threshold probability in the abovementioned treatment threshold approach. By introducing a weight for regret and rejoicing sensitivity, we show the condition under which the threshold probability is decreasing in the weight. In other words, more regret-sensitive agents tend to opt for treatment at lower sickness probabilities. This condition gives us the shape of the function that captures preferences for regret and rejoicing, which is called the "regret–rejoicing function." This shape seems to be reasonable based on the classical paper by Bell [5] because it succeeds in explaining the observed choices, which are inconsistent with EUT.

Regret theory has already been introduced into the treatment threshold approach by Djulbegovic et al. [7] and Hozo and Djulbegovic [8].[5] However, there are two significant differences between our study and earlier studies. The first is that earlier studies assumed the regret function to be linear, whereas this study considers the regret–rejoicing function to be nonlinear. Second, previous studies introduced the concept of "acceptable regret"[6] and examined how regret affects the threshold probability. In contrast, this study determines the threshold probability and examines how regret sensitivity affects it. Thus, this study succeeds in overcoming the problems encountered by earlier studies.[7] The first difference is essential because preferences toward regret and rejoicing can be captured by the shape of the regret–rejoicing function, and a linear regret–rejoicing function can identify EUT.[8] The shape of the regret–rejoicing function is crucial for treatment decisions, and we could obtain the wrong implications from regret theory if the shape was incorrect.

This result has implications in relation to issues surrounding the public provision of medical services. Many OECD countries collect taxes and/or public insurance premiums to provide universal health-care programs (UHCPs). However, this is a controversial issue from both political and public viewpoints. Thus, regret sensitivity might help to explain the following problems related to UHCPs: government spending on medical services is much higher than forecast, and only a small minority of the population enjoys the benefits of UHCPs. We also suggest a solution to this problem.

The rest of this paper is organized as follows. In "Methods" section, we introduce preference representation, obtain the threshold probability, and determine the effect of regret on such a probability. "Results" section presents some of the implications of the results regarding the social problems that occur in the public provision of medical services in OECD countries. We also suggest a solution to these problems based on our analysis. "Discussion" section concludes.

Methods

Regret-sensitive preference representation

Here, we describe regret theory, as formulated by Bell [5] and Loomes and Sugden [6]. An agent has two alternatives: one is chosen and the other is forgone. w_c and w_f denote the consequences of the chosen alternative and the forgone alternative, respectively. In addition, to derive the utility from the actual outcome of the chosen alternative, the agent feels *regret* if the forgone consequence is preferable to the chosen one and *rejoicing* otherwise. We adopt the specific utility form that appears in Theorem 1 of Bell [5]. The utility function of the regret theory has the following form:

$$U(w_c) + k \cdot g\big(U(w_c) - U(w_f)\big) \qquad (1)$$

We call (1) the regret-sensitive utility function and consider an agent to be regret-sensitive if his/her preference is represented by the utility form (1).[9] Here, U is a risk function that is assumed to be continuous and increasing, while g is a regret–rejoicing function that is also assumed to be continuous and increasing. Note that neither convexity nor concavity for both the risk function U and the regret–rejoicing function g is necessary for the analysis.[10]

Next, we consider the case in which the consequence of the forgone alternative is preferable to that of the chosen alternative, that is, $w_c < w_f$. In this case, an agent suffers disutility $k \cdot g(U(w_c) - U(w_f)) < 0$ by regret for his/her choice compared with a better forgone alternative. In the opposite case, that is, $w_c > w_f$, an agent gains utility $k \cdot g(U(w_c) - U(w_f)) > 0$ by rejoicing about his/her choice compared with a worse forgone alternative. A constant, $k \in [0, +\infty)$, expresses how an agent places a weight on the regret–rejoicing term. We sometimes call the agent "agent k" when the weight is k with all other things being identical. The strength of regret sensitivity can be compared using k. A formal definition is as follows.

Definition 1. *Let us consider two agents, $\overline{k}$ and $\underline{k}$. Agent $\overline{k}$ is more regret-sensitive than agent $\underline{k}$ if $\overline{k}$ is more than $\underline{k}$.*

Because agents have the same risk function and regret–rejoicing function, the difference in regret sensitivity among agents can be completely captured by k. We note that the utility function corresponds to EUT for $k = 0$[11], and the original formulation by Bell [2] and Loomes and Sugden [6] for the case that k is normalized to unity.

Treatment decision

We incorporate regret sensitivity into the classical treatment decision under diagnostic risk by Pauker and Kassirer [1, 2]. Let us consider an agent who develops particular symptoms and has a regret-sensitive utility function of (1).[12] Following Pauker and Kassirer [1, 2], we consider the following setting. There are two health states: the agent is either sick (*s*) or healthy (*h*). In addition, there are two treatment alternatives: treatment (*T*) or no treatment (*NT*). The agent needs to choose either *T* or *NT* before knowing his/her true health state. Quality-adjusted life years (QALYs) are determined by the health state and treatment choice.[13] The agent gains utility from the realized QALYs and feels either regret or rejoicing based on the difference in utility between the realized QALYs and the forgone QALYs.

Let Q_h^T (Q_s^T) denote the agent's QALYs when he/she undergoes treatment and is healthy (sick). Similarly, Q_h^{NT} (Q_s^{NT}) denotes the agent's QALYs when he/she does not undergo treatment and is healthy (sick). We assume that $Q_h^{NT} > Q_h^T > Q_s^T > Q_s^{NT}$, and set $U(Q_h^{NT}) = 1$, $U(Q_h^T) = 1\text{-}c$, $U(Q_s^T) = b$, and $U(Q_s^{NT}) = 0$ without any loss of generality. Since the risk function U is increasing, $0 < b < 1 - c < 1$. b can be interpreted as the utility of the therapeutic effect of the right treatment in the sick state. c can be viewed as the disutility of an adverse reaction to the wrong treatment in the healthy state. The agent is sick with probability p and healthy with probability $1 - p$. Under the abovementioned setting, his/her regret-sensitive EU from treatment can be written as

$$\begin{aligned} W_p^T &= p\left[U(Q_s^T) + kg\left(U(Q_s^T)\text{-}U(Q_s^{NT})\right)\right] \\ &\quad +(1\text{-}p)\left[U(Q_h^T) + kg\left(U(Q_h^T)\text{-}U(Q_h^{NT})\right)\right] \\ &= p[b + kg(b)] + (1\text{-}p)[(1\text{-}c) + kg(-c)] \\ &= p[b + c\text{-}1 + kg(b)\text{-}kg(-c)] + 1\text{-}c + kg(-c). \end{aligned}$$

Likewise, his/her regret-sensitive EU from no treatment can be written as

$$\begin{aligned} W_p^{NT} &= p\left[U(Q_s^{NT}) + kg\left(U(Q_s^{NT})\text{-}U(Q_s^T)\right)\right] \\ &\quad +(1\text{-}p)\left[U(Q_h^{NT}) + kg\left(U(Q_h^{NT})\text{-}U(Q_h^T)\right)\right] \\ &= p[0 + kg(-b)] + (1\text{-}p)[1 + kg(c)] \\ &= p[-1 + kg(-b)\text{-}kg(c)] + 1 + kg(c). \end{aligned}$$

Note that both types of regret-sensitive EU are linear functions of sickness probability p.

Regret (rejoicing) is denoted by a negative (positive) sign in the difference between utility under treatment and utility under no treatment.

For all $k \in [0, \infty)$, it is easy to obtain[14]

$$W_0^T < W_0^{NT}, W_1^T > W_1^{NT} \text{ and } \frac{\partial W_p^T}{\partial p} > \frac{\partial W_p^{NT}}{\partial p}$$

These inequalities mean that W_p^T and W_p^{NT} satisfy the single-crossing property, that is, W_p^T crosses W_p^{NT} once from below at a single sickness probability. This is easily understood by viewing Fig. 1, in which the dotted and solid lines represent the regret-sensitive EU from treatment and no treatment, respectively. We denote this probability $p(k)$ to explicitly indicate that it is dependent on regret sensitivity k, and call it the threshold probability. Probability $p(k)$ provides the threshold probability by which the agent decides whether to undergo treatment or not because

$$W_p^T > (=,<) W_p^{NT} \Leftrightarrow p > (=,<) p(k).$$

In other words, the agent makes the treatment decision after comparing the sickness probability with the threshold probability. When the sickness probability is strictly higher (lower) than the threshold probability, the agent makes the decision to undergo (not to undergo) treatment. At threshold probability $p(k)$, agent k is indifferent between treatment and no treatment. Threshold probability $p(k)$ is given by

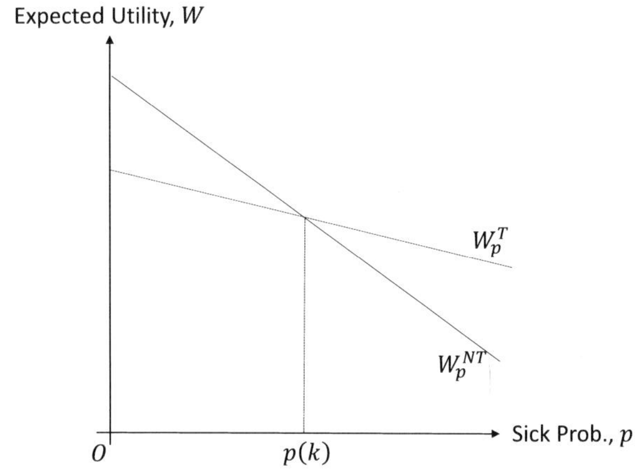

Fig. 1 Sickness probability and regret-sensitive EU. This figure illustrates that the threshold probability, $p(k)$, is the single crossing point between the regret-sensitive EU from treatment (W_p^T) and no treatment (W_p^{NT}), represented by the dotted and solid lines, respectively

$$p(k) = \frac{c + k(g(c) - g(-c))}{b + c + k(g(b) - g(-b)) + k(g(c) - g(-c))}.$$

Results

Here, we examine how regret sensitivity k affects the threshold probability $p(k)$.

The following theorem is our main result.

Theorem 1. *Suppose that the therapeutic effect in the sick state exceeds the adverse reaction in the healthy state, that is, $b \geq c$. The following conditions are equivalent:*

- *$(g(x) - g(-x))/x$ is increasing (decreasing) in x*
- *The threshold probability is decreasing (increasing) in the weight of regret sensitivity, that is, $p(k) \geq (\leq)\, p(\bar{k})$ for all $k, \bar{k}$ with $k \leq \bar{k}$.*

Proof. We denote $G(x) = g(x) - g(-x)$ for notational simplicity. The sign of $dp(k)/dk$ coincides with the sign of its numerator:

$$\begin{aligned} &G(c)(b + c + kG(b) + kG(c)) \\ &\quad -(G(b) + G(c))(c + kG(c)) \\ &\quad = bG(c) - cG(b). \end{aligned}$$

Then,

$$\begin{aligned} \frac{dp(k)}{dk} &\leq (\geq) 0 \Leftrightarrow bG(c) - cG(b) \leq (\geq) 0 \\ &\Leftrightarrow \frac{g(b) - g(-b)}{b} \geq (\leq) \frac{g(c) - g(-c)}{c}. \end{aligned}$$

Since $b \geq c$, the proof is complete.

Note that all of the variables in Theorem 1 (b, c, and x) are measured in utility units. It seems to be an innocuous assumption that the utility from the right treatment exceeds the disutility from the wrong treatment.[15] This effect of regret sensitivity on the threshold probability is dependent on the shape of the regret–rejoicing function g in terms of how regret and rejoicing affect the threshold probability. Which condition, "$(g(x) - g(-x))/x$ is increasing or is decreasing in x," is reasonable? As shown in Bell [5], some choices that cannot be captured by EUT, such as the coexistence of insurance and gambling and probabilistic insurance (Kahneman and Tversky [12]), can be explained when the regret–rejoicing function satisfies the condition whereby $(g(x) - g(-x))/x$ is increasing in x. Once this condition can be recognized from a descriptive viewpoint, introducing regret and rejoicing into the preference representation lowers the threshold probability. In other words, regret sensitivity causes the agent to tend to undergo treatment. In the remainder of this paper, we assume that $(g(x) - g(-x))/x$ is increasing in x.

We provide an intuition of Theorem 1. When the agent undergoes treatment, there are two positions of merit in terms of regret and rejoicing: the agent enjoys rejoicing from making the right decision in the sick state, which is represented by $g(b)$, and avoids regret from making the wrong decision in the sick state, which is represented by $g(-b)$. A similar argument can be applied to the case in which the agent does not undergo treatment, that is, rejoicing is $g(c)$ in the healthy state and regret is $g(-c)$ in the healthy state. From the above-mentioned argument, we can interpret Theorem 1 as follows. When the merit of treatment per utility unit $((g(b) - g(-b))/b)$ is greater than that of no treatment $((g(c) - g(-c))/c)$, the agent has a stronger incentive to undergo treatment, as the regret sensitivity k is larger.

As the EUT case corresponds to $k = 0$, we immediately obtain the following corollary.

Corollary 1. *Suppose that an agent has a regret-sensitive utility function where $(g(x) - g(-x))/x$ is increasing in x. The threshold probability of the regret-sensitive agent is lower than that in the EUT case.*

In addition, we obtain the following intuitive results by simple calculations.

Theorem 2. *Assume that g is differentiable.*

- *The threshold probability is decreasing in the therapeutic effect of the treatment, that is, $\partial p(k)/\partial b \leq 0$.*
- *The threshold probability is increasing in the adverse reaction to the treatment, that is, $\partial p(k)/\partial c \geq 0$.*

Finally, we provide a numerical example. Let us set $g(x) = x^3$, $b = 0.45$, and $c = 0.2$. We can easily confirm that $(g(x) - g(-x))/x$ is increasing in x. Figure 2 shows the relationship between regret sensitivity and the threshold probability. Let us consider the following simple example to obtain an intuitive understanding of the results based on the numerical example. An

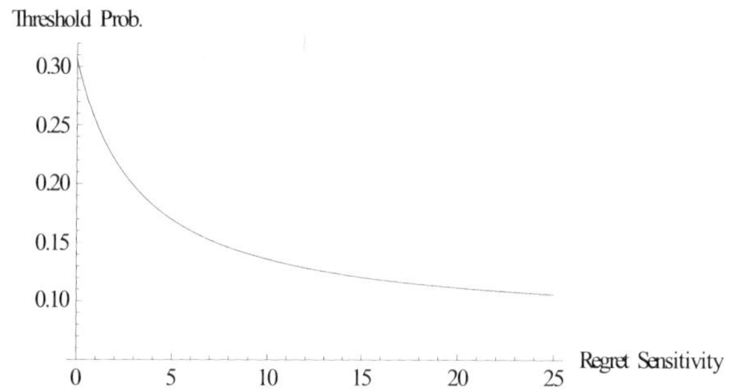

Fig. 2 Regret sensitivity and threshold probability. This figure illustrates the relationship between regret sensitivity (k) and threshold probability. We can confirm the theoretical result presented in Theorem 1. In this numerical example, we set $g(x) = x^3$, $b = 0.45$, and $c = 0.2$

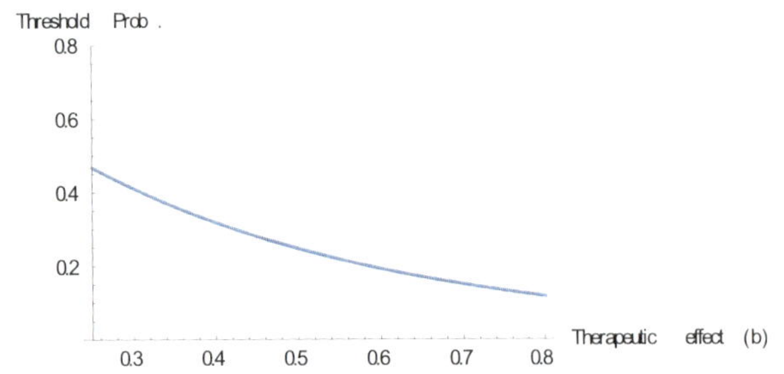

Fig. 3 Therapeutic effect and threshold probability. This figure illustrates that the relationship between therapeutic effect (b) and threshold probability. We can confirm the theoretical result presented in Theorem 2. In this numerical example, we set $g(x) = x^3$, $k = 3$, and $c = 0.2$

agent exhibits cold symptoms such as coughing and having a fever, which may also indicate the possibility of a severe illness such as pneumonia. Medical treatment is the right decision if the agent contracts a severe illness, and the agent gains the therapeutic effect, b. However, treatment is the wrong decision if he/she merely catches a slight cold, and the agent loses the adverse reaction, c. Suppose that the agent estimates the probability of a serious illness at 0.25. From Fig. 2, we conclude that the agent need not visit a doctor to undergo treatment when k is equal to zero, which is the EU case.[16] However, the conclusion may be the opposite in regret theory. The agent should visit a doctor when, for example, k is equal to 3.[17] It is important to classify whether the agent is sophisticated or naïve in terms of his/her regret sensitivity. When the agent is naïve, he/she cannot recognize that the medical decision is dependent on his/her regret sensitivity. We also examine the effect of the therapeutic effect of the treatment (b) and the adverse reaction to the treatment (c) on the threshold probability based on the above numerical example, where we set $k = 3$ (Figs. 3 and 4).

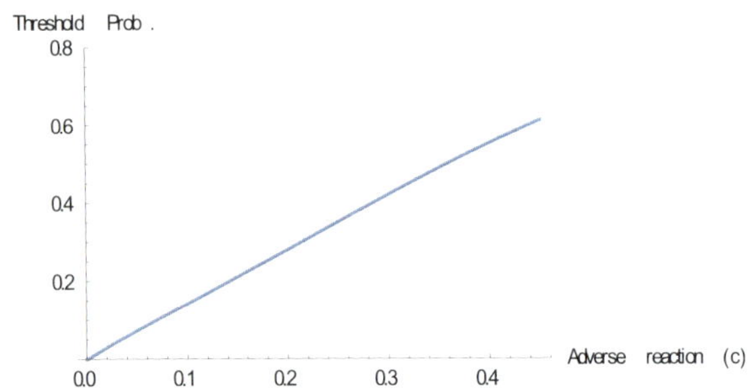

Fig. 4 Adverse reaction and threshold probability. This figure illustrates that the relationship between adverse reaction (c) and threshold probability. We can confirm the theoretical result presented in Theorem 2. In this numerical example, we set $g(x) = x^3$, $k = 3$, and $b = 0.45$

Discussion

Many OECD countries provide public medical services through universal health-care programs (UHCPs). The United States was previously an exception until a UHCP (known as Obamacare) was introduced in 2010.[18] In this section, we demonstrate how regret sensitivity may cause problems in UHCPs and suggest a solution to help mitigate these problems. We discuss two problems: (i) regret sensitivity leads to higher medical costs than the government has forecast and (ii) regret sensitivity causes inequality of benefits from public medical services.

Before proceeding with the exposition, we introduce the notion of willingness to pay (WTP) for treatment, which is defined as the maximum amount an agent can pay to undergo treatment. The threshold probability $p(k)$ can be transformed into a monetary value by $WTP(k)$, which represents the WTP of agent k. From Theorem 1, we show that the WTP of a regret-sensitive agent $\bar{k}$ is higher than that of a less regret-sensitive agent k $(\leq \bar{k})$, *that is,* $WTP(\bar{k}) \geq WTP(k)$.[19]

Under UHCPs, an agent only pays a part of the actual cost of treatment, with the remainder being paid for by subsidies collected from the entire nation through taxes and/or insurance premiums. We call the amount of agents' own payments their "medical expenses," and denote this by ME.[20]

Increases in medical expenses and inequality of benefits

Here, we show that regret sensitivity may increase medical cost the government bears than one the government forecasts. Let us consider agents to be homogeneous, apart from their sickness probabilities, which are uniformly distributed over $[0, 1]$ by normalization. A policymaker determines the subsidy necessary to maximize social welfare and estimates that the optimal proportion of the population undergoing treatment is $1 - p^*$. EUT has traditionally been the dominant tool, and is considered to be a suitable normative criterion in medical decision-making. Based on EUT, the subsidy should be set at $p^* = p(0)$. Recall that $k = 0$ corresponds to EUT. Here, we consider that agents maximize their regret-sensitive EU in reality, even though EUT is the basis of policymaking. The strength of regret sensitivity is denoted by $k > 0$. Given the medical expenses based on EUT, the threshold probability becomes $p(k)$, which is less than $p(0)$. Thus, $1 - p(k)$ of the population undergo treatment. As a result, the government will incur higher medical costs than expected, that is, $p(0) - p(k)$ times the subsidy. The above argument suggests that medical cost the government bear may become too high if regret sensitivity is taken into consideration in medical decision-making.

Regret sensitivity might also lead to inequality of benefits from medical services in UHCPs. Let us assume that agents have different strengths of regret sensitivity $k \in [0, 1]$, and are identical in all other aspects. We denote the WTP for the treatment of agent k as $WTP(k)$. The medical expense, ME, is set as $WTP(0) \leq ME \leq WTP(1)$. There exists k^O such that $ME = WTP(k^O)$. If regret sensitivity k is more (less) than k^O, agent k tends to undergo (not to undergo) treatment because $ME = WTP(k^O) \leq (\geq) WTP(k)$ for $k^O \leq (\geq) k$. This means that agents whose regret sensitivity is greater than k^O can benefit from all of the medical services provided by UHCPs, even though the subsidy is collected from the entire nation, including agents with lower regret sensitivity, that is, $k < k^O$. This inequality causes the only difference in regret sensitivity in our setting. From this observation, UHCPs need some mechanisms by which they can guarantee equality, regardless of the differences in regret sensitivity.

Suggested solution

Here, we suggest a solution to the problems caused by regret sensitivity. In this subsection, we consider the example used in the Results section. Let us consider cold symptoms, which are also related to the probability of a severe illness such as pneumonia. The probability of severe illness is denoted as p. If the agent visits a doctor, he/she gains the benefit (b) of receiving treatment when the illness is severe, but incurs a cost in terms of money and time (c).[21]

Let us consider two agents, $\bar{k}$ and k, with $\bar{k} > k$. We assume the following situation. Both agents display cold symptoms twice a year, and the medical expense lies at $WTP(\bar{k}) > ME > WTP(k)$. In this situation, agent $\bar{k}$ visits a doctor twice a year, but agent k never visits a doctor. As a result, agent $\bar{k}$ can obtain a benefit from UHCPs, but agent k cannot. If the medical expense is set such that it increases with the times to visit a doctor, it may be possible to prevent this inequality caused by regret sensitivity. For example, consider the case in which the medical expense is set to $ME(2) > WTP(\bar{k}) > WTP(k) > ME(1)$, where $ME(i)$ denotes the medical expense of i ($i = 1, 2$) visits to a doctor. In this setting, both agents visit a doctor once a year, so there is no inequality between patient $\bar{k}$ and patient k. This might also reduce medical costs because it prevents highly regret-sensitive agents from visiting a doctor numerous times.

The early detection of serious illness is important. Doctors may find signs of serious illness such as pharyngeal cancer when agents present with what appear to be merely cold symptoms. The possibility of early detection diminishes per examination. Thus, equality of access to medical treatment is important not only for reducing medical costs, but also for the early detection of serious illness in more people.

In this section, we consider the situation in which the decision-maker is an agent. However, a similar argument can also be applied to other situations, for example, where the medical decision is made by the agent's general practitioner (GP). The GP decides whether to refer an agent to a specialist based on their estimation of the likelihood of severe illness following a medical examination of what initially appear to be cold symptoms. When the GP is naïve in relation to regret sensitivity in medical decision-making, some variations to our suggested solution might be promising ways to mitigate the problems. On one hand, the GP is somewhat reluctant to refer an agent to a specialist if he/she does not appear to have a serious illness. On the other hand, the GP is fearful of missing a severe illness. In this situation, the GP might be reluctant to routinely refer the agent to a specialist if the GP is unsure that the agent has a severe illness. This kind of pressure is harmful to a society based on EUT. However, this kind of pressure may be useful in mitigating the problems caused by the presence of regret sensitivity.

Because the example considered in this section is a simplification of the complexity in the real world, we recognize that our suggested solution cannot be directly applied to solving real-world problems. However, this suggested solution might be a useful as a starting point for a discussion on policy intervention in relation to medical treatment to mitigate social problems.

Conclusion

In this study, regret and rejoicing are incorporated into the classical medical decision-making problem presented by Pauker and Kassirer [1, 2]. When the regret–rejoicing function satisfies the condition that $(g(x) - g(-x))/x$ is increasing in x, the threshold probability decreases as a result of regret sensitivity. In other words, agents with higher regret sensitivity tend to opt for more medical treatment.

In a recent study, Felder and Mayrhofer [9] showed that the threshold probability decreases when risk vulnerable agents face comorbidity risk in addition to diagnostic risk. This might explain empirical findings of lower threshold probabilities than those predicted by the classical model of Pauker and Kassirer [1, 2]. It is interesting that we obtain the same result as Felder and Mayrhofer [9], even though our approaches differ.

The limitations of this study are its simple setting, namely, a binary state and a binary choice. While this setting is necessary for the treatment threshold approach, we should relax these assumptions in future research. The binary choice is essential because the original regret theory, which is adopted in this study, causes intransitivity in choices from among more than two alternatives. To avoid this difficulty, we need to adopt modified versions of regret theory satisfying transitivity, for example, the preference representation proposed by Braun and Muermann [10].

It goes without saying that we need a parametric form of regret-sensitive utility function for actual applications. Even though measurement methods to elicit preference parameters of regret theory have been developed, for example by Bleichrodt et al. [11], we need to collect more experimental and empirical evidence to obtain consensus regarding plausible parametric forms of the regret-sensitive utility function. In addition to addressing the limitations of this study, this is an important future line of research regarding the application of regret theory. Qualitative analysis, including that presented in this study, will also play a complementary role in examining the descriptive properties of specific forms of the regret-sensitive utility function.

Endnotes

[1]Comprehensive surveys of medical decision-making were undertaken by Eeckhoudt [12] and Felder and Mayrhofer [13]. Djulbegovic et al. [14] present a review of recent developments in the treatment threshold approach.

[2]Although we adopt "regret theory" in accordance with this custom, the name may be misleading because we must keep in mind that rejoicing is also included in regret theory.

[3]We have borrowed the word "bold" from Bleichrodt and Wakker [15].

[4]Bleichrodt and Wakker [15] provide an excellent survey of the development of regret theory.

[5]A series of studies and other related literature are included in the references therein.

[6]In this approach, ranges of sickness probabilities are determined, in which people feel regret below specified levels by undergoing medical treatment.

[7]As noted in Hozo and Djulbegovic [8] (p. 542), "the complexity of modelling negative regret values and nonlinear value functions in a medical setting makes this original economic definition of regret difficult to apply."

[8]Since the threshold probabilities based on both EUT and the linear regret function coincide, earlier studies needed to adopt a different approach such as acceptable regret.

[9]The regret utility function is cardinal in the sense that it is unique up to the affine transformation.

[10]Because we do not consider any optimization problems in our analysis, no regularity conditions for optimality are necessary.

[11]The regret-sensitive utility function also corresponds to EUT when the regret–rejoicing function is linear.

[12]In general, treatment decisions are not necessarily made by the agent. Decisions might be taken by his/her family, his/her general practitioner (GP), or someone else.

[13]The health outcome is measured in QALYs for ease of exposition. We can adapt any other variables if the health outcome is measurable and unidimensional.

[14]may be positive when regret sensitivity is sufficiently large.

[15]If is less than, we obtain the same statement by reversing either of the conditions.

[16]For ease of exposition, we consider the situation in which an agent decides whether to visit a specialist or not. The same explanation can be applied to other situations by changing roles. For example, an agent goes to see a GP, and the GP makes the decision to refer the agent to a specialist or not.

[17]The threshold probability is 0.25 when is about 1.12.

[18]The Obamacare was reviewed under Trump administration.

[19]A formal argument is presented in the Appendix.

[20]The actual costs are equal to the sum of the medical expenses and subsidies.

[21]Money and time are evaluated in terms of QALYs.

Appendix

In introducing WTP, we consider a bivariate risk function whose first argument is monetary wealth and second argument is QALYs, $U(M, Q)$. The bivariate risk function is assumed to be increasing in both the first and second arguments, that is, U_1, $U_2 > 0$. WTP is defined as the maximum monetary amount agents are willing to pay for treatment. Agent k is endowed with initial wealth M. $WTP(k)$ is referred to as the WTP of agent k. Final wealth can be written as $M^T(k) - M - WTP(k)$ when the agent undergoes treatment and $M^{NT} = M$ when the agent does not undergo treatment. As noted in the main text, utility is set as $U(M^{NT}, Q_h^{NT}) = 1$, $U(M^T, Q_h^T) = 1 - c(k)$, $U(M^T, Q_s^T) = b(k)$, and $U(M^{NT} Q_s^{NT}) = 0$. We retain the assumption that $0 < b(k) < 1 - c(k) < 1$. WTP satisfies the following condition:

$$W_p^T(k, WTP(k)) = p[b(k) + kg(b(k))] + (1-p)$$
$$[(1-c(k)) + kg(-c(k))] = p[kg(-b(k))] + (1-p)$$
$$[1 + kg(c(k))] = W_p^{NT}(k, WTP(k)).$$

Given the WTP, the above condition is identical to the threshold probability.

From Theorem 1, we obtain the following inequality:

$$W_p^T(\bar{k}, WTP(k)) \geq W_p^{NT}(\bar{k}, WTP(k))$$

for all $\bar{k}$ where $\bar{k} \geq k$. This means that agent $\bar{k}$ can pay additional costs to undergo treatment. As a result, we obtain $WTP(\bar{k}) \geq WTP(k)$. We set $k = k$, and $WTP(\bar{k}) \geq WTP(k)$ holds for $\bar{k}$ and k with $\bar{k} \geq k$.

Acknowledgements

The authors thank two anonymous reviewers for their constructive suggestions, and Hideki Iwaki, Thomas Mayrhofer, Isao Miura, Peter Wakker, and the participants at the Foundations of Utility and Risk 2016 and the 2017 Autumn Meeting of the Japan Association for Applied Economics for their helpful comments on earlier versions of this paper.

Funding
This work was partly supported by JSPS Kakenhi Grant Number 17KO3637 (Fujii) 26705004 (Osaki) and The Focused Research of Osaka Sangyo University (Fujii and Osaki).

Authors' contributions
Both authors contributed equally to this work. Both authors also read and approved the final manuscript.

Competing interests
The authors declare that they have no competing interests.

Author details
[1]Faculty of Economics, Osaka Sangyo University, Nakagaito 3-1-1, Daito-shi, Osaka 574-8530, Japan. [2]Faculty of Commerce, Waseda University, Nishi-waseda 1-6-1, Shinjuku-ku, Tokyo 169-8050, Japan.

References
1. Pauker S, Kassirer J. Therapeutic decision making: a cost-benefit analysis. N Engl J Med. 1975;293(5):229–34.
2. Pauker S, Kassirer J. The threshold approach to clinical decision making. N Engl J Med. 1980;302(20):1109–16.
3. Allais M. Le comportement de l'homme rationnel devant le risque: critique des postulats et axiomes de l'Ecole Americaine. Econometrica. 1953;21(4):503–46.
4. Kahneman D, Tversky A. Prospect theory: an analysis of decision under risk. Econometrica. 1979;47(2):263–91.
5. Bell D. Regret in decision making under uncertainty. Oper Res. 1982; 30(5):961–81.
6. Loomes G, Sugden R. Regret theory: an alternative theory of rational choice under uncertainty. Econ J. 1982;92(368):805–24.
7. Djulbegovic B, Hozo I, Schwartz A, McMasters KM. Acceptable regret in medical decision making. Med Hypotheses. 1999;53(3):253–9.
8. Hozo I, Djulbegovic B. When is diagnostic testing inappropriate or irrational? Acceptable regret approach. Med Decis Mak. 2008;28(4):540–53.
9. Felder S, Mayrhofer T. Risk preferences: consequences for test and treatment threholds and optimal cutoffs. Med Decis Mak. 2014;34(1):33–41.
10. Braun M, Muermann A. The impact of regret on the demand for insurance. J Risk Insur. 2004;71(4):737–67.
11. Bleichrodt H, Cillo A, Diecidue E. A quantitative measurement of regret theory. Manag Sci. 2010;56(1):161–75.
12. Eeckhoudt L. Risk and medical decision making. Boston: Kluwer; 2002.
13. Felder S, Mayrhofer T. Medical decision making: a health economic primer. Berlin: Springer; 2011.
14. Djulbegovic B, Ende J, Hamm RM, Mayrhofer T, Hozo I, Pauker SG. When is rational to order a diagnostic test, or prescribe treatment: the threshold model as an explanation of practice variation. Eur J Clin Investig. 2015;45(5):485–93.
15. Bleichrodt H, Wakker PP. Regret theory: a bold alternative to the alternatives. Econ J. 2015;125(583):493–532.

13

Some microeconometric evidence on the relationship between health and income

Amélie Adeline* and Eric Delattre

Abstract

This paper examines the association between income, income inequalities and health inequalities in Europe. The contribution of this paper is to study different hypotheses linking self-perceived health status and income, allowing for the identification of different mechanisms in income-related health inequalities. Using data from the Survey of Health, Ageing and Retirement in Europe (15 countries), we take the advantage of the cross-sectional and longitudinal nature of this rich database to make robust results. The analyses (coefficient estimates as well as average marginal effects) strongly support two hypotheses by showing that (i) income has a positive and concave effect on health (Absolute Income Hypothesis); (ii) income inequalities in a country affect all members in a society (strong version of the Income Inequality Hypothesis). However, our study suggests that, when considering the position of the individual in the income distribution, as well as the interaction between income inequalities and these rankings, one cannot identify individuals the most affected by income inequalities (which should be the least well-off in a society according to the weak version of the Income Inequality Hypothesis). Finally, the robustness of this study is emphasized when implementing a generalized ordered probit to consider the subjective nature of the self-perceived health status to avoid the traps encountered in previous studies.

JEL Classification: I00, I14, D31

Keywords: Health inequalities, Income inequalities, Self-reported health, Europe

Background

The last few years have seen unprecedented attention to an attempt by policy makers, policy advisers and international institutions to reduce health inequalities. To do so, they usually focus on the access to healthcare, given that such policies allow to improve the health of lower income groups [28, 34]. Improving equality of access to healthcare is however not the sole public policy which can favor health equality. In particular, it has been widely said that income and income inequalities are associated to health status; thus, any public policy which influences income and/or income inequalities might influence health. In this way, studying the relationship between income, income inequalities and health is interesting per se. With these elements in mind, this paper confronts on an empirical basis three hypotheses. The first one, called the Absolute Income Hypothesis, was initially introduced by Preston [29] and states that there is a positive and concave relationship between income and health.[1] Higher incomes can provide means for purchasing a better health status. The second one is the strong version of the Income Inequality Hypothesis and it asserts that the health status is determined by income inequalities within a society. Thus, the health of all individuals is affected by an increase or a decrease in income inequalities. The last one, a weak version of the Income Inequality Hypothesis, says that income inequalities are a threat to individuals placed at the lower end of the income distribution. This last hypothesis implies that income inequalities do not impact low income people and high income people in the same magnitude.

Various authors have studied the Absolute Income Hypothesis mainly in the United States, using different health measures, like self-perceived measures [26], life expectancy [10] and other health outcomes [8, 12]. Fiscella and Franks [13], Kennedy et al. [20], Van Doorslaer et al. [32], Wagstaff et al. [33] focus on the strong version of the Income Inequality Hypothesis and show that income inequalities in a society also matter in order to explain

*Correspondence: amelie.adeline@u-cergy.fr
THEMA, University of Cergy-Pontoise, 33 Bd. du Port, 95000 Cergy, France

the average health status measured by self-perceived measures (mostly in the United States). Concerning the weak version of the Income Inequality Hypothesis, there are few empirical studies which investigate it, with the exception of Mellor and Milyo [27] in the United States, Li and Zhu [21] in China or Hildebrand and Van Kerm [15] in Europe. Importantly, the strong version of Income Inequality Hypothesis and the weak version of Income Inequality Hypothesis are non-nested given that the weak version considers the rank of individuals and an interaction term between the rank and the income inequalities index whereas the strong version does not. Thus, both versions can be valid when income inequalities in a society are negatively associated to the health of all individuals, and more particularly the health of people ranked at the lower end of the income distribution. However, the authors previously mentioned focus mainly on one of the versions in the best case (mainly on data from the United States), without comparing them. This paper aims at filling these gaps by looking at the three hypotheses, using the same European data, in order to give more insight about efficient public policies which should be implemented in Europe. Finally, studying these three hypotheses at the same time allows to highlight different mechanisms between health and income.

In this paper, we test the three above hypotheses with the Survey of Health, Ageing, and Retirement in Europe (SHARE), using mainly the fifth wave of this survey (2015 release), as well as the pooled version of the survey in robustness. We use self-perceived health status as our health outcome. This type of subjective measure is sometimes criticized but it is similar to the ones used by Mackenbach et al. [26], Fiscella and Franks [13] and Hildebrand and Van Kerm [15]. Furthermore, some authors show that these subjective measures are not biased [1]. Lastly, even if this type of measure can be criticized because of interpersonal comparison issues, authors prove that some econometric models tackle these problems [22] (see "Robustness checks" subsection for some robustness checks in which we explicitly consider this issue).

The paper is organized as follows. "Literature review: the relationship between income inequalities and health" section presents formally the three hypotheses that we will test empirically. "Method" section describes the SHARE dataset as well as the baseline econometric specification. In "Results" section we present the results and some robustness checks. "Conclusion" section concludes the paper.

Literature review: the relationship between income inequalities and health

Inequalities in health refer to the close relationship between health and membership in a group characterized by incomes, where income is an individual social determinant. This section formally presents the three hypotheses mentioned in the introduction, as well as some related literature. We should mention that, in this literature review, we transcribe terminology employed by authors which reflects causal relationships even if cross-sectional databases are used or some endogeneity might be at play.

The Absolute Income Hypothesis

From an early stage in the debate, the Absolute Income Hypothesis states that the relationship between health and income is positive and concave [29], meaning that people with higher incomes have better health outcomes, but income inequalities have no direct effect on health. As a result, the concavity of the relationship between individual income and health status is a necessary condition to assess the efficiency of redistributive policies, in which transferring a given amount of money from rich people to poor people will result in an improvement of the average health.

The individual-level relation between income and health is specified as follows:

$$h_i = \beta_0 + x_i\beta_1 + x_i^2\beta_2 + Z_i\gamma + \epsilon_i \tag{1}$$

where h_i represents the health status of individual i (objective or subjective measures); x_i is the income of individual i; Z_i is a set of individual specific control variables[2]; and ϵ_i is the error term coming from differences in individual health. The concavity effect is legitimized if β_1 is positive, β_2 is negative, and $\frac{\partial h_i}{\partial x_i} > 0$.

A strong link between health and income has been demonstrated in a large number of empirical studies, and a concave relationship between the two is found. Preston [29] explains that the impact of additional income on mortality is greater among the poor than richer people. Ettner [12], using three US surveys, finds that increases in income improve mental and physical health but also increase alcohol consumption. Then, Mackenbach et al. [26] show that a higher income is associated with better self-assessed health in Europe. Using mortality rates, Cutler et al. [10] conclude the same thing in the United States. Theodossiou and Zangelidis [31], using data on individuals aged between 50 and 65 from six European countries, find a positive but small effect of income on health. More recently, Carrieri and Jones [8] analyze the effect of income on blood-based biomarkers and find a positive and concave effect of income on health.

The strong version of Income Inequality Hypothesis

Some researchers affirm that income inequalities in a society are equally important in determining individual health status. The key difference between the Absolute Income Hypothesis and the strong version of Income Inequality Hypothesis stems from the fact that the latter explicitly considers the effect of income inequalities on health while the former only takes into account the concavity assumption between health and income. Mellor and Milyo [27] specifically define two versions of this hypothesis: the strong version and the weak version. The strong version of the Income Inequality Hypothesis implies that, whatever the level of income, the health of all individuals in a society is equivalently affected by income inequalities in this society. In this way, both the well-off and poor people are impacted by income inequalities. These may be a public bad for all members in a society since income inequalities are a threat to the health of all individuals. We can thus identify an individual effect (a micro part) which is assimilated to the Absolute Income Hypothesis and an aggregate effect (a macro part) which corresponds to the relationship between individual health and income inequalities in a society. Theoretically, the strong version of the Income Inequality Hypothesis is specified as follows:

$$h_{ij} = \beta_0 + x_i\beta_1 + x_i^2\beta_2 + \delta II_j + Z_i\gamma + \epsilon_{ij} \tag{2}$$

which is an expansion of Eq. (1) with the introduction of II_j as a measure of income inequalities in a society j (corresponding to the macro part explained above); where h_{ij} represents the health status of individual i in a society j.

This hypothesis has been empirically tested mainly on data from developed countries (principally in the United States). Tests have been conducted at both the individual level and the aggregate level. At the aggregate level, a number of studies try to demonstrate an association between income inequalities and public health and the results are contrasted [17, 25, 30]. At the individual level, Kawachi et al. [19], Kennedy et al. [20], and Fiscella and Franks [13] all find a negative association between income inequalities and self-perceived health. However, Van Doorslaer et al. [32] find no effect of income inequalities on an objective health measure, the McMaster health utility index, derived from the self-perceived health status. Finally, other authors test the impact of income inequalities on malnutrition [33] or health service use [23] and find contrasted results.

The strong version focuses on the direct ties between health and income inequalities. There are several potential pathways through which income inequalities might be negatively related to an individual's health. Kawachi and Kennedy [18] summarize three plausible mechanisms linking income inequalities to health. The first one is that disinvestment in human capital is linked to income inequalities. In states with high income inequalities, educational outcomes are negatively impacted when a smaller proportion of the state budget is spent on education which creates differences in education and thus in income. High income disparities may translate into lower social spending because interests of richer persons begin to diverge from other people in societies where inequalities rise. Thus, reducing social spending turns into a decrease in life opportunities for poorer people and thus an increase in inequalities (see also [14]). The second mechanism is that income inequalities lead to the erosion of the "features of social organization that facilitate cooperation for mutual benefit". In other words, Kawachi and Kennedy [18] interpret this mechanism as the erosion of the "social capital", corresponding to the set of collective resources an individual can put together. This may be the access to public services, the feeling of security, the characteristics of the relatives or the community solidarity (Grignon et al.: Mesurer l'impact des déterminants non médicaux des inégalités sociales de santé, unpublished). Here we focus on the solidarity argument. This one is important for the maintenance of population health. Kawachi and Kennedy [18] made a study using the General Social Survey where each indicator of social capital (like the degree of mistrust or levels of perceived reciprocity) was correlated with lower mortality rates. An increasing level of mistrust between the members of a society was due to the development of the distance between the well-off's expectation and the ones of poorer people. Unfortunately this result implies a growth of a latent social conflict. As a result, when health is associated to the erosion of social capital, this seems to be towards the transition of social policies which are detrimental to poor people, implying unequal political participation. A lower turnout at elections is perceived among states with low levels of interpersonal trust. These states are less likely to invest in policies that ensure the security of poorer people in a society. Finally less generous states are likely to provide less hospitable environments for these individuals. The last mechanism is that income inequalities are correlated to unhealthiness through stressful social comparisons. In this case, a technique in anthropology called "cultural consensus analysis" is used to take into account the psychosocial effects of social comparisons. Indeed, many communities have a common cultural model of the standard of living. This technique involves interviewing people and observing if individuals succeed in achieving the cultural model of lifestyle. This aspect can be seen as the satisfaction individuals have with their life. However, it should be noticed and not forgiven that a possible endogeneity issue can appear with this mechanism connected to the life satisfaction of individuals.

The weak version of Income Inequality Hypothesis

The second version of the Income Inequality Hypothesis is the weak one. According to this hypothesis, people who are more likely to have poorer health are the ones who feel more economically disadvantaged than their peers in a reference group. As a result, it specifically suggests that only the least well-off are hurt by income inequalities in a society. The damaging effect of these inequalities on health decreases with a person's income rank. Indeed, for an individual, stress and depression leading to illness may be linked to the fact of having a low relative income when compared to another person [9]. The main concern is thus on the difficulties that an individual may face when he is situated at the bottom of the social ladder. Theoretically, the weak version of the Income Inequality Hypothesis is specified as follows:

$$h_{ij} = \beta_0 + x_i\beta_1 + x_i^2\beta_2 + \delta II_j + \theta R_{ij} + \eta R_{ij} * II_j + Z_i\gamma + \epsilon_{ij} \quad (3)$$

which is an expansion of Eq. (2) where we introduce R_{ij} as a person's rank, and the interaction between inequalities and a person's rank ($R_{ij} * II_j$) to allow the effects of income inequalities to vary by the relative income level in a society. The interaction term allows us to know how income inequalities are related to people with lower levels of income, compared to other people. Therefore, this hypothesis suggests that the breadth of the difference between rich people and poor ones accounts for the health. When testing this equation, δ underlines the strong version of the Income Inequality Hypothesis whereas θ and η specifically refer to the weak version. Thus, if the three previous coefficients are significant and have the right signs, then both the strong and the weak version are correct, meaning that everybody's health is associated to income inequalities, and in particular people who are at the lower end of the income distribution. On the other hand, whether only δ (or θ and η respectively) is significant implies that only the strong version (*resp.* the weak version) is satisfied.

As explained in the introduction, only few researches focus on this hypothesis. Mellor and Milyo [27] use data from the Current Population Survey and find no consistent association between income inequalities and individual health. On the other hand, Li and Zhu [21], using data from China, find that income inequalities are detrimental for people who are at the lower end of the income hierarchy. Finally, Hildebrand and Van Kerm [15] also test the hypothesis that income inequalities may affect only the least well-off in a society using the European Community Household Panel but find no evidence supporting it.

Method

The data

The survey

The Survey of Health, Ageing and Retirement in Europe (SHARE) is a multidisciplinary and cross-national panel database of micro data on health, socio-economic status and social and family networks of more than 123,000 individuals aged 50 and over from many European countries and Israel [7]. Since 2004, SHARE asks questions throughout Europe to a sample of households with at least one member who is 50 and older. These households are re-interviewed every two years in the panel. SHARE is part of a context of an ageing population. It is the European Commission which has identified the need for scientific knowledge about ageing people in Europe.[3] In fact, people of the European Innovation Partnership on Active and Health Ageing project estimate that in 2050, one in three Europeans will be over 60 years old and one in ten will be over 85 years old. The SHARE survey was then constructed in the different European countries under the leadership of Professor Axel Börsch-Supan. In addition, SHARE is harmonized with the Health and Retirement Study (in the United States - HRS) and the English Longitudinal Study of Ageing (UK - ELSA).

The first wave (2004-2005, 27,014 individuals) and the second one (2006-2007, 34,393 individuals) were used to collect data on health status, medical consumption, socio-economic status and living conditions. The 2008-2009 survey (Wave 3 - "SHARELIFE") was extended to life stories by collecting information on the history of the respondents. The number of participants increased from 12 countries in wave 1, to 15 (+ Ireland, Israel, Poland and Czech Republic) in wave 2, and the third wave contains information about 14 countries. The fourth wave (2010-2011), is a return to the initial questionnaire of the first two waves. It collects data from 56,675 individuals in 16 European countries. Finally, the fieldwork of the fifth wave of this survey was completed in 2013. The following countries are included in the scientific release of 2015: Austria, Belgium, Switzerland, Czech Republic, Germany, Denmark, Estonia, Spain, France, Israel, Italy, Luxembourg, Netherlands, Sweden, and Slovenia. This wave contains the responses of 63,626 individuals. We focus on the fifth wave [3] in order to have a great number of individuals who come from different countries. Moreover, in order to test and compare the three hypotheses linking health and income, one has to use the same set of observations (e.g. the fifth wave of the SHARE survey). We do not make our analysis using directly the pooled database since all the control explanatory variables are not available in each waves, which is a limitation of this database. Moreover, we also focus on the pooled database (waves 1, 2, 4 [4–6] and 5) in order to make our results more robust (the third wave is not considered in the pooled database since it does not contain the same information as the other ones).

The advantage of the SHARE database is that it has many individual variables on health, socioeconomic status and income to perform this research. However, researchers should be also aware of the potential disadvantage of this database. Indeed, Börsch-Supan et al. [7] explain that in some waves there are a relative low response rates and moderate levels of attrition (even though the overall response rate is high compared to other European and US surveys[4]) which are due to the economic crisis faced by some countries, implying a decrease in the participation rates. Due to this attrition, we thus focus on the fifth wave of this survey instead of the pooled database. Nonetheless, we present the results using the pooled database as a robustness test.

Indexes for the measurement of income inequalities

In this study, we want to underline the effects of income inequalities on health and this is why we need a measurement of income inequalities. The Gini coefficient, as well as the Theil index are two well-known indexes which can be used.

Algebraically, the Gini coefficient is defined as half of the arithmetic average of the absolute differences between all pairs of incomes in a population, and then the total is normalized on mean income. If incomes in a population are distributed completely equally, the Gini value is zero, and if one person has all the incomes in a society, the Gini is one. The Gini coefficient can be illustrated through the Lorenz curve. However, the Gini coefficient does not take into account the income distribution since different Lorenz curves may correspond to the same Gini index.[5] In other words, it does not distinguish between inequalities in low income group and high income ones. Formally, the Gini coefficient is:

$$Gini = \frac{2\sum_i iy_i}{N\sum y_i} - \left(\frac{N+1}{N}\right) \quad (4)$$

with y_i representing the income of the population sorted and ranked, from the lowest decile group to the top decile group, and N representing the total population.

As a result, one of the solution is to use the Theil index which measures income inequalities. The Theil index is:

$$Theil = \frac{1}{N}\sum_i \frac{y_i}{\bar{y}} \ln\left(\frac{y_i}{\bar{y}}\right) \quad (5)$$

where $\bar{y}$ is the mean income per person (or expenditure per capita). In order to normalize the Theil index to vary between zero and one, we divide it by $ln(N)$.[6] It measures a "distance" of the real population and the "ideal" egalitarian state where everyone have the same income.

Since the Gini coefficient does not take into account the income distribution, most of the following tables of results will be displayed using the Theil index.

Descriptive statistics - an overview

In this paper, the data used are from the fifth wave of the SHARE survey. This wave includes responses from 63,626 respondents aged 50 and over, living in 15 different countries. Thus, this survey aims to provide information on health, income, activities and other features of the elderly. In one hand, the variable of interest is the health which is defined in the database as the self-perceived health status. Individuals are asked to classify their health using ordered qualitative labels from "poor" to "excellent. The Fig. 1 characterizes the distribution of the health variable among individuals aged 50 and older by gender for all countries. As we can see the majority of inhabitants reports being in a good health. In the other hand, one of our main determinant of health is the income. This variable can be seen as a proxy for well-being, that is to say a factor which allows individuals to improve the living standards. In the database, it corresponds to the sum of individual imputed

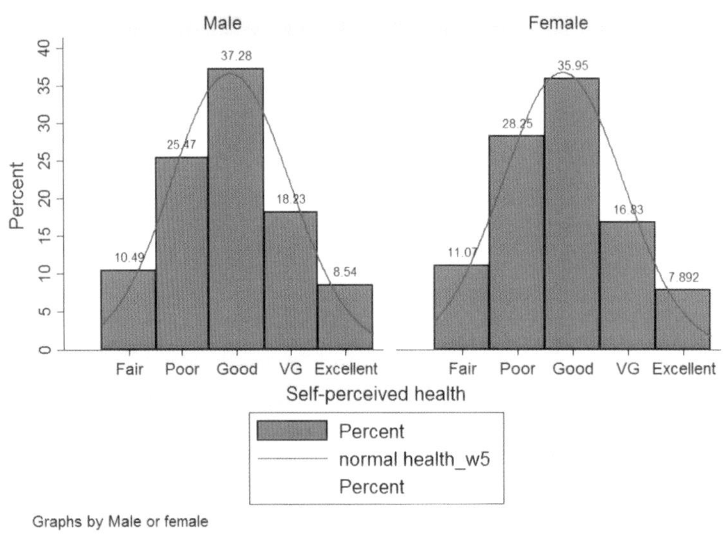

Fig. 1 Self-perceived health in Europe

income for all household components. Figure 2 shows the distribution of income of people aged 50 and over in the fifth wave where the mean is about 36,000€. Moreover, the income inequality hypothesis includes an indicator for the measurement of income inequalities (see Fig. 3). In this paper, we use either the Gini index or the Theil index. The mean of the Gini index in Europe is 0.39 which corresponds to a rather egalitarian society. The mean of the Theil index in Europe is 0.33 which is also rather egalitarian. In our analysis we include others variables such as the age, the marital status, the education, the job situation, dummies for the countries and the gender, and the GDP of the countries (see Tables 2, 3, 4 and 5 in the Appendix for further information). Finally, the pooled data (waves 1, 2, 4 and 5) contains 181,708 observations, where each individual is present on average 2.9 years in the panel.

The ordered probit model

To model the association between self-perceived health and other socioeconomic status and test the hypotheses, we use an ordered probit specification. When the self-perceived health status outcome is denoted as h_i, the model can be stated as:

$$h_i = j \qquad \text{iff} \quad \mu_{j-1} < h_i^* \leq \mu_j, \qquad \text{for} \quad j = 1, 2, 3, 4, 5 \tag{6}$$

The latent variable specification of the model that we estimate can be written as:

$$h_i^* = x_i\beta + \epsilon_i \tag{7}$$

where h_i^* is a latent variable which underlies the self-reported health status[7]; x_i is a set of observed socioeconomic variables; and ϵ_i is an individual-specific error term, which is assumed to be normally distributed.

In this data, the latent outcome h_i^* is not observed. Instead, we observe an indicator of the category in which the latent indicator falls. As a result the observed variable

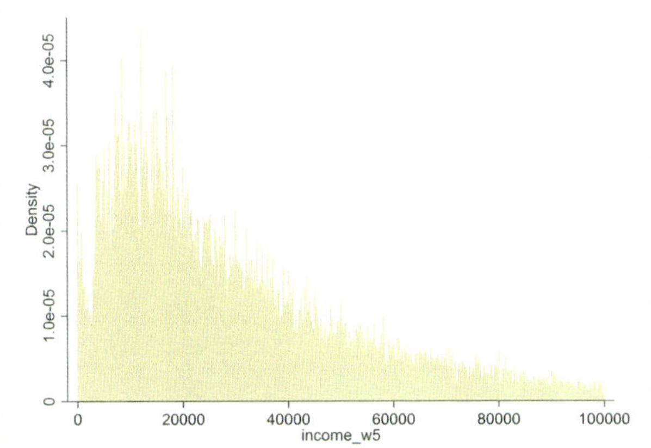

Fig. 2 Distribution of income in Europe

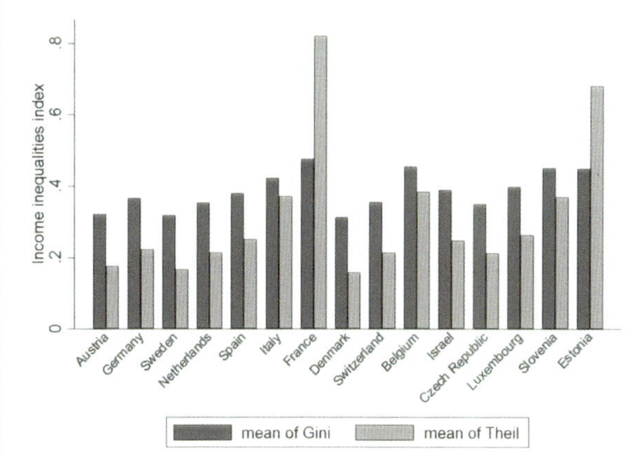

Fig. 3 Income inequalities indexes in Europe

is equal to 1, 2, 3, 4 or 5 for "poor", "fair", "good", "very good" or "excellent" with this probability:

$$P(y = j|x) = F(\mu_j - x_i\beta) - F(\mu_{j-1} - x_i\beta) \tag{8}$$

The interval decision rule is:

1. $h_i = 1$ if $h_i^* \leq \mu_1$;
2. $h_i = 2$ if $\mu_1 < h_i^* \leq \mu_2$;
3. $h_i = 3$ if $\mu_2 < h_i^* \leq \mu_3$;
4. $h_i = 4$ if $\mu_3 < h_i^* \leq \mu_4$;
5. $h_i = 5$ if $h_i^* > \mu_4$.

In this model, the threshold values $(\mu_1, \mu_2, \mu_3, \mu_4)$ are unknown. We do not know the value of the index necessary to shift from very good to excellent. In theory, the threshold values are different for everyone.

Results

Economic results and discussion

Table 1 reports coefficient estimates for all estimated ordered probit models when income inequalities are measured using the Theil index.[8] The fifth wave gives us access to 63,626 observations and we also display results of the pooled database for sake of robustness (see Table 6 in the Appendix section). Results in the first column reports the estimated coefficients for the absolute income hypothesis while results in columns two and three provide tests of both the strong version and the weak version of the income inequality hypothesis.

Coefficients of individual income and income squared provide support for all the hypotheses that there is a positive and concave relationship between income and self-perceived health status. Indeed, coefficients associated to the income variable are all positive and significant and coefficients associated to the income squared variable are all negative and significant. This implies that higher income is related to a better health outcome. As a result, the absolute income hypothesis is verified. Concerning

Table 1 Results of the ordered probit regressions for Wave 5

Variables	Absolute income	IIH	
	Hypothesis	Strong version	Weak version
Income	1.84e-06*** (1.22e-07)	1.84e-06*** (1.20e-07)	1.89e-06*** (1.44e-07)
Income squared	−2.06e-13*** (1.55e-14)	−2.04e-13*** (1.50e-14)	−2.09e-13*** (1.73e-14)
Quintiles of income: Reference - Q5			
Quintile 1			−0.258*** (0.029)
Quintile 2			−0.201*** (0.028)
Quintile 3			−0.115*** (0.027)
Quintile 4			−0.053*** (0.026)
Index of inequalities (II) - Theil		−0.403*** (0.024)	−0.838*** (0.049)
Interaction quintile 1 and II			0.115* (0.069)
Interaction quintile 2 and II			0.114* (0.068)
Interaction quintile 3 and II			0.023 (0.068)
Interaction quintile 4 and II			0.062 (0.068)
GDP		1.99e-06*** (4.53e-07)	0.0001*** (0.049)
Age	0.037*** (0.006)	0.019*** (0.006)	0.037*** (0.006)
Age squared	−0.0004*** (0.00004)	−0.0003*** (0.0004)	−0.0004*** (0.00004)
Years of education	0.034*** (0.001)	0.028*** (0.001)	0.026*** (0.001)
Gender = 1 if women	0.003 (0.009)	0.005 (0.009)	0.007 (0.009)
Marital Status: Reference - Married			
Registered partnership	−0.042 (0.035)	−0.006 (0.035)	0.058* (0.035)
Married, not living with spouse	−0.094** (0.039)	0.004 (0.039)	−0.076** (0.039)
Never married	−0.071*** (0.019)	0.023 (0.019)	0.023 (0.019)
Divorced	−0.045*** (0.015)	0.068*** (0.016)	0.032** (0.018)
Widowed	−0.024* (0.014)	0.055*** (0.015)	0.015 (0.014)
Job Situation: Reference Retired			
Employed	0.253*** (0.014)	0.224*** (0.014)	0.246*** (0.014)
Unemployed	−0.212*** (0.028)	−0.103*** (0.028)	−0.176*** (0.028)
Permanently sick	−1.25*** (0.026)	−1.069*** (0.026)	−1.207*** (0.026)
Home-maker	−0.059*** (0.017)	−0.064*** (0.017)	−0.056*** (0.017)
Other	−0.236*** (0.031)	−1.169*** (0.031)	−0.207*** (0.031)
Mechanisms IIHs:			
1st: % Health expenditure in GDP		0.077*** (0.003)	
2nd: Received help from others		−0.179*** (0.006)	
2nd bis: Given help from others		0.001*** (0.0001)	
3rd: Life satisfaction		0.216*** (0.003)	
Cut-point μ_1	−0.474 (0.216)	0.899 (0.219)	−0.428 (0.215)

Table 1 Results of the ordered probit regressions for Wave 5 *(Continued)*

Cut-point μ_2	0.615 (0.216)	2.076 (0.219)	0.632 (0.215)
Cut-point μ_3	1.746 (0.216)	3.261 (0.219)	1.728 (0.215)
Cut-point μ_4	2.592 (0.216)	4.133 (0.219)	2.548 (0.215)
ME at mean of absolute income on:			
Pr(Poor health)	−2.84e-07*** (1.92e-08)	−2.58e-07*** (1.71e-08)	−3.02e-07*** (2.32e-08)
Pr(Fair health)	−3.06e-07*** (2.05e-08)	−2.97e-07*** (1.95e-08)	−3.24e-07*** (2.49e-08)
Pr(Good health)	8.80e-08*** (6.44e-09)	6.65e-08*** (4.97e-09)	9.56e-08*** (7.80e-09)
Pr(Very good health)	2.65e-07*** (1.78e-08)	2.55e-07*** (1.68e-08)	2.79e-07*** (2.14e-08)
Pr(Excellent health)	2.37e-07*** (1.59e-08)	2.34e-07*** (1.54e-08)	2.51e-07*** (1.92e-08)

For AIH, dummies for countries are included but not reported, and available upon request
***: 1% significant; **: 5% significant; *: 10% significant. Standard deviations are in parentheses, below the coefficients.

income inequalities, coefficients on the Theil index in columns two and three are negative and significantly different from zero. This supports evidence of the strong version of income inequality hypothesis stating that an increase in income inequalities is detrimental to all members of a society, i.e. income inequalities and health are negatively related. Indeed concerning this index, zero represents an egalitarian state, thus the negative relationship between self-perceived health and the indicator of income inequalities is in line with health being better if the index is low. However, results in column three do not give support to the weak version of income inequality hypothesis which states that inequalities are more detrimental to the least well-off in a society. Indeed, we introduce individual rank (by country) and an interaction term between the rank and the index of income inequalities to allow a variation between income level and the effect of income inequalities. In the specification, we choose to follow the framework of Mellor and Milyo [27] who introduced interaction terms between the measurement of income inequalities and dummies variables based on quintiles of income (1 for the lowest income group and 5 for the highest, which is a proxy for the rank). In other words, interaction terms indicate the effect of aggregate income inequalities (at the country level) on self-perceived health status between individuals situated at different levels of the income distribution. Concerning the first two interaction terms ($II_j * Q1$ and $II_j * Q2$), these indicate the effect of aggregate income inequalities (at the country level) on self-perceived health status between the poorest individuals (situated at the lower end of the income distribution) and the richest ones (reference category corresponding to individuals situated at the top of the income distribution). These coefficients are positive and statistically significant, meaning that for the poorest individuals (compared to more well-off individuals), an increase in income inequalities in their country increases self-perceived health status, which is in contradiction with the weak version of the income inequality hypothesis. Concerning the two other interaction terms (third and fourth quintiles, representing people at the middle and almost top of the income distribution), coefficients are not statistically significant meaning that middle and higher income people are not affected at all by an increase in income inequalities. This claim does not support the weak version because this hypothesis states that people at the lower end are the most affected by an increase in income inequalities compared to people at the top of the income distribution. As a result, higher income people should also be affected by income inequalities (at a lower rate). Our qualitative results suggest that for low-income individuals, an increase in income inequalities in their country is positively related to report a better health status. Furthermore, for higher income individuals, an increase in income inequalities in their country is not related to report neither a better nor a lower health status. To conclude, our results do not support the weak version of income inequality hypothesis, but it further invalidates this weak version because our qualitative results quite claim the opposite.

Regarding the mechanisms of Kawachi and Kennedy [18] (Table 1, column two), the disinvestment in human capital (first mechanism) is characterized by the percentage of health expenditure in the GDP.[9] The coefficient associated is positively correlated to health meaning that when governments increase health spending, this has a positive effect on individual health. For the second mechanism, we want to illustrate the interaction between individuals to represent the erosion of social capital. As a result, we choose a variable from the SHARE survey: "received help from others". The coefficient associated to this variable is negative and significant. We can explain this negative association by saying that people who are in bad health are the ones who receive help. In order, to legitimize this explanation, we also do the estimation with the "reverse variable": "given help to others". In this case, the coefficient is positive and significant proving that people in good health offer their help. Then, the last mechanism is about social comparisons. The coefficient associated to this variable ("life satisfaction") is positively linked to health which implies that when individuals are satisfied with their life, they also report having a good health.

In sum, our baseline specifications provide evidence of a statistically significant association between income, income inequalities and health since results are robust to model specifications.

Robustness checks

As a sake of robustness, we also make our entire analysis using the pooled database (see Table 6 in the Appendix section) and the results are very similar to the ones obtained with the fifth wave of the survey.

To give more support to the concavity assumption, we compute, for all three hypotheses, the marginal effects at mean[10] of income on the five outcomes. Results, reported at the end of Table 1, are all significant. On one hand, for the first two outcomes, income has a negative effect on the probability to report either a poor health or a fair health status. On the other hand, there is a positive effect of income on the probability to report being in a good, very good and excellent health (outcomes three to five). These results are obtained following the ordered probit regressions of the three hypotheses, where the quadratic effect of income is investigated (see Eqs. 1, 2 and 3). These results do not validate the concavity assumption but they do show the increasing effect of income on self-perceived health status. We also plot the average marginal effect of income on each outcome for all individuals with a confidence interval, in order to give more support to the concavity effect in the three hypotheses (see Fig. 4). We restrict ourselves to individuals who earn less than 200,000€ per year (which corresponds to more than 99% of the distribution, see Table 4 in the Appendix section for further information on the distribution of income). The following graphs (Fig. 4) concern the absolute income hypothesis.[11] Graph 4a gives the impact of income on the probability to report a poor health. This impact is negative (y-axis is negative), meaning that when income raises, the probability decreases. In addition, the negative impact is stronger for the majority of the population than for individuals who earn very high incomes. In other words, for low incomes, in absolute terms, an additional increase in income has a larger impact on the probability of reporting a poor health than for very high income. This is a low support for the concavity assumption. Graph 4b gives the impact of income on the probability of reporting a fair health status. Conclusion are similar to the ones of graph 4a since the effect is negative. The slight decreases of the curve at the beginning does not impact the conclusion and can be related to large confidence intervals. Graph 4c gives the impact of income on the probability to report a good health status. For almost all the distribution, when income raises, the probability increases. Then, graphs 4d and 4e are more conclusive. Indeed, graph 4d gives the impact of income on the probability to have a very good health. For more than 99% of the income distribution, this impact is positive and decreasing, which might support the concavity assumption. Finally, graph 4e gives the impact of income on the probability of reporting an excellent health status. As previously, when income increases, the probability to have an excellent health increases. However, when we look at people with very high incomes[12], this impact is greater than for the majority of individuals.

Finally, it is important to investigate the robustness of our results by taking into account the subjective nature of the self-perceived health status. Indeed, our baseline specification depends on a dependent variable which is subjective. Self-reported measures give a good amount of information about individual health since people summarize all the health information they have from their practitioners (general practitioners and specialists) and from what they feel [1]. The use of this measure in our specification raises the problem of interpersonal comparisons between people aged 50 and over ("Is the way I consider "good health" the same as you consider this health commodity?". Empirical studies on the relationship between health, income and income inequalities commonly use ordered probit models where the thresholds are constant by assumption. However, one limit is that it restricts the marginal probability effects. In fact the distributional effects are restricted by the specific structure. Then, another limit is that additional individual heterogeneity between individual realizations is not allowed by the distributional assumption. Thus, Boes and Winkelmann [2] and Jones and Schurer [16] both give a solution to these issues with the use of the generalized ordered probit model since it is based on a latent threshold where the thresholds themselves are linear function of the explanatory variables. In other words, previous thresholds of Eq. 8 are now computed by selecting individual characteristics so that they depend on covariates:

$$\mu_{ij} = \widetilde{\mu}_j + x_i'\gamma_j \tag{9}$$

where γ_j is a vector of response specific parameters. We have:

$$\mu_{ij} = \mu_j \qquad \forall_i \in C_j \tag{10}$$

where C_j is the class. With this model, the probabilities are:

$$P(y = j|x) = F(\widetilde{\mu}_j - x_i\beta_j) - F(\widetilde{\mu}_{j-1} - x_i\beta_{j-1}) \tag{11}$$

Now, the effects of covariates on the log-odds are category-specific and this model allows to have more

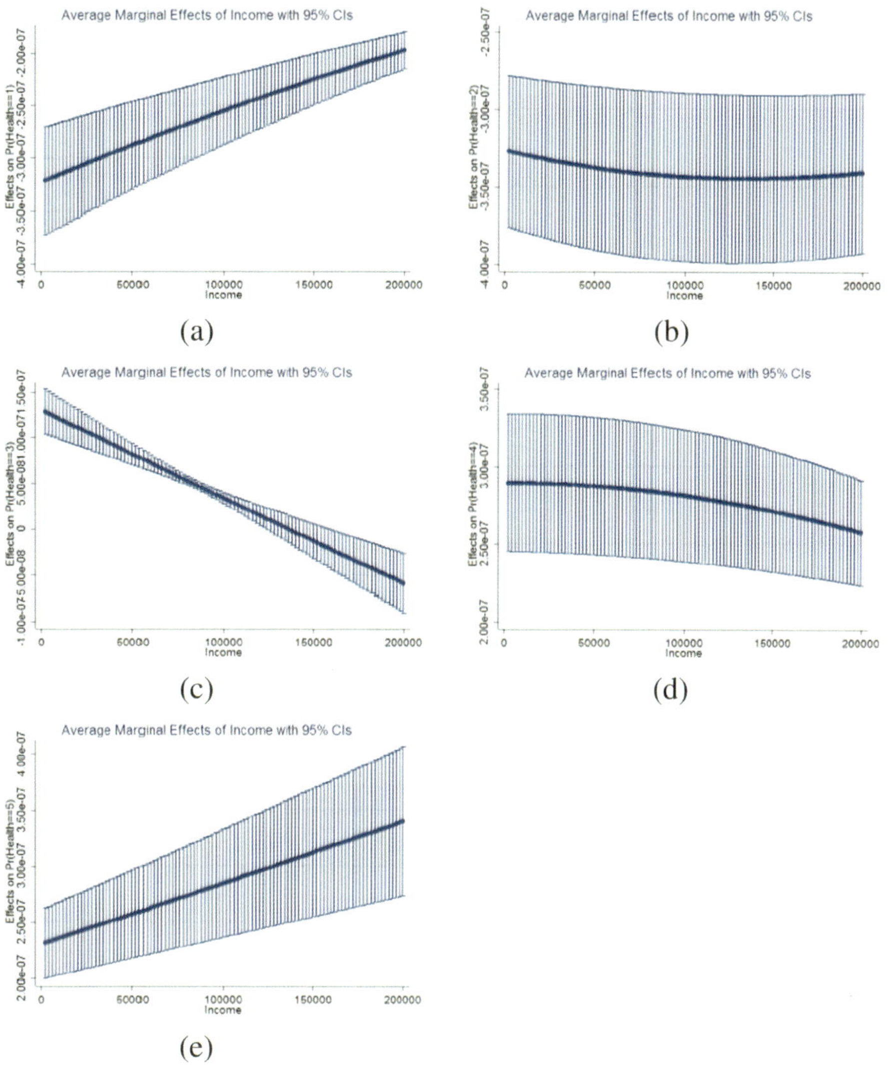

Fig. 4 Average marginal effects of income on health - Absolute Income Hypothesis. **a** Probability to report a poor health; **b** Probability to report a fair health; **c** Probability to report a good health; **d** Probability to report a very good health; **e** Probability to report an excellent health

heterogeneity across individuals. Results concerning the generalized ordered probit model are similar to those obtained from the ordered probit model. All the effects are estimated around each four cut-points (from poor to fair, from fair to good, from good to very good, and from very good to excellent). For all the hypotheses (absolute income hypothesis - Appendix: Table 7, income inequality hypothesis, both versions - Tables 8 and 9 in the Appendix part), the coefficients associated to the variables of interest (income and income squared) do not change significantly in comparison to the results with the ordered probit model. Results are consistent (either with the Theil index or the Gini coefficient for the income inequality hypothesis) as this is proved in previous study [22]. In fact, in the four cut-points, the results legitimize the concavity assumption of income since the coefficients are statistically significant. Moreover, the index of income inequalities is negative and significant which is in line with the strong version of the income inequality hypothesis. Then, concerning the interaction terms, these are not significant for all quintile groups which do not justify the weak version of income inequality hypothesis. Finally, adding some heterogeneity in this model and taking into account the issues of interpersonal comparisons do not modify our previous results.

Conclusion

In this study we underline the hypotheses through which health is associated to income and income inequalities. The aim of this paper is to empirically investigate the evidence for the absolute income hypothesis and both the strong and the weak versions of the income inequality hypothesis for people aged 50 and over in Europe, using data from the SHARE survey. Indeed, we review the relationship on income-related health inequalities where we mention the literature as well as the theoretical and statistical tools needed to carry out this research. Then we present the data used and some descriptive statistics. Finally we show the model specification, the results of the three hypotheses and some robustness tests. This whole work, both the literature study and the establishment of various models led us to estimate different assumptions on the relationship between health and income. This study is one of the first analyzing this relationship through different hypotheses at the same time using the SHARE survey which is a rich database, containing a lot of information on elderly people and countries simultaneously.

We find evidence supporting the absolute income hypothesis which states that people with higher incomes have better health outcomes. We also find evidence supporting the strong version of income inequality hypothesis which argues that inequality affects all members in a society equivalently. In this hypothesis, we find that when there are high income inequalities in a country, people aged 50 and over feel less healthy. However, we do not find evidence supporting the weak version of income inequality hypothesis which states that only the least well-off are hurt by income inequalities in a society. This hypothesis underlines the fact that income inequalities are more detrimental for the health of people with low incomes. Our qualitative results suggest that for low-income individuals, an increase in income inequalities in their country is positively related to report a better health status. Furthermore, for higher income individuals, an increase in income inequalities in their country is not related to report either a better or a lower health status. One limitation is the used of cross-sectional data without investigating possible endogeneity issues. Thus our results highlight statistical associations rather than causal effects. Finally, by implementing the generalized ordered probit, we control for potential problems of interpersonal comparisons and the results are very similar to those found with the ordered probit model.

Results concerning the hypotheses are consistent with the concavity assumption of income on health. Extension would be to highlight causal effects, using other methods, in order to support some political implication. In fact, what is important in determining the health status is more how income is distributed in a society and less the overall health of this society. As a result, the more equally income is distributed, the better the overall health in this society. Concerning political implication, one way to improve health might be to take measures using the redistribution of incomes as a lever. In fact, Lynch et al. [24] argue that, redistributive fiscal and tax policies will help the governments to achieve better population health. Deaton [11] explains that if income inequalities affect health, transfer policies that affect the distribution of incomes would have good effects through individual levels of health. There will be like a virtuous circle in which incomes influence the health status (improving the production possibilities of the economy can be achieved by improving the health) which in turn affects the income.

Endnotes

[1] In this way, redistributing income from rich people to poor people will have an important and positive impact on the health of the poorer people, whereas the richer ones will experience a small decrease in their health.

[2] Such as age, gender, number of years of education, marital status and the job situation. It can also contain countries dummies variables.

[3] See http://ec.europa.eu/ for an explanation of the European Innovation Partnership on Active and Healthy Ageing - A Europe 2020 initiative.

[4] After wave four was completed, the average retention rate over the year was 81%.

[5] For instance, if 50 percent of the population has no income and the other half has the same income, the Gini index is 0.5. The same result can be found with the following analysis which is less unequal. On one hand, 25 percent of total income is shared in the same way by 75 percent of the population, and on he other hand, the remaining 25 percent of the total income is divided by the remaining 25 percent of the population.

[6] It is this normalized index that we use hereafter and that we name the Theil index.

[7] Once h_i^* crosses a certain value you report fair, then poor, then good, then very good, then excellent health.

[8] Results associated to the Gini coefficient are not provided here but they are very similar and available upon request.

[9] Source: OECD website.

[10] We look at the average individual of the database and compute the marginal effects.

[11] We do not include the ones for the income inequality hypothesis (both versions) since the results are very similar and do not change the main conclusion, but these are available upon request.

[12] In this case, people with very high incomes are individuals who earn more than 150,000€ per year, corresponding to less than 2% of the sample.

Appendix

Descriptive Statistics

Table 2 Descriptive statistics of the variables

Variables	Mean	Standard deviation	Minimum	Maximum
Health				
Self-perceived health status ($N = 63626$)	2.85	1.09	1	5
Inequalities				
Gini per country	0.39	0.05	0.31	0.48
Theil per country	0.33	0.19	0.16	0.82
Other Variables				
Income	36,621.21	71,863.78	2	1.00e+07
GDP per country (2013 - Dollar US/capita)	39,726.43	11,543.57	26,160.08	92,781.41
Education	11.12	4.28	1	25
Age	67.12	10.06	50	103

Table 3 Detailed descriptive statistics for the health

Health	Percentage of people
Poor (1)	10.81%
Fair (2)	27.01%
Good (3)	36.52%
Very Good (4)	17.58%
Excellent (5)	8.18%

Table 4 Detailed descriptive statistics for income

Distribution	Income
5%	3,828.99
25%	12,446
50%	24,659.55
75%	46,200
95%	103,897.2

Table 5 Detailed descriptive statistics for the countries

Country	Percentage of people*	GDP - 2013**	Indexes of inequality***	
			Theil index	Gini index
Austria	6.54%	45 132.54	0.1762	0.3222
Germany	8.71%	43 282.31	0.2234	0.3672
Sweden	7.06%	44 585.87	0.1672	0.3183
Netherlands	6.42%	46 749.31	0.2152	0.3543
Spain	9.75%	33 111.45	0.2521	0.3813
Italy	6.88%	34 836.43	0.373	0.4239
France	6.86%	37 617.06	0.8224	0.4772
Denmark	6.37%	43797.23	0.1578	0.3138
Switzerland	4.62%	56 896.91	0.2144	0.3554
Belgium	8.66%	41 863.94	0.3849	0.4545
Czech Republic	8.7%	28 962.64	0.2123	0.3512
Luxembourg	2.5%	92 781.4	0.2649	0.3979
Israel	3.56%	32 504.72	0.2475	0.3906
Slovenia	4.51%	28 675.43	0.3696	0.451
Estonia	8.88%	26 160.08	0.6816	0.4497

*: From each country in the full sample
**: Gross Domestic Product, Total dollar US/capita
***: Values

Additional Econometric Results

Table 6 Results of the ordered probit regressions for the pooled database

Variables	Absolute Income	IIH	
	Hypothesis	Strong Version	Weak Version
Income	1.41e-06*** (4.74e-08)	1.94e-06*** (4.34e-08)	1.16e-06*** (4.76e-08)
Income squared	−1.78e-13*** (1.14e-14)	−2.39e-13*** (1.13e-14)	−1.46e-13*** (1.12e-14)
Quintiles of income: Reference - Q5			
Quintile 1			−0.379*** (0.019)
Quintile 2			−0.288*** (0.019)
Quintile 3			−0.184*** (0.019)
Quintile 4			−0.115*** (0.018)
Index of inequalities (II) - Theil		−0.473*** (0.018)	−0.567*** (0.038)
Interaction quintile 1 and II			0.121* (0.053)
Interaction quintile 2 and II			0.054 (0.053)
Interaction quintile 3 and II			−0.012 (0.052)
Interaction quintile 4 and II			0.053 (0.052)
Interaction quintile 5 and II			Reference
GDP		0.0002*** (3.03e-07)	0.0002*** (3.06e-07)
Age	−0.014*** (0.003)	−0.018*** (0.003)	−0.015*** (0.003)
Age squared	−0.0001*** (0.00002)	−0.0001** (0.0002)	−0.0006*** (0.00002)
Years of education	0.021*** (0.001)	0.019*** (0.0005)	0.017*** (0.001)
Gender = 1 if women	−0.055*** (0.005)	−0.057*** (0.005)	−0.050*** (0.005)
Marital Status: Reference - Married			
Registered partnership	−0.060*** (0.017)	−0.030* (0.017)	−0.026 (0.017)
Married, not living with spouse	−0.098*** (0.009)	−0.087*** (0.009)	−0.091*** (0.009)
Never married	−0.127*** (0.014)	−0.108*** (0.013)	−0.027** (0.014)
Divorced	−0.079*** (0.011)	−0.062*** (0.011)	0.016 (0.011)
Widowed	−0.046*** (0.009)	−0.055*** (0.009)	0.026*** (0.009)
Waves: Reference - Wave 5			
Wave 1	0.139*** (0.009)	0.431*** (0.009)	0.469*** (0.009)
Wave 2	0.094*** (0.009)	0.247*** (0.009)	0.272*** (0.009)
Wave 4	−0.024*** (0.006)	−0.001 (0.006)	0.003 (0.006)
Cut-point μ_1	−2.494 (0.104)	−1.960 (0.104)	−1.976 (0.105)
Cut-point μ_2	−1.46 (0.104)	−0.952 (0.105)	−0.962 (0.105)
Cut-point μ_3	−0.378 (0.104)	0.106 (0.104)	0.102 (0.105)
Cut-point μ_4	0.455 (0.104)	0.919 (0.104)	0.919 (0.105)

For AIH, dummies for countries are included but not reported, and available upon request

***: 1% significant; **: 5% significant; *: 10% significant. Standard deviations are in parentheses, below the coefficients

Table 7 Absolute Income Hypothesis - Generalized ordered probit (Wave 5)

Variables	Health commodities			
	1 to 2	2 to 3	3 to 4	4 to 5
Income	1.99e-06 ***	2.25e-06 ***	3.68e-06 ***	3.81e-06 ***
	(2.76e-07)	(2.00e-07)	(2.44e-07)	(4.44e-07)
Income squared	-2.11e-13 ***	-7.96e-13 ***	-3.26e-13 ***	-5.41e-12 ***
	(2.90e-14)	(1.17e-13)	(4.71e-13)	(1.55e-12)
Age	0.037 ***	0.037 ***	0.026 ***	0.029 ***
	(0.01)	(0.008)	(0.009)	(0.012)
Age squared	-0.0004 ***	-0.0004 ***	-0.0004 ***	-0.0003 ***
	(0.0001)	(0.0001)	(0.0001)	(0.0001)
Years of education	0.031 ***	0.038 ***	0.036 ***	0.024 ***
	(0.002)	(0.001)	(0.001)	(0.002)
Gender = 1 if women	0.066 ***	-0.014	-0.005	-0.002 **
	(0.016)	(0.012)	(0.012)	(0.016)
Marital Status:				
Married, living with spouse	Reference group			
Registered partnership	-0.063	-0.093 **	0.029	-0.027
	(0.069)	(0.046)	(0.045)	(0.057)
Married, not living with spouse	-0.251 ***	-0.112 **	-0.0001	0.118 *
	(0.062)	(0.049)	(0.053)	(0.069)
Never married	-0.048	-0.068 ***	-0.038	-0.065 *
	(0.032)	(0.024)	(0.026)	(0.035)
Divorced	-0.157 ***	-0.059 ***	0.05 ***	0.06 **
	(0.026)	(0.019)	(0.021)	(0.027)
Widowed	-0.017	-0.026	0.002	-0.015
	(0.021)	(0.017)	(0.02)	(0.029)
Job Situation:				
Retired	Reference group			
Employed	0.398 ***	0.312 ***	0.203 ***	0.174 ***
	(0.029)	(0.019)	(0.019)	(0.025)
Unemployed	-0.222 ***	-0.191 ***	-0.233 ***	-0.126 **
	(0.047)	(0.035)	(0.038)	(0.053)
Permanently sick	-1.196 ***	-1.268 ***	-1.307 ***	-0.963 ***
	(0.033)	(0.038)	(0.054)	(0.076)
Home-maker	-0.088 ***	-0.052 **	-0.047 *	-0.006
	(0.029)	(0.022)	(0.025)	(0.035)
Other	-0.354 ***	-0.173 ***	-0.145 ***	-0.017
	(0.041)	(0.037)	(0.046)	(0.064)

Dummies for countries are included but not reported, and available upon request
***: 1% significant; **: 5% significant; *: 10% significant
1 to 2: Poor to Fair; 2 to 3: Fair to Good; 3 to 4: Good to VG; 4 to 5: VG to Excellent

Table 8 IIH, strong version - Generalized ordered probit (Wave 5)

Variables	Health commodities			
	1 to 2	2 to 3	3 to 4	4 to 5
Income	1.75e-06 ***	2.34e-06 ***	3.89e-06 ***	3.20e-06 ***
	(2.69e-07)	(1.97e-07)	(2.38e-07)	(4.42e-07)
Income squared	-1.89e-13 ***	-8.28e-13 ***	-3.75e-12 ***	-5.18e-12 ***
	(2.82e-14)	(1.18e-13)	(4.72e-13)	(1.60e-12)
Index of inequalities (Theil)	-0.095 **	-0.369 ***	-0.7389 ***	-0.4746 ***
	(0.041)	(0.031)	(0.035)	(0.048)
Mechanisms:				
1st: % Health exp. in the GDP	0.059 ***	0.087 ***	0.073 ***	0.082 ***
	(0.005)	(0.004)	(0.004)	(0.006)
2nd: Received help from others	-0.214 ***	-0.193 ***	-0.134 ***	-0.089 ***
	(0.009)	(0.008)	(0.009)	(0.013)
2nb bis: Given help to others	0.001 ***	0.001 ***	0.001 ***	0.001 ***
	(0.0001)	(0.0001)	(0.0001)	(0.0001)
3rd: Life satisfaction	0.195 ***	0.215 ***	0.239 ***	0.238 ***
	(0.004)	(0.003)	(0.004)	(0.006)
GDP	2.52e-06 ***	1.41e-06 **	-4.87e-07	5.94e-07
	(8.66e-07)	(6.04e-07)	(6.36e-07)	(8.72e-07)
Age	0.019 *	0.004	0.013	0.019 *
	(0.01)	(0.008)	(0.009)	(0.012)
Age squared	0.0003 ***	-0.0002 ***	-0.0003 ***	-0.0003 ***
	(0.0001)	(0.0001)	(0.0001)	(0.0001)
Years of education	0.025 ***	0.029 ***	0.028 ***	0.021 ***
	(0.002)	(0.001)	(0.0014)	(0.0018)
Gender = 1 if women	0.069 ***	-0.018	-0.003	-0.0004
	(0.016)	(0.012)	(0.012)	(0.016)
Marital Status:				
Married, living with spouse	Reference group			
Registered partnership	-0.023	-0.053	0.034	0.014
	(0.071)	(0.047)	(0.045)	(0.058)
Married, not living with spouse	-0.131 **	0.005	0.091 *	0.122 *
	(0.065)	(0.051)	(0.054)	(0.072)
Never married	0.033	0.023	0.064 **	0.001
	(0.034)	(0.025)	(0.027)	(0.036)
Divorced	-0.046 *	0.062 ***	0.166 ***	0.122 ***
	(0.028)	(0.021)	(0.022)	(0.028)
Widowed	0.053 **	0.069 ***	0.076 ***	0.022
	(0.023)	(0.018)	(0.022)	(0.031)
Job Situation:				
Retired	Reference group			
Employed	0.344 ***	0.225 ***	0.177 ***	0.176 ***
	(0.03)	(0.019)	(0.019)	(0.025)
Unemployed	-0.141 ***	-0.097 ***	-0.11 ***	0.012
	(0.048)	(0.035)	(0.039)	(0.054)

Table 8 IIH, strong version - Generalized ordered probit (Wave 5) *(Continued)*

Permanently sick	-1.016 ***	-1.121 ***	-1.098 ***	-0.744 ***
	(0.034)	(0.034)	(0.056)	(0.084)
Home-maker	-0.074 ***	-0.033	-0.076 ***	-0.044
	(0.029)	(0.022)	(0.025)	(0.035)
Other	-0.299 ***	-0.114 ***	-0.09 *	0.048
	(0.043)	(0.038)	(0.048)	(0.067)

***: 1% significant; **: 5% significant; *: 10% significant
1 to 2: Poor to Fair; 2 to 3: Fair to Good; 3 to 4: Good to VG; 4 to 5: VG to Excellent

Table 9 IIH, weak version - Generalized ordered probit (Wave 5)

Variables	Health commodities			
	1 to 2	2 to 3	3 to 4	4 to 5
Income	1.97e-06 ***	3.03e-06 ***	5.92e-06 ***	7.65e-06 ***
	(3.06e-07)	(2.43e-07)	(3.15e-07)	(6.10e-07)
Income squared	-2.09e-13 ***	-1.14e-12 ***	-6.03e-12 ***	-1.60e-11 ***
	(3.17e-14)	(1.25e-13)	(5.21e-13)	(1.92e-12)
Index of inequalities (Theil)	-0.319 ***	-0.79 ***	-1.077 ***	-0.899 ***
	(0.101)	(0.065)	(0.065)	(0.084)
Quintile 1	-0.145 ***	-0.195 ***	-0.003	0.07
	(0.055)	(0.039)	(0.043)	(0.059)
Quintile 2	-0.099 *	-0.159 ***	-0.014	0.079
	(0.054)	(0.038)	(0.039)	(0.059)
Quintile 3	-0.061	-0.043	0.018	0.025
	(0.054)	(0.037)	(0.037)	(0.047)
Quintile 4	-0.012	-0.02	0.055	0.023
	(0.056)	(0.036)	(0.034)	(0.043)
Quintile 5	Reference group			
Interaction quintile 1 and II	-0.204 *	0.079	-0.039	0.084
	(0.12)	(0.088)	(0.107)	(0.147)
Interaction quintile 2 and II	-0.162	0.097	0.048	0.029
	(0.123)	(0.087)	(0.101)	(0.138)
Interaction quintile 3 and II	-0.163	-0.048	-0.013	0.144
	(0.125)	(0.088)	(0.098)	(0.129)
Interaction quintile 4 and II	-0.058	0.066	0.001	0.098
	(0.132)	(0.088)	(0.093)	(0.124)
Interaction quintile 5 and II	Reference group			
GDP	0.0001 ***	9.96e-06 ***	3.83e-06 ***	2.17e-06 ***
	(8.30e-07)	(6.31e-07)	(6.99e-07)	(9.91e-07)
Age	0.034 ***	0.023 ***	0.029 ***	0.034 **
	(0.01)	(0.008)	(0.008)	(0.011)
Age squared	-0.0004 ***	-0.0003 ***	-0.0004 ***	-0.0004 ***
	(0.0001)	(0.0001)	(0.0001)	(0.0001)
Years of education	0.025 ***	0.029 ***	0.028 ***	0.022 ***
	(0.002)	(0.001)	(0.001)	(0.002)

Table 9 IIH, weak version - Generalized ordered probit (Wave 5) *(Continued)*

Gender = 1 if women	0.066 ***	-0.016	0.0004	0.007
	(0.015)	(0.011)	(0.012)	(0.016)
Marital Status:				
Married, living with spouse	Reference group			
Registered partnership	0.053	0.023	0.075 *	0.049
	(0.067)	(0.045)	(0.044)	(0.056)
Married, not living with spouse	-0.203 ***	-0.091 *	-0.014	0.052
	(0.061)	(0.049)	(0.052)	(0.068)
Never married	0.034	0.014	0.042	-0.008
	(0.033)	(0.024)	(0.026)	(0.035)
Divorced	-0.079 ***	0.009	0.107 ***	0.085 ***
	(0.027)	(0.02)	(0.021)	(0.027)
Widowed	0.024	0.015	0.019	-0.015
	(0.022)	(0.018)	(0.021)	(0.029)
Job Situation:				
Retired	Reference group			
Employed	0.374 ***	0.251 ***	0.206 ***	0.188 ***
	(0.029)	(0.019)	(0.018)	(0.024)
Unemployed	-0.188 ***	-0.169 ***	-0.221 ***	-0.128 **
	(0.046)	(0.034)	(0.038)	(0.053)
Permanently sick	-1.162 ***	-1.262 ***	-1.245 ***	-0.923 ***
	(0.032)	(0.033)	(0.054)	(0.08)
Home-maker	-0.062 **	-0.021	-0.081 ***	-0.069 **
	(0.027)	(0.021)	(0.024)	(0.034)
Other	-0.317 ***	-0.152 ***	-0.148 ***	-0.017
	(0.041)	(0.037)	(0.046)	(0.064)

***: 1% significant; **: 5% significant; *: 10% significant
1 to 2: Poor to Fair; 2 to 3: Fair to Good; 3 to 4: Good to VG; 4 to 5: VG to Excellent

Acknowledgements
"This paper uses data from SHARE Waves 1, 2, 4 and 5 (DOIs: 10.6103/SHARE.w1.260, 10.6103/SHARE.w2.260, 10.6103/SHARE.w4.111, 10.6103/SHARE.w5.100). The SHARE data collection has been primarily funded by the European Commission through FP5 (QLK6-CT-2001- 00360), FP6 (SHARE-I3: RII-CT-2006-062193, COMPARE: CIT5-CT-2005-028857, SHARELIFE: CIT4-CT-2006- 028812) and FP7 (SHARE-PREP: N 211909, SHARE-LEAP: N 227822, SHARE M4: N 261982). Additional funding from the German Ministry of Education and Research, the U.S. National Institute on Ageing (U01 AG09740-13S2, P01 AG005842, P01 AG08291, P30 AG12815, R21 AG025169, Y1-AG-4553-01, IAG BSR06-11, OGHA 04-064) and from various national funding sources is gratefully acknowledged (see www.share-project.org)." We thank participants of the 5th SHARE User's Conference, the EuHEA conference and the third EuHEA PhD student and supervisor conference, Fabian Gouret and Toni Mora for their helpful comments, as well as Richard Moussa for technical support. We also want to thank two anonymous referees who made very interesting comments.

Authors' contributions
The authors did the research jointly. Both authors read and approved the final manuscript.

Competing interests
Authors declare that they have no competing interests.

References

1. Benitez-Silva H, Buchinsky M, Man Chan H, Cheidvasser S, Rust J. How large is the bias in self-reported disability? J Appl Econom. 2004;19(6): 649–670.
2. Boes S, Winkelmann R. Ordered response models. In: Modern Econometric Analysis. Springer. Allgemeines Statistiches Archiv. 2006; 90(1):167–91.
3. Börsch-Supan A. Survey of Health, Ageing and Retirement in Europe (SHARE) Wave 5. Release version: 5.0.0. SHARE-ERIC Data set. 2016a. doi:10.6103/SHARE.w5.500.
4. Börsch-Supan A. Survey of Health, Ageing and Retirement in Europe (SHARE) Wave 1. Release version: 5.0.0. SHARE-ERIC. Data set. 2016b. doi:10.6103/SHARE.w1.500.
5. Börsch-Supan A. Survey of Health, Ageing and Retirement in Europe (SHARE) Wave 2. Release version: 5.0.0. SHARE-ERIC. Data set. 2016c. doi:10.6103/SHARE.w2.500.
6. Börsch-Supan A. Survey of Health, Ageing and Retirement in Europe (SHARE) Wave 4. Release version: 5.0.0. SHARE-ERIC. Data set. 2016d. doi:10.6103/SHARE.w4.500.
7. Börsch-Supan A, Brandt M, Hunkler C, Kneip T, Korbmacher J, Malter F, Schaan B, Stuck S, Zuber S. Data Resource Profile: the Survey of Health, Ageing and Retirement in Europe (SHARE). Int J Epidemiol. 2013;42(4): 992–1001. doi:10.1093/ije/dyt088.
8. Carrieri V, Jones AM. The income-health relationship "beyond the mean": New evidence from biomarkers. Health Econ. 2017;26(7):937–56.
9. Cohen S, Line S, Manuck SB, Rabin BS, Heise ER, Kaplan JR. Chronic social stress, social status, and susceptibility to upper respiratory infections in nonhuman primates. Psychosom Med. 1997;59(3):213–21.
10. Cutler D, Deaton A, Lleras-Muney A. The determinants of mortality. J Econ Perspect. 2006;20(3):97–120.
11. Deaton A. Health, inequality, and economic development. J Econ Lit. 2003;41(1):113–58.
12. Ettner SL. New evidence on the relationship between income and health. J Health Econ. 1996;15(1):67–85.
13. Fiscella K, Franks P. Individual income, income inequality, health, and mortality: what are the relationships? Health Serv Res. 2000;35:307–18.
14. Grossman M. The relationship between health and schooling: What's new? Tech. rep. National Bureau of Economic Research. 2015.
15. Hildebrand V, Van Kerm P. Income inequality and self-rated health status: evidence from the European Community Household Panel. Demography. 2009;46(4):805–25.
16. Jones AM, Schurer S. How does heterogeneity shape the socioeconomic gradient in health satisfaction? J Appl Econom. 2011;26(4):549–79.
17. Kaplan GA, Pamuk ER, Lynch JW, Cohen RD, Balfour JL. Inequality in income and mortality in the United States: analysis of mortality and potential pathways. Brit Med J. 1996;312(7037):999–1003.
18. Kawachi I, Kennedy BP. Income inequality and health: pathways and mechanisms. Health Serv Res. 1999;34(1):215.
19. Kawachi I, Kennedy BP, Lochner K. Prothrow-Stith. Social capital, income inequality, and mortality. Am J Public Health. 1997;87(9):1491–98.
20. Kennedy BP, Kawachi I, Glass R, Prothrow-Stith D, et al. Income distribution, socioeconomic status, and self rated health in the United States: a multilevel analysis. Brit Med J. 1998;317(7163):917–21.
21. Li H, Zhu Y. Income, income inequality and health: Evidence from china. J Comp Econ. 2006;34(4):668–93.
22. Lindeboom M, Van Doorslaer E. Cut-point shift and index shift in self-reported health. J Health Econ. 2004;23(6):1083–99.
23. Lindelow M. Sometimes more equal than others: how health inequalities depend on the choice of welfare indicator. Health Econ. 2006;15(3): 263–279.
24. Lynch J, Smith GD, Harper S, Hillemeier M, Ross N, Kaplan GA, Wolfson M. Is income inequality a determinant of population health? part 1 - A systematic review. Milbank Q. 2004;82(1):5–99.
25. Lynch JW, Kaplan GA, Pamuk ER, Cohen RD, Heck KE, Balfour JL, Yen IH. Income inequality and mortality in metropolitan areas of the united states. Am J Public Health. 1998;88(7):1074–80.
26. Mackenbach JP, Martikainen P, Looman CW, Dalstra JA, Kunst AE, Lahelma E, Group SW, et al. The shape of the relationship between income and self-assessed health: an international study. Int J Epidemiol. 2005;34(2):286–93.
27. Mellor JM, Milyo J. Income inequality and health status in the United States: evidence from the current population survey. J Hum Resour. 2002;37(3):510–39.
28. Potvin L, Moquet MJ, Jones C. Réduire les inégalités sociales en santé: INPES - coll. Santé en Actions (French national institute on health prevention and education). 2010. p. 380.
29. Preston SH. The changing relation between mortality and level of economic development. Pop Stud. 1975;29(2):231–48.
30. Subramanian S, Kawachi I. Income inequality and health: what have we learned so far? Epidemiol Rev. 2004;26(1):78–91.
31. Theodossiou I, Zangelidis A. The social gradient in health: The effect of absolute income and subjective social status assessment on the individual's health in Europe. Econ Hum Biol. 2009;7(2):229–237.
32. Van Doorslaer E, Koolman X, Jones AM. Explaining income-related inequalities in doctor utilisation in Europe. Health Econ. 2004;13(7): 629–47.
33. Wagstaff A, Van Doorslaer E, Watanabe N. On decomposing the causes of health sector inequalities with an application to malnutrition inequalities in Vietnam. J Econometrics. 2003;112(1):207–23.
34. World Health Organization. WHO: Commission on Social Determinants of Health: final report. 2009.

14

Pay for performance and contractual choice: the case of general practitioners in England

Eleonora Fichera[1] and Mario Pezzino[2*]

Abstract

The Quality and Outcomes Framework (QOF) is a Pay-for-Performance scheme introduced in England in 2004 to reward primary care providers. This incentive scheme provides financial incentives that reward the overall performance of a practice, not individual effort. Consequently, an important question is how the QOF may affect contractual choices, quality provision and doctor mobility in the primary healthcare labour market. The paper provides a simple theoretical model that shows that the introduction and further strengthening of the scheme may have induced practices to compete for the best doctors and modified their choices in terms of contractual agreements with practitioners. We test the implications of this model using a linkage between Doctors Census data and practices' characteristics from 2003 to 2007. We use linear multilevel models with random intercept and we account for sample selection. We find that after the introduction of the QOF efficient doctors are more likely to become partners and mobility among doctors has increased. The strengthening of the scheme in 2005 is associated with an increase in the quality of primary care and a reduction in access to the market for new doctors.

Keywords: P4P, contracts, Primary care, Mobility

JEL Classification: I11, I18, J41

Introduction

The number of GPs in the U.K. has risen by an average of 1.8% each year between 2004 and 2014, but there are still problems in recruiting and retaining GPs into the healthcare market (The Health Foundation [16]). In the U.K. there is also a relative long tradition in the use of Pay-for-Performance (P4P) schemes, but little is known about the sorting and retention effects they might produce (Lazear [9]).

The aim of this paper is to investigate the sorting and retention effects of the only P4P scheme for General Practitioners (GPs) in the U.K., the Quality and Outcomes Framework (QOF). GPs are paid under a mix of capitation and financial incentives including the QOF. The QOF awards an amount of money to practices that achieve certain levels of performance. Such pay is linked to the performance of the practice and may then be internally distributed over to GPs. We examine the effects that the introduction of the QOF in 2004 and its subsequent strengthening in 2005 had on the contractual arrangements, the provision of quality and doctor mobility in the primary healthcare market.

We motivate our empirical analysis with a simple theoretical model with two practices combining three aspects of the primary healthcare sector that together, to our knowledge, have not yet been considered by the literature. These are: i) the altruistic[1] nature of the GP's job; ii) different contractual arrangements (e.g. salaried positions or partnerships) for GPs (National Audit Office [11]); and iii) the multidimensional nature of quality experienced by patients as a mix of the effort of GPs, front desk and nursing staff. In our model each practice serves a representative patient and requires the effort of one doctor to provide healthcare. Doctors may be of two types: efficient and inefficient. If they are efficient, then they are able to provide medical effort at a lower cost than the other type of doctors, the inefficient ones. The model

*Correspondence: mario.pezzino@manchester.ac.uk
[2]University of Manchester, Economics, Arthur Lewis Building Oxford Road, Manchester, M13 9PL, UK
Full list of author information is available at the end of the article

predicts that the behaviour of a salaried doctor will not be affected by the introduction of the P4P scheme, since her remuneration is not quality-dependent. However, the introduction of the QOF may induce practices to compete (offering partnerships) for the best doctors and increase mobility.

We test the empirical implications of this model using a unique linkage between GP Census data from 2003 to 2007 with practices' characteristics in England. We then link these data with information on practices' performance on the QOF. Whilst we find that the introduction of the QOF in 2004 decreased the probability of becoming a partner by one percentage point, more efficient doctors are more likely to be partners. Mobility of doctors increased by two percentage points after the QOF was introduced. But more efficient doctors are less likely to move. And doctors in better practices are also less likely to move. Overall, these results might suggest some evidence of a sorting effect of the QOF with more efficient doctors becoming partners and retention of doctors in higher quality practices. Finally, we find that the strengthening of the scheme in 2005 has produced on average an increase in primary care quality of practices. Over the period between 2004 and 2007 more efficient doctors improve the quality of the practice and if they are also partners they put more effort. However, we observe a *decrease* in GPs' effort connected to the strengthening of the scheme. We interpret this result with the existence of reputational effects as described by the literature on pro-social behaviour and intrinsic motivation.

Background

Literature

Incentive pay is a way to partially overcome information asymmetries in the labour market. The rationale behind P4P is to tie workers' compensation to their output aligning their individual objectives to those of the firm (see for example, Lazear [9]; Prendergast [13]; Ross [15]). If such schemes are introduced in multi-level organisations, there might be two potentially counteracting effects at play. On the one hand, individual agents might free-ride on the team thus weakening the incentive effect of P4P. On the other hand, the sorting effect might cause more able workers to select and stay in performance pay jobs and less able workers to leave these jobs (see for example, Dohmen and Falk [4]; Gielen et al. [6]; Lazear [10]; 2000). According to these studies, in equilibrium workers relocate themselves on the basis of their ability, thus increasing productivity and wages in firms that use P4P schemes.

In this paper we focus on the QOF, an incentive scheme that applied to practices, which has increased doctors' income by 25 percent (NHS Review Body [12]). We examine its effects on doctors' behaviour (e.g. mobility and effort provision) and on practices' behaviour (e.g. contractual arrangements). This is an important issue for the incentive and sorting effects in the GPs' labour market and for the resulting potential inequalities in the provision of healthcare to patients.

The Quality and Outcomes Framework

In the U.K. most healthcare is delivered by the National Health Service (NHS), which is a comprehensive freely available service funded out of general taxation. All citizens are registered with a GP who delivers primary care and acts as gatekeeper for elective secondary care. Primary care practices are typically a group of one to six doctors responsible for a pool of patients. They are independent contractors retaining the surpluses they make as private income.

In early 2000s the terms of two new contracts for GPs remuneration were negotiated (see the National Audit Office [11]). The first contract is the nationally negotiated General Medical Services (GMS), with a mix of capitation, lump sum allowances and P4P schemes, such as the QOF. The capitation payment is based on the number of patients treated by a practice, adjusted for the characteristics of both patients and area where the practice operates. The second contract is the Primary Medical Services (PMS), negotiated between the practice and the local primary care organisation. Under the PMS contract, the practice receives a lump sum payment for the same services provided in the GMS contract (Gravelle et al., [8]). The first three years of this new contract cost about £1.76 billion (National Audit Office [11]).

The new GMS contract was officially introduced on 1st April 2004 with measurement of achievements on 1st April 2005 for the previous 12 months (Roland [14]). In the first two years of the QOF, practices were rewarded on the basis of performance points reported on 146 indicators. The points correspond to an amount of money in pounds sterling (£) claimed annually. Points were awarded on the basis of reported coverage rates above a lower threshold of 40% and an upper threshold that varied depending on the particular indicator (see Doran et al., [5]). The average price per point in 2004 was £76, increasing to £125 in 2005. Thresholds of payments for some indicators increased between 2005 and 2006 so that it was more difficult for a practice to be rewarded the same amount in 2006 as in 2005 if their performance did not change.

Methods

The theoretical model

Let us consider a market where patients are treated by two practices, say practice 1 and 2, located at a positive distance $t > 0$ from each other. Practices need only one doctor to serve their population. Let us suppose that there are two types of doctors: efficient (v) and inefficient (nv). The mass of doctors of type v is equal to $\pi \in [0,1]$, and consequently the mass of doctors of type nv is equal to $(1-\pi)$.

Suppose that the practices know the type of two doctors, each located next to a practice. These doctors' type may be known because they were previously employed.

Practices can however access the labour market and offer a salary to new doctors (whose type will be ex-ante unknown) who receive salary w_i from practice i, $i = 1,2$. The utility of the salaried doctor $z = \{v, nv\}$, who works for practice i, is (superscript N indicates that we are considering the case of new salaried doctors):

$$U_{zi}^N = w_i + Q_{zi} - \gamma_z \frac{e_{zi}^2}{2} + b_i \qquad (1)$$

where Q_{zi} is the total level of quality of care of practice i; $\gamma_z \frac{e_{zi}^2}{2}$ is the doctor's cost of effort[2], with $1 = \gamma_{nv} \geq \gamma_v > 0$ representing the degree of inefficiency of doctor z; e_i is the level of effort invested by the doctor employed by practice i and $b_i \geq 0$ is the benefit the doctor receives from accessing the amenities in the neighbourhood of practice i. Let us assume that the outside option of a new salaried doctor is equal to zero.

Notice the utility in (1) increases with the quality of care Q_{zi}; this captures the assumption that doctors are assumed to be altruistic and care about quality. The quality perceived by patients is the sum of quality improvements given by doctor's effort and practice's investment in facilities and nursing staff:

$$Q_{zi} = q_i + e_{zi} \qquad (2)$$

where q_i is the quality investment of the practice (e.g. nursing staff, front desk, IT).

Practices are run by doctors who have taken a completely profit-oriented managerial position in the practice.

If a practice employs a new doctor its (expected) profit function is given by:

$$\Pi_i^N = m + p\left[\pi Q_{vi} + (1-\pi) Q_{nvi}\right] - w_i - \frac{q_i^2}{2} \qquad (3)$$

where m is a capitation payment, $p \geq 0$ is the quality-related payment based on a P4P scheme, $\frac{q_i^2}{2}$ is the cost function of the practice[3].

The timing unravels as follows.

In stage 1, practices (i.e. managers) choose the contract to offer to the doctor; specifically they may offer a partnership to one of the doctors whose type is known or a salaried contract to a new doctor.

In stage 2, practices choose investment in quality q_i to maximise profits. Doctors who accepted a contract choose the level of effort e_{zi} to maximise utility.

In stage 3, primary health care is provided.

Salaried contract

Let us look first at the provision of care when a practice hires a new doctor.

The effort chosen by the salaried doctor in stage two is simply produced by the satisfaction of first order conditions to maximise (1).

$$\frac{dU_i^N}{de_{zi}} = 0 \Rightarrow e_{zi}^N = \frac{1}{\gamma_z} \qquad (4)$$

Notice that p has no effect on the effort choice of the salaried doctor. This is not surprising, since she receives a remuneration that does not depend on the quality of care.

Similarly the maximisation of profits defines the investment in quality of the practices at stage two.

$$\frac{d\Pi_i^N}{dq_i} = 0 \Rightarrow q_i^N = p \qquad (5)$$

Since the outside option of a new doctor is equal to zero and the resulting utility is strictly positive, practices will set $w_i = 0$.[4] Notice that a positive p is necessary to induce the practice to invest in quality. In equilibrium:

$$\Pi_i^N = \Pi^N = m + \frac{p^2}{2} + \frac{p(\gamma_v + \pi - \gamma_v \pi)}{\gamma_v} \qquad (6)$$

Notice also that, when the practices choose to hire a new doctor, profits increase in m, p, and π, and decrease in γ_v. In addition, if $p = 0$ (i.e. no P4P scheme is in place), then $\Pi_i^N = m$.

Partnership contracts and competition over doctors

Subsection Salaried contract considered the case in which practices decided to hire a new doctor in stage one. However next to each practice lives a doctor whose type is known and who could be offered a partnership. A practice may be also willing to pay a relocation package equal to t and offer a partnership to the doctor located next to the other practice. Similar to the analysis in section Salaried contract, let us study first the provision of care of a practice who employs a partner of type z.

Assuming that a partner will be entitled, in addition to a salary, to equally share profits with the management,[5] the utility of a partner and the remaining profits for the practice are equal to:

$$U_{zi}^{P} = \frac{1}{2}\left[m + pQ_{zi}^{P} - w_{i}^{P} - \frac{q_i^2}{2}\right] + w_i^P + Q_{zi}^P - \gamma_z \frac{e_{zi}^2}{2} + b_i$$

$$\Pi_{zi}^{M} = \frac{1}{2}\left[m + pQ_{zi}^{P} - w_{i}^{Pi} - \frac{q_i^2}{2}\right]$$

Superscripts P and M indicate variables respectively related to a doctor working as a partner and a manager in a partnership.

The simultaneous choice of medical effort and practice quality produces:

$$\begin{cases} \frac{d\Pi_{zi}^{M}}{dq_i} = 0 \\ \frac{dU_{zi}^{P}}{de_{zi}} = 0 \end{cases} \Rightarrow \begin{matrix} q_{zi}^{M} = p \\ e_{zi}^{P} = \frac{2+p}{2\gamma_z} \end{matrix} \tag{7}$$

Comparing (7) with (4) it is clear that $e_{zi}^{P} \geq e_{zi}^{N}$ (this is the effect of the incentive of the P4P scheme). Not surprisingly, the practice investment is not directly affected by the partnership and $q_{zi}^{M} = q_i^N$. In addition, without the P4P scheme, i.e. $p = 0$, practice quality would be $q_{zi}^{N} = q_{zi}^{M} = 0$.

The study of the expressions in (4), (5) and (7) produces a testable implication: *an increase in the QOF price per-quality-point (i.e. higher p) may increase medical effort and practice quality.*

The utility of the partner in equilibrium is given by

$$U_{zi}^{P} = b_i + \frac{(p+2)^2}{8\gamma_z} + \frac{(2m + p^2 + 2w_i^P + 4p)}{4}$$

$U_{zi}^{P} > 0$. Let us suppose again that the outside option of the doctor is sufficiently low to allow practices to offer $w_i^P = 0$. Remaining equilibrium profits for the manager are given by

$$\Pi_{zi}^{M} = \frac{\gamma_z(2m + p^2) + p(p+2)}{4\gamma_z}$$

An increase in p (P4P incentive) has a positive effect on quality (both Q_{zi}^P and e_{zi}^P), partner's utility and practice's profits. Notice that if $p = 0$ (i.e. no P4P scheme is in place) then $\Pi_{zi}^{M} = \frac{m}{2} < \Pi^N = m$. In other words, without a P4P scheme, it is not desirable for a profit-oriented practice to offer a partnership. This implies that with the introduction of P4P incentives practices become more concerned about the ability of the doctors. Consequently, they will consider offering partnerships and eventually compete to attract the best doctors.

This provides another testable implication: *the introduction of the QOF ($p > 0$ compared to $p = 0$) may have created mobility among doctors.*

In stage one a practice needs to choose whether to offer a partnership to (either) of the two old doctors or access the labor market.

Three scenarios may exist: (i) both old doctors are of type v, (ii) both old doctors are of type nv, (iii) the old doctor in practice 1 is of type v, while the old doctor in practice 2 is of type nv.[6] Due to the existence of relocation costs t, in cases (i) and (ii) the practices will not find profitable to offer a partnership to the doctors located in another region. There is not competition for doctors is case (i) and (ii) and, therefore, we discard these scenarios. Relocation will be feasible instead in case (iii) and this will be the focus of our analysis.

In any case, in stage one a practice will consider to offer a partnership to the local doctor if $\Pi_{zi}^{M} > \max\{0, \Pi^N\}$. The necessary condition is satisfied in the subset of the parameters S, where:

$$S \equiv S_1 \cup S_2$$

and

$$S_1 = \left[(m,p,\gamma_z)\middle|0 \leq m < \bar{m}, p > \bar{p}, 0 < \gamma_z < 1, \frac{1-2\gamma_z}{2(1-\gamma_z)} < \pi < 1\right]$$

$$S_2 = \left[(m,p,\gamma_z)\middle|0 \leq m < \bar{m}, p > 0, 0 < \gamma_z < 1, 0 < \pi < \frac{1-2\gamma_z}{2(1-\gamma_z)}\right]$$

$$\bar{m} = \frac{p(p - \gamma_z p + 2(1 + 2\gamma_z(-1+\pi) - 2\pi))}{2\gamma_z}$$

$$\text{and } \bar{p} = \frac{2(2\pi - 1 - 2\gamma_z(1-\pi))}{1-\gamma_z}$$

It follows that a practice will offer a partnership only if the probability to hire an efficient new doctor is low or if the P4P incentive is sufficiently strong to enhance the performance for the doctor and, consequently, profits. Notice that $\gamma_{nv} = 1$ does not belong to sets S_1 nor S_2. This means that $\Pi_{nvi}^{M} < \Pi^N$. In other words, no practice will offer a partnership to an inefficient doctor.

This provides another testable implication: *efficient doctors are more likely to be offered a partnership.*

Focusing our attention on parameters in S, simple and intuitive comparative statics analysis on $\left(\Pi_{vi}^{M} - \Pi^N\right)$ shows that an increase in π (the probability to hire an efficient new doctor), in γ_v (i.e. less efficient to provide effort for type v doctors) or in the capitation payment m reduce the profitability of offering a partnership and may increase turn-over. An increase in p, instead, induces a practice to offer a partnership to the local efficient doctor. This last result implies that *an increase in p reduces access to the job market to new (salaried) doctors,* another testable implication.

Let us focus our attention to the case in which an asymmetric allocation of doctors may induce practices to compete for the best doctors. Let us assume for example that an efficient doctor is located next to practice 1 and an inefficient one is located next to practice 2.

Let us restrict our attention to the following subset of parameters:

$$\hat{S} \equiv S \cap \left[t | 0 < t < \Pi_{vi}^{M} - \Pi_{nvi}^{M} \right]$$

Set $\hat{S}$ ensures that relocation costs are sufficiently small to make relocation of an efficient doctor feasible.

Practice 1 may face competition from practice 2 over the services of the efficient doctor and therefore may have to offer a higher salary in order to outbid the rival. Define $\tilde{\Pi}_{v1}^{M}$ the profits earned by practice 1 hiring the efficient doctor when practice 2 is also offering a partnership to the same doctor. Practice 1 will offer a partnership to doctor v if:

$$\tilde{\Pi}_{v1}^{M} \geq \max \left\{ 0, \Pi^{N} \right\}$$

where

$$\tilde{\Pi}_{v1}^{M} = \max \Pi_{v1}^{M}$$
$$\text{s.t.} U_{v1}^{P}(w_1) \geq U_{v2}^{P}(w_2)$$

Constraint $U_{v1}^{P}(w_1) \geq U_{v2}^{P}(w_2)$ requires that the efficient doctor will not be worse off accepting a partnership by practice 1 rather than practice 2. Using expressions (7), the condition simplifies to

$$w_1 \geq w_2 - 2(b_1 - b_2) \tag{8}$$

The highest salary that practice 2 will be willing to offer to the vocational doctor is

$$\bar{w}_2 : \max \Pi_{v2}^{M} - t = \max \Pi^{N} \tag{9}$$

It follows that $\bar{w}_2 = \frac{p^2 - \gamma_v(2m + p^2 + 4t) + 2p(1 + 2\gamma_v(-1 + \pi) - 2\pi)}{2\gamma_v} \geq 0$ for parameters in $\hat{S}$.

The salary that practice 1 has to guarantee to the local efficient doctor to beat competition from practice 2 is

$$\bar{w}_1 = \bar{w}_2 - 2(b_1 - b_2) = \frac{p^2 - \gamma_v(4b_1 - 4b_2 + 2m + p^2 + 4t) + 2p(1 + 2\gamma_v(-1 + \pi) - 2\pi)}{2\gamma_v}$$

Simple comparative statics analysis shows that $\frac{d\bar{w}_1}{dp} > 0$ (an increase in p increases the performance of the partner and, therefore, the willingness to pay of practice 2) and $\frac{d\bar{w}_1}{db_2} > 0$ (if the neighbourhood of practice 2 provides attractive amenities, practice 1 needs to reward the efficient doctor more to convince her to stay); also $\frac{d\bar{w}_1}{dm} < 0$, $\frac{d\bar{w}_1}{d\gamma_v} < 0$, $\frac{d\bar{w}_1}{d\pi} < 0$ (increases in m, γ_v and π make less desirable for practice 2 the option of hiring a new doctor and, consequently, practice 1 can reduce the salary offered to the efficient doctor[7]); $\frac{d\bar{w}_1}{dt} < 0$, $\frac{d\bar{w}_1}{db_1} < 0$ (an increase in t or b_1 makes more difficult for practice 2 to attract the efficient doctor).

The profits obtained by practice 1 when offering the partnership to the local efficient doctor are:

$$\tilde{\Pi}_{v1}^{M} = b_1 - b_2 + m + t + \frac{p}{2}\frac{p + 2(\gamma_v + \pi - \gamma_v \pi)}{\gamma_v} \tag{10}$$

Finally

$$\tilde{\Pi}_{v1}^{M} - \Pi^{N} = b_1 - b_2 + t \tag{11}$$

Mobility (in our example the relocation of the efficient doctor from practice 1 to practice 2) ultimately depends on the relocation costs and the characteristics of the areas where the two practices operate. Indeed mobility will increase if the relocation costs or the workplace quality differential $(b_1 - b_2)$ decrease. The P4P scheme does not directly affect the willingness to pay of practice 1 to retain the efficient doctor. Since the scheme offers the same incentives to both practices, an increase in p equally induces both practices to compete for the efficient doctor. The scheme, however, may have an effect on the welfare of the efficient doctor. In fact, the efficient doctor may be better off because of the competition from practice 2. The increase in utility (compared to a partnership in practice 1 without competition) depends on ultimately in $\bar{w}_1$.

Empirical strategy

The above-described theoretical model motivates our empirical strategy by providing the following testable implications:

1. Efficient doctors are more likely to be offered a partnership.
2. The introduction of the QOF ($p > 0$ compared to $p = 0$) may have created mobility among doctors.
3. An increase in the QOF price per-quality-point (i.e. higher p) may have (i) increased medical effort and practice quality, (ii) decreased access to the job market to new (salaried) doctors to replace inefficient colleagues.

As a result, the empirical strategy focuses on how to model efficiency, partnership, mobility and access of new doctors to the healthcare market. Efficiency can be modelled as a function of an observed component, e.g. experience, and an unobserved one, e.g. ability. Ideally, we would need a single data source with a large longitudinal sample where we have sufficient doctors' mobility and we measure wage as proxy for efficiency. Since such source of data is not available, we have to use age as proxy for efficiency in the General Medical Services (GMS) Statistics Databases. In reality there are complex interactions between experience and efficiency so it is not an unreasonable assumption. We can test whether age is positively correlated with practices' quality on a sample of single-handed practices in order to attribute efficiency to a single doctor rather than to the average doctor in a practice. We estimate three separate pooled linear regression models. These models can be formally described as follows:

$$y_{ijt} = a + bx_{ij(t-1)} + dw_{ij(t-1)} + gz_{j(t-1)} + \epsilon_{ijt} \quad (12)$$

where y indicates the proportion of total QOF points practice j achieves. The subscript $i = 1, \ldots, N$ indicates each of the N doctors, $j = 1, \ldots, N$ indicates each practice and $t = 2004, 2005$. Demographic characteristics of doctor i, including age, are denoted by $x_{ij(t-1)}$, $w_{ij(t-1)}$ is doctor's i income in practice j and $z_{j(t-1)}$ are practice j characteristics. ϵ_{ijt} indicates the residual of equation (12). We then test the implications of the theoretical model using pooled linear probability models and random intercept multilevel models[8], accounting for sample selection bias in the mobility equation.

The first and second testable implications are modelled as the probability of being a partner or to move to another practice:

$$y_{ijt} = a_i + bx_{ij(t-1)} + gz_{j(t-1)} + \epsilon_{ijt} \quad (13)$$

where as in Eq. 12 i and j indicate the doctor and practice, respectively; $t = 2003, \ldots, 2007$, where $y_{ijt} = 1$ indicates whether the doctor is a partner or has moved to another practice. We argue that a_i captures the unobserved component of efficiency, the ability of doctor i. The time-variant error term is denoted as ϵ_{ijt} which also includes practice effects d_j.

To test the second implication of the theory, we model mobility as a two stages Heckman model. The first stage regression is essentially the same as Eq. 13 with y_{ijt} representing the realised value of doctors' propensity to stay in the health care job market. The exclusion restriction of the first stage regression is the number of years to statutory retirement depending on the time of the survey. Statutory retirement does not vary by practice and should not affect the probability of changing practice [9]. From each year's probit model we calculate the Inverse Mills Ratio (IMR) as the ratio of the probability density function to the cumulative distribution function. We then "stack" all IMRs and include the time-variant IMR into the second stage random intercept multilevel model of mobility. Conditional on staying in the market, doctors might want to stay in the same practice or to move practices which is formalised with the inclusion of the time-varying IMR as additional covariate. In these specifications we include 2003 as a pre-QOF year because we want to test the effect of the introduction of a new performance scheme on the contractual choice and mobility of doctors.

Finally, we test the third implication of the theoretical model by examining whether the price increase induced by the QOF is associated with an increase of medical effort (measured by the workload of a doctor or full-time equivalence (FTE)), practice quality (measured by the proportion of total QOF points) and a decrease in access of new doctors in the market. The first two models can be formalised as follows:

$$y_{ijt} = \alpha_i + \beta x_{ij(t-1)} + \gamma z_{j(t-1)} + \epsilon_{ijt} \quad (14)$$

where y_{ijt} indicates doctors' effort measured by their FTE and the proportion of total QOF points practice j achieves. The other covariates are the same as those described above, but $t = 2004, \ldots, 2007$. The third model is formally the same as the one in Equation 13 with y_{ijt} indicating whether a new doctor entered the market.

Robustness checks

One potential threat to our empirical strategy is the identification of the effect of the QOF on doctors' mobility from a before and after comparison as the P4P scheme applied to all practices. We can indirectly test the robustness of the results of the 2005 price increase using a similar price change that occurred in 2006. We use the exogenous price shock determined by the increase in threshold levels in 2006, constructed as a potential income loss for each practice, and test its effect on doctors' effort, access of new doctors in the market and mobility. If the before/after comparison was not biased by other policies then we would expect this price decrease to generate similar results as before (but with opposite sign). We highlight a caveat. As this price decrease only applied to some indicators of cardiovascular diseases (CVD), there could be effort diversion to similar tasks for which payments remained unchanged. As an additional robustness check we consider the full set of CVD indicators for which effort diversion might have occurred. More formally, we estimate:

$$\Delta y_{ij} = b\Delta x_{ij} + \theta \Delta S_{ij} + g\Delta z_j + \epsilon_{ijt} \quad (15)$$

where the unobserved component α_i is differenced out and Δy_{ij} indicates the change in FTE, access to the market of new doctors and mobility. We estimate the change in mobility separately for the top and bottom performers, measured as practice performance in 2004. Δx_{ij} includes the same characteristics as in Eq. (14), but age. ΔS_{ij} is the exogenous price shock between 2005 and 2006.

Finally, models of partnership, mobility and access to the healthcare job market could be estimated as non-linear models because the outcome variables are binary. The latent propensity to be a partner, to move to another practice or to access the healthcare job market can be modelled as:

$$y^*_{ijt} = a_i + bx_{ij(t-1)} + gz_{j(t-1)} + \epsilon_{ijt} \quad (16)$$

where, as in Eq. 12, i and j indicate the doctor and practice, respectively; $t = 2003, \ldots, 2007$, and $y_{ijt} = 1.(y^*_{ijt} > 0)$.

Data and summary statistics

Data sources

Our analysis is based on two data sources: i) the General Practitioners' Worklife Survey (GP WLS); and ii) the General Medical Services (GMS) Statistics Databases to which we link geodata and measures of practices' quality. We use multiple data sources to combine their relative strengths because the GP WLS records doctors' income, but as a small longitudinal sample it does not contain a large sample of doctors who move. The GMS database instead contains information on all doctors in England, but does not record their income.

We use the 2004 and 2005 longitudinal samples of about 2000 doctors from the GP WLS, a postal survey of GPs' working lives undertaken by the National Primary Care Research and Development Centre. The questionnaire contains information on personal characteristics of the GPs, their job satisfaction and some characteristics of the practices.

The main data source are the GMS Statistics Databases from 2003 to 2007. They are annual Censuses of GPs in post at each September each year. They contain information on practice codes, Primary Care Trusts (PCTs) codes, GPs age, gender and country of qualification; GP type (i.e. salaried or partner), full-time equivalence (FTE) (including hours if available). They also include information on practice contract, whether it is a dispensing practice, its list size by age-group and gender.

Any doctor who treats patients is required by the law to register with the General Medical Council (GMC) to obtain a licence to practice. Once registered, doctors receive a GMC reference number that uniquely identifies them. This number has been used to trace doctors in the yearly Censuses so that our final dataset contains a description of characteristics and movements of doctors from 2003 to 2007.

Practice postcodes have been used to calculate distances and to link local areas characteristics such as the Local Income Scheme Index (LISI) to this data. LISI is a direct measure of practice list deprivation derived from prescription data.

Finally, we link practice codes to the Health and Social Care Information centre database containing numerators, denominators and number of points that each practice has obtained on all QOF indicators from 2004 onwards.

Summary statistics

Because income is recorded in the GP WLS in eight intervals from less than £25,000 to more than £150,000, we recode it as a continuous variable by assigning each doctor the mid value of the income interval they report. The average income in our GP WLS (2004-2005) sample is about £73,311. On average, doctors report to work about 44 hours per week as GP[10].

We also consider a number of practices' and doctors' characteristics from the GMS database (2003-2007). We use FTE of doctors as measure of their effort (i.e. parameter e_{zi} in the theoretical model). FTE indicates the workload of a doctor on a scale from 0 to 100 where 100 indicates the doctor is employed as full-time worker in the practice and 50 signals that the worker is only half-time. Table 1 reports that on average between 2003 and 2007 doctors work almost 91 percent of their working time. But there is quite a high standard deviation indicating differences between doctors. The FTE in the GP WLS (calculated from the self-reported weekly hours of work) is about 97 percent.

Table 1 Description of the variables in the empirical models 2003-2007

Variable	Obs.	Mean	Std. dev.	Min.	Max.
Outcome variables:					
Principal	171,212	0.82		0.00	1.00
Mobility (old doctors)	141,930	0.06		0.00	1.00
New doctors	171,212	0.17		0.00	1.00
Exit	171,212	0.06		0.00	1.00
FTE	171,212	90.77	17.93	11.00	100.00
Proportion total QOF points	138,303	96.97	5.68	10.00	100.00
Independent variables:					
Age	171,212	45.18	9.74	23.00	85.00
Female	171,212	0.42		0.00	1.00
Practice years	171,212	28.92	6.26	0.00	32.99
Total population (/1,000)	171,204	8.77	4.51	0.00	37.61
LISI	170,930	11.23	7.41	0.00	90.00
Proportion female 65-74	171,212	4.23	1.26	0.00	33.33
Proportion female 75+	171,212	4.62	1.73	0.00	16.10
Proportion male 65-74	171,212	3.91	1.17	0.00	33.33
Proportion male 75+	171,212	2.89	1.19	0.00	100.00
Distance to the best practice	171,212	8.76	16.32	0.01	390.33
Price shock	35,043	-1.41	3.74	-36.86	0

Note: price shock refers to 2005/06

Contractual status is available in the GMS data and records whether the doctor is partner or salaried. On average in our sample 82 percent of doctors work as partners.

We use the GMC reference code in the GMS data to identify new and old doctors. On average about seven percent of doctors between 2003 and 2007 are newly qualified, about six percent exit the healthcare job market or, if they don't exit the market, they move practice.

Our measure of quality (i.e. the parameter Q in the theoretical model) is practice performance in the QOF as measured by the proportion of total points achieved by the practice. The revenue the practice earns varies linearly between lower and upper thresholds of coverage, called "achievement" $A \in [0, 1]$. It indicates the proportion of eligible patients for which a specific measurement of quality has been achieved. No money is received by the practice if achievement is less than or equal to the lower threshold and the maximum revenue is received if the practice is on or above the upper threshold [see Gravelle et al. ([8]); Doran et al. (2011) for further details]. Practices performed quite well as the proportion of total points they achieved in the QOF is almost 97 percent. The low standard deviation indicates small differences between practices.

We select a number of control variables that vary among doctors and practices. On the doctor's side, we consider gender and age in years. Approximately 42 percent of doctors are female and the average age of doctors is 45 years old (with a standard deviation of 9 years). We show that age indicates doctors' experience which is an important component of doctors' efficiency parameter (i.e. parameter γ_z).

On the practice's side, we consider the number of years the practice exists, the size of its population and the proportion of its female and male population aged 65 or over. Practice years is calculated as difference between current and opening date. On average, practices have been in business for about 29 years, but there is a standard deviation of about 6 years. On average, about four percent of the practice population is aged 65 or over. A practice could also have up to a third of its population that is aged 65 or over. We also consider a measure of deprivation based on prescribing in general practice, the LISI (i.e. parameter b_i in the theoretical model). More than 80 percent of prescription by NHS GPs in England are exempt from charges. Most of such exemptions are made on the basis of age and specific diseases. However, 12.1 percent of items are exempt because of low income. LISI includes recipients (and their dependents) of family credit and income support and others who qualify because of low income. It indicates the proportion of total cost in a practice going to patients who are exempt for these reasons. On average, eleven percent of a practice's cost goes to patients with low income, but there is quite a large variation between practices. Practices in deprived areas may have to incur to 90 percent of their costs to poorer patients.

We use the postcode to obtain the latitude and longitude of each practice. We then calculate the Vincenty (1975) distance to the 10 closest practices. Vincenty's formula is used in geodesy to calculate the distance between two points on the assumption that the figure of the Earth is an oblate spheroid rather than spherical. We then calculate the distance (in miles) of the most distant practice amongst the closest 10 practices. We select the distance to the best practice (measured by its QOF points) that is the most further away amongst the 10 selected practices. Under the assumption that relocation costs increase with distance, this is an empirical proxy for parameter t in the theoretical model. We recognise, however, that attractiveness of a practice is determined by other occupation characteristics (i.e. wages) offered to the doctor that we cannot observe. On average, the best practice is at about nine miles distance, but there is a standard deviation of about 16 miles.

Finally, we select four indicators for the management of cardiovascular diseases (CVD), the only ones for which there was an increase in the threshold levels and/or a decrease in the number of points from 2005 to 2006. This change corresponds to a price decrease as practices were paid less in 2006 if they performed the same as in 2005. These indicators measure whether practices successfully manage CVD by keeping blood pressure and cholesterol under the recommended levels. We aggregate them into a CVD control indicator. For an average practice, these indicators were worth about £5,395 in 2006. We then define the exogenous price shock to be the difference between what practices would receive if they continued to provide the same quality in 2006 as they did in 2005 but with the new 2006 thresholds and what they actually received in 2005. The size of the negative price shock can be as high as 37% and on average practices could lose up to 1% in 2006 if they performed in 2006 the same as they did in 2005.

Results and discussion

Before we discuss our results we explain how we measure efficiency. In Table 2 we report estimates of Eq. 12, the pooled regression models of practice quality measured as the proportion of total QOF points. We indirectly show that age is a proxy for doctor's efficiency with three separate models. First, in model I, estimated on the GMS database, we find that in single-handed

Table 2 Pooled linear models of determinants of practices' quality (2004–2005)

	GMS:		GP worklife survey:
	Model I	Model II	Model III
Age	0.84***	0.24***	0.33**
	(0.23)	(0.03)	(0.14)
Age squared	-0.01***	-0.003***	-0.004**
	(0.002)	(0.0003)	(0.002)
Female	0.70	0.09*	0.10
	(0.52)	(0.05)	(0.20)
FTE	0.04	-0.01***	-0.01***
	(0.03)	(0.001)	(0.005)
Income	-	-	0.000
			(0.000)
Distance to the best practice	0.07	0.01**	0.01***
	(0.06)	(0.002)	(0.003)
Total population	0.71***	0.12***	0.10***
	(0.25)	(0.01)	(0.03)
LISI	-0.15***	-0.10***	-0.09***
	(0.04)	(0.01)	(0.03)
Proportion female 65-74	0.75**	0.66***	0.39*
	(0.37)	(0.11)	(0.23)
Proportion female 75+	0.06	0.14**	0.27*
	(0.24)	(0.07)	(0.15)
Proportion male 65-74	-0.20	-0.53***	-0.22
	(0.38)	(0.12)	(0.28)
Proportion male 75+	-1.06**	-0.33***	-0.52
	(0.44)	(0.12)	(0.34)
Practice years	-0.04	0.03***	0.03
	(0.02)	(0.01)	(0.02)
Constant	74.19***	92.78***	90.35***
	(6.07)	(0.74)	(3.21)
N. observations	1652	31,551	1971
N. practices	1652	8192	1659

Note: Model I on single practices, Models II-III on all practices
***$p < 0.01$; **$p < 0.05$; *$p < 0.10$

practices an increase of doctor's age is associated with a better performance of the practice. But this association is non-linear as it is characterised by an inverted-U shape with a decline after the age of 42. The same non-linear relation between age and quality of the practice can be found in Model II using the full sample of practices. However, one limitation is that age could capture the effect of omitted factors such as income. In Model III, estimated on the GP WLS sample, we show that even after controlling for doctors' income, age statistically significantly affects practices' quality. As doctors gain more experience they improve practices performance up to the age of 41 after which their efficiency starts declining.

We report results of the three testable implications in four tables. The first and second testable implication around doctor efficiency, partnership and mobility are reported in Table 3. Results on the third testable implications are reported in Tables 4, 5 and 6.

In Table 3 we report two models of the partnership equation that show results of the first testable implication. Model I is a pooled linear regression and Model II is a random intercept multilevel model where doctors are nested in practices. Both models show that more efficient doctors, where efficiency is proxied by age, are more likely to become partners up to the age of 35 after which the probability of becoming a partner declines. Model II indicates that with a one year of additional experience there is an increase in the probability of becoming a partner by five percentage points when ability is accounted for, compared to seven percentage points when ability was unaccounted for in Model I. Effort is a statistical significant factor in explaining the probability to become a partner. We show that the introduction of the QOF in 2004 decreased the probability of becoming a partner by one percentage point.

There is no evidence of sample selection in the mobility equation[11]. Mobility decreases with age as presumably the costs of moving become higher. An additional year decreases the probability of moving by six percentage points. A doctor working in a practice that performs better in terms of QOF points is less likely to move. A ten percentage point increase in the proportion of total QOF points decreases the probability of moving practices by 0.4 percentage point. But we observe a raise of mobility over time, in 2004 with the introduction of the QOF there is an increase in the probability of moving by two percentage points.

Models I-III in Table 4 report the estimates for the third testable implication on the medical effort, the quality of the practice and access of new doctors in the market. We find evidence of a decrease in medical effort (variable e_{zi} in the model) associated with the increase in the QOF price introduced in 2005. In Model II we find however an increase in the proportion of total QOF points achieved by practices. This result may be explained by the possible effects that forms of *intrinsic motivation* play in the market. Indeed theoretical contributions (Bénabou and Tirole [1]) and industry practioners[12] have argued that doctors' effort may not simply be the result of financial decisions, but also the product of social/reputational considerations. If reputation and pro-social behaviour is important to doctors, the introduction

Table 3 Linear probability models of partnership and mobility (2003–2007)

	Partnership:		Mobility:
	Model I	Model II	Model I
Age	0.07***	0.05***	-0.06***
	(0.001)	(0.001)	(0.01)
Age squared	-0.001***	-0.0004***	0.001***
	(0.00001)	(0.00001)	(0.00005)
Female	-0.06***	-0.12***	0.009***
	(0.003)	(0.004)	(0.002)
Prop. total QOF points	-	-	-0.0004***
			(0.0001)
FTE	0.003***	0.001***	0.001***
	(0.0001)	(0.00004)	(0.0001)
Distance to the best practice	0.0001	-0.00006	-0.00004
	(0.0001)	(0.00003)	(0.00004)
Total population	0.009	0.002***	-0.002***
	(0.001)	(0.0004)	(0.0002)
LISI	-0.0003	-0.001***	0.001***
	(0.0002)	(0.0002)	(0.0002)
Proportion female 65-74	0.01***	0.004**	-0.001
	(0.003)	(0.002)	(0.002)
Proportion female 75+	0.004	0.002**	-0.003***
	(0.003)	(0.002)	(0.001)
Proportion male 65-74	-0.001**	-0.0004	0.003
	(0.003)	(0.002)	(0.002)
Proportion male 75+	-0.01*	-0.0001	0.003*
	(0.003)	(0.001)	(0.001)
Practice years	0.002***	0.002***	-0.001***
	(0.0003)	(0.0003)	(0.0002)
Practice size	-0.02***	-0.01***	-0.002***
	(0.001)	(0.0004)	(0.001)
2004	-0.04***	-0.01***	0.02***
	(0.002)	(0.001)	(0.003)
2005	-0.06***	-0.01***	0.02***
	(0.002)	(0.001)	(0.002)
2006	-0.12***	-0.06***	0.03***
	(0.003)	(0.002)	(0.002)
2007	-0.15	-0.07***	-
	(0.003)	(0.002)	
Inverse Mills' ratio	-	-	-0.04
			(0.05)
Constant	-1.18***	-0.55***	1.60***
	(0.03)	(0.02)	(0.02)
N. observations	141,529	141,529	141,529
N. practices	8507	8507	8507

Note: Model I is a pooled linear regression and Model II is a random intercept multilevel model
Model I of Mobility is second stage of Heckman model
$^{***}p < 0.01$; $^{**}p < 0.05$; $^{*}p < 0.10$

Table 4 Linear models of doctors' effort, practice quality and access of new doctors (2004–2007)

	Model I: FTE	Model II: Proportion of total QOF points	Model III: Access of new doctors
Age	0.36***	0.17***	-0.01***
	(0.06)	(0.02)	(0.0002)
Age squared	-0.01***	-0.002***	-
	(0.001)	(0.0002)	
Female	-0.12***	0.16***	-0.02***
	(0.002)	(0.05)	(0.003)
Being a partner	-0.07***	-	-
	(0.01)		
Age* Being a partner	0.004***	-	-
	(0.0002)		
Distance to the best practice	-0.02***	0.001	-0.00004
	(0.002)	(0.001)	(0.0001)
Total population	0.50***	0.01	-0.01***
	(0.02)	(0.01)	(0.001)
LISI	0.04***	-0.11***	0.001**
	(0.01)	(0.003)	(0.0002)
Proportion female 65-74	0.45***	0.52***	-0.001**
	(0.14)	(0.04)	(0.003)
Proportion female 75+	-0.34***	0.05*	-0.001
	(0.08)	(0.02)	(0.002)
Proportion male 65-74	0.10	-0.48***	0.004
	(0.13)	(0.04)	(0.003)
Proportion male 75+	-0.05	-0.07**	0.001
	(0.09)	(0.03)	(0.004)
Practice years	-0.03***	0.04***	-0.0005*
	(0.01)	(0.004)	(0.0003)
Practice size	-0.58***	0.23***	0.01***
	(0.03)	(0.01)	(0.001)
2005	-0.16**	3.40***	-0.04***
	(0.08)	(0.03)	(0.002)
2006	4.39***	3.54***	-0.06***
	(0.09)	(0.03)	(0.002)
2007	4.09***	3.69***	-0.07***
	(0.94)	(0.03)	(0.002)
Constant	83.25***	90.43***	0.87***
	(1.37)	(0.42)	(0.01)
N. observations	126,930	126,626	102,325
N. practices	8504	8472	5033

Note: Models I and II are linear random intercept multilevel models. Partner and female in Model I
are on a 0-100 scale. Model III is a linear probability random intercept multilevel model. $^{***}p < 0.01$; $^{**}p < 0.05$; $^{*}p < 0.10$

Table 5 First-differenced models with exogenous price shock (2005–2006)

	Model I: Change in FTE	Model II: Change in access of new doctors
Price shock	0.10***	0.001
	(0.03)	(0.0005)
Change in distance to the best practice	-0.05***	0.001
	(0.01)	(0.0001)
Change in total population	0.40***	-0.02***
	(0.09)	(0.002)
Change in LISI	-0.01	-0.002
	(0.03)	(0.001)
Change in proportion female 65-74	1.10**	0.06***
	(0.50)	(0.02)
Change in proportion female 75+	-0.43	0.06***
	(0.34)	(0.01)
Change in proportion male 65-74	-0.03	0.01
	(0.49)	(0.01)
Change in proportion male 75+	-0.66	-0.16
	(0.63)	(0.02)
Change in practice size	-0.16	0.03***
	(0.11)	(0.003)
Constant	3.45***	-0.01***
	(0.14)	(0.003)
N. observations	34,954	25,905
N. practices	8119	4756

***$p < 0.01$; **$p < 0.05$; *$p < 0.10$

Table 6 First-differenced models with exogenous price shock (2005–2006)

	Model I: bottom quintile Change in mobility	Model II: top quintile Change in mobility
Price shock	-0.0003	-0.0003
	(0.001)	(0.003)
Change of distance to the best practice	-0.0001	0.0003
	(0.0003)	(0.0002)
Change in total population	-0.03***	0.01
	(0.01)	(0.01)
Change in LISI	0.004**	-0.003
	(0.002)	(0.003)
Change in proportion female 65-74	-0.04	-0.09**
	(0.03)	(0.04)
Change in proportion female 75+	-0.005	-0.04
	(0.03)	(0.04)
Change in proportion male 65-74	0.01	0.02
	(0.03)	(0.04)
Change in proportion male 75+	0.01	0.16***
	(0.03)	(0.05)
Change in practice size	-0.01*	-0.00004
	(0.01)	(0.004)
Inverse Mills' ratio	0.45***	0.13
	(0.11)	(0.12)
Constant	-0.08***	-0.04***
	(0.01)	(0.02)
N. observations	5967	5384
N. practices	2282	1151

***$p < 0.01$; **$p < 0.05$; *$p < 0.10$

of a P4P scheme may induce doctors to reduce their effort in those tasks that receive a financial incentive to avoid being recognised as greedy. Practice management instead may be less affected by reputational/pro-social considerations, and may react positively to the introduction of a P4P scheme. In model I there is also evidence that more efficient doctors work more, but this association declines as they get older. Effort provision varies by contractual arrangement as more efficient partners put more effort. The more distant the nearest best QOF practice is, the less effort doctors put, indicating either less competition or lower demand for services.

Finally, in Model III we report estimates of the linear probability model of access to the market of new doctors. All covariates are contemporaneous because we don't observe the characteristics of doctors prior to their entrance in the healthcare job market. In this specification we compare 2005 with 2004 as we want to test the effect of a price increase in the QOF on the likelihood that doctors enter the market. We show there is no evidence that an increase in the QOF price in 2005 has increased doctors' access to the healthcare job market. Actually, compared to 2004 in 2005 the probability that a new doctor enters the market *decreases* by four percentage points.

The results in Tables 5 and 6 report the effect of the price shock in 2005. We find results symmetric to the previous ones with an increase of doctors effort and access to the market of new doctors, although the latter is not statistically significant. There is statistically significant effect on mobility for either top or bottom practices based on their performance in 2004. We replicate this analysis using the exogenous price shock on all CVD indicators and find similar results which are available on request.

In Table 7 in the Appendix we show that our results on partnership, mobility and access to the healthcare job market are unaffected by the linear specification because the coefficients of the non-linear models are qualitatively similar.

Conclusions

There is a lack of research on the sorting and retention effects that P4P may produce. In this paper we focus on the only P4P scheme for General Practitioners in England, the Quality and Outcomes framework (QOF).

We have developed a simple two-practice theoretical model where we account for doctors' altruism, different contractual arrangements and multidimensional quality. The model predicts more efficient doctors should be more likely to be offered a partnership. The QOF may induce less turn-over and generate more mobility among more efficient doctors.

We have then tested the empirical implications of this model using a unique linkage between doctors Census data from 2003 to 2007, practices' characteristics and quality as measured by the QOF in England. After controlling for doctors' unobserved heterogeneity in multilevel models where doctors are nested in practices, we have found that the QOF is associated with a two percentage point increase in mobility. We have also found that the introduction of the QOF is associated with a decrease in the probability of becoming a partner by one percentage point, but more efficient doctors are more likely to become partners. More efficient doctors improve the quality of the practice and if they are also partners they put more effort.

Despite the relative richness of the data, our study has some limitations. Firstly, as the QOF applied to all practices in England we identify its effect off time dummies. However, the National Audit Office Report [11] does not highlight any policy other than the QOF that was introduced in England between 2004 and 2005. We have also checked the robustness of our results using the 2006 negative price shock which is exogenous to the individual doctor's behaviour and we found similar results. Secondly, we cannot measure wages at the same time as mobility. We had to resort to an indirect method arguing that age can proxy for experience, a component of efficiency. We have shown this holds in single handed practices where practice quality is doctor's quality. However, this relies on the assumption that the only factor that affects practices' quality is doctors' effort and not the effort of other staff.

Endnotes

[1] See for example Glazer [7]. In the rest of the paper will use the terms devotion, vocation, motivation and altruism interchangebly.

[2] The assumption that the cost of effort is described by a quadratic function is commonly adopted in the literature (see for example Brekke and Sørgard [3] and Zweifel et al. [18]). The convexity of the cost function captures an opportunity cost concept, i.e. the idea that an additional unit of time/effort spent at work increases the value of leisure.

[3] The assumption that health care providers face a convex function is standard. Convexity captures that idea that practices face a capacity constraintthere are physical limitations in physical resources. See for example Brekke et al. [2].

[4] If the doctors had an outside option ensuring a monetary reward greater than zero, then practices would have to consider the satisfaction of a participation constraint and, in case of a binding constraint, the fact that equilibrium profits would depend on the monetary remuneration of the outside option. Qualitatively the results of the model remain unchanged.

[5] The assumption that the partners of a practice equally share profits is clearly a simplification. Nonetheless, given the lack of information in the data available to us, it is an innocent assumption.

[6] The opposite case where type v is located next to practice 2 is completely symmetric to case (iii).

[7] A very recent debate in the news seems to point out that m may have been reduced in the last few years. http://www.bbc.co.uk/news/uk-politics-24362902.

[8] Multilevel models are used because doctors are nested in practices.

[9] We test the exclusion restriction assumption by including the number of years to statutory retirement directly in the mobility equation. We find that it does not statistically significantly affect mobility.

[10] These statistics are not reported in Table 1 as they are not part of our main analysis.

[11] We do not report the results of the year-by-year first stage probit selection model, but these can be made available on request.

[12] http://www.telegraph.co.uk/news/health/news/11177632/Anger-over-cash-for-diagnoses-dementia-plan.html

Appendix A: Additional model specifications

Table 7 Probit models of partnership, mobility and access of new doctors)

	Model I Partnership:	Model II Mobility:	Model III Access of new doctors:
Age	1.03***	-0.33***	-0.22***
	(0.02)	(0.01)	(0.01)
Age squared	-0.01***	0.003***	-
	(0.0002)	(0.00001)	
Female	-1.48***	0.03	-0.07
	(0.04)	(0.02)	(0.04)
Prop. total QOF points	-	-0.01***	-0.001
		(0.002)	(0.001)
FTE	0.02***	0.003***	-
	(0.001)	(0.001)	
Distance to the best practice	0.002*	-0.001	-0.001
	(0.001)	(0.001)	(0.001)
Total population	0.13***	0.02***	-
	(0.01)	(0.005)	
LISI	0.004	0.002	0.01**
	(0.003)	(0.001)	(0.003)
Proportion female 65-74	0.16***	-0.02	-0.13***
	(0.05)	(0.02)	(0.05)
Proportion female 75+	0.05*	-0.04***	-0.01
	(0.03)	(0.01)	(0.03)
Proportion male 65-74	-0.08*	0.05**	0.09*
	(0.05)	(0.02)	(0.05)
Proportion male 75+	-0.06	0.02	0.03
	(0.05)	(0.01)	(0.06)
Practice years	0.02***	-0.008***	-0.01**
	(0.003)	(0.001)	(0.004)
Practice size	-0.23***	-0.06***	0.17***
	(0.01)	(0.01)	(0.009)
2004	-1.96***	-0.01***	-
	(0.18)	(0.001)	
2005	-2.02***	-0.01***	-0.88***
	(0.18)	(0.001)	(0.03)
2006	-3.00***	-0.06***	-1.65***
	(0.19)	(0.002)	(0.05)
2007	-3.35	-0.07***	-2.68***
	(0.19)	(0.002)	(0.07)
Inverse Mills' ratio	-	5.25***	
		(0.62)	
Constant	-20.64***	6.96***	7.49***
	(0.03)	(0.25)	(0.21)
N. observations	141,529	126,626	102,325
N. practices	8507	8507	5033

$^{***}p < 0.01$; $^{**}p < 0.05$; $^{*}p < 0.10$

Acknowledgements

We are grateful to participants to the Nordic Health Economists' Study Group (NHESG) meeting in Reykjavik 2014 and the European Association for Research in Industrial Economics (EARIE) in Milan 2014 for helpful comments and suggestions. We thankfully acknowledge NIHR support from grant RMOFS 2012/07. Eleonora Fichera acknowledges financial support from the MRC Early Career Fellowship in Economics of Health (MR/K021583/1). Finally, we are grateful to two anonymous referees for helpful comments and suggestions. The views expressed in this publication are those of the authors and not necessarily those of the National Institute for Health Research.

Authors' contributions

MP and EF equally led the research project. MP contributed to the literature review and produced the theoretical model. EF contributed to the literature review, the model design and the empirical analysis. Both authors read and approved the manuscript.

Competing interests

We confirm that this manuscript describes original work and has neither been published elsewhere nor is under consideration by any other journal. All authors have approved the manuscript and agree with its submission to Health Economics Review. The study funders played no role in the analysis and interpretation of the data or preparation of the manuscript. The study authors have no competing interests.

Author details

[1]University of Manchester, Manchester Centre for Health Economics, Jean McFarlane Building, Oxford Road, Manchester M13 9PL, UK. [2]University of Manchester, Economics, Arthur Lewis Building Oxford Road, Manchester, M13 9PL, UK.

References

1. Bénabou R, Tirole J. Incentives and Prosocial Behavior. Am Econ Rev. 2006;96(5):1652–78.
2. Brekke K, Nuscheler R, Straume OR. Gatekeeping in health care. J Health Econ. 2007;26(1):149–70.
3. Brekke K, Sørgard L. Public VS private health care in a natioanl health service. Health Econ. 2007;16:579–601.
4. Dohmen T, Falk A. Performance pay and multidimensional sorting: productivity, preferences, and gender. Am Econ Rev. 2011;101:556–90.
5. Doran T, Kontopantelis E, Valderas JM, Campbell S, Roland M, Salisbury C, Reeves D. Effect of financial incentives on incentivised and non-incentivised clinical activities: longitudinal analysis of data from the UK Quality and Outcomes Framework. BMJ. 2011;342:d3590. Available at http://www.bmj.com/content/342/bmj.d3590.
6. Gielen AC, Kerkhofs MJM, van Ours JC. How performance related pay affects productivity and employment. J Popul Econ. 2009;23:291–301.
7. Glazer A. Motivating devoted workers. Int J Ind Organ. 2004;22(3):427–40.
8. Gravelle H, Sutton M, Ma A. Doctor behaviour under a pay for performance contract: treating, cheating and case finding? Econ J. 2010;120:F129—56.
9. Lazear EP. Output-based pay: incentives, retention or sorting? In: Solomon WP, editor. Accounting for Worker Well-Being (Research in Labor Economics, Volume 23). Emerald Group Publishing Limited; 2004. p. 1–25.
10. Lazear E. Performance Pay and Productivity. Am Econ Rev. 2000;90(5): 1346–61.
11. National Audit Office. NHS Pay Modernisation: New Contracts for General Practice Services in England Report by the Controller and Auditor General | HC 307 Session. 20082007–2008. https://www.nao.org.uk/wp-content/uploads/2008/02/0708307.pdf. Accessed Jan 2017.
12. NHS Review Body. Twenty-Third Report, 2008. Available at: http://www.aop.org.uk/uploads/hospital-optometry/23rd-nhs-pay-review-body-report-2009-10.pdf. Last Accessed 22 Mar 2015.
13. Prendergast C. The provision of incentives in firms. J Econ Lit. 1999;37(1): 7–63.
14. Roland M. Linking physician pay to quality of care: a major experiment in the UK. N Engl J Med. 2004;351:1448–54.

15. Ross S. The economic theory of agency: the principal's problem. Am Econ Rev. 1973;63:134–9.
16. The Health Foundation. Staffing matters; funding counts - Pressure point. GP recruitment and retention. Retrieved from: Can the recruitment, retention and distribution of GPs be improved; 2016. http://www.health.org.uk/sites/health/files/SMFCGPRetention.pdf. Accessed Jan 2017.
17. Vincenty T. Direct and inverse solutions of geodesics on the ellipsoid with application of nested equations. Survey Review. 1975;23(176):88–93.
18. Zweifel P, Breyer F, Kifmann M. Health Economics, Second Edition. Heidelberg: Springer; 2009.

15

Economic evaluation of 2014 cholera outbreak in Ghana: a household cost analysis

Dziedzom Kwesi Awalime[1,2*], Bernard Bright K. Davies-Teye[2], Linda A. Vanotoo[2], Nkechi S. Owoo[1] and Edward Nketiah-Amponsah[1]

Abstract

Introduction: Ghana experienced its worst cholera outbreak in three decades in 2014. Evidence of cholera economic costs on affected households has been limited. This study aimed at determining economic costs on households affected by the cholera outbreak in a Coastal Region of Ghana.

Methods: Two districts; High and Low Incidence Areas (HIA and LIA) were selected in comparative cost analysis and disease impact on affected households assessed based on scientifically documented economic indicators. A total of 418 (282 HIA and 136 LIA) households that experienced at least one case of cholera infection were interviewed. Direct and indirect costs were estimated. Correlates of household's cholera infection were estimated using Tobit Regression model in STATA 13.

Results: Average direct cost to households in HIA amounted to USD 106.88, almost 2 folds higher than LIA (USD 62.02). Potential cost saving of an episode of cholera is USD 99,201.28 in LIA and raises almost 8 folds in HIA (USD 782,611.60). Households in lowest income category had the highest incidence of cholera (0.073) compared to other categories plus other factors were significant in explaining cholera incidence.

Conclusions: The study showed considerable differences in HIA and LIA costs with higher household economic impact of cholera on the lowest income category. Results underscore the need for pragmatic policy interventions to avert recurrent outbreaks and emphasis huge potential cost saving with reducing cholera cases.

Keywords: Cholera, HIA, LIA, Cost of illness, Household, Ghana

Background

Economic measurements of disease complement clinical and epidemiological approaches in disease burden assessment. Economic analyses seek to address a number of policy questions on consequences of disease or injury [1]. Economic measurements ultimately translate into cost-savings with reduction of adverse health effects.

Health 'shocks' such as unexpected health expenditures, reduced functional capacity and lost income and productivity are primary risk factors for health impoverishment [2, 3]. These factors pose a great burden on households which experience diseases such as cholera that presents symptoms only after patient is acutely ill.

"Cholera represents an estimated burden of 1.3 to 4.0 million cases, and 21,000 to 143,000 deaths per year worldwide" [4]. However, there could be as much as 100,000 to 120,000 cholera deaths every year but countries normally fail to report actual numbers due to fear of external economic implications on sectors like trade and tourism [4]. These numbers are corroborated by Ali et al. [5].

In parts of Ghana, cholera is now endemic and the country experiences outbreaks about every 5 years. In 2014, Ghana together with Nigeria and DR Congo reported 83% of all cases in Sub-Saharan Africa [6]. In that

* Correspondence: dawalime@gmail.com
[1]Economics Department, University of Ghana, Legon, P. O. Box LG 25, Accra, Ghana
[2]Ghana Health Service, Regional Health Directorate, P. O. Box 184, Accra, Greater Accra Region, Ghana

same year, Ghana experienced its worst outbreak in three decades reporting 28,944 cases including 243 deaths coming only second to Nigeria in infection rates [6, 7].

Research on cholera in Ghana has focused more on epidemiology of outbreaks and little emphasis on economic costs. Studies which identify socio-economic factors [8–10] are not detailed but provide mostly socio-economic linkages.

This study estimated comparative cholera costs in high and low incidence areas (HIA & LIA) plus correlates among cholera affected households. These provide empirical evidence to a lean literature on economic evaluations of cholera.

Methods

The study used Cost-of-Illness approach by Rice [11] including WHO guidelines [1] for estimating economic consequences of disease and injury. This guided the assessment of household costs. Data on direct and indirect cost implications were collected using structured questionnaires.

Study sites

The study was conducted in La-Dadekotopon and Shai-Osudoku districts within the Greater Accra Region. Historically, the region has become the epicenter for cholera outbreaks in the country. At the end of 2014, La-Dadekotopon and Shai-Osudoku documented 1907 and 315 cholera cases respectively. These districts ranked second and eighth respectively among the top ten districts that reported cases and where selected as high and low incidence districts respectively. Distinctive feature of these areas are that one is urban, highly polluted indigenes with mostly poor communities whilst the other is rural sparely populated mixed communities. These inherent differences help to understand the incidence and costs implications within these areas.

Data and sampling

Patient data was obtained from the Ghana Health Service line list for cholera outbreak. This contained names, place of residence, sex, age, laboratory test result, outcome of treatment and the telephone contact of patient. GHS used this database in contact tracing of cases and this same tool was used in tracing patients to their households. For the purposes of this study, population was defined as all positive cases of cholera reported from a particular district. These formed the basis of inclusion criteria with all other households excluded for no documented cases at the health facilities.

Random sampling procedure was adopted in selecting 418 households; 282 and 136 from a HIA and LIA respectively. More specifically, households were randomly selected from patient population database using a calculated sampling interval to help answer the research objectives of this study. Data collection was primary through interviews. Patients who were untraceable where replaced by new ones who were sampled through the same random selection process, traced and interviewed. There was over 90% response rate and those who refuse to grant interview were also replaced. All questionnaires were retrieved and data entered for analysis.

Cost estimation

Direct costs

Direct costs included; first aid, cost of transportation for patient and caregiver, consultation fees, drugs purchased, laboratory cost, facility admission cost (hoteling cost), under-the-table payments (unofficial payments), feeding costs (special diet and water) and burial costs (supervised burial) in the event of death. An accounting process was followed where all costs attributing to various components were summed to obtain the disease cost. Costs were separated based on low and high incidence area costs.

Indirect costs

The method adopted for measuring indirect cost (opportunity cost of ailment) was similar to that adopted by Sarker et al. [12]. This was done by computing the average household earnings as the base for determining the opportunity cost for the household. This average was then multiplied by the time component spent by the patient or caregiver for the time spent in travelling to and fro health facility, on admission and recovery after discharge. The time components include; travel time to facility, time spent at facility till discharge and work or school days lost after discharge. Waiting time with cholera treatment is reduced to zero because all cases brought into facilities are treated as emergencies and hence are not significant to this study. To ensure time loss estimates are not overweighed, during data collection only actively employed patients and caregivers were assumed to be losing productive hours and unemployed patients and caregivers time loss assumed to be zero.

Cholera correlates

The study further examined relationship between cholera affected households using Tobit Regression model by observing the relevance of income categories and other household characteristics in relation to the proportion of household infection. Household's characteristics were examined within this framework, testing which income groupings bore the greatest burden of the outbreak.

The empirical model is specified as:

$$iC = \beta_0 + \beta_1 INC + \beta_2 SEX + \beta_3 MS + \beta_4 RHH + \beta_5 AGE + \beta_6 EDU + \beta_7 HI + \beta_8 DWS$$

iC = proportion of Household members Infected (number of infected persons divided by total household size).

INC= income category (categorical dummy; base: income above GH¢750; USD 234.38).

SEX= sex (dummy variable; base: male).

MS= marital status (dummy variable; base: married).

RHH = relationship with household head (categorical dummy; base: Other dependents); head of household, spouse, daughter or son.

AG = age (continuous variable).

EDU = education (categorical dummy; base: highest education (above Secondary); none, basic, secondary/technical/vocational.

HI = health insurance status (dummy variable; base: not insured).

DWS = drinking water source (categorical dummy; base: Inside Plumbing/Inside Standpipe); water vendor, neighbouring house, public standpipe and others.

Results and discussion

The total direct cost incurred by households in the HIA and LIA amounted to GH¢96,444.30 (USD 30,138.84) and GH¢26,991.30 (USD 8434.78) respectively (see Fig. 1 and Table 1). Treatment costs in both high and low incidence districts formed the highest cost driver for households. When admissions costs were added, facility costs formed over 70% of all direct costs. These costs have important implications for the health system because during the outbreak, cholera treatment was declared free but this outcome shows the contrary. In the HIA, direct cost composition showed treatment cost (49.49%) as the largest component of the direct cost, followed by admission cost (23.47%), transportation for both patient and caregiver (12.63%), feeding (12.09%) then first aid (2.32%) (see Table 1).

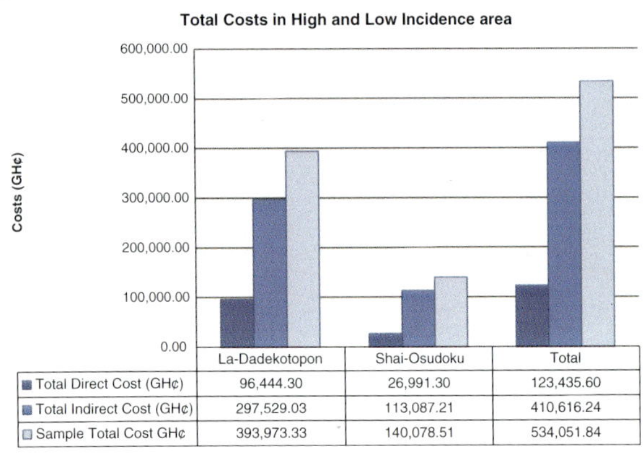

	La-Dadekotopon	Shai-Osudoku	Total
Total Direct Cost (GH¢)	96,444.30	26,991.30	123,435.60
Total Indirect Cost (GH¢)	297,529.03	113,087.21	410,616.24
Sample Total Cost GH¢	393,973.33	140,078.51	534,051.84

Fig. 1 Total Costs in High and Low cholera incidence areas

From Table 2 on average it cost a household in a HIA GH¢342.00 (USD 106.88) and GH¢198.47 (USD 62.02) in a LIA to seek treatment. When compared to average costs reported by Sarker et al. [12] in Bangladesh (USD 30.40) average costs are two folds higher in the LIA and more than three folds higher in the HIA.

The average daily wage for households in the LIA was GH¢26.90, higher than in the HIA (GH¢22.80). On the other hand the average household size in LIA (3.6) is marginally smaller compared to HIA (3.7). These statistics have important bearings on the estimation of indirect costs within these two districts. Higher wages mean greater opportunity cost for lost man hours and household size influences the average household income; larger households mean lower per capita income and greater burden of the disease on that household.

In both districts, days missed by patients during recovery formed the largest composition of indirect costs but was 1% higher in HIA. Indirect costs associated with travel time were insignificant for both districts and is explained by existence of fairly easier access to transportation means in both districts (see Fig. 2). Average admission days was the same for both districts (3 days) but admission days formed a larger proportion of total indirect cost in the LIA (25%) than the HIA (19%) and in consonance, patients from LIA spent 2 days lesser away from normal daily activities than in the HIA (7 days). These suggest that complete recovery was faster and better in the LIA than the HIA.

From Table 3 an average of 25 days were missed in total by patients and caregivers away from their normal economic activities in the LIA but almost doubled in the HIA (48 days). This translated into GH¢1055.07 (USD 329.71) and GH¢831.52 (USD 259.85) average indirect cost for selected sample in the HIA and LIA respectively. Indirect costs in HIA were greater for all components than in LIA with the exception of productive days missed by caregivers. Total productivity loss by patients was GH¢ 141, 656.40 (USD 44,287.63) and GH ¢ 52,858.50 (USD 16,518.28) in HIA and LIA respectively. That of caregivers was GH¢56,293.20 (USD 17,591.63) (HIA) and GH¢28,809.90 (USD 9003.09) (HIA). Together these costs formed over 70% of indirect cost composition.

Table 1 Direct costs in high and low cholera incidence area

Direct Cost	La-Dadekotopon		Shai-Osudoku		Total	
	GH¢	USD$	GH¢	USD$	GH¢	USD$
First Aid	2236.60 (2.32)	698.94	283.80 (1.05)	88.69	3219.34 (2.10)	1006.04
Treatment at Facility	47,729.00 (49.49)	14,915.31	12,885.00 (47.74)	4026.56	75,529.31 (49.18)	23,602.91
Feeding	11,658.00 (12.09)	3643.13	3684.00 (13.65)	1151.25	18,985.13 (12.36)	5932.85
Admission	22,637.00 (23.47)	7074.06	6470.00 (23.97)	2021.88	36,181.06 (23.56)	11,306.58
Transportation (Patient)	5912.00 (6.13)	1847.50	1410.00 (5.22)	440.63	9169.50 (5.97)	2865.47
Transportation (Caregiver)	6271.70 (6.50)	1959.91	2258.50 (8.37)	705.78	10,490.11 (6.83)	3278.16
Total	96,444.30	30,138.84	26,991.30	8434.78	123,435.60	38,573.63

Bracket figures are percentages
Exchange rate: 1USD = GH¢3.20 (Exchange rate as at December 31, 2014)

From Fig. 1 total cost to households were GH¢ 393,973.33 (USD 123,116.67) and GH¢140,078.51 (USD 43,774.53) for sample selected in HIA and LIA districts respectively. In HIA indirect costs was markedly greater (above GH¢200,000 (USD 62,500) more) but in LIA just slightly above GH¢100,000 (USD 31,250).

In total, 2222 cholera cases were reported in health facilities; HIA (1907) and LIA (315). When costs are projected for the total number of cases reported for both districts, the total cost of the 2014 cholera outbreak in a high incidence situation is GH¢ 2,504,357.12 (USD 782,611.60) and GH¢317,444.10 (USD 99,201.28) for lower incidence (see Fig. 3). Hence, if high incidence cases are reduced to levels of a lower incidence scenario, cost saving will be GH ¢2,186,913.02 (USD 683,410.32).

Per capita costs within these areas amounts to GH¢ 1313.24 (USD 410.39) in the HIA and falls to GH¢ 1007.76 (USD 314.93) in the LIA (see Fig. 4).

The regression result from Table 4 supports the fact that the impact of cholera is felt largest by the lower income categories. Compared to the highest income bracket, households in the least income bracket are 7% points more likely to experience a higher cholera incidence. For households within income brackets 3 and 4, there is a 6% points higher likely of infection compared with those in the highest income bracket. All are statistically significant at 10%. These results corroborate the percentages in the cross-tabulation on the infection rates among these income categories. Both Borroto & Martinez-Piedra [13] and Talavera & Pérez [14] studies support impacts of cholera being heaviest on the least income people.

Table 2 Individual and household direct average costs

	Individual Average Direct Cost				HH Average Direct Cost			
	La-Dadekotopon		Shai-Osudoku		La-Dadekotopon		Shai-Osudoku	
	GH¢	USD	GH¢	USD	GH¢	USD	GH¢	USD
First Aid	7.46	2.33	2.04	0.64	7.93	2.48	2.09	0.65
Treatment	159.10	49.72	92.70	28.97	169.25	52.89	94.74	29.61
Feeding	38.86	12.14	26.50	8.28	41.34	12.92	27.09	8.47
Admission	75.46	23.58	46.55	14.55	80.27	25.09	47.57	14.87
Transportation (Patient)	19.71	6.16	10.14	3.17	20.96	6.55	10.37	3.24
Transportation (Caregiver)	20.91	6.53	16.25	5.08	22.24	6.95	16.61	5.19
Total	321.48	100.46	194.18	60.68	342.00	106.88	198.47	62.02

*Exchange rate: 1USD = GH¢3.20 (Exchange rate as at December 31, 2014)
Source: Survey Data; Author's computation from Excel

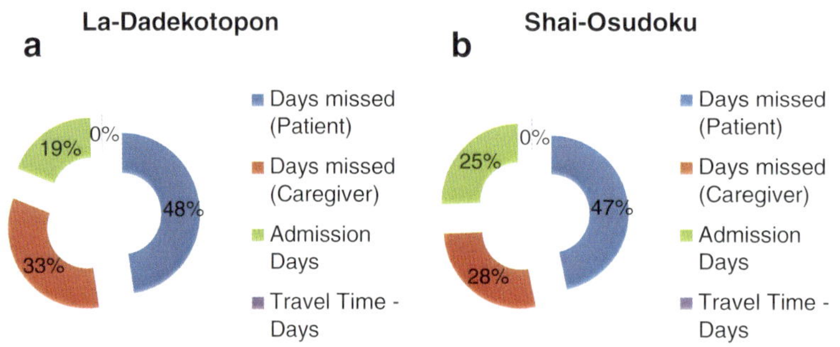

Fig. 2 a and **b** Indirect Cost Composition in high and low incidence areas

Households with unmarried persons have 14% likely incidence than their married counterparts. In 2013, an Oxfam research report on gender and vulnerability to cholera in Sierra Leone showed higher infection among unmarried males compared to married males [15].

Within the household composition, the impact of cholera was highest among dependents of household heads in the sample. There was 15% higher cholera incidence among this group in relation to the head of household. Spouses however had 4% less likely incidence of the disease.

Among adults is a higher tendency to eat away from home and mostly from unregulated commercial food vender around their places of work. The regression shows that with an additional year in age of a household member, there is 0.2% points higher likelihood of cholera infection at 1% significance level. However, Deen et al. [16] in a study of three cholera endemic areas (Jakarta, Kolkata and Biera) found that in all three areas, the impact of the disease was highest among children under five. There seems to be some contextual underpinnings accounting for these mixed results from these two different studies. This can however be understood through future investigation.

Within household composition, cholera impact was greatest among household heads' dependents. A 15% higher proportion of cholera incidence was among this group in compared to household head. Spouses however had 4% less incidence of the disease during the outbreak.

The incidence of cholera and sources of water cannot be exaggerated and studies such as Crooks & Hailegiorgis [17] support this fact. The safest source of drinking water as stipulated by the WHO is piped water on premises. Nketiah-Amponsah et al.'s [18] study's the socioeconomic determinants of drinking water source in Ghana and found that income increases access to piped water in residence by 29 percentage points. Asante [19] also found a significant statistical relationship between income and access to safe or portable water. Based on these, inside plumbing and inside standpipe was set as the reference

Table 3 Days missed by patients and caregivers with indirect costs in high and low incidence areas

		Days missed (Patient)	Days missed (Caregiver)	Admission Days	Travel Time (Days)	Total Missed Days
La-Dadekopon		2071	1451	823	5	14,409
	Average	*6.90*	*4.84*	*2.74*	*0.02*	*48.03*
Shai-Osudoku		655	388	357	1	6816
	Average	*4.71*	*1.41*	*2.57*	*0.00*	*24.79*
	Total	2726	1839	1180	6	5751
		GH¢	GH¢	GH¢	GH¢	GH¢
La-Dadekopon	HH Total Indirect Cost	141,656.40	56,293.20	99,248.40	331.03	297,529.03
Shai-Osudoku	HH Total Indirect Cost	52,858.50	28,809.90	31,311.60	107.21	113,087.21
La-Dadekopon	HH Average Indirect Cost	502.33	199.62	351.94	1.17	1055.07
Shai-Osudoku	HH Average Indirect Cost	388.67	211.84	230.23	0.79	831.52
	Difference	113.66	−12.22	121.71	0.39	223.54

Source: Survey Data; Author's computation from Excel

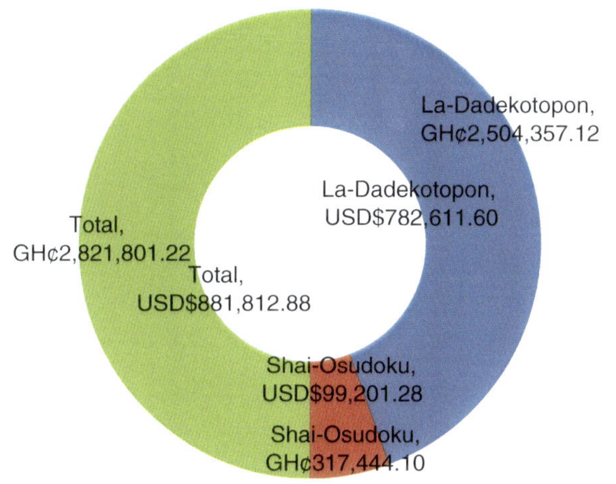

Fig. 3 Total Cost of 2014's Cholera Outbreak in High and Low Incidence Area

base for which other sources were compared. In the sample for this study, close to 70% of the households get their drinking water from a piped source, that is, an inside plumbing or in-house stand pipe (27.5%), tab water in neighbouring house (18.1) or public stand pipe (42.0%). These together formed 87.6% of drinking water sources that qualified as portable sources. The only water source that showed significance in relation to infection of cholera was water from neighbouring house. There was 5.8% higher cholera incidence in households that had their water sources from a neighbouring house as compared to household having inside plumbing as source of drinking water.

Conclusion

Facility costs incurred by households formed the highest cost drivers (forming over 70% of all direct costs in both HIA and LIA) regardless of the government intervention of free treatment of cholera. HIA showed four times higher direct cost to households (GH¢96,444.30; USD 30,138.84) compared to LIA (GH¢26,991.30 or USD 8434.78), representing four folds increased cost when incidence rises from low to high incidence scenario. Average costs in these scenarios saw a 25% increase of costs in HIA households mostly resulting from increased out-of-pocket payments due to medical supply shortages in health facilities within HIA. In both districts, indirect costs were important and higher than direct costs. It was over 50% higher for both districts (51.0% and 61.4% higher in HIA and LIA respectively). In HIA, patients spent an additional 7 days in recovery after discharge from hospital but reduced to 5 days in the LIA. Total cost saving in averting an episode of cholera amounts to GH¢2,504,357.12 (USD 782,611.60) in HIA but rises 8 folds in a LIA scenario GH¢ 317,444.10 (USD 99,201.28). Factors such as income quintile, marital status, age and some drinking water sources were significant correlates with the incidence of cholera.

One limitation of this study is its assumption of unemployed patients or caregivers having zero indirect costs, but since illness and caring for the sick can prevent job hunting or accepting offers of work this is a limitation.

Also, not all sampled cases could be traced and interviewed so had to be replaced. This formed about 10% of all selected cases.

Significance for public health

Cholera is a disease of poverty and continues to cause much strain on the resources of the health system as well as poor homes. The ease of spread and resulting costs cannot be downplayed. Cost analysis of cholera provides a key indicator of the

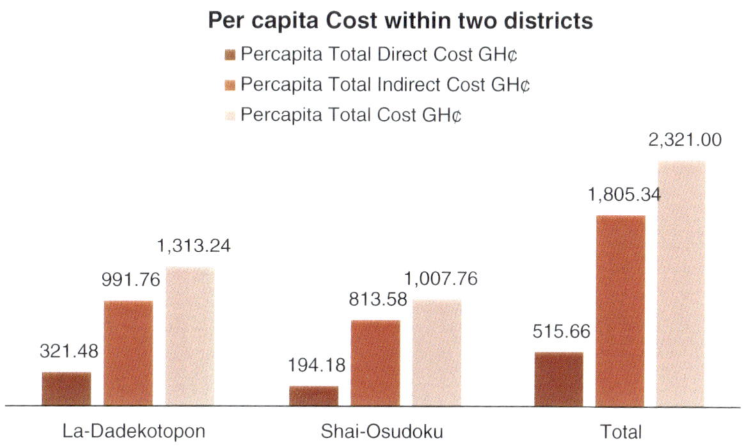

Fig. 4 Per capita cost in High and Low incidence area

Table 4 Tobit regression output showing coefficients, marginal effects for censored sample, standard errors and *p*-values

	Tobit Regression			Censored Sample		
Proportion of HH	Coef.	Std. Err.	P > t	dy/dx	Std. Err.	P > z
Income Grouping (Above GH¢750)						
C1: No Income	0.073**	0.032	0.022	0.019**	0.009	0.036
C2: Less than GH¢100	0.002	0.033	0.960	0.000	0.009	0.960
C3: >GH¢100 < GH¢350	0.059**	0.030	0.050	0.019**	0.009	0.037
C4: >GH¢350 < GH¢750	0.061**	0.030	0.042	0.019**	0.009	0.031
Sex (Male)						
Female	0.004	0.012	0.760	0.001	0.003	0.760
Marital Status (Married)						
Not married	0.137***	0.015	0.000	0.035***	0.004	0.000
Relationship with HH Head (Other Dependents)						
Head of HH	0.002	0.018	0.925	0.001	0.006	0.925
Spouse	−0.043*	0.022	0.054	−0.015*	0.008	0.059
Son/Daughter	0.146***	0.016	0.000	0.038***	0.004	0.000
Age	0.002***	0.000	0.000	0.001***	0.000	0.000
Education (Higher)						
None	0.008	0.036	0.820	0.002	0.009	0.822
Basic	0.017	0.034	0.619	0.005	0.009	0.610
Sec/Tec/Voc.	0.038	0.035	0.283	0.010	0.009	0.260
NHIS Enrolled (Yes)						
No	−0.015	0.011	0.167	−0.004	0.003	0.168
Drinking Water Source (Inside Plumbing/Standpipe)						
Water vendor	0.015	0.021	0.486	0.004	0.006	0.492
Neighbouring hse pipe	0.058***	0.016	0.000	0.016***	0.005	0.000
Public Standpipe	0.019	0.013	0.143	0.005	0.003	0.140
Other sources	0.004	0.027	0.879	0.001	0.007	0.880
Tobit regression		Number of obs = 1543				
		LR chi2(18) = 315.16				
		Prob > chi2 = 0.0000				
Log likelihood = −3801.5065		Pseudo R2 = 0.0398				

Significance levels = ***$p < 0.01$, **$p < 0.05$, *$p < 0.1$

financial strain on poor families when dealing with such menace.

- GHS must ensure the full and continuous implementation of its free cholera treatment.
- Need for social intervention policies such as free feeding or income compensations to mitigate impact.
- Importance of education on symptoms, first aid and need for early treatment by Information Services Department.
- Disparities of infection rates among different income groups plus other demographic variables highlights issues of discrimination and inequitable distribution of resources.

Abbreviations

DHRC: Dodowa Health Research Centre; GHS: Ghana Health Service; GSS: Ghana Statistical Service; HIA: High incidence area; ISSER: Institute of Statistical Social and Economic Research; LIA: Low incidence area; WHO: World Health Organization

Acknowledgements

We are much grateful to Noguchi Memorial Institute for Medical Research for financial support through the Post-doctoral office that aided the facilitation this study. We also thank Ghana Health Service (GHS), Greater Accra Regional Health Directorate for providing initial household data and other useful resources for the study. As well as the La-Dadekotopong and Shai-Osudoku District Hospitals and the Dodowa Health Research Institute (DHRI) for use of their facility.

Funding

A grant was won by the lead author from the Noguchi Memorial Institute for Medical Research, Legon Ghana. This grant was to aid data collection and was not conditioned to influence the design, collection of data, analysis, interpretation and writing of manuscript.
This funding was provided under the Post-Doctoral Office of Sponsored Research which gives an annual grant to master students to support and aid quality research and mitigate financial constraints.

Sponsorship
Noguchi Memorial Institute for Medical Research; Post-Doctoral Office.

Authors' contributions
Dziedzom Awalime identified the topic to research. Dziedzom Awalime, Nkechi Owoo and Edward Nketiah-Amponsah planned the study, executed the study and analyzed the data. Bright Davies-Teye & Vanotoo critically reviewed the paper and provided certain sections of the data required. All authors wrote the paper.

Competing interests
All data collected for use in the study was proprietary work from authors. All models and methodology adopted from other sources are duly recognized and cited. The authors declare that they have no competing interests.

References

1. World Health Organization. WHO guide to identifying the economic consequences of disease and injury; 2009.
2. World Health Organization. The world health report 1999: making a difference. Geneva: World Health Organization; 1999.
3. Xu K, Evans DB, Kawabata K, Zeramdini R, Klavus J, Murray CJ. Household catastrophic health expenditure: a multicountry analysis. Lancet. 2003;362(9378):111–7.
4. World Health Organization. Weekly Epidemiological Record. 2015. Available from: http://www.who.int/wer/2015/wer9040.pdf?ua=1. [Accessed 24 Nov 2016].
5. Ali M, Lopez AL, You Y, Kim YE, Sah B, Maskery B, Clemens J. The global burden of cholera. Bull World Health Organ. 2012;90(3):209–18.
6. World Health Organization. WHO Outbreak Bulletin. 2014;4(4). Available from: https://reliefweb.int/sites/reliefweb.int/files/resources/outbreak_bulletin_issue_4_-september_2014.pdf. [Accessed 24 Nov 2016].
7. Ghana Health Service. Report on cholera outbreak in the Greater Accra Region: June to December, 2014. Accra: Ghana Health Service; 2015.
8. Dotse E, Odoom JK, Opare JK, Davies-Teye BBK. Outbreak of cholera, Greater Accra region Ghana 2014. J Sci Res Rep. 2016;9:3.
9. Davies-Teye BB, Vanotoo L, Yabani JB, Kwaakye-Maclean C. Socio-economic factors associated with cholera outbreak in Southern Ghana, 2012: a case-control study. Int J Epidemiol. 2015;44(suppl 1):i188.
10. De Magny GC, Cazelles B, Guégan JF. Cholera threat to humans in Ghana is influenced by both global and regional climatic variability. EcoHealth. 2006;3(4):223–31.
11. Rice DP. Estimating the cost of illness (health economics series no. 6, PHS no. 947-6). Washington, DC: US Government Printing Office; 1966.
12. Sarker AR, Islam Z, Khan IA, Saha A, Chowdhury F, Khan AI, Qadri F, Khan JAM. Cost of illness for cholera in a high risk urban area in Bangladesh: an analysis from household perspective. Infect Dis. 2013;13:518.
13. Borroto RJ, Martinez-Piedra R. Geographical patterns of cholera in Mexico, 1991–1996. Int J Epidemiol. 2000;29(4):764–72.
14. Talavera A, Perez EM. Is cholera disease associated with poverty? J Infect Dev Ctries. 2009;3(06):408–11.
15. Rancourt N. Gender and Vulnerability to Cholera in Sierra Leone: Gender analysis of the 2012 cholera outbreak and an assessment of Oxfam's response. 2013.
16. Deen JL, Von Seidlein L, Sur D, Agtini M, Lucas ME, Lopez AL, Kim DR, Ali M, Clemens JD. The high burden of cholera in children: comparison of incidence from endemic areas in Asia and Africa. PLoS Negl Trop Dis. 2008;2(2):e173.
17. Crooks AT, Hailegiorgis AB. An agent-based modeling approach applied to the spread of cholera. Environ Model Softw. 2014;62:164–77.
18. Nketiah-Amponsah E, Aidam PW, Senadza B. Socio-economic determinants of sources of drinking water: some insight from Ghana. Conference on International Research on Food Security, Natural Resource Management and Rural Development, University of Hamburg; 2009.
19. Asante FA. Economic analysis of decentralisation in rural Ghana. Peter Lang; Frankfurt am Main. 2003.

16

Hospital physician payment mechanisms in Austria: do they provide gateways to institutional corruption?

Margit Sommersguter-Reichmann[1] and Adolf Stepan[2*]

Abstract

Institutional corruption in the health care sector has gained considerable attention during recent years, as it acknowledges the fact that service providers who are acting in accordance with the institutional and environmental settings can nevertheless undermine a health care system's purposes as a result of the (financial) conflicts of interest to which the service providers are exposed. The present analysis aims to contribute to the examination of institutional corruption in the health sector by analyzing whether the current payment mechanism of separately remunerating salaried hospital physicians for treating supplementary insured patients in public hospitals, in combination with the public hospital physician's possibility of taking up dual practice as a self-employed physician with a private practice and/or as an attending physician in private hospitals, has the potential to undermine the primary purposes of the Austrian public health care system. Based on the analysis of the institutional design of the Austrian public hospital sector, legal provisions and directives have been identified, which have the potential to promote conduct on the part of the public hospital physician that systematically undermines the achievement of the Austrian public health system's primary purposes.

Background

Analyses regarding the interplay between hospitals' and physicians' financial incentives and the quantity and quality of health care supply and expenditure have a long history. The relevant contributions can be divided broadly into two major streams: first there are those that concentrate on the direct link between different payment systems and service provision in terms of the volume and range of services, technology use and service quality, and second there are contributions that choose a broader perspective by taking into account the conflicts of interest that the service providers face in light of the legal and institutional settings.

The impact that conflicts of interest may exert on the conduct of health care professionals has been investigated in the medical literature since the 1980s [1], followed by an intensive examination by social scientists, (health) economists, lawyers and ethicists. According to Rodwin [2], p. 9, physicians are confronted with conflicts of interest whenever '[...] their interests [...] compromise their independent judgment [...].' Thompson [3], p. 137, clarified a conflict of interest as '[...] a set of circumstances that are reasonably believed to create a substantial risk that professional judgment of a primary interest will be unduly influenced by a secondary interest.' There is a broad consensus that the primary interest of physicians should be to act in the best interests of the patient, particularly as the relationship between physician and patient is often considered to be fiduciary [4]. Physicians' secondary interests comprise, among others, professional or scientific recognition, continuing professional education and specialization, as well as financial gain. Koelewijn et al. [5] investigated various personal interests of hospital physicians in the Netherlands, which ranged from helping patients as well as possible – supposedly the primary interest – to having a say in work and to earning a good income. Among the ten major interests under investigation, helping patients in the best possible way ranked first while earning a good income was the fifth most important interest. Jegers et al. [6] analyzed remuneration per service (so-called fee-for-service, FFS), per

* Correspondence: adolf.stepan@tuwien.ac.at
[2]Institute of Management Science, Technical University Vienna, Theresianumgasse 27, A-1040 Vienna, Austria
Full list of author information is available at the end of the article

day, per case (diagnoses-related group, DRG), per patient (capitation) and per period (global budget) and concluded that service providers do indeed respond to financial incentives, so – depending on the type of financial incentive – effects on the volume, range, frequency and continuity of services, number of hospitalizations, length of stay (LOS) and (self-) referrals can be observed. Similar results can be found in the relevant literature [7–16], also considering the effects on quality and risk selection [17–20].

The broader literature stream that problematizes the fact that a physician who is acting in accordance with the legal and institutional settings can nevertheless undermine a system's purposes as a result of the (financial) conflicts of interest to which he or she is exposed dates back to the early work on congressional ethics by Thompson, who identified conduct on behalf of congressional members, which '[...] under certain conditions is a necessary or even desirable part of institutional duties [...]' and '[...] has a tendency to damage the legislature of the democratic process' [21], p. 7. More generally speaking, this phenomenon describes a situation in which the institutional setting produces incentives that create conflicts of interest and subsequently promote behavior on the part of those who perform the duties within the institution that systemically compromises the institution's purposes. Thompson [21] termed this phenomenon institutional corruption. Lessig [22], p. 553, further elaborated that institutional corruption exists '[...] when there is a systemic and strategic influence which is legal, or even currently ethical, that undermines the institution's effectiveness by diverting it from its purpose or weakening its ability to achieve its purpose [...].' Currently, a lively discussion about the 'ultimate' definition of institutional corruption is ongoing [21, 23–25] and so far has resulted in a range of definitional approaches. Marks [26], p. 11, however, noted that a broader perspective regarding institutional corruption may be useful because '[...] one definition works better in some contexts and not so well in others.' For this contribution, a symbiosis of Thompson's and Lessig's definitions of institutional corruption is used as we see institutional corruption as a situation in which the institutional design produces incentives for those who perform the duties within the institution that create conflicts of interest and subsequently promote behavior that systemically and strategically influences the institution's effectiveness by diverting it from its purposes.

Systemic dependencies and informal practices in health care that have the potential to distort a health care system's societal mission through institutional corruption have only occasionally been investigated in the relevant literature. Most studies have focused on the pharmaceutical industry [27–30] and clinical research [31–33], as well as medical care provision in general [34–37]. Rodwin [27] highlighted the influence of the pharmaceutical industry on medical research, publications and key stakeholders. Gagnon [28] problematized the misalignment of the pharmaceutical industry's financial interests with the purposes of the health care system, which allows institutional corruption to breed, while Light et al. [29] provided evidence that, during the last decades, pharmaceutical firms have mainly developed minor-variation new drugs instead of investing in clinically superior new drugs following several systemic dependencies, such as inadequate monitoring by and commercialization of the Food and Drug Administration. Whitaker and Cosgrove [30] investigated the influence of the pharmaceutical industry on the American Psychiatry Association. Wilmshurst [31] emphasized the key role of medical schools and universities in setting standards for clinical research, and Redman [32] drew attention to the research ethics in biomedical research. Emanuel and Steiner [33] investigated institutional conflicts of interest and potential remedies in the context of clinical research. Ensor [34] analyzed 'endemic' corruption in the form of informal payments for health care services in transition economies. Informal payments coincide – at least to a certain extent – with institutional corruption, as they are '[...] part of daily life to the point at which it is no longer considered illegitimate' [34], p. 244. García-Prado and González [35] examined the consequences of dual practice for health care in terms of access, efficiency and quality because the complexity of the financial incentives and the possible conflicts of interest are likely to increase when physicians work at the same time in the public and the private sectors. They concluded that a statement on the net effects of dual practice is difficult to make as a result of the limited empirical evidence on these issues. Socha and Bech [36] predominantly found arguments supporting the negative effects of dual practice, among which were an increased focus on and effort in private practice at the expense of public health care provision resulting from the higher income in private practice, an increase in public waiting lists to stimulate the demand for equivalent private services, the redirection of profitable patients from public waiting lists to private practice, the overprovision of health services in the public sector to obtain a good reputation for treating patients in the private sector and the use of public resources for privately offered medical services. In relation to dual practice, Ferrinho et al. [37] identified financial and other barriers to access to health services resulting from the predatory behavior of clinicians who generate additional demand for their own privately offered services, the absenteeism of clinicians in public institutions due to the competition for time, the emergence of (financial) conflicts of interest, which are supposed to result in poor quality of publicly provided services, the outflow of public resources for providing services in private practice and the corruption in the health care sector.

While combating individual corruption, that is, illegal individual behavior, has a long history in health care (see, e.g., [34, 38–40], the analysis of institutional corruption has only recently become the focus of scientific research. As reasons for the neglect of institutional corruption, Thompson [24], p. 19, listed the following: 1) institutional corruption is closely related to conduct, which is part of the job, 2) there is a common perception that no solution to this problem exists, 3) there is predominantly a concentration on personal misconduct rather than institutional failures on the part of the public and the media and 4) individual corruption still dominates.

The current analysis is intended to contribute to the examination of institutional corruption in the health sector by investigating whether the Austrian health care system is prone to institutional corruption. In particular, we analyze whether the current payment mechanism of remunerating salaried public hospital physicians separately for treating supplementary-insured patients in public hospitals, in combination with public hospital physicians' possibility of taking up dual practice as self-employed physician with private practice and/or as attending physician in private hospitals, provides a systemic and strategic influence that undermines the health care system by diverting it from its purposes [23]. Following the theory of institutional corruption, we first identify the primary purposes of the Austrian public health care system. Next, we scrutinize the institutional design regarding special fees and dual practice in the public hospital sector to identify provisions that potentially promote behavior on the part of the public hospital physician that may systematically undermine the primary purposes of the Austrian public health care system.

The research question is motivated as follows. Special fees are an important source of income for public hospital physicians; they are legitimate but may introduce (financial) conflicts of interest on the part of public hospital physicians, so there may be a substantial risk that their financial interests will weaken the ability to achieve the ascribed purposes of the Austrian health care system. The diversion from the primary purpose(s) of the health care system may even be aggravated by the public hospital physician's opportunity to take up dual practice as a self-employed physician with private practice and/or as attending physician in private hospitals as a result of the possible conflicts of interest the physician may face when providing services in different settings in which different remuneration systems are likely.

We focus on special fees in combination with the above-mentioned dual practice options, because we suspect several adverse effects on health care expenditure and patient care (e.g. two-tier medicine and/or inefficiency in service provision), which are the final result of a failure of the institutional design rather than individual misconduct. Undoubtedly, many more manifestations of corrupt behavior, such as bribery, procurement corruption, improper marketing relations, misuse of high level positions, undue reimbursement claims and fraud and embezzlement [38] – whether in the form of individual corruption, institutional corruption or a combination of the two – are worth analyzing. Covering all potential manifestations of corrupt behavior, however, is beyond the scope of this paper. Given a loss to corruption estimated to range between €1.1 and €3.6 billion in Austria [41], the identification of potential gateways to corruption, however, should be a priority issue.

The remaining part of the paper is structured as follows. In Section 2 the characteristics of the Austrian public hospital sector and the institutional design approach of Oliveira [42], which has been chosen to investigate potential gateways to institutional corruption in the Austrian health care system, are presented. The primary purposes, institutional design and potential gateways to institutional corruption resulting from the payment of special fees to public hospital physicians in combination with the above mentioned dual practice options in Austria are introduced and discussed in Section 3. The paper concludes with a short summary, discusses the shortcomings and provides prospects for future research.

Methods

The Austrian public hospital sector

The Austrian health care system is based on the principles of solidarity, universal, equal and low-threshold access to health services, high quality and efficiency in service delivery [43]. The legally specified responsibilities for the health sector are split between the federal government, the state governments and the statutory health insurance (SHI) funds: while the federal government is responsible for the framework legislation, the implementation and enforcement of regulations are the responsibility of the state governments, which are also in charge of the relevant hospital sector. The self-governing SHI funds have been delegated the competencies for health care services provided outside hospitals. The split of competencies has resulted in a highly fragmented, complex and partly opaque health care system with regard to the delivery and financing of health services.

The Austrian hospital population can be classified according to different (partly overlapping) structural features, such as the care sector (acute, non-acute), care type (general, specialized), care level (standard, extended, maximum, specialized), hospital type (general, specialized), type of financing (DRG-based, not DRG-based), legal status (with/without public law status), benefit status (not-for-profit, for-profit) and ownership type (public, private). According to the Austrian Federal Hospitals Act (KAKuG), the legal status is decisive for the distinction between public and private hospitals: Public hospitals are general and specialized acute care hospitals and nursing facilities for chronically ill patients which are granted public law status. Public law status, which requires the hospital, among others, to be run on a not-for-profit basis (irrespective of the type of ownership), imposes additional obligations (e.g. to charge only officially fixed tariffs) on the hospital in exchange for additional rights (e.g. the right to subsidies in the case of deficits) [44]. In 2017 113 hospitals (41% of all hospitals) operated under public law status, providing around 67% of the overall hospital bed capacity. Of these 113 public hospitals, 105 hospitals were acute care hospitals which were eligible for public financing through state health funds. The state health funds allocate a more or less fixed budget, which mainly comprises predefined percentages of sales taxes and valorized contributions of SHI funds, on a DRG basis. The remaining eight hospitals were not DRG-financed facilities for the chronically ill (mainly financed out of SHI). Of the 161 private hospitals, i.e. of the hospitals without public law status, 40 hospitals were non-profit hospitals (comprising DRG-funded and not DRG-funded facilities) and 121 hospitals were for-profit hospitals [45]. Private, for-profit hospitals (private hospitals henceforth) also receive public funds (mainly SHI contributions) through a private hospitals' fund for services provided to socially insured patients that are covered by the SHI scheme.

Public (and private non-profit) hospitals may be authorized through state legislation to run a special class in addition to the general class and to approve further fees, so-called special fees, for the treatment in the special class [46]. The special class is supposed to cover increased patient demands regarding accommodation (one- or two-bed room) and food as well as free choice of the employed public hospital physician (mostly senior doctors or department heads). Each of the nine Austrian states has made use of the right to authorize a special class in public hospitals and to approve additional charges in the form of special fees.

The special fees are usually covered through private hospital cost insurance (also termed supplementary health insurance, as medical care as such is publicly funded, irrespective of whether it is provided in the general or the special class). In 2015 around 36% of the Austrian population had taken out some form of supplementary health insurance. Approximately 56% of these supplementary-insured Austrians were covered through private hospital cost insurance [47]. In 2014 the expenditures of supplementary health insurance on hospitals amounted to 7% of the public expenditure on hospitals [48].

Operating a special class in public hospitals has frequently been justified as follows. Salaries in the public health care sector are perceived as low. Special fees, which comprise – among others – a hospital and a physician fee, are supposed to ensure the commitment of highly qualified medical staff to the public sector [49]. This 'one-size-fits-all' justification, however, is problematic, because the share of special fees and therefore the compensating effect regarding the salary vary considerably across hospitals, disciplines and qualification levels [50].

Public hospital services are supplied by health professionals, ranging from hospital physicians to nurses and to lab assistants. Except for university hospitals, which carry out research and teaching tasks in addition to providing public health services and in which employees of medical universities also provide public services, hospital physicians are employed by the respective hospital owner, which is in most cases a hospital company owned by the state or the municipality (public ownership) or a religious order (private ownership). Public hospital physicians receive a salary and an additional variable income, comprising, among others, special fees for the treatment of supplementary-insured patients in the special class. A study in 2014 revealed the following average shares of the yearly income of a public hospital physician: basic salary (42%), allowances, such as length-of-service or hardship allowance (12%), overtime compensation (17%), outpatient fees (8%) and physician fees (21%). The actual shares, however, may differ considerably, depending – among others – on the age and the medical field of the physician [50].

Public hospital physicians may be authorized by their employer to perform dual practice as a self-employed physician with a private practice and/or as an attending physician in private hospitals. The type and extent of dual practice of employed hospital physicians may vary considerably across states, hospitals and hospital physicians, depending, among others, on how dual practice is regulated. The dual practice of employees of medical universities, for example, is regulated by federal law (the Civil Servants Act (BDG)) or collective and operating agreements, while the dual practice of employees of privately owned public hospitals is regulated in the respective employment contract.

Supplementary-insured patients have several options to consult a senior public hospital physician: directly in his/her private practice (if additionally self-employed), indirectly via the outpatient department of the public hospital, directly in the private hospital (if he/she is also an attending physician) or indirectly through referral by another physician. The fact that public hospital physicians are allowed to offer medical services in different settings, in which they are most likely to be remunerated differently, may have an impact on medical decisions in terms of the volume, range, frequency and timing of medical services. It can also affect the setting in which specific services are offered.

Rarely available state-specific data regarding the income of chief public hospital physicians have revealed that the size of the special fees is considerable (Table 1) and even increases over time. Average income data have shown the considerable size of chief hospital physicians' financial gain from special fees, as they are able to increase their income by more than double. The system of special fees may therefore introduce considerable conflicts of interest, as hospital physicians are 'rewarded' for treating supplementary-insured patients. As public hospitals benefit from special fees as well, strategic alliances may emerge.

The institutional design approach

Oliveira [42] suggested a stepwise procedure (Fig. 1) to investigate institutional corruption. In the first step, the units under analysis have to be determined. Next, the ascribed purposes of these units need to be identified. The constituent elements of an institution are frequently described in terms of vision or mission statements, while implementation is frequently asserted through bylaws and strategy plans. These implementation issues are addressed in the third step, which analyzes the institutional design in terms of the breakdown and motivation structure. This step follows a typical procedure in practice in which regular reviews of implementation strategies take place to identify any intentional or unintentional deviation from the primary purposes. These review practices are important, because they help to disclose whether groups (e.g. staff categories) within or outside the institution (e.g. lobbies) are pursuing goals other than the primary purposes without disclosing their behavior to the primary target group of the institution. The assessment of actually achieved or presumably resulting goals, given the institutional design, is the subject of the fourth step. If there is a discrepancy between the ascribed purposes and the actually achieved or presumably resulting goals, statements can be made regarding the existence of (gateways to) institutional corruption. The approach proposed by Oliveira therefore illustrates that, apart from identifying institutional corruption, it is important to be able to trace how, that is, through which channels, institutional corruption has developed, and whether it is the result of inappropriate rule making, probably influenced by external advisory bodies, or rule-gaming decisions by-passing the existing rules [51].

In our case the focus lies on public hospitals and public hospital physicians in particular. It has to be considered, however, that these service providers are embedded within a hierarchical legal system, in which the ascribed purposes of public hospitals are defined at the level of the constitutional law. The framework legislation, that is, federal laws, may also outline mission statements, which are tantamount to primary purposes. The institutional design in terms of the breakdown and motivation structure at the public hospital level is heavily defined by state laws and regulations, because the states are responsible for hospital care. The states are therefore supposed to implement the primary purposes outlined in the framework legislation at the federal level in appropriate goals at the state and, thus, public hospital level. If the institutional design promotes behavior that actually or presumably leads to a deviation from the primary purposes, institutional corruption and potential gateways to institutional corruption are identified.

The evaluation of outcomes, however, can be based on various approaches. First, if relevant data are available, an empirical analysis of them is obvious to assess the actual outcome. Alternatively, relevant knowledge from the scientific literature can be used to draw conclusions on possible outcomes in light of the breakdown and motivation structure. The latter approach is chosen for this contribution due to a lack of access to relevant data and missing data for Austria.

Results and discussion

Units of analysis, primary purposes and institutional design

The examination of the Austrian health care system for institutional corruption started in the first step with the definition of the units of analysis, which comprise public acute care hospitals (public hospitals henceforth) as defined in section 2.a and public hospital physicians. Since there are differences regarding the design of the regulations concerning the special fees across the nine states and the presentation of the nine state laws is beyond the scope of this paper, the provisions for a single state (Styria) are outlined representatively.

Table 1 Average income components

State	Year	Average gross income in thousand € (deflated to 1994 prices)	
		Salary	Special fee
Styria [63]	1994	75.7	61.7
Styria [59]	2003	91.9 (79.2)	91.4 (78.7)
Upper Austria [50]	2014	104.0 (71.5)	156.0 (107.2)

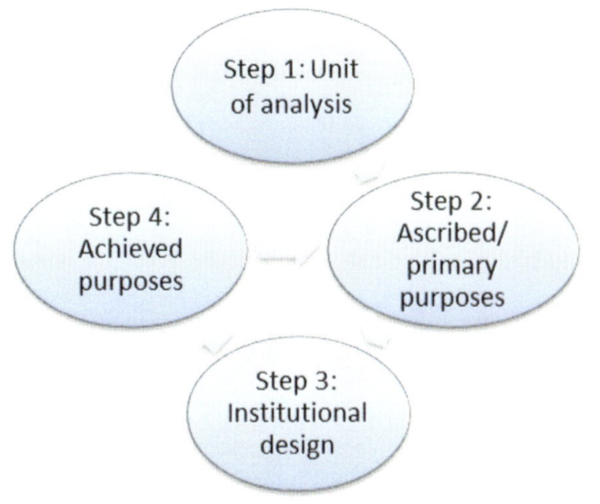

Fig. 1 Operationalizing institutional corruption

As regards the Austrian hospital sector, we identified as primary purposes the goals for the overall health care system outlined in the preambles of Austrian laws and related resolutions. The preamble of the 15a Agreement 'Health Care Organization and Financing' outlines that the parties (i.e. the federal and the state governments) commit themselves to comprehensive medical care for all people, regardless of age and income, based on the principles of solidarity, equal access to health services and high quality and efficiency in service delivery [43]. In 2011 the Federal Health Commission and the Austrian Council of Ministers initiated the formulation of overall health targets for Austria. Finally, 10 health targets, which mainly aim to increase the years of healthy life instead of only responding to illnesses, were officially approved following a target-setting process involving all the relevant stakeholders. Targets 2 and 10 are directly related to the major principles of the Austrian health policy as outlined in the 15a Agreement 'Health Care Organization and Financing': target 2 is to promote fair and equal opportunities in health, irrespective of gender, socio-economic group, ethnic origin and age, and target 10 aims to secure sustainable and efficient health care services of high quality for all [52]. In its preamble the 15a Agreement 'Target Control Health' [53] emphasizes the focus on these guiding principles for the Austrian health policy and public health principles. Based on these laws and the resolution regarding the Austrian health targets, we identified 'good health,' 'equity' and 'efficiency' as the primary purposes of the Austrian health care system, and we assume that they are also valid for the service providers who operate within the public health care system. 'Good health' is a typically intrinsic goal, while 'equity' and 'efficiency' are instrumental goals, meaning that, if achieved, they prepare the way for achieving 'good health.'

These universal statements need to be translated into explicit directives so that they can be used as a baseline for service providers. We therefore first examined the concrete formulations at the federal level that set up the framework for the respective provisions regarding the special fees at the state level. Table 2 summarizes the provisions of the federal and state laws, regulations and treaties that put the primary purposes into explicit terms, that are considered potentially to exert an impact (positively or negatively) on one or more of the primary purposes and that are, to a certain extent, related to the issue of special fees. Assignments to primary purposes are made in accordance with what we considered to be the main purpose(s) of the relevant provision.

Regarding the purpose of 'good health,' public hospitals have to admit anyone in need of medical care, have to treat a patient as long as medically necessary and have to decide on the medical treatment based on medical grounds solely. Some of these provisions can also be related to the purpose of 'equity,' particularly the fundamental principles that no one in need of care must be rejected and no discrimination must be made according to the insurance status of the patient. 'Efficiency' is of considerable importance, because compliance with efficiency secures the financial stability of the health care system. Efficiency-related provisions are found in the 15a Agreement 'Target Control Health,' which emphasizes the importance of treatment at the best point of service, that is, cost-effective and efficient service provision that guarantees high-quality medical and nursing care at the right time and in the right place, the importance of coordination between different service providers, the relief of the cost-intensive Austrian inpatient sector and the development of remuneration systems that are compatible with the Austrian health targets.

For certain provisions, however, it is a priori unclear whether a positive or a negative effect on the primary purposes dominates. These include, inter alia, the prohibition of extra payments of hospital staff, which per se promotes equity and efficiency efforts. As the respective provision excludes special fees and separate fees (§46), which chief university physicians may require in addition to the possibility of charging special fees pursuant to §§16 and 27 (4) of the KAKuG, the primary purposes of equity and efficiency may be undermined considerably. Similar arguments are valid for the restriction of the number of special-class beds to 25% of the overall bed capacity: on the one hand, special-class beds cannot be increased arbitrarily; on the other hand, a 25% limit may increase the overall bed capacity or hinder the capacity-reducing efforts. With regard to the implementation of the special class in general, a positive effect in terms of generating additional revenue is prevalent; a negative effect is expected from additionally remunerating hospital

Table 2 Directives outlined in federal and state laws

Federal laws	Good health	Equity	Efficiency	State laws, regulations and treaties
15a Agreement 'Target Control Health'				State treaty 'Target Control Health' [64]
Art. 5 (1–2) Provision of medical care at the 'best point of service'			+	Definition of public service obligations for all care levels (primary, hospital outpatient and inpatient care) and launching implementation
Art. 5 (2–3) Coordination of services across all sectors, offering of patient-oriented and needs-based services and prevention or reduction of parallel structures	+	+	+	Development of interdisciplinary forms of care in the ambulatory setting
Art. 5 (3–2) Relief of the inpatient sector in hospitals through medically and economically justified relocation of services to day care and ambulatory care		+	+	
Art. 5 (3–7) Development of remuneration schemes, which guarantee service provision at the best point of service			+	Participation at the federal level in developing incentives to promote outpatient care
Federal Hospitals Act (KAKuG)				Styrian Hospitals Act (StKAG)
§16 Non-profit hospitals must				§51 adopts §16 KAKuG
• admit everyone in need of medical care in accordance with the hospital's facilities	+	+		
• accommodate every patient as long as medically required	+	+	+	
• ensure that medical treatment, irrespective of accommodation in the special class, is based on the medical condition of the patient solely [...]	+	+	+	
• secure that the staff, notwithstanding §27 (4) and §46 (1), must not be remunerated by patients or their family members		+/−	+/−	
• not run more than 25% of the total beds as special-class beds		+/−	+/−	
§22 (2): Public hospitals are obliged to admit any socially insured patients	+	+		§87 (1) adopts §22 (2) KAKuG
§27 (4-1) State legislation has to determine				
• whether and		+/−	+/−	§66 regulates the prerequisites for implementation of the special class
• what further charges may be levied in the special class		+/−	+/−	§75 regulates special fees
§46 (1) The department heads of university hospitals may agree a separate fee with special-class patients [...], irrespective of the special-class patients' obligations to pay special fees [...], if these patients request treatment by the department head. This separate fee is not subject to §27 (4) [...].		+/−	+/−	

physicians for providing medical care in the special class, which, in turn, must not be different from the medical care provided in the general class.

The legal provisions, which regulate the hospital and the physician fees of the state-owned public hospitals in Styria (and which provide about 91% of the public hospital bed capacity in Styria [45]) are complex and outlined in Table 3. Public hospitals are allowed to run a special class if there is a sufficient (absolute) number of beds in the general class. If accommodation in the special class is requested, hospital and physician fees apply. The hospital fee is levied to compensate for the extra costs for material and personnel in the special class and is made up of different compensation systems, ranging from a percentage of the relevant DRG fee to flat fees. The hospital owner retains the entire hospital fee. Although there shall not be any difference in medical treatment between the general class and the special class, a physician fee applies if the patient requests medical treatment in the special class. As differences in medical care are prohibited by law, there has been a lively discussion in the scientific literature what exactly the supplementary-insured patient receives in return for the physician fee [54]. Both the hospital and the physicians benefit from the physician fee. The public hospital currently receives a hospital share totaling 19%, while the physicians involved in the treatment of special-class patients receive the remaining 81% (physician share). The physician share is then divided between the affiliated physicians. The allocation procedure, which is governed by regulation and, thus, obligatory for the employees of the public

Table 3 Regulations regarding special fees in Styria

Special fees (StKAG)			
Public hospitals may run a special class in addition to the general class [...] if the hospital provides a sufficient number of beds in the general class, particularly for those who cannot be denied hospital care. [...] There shall not be any difference in medical care. The special class has to meet higher demands in terms of food and accommodation. (§66) Special fees comprise the hospital fee, the physician fee and the midwife fee in the special class and the outpatient fee.[a] (§76)			
Outpatient care and financing	Inpatient care and financing		
Lump-sum compensation (socially insured) Special fees (self-payers only)	DRG/case fees (general class; socially insured) DRG/case fees and special fees (special class; supplementary-insured)		
	Special fees comprise [65]		
	Hospital fee	Physician fee	
	– compensation for extra costs (material, personnel) in the special class – tariffication predominantly based on flat fees and fees as a percentage of the DRG fees	– compensation for medical care provided by the department head and affiliated physicians in the special class – tariffication predominantly based on specific fees (for surgical interventions, diagnostic imaging, radiotherapy treatments), fee/day (conservative treatments), surcharges and flat fees (e.g. lab tests)	
		decomposes into [66]	
	Hospital share 100%	Hospital share 19%	Physician share 81%

[a]Midwife and outpatient fees are no longer considered

state-owned hospitals, follows a complex scoring method that takes the hierarchical position, seniority and special qualifications of the physicians into account [55].

The breakdown and motivation structure with regard to the special class provides financial incentives for hospitals and hospital physicians to treat special-class patients. The question therefore arises of whether the service providers have the opportunity to boost their income through special fees, that is, whether hospital physicians can influence the demand for treatment in the special class. The widespread possibility of dual practice for (senior) hospital physicians paves the way to influencing the demand regarding elective services.

Usually, dual practice requires authorization from the employer and is limited in time. Regarding dual practice, there may be differences depending on the type of ownership across public hospitals: while privately owned hospitals usually regulate dual practice options individually under employment contracts (non-competition clause), the dual practice of physicians of the state-owned public hospitals (and the medical university) is subject to two different sources of law in Styria, the Civil Servants Act (BDG) and the Styrian Civil Servants and Pay Act (Stmk L-DBR). The BDG outlines that dual practice is any activity pursued outside employment and must not be performed if it hinders the physician from fulfilling his official duties, causes the presumption of partiality or endangers other essential interests of the service. The civil servant (i.e. the hospital physician) is obliged to notify the employer about any dual practice. The Stmk L-DBR adopts these provisions and further states that the employed physician may pursue a medical activity in another hospital or may use hospital equipment and staff only if authorized by the employer. These regulations offer the opportunity to perform dual practice and, therefore, to influence the demand in the settings in which physicians operate.

Gateways to institutional corruption

Rodwin [2], p. 10, pointed out in quite an early study that self-employed physicians are entrepreneurs just like any other freelancers, meaning that they sell services to generate income, while the employment of physicians typically precludes entrepreneurship. The institutional setting in the Austrian hospital sector, however, opens up a broad spectrum of opportunities for physicians employed in public hospitals to act in an entrepreneurial manner. Public hospital physicians can influence their overall income by pushing their variable income components, such as the physician fee for the treatment in the special class of the public hospital, and the income resulting from authorized dual practice as self-employed physician and/or as attending physician in private hospitals.

The employed public hospital physician can proactively influence the occupancy of the special class through the referral of supplementary-insured patients from outpatient to inpatient care, because hospital and physician fees are restricted to inpatient services. This may be attractive whenever there is void capacity in the special class. This activity can boost physician income but may impede any attempts to relieve the inpatient sector because any reduction of the total bed capacity is tantamount to income loss for both the hospital owner and the hospital physician because the special-class bed capacity is linked to total bed capacity (25% rule). In addition, the tariffication of hospital and physician fees reveals that pay per intervention and pay per day are predominantly used to remunerate hospitals and hospital physicians for providing special-class services. Following the findings of relevant scientific studies [6, 8–10, 13, 16], these payment forms are likely to increase the volume and range of services. The restriction of hospital and physician fees to inpatient care and their tariffication are likely to threaten any attempts to provide services effectively and efficiently at the best point of service.

If any of the dual practice options outlined above is performed in addition to the employment in a public hospital, we assume that the extra work is pursued to increase the public hospital physician's income. Although dual practice may lead to considerably adverse effects [36, 37] the institutional design of the Austrian public hospital sector permits different types of dual practice. As a consequence, intricate structures evolve regarding the flow of funds and patients and the activity that hospital physicians may undertake in the context of physician fees (Fig. 2).

A public hospital physician may be authorized to pursue dual practice as a non-contracted physician or – in rare cases – even as a contracted physician with a private practice. If a patient attends a contracted physician, the services provided are directly settled with the SHI fund (mostly on a FFS basis) that individually contracts with the respective physician. The SHI funds directly regulate the number of contracted physicians through the number of contracts offered. Patients may also attend a non-contracted physician directly. In that case they have to pay in advance and receive reimbursement to the amount of 80% of the tariff that the SHI fund would have paid for this service to a contracted physician. The SHI funds have no opportunity to regulate the supply with non-contracted physicians directly. In the context of special fees, the dual practice as a (non-)contracted physician with a private practice opens up the possibility not only of acquiring income in the form of physician fees through (self-) referral from private practice to the special class in the public hospital but also of acquiring additional income as a self-employed physician through, for example, reverse referral from the special class to private practice for medical aftercare. In Vienna, for example, referral from private practice to the special class is rewarded through 'bringer solutions' [56]; that is, hospital physicians are financially better off (in terms of the physician share) when they refer patients from private practice to the special class. While this may impede attempts to relieve the inpatient sector, proponents of this solution argue that it strengthens the competitiveness of the public hospital sector if the patient would otherwise have been admitted to a private hospital. This argument, however, presumes that there is no physician-induced demand and that inpatient care is the 'best point' for service provision. Empirical evidence on this issue is lacking in Austria. A potential approach to investigating this question could be to undertake, for a selection of comparable diagnoses, a comparison of the referral behavior of hospital physicians who run a private practice with

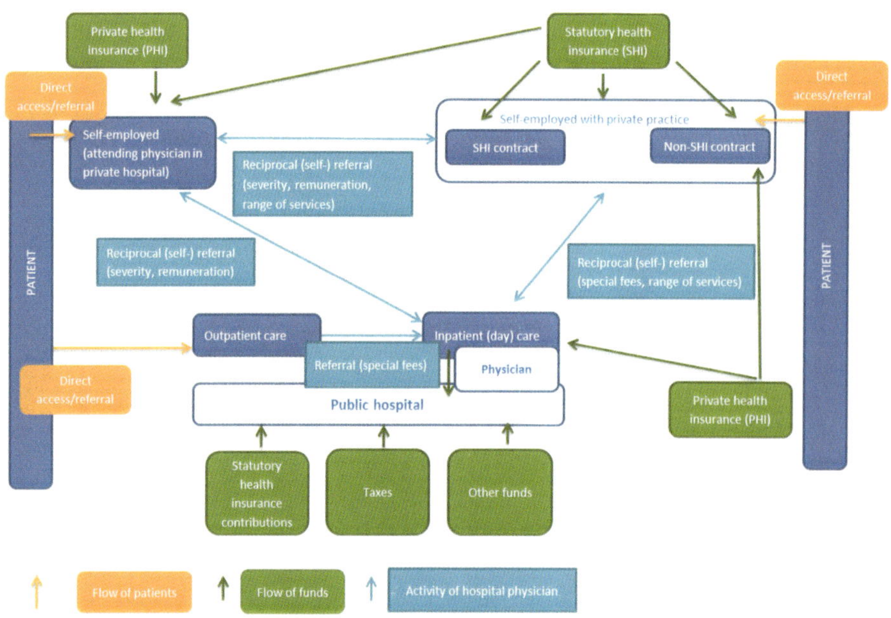

Fig. 2 Interplay between hospital physicians' activities in the presence of physician fees and dual practice

that of contracted and non-contracted self-employed physicians without any affiliation to a hospital. This issue, however, is challenging due to the different accounting systems that apply to contracted and non-contracted physicians and the different accounting systems between the 19 SHI funds.

The analysis of the referral behavior can also be used to investigate whether the current institutional design systematically promotes a two-tier medical system: the differences in the waiting times, access, range and volume of services between socially and supplementary-insured patients, adjusted for diagnosis and age, would indicate that the current institutional design promotes behavior that undermines the system's equity purpose. Differences in waiting times for elective treatments between socially and supplementary-insured inpatients, however, have already been disclosed [57]. Another study revealed a higher number of lab tests and a greater frequency of express lab tests for supplementary-insured patients [58]. Further sparse empirical evidence regarding the impact of supplementary health insurance on 'good health,' 'equity' and 'efficiency' is available through the Audit Court Reports, but the results are mainly snapshots, particularly as the findings are mostly by-products of audit assignments, the aim of which differs from the current research question. One Audit Court Report [59] revealed differences in the average LOS between socially and supplementary-insured inpatients in university hospitals in 2004 (Vienna +1.6 days, Graz +1.8 days and Innsbruck +1.5 days in the case of supplementary health insurance), which mainly occurred in orthopedic and vascular surgery departments. In 2008 the Vienna Audit Court investigated differences in assignments of elective surgeries between socially and supplementary-insured patients in the departments of orthopedics and ophthalmology, in which differences were found regarding the registration for and planning of elective surgeries [60].

Public hospital physicians may also be authorized to provide medical services as attending physicians in private hospitals. Dual practice in private hospitals is sometimes handled more restrictively (e.g. conditional on the explicit patient wish [61]), because dual practice in private hospitals competes directly with public hospitals. If dual practice as an attending physician in private hospitals is authorized and the hospital physician decides to treat a patient in the private hospital, financial resources (the hospital fee and the hospital share) are withdrawn from the public hospital. As only public hospitals are obliged to admit socially insured patients, private hospitals have a decisive strategic advantage, as they may cherry pick financially attractive patients, which, in turn, may be mirrored in the amount of remuneration that the public hospital physician receives for providing services as an attending physician in the private hospital. In the case of dual practice in private hospitals, reciprocal referral between the private and the public hospital may occur, probably depending on the severity of the illness (usually, the more severe the more appropriate the public hospital so that more complex and more expensive services then have to be provided in the public hospital) and the financial consequences for the hospital physician of treating patients in either of the two hospitals. The complexity of the referral behavior further increases if the public hospital physician works as a self-employed physician in private practice in addition to dual practice in private hospitals. Another Audit Court Report revealed that 3700 of the 32,300 employees of the Vienna Hospital Association (the main owner of public hospitals in Vienna), that is, around 11.5%, had indicated that they had engaged in dual practice in 2006. With regard to the 165 medical directors and department heads, 148, that is, 89.7%, performed dual practice [62]. Such activities may seriously impair attempts to coordinate services efficiently and effectively in all sectors and to prevent parallel structures. Further negative effects, such as increases in public waiting lists, may result from the potential absenteeism of department heads in public hospitals as a consequence of providing services in private hospitals as outlined in the relevant literature [37]. Previous reports have revealed that chief physicians had the opportunity to perform services outside the hospital starting in the early afternoon due to highly flexible work time regulation and a lack of transparency regarding timekeeping [61, 62].

Summing up, the analysis of the institutional design of the public hospital sector with regard to special-fee payment and dual practice, in combination with the knowledge from the relevant scientific literature and the sparsely available Austrian-specific studies, has revealed that there are several gateways to institutional corruption in Austria. Table 4 summarizes potential conduct as a result of legal regulations that has the potential to put the achievement of the purposes of 'good health,' 'equity' and 'efficiency' at risk.

Conclusions

The aim of this paper was to investigate whether the Austrian health care system is prone to institutional corruption and, if so, through which channels institutional corruption has developed. Institutional corruption may arise as a consequence of the emergence of (financial) conflicts of interest that result from the institutional design and that enforce the tension between physicians' fiduciary task of acting in the best interests of the patient and their financial interests. Medical decisions that are made in favor of physicians' financial benefit usually do not harm patients directly, as their effects are rather indirect: inefficient resource use as a consequence of supplier-induced demand (concerning the volume, range and frequency of services), inequity as a consequence of

Table 4 Potential gateways to institutional corruption

Breakdown/motivation structure according to federal/state laws	potentially promotes	puts at risk
• Existence of a physician fee per se	prioritization of supplementary- insured patients, increasing/by-passing public waiting lists	equal treatment for equal needs in terms of volume, range, timing and access
• Restriction of hospital and physician fees to inpatient (day) care	inpatient care of outpatient (ambulatory) care	service provision at the 'best point of service' and relief of the inpatient sector
• Limiting the special-class bed capacity to 25% of the overall bed capacity	high capacity utilization	reasonable reduction in the overall bed capacity and capacity-reducing innovations
• Tariffication of physician fees	overprovision of medical services, prolongation of length of stay	equal and efficient service provision
• Possibility of dual practice	redirection of profitable patients to private practice/private hospital overprovision of medical services through self-referral focus on private practice at the expense of public health care provision misuse of public resources for privately offered medical services absenteeism outflow of public hospitals' resources to private hospitals	service provision at the 'best point of service,' coordinated service provision, prevention and decrease of parallel structures and relief of the inpatient sector

a two-tier medicine system (concerning the range, timing and continuity of and access to medical services) and, subsequently, impairment of the population's good health if the financial viability of the overall health care system suffers and equal access for equal needs cannot be guaranteed.

The paper focused on special fees in the form of physician fees, because they represent an important source of additional income for employed public hospital physicians. Physician fees are paid for treating supplementary-insured patients in the special class of public hospitals. The impact of dual practice was also taken into consideration, because dual practice as self-employed physician or attending physician in private hospitals opens up a broad spectrum of opportunities for employed hospital physicians to act in an entrepreneurial manner, which, in turn, is supposed to interact with the service provision provided in the special class of the public hospital.

The institutional design, which regulates special fees and dual practice in the public hospital sector in Austria, has grown historically in an attempt to contribute to the financing of the public health sector and to commit highly qualified physicians to the public hospital sector. The rule-making resulted in extremely complex and further proliferating amendments to the respective regulations. The institutional design, however, has been put into place without clearly and comprehensively addressing and assessing the overall consequences for the purposes of the health care system as can be seen by the potential gateways to institutional corruption which have been identified for a single Austrian state. The results showed that there are in fact legal provisions and directives, which have the potential to promote behavior on the part of the employed public hospital physician that systematically undermines the achievement of the Austrian public health system's primary purposes of 'good health,' 'equity' and 'efficiency.' This corresponds to the definition of 'institutional corruption' in the relevant literature. In particular, linking the additional income of public hospital physicians in terms of physician fees to inpatient capacity utilization and paying fees per intervention and/or day bears the risk of inefficient service provision as a result of potential supplier-induced demand and overprovision of services. Restricting the payment of special fees to inpatient care and authorizing dual practice, especially in private hospitals, puts at risk the service provision at the best point of service and the relief of the cost-intensive inpatient sector. Paying physician fees to employed hospital physicians at all may lead to two-tier medicine in the form of prioritizing the supplementary-insured patients and/or increasing or by-passing public waiting lists. Following some rare Austria-specific studies and general findings in the relevant scientific literature, the emergence and existence, respectively, of two-tier medicine seem likely.

While the prevailing contribution identified only potential gateways to institutional corruption following the lack of access to empirical data and missing data, future research needs to concentrate on the actual effects on the medical decisions of public hospital physicians caused by the conflicts of interest resulting from the institutional design regulating physician fees and dual practice. The hypotheses, which were derived on the basis of the rarely available data for Austria and the general findings in the relevant literature, clearly need to be tested empirically. In other words, a reliable and accessible database covering relevant information regarding, for example, the revenues/ income from special fees at the hospital and the physician level, and across medical disciplines, the type and extent of dual practice of public hospital physicians, the service provision in terms of the volume, range and timing of services inside and outside the hospital, the referral and timing of referrals and the waiting times for medical treatment, each disaggregated by the insurance status of the patient, is required to assess reliably the actual effects of the current institutional design on the ascribed purposes of the Austrian public health care system.

Empirical evidence regarding the actual effects is a prerequisite for the development of reform proposals in terms of conflict regulation, should the hypotheses regarding institutional corruption prove to be true. If there is still commitment to the current primary purposes of 'good health,' 'equity' and 'efficiency,' possible options for reform range from reshaping the payment system of public hospital physicians towards higher salaries as compensation for variable income components (physician fees) to changing the tariffication and/or allocation of physician fees and to reregulating the options regarding the dual practice of employed public hospital physicians, particularly in private hospitals. It might, however, also become necessary to reregulate the service provision of self-employed physicians and the organization of SHI: starting points range from revising the organization and financing of primary health care to overthinking the overall number of contracts offered in the present system and to uniting the SHI funds (or even all the social security funds) to avoid differences in the accounting systems and in the benefits and contributions between the socially insured. If, however, there is no longer commitment to the purposes of 'good health,' 'equity' and 'efficiency' or the purposes can no longer be maintained, further options may emerge. Final considerations and recommendations can only be made if the nature and extent of the alleged negative effects of physician fees and dual practice on the primary purposes of the Austrian health care system are determined comprehensively.

Acknowledgements
We would like to thank the Brocher Foundation for organizing the inspiring work in the context of ethical physician remuneration. We would also like to thank Mark Rodwin for his motivating comments on a previous version of the paper and two anonymous referees for their recommendations on how to improve the paper.

Funding
Adolf Stepan was partly funded by the Brocher Foundation. The other co-author did not receive any specific grant from funding agencies in the public, commercial, or not-for-profit sectors.

Authors' contributions
Both authors have equally (50%) contributed to the prevailing paper. Both authors read and approved the final manuscript.

Competing interests
The authors declare that they have no competing interests.

Author details
[1]Department of Finance, Karl-Franzens University Graz, Resowi G2, A-8010 Graz, Austria. [2]Institute of Management Science, Technical University Vienna, Theresianumgasse 27, A-1040 Vienna, Austria.

References
1. Thompson D. Restoring responsibility: ethics in government, business, and healthcare. Cambridge, New York: Cambridge University Press; 2005.
2. Rodwin M. Medicine, money, and morals: physicians' conflicts of interest. New York: Oxford University Press; 1993.
3. Thompson D. The challenge of conflict of interest in medicine. Z Evid Fortb Qual Gesundhwes. 2009;103:136–40.
4. Hafemeister T, Gulbrandsen R. The fiduciary obligation of physicians to 'Just Say No' if an 'informed' patient demands services that are not medically indicated. Seton Hall Law Rev. 2009;39:335–86.
5. Koelewijn W, Ehrenhard M, Groen A, van Harten W. Exploring personal interests of physicians in hospitals and specialty clinics. Soc Sci Med. 2014;100:93–8.
6. Jegers M, Kesteloot K, de Graeve D, Gilles W. A typology for provider payment systems in health care. Health Policy. 2002;60:255–73.
7. Bolz N, Iorio R. Bundled payments: our experience at an academic medical center. J Arthroplasty. 2016;31:932–5.
8. Chaix-Couturier C, Durand-Zaleski I, Jolly D, Durieux P. Effects of financial incentives on medical practice: results from a systematic review of the literature and methodological issues. Int J Qual Health Care. 2000;12:133–42.
9. Chen C, Dong W, Shen J, Cochran C, Wang Y. Is the prescribing behavior of Chinese physicians driven by financial incentives? Soc Sci Med. 2014;120:40–8.
10. Clemens J, Gottlieb J. Do physicians' financial incentives affect medical treatment and patient health? American Econ Rev. 2014;104:1320–49.
11. Hennig-Schmidt H, Selten R, Wiesen D. How payment systems affect physicians' provision behavior: an experimental investigation. J Health Econ. 2011;30:637–46.
12. Kim J, Shin D, Chae J, Park S. Impact of the new payment system on laparoscopic appendectomy in Korea. J Surg Res. 2015;199:338–44.
13. Moreno-Serra R, Wagstaff A. System-wide impacts of hospital payment reforms: evidence from central and eastern Europe and central Asia. J Health Econ. 2010;29:585–602.
14. Shigeoka H, Fushimi K. Supplier-induced demand for newborn treatment: evidence from Japan. J Health Econ. 2014;2014(35):162–78.
15. Waters H, Hussey P. Pricing health services for purchasers: a review of methods and experiences. Health Policy. 2004;70:175–84.
16. Echevin D, Fortin B. Physician payment mechanisms, hospital length of stay and risk of readmission: evidence from a natural experiment. J Health Econ. 2014;36:112–24.
17. Kantarevic J, Kralj B. Risk selection and cost shifting in a prospective physician payment system: evidence from Ontario. Health Policy. 2014;115:249–57.
18. Lindenauer P, Remus D, Roman S, Rothberg M, Benjamin E, Ma A, et al. Public reporting and pay for performance in hospital quality improvement. N Engl J Med. 2007;336:486–96.
19. Perelman J, Closon M. Hospital response to prospective financing of in-patient days: the Belgian case. Health Policy. 2007;84:200–9.
20. Ellis R, McGuire T. Hospital response to prospective payment: moral hazard, selection, and practice-style effects. J Health Econ. 1996;15:257–77.
21. Thompson D. Ethics in congress: from individual to institutional corruption. Washington, DC: Brookings Inst; 1995.

22. Lessig L. "Institutional corruption" defined. J Law Med Ethics. 2013;41:553–5.
23. Lessing L. Institutional corruptions. Edmond J Safra Center for Ethics. 2013. http://ethics.harvard.edu/working-papers-series . Accessed 15 Aug 2016.
24. Thompson D. Two concepts of corruption. Edmond J Safra Center for Ethics. 2013. http://ethics.harvard.edu/working-papers-series. Accessed 15 Aug 2016.
25. Light D. Strengthening the theory of institutional corruptions: broadening, clarifying, and measuring. Edmond J Safra Center for Ethics. 2013. http://ethics.harvard.edu/working-papers-series . Accessed 15 Aug 2016.
26. Marks J. What's the big deal? The ethics of public-private partnerships related to food and health. Edmond J Safra Center for Ethics. 2013. http://ethics.harvard.edu/working-papers-series . Accessed 15 Aug 2016.
27. Rodwin M. Institutional corruption and the pharmaceutical policy. J Law Med Ethics. 2013;41:544–52.
28. Gagnon M. Corruption of pharmaceutical markets: addressing the misalignment of financial incentives and public health. J Law Med Ethics. 2013;41:571–80.
29. Light D, Lexchin J, Darrow J. Institutional corruption of the pharmaceuticals and the myth of safe and effective drugs. J Law Med Ethics. 2013;41:590–600.
30. Whitaker R, Cosgrove L. Psychiatry under the influence: institutional corruption, social injury, and prescriptions for reform. New York: Palgrave Macmillan; 2015.
31. Wilmshurst P. Institutional corruption in medicine. BMJ. 2002;325:1232–5.
32. Redman B. Are the biomedical sciences sliding toward institutional corruption? And why didn't we notice it? Edmond J Safra Center for Ethics. 2015. http://ethics.harvard.edu/working-papers-series . Accessed 15 Aug 2016.
33. Emanuel J, Steiner D. Institutional conflict of interest. N Engl J Med. 1995;26:262–7.
34. Ensor T. Informal payments for health care in transition economies. Soc Sci Med. 2004;58:237–46.
35. García-Prado A, González P. Whom do physicians work for? An analysis of dual practice in the health sector. J Health Polit Policy Law. 2011;36:265–94.
36. Socha K, Bech M. Physician dual practice: a review of the literature. Health Policy. 2011;102:1–7
37. Ferrinho P, van Lerberghe W, Fronteira I, Hipólito F, Biscaia A. Dual practice in the health sector: review of the evidence. Hum Resour Health. 2004;2:2–14.
38. European Commission. Study on corruption in the healthcare sector. European Union. 2013. https://www.stt.lt/documents/soc_tyrimai/20131219_study_on_corruption_in_the_healthcare_sector_en.pdf . Accessed 1 Feb 2017.
39. Transparency International. Global corruption report 2006: corruption and health. 2006. https://www.transparency.org/whatwedo/publication/global_corruption_report_2006_corruption_and_health. Accessed 1 Feb 2017.
40. Vian T. Review of corruption in the health sector: theory, methods and interventions. Health Policy Plan. 2008;23:83–94.
41. Sommersguter-Reichmann M, Wild C, Stepan A, Reichmann G, Fried A. Individual and institutional corruption in health care: various definitions and typologies, and relevant examples from Austria. Working Paper Graz/Wien. 2016
42. Oliveira G. Institutional corruption as a problem of institutional design: a general framework. Edmond J Safra Center for Ethics. 2014. http://ethics.harvard.edu/working-papers-series . Accessed 15 Aug 2016.
43. Vereinbarung gemäß Art. 15a B-VG über die Organisation und Finanzierung des Gesundheitswesens; BGBl. I Nr. 199. 2013.
44. Steiner P. Das sog "Öffentlichkeitsrecht" im Krankenanstaltenrecht. Recht der Medizin. 2009;45:89–93.
45. Bundesministerium für Gesundheit. Krankenanstalten in Österreich. 2017. http://www.bmgf.gv.at/home/Gesundheit/Krankenanstalten/Krankenanstalten_und_selbststaendige_Ambulatorien_in_Oesterreich/Krankenanstalten_in_Oesterreich. Accessed 23 Feb 2017.
46. Stöger K. §§ 27-32 KAKuG. In: Neumayr M, Resch R, Wallner F, editors. Gmundner Kommentar zum Gesundheitsrecht. Wien: Manz; 2016
47. Versicherungsverband Österreich. Jahresbericht 2015. 2016. http://www.vvo.at. Accessed 15 Aug 2016
48. Statistik Austria. Current expenditure on health care by providers and financing schemes in Austria, 2014 (in million euros): Statistik Austria. https://www.statistik.at/. Accessed 12 Jan 2017.
49. Hofmarcher MM. Das österreichische Gesundheitssystem: Akteure, Daten, Analysen. Berlin: MWV Medizinisch Wiss. Verl.-Ges; 2013.
50. Amt der oberösterreichischen Landesregierung. Aktuelles zu Verhandlungen zum Krankenanstalten-Arbeitszeitgesetz: Information zur Pressekonferenz am 23.12.2014. 2014. www.land-oberoesterreich.gv.at/Mediendateien/LK/pku_krankenanstalten_arbeitszeitgesetz.pdf. Accessed 24 Jun 2016.
51. Salter M. Lawful but corrupt: gaming and the problem of institutional corruption in the private sector. 2010. http://www.hbs.edu/research/pdf/11-060.pdf. Accessed 15 Aug 2016.
52. Bundesministerium für Gesundheit. Rahmen-Gesundheitsziele. 2015. http://www.gesundheitsziele-oesterreich.at/wp-content/uploads/2015/11/RGZ_Langfassung_20150915.pdf. Accessed 29 June 2016.
53. Vereinbarung gemäß Art. 15a B-VG Zielsteuerung-Gesundheit. BGBl. I Nr. 200, 2013. 2013.
54. Wallner F. Zivilrechtliche Aspekte der Arzthonorare in öffentlichen Krankenanstalten. Recht der Medizin. 2015;140:227–41.
55. Verordnung der Steiermärkischen Landesregierung vom 16. Juni 2016 über die Bemessung der Arzthonorare (Honorarpunkte-Verordnung 2016): LGBl. Nr. 72/2016
56. Ärztekammer Wien. Richtlinien 2014 betreffend ärztliche Sonderklassehonorare in Wien. 2014. http://www.aekwien.at/sonderklasse-info. Accessed 23 Feb 2017.
57. Czypionka T, Kraus M, Röhrling G. Wartezeiten auf Elektivoperationen: Neues zur Frage der Transparenz? Health System Watch. 2013;II:1–16.
58. Painold J. Qualitätsmanagement und Leistungscontrolling in Krankenanstalten. Graz: Technische Universität Graz; 2006.
59. Rechnungshof. Bericht des Rechnungshofes: Allgemeines Krankenhaus der Stadt Wien–Universitätskliniken Landeskrankenhaus Graz–Universitätsklinikum Landeskrankenhaus–Universitätskliniken Innsbruck Sondergebühren und Arzthonorare Allgemeines Krankenhaus der Stadt Wien–Universitätskliniken mit dem Schwerpunkt Klinisches Institut für Pathologie Prinz Eugen–Studienstiftung der Stadt Wien. 2006. http://www.rechnungshof.gv.at/fileadmin/downloads/2006/berichte/berichte_laender/wien/Wien_2006_04.pdf. Accessed 7 Jul 2016.
60. Kontrollamt der Stadt Wien. Unternehmung "Wiener Krankenanstaltenverbund", Vergabe von Terminen für Elektivoperationen, insbesondere für Implantationen von Hüft-bzw. Knieendoprothesen und Kataraktoperationen an Patientinnen Patienten in den Krankenanstalten der Unternehmung "Wiener Krankenanstaltenverbund". 2008. http://www.stadtrechnungshof.wien.at/berichte/2008/lang/03-05-KA-II-K-18-7.pdf. Accessed 23 Feb 2017.
61. Kontrollamt der Stadt Wien. Kontrollamt der Stadt Wien, "Unternehmung "Wiener Unternehmung "Wiener Krankenanstaltenverbund", Prüfung betreffend Transparenzmängel im öffentlichen Gesundheitswesen der Gemeinde Wien: Tätigkeitsbericht; 2009. http://www.stadtrechnungshof.wien.at/berichte/2009/lang/03-02-KA-II-K-19-7.pdf.Accessed 23 Feb 2017.
62. Kontrollamt der Stadt Wien. Unternehmung "Wiener Krankenanstaltenverbund", Prüfung der Nebenbeschäftigungen von Ärztinnen und Ärzten der Teilunternehmungen "Krankenanstalten der Stadt Wien" und "Pflegeheime der Stadt Wien". 2007. http://www.stadtrechnungshof.wien.at/berichte/2007/lang/4-07-KA-II-KAV-5-7.pdf. Accessed 23 Feb 2017.
63. Rechnungshof. Wahrnehmungsbericht des Rechnungshofes über Teilgebiete der Gebarung der Krankenanstalten im Land Steiermark betreffend die Bezüge, Gebühren und Honorare der Ärzte. 1997. http://www.rechnungshof.gv.at/fileadmin/downloads/1997/berichte/berichte_laender/steiermark/Steiermark_1997_4.pdf. Accessed 23 Feb 2017.
64. Landes-Zielsteuerungsvertrag: Zielsteuerung-Gesundheit abgeschlossen zwischen dem Land Steiermark und den Trägern der gesetzlichen Krankenversicherung. http://www.landtag.steiermark.at/cms/dokumente/11407021_73552632/2d81c367/16_2300_1_BE.pdf. Accessed 1 Feb 2017.
65. Verordnung der Steiermärkischen Landesregierung vom 31. Jänner 2013 über die Festsetzung der Sondergebühren in der Sonderklasse der Landeskrankenanstalten: LGBl. Nr. 9/2016.
66. Verordnung der Steiermärkischen Landesregierung vom 15. März 1999 über den Anstaltsanteil an den Arztgebühren und die Aufteilung der Arztgebühren zwischen dem Land und dem Rechtsträger der Steiermärkischen Landeskrankenanstalten: LGBl. Nr. 83/2004 Stück 30.

17

Factors for healthcare utilization and effect of mutual health insurance on healthcare utilization in rural communities of South Achefer Woreda, North West, Ethiopia

Hiwot Tilahun[2], Desta Debalkie Atnafu[1*], Geta Asrade[3], Amare Minyihun[3] and Yihun Mulugeta Alemu[1]

Abstract

Objective: To identify factors for healthcare utilization and to describe effect of Mutual Health Insurance on health service utilization in rural community in South Achefer, North West Ethiopia.

Methods: Across-sectional study was conducted. A total of 652 households consented to participate in the study (326 insured and 326 uninsured households). Propensity score matching was used to explain possible differences in the baseline variables between enrolled and un-enrolled households. Logistic regression analysis was used to identify factors for healthcare utilization.

Results: Healthcare utilization among insured households was 50.5% (95% CI: 44.8%, 56.2%). Whilst among uninsured households, healthcare utilization was 29.3% (95% CI: 24.11, 34.47). In general, the overall healthcare utilization was 39.89% (95% CI: 35.7, 43.8). The overall increase in patient-attendance given illness among insured households was 25.2% higher compared with uninsured (t = 4.94, 95% CI: 0.145, 0.359). Educated (primary and above) (AOR = 1.84; 95% CI: 1.14, 2.98), chronic patient (AOR = 1.86; 95% CI: 1.13, 3.06), first choice was health facilities at the point of illness (AOR = 6.33; 95% CI: 2.97–13.51), rich (AOR = 2.1; 95%CI: 1.29, 3.43), and insured (AOR = 2.16; 95% CI: 1.45, 3.23) were independently associated with increased healthcare utilization.

Conclusion: Enrolment to mutual health insurance increases healthcare utilization. Presence of illness in the households, household earnings, educational status, first choice of treatment at point of illness, and membership to Mutual Health Insurance scheme should be targeted during escalating of healthcare utilization.

Keywords: Insurance, Enrolment, Effect, Mutual, Health, Achefere, Ethiopia

Background

Globally an approximate of 44 million households (150 million people) faced catastrophic healthcare expenditure [1]. Each year, a total of 25 million households (100 million people) are pushed into deep poverty because of out of pocket healthcare spending [2]. Over 90% of healthcare expenditure catastrophes occurred in resource limited settings [3, 4].

Ethiopia is one of the highest disease burden countries [5] where utilization of facility based healthcare is very low [6]. Low level healthcare utilization might be linked with impoverished healthservices [7, 8]. Healthcare utilizations are also overwhelmed by inadequate and low quality healthcare because of limited resources and absence of dedicated healthcare financing scheme [9].

Out of pocket healthcare expenditure is one of the major problems in resource limited countries like Ethiopia [10, 11]. About 37% of the national healthcare expenditure in Ethiopia was covered due to out of pocket payments [11]. As a result of this direct way of expense, most patients were unable to afford the amount of financial expenditures for utilizing a given healthcare. Hence, they were enforced to take self-administered local medicines, and go to traditional healers or simply waiting the last

* Correspondence: destad2a@gmail.com
[1]School of Public Health, College of Medicine and Health Sciences, Bahir Dar University, Bahir Dar City, Ethiopia
Full list of author information is available at the end of the article

date of their alive [12]. However, prepayment health insurance scheme; a best solution for financial barriers of payments made at point of healthcare use; addressed healthcare financial challenges [13]. There for, moving away from out of pocket charges for healthcare is an important step towards averting the financial ruin associated with medical care [14, 15].

Furthermore, for the last several years, unimproved healthcare services and financial burdens of healthcare are the main issues of Ethiopian people which associated with low coverage of health insurance, below 1% [2, 11]. According to Ethiopian demographic and health survey (EDHS) 2016, more than 95% of females and 94% of males were not also enclosed by any type of health insurance. Only about 1.2% of the citizens can access health insurance from both private and public agencies [13]. It is because of the fact that the fifth national health accounts of the country recommended a need to mobilize more resources for health to improve the quality, equity and access to healthcare. This has been made the focus of the national health sector transformation plan of 2015/16–2019/20. Consequently, the government of Ethiopia is currently undertaking strategies to increase government budget in the sector [11] via healthcare financing [2].

After the strategies, the following financial protection schemes were introduced: systematizing fee waivers system; revenue retention and utilizations; standardizing exemption services and initiations of health insurance [mutual health insurance (MHIS) and social health insurance (SHI)]. However, social health insurance which would suppose to cover 10.46% of the population in the formal sectors is a compulsory one. Whilst, mutual health insurance scheme was proposed to address 83.6% of Ethiopian citizens who are engaged in informal sectors; mainly the rural residents [11]. The policy agenda of health insurances coverage is aimed to deliver equitable access; to sustainable quality of healthcare, to decrease financial barrier; and to develop social inclusion for households in the health sector. Unlike social health insurance, membership in mutual health insurance scheme is based on voluntary decisions which are made by households. A household contributed an amount of 10.4 US$ per annum to join mutual health insurance scheme. Nonetheless, the amount of money contributed to the mutual health insurance might vary from year to year or based on nature of household's income. The mutual health insurance scheme benefit package covers all outpatient and inpatient services at all levels of the health facilities except for dentures, eyeglasses, and cosmetic healthcare services. In Ethiopia, despite remarkable benefits, less than 1% of people are enclosed by social health insurance, and the same percentage covered by employer-based insurance [9, 12].

The effects of health insurance on healthcare utilization and factors for healthcare utilization are not well described in resource limited settings particularly Ethiopia. This study aims to determine effects of mutual health insurance on healthcare utilization and to identify factors for healthcare utilization in rural community in South Achefer, North West Ethiopia.

Methods

Study design and setting

We conducted a cross-sectional study from February to March, 2016 in rural community of South Achefer, Northwest Ethiopia. In 20 kebeles, a total of 36,204 households were identified; of which 12,612(35%) households were enrolled to mutual health insurance [16].

Goals and challenges of the empirical analysis

House to house, community-based survey was conducted in South Achefer district. The objectives of this study were to determine healthcare utilization among insured and uninsured households and to identify factors linked with healthcare utilization. The main methodological challenges could be selection bias and variable omission because of unobserved heterogeneity during matching. Heterogeneity is a variation across individual units of observations, and the variation can't be observed. The term heterogeneity refers to differences across the units being studied. For example, in an insurance model, members with non-members are assumed to differ from one another is said to have heterogeneous agents. We might have an omitted variable (as is often with cases of causal inference and selection bias) that we say we have endogeneity caused by unobserved heterogeneity. The effect of unobserved heterogeneity is endogeneity that is correlation between explanatory variables and error term. Unobserved heterogeneity is one instance in where correlation between observables and unobservable may be expected. In addition to the observed variables under study, there are other relevant variables which are unobserved, but correlated with the observed variables. Mutual health insurance scheme was voluntary based which could lead people to self-select themselves in to a particular group (either being insured or uninsured) [7, 14, 15]. Therefore, we applied a technique called propensity score matching to account for potential differences in background characteristics between insured and uninsured so that difference in the outcome of interest could be attributed to the intervention itself.

Sampling and study participants

The study was designed to have 80% statistical power in order to get adequate sample size for justifiable statistical significant given efficient resource utilization. The level of significance was taken 5%. The ratio of insured to uninsured was 1:1. Assuming the proportion of health service utilization was 35% for insured households and 20% for uninsured household [17]. The sample size was estimated to be 296 for insured and 296 for uninsured households. The non-response rate of 10% was taken. The design effect was determined to be two for having two stages in selecting study subjects, the resulting sample size was 652 (326 insured and 326 uninsured households). The sample size was calculated for different objectives and the largest sample estimate was taken.

Sampling procedure

In this study, for large clusters of population, multi-stage sampling procedure was appropriate. Multi-stage sampling could divide large clusters of population into smaller clusters in several stages in order to make primary data collection manageable and cost wise. Of 20 Kebeles, six Kebeles were randomly selected from the South Achefer district. A total of 652 households were identified from six Kebeles. Proportional allocation of households per kebele was employed. Sampled households (insured and uninsured) were selected systematically from each Kebele.

Data collection and study variables

Ten trained diploma graduate data collectors conducted face to face interviews with household heads. The data collection tools were structured questionnaires that were prepared in English, translated into Amharic and back translated to check its consistency. Pre-test was conducted for reliability and ease of understanding. We measured all variables at the household level. Enrollment to mutual health insurance was at the household level. Health services utilization was the dependent variable. Independent variables were age, sex, education, family size, distance from health institutions, insurance membership, wealth index, first choice place for treatment, chronic illness and health seeking behavior.

Operational definitions

Utilization of healthcare was defined as health facilities visits by members of households at least once in the last 6 months for health services (diagnostic or treatment). Perceived health status was respondent's report about their health status that was assigned numerical values according to the following scale: very good = 5, good = 4 medium =3 poor =2 and very poor = 1. Perceived quality of care was the extent of respondent's view on the quality of healthcare delivery; it was measured by Likert scale questions. Chronic illness is a disease condition that lasts more than three months. Household wealth index was measured by using principal component analysis and categorized as poor, medium and rich. Households indexed in the mustered book of mutual health insurances schemes were recruited as insured while households which were not indexed to mutual health insurance schemes were recruited as uninsured.

Data analysis

Data were entered into Epi-info and analysis was performed by using STATA. Frequencies and proportions were used to describe the respondents in relation to the studied variables. To identify factors associated with healthcare utilization, logistic regression models were used. A bi-variable logistic regression model was fitted for each explanatory variable to identify the existence of associations among candidate and outcome variables. Multivariable logistic regression analysis (backward stepwise) was used to identify independent predictors for healthcare utilizations. All variables whose crude odds ratios greater than 0.2 in the bi-variable logistic regression model were fitted in to multivariable logistic regression model. An odds ratio with 95% confidence interval was used to measure the strength of association and identify statistically significant results. Propensity score matching was used to explain possible differences in the baseline variables between enrolled and un-enrolled households. In this data set a good-quality matching was observed since mean absolute bias was 4% which was < 5%. Therefore, the variation in healthcare utilization was due to average impact of mutual health insurance itself.

Ethical considerations

Ethical approval from the University of Gondar Ethics committee was obtained. In addition, ethical endorsement from Amhara Regional Health Bureau Research Core Process Unit was approved. Written permission to conduct the study was obtained from each Kebele administration involved in the study. The data collectors took written informed consent from household heads.

Results

Socio-demographic and other characteristics of respondents

A total of 594 households participated in the study with a response rate of 91.1%. The average age of the respondents was 47.5 years (±14.6SD). Table 1 presents socio-demographic characteristics of study participants, enabling and needs factors. Among study subjects, more female household heads (47%) were utilizing healthcare services than male household heads (36%). Among respondents who were not able to write and read, higher percentage (68%) were not utilizing health care service than respondents who were able to write and read (51%). A considerable percentage of household heads who traveled less than five kilometers to reach the nearest health institutions (43%) were utilizing health services than household heads who traveled five kilometers and above (37%). Higher proportion of respondents with chronic

Table 1 Presentation of characteristics of study participants by health service utilization in rural communities of South Achefer, March 2016 ($n = 594$)

Variables	Health service utilization	
	No (%)	Yes (%)
Sex of respondents		
Male	249(64)	143(36)
Female	108(53)	94(47)
Educational level		
Unable to read & write	259(68)	120(32)
Able to read & write	42(51)	41(49)
Primary education and above	56(42)	76(58)
Family size		
< 5	159(63)	93(37)
≥ 5	198(58)	144(42)
Distance from health facilities in kilo meters		
< 5	184(57)	137(43)
≥ 5	173(63)	100(37)
Chronic illness		
No	307 (62.6)	183 (37.4)
Yes	50 (48)	54(52)
Household wealth index		
Poor	140(70.7)	58(29.3)
Medium	120(60.6)	78(39.4)
Rich	97(48.9)	101(54.1)
First choice place for treatment at the point of illness		
Health institution	273(54.6)	227(55.4)
Traditional healer	84(89)	10(11)
Perceived health status		
Poor	64(71)	26 (29)
Medium	185 (67)	92 (33)
Good	81 (58)	58(42)
Very good	27(31)	61(69)
Enrollment to mutual health insurance		
No	210(72)	87(28)
Yes	147(49)	150(52)

illness in the households (52%) were utilized the health services than households without chronically ill respondents (37.4%) (Table 1).

Multilevel logistic regression

Respondents, whose educational level was primary and above, were more likely to utilize health service (AOR = 1.84; 95% CI: 1.14, 2.98) than respondents who did not write and read. Households with presence of a chronic patient were more likely to utilize health services (AOR = 1.86; 95% CI: 1.13, 3.06) than its counter parts. Households, whose wealth index was categorized as rich, were more likely to utilize health service (AOR = 2.1; 95%CI: 1.29, 3.43) than households, whose wealth index was categorized as poor. Respondents whose first choice was health institution for treatment at the point of illness were more likely to utilize health service (AOR = 6.33; 95% CI: 2.97, 13.51) than household heads whose first choice was traditional healer. Respondents with poor perceived health status were less likely to utilize health service (AOR = 0.33; 95% CI: 0.18, 0.61) than respondents with perceived health status of very good. Households who enrolled to mutual health insurance scheme were more likely to utilize health service (AOR = 2.16; 95% CI: 1.45, 3.23) compared to households who did not enrolled to mutual health insurance scheme (Table 2).

Effect of mutual health insurance on health service utilization

Before matching was computed, healthcare utilization is significantly higher in households which were enrolled to mutual health insurance (50.5%) than households which were not enrolled to mutual health insurance (29.3%) ($t = 5.4$, p-value< 0.001). To minimize self-selection bias of insurance uptake, nearest neighborhood matching was done between who were enrolled (treated) to mutual health insurance ($n = 297$) and who were not enrolled (control) to mutual health insurance ($n = 218$). The average treatment effect on the treated group was 0.252 ($t = 4.94$, 95% CI: 0.14–0.35). Being a member to mutual health insurance contributed approximately 25.2% point increase healthcare utilization. The average incremental effect on healthcare utilization was because of enrollment to mutual health insurance scheme (Table 3).

Discussion

Enrolment to healthcare insurance increases use of healthcare in various settings [15, 18]. In Ethiopia (37%) of households are reliance on out of packet spending; health insurance coverage remains low [11, 13, 15]. This study determined the effect of mutual health insurance on healthcare utilization and identified factors associated with healthcare utilization.

Health insurance scheme is a crucial strategy for financial protection of many households [14]. Mutual health insurance scheme prevents financial hardship during illness. Mutual health insurance scheme increases healthcare utilization [13]. This study shown that the overall health service utilization rate in the past 6 month was 39.9% (95% CI: 35.7,43.8) which was consistent with the study conducted in Amhara region (38.7%) [19]. However, our study finding was lower than the study finding of Federal Ministry of Health (48%) and the study finding in Jimma Zone (54.76%) [20]. Difference in effect of mutual health insurance on healthcare utilization could

Table 2 Factors associated with utilization of health service in South Achefere, March 2016 ($N = 594$)

Variables	Health service utilization		COR (95% CI)	AOR (95% CI)
	No	Yes		
Sex of respondents				
Male	249	143	1.00	1.00
Female	108	94	1.52 (1.07–2.14)	1.47 (0.97–2.22)
Educational level				
Unable to read & write	259	120	1.00	1.00
Able to read &write	42	41	2.11 (1.30–3.41)	1.75 (1.003–3.06)[a]
Primary education and above	56	76	2.93 (1.95–4.40)	1.84 (1.14–2.98)[a]
Family size				
< 5	159	93	1.00	1.00
≥ 5	198	144	1.35(0.92–1.98)	1.31(0.83–2.07)
Distance from health facilities in kilo meters				
< 5	184	137	1.29(0.93–1.79)	1.47(0.98,2.2)
≥ 5	173	100	1.00	1.00
Chronic illness				
No	307	183	1.00	1.00
Yes	50	54	1.81 (1.18–2.77)	1.86 (1.13–3.06)[a]
Household wealth index				
Poor	140	58	1.00	1.00
Medium	120	78	1.57 (1.03–2.384)	1.52(0.94–2.46)
Rich	97	101	2.52(1.66–3.8)	2.1(1.29–3.43)[a]
First choice place for treatment at the point of illness				
Health institution	273	227	1.00	6.33(2.97–13.51)[a]
Traditional healer	84	10	6.99(3.54–13.77)	1.00
Perceived health status				
Poor	64	26	0.15 (0.07–0.29)	0.18 (0.09–0.4)[a]
Medium	185	92	0.22 (0.13–0.37)	0.28 (0.16–0.51)[a]
Good	81	58	0.32 (0.18–0.56)	0.33 (0.18–0.61)[a]
Very good	27	61	1.00	1.00
Enrolment to mutual health insurance				
No	210	87	1.00	1.00
Yes	147	150	2.46(1.76–3.45)	2.16 (1.45–3.23)[a]

COR Crude odds ratio
AOR Adjusted odds ratio
[a]= Independently significant at α 0.05

be attributed to difference in health seeking behaviour, severity of illness, healthcare coverage and perception to healthcare quality of various settings.

Before matching, the percentage value of healthcare utilization is significantly higher in mutual health insurance enrolled group (50.5%) than the non-enrolled (29.3%) ($t = 5.4$, p-value< 0.001). This finding was consistent to study findings in Burkina Faso; the percentage of health-care utilization was 37% among insured and 12% among uninsured. Similarly, the study showed that the proportion

Table 3 The average treatment effect of mutual health insurance on healthcare utilization, South Achefer Woreda, March 2016 ($n = 594$)

Outcome	Means before matching		Difference	p-value	ATT	S. E	T	95% CI		No. of cases	
	Insured	Uninsured								Insured	Uninsured
HSU	0.505	0.293	0.212	< 0.001	0.252	0.05	4.9	0.14	0.35	297	218

HSU Health service utilization, *ATT* Average treatment effect on treated, *S.E* Standard error, *t* Student's t distribution

of unmatched women who visited at least one antenatal care was higher among insured women than uninsured women [15]. The matching estimator of this study showed that household participated in the mutual health insurance contributed a 25.2% ($t = 4.94$; 95% CI: 0.14, 0.35) increase in healthcare utilization. This finding was higher in magnitude than the finding in Rwanda (15%) [21].

Community health insurance program in Ethiopia aimed to enhance healthcare utilization. In this study mutual health insurance increased healthcare utilization. This was consistent with the study finding in Burkina Faso, Nuna district where the level of health service utilization were higher among insured groups [22]. Community health insurance motivates participants to attend more healthcares.

Low income earned households were less likely to utilize healthcare than households earned higher income [23–25]. In this study, households which were categorized as rich were more likely utilize healthcare than households whose wealth index was categorized as poor. Our study finding was consistent with a study conducted in Rwanda [26] and China [27] which showed that high income farmers were more likely to utilize outpatient services than low income farmers. This is because of the perceived cost of premium and treatment. Respondents whose wealth index rich were able and afford to pay the premium for enrolment as reduction of marginal utility of wealth and likely to consume more healthcares due to moral hazard. In addition, higher income groups, who feared loss of their money due to illness (indirect cost of illness or production loss) had shown alert for increased demand in healthcare utilization by contributing premium in their insurance [28].

In this study, the utilization of health services by respondents observed their health poor was too low (28.9%). This is lower than reported in Amhara region (38.7%) [19], in Jimma (52.9%) [20]. The probable reason for not utilizing modern healthcare service by those perceived their health poor was a need for treatment made at home due to traditional healers followed by reduction in cost of transportation and treatment given shortage of money. There were a massive known practices of traditional medicines found at home made off local knowledge from herbal leaf given by traditional healers [29]. It is also possible to note that the community healthcare seeking behavior is compromised and result in lower adverse selection given an efficient and effective insurance program.

A study finding in Ghana identified that enrollment to national health insurance increase their preference of healthcare provided at healthcare facility than at home or traditional healers [30]. The same is also true in the case of study conducted in Burikina Faso [31]. Similarly, our research report showed that respondents who were enrolled to mutual health insurance were less likely to visit traditional healer compared with uninsured. Enrollments into mutual health insurance could ensure healthcare preference to facility based healthcare than traditional healers [32]. Uninsured households refrain from facilities based healthcare (hospital, health center) and might increase attendance for traditional healer given lower service cost of healings and transportation compared to healthcare facilities did [32]. In general, the decision to visit a traditional healer is not an easily job of whither to select a given provider or not, nonetheless it is the matter of choice made between able and afford to buy a given healing.

Limitations

As we conducted cross-sectional study, factors do not establish temporal relationship. Selection bias due to matching may result in variable omission; unobserved heterogeneity could be exhibited. An important source of potential bias did exist as participation. In general, mutual health insurance scheme was voluntary which could lead people to self-select themselves in to a particular group (either being insured or uninsured). This results in endogeneity.

Conclusion

Enrolment to mutual health insurance increases healthcare utilization. Presence of illness in the households, household earnings, educational status, first choice of treatment at point of illness, and membership to mutual health insurance scheme should be targeted during escalating of healthcare utilization.

Abbreviations

AOR: Adjusted odds ratio; CI: Confidence interval; COR: Crude odds ratio; EDHS: Ethiopian demographic and health survey; MHIS: Mutual health insurance scheme; SD: Standard deviations; SHI: Social health insurance; t: Students' t distribution; US: United states

Acknowledgements

The authors gratefully acknowledge Gondar University, data collectors and study participants involved in the study.

Funding

Gondar University funded this article. The funder had no role in design, analysis, wrote paper, manuscript preparation or decision for publication.

Authors' contributions

Conceived and designed the experiments: HT, DDA, GA, AM, and YMA. Performed the experiments: HT, DDA, GA, AM, and YMA. Analyzed the data: HT, DDA, GA, AM, and YMA. Contributed materials/ analysis tools: HT, DDA, GA, AM, and YMA. Wrote the paper: HT, DDA, GA, AM, and YMA. All authors have read and approved the final version of this manuscript.

Competing interests

The authors have declared that no competing interests exist.

Author details

[1]School of Public Health, College of Medicine and Health Sciences, Bahir Dar University, Bahir Dar City, Ethiopia. [2]Curative and Rehabilitative Core Process, Amhara Regional Health Bureau, Bahir Dar City, Ethiopia. [3]Institute of Public Health, College of Medicine and Health Sciences, University of Gondar, Gondar City, Ethiopia.

References

1. World Health Organization (2005) Design health financing system to reduce health catastrophe. WHO, 2005. http://www.who.int/health_financing/pb_2.pdf.
2. WHO Library Cataloguing-in-Publication Data (2010) Health Systems Financing; the Path to Universal Coverage. WHO, 2010. http://www.who.int/whr/2010/cover_en.pdf?ua=1.
3. Xu K, Evans DB, Carrin G, Aguilar-Rivera AM, Musgrove P, et al. Protecting households from catastrophic health spending. Health Aff (Millwood). 2007;26:972–83.
4. Ikegami, Naoki. (2014) Universal Health Coverage for Inclusive and Sustainable Development: Lessons from Japan. A World Bank study. Washington, DC: World Bank. © World Bank. http://www.who.int/whr/2010/cover_en.pdf?ua=1.
5. Xu K, Evans DB, Kawabata K, Zeramdini R, Klavus J, et al. Household catastrophic health expenditure: a multicountry analysis. Lancet. 2003;362:111–7.
6. Mebratie AD, Sparrow R, Yilma Z, Alemu G, Bedi AS. Dropping out of Ethiopia's community-based health insurance scheme. Health Policy Plan. 2015;30:1296–306.
7. Carrin G, Waelkens MP, Criel B. Community-based health insurance in developing countries: a study of its contribution to the performance of health financing systems. Trop Med Int Health. 2005;10:799–811.
8. Spaan E, Mathijssen J, Tromp N, McBain F, ten Have A, et al. The impact of health insurance in Africa and Asia: a systematic review. Bull World Health Organ. 2012;90:685–92.
9. Ali EE. Health care financing in Ethiopia: implications on access to essential medicines. Value Health Reg Issues. 2014;4:37–40.
10. Derseh A, Sparrow R, Yilma Z, Alemu G, Bedi AS. Enrollment in Ethiopia's community-based health insurance scheme. World Dev. 2015;74:58–76.
11. Ethiopian Health Insurance Agency (2015) Evaluation of Community-Based Health Insurance Pilot Schemes in Ethiopia Final Report: Ministry of Health, Ethiopia.
12. Shigute Z, Mebratie AD, Sparrow R, Yilma Z, Alemu G, et al. Uptake of health insurance and the productive safety net program in rural Ethiopia. Soc Sci Med. 2017;176:133–41.
13. USAID (2015) Ethiopia's Community-based Health Insurance: A Step on the Road to Universal Health Coverage: USAID, 2015.
14. Saksena P, Antunes AF, Xu K, Musango L, Carrin G. Mutual health insurance in Rwanda: evidence on access to care and financial risk protection. Health Policy. 2011;99:203–9.
15. Wang W, Temsah G, Mallick L. The impact of health insurance on maternal healthcare utilization: evidence from Ghana, Indonesia and Rwanda. Health Policy Plan. 2016;32:366–75.
16. Jacobs B, Bigdeli M, van Pelt M, Ir P, Salze C, et al. Bridging community-based health insurance and social protection for health care--a step in the direction of universal coverage? Trop Med Int Health. 2008;13:140–3.
17. Mebratie AD, Van de Poel E, Yilma Z, Abebaw D, Alemu G, et al. Healthcare-seeking behaviour in rural Ethiopia: evidence from clinical vignettes. BMJ Open. 2014;4:e004020.
18. Aggarwal A. Impact evaluation of India's 'Yeshasvini' community-based health insurance programme. Health Econ. 2010;19(Suppl):5–35.
19. Fantahun M, Degu G. Health service utilization in Amhara region of Ethiopia. Ethiop J Health Dev. 2003;17:141–7.
20. Girma F, Jira C, Girma B. Health Services Utilization and Associated Factors in Jimma Zone, South West Ethiopia. Ethiop J Health Sci. 2011;21:85–94.
21. Musango L, Orem JN, Elovainio R, Kirigia J. Moving from ideas to action - developing health financing systems towards universal coverage in Africa. BMC Int Health Hum Rights. 2012;12:30.
22. Hounton S, Byass P, Kouyate B. Assessing effectiveness of a mutual health insurance in rural Burkina Faso. MBC Health Serv Res. 2012;12:363.
23. Kahneman D, Tversky A. Prospect theory: an analysis of decision under risk. Econometrica. 1979;47:263–92.
24. Arrow KJ. Uncertainty and the welfare economics of medical care. 1963. Bull World Health Organ. 2004;82:141–9.
25. Dixon J, Tenkorang EY, Luginaah IN, Kuuire VZ, Boateng GO. National health insurance scheme enrolment and antenatal care among women in Ghana: is there any relationship? Trop Med Int Health. 2014;19:98–106.
26. Saksena P, Antunes AF, Xu K, Musango L, Carrin G. Impact of mutual health insurance on access to health care and financial risk protection in Rwanda: world health report background paper, no 6; 2010.
27. Wang H, Yip W, Zhang L, Wang L, Hsiao W. Community-based health insurance in poor rural China: the distribution of net benefits. Health Policy Plan. 2005;20:366–74.
28. Benitez-Silva H, Ni H. Health status and health dynamics in an empirical model of expected longevity. J Health Econ. 2008;27:564–84.
29. WHO. Traditional Medicine Strategy 2002–2005. Geneva: World Health Organization; 2002.
30. Blanchet NJ, Fink G, Osei-Akoto I. The effect of Ghana's National Health Insurance Scheme on health care utilisation. Ghana Med J. 2012;46:76–84.
31. Gnawali DP, Pokhrel S, Siéc A, Sanonc M, Allegri MD, et al. The effect of community-based health insurance on the utilization of modern health care services: evidence from Burkina Faso. Health Policy Plan. 2009;90:214–22.
32. De Allegri M, Sanon M, Bridges J, Sauerborn R. Understanding consumers' preferences and decision to enroll in community based health insurance in rural West Africa. Health Policy. 2006;76(1):58–71.

18

A systematic review about costing methodology in robotic surgery: evidence for low quality in most of the studies

Malene Korsholm[1,2,5,6,7*], Jan Sørensen[2,3], Ole Mogensen[4,5], Chunsen Wu[1,5], Kamilla Karlsen[1,5] and Pernille T. Jensen[1,5]

Abstract

Objectives: The main objective of this review was to evaluate the methodological design in studies reporting resource use and costs related to robotic surgery in gynecology.

Methods: Systematic searches were performed in the databases PubMed, Embase, Scopus, and The Centre for Reviews and Dissemination database for relevant studies before May 2016. The quality of the methodological design was assessed with items regarding methodology from the Consolidated Health Economic Evaluation Reporting Standards (CHEERS). The systematic review was reported according to the PRISMA guidelines.

Results: Thirty-two relevant studies were included. None of the reviewed studied fully complied with the CHEERS methodological checklist. *Background and objectives*, *Target population and subgroups* and *Setting and location* were covered in sufficient details in all studies whereas the *Study perspective*, *Justification of the time horizon*, *Discount rate*, and *Estimating resources and costs* were covered in less than 50%. Most of the studies (29/32) used the health care sector perspective whereas the societal perspective was applied in three studies. The time horizon was stated in 18/32 of the studies.

Conclusions: The methodological quality of studies evaluating costs of robotic surgery was low. The longest follow-up was 4 months and in general, the use of detailed cost data were lacking in most of the investigations. Key determinants, such as purchasing, maintenance costs of the robotic platform, and the use of surgical equipment, were rarely reported. If health care cost analyses lack transparency regarding cost drivers included it may not provide a true foundation for decision-making.

Keywords: Economics, Robot-assisted laparoscopy, Cost analysis, Gynecologic surgery

Background

Previous systematic reviews comparing the cost-effectiveness of Robotic Minimally Invasive Surgery (RMIS) with other surgical modalities found higher costs associated with RMIS. However, the conclusions were based on limited evidence due to heterogeneity in study designs, methodology, and time follow-up after surgery [1–4]. In a recent review, key determinants causing higher costs of RMIS compared to open- and laparoscopic surgery were purchase and maintenance cost of the robot, surgical equipment, and additional costs related to longer operation time. The costs were, to a lesser extent, affected by the lifespan of the robotic platform and the annual number of robotic procedures [2].

The guiding principle for cost analysis is to identify the "opportunity costs", defined as the value of the next best option [5]. Cost analyses are context specific and often limited by the availability of data. Lack of adherence to guiding principles and standards decreases transparency and quality of cost analyses [6] which may lead to wrong conclusions and decisions based on an insufficient foundation.

The aim of the present systematic review was to evaluate the methodological design employed in studies of resource

* Correspondence: malene.korsholm@rsyd.dk
[1]Department of Gynecology and Obstetrics, Faculty of Health Sciences, Odense University Hospital, Clinical Institute, University of Southern Denmark, Odense, Denmark
[2]Danish Centre for Health Economics (DaCHE), Department of Public Health, University of Southern Denmark, Odense, Denmark
Full list of author information is available at the end of the article

use and costs related to RMIS within gynecology. We furthermore assed if the reporting quality complied with the Consolidated Health Economic Evaluation Reporting Standards (CHEERS) statement [7]. Hence, the focus was not to evaluate the cost of RMIS compared with other surgical modalities, but primarily to evaluate different methodological choices that may influence the validity of cost analyses.

Methods

The systematic review was reported according to the Preferred Reporting Items for Systematic Review and Meta-Analyses (PRISMA) guidelines [8].

Eligibility criteria

We included randomized controlled trials, prospective and retrospective cohorts, and case-control studies comparing the cost of hysterectomy conducted with RMIS versus laparoscopic, open, and vaginal access.

Search

A systematic search was performed in the databases PubMed, EMBASE, Scopus, and The Centre for Reviews and Dissemination (CRD) database for relevant studies before May 2016 with assistance of a librarian. No language or date limits were imposed in the search. MK developed the PubMed search strategy with input from JS and PTJ. After the PubMed strategy was made, it was adapted to the syntax and subject headings of the other databases. Reference lists of included studies were examined for additional references [9].

Study selection

Two authors (MK and KK) independently screened the titles and abstracts and obtained full text of all studies for the reviewing in Covidence [10]. Covidence is a component of Cochrane's review production, a web-based systematic review tool designed to facilitate the process of screening and enables two reviewers to work efficiently through the steps of a systematic review [10]. The same two authors examined the full text articles and selected studies according to the inclusion criteria. Any inconsistency in the identification of potentially relevant papers was discussed until consensus.

Data collection process

The CHEERS recommendations attempt to optimize reporting of health economic evaluations and consist of 24 items. We selected eight items from the CHEERS recommendations which were specifically related to the methodological design and assessed important for the reporting of costs [7]. The methodological Items included: 1) Background and objectives, 2) Target population and subgroups, 3) Setting and location, 4) Study perspective, 5) Comparators, 6) Time horizon, 7) Discount rate, 8) Estimating resources and costs. Further, we included items related to cost aspects associated to the robotic platform. The chosen items were translated into 12 questions, against which each study was assessed and marked either "yes", "partly", and "not available" and specification of the time follow-up after surgery (Table 1). MK and KK evaluated the quality of the methodological design in all studies independently [7]. The same authors examined their findings and any disagreement was discussed until consensus.

Table 1 Questions from CHEERS checklist

Section/items	Items No	Questions
Introduction		
Background and objectives	3	Was an explicit statement of the broader context provided for the study?
		Were the study questions and its relevance for health policy or practice decisions presented?
Methods		
Target population and subgroups	4	Were the analyzed characteristics of the base case population and subgroups described, including why they were chosen?
Setting and location	5	Were relevant aspects of the system(s) stated in which the decision(s) needed to be made?
Study perspective	6	Was the perspective of the study described and related to the costs being evaluated?
Comparators	7	Were the compared interventions or strategies describe and was it stated why they were chosen?
Time horizon	8	What was the time horizon?
		Was the time horizon justified?
Discount rate	9	If relevant, which discount rate was applied?[a]
Estimating resources and costs	13	Was micro-costing applied?
		Was the costs of purchasing the RMIS platform included?
		Were the maintainance costs of RMIS reported (incl. depreciation and number of procedures)?

[a]NA: If time horizon is not more than a year

Results

Study selection

We identified 763 references of which 32 met the inclusion criteria. The search, screening and exclusions are given in Fig. 1.

Study characteristics

The cost studies (Table 2) were published from 2008 to 2016 and originated from the U.S. (n = 21), Europe (n = 9), and Canada (n = 2). In three studies, the cost analyses were conducted within the framework of a cost-minimization analysis [11, 12], one study used a cost-benefit framework [13] and one study used activity based costing [14]. The remaining studies reported on costing analyses.

Results of individual studies

A visual presentation of the CHEERS criteria and the ranking of the quality assessment are shown in Table 3. All 12 questions from the CHEERS recommendations were marked either "yes", "partly", and "not available" for each study. A "yes" was given 1 point, "partly" a ½ point and "not available" none points.

None of the studies reported all 12 questions; one study (3%) was given 9.5 point [15], six studies (18.8%) 8–8.5 points [14, 16–20], three studies (9.4%) 7.5 point [12, 21, 22], three studies (9.4%) 6–6.5 points [23–25], fourteen studies (43.8%) 5–5.5 points [9, 26–37] and five studies (12.5%) 4.5 point [13, 38–41].

Results from the 12 questions

"Background and objectives", "Target population and subgroups" and "Setting and location" were described in all studies. Comparators were partly described in most studies (30/32) but were fully reported in two studies only. The *study perspective* was clearly stated in seven studies but was not mentioned in 23 studies and only

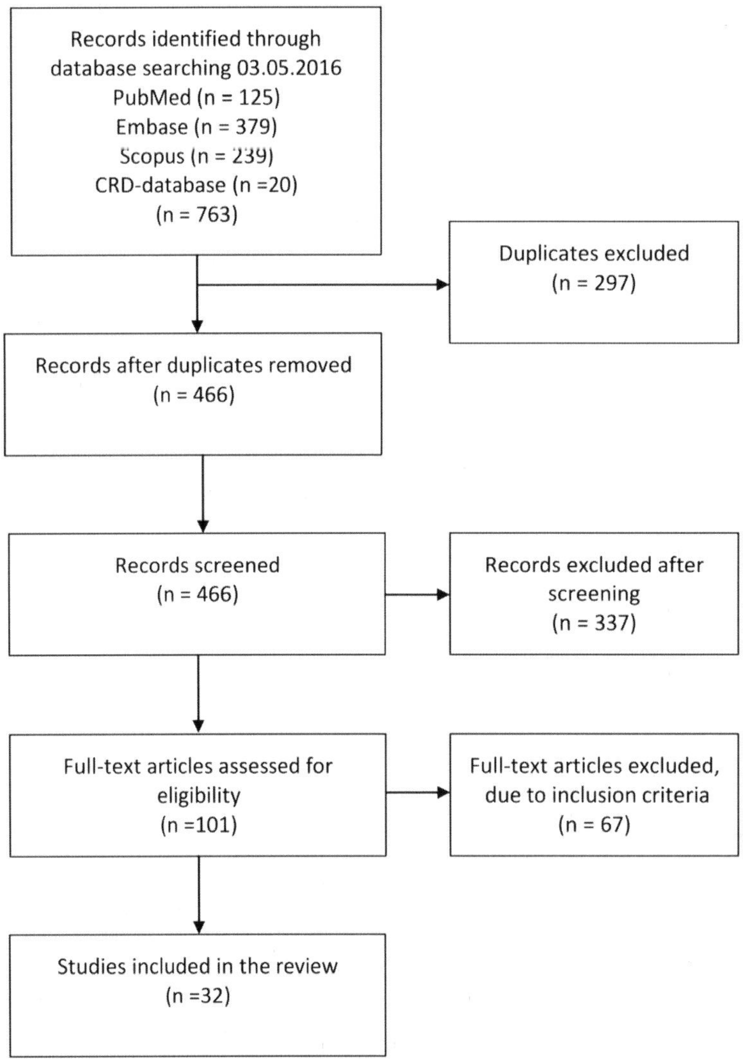

Fig. 1 PRISMA flow chart for selection of included studies

Table 2 Characteristics of included studies

First author, country and year	Women (N)	Year of inclusion	Design	Economic evaluation	Data collection	Level
Bogani, G. (2016) U.S. [26]	251	2007–2012	Retrospective	Cost study	Chart review	Individual
Brooks, RA. (2016) U.S. [27]	6560	2010	Retrospective	Cost study	National database	Not individual
Fader, AN. (2016) U.S. [23]	32,560	2007–2011	Retrospective	Cost study	National database	Not individual
Hachem, LE. (2016) U.S. [9]	92	2013–2014	Retrospective	Cost study	Chart review	Individual
Winter, ML. (2015) U.S. [20]	183	2013	Retrospective	Cost study	Chart review	Individual
Chan, JK. (2015) U.S. [28]	1087	2011	Retrospective	Cost study	National database	Not individual
Herling, SF. (2015) Denmark [14]	360	2006–2014	Retrospective	Activity-based cost analysis	Chart review and national database	Individual
Eklind, S. (2014) Sweden [16]	88	2010–2012	Prospective	Cost study	Prospective	Individual
Shepherd, JP. (2014) U.S. [29]	4871	2011–2013	Retrospective	Cost study	Local database	Not individual
Teljeur, C. (2014) Ireland [12]	NA	NA	Retrospective	Cost-minimization analysis	Local databases, review of the literature	Not individual
Wright, JD. (2014) U.S. [30]	180,230	2006–2012	Retrospective	Cost study	Chart review	Not individual
Woelk, JL. (2014) U.S. [31]	892	2007–2009	Retrospective	Cost study	Local database and chart review	Individual
Lönnerfors, C. (2014) Sweden [17]	122	2010–2013	RCT	Cost study	Prospective	Individual
Reynisson, P. (2013) Sweden [18]	231	Jan. 2001-Feb. 2012	Retrospective	Cost study	Chart review	Individual
Desille-Gbaguidi, H. (2013) France [15]	57	2008–2011	Retrospective	Cost study	Chart review	Individual
Rosero, EB. (2013) U.S. [32]	804,551	2009–2010	Retrospective	Cost study	National database	Not individual
Wright, JD. (2013) U.S. [33]	264,758	2007–2010	Retrospective	Cost study	National database	Not individual
Turunen, H. (2013) Finland [38]	217	2009–2013	Retrospective	Cost study	Chart review	Individual
Yu, X. (2013) U.S. [39]	2247	2008–2009	Retrospective	Cost study	Local database	Not individual
Coronado, PJ. (2012) Spain [13]	347	2003–2011	Prospective and retrospective	Cost-benefit	Chart review	Individual
Wright, KN. (2012) U.S. [48]	688	2009	Retrospective	NA	Chart review	Individual
Wright, JD. (2012) U.S. [34]	2464	2008–2010	Retrospective	NA	National database	Not individual
Scribner, DR. (2012), U.S. [21]	76	2005–2009	Retrospective	NA	Chart review	Individual
Lau, S. (2012) Canada [19]	303	2003–2010	Prospective and retrospective	NA	Prospective collection and chart review	Individual
Venkat, P. (2012) U.S. [25]	54	2008–2010	Retrospective	NA	Chart review	Individual
Shah, N. (2011) U.S. [24]	234	2009	Retrospective	Cost-minimization analysis	Chart review	Individual
Jonsdottir, GM. (2011) U.S. [35]	2133	2006–2009	Retrospective	NA	Chart review	Individual
Holtz, DO. (2010) U.S. [40]	33	2005–2006	Retrospective	NA	Chart review	Individual
Pasic, RP. (2010) U.S. [36]	36,188	2007–2008	Retrospective	NA	National database	Not individual
Halliday, D. (2010) Canada [22]	40	2003–2009	Prospective and retrospective	NA	Prospective collection and chart review	Individual
Sarlos, D. (2010) Switzerland [41]	80	2007–2009	Prospective and retrospective	NA	Prospective collection and chart review	Individual
Bell, MC. (2008) U.S. [37]	110	2000–2007	Retrospective	NA	Chart review	Individual

Table 3 Results from CHEERS checklist.

First author and year	Background and objectives		Target population & subgroups	Setting and location	Study perspective	Comparators	Time horizon	Time horizon	Discount rate	Estimating resources and costs		
Bogani, G. (2016)							30 days					
Brooks, RA. (2016)							Inpatient					
Fader, AN. (2016)							Inpatient					
Hachem, LE. (2016)							6 weeks					
Winter, ML. (2015)							Inpatient					
Chan, J.K.(2015)							Inpatient					
Herling, SF. (2015)							4 months					
Eklind, S. (2015)							3 months					
Shepherd, JP. (2014)												
Teljeur, C. (2014)												
Wright, JD. (2014)												
Woelk, J.L. (2014)							6 weeks					
Lönnerfors, C. (2014)							4 months					
Reynisson, P. (2013)							3 months					
Desille-Gbaguidi, H. (2013)							2 months					
Rosero, EB. (2013)							Inpatient					
Wright, JD. (2013)							Inpatient					
Turunen, H. (2013)												
Yu, X. (2013)												
Coronado, PJ. (2012)												
Wright, KN. (2012)												
Wright, JD. (2012)							2 months					
Scribner, DR. (2012)							30 days					
Lau, S. (2012)							2 years					
Venkat, P. (2012)												
Shah, NT. (2011)												
Jonsdottir, GM. (2011)												
Holtz, D. O. (2010)												
Pasic, R. P. (2010)							30 days					
Halliday, D. (2010)												
Sarlos, D. (2010)												
Bell, MC. (2008)												

Reported, Partly reported, Not reported

partly mentioned in two studies. Most of the studies (n = 29) used the health care sector perspective whereas the societal perspective was applied in three studies only [24, 35, 37]. The societal perspective included return to work/normal daily activity and estimated lost wages [24, 35, 37]. The time horizon was stated in 18/32 studies but none provided a reason for their choice of time horizon. Most studies reported from the inpatient stay (n = 6) and the time horizon ranged from inpatient stay to 4 months after discharge. One study measured the cancer recurrence rate 2 years after surgery but did not report the cost of the recurrence [19].

Seven studies estimated *Resources and costs* by micro-costing (collection of detailed data on resources used to assess costs of an activity) reporting detailed data from a single hospital. The majority of cost items derived from surgery and included the purchase and maintenance costs of the robotic platform with depreciation and yearly number of procedures [14–19, 22]. One of the seven studies combined micro-costing with gross-costing using hospital charge data but did not include detailed data on resource use [14]. The discount rate was not reported in any of the studies due to the short time horizon applied. The depreciation period of the robotic lifespan ranged from five to 10 years in 8/32 of the studies and [12, 14–16, 18, 19, 22, 37] 7 years was most frequently used (n = 5). The number of annual robotic procedures ranged from 234 to 400 and was reported in five studies [12, 14, 16–18]. The service agreement costs of 10% of the purchasing prize of the robot were reported in five studies only [12, 15, 19, 22, 37].

From the index hospitalization *Equipment costs* were the most common included cost items reported from the operation (n = 18) and the exact numbers of operation equipment costs were reported in six studies [9, 12, 14, 16, 17, 42]. Other costs included: costs of the operating room (n = 18), room and board (costs of regular room and any intensive care unit stay) (n = 14), other cost categories (e.g. pathology, laboratory, central supply, pharmacy, and infusion) (n = 14), operation time and costs of anesthesia (n = 13). Less frequently included costs were cleaning and sterilizing equipment (n = 4). Other reported costs not related to the index hospitalization were costs of the patient being morbidly obese and insurance coverage (n = 3). An overview of reported costs is presented in Fig. 2.

Discussion

Our study showed that only few cost studies complied with the methodological items recommended by the CHEERS checklist. We identified critical design issues.. Ideally, a broader cost perspective is recommended to clarify resource use from hospitalization and outside the healthcare system. The time horizon should include resource consumption and costs following the intervention e.g. include rehabilitation.

Only few studies [11, 37, 43] included the societal perspective thus avoiding potentially important cost elements such as estimated costs related to the use of patient time e.g. return to labor market, transportation, and costs from the non-health care sector. Collecting costs from the hospital perspective, only short-term cost implications are considered. When the loss of productivity or other patient related use outside the hospital is not included; additional costs or savings of the surgical procedure will not be elucidated. The societal perspective includes both short- and long-term outcomes. If costs outside the

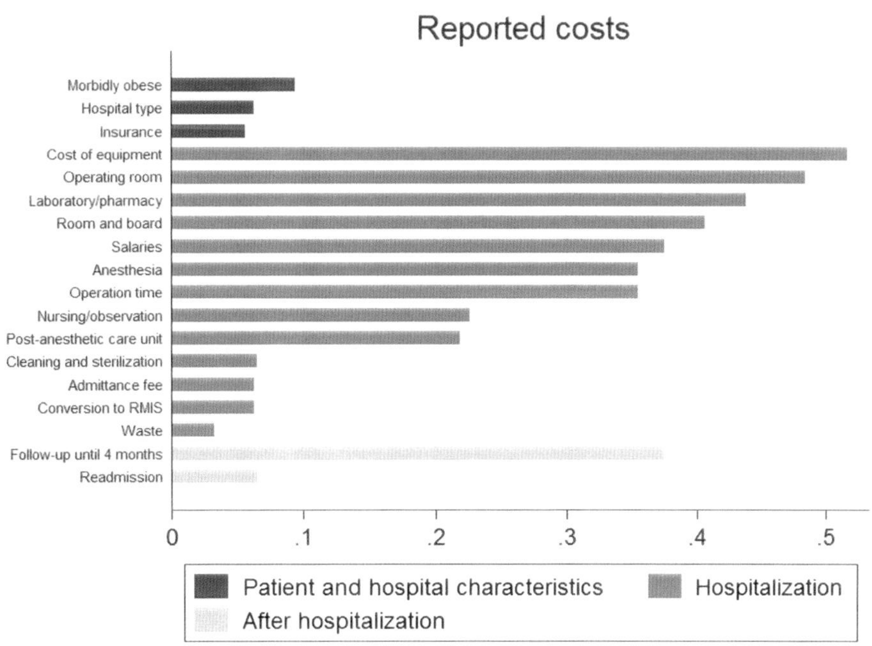

Fig. 2 Reported costs from included studies

hospital are not included, investments with high purchasing costs may seem less attractive.

The time horizon was reported in a few studies and most often costs from the inpatient stay and up to 4 months after surgery was given. With a short follow-up time after surgery cost drivers as rehabilitation and return to work are missing and all costs and effects from surgery are therefore not displayed [3, 44, 45].

Most of the studies used gross-costing based on data from records, chart reviews, or databases. However, when comparing RMIS with other surgical procedures, gross-costing lacks specificity and primarily defines a total budget instead of detailed data. In a pragmatic world, micro-costing is possible from a single hospital, whereas gross-costing data may be the only available data suitable to perform large-scale analyses. Micro-costing is desirable but may be very costly and time consuming to collect. If health care cost analyses have omitted clarity of which cost items they have included it may have a great impact on the transparency and hence the conclusions being used for decision making. Costs of operative procedures should be transparent and state which cost drivers are included and whether indirect costs such as cleaning and staff salary are included in the calculation. It may be difficult to rank the most important cost items in cost studies depending of the aim and data available. One of the most crucial cost items is the purchasing and maintenance costs of the robotic platform. This will affect the result and should be very clearly stated. The operation time may seem as an important cost item, where the exact time can influence the overall costs. When using charges, the overall costs are often based on an average of utensils, staff salary and operation time etc. for the specific operation and it is not possible to measure the smaller variations in time consumption. Even though robotic operations have shorter length of stay compared to open surgery, the taxes may seem unaffected. Hospitals are paid a fixed price for each patient treated.

The purchase of the robotic platform and the maintenance costs were rarely included although they represent an important opportunity costs and have a potential to display major impact on the cost analyses. An increased number of operations per year will decrease the cost per operation [2, 3] but only a few studies included the number of annual procedures or procedures performed per robotic platform. Of notice, Reynisson, P. et al. reported twice as high in-patient charge compared to other studies due to a minor depreciation time of the robot and a decreased number of yearly operations [18]. They also reported investment and equipment costs to be lower in North America than in Europe which should be taken into account when comparing the costs between countries [18].

Staff salaries may represent the most expensive cost driver when estimating the total costs. Only one study included staff salaries as a transparent cost estimation, dividing the time spent on the operation by the hourly wage [14]. A study by Lonnerfors, C. et al. defined major cost drivers influencing the hospital costs as duration of operating time and length of inpatient stay [17]. The majority of the studies did not report key cost items thus decreasing the generalizability.

Hospital charges based on what a health care provider bills for the service may be easily obtained from databases. However, hospital charges do not reflect the actual expenses; rather they represent local estimations of costs related to specific procedures. There can be great variations in the charges due to either over- or underestimation of the actual costs of hospital care, time variation, or variation in profit [32, 46]. Hence, use of the charging system may be inappropriate and prevent comparisons across countries or institutions due to variations in organizational structures, range of health care facilities, and different budgets.

Several studies have documented that great expertise with RMIS improves the surgical outcome in terms of decreased operation time, shorter length of stay and a decrease in readmissions [18, 26, 34, 38]. Many of the studies mentioned the importance of the learning curve of RMIS but did not adjust for it in the analysis. Laursen et al. examined the costs of RMIS in 7670 women over a period of 7 years showing costs to depend on the learning curve of RMIS [47]. Hence, although difficult to account for, the learning curve may represent an important cost driver.

Conclusions

Inadequate reporting of the study perspective, short time horizon, and use of charge data decreased the methodological quality in studies of resource use and costs related to RMIS within gynecology. Few studies complied with the methodological items in the CHEERS checklist and the methodological quality was generally assessed low. If the results lack transparency of included cost elements it can lead to incorrect incentives for decision makers leading to inefficient allocation of hospital resources.

Acknowledgments

The author acknowledges Herdis Foverskov, The Medical Research Library at Odense University Hospital for competent advice in systematic search strategies. We would like to thank Asbjørn Hrobjartsson, Centre for Evidence-Based Medicine Odense (CEBMO), Odense University Hospital, Odense, Denmark for competent advice regarding the methodology in systematic reviews.

Authors' contributions

MK is the principal author and was responsible for designing and planning the study, designing the search strategy, searching the literature databases, screening article titles and abstracts, discussing full-text articles to decide on the articles included, measuring and analyzing the reporting quality of all studies, making the table and figures, and writing and revising the manuscript. JS contributed to the design and conduct of this study by discussing the objective, design and various methodological issues during the process, including the search strategy, inclusion criteria, and the data extraction. He supported the analysis, revised, and commended on earlier drafts of the manuscript. OM was responsible for designing and planning the study, and writing and revising the manuscript. CW was responsible for designing and planning the study, conducting data analysis, competent feedback during the process, and writing and revising the manuscript. KK was responsible for screening article titles and abstracts, discussing full-text articles and selecting the studies to include, measuring and analyzing the reporting quality of all studies, and writing and revising the manuscript. PTJ contributed with outlining the article, outlined the progression and competent feedback during the process, was responsible for designing and planning the study, discussing the inclusion criteria and deciding which articles to include, conducting data analysis, and writing and revising the manuscript. All authors critically reviewed the article and approved the final version.

Competing interests

The authors declare that they have no competing interests.

Author details

[1]Department of Gynecology and Obstetrics, Faculty of Health Sciences, Odense University Hospital, Clinical Institute, University of Southern Denmark, Odense, Denmark. [2]Danish Centre for Health Economics (DaCHE), Department of Public Health, University of Southern Denmark, Odense, Denmark. [3]Healthcare Outcomes Research Centre, Royal College of Surgeons in Ireland, Dublin, Ireland. [4]Department of Pelvic Cancer, Karolinska University Hospital and Karolinska Institute, Stockholm, Sweden. [5]Clinical Institute, University of Southern Denmark, Odense, Denmark. [6]Center of Evidence-Based Medicine Odense (CEBMO), Odense University Hospital, Clinical Institute, University of Southern Denmark, Odense, Denmark. [7]Research Unit of Gynecology and Obstetrics, University of Southern Denmark, Odense University Hospital, Kløvervænget 10, 10th Floor, 5000 Odense, Denmark.

References

1. Pynna K, Vuorela P, Lodenius L, Paavonen J, Roine RP, Rasanen P. Cost-effectiveness of hysterectomy for benign gynecological conditions: a systematic review. Acta Obstet Gynecol Scand. 2014;93(3):225–32.
2. Tandogdu Z, Vale L, Fraser C, Ramsay C. A systematic review of economic evaluations of the use of robotic assisted laparoscopy in surgery compared with open or laparoscopic surgery. Appl Health Econ Health Policy. 2015; 13(5):457–67.
3. Iavazzo C, Papadopoulou EK, Gkegkes ID. Cost assessment of robotics in gynecologic surgery: a systematic review. J Obstet Gynaecol Res. 2014; 40(11):2125–34.
4. Tapper AM, Hannola M, Zeitlin R, Isojarvi J, Sintonen H, Ikonen TS. A systematic review and cost analysis of robot-assisted hysterectomy in malignant and benign conditions. Eur J Obstet Gynecol Reprod Biol. 2014; 177:1–10.
5. Fuertes-Guiro F, Girabent-Farres M, Viteri-Velasco E. Opportunity cost in the economic evaluation of da Vinci robotic assisted surgery. Eur J Health Econ. 2016;17(3):245–56.
6. Walker DG, Wilson RF, Sharma R, Bridges J, Niessen L, Bass EB, et al. AHRQ methods for effective health care. Best practices for conducting economic evaluations in health care: a systematic review of quality assessment tools. Rockville (MD): Agency for Healthcare Research and Quality (US); 2012.
7. Husereau D, Drummond M, Petrou S, Carswell C, Moher D, Greenberg D, et al. Consolidated health economic evaluation reporting standards (CHEERS)--explanation and elaboration: a report of the ISPOR health economic evaluation publication guidelines good reporting practices task force. Value Health. 2013;16(2):231–50.
8. Moher D, Liberati A, Tetzlaff J, Altman DG. Preferred reporting items for systematic reviews and meta-analyses: the PRISMA statement. Int J Surg (London, England). 2010;8(5):336–41.
9. El Hachem L, Andikyan V, Mathews S, Friedman K, Poeran J, Shieh K, et al. Robotic Single- Site and Conventional Laparoscopic Surgery in Gynecology: Clinical Outcomes and Cost Analysis of a Matched Case-Control Study. 2016.
10. Cochrane Pw. Covidence https://www.covidence.org/about-us.
11. Shah NT, Wright KN, Jonsdottir GM, Jorgensen S, Einarsson JI, Muto MG. The feasibility of societal cost equivalence between robotic hysterectomy and alternate hysterectomy methods for endometrial Cancer. Obstet Gynecol Int. 2011;2011:570464.
12. Teljeur C, O'Neill M, Moran PS, Harrington P, Flattery M, Murphy L, et al. Economic evaluation of robot-assisted hysterectomy: a cost-minimisation analysis. BJOG. 2014;121(12):1546–53.
13. Coronado PJ, Herraiz MA, Magrina JF, Fasero M, Vidart JA. Comparison of perioperative outcomes and cost of robotic-assisted laparoscopy, laparoscopy and laparotomy for endometrial cancer. Eur J Obstet Gynecol Reprod Biol. 2012;165(2):289–94.
14. Herling SF, Palle C, Moller AM, Thomsen T, Sorensen J. Cost-analysis of robotic-assisted laparoscopic hysterectomy versus total abdominal hysterectomy for women with endometrial cancer and atypical complex hyperplasia. Acta Obstet Gynecol Scand. 2016;95(3):299–308.
15. Desille-Gbaguidi H, Hebert T, Paternotte-Villemagne J, Gaborit C, Rush E, Body G. Overall care cost comparison between robotic and laparoscopic surgery for endometrial and cervical cancer. Eur J Obstet Gynecol Reprod Biol. 2013;171(2):348–52.
16. Eklind S, Lindfors A, Sjoli P, Dahm-Kahler P. A prospective, comparative study on robotic versus open-surgery hysterectomy and pelvic lymphadenectomy for endometrial carcinoma. Int J Gynecol Cancer. 2015; 25(2):250–6.
17. Lonnerfors C, Reynisson P, Persson J. A randomized trial comparing vaginal and laparoscopic hysterectomy vs robot-assisted hysterectomy. J Minim Invasive Gynecol. 2015;22(1):78–86.
18. Reynisson P, Persson J. Hospital costs for robot-assisted laparoscopic radical hysterectomy and pelvic lymphadenectomy. Gynecol Oncol. 2013;130(1):95–9.
19. Lau S, Vaknin Z, Ramana-Kumar AV, Halliday D, Franco EL, Gotlieb WH. Outcomes and cost comparisons after introducing a robotics program for endometrial cancer surgery. Obstet Gynecol. 2012;119(4):717–24.
20. Winter ML, Leu SY, Lagrew DC Jr, Bustillo G. Cost comparison of robotic-assisted laparoscopic hysterectomy versus standard laparoscopic hysterectomy. J Robot Surg. 2015;9(4):269–75.
21. Scribner DR, Andre T, Lara-Torre E, Weiss PM. Cost analysis of robotic versus standard laparoscopic hysterectomies: a preliminary analysis. J Gynecol Surg. 2012;28(4):255–61.
22. Halliday D, Lau S, Vaknin Z, Deland C, Levental M, McNamara E, et al. Robotic radical hysterectomy: comparison of outcomes and cost. J Robot Surg. 2010;4(4):211–6.
23. Fader AN, Weise RM, Sinno AK, Tanner EJ, 3rd, Borah BJ, Moriarty JP, et al. Utilization of minimally invasive surgery in endometrial cancer Care: A quality and cost disparity. Obstet Gynecol. 2016;127(1):91–100.
24. Shah N, Wright K, Jonsdottir G, Jorgensen S, Einarrson J, Muto M. Comparing robotic hysterectomy with alternate operative strategies for endometrial cancer: a feasibility analysis of cost equivalence from the societal perspective. Gynecol Oncol. 2011;120:S125–S6.
25. Venkat P, Chen LM, Young-Lin N, Kiet TK, Young G, Amatori D, et al. An economic analysis of robotic versus laparoscopic surgery for endometrial cancer: costs, charges and reimbursements to hospitals and professionals. Gynecol Oncol. 2012;125(1):237–40.
26. Bogani G, Multinu F, Dowdy SC, Cliby WA, Wilson TO, Gostout BS, et al. Incorporating robotic-assisted surgery for endometrial cancer staging: analysis of morbidity and costs. Gynecol Oncol. 2016;141(2):218–24.
27. Brooks RA, Blansit K, Young-Lin N, Usach I, Chen LM, Yu X, et al. The economic impact of surgical care for morbidly obese endometrial cancer patients: a nationwide study. Am J Obstet Gynecol. 2016;214(4):498.
28. Chan JK, Gardner AB, Taylor K, Thompson CA, Blansit K, Yu X, et al. Robotic versus laparoscopic versus open surgery in morbidly obese endometrial cancer patients - a comparative analysis of total charges and complication rates. Gynecol Oncol. 2015;139(2):300–5.
29. Shepherd JP, Ahn K, Kantartzis KL, Bonidie MJ, Lee T. Minimizing hysterectomy costs transitioning from open to minimally invasive techniques. J Minim Invasive Gynecol. 2014;21(2 SUPPL. 1):S7–8.

30. Wright JD, Ananth CV, Tergas AI, Herzog TJ, Burke WM, Lewin SN, et al. An economic analysis of robotically assisted hysterectomy. Obstet Gynecol. 2014;123(5):1038–48.
31. Woelk JL, Borah BJ, Trabuco EC, Heien HC, Gebhart JB. Cost differences among robotic, vaginal, and abdominal hysterectomy. Obstet Gynecol. 2014;123(2 Pt 1):255–62.
32. Rosero EB, Kho KA, Joshi GP, Giesecke M, Schaffer JI. Comparison of robotic and laparoscopic hysterectomy for benign gynecologic disease. Obstet Gynecol. 2013;122(4):778–86.
33. Wright JD, Ananth CV, Lewin SN, Burke WM, Lu YS, Neugut AI, et al. Robotically assisted vs laparoscopic hysterectomy among women with benign gynecologic disease. JAMA. 2013;309(7):689–98.
34. Wright JD, Burke WM, Wilde ET, Lewin SN, Charles AS, Kim JH, et al. Comparative effectiveness of robotic versus laparoscopic hysterectomy for endometrial cancer. J Clin Oncol. 2012;30(8):783–91.
35. Jonsdottir GM, Jorgensen S, Cohen SL, Wright KN, Shah NT, Chavan N, et al. Increasing minimally invasive hysterectomy: effect on cost and complications. Obstet Gynecol. 2011;117(5):1142–9.
36. Pasic RP, Rizzo JA, Fang H, Ross S, Moore M, Gunnarsson C. Comparing robot-assisted with conventional laparoscopic hysterectomy: impact on cost and clinical outcomes. J Minim Invasive Gynecol. 2010;17(6):730–8.
37. Bell MC, Torgerson J, Seshadri-Kreaden U, Suttle AW, Hunt S. Comparison of outcomes and cost for endometrial cancer staging via traditional laparotomy, standard laparoscopy and robotic techniques. Gynecol Oncol. 2008;111(3):407–11.
38. Turunen H, Pakarinen P, Sjöberg J, Loukovaara M. Laparoscopic vs robotic-assisted surgery for endometrial carcinoma in a Centre with long laparoscopic experience. J Obstet Gynaecol. 2013;33(7):720–4.
39. Yu X, Lum D, Kiet TK, Fuh KC, Orr J, Jr., Brooks RA, et al. Utilization of and charges for robotic versus laparoscopic versus open surgery for endometrial cancer. J Surg Oncol. 2013;107(6):653–8
40. Holtz DO, Miroshnichenko G, Finnegan MO, Chernick M, Dunton CJ. Endometrial cancer surgery costs: robot vs laparoscopy. J Minim Invasive Gynecol. 2010;17(4):500–3.
41. Sarlos D, Kots L, Stevanovic N, Schaer G. Robotic hysterectomy versus conventional laparoscopic hysterectomy: outcome and cost analyses of a matched case-control study. Eur J Obstet Gynecol Reprod Biol. 2010; 150(1):92–6.
42. Lee T, Shepherd JP, Kantartzis KL, Ahn KH, Bonidie MJ. Cost analysis when open surgeons perform minimally invasive hysterectomy. J Soc Laparoendosc Surg. 2014;18(4)
43. Jonsdottir G, Jorgensen S, Cohen S, Wright K, Shah N, Chavan N, et al. Increasing minimally invasive hysterectomy. Effects on cost and complications. Acta Obstet Gynecol Scand. 2012;91:14.
44. Liu H, Lawrie TA, Lu D, Song H, Wang L, Shi G. Robot-assisted surgery in gynaecology. The Cochrane database of systematic reviews. 2014;(12): Cd011422.
45. Gala RB, Margulies R, Steinberg A, Murphy M, Lukban J, Jeppson P, et al. Systematic review of robotic surgery in gynecology: robotic techniques compared with laparoscopy and laparotomy. J Minim Invasive Gynecol. 2014;21(3):353–61.
46. Swan K, Advincula AP. Understanding the financial impact of robotics in gynecologic surgery. Clin Obstet Gynecol. 2011;54(3):449–57.
47. Laursen KR, Hyldgard VB, Jensen PT, Sogaard R. Health care cost consequences of using robot technology for hysterectomy: a register-based study of consecutive patients during 2006- 2013. J Robot Surg. 2017.

19

Volume-outcome relationship and minimum volume regulations in the German hospital sector – evidence from nationwide administrative hospital data for the years 2005–2007

Corinna Hentschker[1*], Roman Mennicken[2], Antonius Reifferscheid[3], Jürgen Wasem[3] and Ansgar Wübker[4*]

Abstract

Background: This paper analyses the volume-outcome relationship and the effects of minimum volume regulations in the German hospital sector.

Methods: We use a full sample of administrative data from the unselected, complete German hospital population for the years 2005 to 2007. We apply regression methods to analyze the association between volume and hospital quality. We measure hospital quality with a binary variable, which indicates whether the patient has died in hospital. Using simulation techniques we examine the impact of the minimum volume regulations on the accessibility of hospital services.

Results: We find a highly significant negative relationship between case volume and mortality for complex interventions at the pancreas and oesophagus as well as for knee replacement. For liver, kidney and stem cell transplantation as well as for CABG we could not find a strong association between volume and quality. Access to hospital care is only moderately affected by minimum volume regulations.

Conclusion: The effectiveness of minimum volume regulations depends on the type of intervention. Depending on the type of intervention, quality gains can be expected at the cost of slightly decreased access to care.

Keywords: Volume, Hospital quality, Mortality, Access to care

JEL classification: I12, I18

Background

Since the study of Luft et al. [1] the relationship between case volume and outcome-quality has been debated in the scientific literature. The international literature provides broad evidence for the volume-outcome relationship for various conditions in several disciplines - e.g. transplantation medicine, cardiology, orthopedics, neurosurgery, oncology, urology and neonatology (Halm et al. [2]; Gandjour et al. [3]; Chowdhury et al. [4]). The majority of these studies indicates that hospitals, which perform more (surgical) procedures, tend to have better outcomes than hospitals that perform fewer.

Due to these international findings, minimum volume regulations were implemented by German hospital policy in 2004. The idea behind these regulations is to exclude hospitals with bad outcomes caused from not performing certain procedures frequently enough. Currently, they are defined for seven conditions (since 2004: liver transplantation, kidney transplantation, complex oesophagus interventions, complex pancreas interventions and stem cell

* Correspondence: Corinna.Hentschker@rwi-essen.de; Corinna.Hentschker@RWI.de; Ansgar.Wuebker@rwi-essen.de
[1]Essen, Germany
[4]RWI, RUB and Leibniz Science Campus Ruhr, Hohenzollernstraße 1-3, 45127 Essen, Germany
Full list of author information is available at the end of the article

transplantation, followed by knee replacement (2006) and premature births (2010)).

However, for Germany credible empirical evidence on the volume-outcome relationship for these services is rare. Recently, Nimptsch et al. [5] assessed the association between minimum caseload requirements and in-hospital mortality in Germany. Using hospital discharge data from 2006 to 2013 and applying regression methods they found that adjusted in-hospital mortality in hospitals with a caseload above minimum volume threshold is significantly lower than in hospitals with a caseload below the threshold for four indications (esophageal surgery, pancreatic surgery, kidney transplantation and total knee replacement). For liver transplantation, no significant difference in adjusted mortality was found and for stem cell transplantation a positive association was found. Other existing studies focus on knee replacement and pancreatic surgery. Results indicate reduced wound infection rates with increasing case volumes for knee replacement (Geraedts et al. [6], Ohrmann et al. [7]). Recently, Krautz et al. [8] found, that patients who are undergoing major pancreatic resections have improved outcomes if they are admitted to higher volume hospitals. Other German studies focus on different conditions (Hentschker and Mennicken [9], Hentschker and Mennicken [10]) that are not included in the regulations.

Moreover, the potential impact of minimum volume regulations in Germany is scarce. Existing evidence suggest, that so far, in Germany minimum volume regulations have never been executed in the intended way (de Cruppé et al. [11], de Cruppé et al. [12], Peschke et al. [13], de Cruppé et al. [14], de Cruppé and Geraedts [15]). This can be partially explained by some exceptions from minimum volume regulations, for example to ensure access to hospital services. However, several hospitals treat patients in minimum volume conditions without achieving the minimum volume threshold and without fulfilling any legal exception. This shows that the regulation is not executed in the intended way. However, in the Hospital Structures Act in 2016 minimum volume regulations shall be drawn up in a legally secured manner.

This paper analyses the volume-outcome relationship and assesses the minimum volume regulations in the German hospital sector. It contributes to the literature in the following ways. First, it is one of the first studies (besides Nimptsch et al. [8]) which systematically evaluate the volume-outcome relationship for seven conditions that are affected by the German minimum volume regulations. This is important, as it is not clear whether results from other health systems are transferable to the German context and credible national empirical evidence is necessary. In comparison to Nimptsch et al. [8] we extend their assessment by not only comparing outcomes for hospitals below and above the minimum-volume thresholds, thus directly focusing on the general volume-outcome relationship for these indications. In this context, we analyze the relationship between volume and outcome with alternative econometric specifications (e.g. by different volume tertiles). Additionally, we simulate the consequences of withdrawing hospitals from performing a specific services for hospital access for different "hospital closure scenarios". Moreover, we focus on an early period shortly after the introduction of minimum volume regulations. This focus might provide an assessment of the volume-outcome relationship to a quite unselective sample of the whole German hospital market, as hospitals did not adhere to the minimum volume regulation shortly after the introduction (see de Cruppé et al. [11] and Peschke et al.13]).

Second, despite international evidence generally supporting a positive volume outcome relationship (e.g. Halm et al. [2]), the magnitude of the associations differs widely across studies and the clinical and policy relevance of these findings is complicated by methodological limitations of many studies. For example, studies have shortcomings in controlling for differences in patient disease severity between high and low volume hospitals (e.g. Halm et al. [2], Gandjour et al. [3], Chowdhury et al. [4]). Our study uses comprehensive administrative data containing detailed information on patient health status. Third, our study uses a full sample of data from the unselected, complete German hospital population. This allows us to examine actual hospital case volumes. Existing studies are generally restricted to a specific group, e.g. Medicare patients (e.g. Barker, Rosenthal and Cram [16]). Fourth, by simulating whether minimum volume standards affect patient travel times, the study also sheds light on whether a trade-off exists between potential quality gains and reduced access to care for the regulated procedures. This potential trade-off is a major concern for German health policy. Withdrawing hospitals not meeting the minimum volume standards from performing the procedures has been studied by de Cruppé et al. [12] 2007, de Cruppé et al. [17], Geraedts et al. [18], Geraedts et al. [19] or Hentschker and Mennicken [9]. In comparison to these studies we do not only provide comparisons of travel times for the whole patient population in each condition, but also for the specific group of affected patients, i.e. patients with increasing travel times due to the closure of the nearest hospital in the specific service. This specific focus including only the people affected provides additional insights of the impact of minimum volume regulations on access to care.

Methods

Data and econometric model

The analysis is based on an administrative data set for the years 2005, 2006, and 2007.[1] It is a sample of all inpatients in Germany (around 16.0 million (2005) to 16.6 million DRG-inpatients per year) - except psychiatric cases -

treated in around 1700 hospitals. The data set includes detailed information on the patient; for example, age, gender, length of stay, diagnosis, procedure codes, patient admission date, and whether the patient died in the hospital (mortality as discharge reason). Moreover, structural information about each hospital is provided: ownership type, numbers of beds and teaching status.

This analysis focuses on six conditions which were governed by minimum volume regulations during the investigation period: liver transplantation (liver), kidney transplantation (kidney), oesophagus interventions (oesophagus), pancreas interventions (pancreas), stem cell transplantation (stem cell), and knee replacement (knee). Additionally, coronary artery bypass graft (CABG) surgery is also part of minimum volume regulations since its introduction, but minimum volume thresholds were never defined (G-BA [20], G-BA [21], G-BA [22]). For this reason CABG is also considered in this study to potentially derive policy implications for this condition. In the USA, the Leapfrog Group (2011) [23] recommends 450 CABG procedures per hospital. Such a minimum volume threshold seemed too high for the German actual medical care situation, with generally much smaller hospitals compared to the USA. For this reason, we choose a minimum volume threshold of 200.

Our analyzed conditions are identified with the procedure codes of the Federal Joint Committee (G-BA [20], G-BA [21], G-BA [22]). For CABG we use the definition of Mansky et al. [24]. Due to yearly updates of the minimum volume regulations of the Federal Joint Committee, procedure codes change slightly during the observation period. For example there are two additional procedure codes in 2007 for the definition of knee replacements. Therefore, the relevant conditions are identified by using the procedure codes of the respective year. We have to exclude patients with missing patient characteristics. Furthermore, we drop patients with discharge reason transfer (to another hospital) because we cannot determine the outcome of these patients.

We use in-hospital mortality as outcome measure in our analysis. Mortality is the most frequently used endpoint for volume-outcome analyses because it is the most severe clinical outcome (e.g. Cash et al. [25]; Fechner et al. [26]; Smith et al. [27]). Compared to other outcomes, mortality has the advantage of its robustness against hospitals' individual coding behavior (AOK-Bundesverband et al. [28]). However, mortality is also a rare event – at least for certain conditions. This impedes the identification of statistically meaningful differences for hospitals with low case numbers. According to the literature, one possible approach is to eliminate hospitals with less than five expected death per year (Ash et al. [29]). However, this approach appears less rewarding in the context of the study due to its focus on hospitals with very low case volumes. To account for this, we choose three functional forms of case volume. First, we use the logarithm of case volume, which accounts for a decreasing effect of case volume on outcome with increasing volume. Second, we classify the case volume of hospitals in tertiles, which ensures a sufficient number of patients in every group (Hentschker and Mennicken [10]). In every tertile are approximately the same number of patients and we can distinguish between patients who are treated in low, medium, and high volume hospitals. Third, we specify a binary variable, which is 1 for patients who are treated in hospitals that achieve the minimum volume threshold and 0 otherwise. This variable should reflect whether the minimum volume thresholds have a significant impact on mortality.

To account for other factors which influence mortality besides case volume, we include several covariates in our empirical model. To reflect the impact of patient-specific factors on mortality risk, information on age, gender and especially the comorbidity of the patient must be considered. To account for number and severity of the comorbidities, we use the Charlson Comorbidity Index (CCI). The CCI considers 17 different comorbidities, each with a specific severity weight, which add to a total comorbidity score. A higher comorbidity score reflects a higher severity of illness, which is associated with an increased mortality risk (Charlson et al. [30]). Depending on their comorbidity score patients are divided into four risk-groups: CCI = 0, CCI = 1–2, CCI = 3–4, or CCI > = 5. Furthermore, it is controlled for different main diagnosis within one condition and the admission status (scheduled admission, emergency, transfer). Additionally, we include a binary variable for weekend or holiday admissions, because of a potentially higher mortality risk during those days (Cram et al. [31]).

Moreover, several hospital characteristics besides case volume are included in the model. Referring to Milcent [32], information about the ownership type is considered. Furthermore, university hospitals are represented by a binary indicator variable, because of tendencies to treat patients with more severe (co-)morbidities (Heyder [33]). To account for within-hospital correlation of mortality, standard errors are clustered at hospital level. Referring to Hentschker and Mennicken [8] we estimate the effect of volume on outcome with the following regression:

$$y_{ih} = \alpha_0 + vol_h\beta_1 + \mathbf{x}'_{ih}\beta_2 + \mathbf{k}'_h\beta_3 + \varepsilon_{ih}$$

y_{ij}	= mortality
α_0	= constant
vol_h	= case volume
β	= regression coefficients
x'_{ih}	= vector of patient characteristics
k'_h	= vector of hospital characteristics
ε_{ih}	= error term
i	= patient index
h	= hospital index

This linear probability model is estimated by ordinary least squares. Our dependent variable y_{ih} is specified as a binary variable, 1 if patient died in hospital and 0 otherwise, for every patient i in hospital h. Case volume *vol* is specified depending on the functional form in the three different specifications. As mentioned above procedure codes change slightly during the observation period. Therefore we apply regressions for each year separately and do not exploit variation over time in our empirical specifications.[2]

Accessibility analysis

In addition to the econometric analysis of the volume-outcome relationship, the impact of the minimum volume regulations on the accessibility of hospital services is examined [34]. Accessibility to hospital services is measured by travel times of patients to the according hospitals with different indicators. On the one hand we calculate actual travel times of patients to hospitals, i.e. travel of patient to the hospital they chose ("Status-quo-scenario"). On the other hand we calculate minimum travel times for different closing scenarios. In the closings scenarios we simulate that hospitals below the minimum volume thresholds are excluded from providing care (as described below). As we have the individual ZIP codes of all patients, we show changes in average travel times for all patients within a ZIP code area. We use over 8000 residential 5-digit ZIP code areas in Germany. To calculate travel times, we use the Stata command "traveltime". We follow the approach of Hentschker and Mennicken (2015) [9]. As a first step, hospitals not achieving minimum volume thresholds are identified. The patients of these hospitals have to be redistributed to other hospitals which still provide the specific service. This implies longer travel times for the affected patients.

Sometimes patients do not choose the nearest hospital for treatment. This can lead to decreasing travel times in the simulation. Because we are interested in changes in access due to the minimum volume regulations, we assign minimum travel times to the patients, irrespective of whether the patient has been treated in the nearest hospital providing the respective procedure. For the following simulations, we exclude hospitals with a case volume below three cases. These hospitals are not relevant for care provision and should therefore not enter the simulation process. Additionally, we have to exclude patients with missing ZIP code, because we cannot assign travel times to hospitals for these patients.

Concerning the redistribution of patients, two different closure-scenarios are applied. The first scenario, "immediate closure", models a simultaneous market exit of all hospitals not achieving the minimum volume threshold in the respective condition. The affected patients are allocated to the next nearest hospital from their place of residence which provides the same treatment. The second scenario, "successive closure", models an iterative closing process. In each step the hospital with the smallest case volume is closed for the specific hospital service, and its patients are diverted to the next nearest hospital. This process is repeated until all hospitals achieve the minimum volume threshold for the specific condition. The main difference between the two scenarios is the opportunity for hospitals below the minimum volume threshold in the successive closure scenario to profit from the closure of the other hospitals with even lower case volumes and, hence, to increase case volume to the required threshold. We consider this scenario as the more realistic one.

Additionally to Hentschker and Mennicken (2015) [9], we do not only provide comparisons of travel times for the whole patient population in each condition, but also for the specific group of affected patients, i.e. patients with increasing travel times due to the closure of the nearest hospital in the specific service. This specific focus including only the people affected provides a more realistic insight of the impact of minimum volume regulations on access to care.

Results

Descriptive analysis

Table 1 summarizes number of patients and hospitals for each condition for every year. For most conditions the total number of patients increases from 2005 to 2007. Knee replacements are the largest subsample with over 120,000 patients treated in around 1000 hospitals each year, whereas liver transplantations are the condition with the smallest total case volume and the lowest number of hospitals. The amount of hospitals not achieving the minimum volumes varies by condition from 5% (kidney transplantation) to 75% (interventions at the oesophagus). Moreover, the changes of minimum volume thresholds in 2006 increased the share of hospitals not achieving minimum volume thresholds, but the number of hospitals providing the respective services stayed relatively constant. Although several hospitals fail to achieve minimum volumes, the vast majority of the patients are treated in hospitals achieving the required minimum volume threshold. Overall, the number of hospitals and the case volumes correspond with the data reported by other studies (Peschke et al. [14]; Geraedts et al. [24]; de Cruppé et al. [35]).

Table 2 shows descriptive statistics of patient and hospital characteristics in 2007 and comprises only patients which are also included in the regressions, i.e. patients with missing patient characteristics and discharge reason transfer are excluded. The diagnosis specific main diagnoses are shown in the Appendix in

Table 1 Overview of number of patients and hospitals for all conditions from 2005 to 2007

Condition	Year	Number of patients	Number of hospitals	Average case volume	Minimum volume threshold	Hospitals achieving minimum volume threshold (%)	Patients treated in these hospitals (%)
Liver transplantation	2005	941	22	42.8	10	81.8	96.2
	2006	1005	22	45.7	20	68.2	89.8
	2007	1118	22	50.8	20	77.3	94.5
Kidney transplantation	2005	2627	42	62.5	20	92.9	97.9
	2006	2728	42	65.0	25	90.5	97.8
	2007	2902	42	69.1	25	95.2	98.6
Complex interventions at the oesophagus	2005	3063	436	7.0	5	36.2	79.5
	2006	3249	411	7.9	10	25.1	63.1
	2007	3361	437	7.7	10	24.0	64.5
Complex interventions at the pancreas	2005	7795	708	11.0	5	47.0	88.5
	2006	8330	712	11.7	10	32.2	77.9
	2007	9152	691	13.2	10	40.1	82.3
Stem cell transplantation	2005	5522	102	54.1	12	70.6	97.5
	2006	5940	94	63.2	25	61.7	91.5
	2007	5744	101	56.9	25	60.4	92.5
Knee replacement	2005	118,269	1055	112.1	–	–	–
	2006	124,693	1017	122.6	50	78.2	96.0
	2007	134,782	1004	134.2	50	83.8	97.2
CABG	2005	43,501	95	457.9	(200)[a]	77.9	99.1
	2006	39,254	102	384.8	(200)[a]	69.6	97.8
	2007	38,569	101	381.9	(200)[a]	69.3	96.5

Note: [a] No official minimum volume threshold exists; a hypothetical minimum volume threshold of 200 is assumed

Table 5. In-hospital mortality varies by condition from 0.1% (knee replacements) to 17.7% (liver transplantations). On the one hand, the low mortality rates of knee replacements and CABG impede analysis of volume-outcome relations. On the other hand, the high case volumes in these conditions are advantageous from a statistical point of view. Patients receiving liver, kidney or stem cell transplantations are on average 50 years old. For all other conditions the average age is above 60 years. Besides knee replacement, male patients are more prevalent in all other conditions. In general, admission on weekend/holiday is more likely for conditions with a higher share of emergency cases. Again, knee replacement is an exception with the lowest emergency rate and yet still 17.5% weekend/holiday admissions. Moreover, the conditions with the highest mortality rates (liver, pancreas, oesophagus) also have the highest comorbidity score with a quarter of patients having a CCI-score above five. The university status of the hospitals is important for liver and kidney transplantations with the vast majority of patients being treated at university hospitals. One third of stem cell transplantations and CABG are performed in university hospitals. As university hospitals mostly have a public owner, the percentage of public hospitals is very high for these conditions.

Results of the econometric model

Table 3 shows the estimation results for each condition for every year. We find different results for the conditions. We find a highly significant negative relationship between case volume and mortality for complex interventions at the pancreas and oesophagus as well as for knee replacement supporting the volume-outcome relationship. For example, for complex pancreas interventions we find the following results. The left column shows results of the log specification for case volume. The coefficient of −0.028 (year 2007) indicates that an increase of 1% in case volume reduces the probability of death by 0.028 percentage points. More precisely: a patient who is treated in a hospital with 10 cases has a probability of death of 12.8% (not shown in the table). An increase of 10 cases reduces the probability of death by 1.9 pp. to 10.9%. For the calculation of the changes in the probability of death, we take the "average" patient and set all variables of the model except case volume at

Table 2 Descriptive statistics of patient and hospital characteristics (2007)

	Liver	Kidney	Oesophagus	Pancreas	Stem cell	Knee	CABG
Patient level							
Number of patients	1064	2885	3190	8854	5687	132,195	27,644
Mortality rate (%)	18.6%	1.8%	11.8%	10.1%	5.9%	0.1%	3.2%
Age (mean)	48.1	49.7	62.8	62.1	48.4	69.7	66.4
Male (%)	63.3%	62.3%	75.9%	57.5%	62.4%	32.3%	78.3%
Admission reason (%)							
Scheduled	32.6%	34.6%	80.9%	68.9%	80.2%	95.2%	63.2%
Emergency	52.7%	60.3%	13.6%	23.3%	14.1%	4.5%	9.3%
Transfer	14.7%	5.0%	5.5%	7.8%	5.7%	0.3%	27.5%
Weekend/holiday admission (%)	22.4%	24.1%	9.3%	12.1%	5.0%	17.5%	7.7%
Charlson comorbidity index (%)							
0	8.6%	18.7%	17.9%	27.1%	47.0%	65.2%	31.7%
1–2	22.7%	47.9%	35.0%	34.3%	28.4%	30.4%	46.8%
3–4	40.0%	26.3%	20.5%	16.2%	9.4%	3.7%	16.4%
> =5	28.7%	7.1%	26.6%	22.5%	15.2%	0.6%	5.1%
Hospital level							
Number of hospitals	22	42	415	680	100	999	98
Case volume (mean)	50.8	69.1	8.0	13.4	57.4	134.2	393.5
Ownership (%)							
Public	100.0%	95.2%	46.3%	45.0%	68.0%	42.2%	55.1%
Private non-profit	0.0%	2.4%	41.4%	42.2%	16.0%	40.0%	18.4%
Private for-profit	0.0%	2.4%	12.3%	12.8%	16.0%	17.7%	26.5%
University hospital (%)	95.5%	78.6%	9.2%	5.4%	35.0%	3.6%	34.7%

their means. The middle columns display that for example in the year 2007 hospitals in the middle tertile (highest tertile) of case volumes have a 3.87 percentage points (5.03 percentage points) lower mortality rate than the hospitals in the lowest tertile. The right column shows that hospitals above the minimum-volume thresholds have a 5.97 percentage points lower mortality rate than hospitals below the minimum-volume threshold. These numbers relate again to complex pancreas interventions for the year 2007.

In sum, the effect of case volume on mortality for pancreas interventions is of substantial size. The effects are of similar magnitude for complex interventions at oesophagus. It is much lower and close to zero for knee replacements, because of the low overall mortality rate in this condition.

In contrast, for liver and kidney transplantation as well as for CABG only few statistically significant negative coefficients between the case volume and mortality are identified which cannot support a volume-outcome relationship. Also for stem cell transplantation we could not find any evidence of a relationship between volume and outcome.

Results of the accessibility analysis

The observed travel times and the minimum travel times for status quo and both closing scenarios are presented in Table 4. The travel times were calculated for the whole patient population in each condition as well as only for the patients affected, i.e. patients with increasing travel times due to the closure of the hospital in the specific service. Table 4 reads as follows: The four column on the right hand side of Table 4 provide information for the whole patients. For example, actual travel time for Liver patients was 69 min. Minimum travel times for Liver patients are on average 45 min in status quo with a maximum of 166 min to the nearest hospital. Ninety-five percent of all patients in our sample would reach a hospital within 98 min. In this baseline scenario, all 22 hospital still provide services. In scenario 1 "immediate closure", the five hospitals of the first quintile lose its authorization to treat Liver patients leaving 17 hospitals in the sample. This scenario leads to an increase in average travel time by more than 4 min. The maximum travel time in this scenario would be 167 min with a 95% percentile of 106 min. In comparison with scenario 1, a stepwise introduction (scenario "successive closure") has a similar impact on travel times. Average

Table 3 Results of the econometric models

Condition	Year	OLS with logarithm of case volume		OLS with case volume tertiles (reference group: low case volume)				OLS with binary variable whether minimum volume threshold is achieved		Number of	
				Medium case volume		High case volume					
		Coeff.	S.E.	Coeff.	S.E.	Coeff.	S.E.	Coeff.	S.E.	Hospitals	Patients
Liver	2005	−0.0324*	(0.0175)	−0.0118	(0.0518)	−0.0513	(0.0354)	−0.0531	(0.0588)	22	906
	2006	−0.0331	(0.0267)	−0.0027	(0.0356)	−0.0441	(0.0513)	−0.0383	(0.0448)	22	965
	2007	−0.0414	(0.0255)	−0.0263	(0.0520)	−0.0279	(0.0381)	−0.1285*	(0.0732)	22	1064
Kidney	2005	−0.0026	(0.0067)	0.0017	(0.0057)	−0.0010	(0.0066)	−0.0035	(0.0129)	42	2610
	2006	0.0001	(0.0055)	−0.0043	(0.0062)	0.0050	(0.0059)	−0.0013	(0.0128)	42	2699
	2007	−0.0102	(0.0064)	−0.0070	(0.0074)	−0.0065	(0.0072)	−0.0539***	(0.0156)	42	2885
Oesophagus	2005	−0.0292***	(0.0081)	−0.0098	(0.0166)	−0.0445*	(0.0250)	−0.0476***	(0.0177)	428	2898
	2006	−0.0306***	(0.0074)	−0.0284*	(0.0166)	−0.0668***	(0.0203)	−0.0422***	(0.0157)	405	3107
	2007	−0.0267***	(0.0075)	−0.0159	(0.0157)	−0.0262	(0.0203)	−0.0186	(0.0147)	415	3190
Pancreas	2005	−0.0268***	(0.0050)	−0.0494***	(0.0103)	−0.0776***	(0.0135)	−0.0586***	(0.0133)	696	7480
	2006	−0.0280***	(0.0053)	−0.0372***	(0.0105)	−0.0568***	(0.0161)	−0.0632***	(0.0112)	702	8031
	2007	−0.0280***	(0.0051)	−0.0387***	(0.0095)	−0.0503***	(0.0150)	−0.0597***	(0.0112)	680	8854
Stem cell	2005	0.0033	(0.0053)	0.0123	(0.0140)	0.0044	(0.0109)	−0.0011	(0.0184)	100	5489
	2006	0.0042	(0.0085)	0.0383**	(0.0166)	0.0043	(0.0164)	0.0139	(0.0151)	94	5883
	2007	0.0056	(0.0059)	0.0290**	(0.0130)	0.0126	(0.0139)	0.0258*	(0.0134)	100	5687
Knee	2005	−0.0005***	(0.0002)	−0.0002	(0.0003)	−0.0006*	(0.0003)			1047	115,401
	2006	−0.0007***	(0.0002)	−0.0009***	(0.0003)	−0.0012***	(0.0003)	−0.0026***	(0.0010)	1008	122,150
	2007	−0.0004***	(0.0002)	−0.0003	(0.0003)	−0.0006**	(0.0002)	−0.0005	(0.0008)	999	132,195
CABG	2005	−0.0011	(0.0046)	−0.0008	(0.0086)	−0.0064	(0.0078)	0.0012	(0.0105)	94	30,633
	2006	−0.0009	(0.0050)	0.0004	(0.0070)	−0.0037	(0.0081)	−0.0021	(0.0099)	101	27,891
	2007	−0.0103***	(0.0037)	−0.0052	(0.0055)	−0.0107*	(0.0061)	−0.0157*	(0.0094)	98	27,644

Note: The table shows the effect of case volume on mortality for different specifications of case volume. All regressions are estimated with the following covariates: age, male, charlson comorbidity index (1–2, 3–4, > = 5), admission reason (emergency, transfer), weekend/holiday admission, diagnosis specific main diagnoses, ownership (private not-for-profit, private for-profit), and university hospital. The tertiles divide the sample in three parts based on the case volume of hospitals. Hence, it is possible to distinguish patients treated in low, medium and high volume hospitals

*Significant at 10%, **Significant at 5%, ***Significant at 1%

travel times are around 48 min with a maximum time of 167 min. Ninety-five percent of the patients reach the nearest hospital within 106 min. The four columns on the left hand side of Table 4 present the according information for the patients that are really affected by the closure. It becomes obvious that for the affected patients travel time increases strongly by hospital closure. E.g. for affected people minimum average travel time increases sharply from 36 min in the status quo to 70 min in the immediate closure scenario and to 68 min in the successive closure scenario.

Generally, the impact of hospital closures for liver, kidney and stem cell transplantations are rather small in the whole population. Median minimum travel times increase only by 2 min maximum when comparing status quo and successive closure scenario. If only affected patients are considered, the closure of even a small number of hospitals leads to a strong increase in travel times. However, it is observable that in some regions already in the status quo patients need more than 75 min to the nearest hospital (see Fig. 1) and hence, after the hospital closures only slight deteriorations in access are noticeable. Moreover, the access to hospital services is graphically depicted to show differences in access in different regions.

In contrast to the transplantations, travel times are much lower for interventions at the oesophagus and pancreas. The closure of hospital below the minimum volume threshold leads to an increase in median travel times of 2 to 4 min. This is quite a small increase considering the fact that a substantial part of hospitals do not achieve the minimum volume threshold. However, closing affects regions differently; in particular, for interventions at the oesophagus, access deteriorates enormously in many regions in Germany (see Fig. 1), i.e. in many regions patients need more than 30 min to reach the nearest hospital after stepwise introduction of the minimum volume threshold.

Table 4 Results of the accessibility analysis for 2007

	All patients				Affected patients			
	Observed travel time	Minimum travel time			Observed travel time	Minimum travel time		
		Status quo	Immediate closure	Successive closure		Status quo	Immediate closure	Successive closure
Liver								
Average	69.0	45.0	49.3	48.4	43.7	36.2	70.0	67.8
Standard deviation	67.9	28.1	30.4	30.2	42.7	25.6	34.4	39.6
Minimum	2	2	2	2	4	4	13	13
Maximum	497	166	167	167	276	108	167	167
25% percentile	26	23	25	25	17	16	48	35
50% percentile	49	41	45	43	32.5	30.5	63.5	56
75% percentile	89	60	67	65	57	48	88	93
95% percentile	193	98	106	106	106	85	126	128
Min volume threshold	9	9	21	21				
Number of hospitals	22	22	17	18				
Number of patients	1041	1041	1041	1041	62	62	62	49
Kidney								
Average	52.4	38.2	38.9	38.9	36.8	32.6	50.7	50.7
SD	41.6	23.5	23.8	23.8	18.8	15.5	15.5	15.5
Minimum	2	2	2	2	5	5	23	23
Maximum	451	130	130	130	83	61	82	82
25% percentile	23	19	20	20	25	25	41	41
50% percentile	43	33	34	34	38	34	53	53
75% percentile	71	54	55	55	48	45	61	61
95% percentile	125	84	84	84	61	55	72	72
Min volume threshold	19	19	26	26				
Number of hospitals	42	42	40	40				
Number of patients	2835	2835	2835	2835	41	41	41	41
Oesophagus								
Average	35.7	19.6	26.2	23.5	24.6	16.0	29.5	26.1
SD	44.9	13.9	17.6	16.1	36.4	11.9	18.0	16.6
Minimum	0	0	0	0	0	0	2	0
Maximum	495	85	107	104	395	64	100	85
25% percentile	12	9	12	11	9	7	15	13
50% percentile	22.5	16	22	20	16	13	25	22
75% percentile	43	27	37	34	27	21	41	36
95% percentile	102	47	60	56	69	39	63	59
Min volume threshold	3	3	11	10				
Number of hospitals	270	270	117	150				
Number of patients	3080	3080	3080	3080	842	842	842	598
Pancreas								
Average	33.2	15.6	19.1	18.1	17.4	12.8	24.4	22.9
SD	43.2	10.6	13.0	12.5	21.8	9.0	14.5	14.1
Minimum	0	0	0	0	0	0	1	1
Maximum	535	84	89	87	324	58	85	67

Table 4 Results of the accessibility analysis for 2007 *(Continued)*

	All patients				Affected patients			
	Observed travel time	Minimum travel time			Observed travel time	Minimum travel time		
		Status quo	Immediate closure	Successive closure		Status quo	Immediate closure	Successive closure
25% percentile	11	7	9	9	7	6	12	12
50% percentile	19	13	16	15	13	11	21	20
75% percentile	38	21	27	25	21	17	34	31
95% percentile	104	36	44	43	43	30	52	51
Min volume threshold	3	3	10	10				
Number of hospitals	502	502	303	338				
Number of patients	8733	8733	8733	8733	1111	1111	1111	829
Stem cell								
Average	51.4	30.7	33.2	32.5	37.2	25.3	39.3	37.1
SD	49.6	19.8	20.7	20.5	39.6	16.3	19.4	19.8
Minimum	0	0	0	0	2	1	4	4
Maximum	481	117	117	117	251	109	109	109
25% percentile	20	15	16	16	16	14	23	21
50% percentile	39	26	29	28	26	22	37	34
75% percentile	65	42	46	45	44	32	52	50
95% percentile	138	70	73	72	113	58	73	72
Min volume threshold	4	4	25	25				
Number of hospitals	90	90	65	68				
Number of patients	5517	5517	5517	5517	317	317	317	264
Knee								
Average	26.7	12.9	13.6	13.5	22.3	11.8	16.8	16.5
SD	32.1	7.8	8.2	8.1	30.2	7.3	9.2	8.9
Minimum	0	0	0	0	0	0	0	0
Maximum	553	92	92	92	465	46	62	53
25% percentile	11	7	7	7	9	6	10	10
50% percentile	19	11	12	12	15	10	16	15
75% percentile	31	18	18	18	25	16	22	22
95% percentile	68	27	29	29	60	26	34	34
Min volume threshold	3	3	50	50				
Number of hospitals	974	974	845	853				
Number of patients	133,389	133,389	133,389	133,389	3290	3290	3290	2924
CABG								
Average	45.1	31.3	32.5	32.5	45.2	29.7	49.5	48.6
SD	38.8	18.5	19.3	19.2	46.9	19.2	25.4	24.7
Minimum	0	0	0	0	0	0	2	2
Maximum	497	113	113	113	458	96	110	106
25% percentile	19	17	17	17	16	15	29	27
50% percentile	34	28	28	28	29	25	48	49
75% percentile	59	43	45	45	62	41	65	65
95% percentile	113	66	69	68	132	68	96	92

Table 4 Results of the accessibility analysis for 2007 *(Continued)*

	All patients				Affected patients			
	Observed travel time	Minimum travel time			Observed travel time	Minimum travel time		
		Status quo	Immediate closure	Successive closure		Status quo	Immediate closure	Successive closure
Min volume threshold	3	3	200	200				
Number of hospitals	83	83	71	72				
Number of patients	37,965	37,965	37,965	37,965	1133	1133	1133	943

More than 950 hospitals provide knee replacements. The closure of hospitals not achieving the minimum volume regulations threshold does not lead to any deterioration in access. For directly affected patients, travel time increases by 4 min. We again see some regional variation in access to this treatment. In some regions patients need longer than 30 min to reach a hospital, but this is not a result of the simulation; it is already the situation in the status quo.

CABG has a high case volume with a comparably low number of hospitals treating this condition. Considering all patients, no increase in median travel times is observable after closure of hospitals below the minimum volume thresholds. However, affected patients have an increase in median travel time of 24 min which is comparable to the increase in travel times by liver transplantations. Even before the simulation, in some regions patients need more than 60 min to reach a CABG hospital. Access has deteriorated after the simulations in some regions.

In summary, the impact of hospital closures on travel time is generally higher i) the lower the number of existing hospitals is and ii) the higher the number of closures is. It makes a substantial difference whether all patients are considered or whether only affected patients are analyzed. Particularly for the latter, we see a strong impact from hospital closures. Finally, regions are affected differently by closings.

Discussion/limitations

This study has two major strengths: First, the study conducts a comprehensive analysis for seven conditions, which includes the investigation of volume-outcome relationship as well as service accessibility. Second, the data set represents a complete sample of all German inpatients for three consecutive years including detailed information on patient health status. Moreover, although mortality is the most common quality outcome, some volume-outcome studies include further quality measures. However, no reliable information was available regarding other quality outcomes (e.g. complications). Further studies should take other outcome variables such as complication rates or other quality indicators into account. With regard to risk the control variables (age, sex and comorbidities, etc.) should cover central patient-related risk factors. For particular conditions, additional clinical data could be useful. For example the "Model for End-stage Liver Disease" (MELD)-Score, that represents the degree of severity of a liver disease (Wiesner et al. [36]), could improve risk-adjustment for the condition "liver transplantation". Regarding the controls on the hospital level, further structural factors (e.g. technical equipment/infrastructure) may be appropriate, but were not available.

Another limitation is that our results show only a correlation between case volume and mortality. Further research might exploit the question of causality more deeply. One approach would be an instrumental variable strategy as done by Hentschker and Mennicken [10] or Seider et al. [37]. The volume-outcome relationship can be explained by two hypotheses with reverse causality directions. The practice-makes-perfect hypothesis assumes that a high case volume leads to better outcomes due to learning effects and with this the improvement of skills. In contrast, the selective-referral hypothesis states that a good outcome leads to higher case volumes. The idea behind this hypothesis is the assumption that, for example, primary physicians know where the quality hospitals are. Another bias can occur due to unobserved patient heterogeneity (omitted variable bias). If we are not able to control for all patient characteristics which are correlated with volume and the outcome variable our results will be biased [10]. An instrumental variable approach might correct for reverse causality and omitted variable bias, but we did not find valid instruments. Moreover, the analysis relies on 10 year old data. Due to data access limitations, we were not able not run an analysis with current data. However, even if meanwhile some changes in the hospital sector occurred, we are confident that the underlying relationships driving the results are still existent. Moreover, as we focus on a time period at an early period of minimum volume regulation in Germany and studies indicate (e.g. that at least at that time) this regulation was not effective in

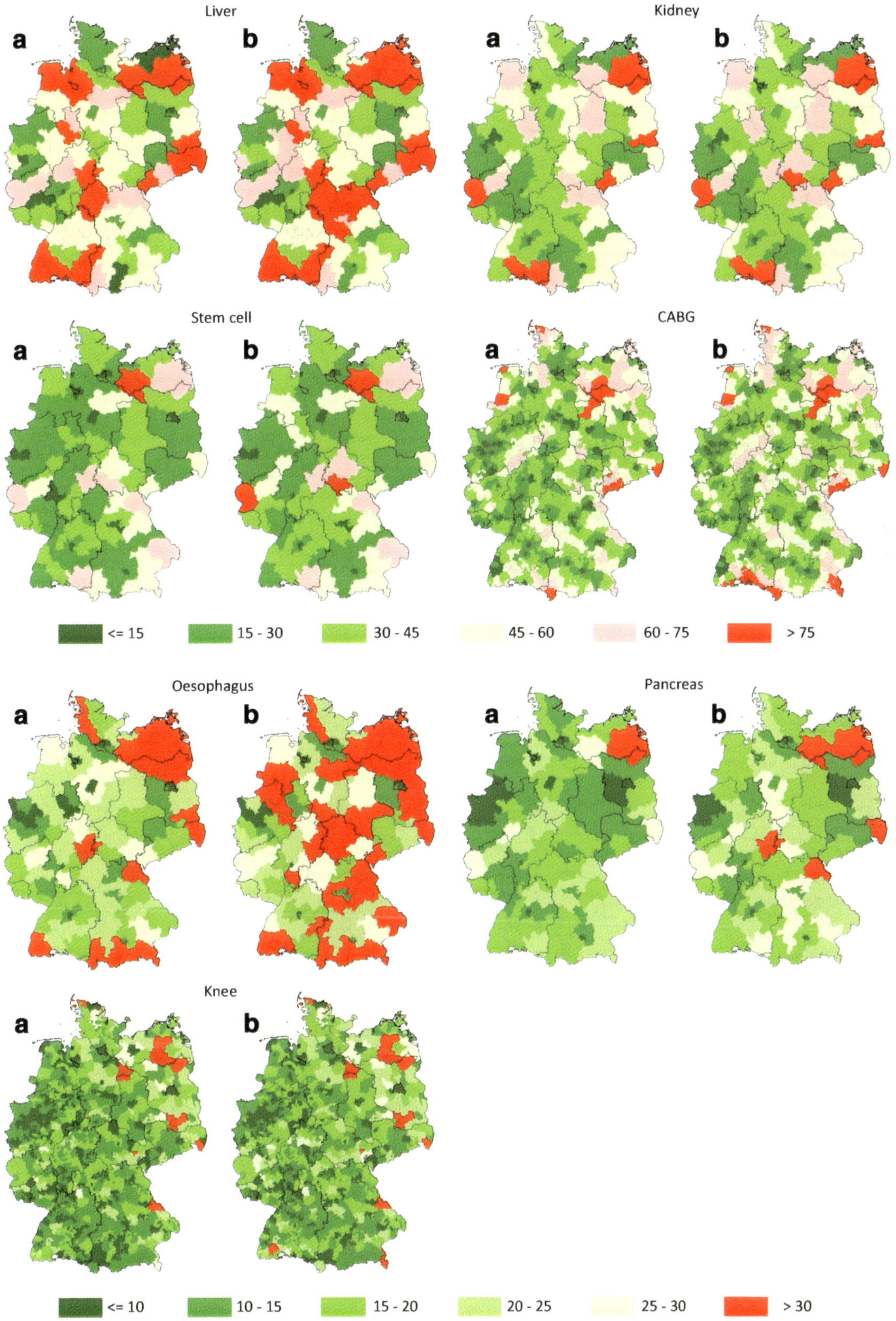

Fig. 1 Minimum travel times in minutes in Status quo (**a**) and after stepwise introduction of the minimum volume threshold (**b**), 2007

Germany. Thus, focusing on this period has the advantage that we are able to assess the volume-outcome relationship on a quite unselected (i.e. not by minimum thresholds affected) hospital population. Finally, our analysis relies on in-hospital mortality and just reflects the time within the hospital. Future studies might additionally consider outpatient mortality and other outcomes like complications.

Conclusion

This study constitutes a comprehensive analysis of minimum volume regulations in Germany. Based on a full sample of all inpatients from 2005 to 2007, volume-outcome relationships are investigated for seven conditions. This study partially confirms international evidence on volume-outcome relationships. In particular, significant negative associations between case volume and in-hospital mortality are identified for oesophagus interventions, pancreas interventions, and knee replacements. For the other conditions, no clear volume-outcome relationship could be identified. This confirms generally results from Nimptsch et al. [7] who focus directly on the minimum volume thresholds and find also a significant negative relationship for kidney transplantations.

Moreover, we found that a relevant share of hospitals did not achieve minimum volume thresholds in each year but still provided these services. Thus, in the study period the introduction of minimum volume regulations seemed to have a limited impact on the supply side. The amount of hospitals not achieving the minimum volume thresholds varies by condition from 5% to 75%. Also, the modification of the thresholds in 2006 did not show relevant effects. These results correspond with other investigations [10, 15]. However, our findings demonstrate the potential steering effect minimum volumes could have if minimum volumes would be strictly implemented in Germany. Moreover, the accessibility analysis shows that a strict implementation of the minimum volume regulations could also result in a reduced accessibility of hospital in certain regions, particularly for oesophagus interventions in Eastern Germany. In general, patients show a high mobility, as the observed travel times are noticeably higher than the minimum travel times.

Recent legislative changes in Germany prohibiting compensation of services in hospitals that do not reach the minimum volume threshold will probably increase the proportion of hospitals which are compliant with the minimum volume regulations. Based on our findings, these regulations might induce quality gains at the cost of moderately decreased access to these services.

In comparison to other countries the German minimum volume standards appear relatively moderate. For example the threshold in the Netherlands for interventions at the oesophagus and pancreas is 20 [38, 39]. In France there is even a threshold of 30 for pancreatic resections [39]. We observed significant negative associations between case volume and in-hospital mortality for these indications. Consequently, an adjustment of these standards should be discussed.

Endnotes

[1]The administrative data of §21 KHEntgG was used as part of a cooperation agreement for the further development of the DRG-system from April, 1st 2011 between the RWI and the BKK Federal Association.

[2]For example, the numbers of knee replacement for 2006 and 2007 are not comparable due to a change in the definition of procedure codes by G-BA. In 2007 two additional procedure codes (5–822.a and 5–822.b) were used for the definition of knee replacement which could yield to an increase in the total number of knee replacements. We do not know exactly whether and to what extent these new procedure codes are responsible for the increase. As a

Appendix

Table 5 Main diagnoses of the conditions

Main diagnosis	Share
Liver transplantation	
Diseases of liver	55.8%
Malignant neoplasms of liver	16.9%
Liver donor	4.4%
Other main diagnosis	22.8%
Kidney transplantation	
Chronic kidney disease	93.2%
Other main diagnosis	6.8%
Complex interventions at the oesophagus	
Malignant neoplasms of oesophagus or stomach	88.8%
Other diseases of oesophagus or gastric ulcer	5.6%
Other main diagnosis	5.5%
Complex interventions at the pancreas	
Malignant neoplasms of pancreas	50.5%
Other disease of pancreas	22.6%
Malignant neoplasm of stomach, small intestine, or colon	8.3%
Other main diagnosis	18.6%
Stem cell transplantation	
Multiple myeloma and malignant plasma cell neoplasms, myeloid or lymphoid leukaemia	60.7%
Lymphoma	20.5%
Malignant neoplasms of testis	4.5%
Other main diagnosis	14.2%

Note: No covariates for knee replacement included, 98% of the patients have the main diagnosis arthrosis of knee. No covariates for CABG included, 98% of the patients have the main diagnosis chronic ischaemic heart disease or angina pectoris

comparison of total case volume between the years might be misleading, we abstain from exploiting longitudinal data in our analysis.

Abbreviations

Coeff: Coefficient; OLS: Ordinary Least Squares; S.E.: Standard Error

Acknowledgements

We thank Klaus Focke, Uwe Mehlhorn and Daniel Viehweg from the BKK Federal Association. Furthermore, we thank Maryna Ivets, Vanessa Kuske Dominik Thomas and Nicolas Wick for helpful remarks as well as. The administrative data of §21 KHEntgG was used as part of a cooperation agreement for the further development of the DRG-system from April, 1st 2011 between the RWI and the BKK Federal Association. The opinions of the authors expressed in this article do not necessarily reflect the views of the affiliated institutions. The publication of this article was funded by the Open Access Fund of the Leibniz Association.

Funding

The background study was financed by the Bundesministerium für Bildung und Forschung.

Authors' contributions

CH participated in the study design, methods, collection of the data, quantitative analysis and interpretation of data, and contributed to the manuscript. RM participated in the study design, methods, collection of the data, and contributed to the manuscript. AR participated in the interpretation of data. He mainly prepared the manuscript. JW discussed the study design and contributed to the manuscript. AW participated in the study design, interpretation of data, and contributed to the manuscript. All authors reviewed and approved the final manuscript.

Competing interests

The authors declare that there is no competing interest.

Author details

[1]Essen, Germany. [2]FOM University of Applied Sciences, Essen Landschaftsverband Rheinland, Cologne, Germany. [3]University Duisburg-Essen, Essen, Germany. [4]RWI, RUB and Leibniz Science Campus Ruhr, Hohenzollernstraße 1-3, 45127 Essen, Germany.

References

1. Luft HS, Bunker JP, Enthoven AC. Should operations be regionalized? The empirical relation between surgical volume and mortality. New Engl J Med. 1979;301(25):1364–9.
2. Halm EA, Lee C, Chassin MR. Is volume related to outcome in health care? A systematic review and methodologic critique of the literature. Ann Intern Med. 2002;137(6):511–20.
3. Gandjour A, Bannenberg A, Lauterbach KW. Threshold volumes associated with higher survival in health care – A systematic review. Med Care. 2003; 41(10):1129–41.
4. Chowdhury MM, Dagash H, Pierro A. A systematic review of the impact of volume of surgery and specialization on patient outcome. Brit J Surg. 2007; 94:145–61.
5. Nimptsch, U., Peschke, D., Mansky, T. Mindestmengen und Krankenhaussterblichkeit – Beobachtungsstudie mit deutschlandweiten Krankenhausabrechnungsdaten von 2006 bis 2013. [Minimum Caseload Requirements and In-hospital Mortality: Observational Study using Nationwide Hospital Discharge Data from 2006 to 2013.]. Gesundheitswesen. April 2016. doi:https://doi.org/10.1055/s-0042-100731.
6. Geraedts M, de Cruppé W, Blum K, Ohmann C. Umsetzung und Auswirkungen der Mindestmengen. Deutsches Ärzteblatt. 2008;105(51–52):890–6.
7. Ohmann C, Verde PE, Blum K, Fischer B, de Cruppé W, Geraedts M. Two short-term outcomes after instituting a national regulation regarding minimum procedural volumes for total knee replacement. J Bone Joint Surg Am. 2010;92(3):629–38.
8. Krautz, C., Nimptsch, U., Weber, G.F., Mansky T, Grützmann R. Effect of hospital volume on in-hospital morbidity and mortality following pancreatic surgery in Germany. Ann Surg (2017); Publish Ahead of Print. doi:https://doi.org/10.1097/SLA.0000000000002248.
9. Hentschker C, Mennicken R. The volume-outcome relationship and minimum volume standards – empirical evidence for Germany. Health Econ. 2015;24(6):644–58.
10. Hentschker, C., and Mennicken, R.: The volume-outcome relationship revisited: practice indeed makes perfect. Health Serv Res (2017) Publish Ahead of Print online: Sep 4. doi: https://doi.org/10.1111/1475-6773.12696.
11. de Cruppé W, Malik M, Geraedts M. Achieving minimum caseload requirements: an analysis of hospital quality control reports from 2004-2010. [Umsetzung der Mindestmengenvorgaben – analyse der Krankenhausqualitätsberichte Eine retrospektive Studie der Jahre 2004–2010]. Dtsch Arztebl Int. 2014;111(33–34):549–55. https://doi.org/10.3238/arztebl.2014.0549.
12. de Cruppé W, Malik M, Geraedts M. Minimum volume standards in German hospitals: do they get along with procedure centralization? A retrospective longitudinal data analysis. BMC Health Serv Res. 2015;15(1):1.
13. Peschke D, Nimptsch U, Mansky T. Achieving minimum caseload requirements: an analysis of hospital discharge data from 2005–2011. Dtsch Arztebl Int. 2014;111:556–63.
14. De Cruppé W, Ohmann C, Blum K, Geraedts M. Evaluating compulsory minimum volume standards in Germany: how many hospitals were compliant in 2004? BMC Health Serv Res. 2007;7(165).
15. de Cruppé W, Geraedts M. Wie konstant halten Krankenhäuser die Mindestmengenvorgaben ein? Eine retrospektive, längsschnittliche Datenanalyse der Jahre 2006, 2008 und 2010. [How Steady are Hospitals in Complying with Minimum Volume Standards? A Retrospective Longitudinal Data Analysis of the Years 2006, 2008, and 2010.]. Zentralbl Chir. 2016; 141(04):425–32.
16. Barker D, Rosenthal G, Cram P. Simultaneous relationships between procedure volume and mortality: do they bias studies of mortality at specialty hospitals? Health Econ. 2011;20(5):505–18.
17. de Cruppé W, Ohmann C, Blum K, Geraedts M. Auswirkung der Mindestmengenvereinbarung auf die stationäre Versorgungsstruktur. [Influence of minimum volumes on the structure of inpatient care.]. Gesundheitswesen. 2008;70(1):9–17.
18. Geraedts M, de Cruppé W, Blum K, Ohmann C. Distanzen zu Krankenhäusern mit Mindestmengen-relevanten Eingriffen 2004 bis 2006. [Distances to Hospitals Performing Minimum Volume Relevant Procedures in Germany 2004 to 2006.]. Das Gesundheitswesen. 2010;72:271–8.
19. Geraedts M, Kühnen C, de Cruppé W, Blum K, Ohmann C. Unterschreitungen der Mindestmengen 2004: Begründungen und Konsequenzen. [Hospitals Failing Minimum Volumes in 2004: Reasons and Consequences.]. Das Gesundheitswesen. 2008;70(02):63–7.
20. G-BA, Gemeinsamer Bundesausschuss: Vereinbarung des Gemeinsamen Bundesausschusses gem. §137 Abs. 1 Satz 3 SGB V für nach § 108 SGB V zugelassene Krankenhäuser (Mindestmengenvereinbarung) in Kraft getreten am 01. Januar 2005 (2005).
21. G-BA, Gemeinsamer Bundesausschuss: Vereinbarung des Gemeinsamen Bundesausschusses gem. §137 Abs. 1 Satz 3 SGB V für nach § 108 SGB V

zugelassene Krankenhäuser (Mindestmengenvereinbarung) in Kraft getreten am 21. März 2006 (2006).

22. G-BA, Gemeinsamer Bundesausschuss: Vereinbarung des Gemeinsamen Bundesausschusses gem. §137 Abs. 1 Satz 3 SGB V für nach § 108 SGB V zugelassene Krankenhäuser (Mindestmengenvereinbarung) in Kraft getreten am 01. Januar 2007 (2007).
23. Leapfrog Group. Factsheet – evidence-based hospital referral, revision 03/21/11. Washington DC: Leapfrog Group; 2011.
24. Mansky T, Niptsch U, Winklmair C, Vogel C, Hellerhoff F. G-IQI – German inpatient quality indicators (version 3.1). Berlin: Technische Universität Berlin; 2011.
25. Cash H, Slowinski T, Buechler A, Grimm A, Friedersdorff F, Schmidt D, Miller K, Giessing M, Fuller TF. Impact of surgeon experience on complication rates and functional outcomes of 484 deceased donor renal transplants: a single-Centre retrospective study. BJU Int. 2012;110(8b):E368–73.
26. Fechner G, Seifert I, Hauser S, Müller SC. Impact of a learning curve model in kidney transplantation on functional outcome and surgical complications in a small volume Centre: does size really matter? Int Urol Nephrol. 2012;44:1411–5.
27. Smith BR, Hinojosa MW, Reavis KM, Nguyen NT. Outcomes of esophagostomy according to surgeon's training: general vs. thoracic. J Gastrointest Surg. 2008;12:1907–11.
28. AOK-Bundesverband, Forschungs- und Entwicklungsinstitut für das Sozial- und Gesundheitswesen Sachsen-Anhalt (FEISA), HELIOS Kliniken and Wissenschaftliches Institut der AOK (WIdO). Qualitätssicherung der stationären Versorgung mit Routinedaten (QSR), Abschlussbericht, Bonn. 2007.
29. Ash AS, Posner MA, Speckman J, Franco S, Yacht AC, Bramwell L. Using claims data to examine mortality trend following hospitalization for heart attack in medicare. Health Serv Res. 2003;38(5):1253–62.
30. Charlson ME, Pompei P, Ales KL, MacKenzie CR. A new method of classifying prognostic comorbidity in longitudinal studies: development and validation. J Chronic Dis. 1987;40(5):373–83.
31 Cram P, Hillis SL, Barnett M, Rosenthal GE. Effects of weekend admission and hospital teaching status on in-hospital mortality. Am J Med. 2004;117(3):151–7.
32. Milcent C. Hospital ownership, reimbursement systems and mortality rates. Health Econ. 2005;14(11):1151–68.
33. Heyder R. Die Bedeutung der Universitätskliniken in der regionalen und überregionalen Versorgung. In: Klauber J, Geraedts M, Friedrich J, Wasem J, editors. Krankenhaus-Report 2015: Strukturwandel. Stuttgart: Schattauer-Verlag; 2015. p. 99–114.
34. Geraedts M, de Cruppé W, Blum K, Ohmann C. Distanzen zu Krankenhäusern mit mindestmengen-relevanten Eingriffen 2004 bis 2006. Gesundheitswesen. 2010;72:271–8.
35. de Cruppé, W., Ohmann, C., Blum, K., and Geraedts; M.: Auswirkung der Mindestmengenvereinbarung auf die stationäre Versorgungsstruktur. Gesundheitswesen. 70: 9–17 (2008).
36. Wiesner R, Edwards E, Freeman R, Harper A, Kim R, Kamath P, Kremers W, Lake J, Howard T, Merion RM, Wolfe RA, Krom R. Model for end-stage liver disease (MELD) and allocation of donor livers. Gastroenterology. 2003;124(1):91–6.
37. Seider, H., Gaynor, M. and Vogt, W. B.: Volume-outcome and antitrust in US health care markets, Unpublished working paper (2004).
38. Mesman R, Faber MJ, Berden BJJM, Westert GP. Evaluation of minimum volume standards for surgery in the Netherlands (2003–2017): a successful policy? Health Policy. 2017;121(12):1263–73.
39. Krautz C, Denz A, Weber GF, Gruetzmann R. Influence of hospital volume effects and minimum caseload requirements on quality of Care in Pancreatic Surgery in Germany. Visceral Medicine. 2017;33(2):131–4.

Permissions

All chapters in this book were first published in HER, by BioMed Central; hereby published with permission under the Creative Commons Attribution License or equivalent. Every chapter published in this book has been scrutinized by our experts. Their significance has been extensively debated. The topics covered herein carry significant findings which will fuel the growth of the discipline. They may even be implemented as practical applications or may be referred to as a beginning point for another development.

The contributors of this book come from diverse backgrounds, making this book a truly international effort. This book will bring forth new frontiers with its revolutionizing research information and detailed analysis of the nascent developments around the world.

We would like to thank all the contributing authors for lending their expertise to make the book truly unique. They have played a crucial role in the development of this book. Without their invaluable contributions this book wouldn't have been possible. They have made vital efforts to compile up to date information on the varied aspects of this subject to make this book a valuable addition to the collection of many professionals and students.

This book was conceptualized with the vision of imparting up-to-date information and advanced data in this field. To ensure the same, a matchless editorial board was set up. Every individual on the board went through rigorous rounds of assessment to prove their worth. After which they invested a large part of their time researching and compiling the most relevant data for our readers.

The editorial board has been involved in producing this book since its inception. They have spent rigorous hours researching and exploring the diverse topics which have resulted in the successful publishing of this book. They have passed on their knowledge of decades through this book. To expedite this challenging task, the publisher supported the team at every step. A small team of assistant editors was also appointed to further simplify the editing procedure and attain best results for the readers.

Apart from the editorial board, the designing team has also invested a significant amount of their time in understanding the subject and creating the most relevant covers. They scrutinized every image to scout for the most suitable representation of the subject and create an appropriate cover for the book.

The publishing team has been an ardent support to the editorial, designing and production team. Their endless efforts to recruit the best for this project, has resulted in the accomplishment of this book. They are a veteran in the field of academics and their pool of knowledge is as vast as their experience in printing. Their expertise and guidance has proved useful at every step. Their uncompromising quality standards have made this book an exceptional effort. Their encouragement from time to time has been an inspiration for everyone.

The publisher and the editorial board hope that this book will prove to be a valuable piece of knowledge for researchers, students, practitioners and scholars across the globe.

List of Contributors

Serge Mandiefe Piabuo and Julius Chupezi Tieguhong
World Agroforestry Centre (ICRAF), Yaounde, Cameroon

Debashish Kundu and Sarabjit Chadha
International Union Against Tuberculosis and Lung Disease (The Union), South-East Asia Office, C-6, Qutub Institutional Area, New Delhi 110016, India

Nandini Sharma
Department of Community Medicine, Maulana Azad Medical College, New Delhi, India

Samia Laokri
Universite Libre de Bruxelles, Brussels, Belgium

George Awungafac
African Society of Laboratory Medicine; Ministry of Health, Cameroon, Yaoundé, Cameroon

Lai Jiang
Center for Instructional Psychology and Technology, Faculty of Psychology and Education Science, KU Leuven, Leuven, Belgium

Miqdad Asaria
Global Health and Development, Imperial College London; Centre for Health Economics, University of York, York, United Kingdom

Tinna Laufey Ásgeirsdóttir and Hildur Margrét Jóhannsdóttir
Department of Economics, University of Iceland, Oddi v/Sturlugotu, Reykjavík, Iceland

Harm Hoekstra, Willem-Jan Metsemakers and Stefaan Nijs
Department of Trauma Surgery, University Hospitals Leuven, Herestraat 49, B-3000 Leuven, Belgium

Harm Hoekstra and and Stefaan Nijs
Department of Development and Regeneration, KU Leuven - University of Leuven, B-3000 Leuven, Belgium

Bart Smeets
Dataroots, B-1040 Brussels, Belgium

Anne-Cécile Spitz
Faculty of Medicine, KU Leuven - University of Leuven, B-3000 Leuven, Belgium

Frank Gyimah Sackey and Peter N. Amponsah
Catholic University College of Ghana, Sunyani, Ghana

Klaus Kaier, Philip Hehn, Dieter Hauschke and Lioudmila Bogatyreva
Institute for Medical Biometry and Statistics, Faculty of Medicine and Medical Center – University of Freiburg, Stefan-Meier-Str 26, 79104 Freiburg, Germany

Silvia Hils, Anja Schmid, , Bernd Jänigen and Przemyslaw Pisarski
Transplantation Center, Department of General and Visceral Surgery, Medical Center, Faculty of Medicine, University of Freiburg, Hugstetter Str 55, 79106 Freiburg, Germany

Stefan Fetzer
Faculty of Economics, Aalen University, Beethovenstraße 1, 73430 Aalen, Germany

Robert Stefko
Faculty of Management, The University of Presov, Presov, Slovakia

Beata Gavurova and Kristina Kocisova
Faculty of Economics, Technical University of Kosice, Kosice, Slovakia

Monica Lambon-Quayefio and Nkechi S. Owoo
Economics Department, University of Ghana, Accra, Ghana

Katharina Schley
University of Goettingen, Humboldtallee 3, 37073 Göttingen, Germany

Camilla Sortsø and Jørgen Lauridsen
Centre of Health Economics Research (COHERE), Department of Business and Economics, University of Southern Denmark, Campusvej 55, DK-5s30 Odense M, Denmark

Camilla Sortsø, Martha Emneus, Anders Green and Peter Bjødstrup Jensen
Institute of Applied Economics and Health Research (ApEHR), Copenhagen, Denmark

Anders Green
Odense Patient data Explorative Network (OPEN), Odense University Hospital and University of Southern Denmark, Copenhagen, Denmark

Kjell Hausken
Faculty of Social Sciences, University of Stavanger, 4036 Stavanger, Norway

Mthuli Ncube
Blavatnik School of Government and Fellow, St Antony's College, University of Oxford, Radcliffe Observatory Quarter, Oxford OX2 6GG, UK

Yoichiro Fujii
Faculty of Economics, Osaka Sangyo University, Nakagaito 3-1-1, Daito-shi, Osaka 574-8530, Japan

Yusuke Osaki
Faculty of Commerce, Waseda University, Nishi-waseda 1-6-1, Shinjuku-ku, Tokyo 169-8050, Japan

Amélie Adeline and Eric Delattre
THEMA, University of Cergy-Pontoise, 33 Bd. du Port, 95000 Cergy, France

Eleonora Fichera
University of Manchester, Manchester Centre for Health Economics, Jean McFarlane Building, Oxford Road, Manchester M13 9PL, UK

Mario Pezzino
University of Manchester, Economics, Arthur Lewis Building Oxford Road, Manchester, M13 9PL, UK

Dziedzom Kwesi Awalime, Nkechi S. Owoo and Edward Nketiah-Amponsah
Economics Department, University of Ghana, Legon, Accra, Ghana

Dziedzom Kwesi Awalime, Bernard Bright K. Davies-Teye and Linda A. Vanotoo
Ghana Health Service, Regional Health Directorate, Accra, Greater Accra Region, Ghana

Margit Sommersguter-Reichmann
Department of Finance, Karl-Franzens University Graz, Resowi G2, A-8010 Graz, Austria

Adolf Stepan
Institute of Management Science, Technical University Vienna, Theresianumgasse 27, A-1040 Vienna, Austria

Desta Debalkie Atnafu and Yihun Mulugeta Alemu
School of Public Health, College of Medicine and Health Sciences, Bahir Dar University, Bahir Dar City, Ethiopia

Hiwot Tilahun
Curative and Rehabilitative Core Process, Amhara Regional Health Bureau, Bahir Dar City, Ethiopia

Geta Asrade and Amare Minyihun
Institute of Public Health, College of Medicine and Health Sciences, University of Gondar, Gondar City, Ethiopia

Malene Korsholm, Chunsen Wu, Kamilla Karlsen and Pernille T. Jensen
Department of Gynecology and Obstetrics, Faculty of Health Sciences, Odense University Hospital, Clinical Institute, University of Southern Denmark, Odense, Denmark

Malene Korsholm and Jan Sørensen
Danish Centre for Health Economics (DaCHE), Department of Public Health, University of Southern Denmark, Odense, Denmark

Jan Sørensen
Healthcare Outcomes Research Centre, Royal College of Surgeons in Ireland, Dublin, Ireland

Ole Mogensen
Department of Pelvic Cancer, Karolinska University Hospital and Karolinska Institute, Stockholm, Sweden

Malene Korsholm, OleMogensen, ChunsenWu, Kamilla Karlsen and Pernille T. Jensen
Clinical Institute, University of Southern Denmark, Odense, Denmark

Malene Korsholm
Center of Evidence-Based Medicine Odense (CEBMO), Odense University Hospital, Clinical Institute, University of Southern Denmark, Odense, Denmark
Research Unit of Gynecology and Obstetrics, University of Southern Denmark, Odense University Hospital, Kløvervænget 10, 10th Floor, 5000 Odense, Denmark

Corinna Hentschker
Essen, Germany

Roman Mennicken
FOM University of Applied Sciences, Essen
Landschaftsverband Rheinland, Cologne, Germany

Antonius Reifferscheid and Jürgen Wasem
University Duisburg-Essen, Essen, Germany

Ansgar Wübker
RWI, RUB and Leibniz Science Campus Ruhr, Hohenzollernstraße 1-3, 45127 Essen, Germany

Index